THE LAWS OF THE KINGS OF ENGLAND
FROM EDMUND TO HENRY I

CAMBRIDGE
UNIVERSITY PRESS
LONDON: FETTER LANE

NEW YORK
The Macmillan Co.

BOMBAY, CALCUTTA and MADRAS
Macmillan and Co., Ltd.

TORONTO
The Macmillan Co. of Canada, Ltd.

TOKYO
Maruzen-Kabushiki-Kaisha

All rights reserved

THE LAWS OF THE KINGS OF ENGLAND FROM EDMUND TO HENRY I

Edited and Translated

by

A. J. ROBERTSON, M.A.

CAMBRIDGE
AT THE UNIVERSITY PRESS
1925

CAMBRIDGE UNIVERSITY PRESS
Cambridge, New York, Melbourne, Madrid, Cape Town, Singapore,
São Paulo, Delhi, Dubai, Tokyo

Cambridge University Press
The Edinburgh Building, Cambridge CB2 8RU, UK

Published in the United States of America by Cambridge University Press, New York

www.cambridge.org
Information on this title: www.cambridge.org/9780521153195

© Cambridge University Press 1925

This publication is in copyright. Subject to statutory exception
and to the provisions of relevant collective licensing agreements,
no reproduction of any part may take place without the written
permission of Cambridge University Press.

First published 1925
This digitally printed version 2009

A catalogue record for this publication is available from the British Library

ISBN 978-0-521-15319-5 Paperback

Cambridge University Press has no responsibility for the persistence or
accuracy of URLs for external or third-party internet websites referred to in
this publication, and does not guarantee that any content on such websites is,
or will remain, accurate or appropriate.

PREFACE

THIS edition of *The Laws of the Kings of England from Edmund to Henry I* has been prepared on the same plan as the preceding volume, *The Laws of the Earliest English Kings*, edited and translated by F. L. Attenborough, Cambridge, 1922. It was at first intended to include in it only the laws of the later Anglo-Saxon period, but it was afterwards thought advisable to add those of William I and Henry I (including the compilation known as the *Leis Willelme*) because of their intimate connection with the period immediately preceding.

In the preparation of this edition much assistance has been derived from Professor Liebermann's monumental work, *Die Gesetze der Angelsachsen*, Halle, 1903–16, and I take this opportunity of expressing my indebtedness to it. In the division and numbering of the sections I have almost invariably followed his example, and I have seldom had occasion to correct his readings; in only one case (I Edgar 2; see Notes) is the interpretation of a passage affected thereby. His work has superseded all previous editions. I have, however, made considerable use of Schmid's second edition, *Die Gesetze der Angelsachsen*, Leipzig, 1858, and have occasionally preferred his interpretation of a passage to that given by Liebermann.

It has been impossible within the limits of a small volume such as this to enter into a detailed discussion of disputed points, and in many cases I have been unable to do more than give references to the work of Liebermann and other authorities on the period. Readers who desire to make a more detailed study are referred to Liebermann's edition which is indispensable for such questions as the history of the texts and their relationship with one another, as well as for the terminology of the laws and Anglo-Saxon legal antiquities in general.

As the preparation of this edition was begun in Cambridge I decided to take as much of my text as possible from the manuscripts most easily accessible, namely those in Corpus Christi College. In addition I have collated the manuscripts in the

British Museum; and in all cases I have examined the originals of the texts given here except those derived from MSS Christina Regina 946 in the Vatican, Rome, and Holkham 228. For the latter, which was unfortunately inaccessible to me, I am indebted to Liebermann's edition and to Matzke, *Les Lois de Guillaume le Conquérant en français et en latin*, 1899; for the former to Liebermann's edition alone.

My thanks are due to all those who have kindly allowed me to consult the manuscripts required at Corpus Christi College, Cambridge, the Bodleian Library and Corpus Christi College, Oxford, Rochester Cathedral, York Minster, St Paul's Cathedral, the John Rylands Library, Manchester, and Keswick Hall, Norwich.

I desire likewise to express my thanks to the Carnegie Trust for their award of a Research Scholarship which I held at Girton College, Cambridge; also to the Syndics of the University Press for undertaking the publication of the book and to the staff for the care with which both the printing and the corrections have been carried out. I am also under great obligations to Mr Attenborough and all those who have helped me in the preparation of this edition. I wish most particularly to express my gratitude to Professor and Mrs Chadwick for their generous assistance; without their inspiration and help it would have been impossible for me to complete such a piece of work.

A. J. R.

February, 1925.

CONTENTS

	PAGE
PREFACE	v
LIST OF ABBREVIATIONS	ix
THE LAWS OF EDMUND AND OF EDGAR	1
Introduction	3
I Edmund	6
II ,,	8
III ,,	12
I Edgar	16
II ,,	20
III ,,	24
IV ,,	28
PROMISSIO REGIS	
Introduction	40
Text	42
THE LAWS OF ÆTHELRED	45
Introduction	47
I Æthelred	52
II ,,	56
III ,,	64
IV ,,	70
V ,,	78
VI ,,	90
VII ,,	108
VII ,, (A.-S.)	114
VIII ,,	116
IX, X ,,	130
THE LAWS OF CANUTE	135
Introduction	137
Proclamation of 1020	140
,, ,, 1027	146
I Canute	154
II ,,	174

CONTENTS

	PAGE
THE LAWS OF WILLIAM I AND OF HENRY I . . .	221
Introduction	223
William I: London Charter	230
Regulations regarding Exculpation . . .	232
Episcopal Laws	234
Ten Articles	238
Articuli Retractati	244
The (so-called) Laws of William I	252
Henry I: Coronation Charter	276
Decree concerning the Coinage	284
Decree concerning the County and Hundred Courts	286
London Charter	288
NOTES:	
To the Laws of Edmund and of Edgar . . .	295
To the Coronation Oath	311
To the Laws of Æthelred	312
To the Laws of Canute	343
To the Laws of William I and of Henry I . .	360
INDEX	376

LIST OF ABBREVIATIONS

1. **Anglo-Saxon Manuscripts.** (See Liebermann, I. p. xviii ff.)
    A......British Museum, Harley 55.
        f. 3 b. II, III Edg.; f. 5. I, II Cn.
    B......Corpus Christi College, Cambridge, 383.
        p. 2. I Edg.; p. 3. I Atr.; p. 43. I, II Cn. (beginning at I 14, 2);
        p. 78. I, II Edm.; p. 88. II Atr.
    C......Corpus Christi College, Cambridge, 265.
        p. 222. IV Edg.
    Cp ...British Museum, Cotton Cleopatra B XIII.
        f. 56. Cor. Oath.
    D......Corpus Christi College, Cambridge, 201.
        p. 30. VII Atr.; p. 46. II, III Edg.; p. 48. V Atr.; p. 93. VIII Atr.;
        p. 96. I Edm.; p. 126. Fragments of I, II Cn.; p. 128. VI Atr.
        16–49.
    F......British Museum, Cotton Nero E I.
        f. 185 b. IV Edg.
    G......British Museum, Cotton Nero A I.
        f. 1. I, II Cn.; f. 41. II, III Edg.; f. 87 b. I Edm. Pre.; f. 88.
        III Edg. (G_2); f. 89. V Atr.; f. 95 b. VIII Atr., 1–5; f. 116 b.
        V Atr. (G_2).
    H......Textus Roffensis, Rochester Cathedral.
        f. 44. I, II Edm.; f. 46. 1 Atr.; f. 47. Wl. lad; f. 48. III Atr.
    Ju ...Oxford Bodley, Junius 60.
        Cor. Oath copied from British Museum, Cotton Vitellius A VII.
    K......British Museum, Cotton Claudius A III.
        f. 33 b. VI Atr.
    Vr. ...Vatican, Rome, Christina regina 946.
        f. 75 b. X Atr.
    York..Minster Library, Eleventh Century Gospels and other documents.
        f. 152. Cn. 1020.

2. **Latin Manuscripts.**
    (a) Containing the Quadripartitus.
        Rs......John Rylands Library, Manchester, 155 (formerly 174).
        K ......British Museum, Cotton Claudius D II.
        Co......Corpus Christi College, Cambridge, 70.
        Or......Oriel College, Oxford, 46.
    These four compose the 'London' group (see Liebermann, I. p. xxxiv s.v. *Lond.*) and represent the earliest form of the Quadripartitus (see *ibid.* pp. xxxviii, 529).

2. Latin Manuscripts, *continued.*
   (*a*) Containing the Quadripartitus, *continued.*
   Dm ...British Museum, Cotton Domitian VIII.
   R ......British Museum, Regius 11, B II.
   T ......British Museum, Cotton Titus A XXVII.
   These three form a group.
   Br ......'Johannis Brompton Jorevallensis Chronicon' (see Liebermann, I. p. xix), preserved in two fifteenth century MSS—Corpus Christi College, Cambridge, 96 and British Museum, Tiberius C XIII.
   Hk......Holkham 228, the property of the Earl of Leicester.
   M ......Macro, the property of the Gurney family at Keswick Hall, near Norwich.
   These three also form a group.

   (*b*) Containing the Tripartita (see Liebermann, I. p. xli).
   Ba......The property of the Marquess of Bath.
   Cb......Bibliothèque Nationale, Paris, Lat. 4771.
   Gr......Gray's Inn, London, 9.
   Hv ...Chronica Rogeri de Hoveden.
   Hy ...British Museum, Harley 1348.
   La......London Lambeth, 179.
   Lb......London Lambeth, 118.
   Pe......Swaffham's Register, Peterborough Cathedral.
   Ph......Phillipps MS 8079, now Cambridge University, 3392.
   Ra......British Museum, Regius 13 A XVIII.
   Rc......British Museum, Regius 13 C II.
   Va......Vatican, Rome, Christina regina 587.
   Vi ......British Museum, Cotton Vitellius A XIII.
   A later version is found in Rs, K_2 (Cotton Claudius D II), Co, Or.

   (*c*) Miscellaneous.
   Ce ....Corpus Christi College, Cambridge, 476.
         f. 160. Hn. Lond.
   Cust ......Liber Custumarum, Guildhall, London.
         f. 13 b. Hn. cor.; f. 14 b. and f. 187. Hn. Lond.
   El ....Liber Albus, Guildhall, London.
         f. 40. Excerptum from Hn. Lond.
   E IV......Patent roll of a. 2 Edward IV, pt 5, Public Record Office, London.
         Inspeximus of Hn. Lond.
   Gl ....Registrum episcopatus Glasguensis.
         f. 25. Hn. cor.
   H ....See above.
         f. 80. Wl. art.; f. 96. Hn. cor.

LIST OF ABBREVIATIONS

2. Latin Manuscripts, *continued*.
    (c) Miscellaneous, *continued*.
    - Hg.........British Museum, Hargrave 313.
        f. 99. Wl. art. retr.; Wl. lad; Hn. cor.; f. 100. Hn. mon.; Hn. com.
    - Hl.........British Museum, Harley 458.
        f. 1. Hn. cor.
    - Horn......Liber Horn, Guildhall, London.
        f. 205 b and 362. Wl. Lond.; f. 362 b. Hn. Lond.
    - Insp.......Rot. Inspeximus Chartarum, Public Record Office, London.
        Ann. 1378. Wl. ep.
    - Lc.........Registrum Antiquissimum Remigii, Lincoln Cathedral.
        f. 1 and 9. Wl. ep.
    - Lp.........Liber pilosus S. Pauli cathedralis Londoniensis.
        f. 1. Wl. ep.
    - Ox.........Corpus Christi College, Oxford, 157.
        p. 329. Cn. 1027.
    - Rl.........Oxford Bodley, Rawlinson C 641.
        f. 43. Hn. cor.; f. 44. Wl. art.
    - S ....British Museum, Harley 746.
        f. 55 b. Leis Wl.; f. 59. Hn. cor.
    - Sc.........Scaccarii Liber Rubeus, Public Record Office, London.
        f. 162 b. Wl. art. retr.; f. 163. Wl. lad; f. 163 b. Hn. cor., Hn. mon.; f. 164. Hn. com.

3. Anglo-French Manuscripts.
    - Cu ......Cambridge University Ee I. 1.
        f. 3. Wl. art. (French version).
    - Hk......See above.
        f. 141. Leis Wl. (incomplete).

4. Editions (see Liebermann, I. p. xlv f.)
    - Ld...............William Lambarde Αρχαιονομια (London, 1568) republished with additions by A. Wheelock (Cambridge, 1644).
    - Wilkins ......*Leges Anglo-Saxonicae*, edited by D. Wilkins (London, 1721).
    - Price } ......An edition of the Laws prepared for the Commissioners of the Public Records by Richard Price but left unfinished at his death and completed by B. Thorpe; published under the title of *Ancient Laws and Institutes of England* (London, 1840). The references are to the octavo edition.
    - Thorpe

xii LIST OF ABBREVIATIONS

4. Editions, *continued*.
    Schmid.........*Die Gesetze der Angelsachsen* by R. Schmid, 1st Edition, Leipzig, 1832; 2nd Edition, 1858. The references are to the second edition.
    Liebermann...*Die Gesetze der Angelsachsen* by F. Liebermann (Halle, 1903–1916).

5. Names of Kings.
    A. & G....Alfred and Guthrum.
    Abt. ....Æthelbert.
    Af. ...... Alfred.
    As..........Æthelstan.
    Atr. ....Æthelred.
    Cn. ......Canute.
        Cn. 1020... Canute's Proclamation of 1020.
        Cn. 1027... Canute's Proclamation of 1027.
        Cons. ......Consiliatio Cnuti.
        Inst..........Instituta Cnuti.
    E. & G....Edward and Guthrum.
    Edg. ......Edgar.
    Edm.......Edmund.
    Edw.......Edward.
    ECf. ......Edward the Confessor.
    Hl..........Hlothhere and Eadric.
    Hn. ......Henry I.
        Hn. com. ...Decree of Henry I concerning the County and Hundred Courts.
        Hn. cor. ...Coronation Charter of Henry I.
        Hn. Lond....London Charter of Henry I.
        Hn. mon. ...Decree of Henry I concerning the Coinage.
    In. ...Ine.
    Wi....Wihtred.
    Wl....William I.
        Wl. art. ....The Ten Articles of Wm I.
        Wl. art. retr....Willelmi articuli retractati.
        Wl. ep. ....The Episcopal Laws of Wm I.
        Wl. lad ....Regulations regarding Exculpation.
        Wl. Lond. ......The London Charter of Wm I.
        Leis Wl..........The Laws of Wm I.

6. Legal Documents.
    Að............*Be Mirciscan Aðe.*
    Be Blas......*Be Blaserum and be Morðslihtum.*
    Be Griðe ...*Be Griðe and be Munde.*
    Be Wer. ...*Be Wergilde.*

LIST OF ABBREVIATIONS xiii

6. Legal Documents, *continued.*
   Duns. ......Ordinance with regard to the *Dunsæte.*
   Episcopus...De Officio Episcopi.
   Geþyncðo ...*Be Leode Geþincðum.*
   Had. ....*Hadbot.*
   Jud. Dei ...*Judicium Dei.*
   Lib. Lond....Libertas Londoniensis.
   N.P.L. ......*Norðhymbra Preosta Lagu.*

7. Miscellaneous.
   Birch ....Birch, *Cartularium Saxonicum.*
   Brunner ....Brunner, *Deutsche Rechtsgeschichte.*
   BT. ....Bosworth and Toller, *Anglo-Saxon Dictionary.*
   Davis, *Reg. Agnorm.* ....Davis, *Regesta Regum Anglo-Normannorum.*
   DB ....Domesday Book.
   Du Cange........................Du Cange, *Glossarium.*
   E.H.R. ....English Historical Review.
   H.L.R. ....Harvard Law Review.
   Kemble ....Kemble, *Codex Diplomaticus Aevi Saxonici.*
   P. and M.........................Pollock and Maitland, *History of English Law.*
   Stubbs, *Reg. Sacr. Anglic.*....Stubbs, *Registrum Sacrum Anglicanum,* Second Edition.
   Thorpe, *Dipl.* ....Thorpe, *Diplomatarium Aevi Saxonici.*

THE LAWS OF EDMUND AND OF EDGAR

THE LAWS OF EDMUND

THREE SERIES of laws issued by Edmund are extant. Earlier editors, following MSS H and B, regarded I and II Edmund as parts of the same code (cf. II and III Edgar, I and II Canute), but Schmid pointed out that in MS D only I Edmund is given, and Liebermann, arguing from internal evidence (e.g. the existence of a special preamble for II Edmund where the king's name is repeated; see further *Gesetze*, III. p. 125), also supports the view that they are two separate codes.

I Edmund was promulgated at a Council which met at London at Easter. The year cannot be exactly determined, but the earliest possible date, as Liebermann points out, seems to be 942; for it was in that year that Oda became Archbishop of Canterbury (see Stubbs, *Registr. Sacr. Angl.* p. 25). In the year 943 Archbishop Wulfstan supported Anlaf (see *Sax. Chr.* D), but his signature is again affixed to royal documents in 944 (see Kemble, Nos. 399–402; Birch, Nos. 791 f., 794 f., 798 f.), 945 (Birch, 803, 807) and 946 (Kemble, 406, 409; Birch, 816). The code must be referred therefore to the years 942 or 944–6. It is distinctly ecclesiastical in tone and suggests comparison with the *Constitutiones Odonis* (Spelman, *Concilia* I. pp. 415 ff.).

II Edmund offers no evidence as to the time or place of its promulgation. It is notable for its regulations with regard to vendetta, and seems to be closely connected with the fragment entitled *Be Wergilde* (see Notes).

III Edmund likewise contains no indication as to its date, but it was promulgated at *Culinton*, i.e. probably Colyton in Devonshire (see Notes). An oath of allegiance to the king is demanded from all his subjects. It contains also various regulations with regard to theft, the tracking of unknown cattle etc., which are based upon earlier laws, especially II Edward and II–VI Æthelstan.

I Edmund is contained in MSS D (C.C.C. 201), H (Textus Roffensis) and B (C.C.C. 383) as well as in Lambarde's edition and in the Quadripartitus. Part of the preamble is also found in G (Brit. Mus. Cotton Nero A 1). II is found in H and B, in Lambarde's edition and in the Quadripartitus, while III has been preserved only in the Quadripartitus. For the relationship of the various MSS see Liebermann, III. pp. 124, 126, 128.

THE LAWS OF EDGAR

King Edgar is definitely named in the preambles to two series of laws, the first of which consists of two codes, an ecclesiastical and a secular. A fourth code dealing with the administration of the hundred is in general attributed to him also, and referred to as I Edgar. No king's name is mentioned in it, but it is obviously later than the time of Edmund (cf. cap. 2).

The only one of these codes which can be dated with any certainty is IV Edgar. The references which it contains to a severe plague and to Æthelwine and Oslac suggest that it belongs to the year 962 or 963 (see Notes and Liebermann, III. p. 138). Internal evidence (see Notes) shows that it was preceded in time by II and III Edgar, and also by the code to which the title I Edgar is given.

The evidence adduced for attributing this nameless code to Edgar is fully stated and discussed by Liebermann (see III. pp. 130–1). He draws attention to the injunction in III Edg. 5 that the hundred court shall be attended "as has been previously ordained," and notes the connection between III Edg. 7, 1 and cap. 2, 1 of the nameless code. He points out also the entire lack of evidence for the promulgation of any codes of law by either Edred or Edwig, but acknowledges the scantiness of the sources for such evidence. The fact that in IV cap. 2 *a* Edgar refers to the prerogatives of his father, and makes no mention of his immediate predecessors, is a further, though not very strong, argument in support of the view that neither of these two kings issued any laws. His conclusion, however, is that this nameless code can be dated for certain only between the years 946 and about 961. With the exception of the last two clauses (see Notes) the regulations bear upon the administration of the hundred.

The code divided by editors into II and III Edgar was apparently promulgated at Andover (cf. IV Edg. 1, 4). II deals exclusively with ecclesiastical affairs and particularly with the payment of church dues. It shows resemblances to passages in the so-called Canons enacted under King Edgar (see Thorpe, *Anc. Laws*, II. pp. 244–288). III draws a good deal upon earlier laws, especially I and II Edward and I and II Æthelstan. It contains definite and clearly stated regulations regarding the administration of justice, the meetings of the borough and county courts, the general employment of the surety system, and the establishment of uniform weights and measures.

IV is described not as a *gerædnis* but as a *gewrit* and was issued at a place called *Wihtbordesstan* which has not been satisfactorily identified (see Liebermann, III. p. 139). The style of the code is noteworthy, especially in the first part which deals with ecclesiastical affairs and reads like a homily. The secular half assures autonomy to the Danes, but at the same time enforces the observance of certain regulations in every part of the realm. The secular decrees of Edgar are as a whole notably progressive.

Three copies of I are extant, namely an A.S. text in MS B and two Latin translations in the Quadripartitus and the Consiliatio Cnuti respectively. II and III are preserved in MSS G, A (Brit. Mus. Harley 55), D, in Lambarde's edition and in Somner's transcript, while a Latin translation is found in the Quadripartitus, and a few clauses appear in the Instituta Cnuti. Two A.S. copies of IV are extant in MSS F (Brit. Mus. Cotton Nero E 1) and C (C.C.C. 265, p. 222), both dating from about 1030–60, while a Latin version which follows C is found also in C.C.C. 265, p. 217. For the relationship between the various texts see Liebermann, III. pp. 130, 133 f., 138.

The following text has been taken from MS D in the case of I Edm., II and III Edg.; from MS B in the case of II Edm. and I Edg.; and from MS C in the case of IV Edg.

I EDMUND

Her onginneð Eadmundes gerædnes[1].

Eadmund cyngc gesamnode micelne sinoð to Lundenbirig on ða halgan easterlican tíd ægðer ge godcundra háda ge worldcundra; ðar wæs Óda arcebiscop[2] 7 Wulfstan arcebiscop 7 manega oðre biscopas smeagende ymbon heora sawla ræd[3] 7 þara þe him underþeodde wæron.

1. [Be gehadeda manna clænnisse.][4]

Ðæt is æres[t][5] þæt hi budon[6], þæt þa halgan hadas þe Godes folc læron sculon lifes bisne, ðæt hi heora clænnesse healdan be heora hade, swa werhades swa wifhades, swa hwaðer swa hit sy. 7 gif hi swa ne don, þonne syn hi þæs wyrðe þe on ðam canone cweð, and þæt[7] hi þolian worldæhta 7 gehalgodre legerstowe, buton hi gebetan.

2. [Be teoþungum 7 cyricsceatum.]

Teoðunge we bebeodað ælcum Cristene[8] men be his Cristendóme, and ciricsceat 7 Romfeoh 7 sulhælmessan[9]. And gif hit hwa don nelle, si he amansumod.

3. [Be monslihte.]

Gif hwa Cristenes mannes blód ageote, ne cume he na on ðæs cyninges neawiste[10], ær he on dædbote ga, swa him biscop tæce 7 his scrift him wisige.

4. [Be nunna hæmede 7 forlygre.]

Se þe wið nunnan hæme, gehalgodre legerstowe ne sy he wyrðe—buton he gebete—þe ma þe manslaga; þæt ilce we cwædon be æwbrice.

5. [Be cyricena gebetunge.]

Eac we gecwædon, þæt ælc biscop béte Godes hus on his agenum, 7 eac þone cyningc minegige, þæt ealle Godes circan syn wel behworfene[11], swa us micel þearf is.

6. [Be mánsworum 7 liblacum.]

Ða ðe mansweriað 7 liblac wyrcað beon[12] hi a fram ælcum Godes dæle aworpene, buton hi to rihtre dædbote gecirran þe geornor[13].

---

[1] *Eadmundes cyninges asetnysse* H; om. B.   [2] Om. H, B, Ld.
[3] *saul ared* B; *sawla ared* Ld.
[4] The Rubrics in this code are found in Ld. only.   [5] H, B; *æres* D.
[6] *þ. h. b.* om. H, B, Ld.   [7] *cwæð: ðæt is* H, B, Ld.   [8] *Cristenum* H, B, Ld.
[9] *c. 7 ælmesfeoh* H, B, Ld.   [10] *ánsyne* H; *neawæste, gyf he cyninges man sy* B, Ld.
[11] *behweorfene* H; *behwofene* B; *behofene* Ld.
[12] *syn* H, B, Ld.   [13] *þ. g.* om. H, B, Ld.

I EDMUND

Here begins Edmund's ordinance.

King Edmund has convened at London, during the holy season of Easter, a great assembly both of the ecclesiastical and secular estates. Archbishop Oda[1] and Archbishop Wulfstan[2] and many other bishops have there been taking counsel for the welfare of their [own] souls and [the souls] of those who have been placed under their charge.

1. This is their first injunction: that those in holy orders whose duty it is to teach God's people by the example of their life[1] should observe the celibacy befitting their estate, whether they be men or women. If they fail to do so, they shall incur that which is ordained in the canon, and[2] they shall forfeit their worldly possessions and burial in consecrated ground, unless they make amends.

2. We enjoin upon every Christian man, in accordance with his Christian profession, to pay tithes[1] and church-dues[2] and Peter's Pence and plough-alms[3]. And if anyone refuses to do so, he shall be excommunicated.

3. If anyone sheds the blood of a Christian man[1], he shall not come anywhere near[2] the king[3] until he proceeds to do penance, as the bishop appoints for him or[4] his confessor directs him.

4 He who has intercourse with a nun, unless he make amends, shall not be allowed burial in consecrated ground any more than a homicide. We have decreed the same with regard to adultery.

5. Likewise we have ordained that every bishop shall restore[1] the houses of God on his own property[2], and also exhort the king that all God's churches be well put in order, as we have much need [that they be].

6. Those who commit perjury[1] and practise sorcery[2] shall be cast out for ever from the fellowship of God[3], unless they proceed with special zeal to undertake the prescribed penance.

II EDMUND

Eadmund cyning cyð eallum folce, ge yldrum ge gingrum, ðe on his anwealde syn[1], ðæt ic smeade mid minra witena geðeahte, ge god[cund]ra hada[2] ge læwedra, ærest, hu ic mæhte Cristendomes mest aræran.

§ 1. Ðonne ðuhte us ærest mæst ðearf, þæt we ure gesibsumnesse 7 geþwærnesse fæstlicost us betweonan heoldan gynd ealne minne anwald. Me egleð swyðe 7 us eallum ða unrihtlican 7 mænigfealdan gefeoht ðe betwux us sylfum syndun; ðonne cwæde we:

1. [Be manslihte.][3]
Gif hwa heonanforð ænigne man ofslea, þæt he wege sylf ða fæhðe, butan he hy[4] mid freonda fylste binnan twelf monðum forgylde be fullan were, sy swa boren swa he sy.

§ 1. Gyf hine ðonne seo mægð forlæte 7 him foregyldan nellen, ðonne wille ic þæt eal seo mægð sy unfah, butan ðam hand[d]ædan[5], gif[6] hy him syððan ne doð mete ne munde.

§ 2. Gif ðonne syððan hwilc his maga hine feormie, ðonne beo he scyldig ealles ðæs þe he age wið ðone cyning, 7 wege ða fæhðe wið þa mægðe, forðam hi hine forsocan ær.

§ 3. Gyf ðonne[7] of ðære [oðre][8] mægðe hwa wrace do on ænigum oðrum men butan on ðam rihthanddædan, sy he gefah wið ðone cyning 7 wið ealle his frynd 7 ðolie ealles ðæs he age.

2. [Be ðon ðe mon oþerne on cyricean gesece oþþe on cyninges burh.]
Gif hwa cyrcan gesece oððe mine burh 7 hine man ðær sece oððe yflige—ða ðe ðæt don[9] syn ðæs ylcon scyldige ðe hit her beforan cweð.

3. [Be fyhtwite 7 manbote.]
7 ic nelle þæt ænig fyhtewite oððe manbot[10] forgifen sy.

---

[1] synd H. [2] godra hada B, Ld; hadedra H.
[3] The Rubrics in this code are found in Ld. only. [4] him Ld.
[5] H; handædan B, Ld. [6] 7 hi Ld.
[7] hwa ðonne on ðær mægþ wræce dô Ld.
[8] H. [9] doð H. [10] H; manbote B, Ld.

II EDMUND

I, King Edmund[1], inform all people, both high and low[2], who are under my authority, that I have been considering, with the advice of my councillors both ecclesiastical and lay, first of all how I could best promote Christianity[3].

§ 1. Now, it has seemed to us first of all especially needful that we steadfastly maintain peace and concord among ourselves throughout all my dominion. I myself and all of us are greatly distressed by the manifold illegal deeds of violence which are in our midst[1]. We have therefore decreed:

1. Henceforth, if anyone slay a man, he shall himself [alone] bear the vendetta, unless with the help of his friends he pay composition for it, within twelve months[1], to the full amount of the slain man's wergeld, according to his inherited rank.

    § 1. If, however, his kindred abandon him and will not pay compensation on his behalf, it is my will that, if afterwards they give him neither food nor shelter[1], all the kindred, except the delinquent, shall be free from vendetta.

    § 2. If, however, any of his kinsmen harbour him thereafter, then, inasmuch as they had previously disclaimed him, that kinsman shall forfeit all his property to the king, and shall incur vendetta with the kin [of the slain man].

    § 3. If, however, anyone from the other kindred take vengeance on any man other than the actual delinquent, he shall incur the hostility of the king and of all his friends[1], and shall suffer the loss of all that he possesses.

2[1]. If anyone flees [for sanctuary] to a church or to my premises[2], and anyone attacks or injures him there, those who do so shall incur the penalty[3] which has already been stated.

3. My will is that no fine for fighting[1] or compensation for a slain dependent[2] be remitted.

II EDMUND

4. [Be blodgeote.]

Eac ic cyðe, þæt ic nelle socne habban [þone ðe mannes blod geote]¹ to minum hirede, ær he hæbbe g[od]cunde² bote underfangen³ 7 wið ða mægðe gebet⁴—on bote befangen— 7 to ælcum rihte gebogen, swa biscop him tæce ðe hit on his scyre sy.

5. [Þæncunge ðæm ðe wið ðyfþe fylstaþ.]

Eac ic ðancie Gode 7 eow eallum, ðe me fylston⁵, ðæs friðes ðe we nu habbað æt ðam ðyfðam⁶; ðonne gelyfe ic to eow, þæt ge willan fylstan to ðyssum swa micle bet, swa us is eallum mare ðearf ðæt hit gehealden sy.

6. [Be mundbryce 7 hamsocne.]

Eac we cwædon be mundbryce 7 be hamsocnum: se ðe hit ofer ðis do, þæt he þolie ealles ðæs he age 7 sy on cyniges dome hwæðer he lif age.

7. [Be fæhþe.]

Witan scylon fæhðe sectan⁷: ærest æfter folcrihte slaga⁸ sceal his forspecan⁹ on hand syllan 7 se forspeca magum, þæt se slaga wille betan wið mægðe.

§ 1. Ðonne syððan gebyreð þæt man sylle ðæs slagan forspecan on hand, þæt se slaga mote mid griðe nyr 7 sylf wæres¹⁰ weddian.

§ 2. Ðonne he ðæs beweddad hæbbe, ðone finde he ðærto wæreborh.

§ 3. Ðonne þæt gedon sy, ðonne rære man cyninges munde; of ðam dæge on XXI nihton gylde man healsfang; ðæs on XXI nihton manbote; ðæs on XXI nihton¹¹ ðæs weres ðæt frumgyld.

---

[1] Om. B, H; *þon ðe m. b. geate* Ld. [2] H, Ld; *gec.* B. [3] H, Ld; *-gan* B.
[4] *ðam ægðe gebet* B; *þā ægðer gebet* H; *ðæm mægðe gebete* Ld.
[5] *wel f.* H. [6] *æt ð. ðyfþe gesette* Ld. [7] *settan* Ld.
[8] Ld; *-rihtes laga* B, H. [9] *forspræcan* Ld. [10] *weres* Ld.
[11] *nih'* B; *niht* H, Ld.

CAP. 4–7   11

4¹. Further, I declare that I forbid anyone [who commits homicide]² to have right of access³ to my household, until he has undertaken to make amends as the church requires, and has made—or set about making⁴—reparation to the kin, and has submitted to every legal penalty prescribed by the bishop in whose diocese it is.

5¹. Further, I thank God and all of you, who have given me full support, for the immunity from thefts which we now enjoy. I therefore confidently expect of you, that you will be all the more willing to give your support towards this [maintenance of the public peace]², in proportion as its observance is a more urgent matter for us all.

6. Further, with respect to violation of [the king's]¹ 'mund' and attacks on a man's house², we have ordained that he who commits either of these after this shall forfeit all that he possesses, and it shall be for the king to decide whether his life shall be preserved.

7¹. The authorities² must put a stop to³ vendettas. First, according to public law, the slayer shall give security to⁴ his advocate⁵, and the advocate to the kinsmen [of the slain man], that he (the slayer) will make reparation to the kindred.

§ 1. After that it is incumbent upon the kin of the slain man to give security to the slayer's advocate, that he (the slayer) may approach¹ under safe-conduct² and pledge himself to pay the wergeld.

§ 2. When he has pledged himself to this, he shall find a surety for the payment of the wergeld.

§ 3. When that is done, the king's 'mund'¹ shall be established. In twenty-one days from that time *healsfang*² shall be paid; in twenty-one days after that 'manbot' (the compensation due to the slain man's lord), and twenty-one days after that the first instalment of the wergeld.

III EDMUND[1]

[2][I. De juratione[3] quae fiebat Eadmundo regi. II. De fure[4]. III. Qui[5] alterius hominem receperit vel ad dampnum aliquem manutenuerit. IIII. De servo fure. V. Ignotum[6] pecus non emendum sine testimonio. VI. De investigando pecore furato. VII. Ut quisque[7] suos faciat credibiles; et de infamatis; et de eis[8] qui haec praecepta negligunt.]

Haec est institutio quam Eadmundus rex et episcopi sui cum sapientibus suis instituerunt apud Culintonam de pace et juramento faciendo[9].

1. Imprimis, ut omnes jurent in nomine Domini, pro quo sanctum[9] illud sanctum est, fidelitatem Eadmundo regi, sicut homo debet esse fidelis domino suo, sine omni controversia et seductione[10], in manifesto, in occulto, et[11] in amando quod amabit, nolendo quod nolet; et[12] a die qua[13] juramentum hoc dabitur, ut nemo concelet hoc in fratre vel proximo suo plus quam in extraneo.

2. Vult etiam, ut ubi fur pro certo cognoscetur, twelfhindi et twihindi[14] consocientur et exuperent eum[15] vivum vel mortuum, alterutrum quod poterunt; et qui aliquem eorum infaidiabit qui in ea quaestione fuerint[16], sit inimicus regis et omnium amicorum eius[17]; et si quis adire negaverit et coadjuvare nolit, emendet regi cxx s.—vel secundum hoc perneget quod nescivit—et hundreto xxx s.

3. Et nolo ut aliquis recipiat alterius hominem, priusquam quietus sit erga omnem manum quae[18] rectum quaerat ab eo; et qui aliquem manutenebit et firmabit ad dampnum faciendum, custodiat, ut repraesentet eum ad emendandum, vel ipse componat quod alius componere debebat[19].

---

[1] *Instituta regis Ædmundi suorumque hic incipiunt* T.
[2] This table of contents is found in M, Hk, Br but not in T.
[3] *sacramento fidelitatis regi Edmundo faciendo* Br.
[4] *furibus capiendis* Br.   [5] *De illo qui* Br.
[6] *De illis qui emunt ignota pecora s. t.* Br.   [7] *Quisquis homines suos* Br.
[8] *haec p. negligentibus* Br.   [9] Om. T.   [10] *seditione* Br.   [11] Om. Br.
[12] Om. M, T.   [13] *ad te qua* M, *quam* Hk; *antequam* Br.
[14] *et twih.* om. Hk; *twifhindi* M, Br; *twifhyndi* T.   [15] *eum in* T.
[16] *fuerit* T.   [17] *eorum* M, Hk, Br.   [18] *qui* T.   [19] *debeat* Hk, *Br*.

III EDMUND

These are the provisions for the preservation of public peace[1] and the swearing of allegiance which have been instituted at Colyton[2] by King Edmund and his bishops, together with his councillors.

1. In the first place, all shall swear in the name of the Lord, before whom that holy thing is holy[1], that they will be faithful to King Edmund[2], even as it behoves a man to be faithful to his lord, without any dispute or dissension[3], openly or in secret[4], favouring what he favours and discountenancing what he discountenances[5]. And from the day on which[6] this oath shall be rendered, let no-one conceal the breach of it in a brother or a relation of his, any more than in a stranger.

2[1]. Further, it is his will, that where a man is proved to be a thief, nobles and commoners shall unite and seize him, alive or dead, whichever they can. And he who institutes a vendetta against any of those who have been concerned in that pursuit shall incur the hostility of the king and of all his friends[2], and if anyone shall refuse to come forward and lend his assistance, he shall pay 120 shillings to the king[3]— or deny knowledge of the affair by an oath of equivalent value—and 30 shillings to the hundred[4].

3[1]. And it is my will that no-one receive [into his service] one who has been in the service of another man, until he be quit [of all charges preferred against him] from any quarter where justice is sought from him; and he who shall support and harbour anyone who perpetrates crime[2] shall see to it that[3] he bring him to make compensation, or shall himself pay what is due from the other.

4. Et dictum est[1] de servis: si qui[2] furentur[3], senior ex eis capiatur et occidatur vel suspendatur, et aliorum singuli verberentur ter et extoppentur[4], et truncetur minimus digitus in signum.

5. Et nemo barganniet vel ignotum pecus recipiat qui non habeat testimonium summi praepositi vel sacerdotis vel hordarii[5] vel portirevae.

6. Et dictum est de investigatione[6] et quaesitione [pecoris furati][7], ut[8] ad villam pervestigetur, et non sit foristeallum aliquod[9] illi vel aliqua prohibitio itineris vel quaestionis.

§ 1. Et si vestigium illud de terra illa[10] non possit educi, quaeratur ubicunque suspectum fuerit ac dubium.

§ 2. Et si aliquis accusetur illic, adlegiet se sicut ad hoc pertinebit, et [stet ipsum pro superjuramento. Et qui quaesitionem huiusmodi prohibebit][11] reddat captale et regi cxx s. Et si quis refragaverit et[12] resistat et rectum facere nolit, emendet regi cxx s.

7. Et omnis homo credibiles faciat homines suos et omnes qui in pace et terra sua sunt.

§ 1. Et omnes infamati et accusationibus ingravati sub plegio redigantur.

§ 2. Et praepositus vel tainus, comes vel villanus, qui hoc facere nolet aut[13] disperdet, emendet cxx sol. et sit dignus eorum quae supra dicta[14] sunt.

---

[1] *d. e.* om. Br.   [2] *qui si* M, Hk; *qui* om. T.   [3] *f. simul ut* T.
[4] M, Hk; *-torp-* Br; *-top-* T.   [5] *ordalii* M, Hk, Br.
[6] *vestigatione* Hk, T.   [7] Om. M, Hk, T.   [8] Hk, Br, T; *non* M.
[9] Hk, Br, T; *-quid* M.   [10] *ipsa* T.   [11] Om. M, Hk, Br.
[12] *vel* T.   [13] *ad* M, Hk; *ac* T.   [14] *qui s. dicti* T.

4. And we have declared with regard to slaves that, if a number of them commit theft, their leader shall be captured and slain, or hanged, and each of the others shall be scourged three times and have his scalp removed[1] and his little finger mutilated as a token of his guilt.

5[1]. And no-one shall make a purchase or receive strange cattle unless he has as witness the high-reeve or the priest or the treasurer or the town-reeve[2].

6. And we have declared with regard to the tracking and pursuit of stolen cattle, that thorough investigation shall be made at the village[1], and that no obstacle shall be placed in the way thereof[2] or anything to prevent the pursuit and search[3].

§ 1[1]. And if the track cannot be followed beyond the bounds of that estate, search shall be made wherever suspicion or doubt attaches.

§ 2. And if anyone is accused there, he shall clear himself in the manner required by the case, and the track shall serve as an oath[1] on behalf [of the accuser]; and he who hinders a search of this kind shall pay the value of the stock and 120 shillings to the king[2]. And if anyone offers opposition and resistance and refuses to comply with the law, he shall pay a fine of 120 shillings to the king.

7[1]. And every man shall act as surety for his men and for all those who are under his protection and on his estate[2].

§ 1[1]. And all men of ill repute and those who have been frequently accused[2] shall be placed under surety.

§ 2[1]. And the reeve or the thegn, the noble or commoner[2] who refuses to do this, or disregards it, shall pay a fine of 120 shillings, and incur the penalties which have been stated above[3].

I EDGAR

Ðis is seo gerædnyss hu mon þæt[1] hundred haldan sceal.

1. Ærest, þæt hi heo gegaderian á ymb feower wucan, 7 wyrce ælc man oðrum riht.

2. Þæt men[2] faran on cryd æfter ðeofan[3]. Gyf neod on handa stande, cyðe hit man ðam hundredesmen, 7 he syððan ðam teoðingmannum; 7 faran ealle forð, ðær him God wisige, þæt hi tocuman moton; do ðam ðeofe his riht, swa hit ær Eadmundes cwide wæs.

    § 1. 7 sylle mon þæt ceapgyld ðam ðe þæt yrfe age; 7 dǽle man þæt oðer on twa—healf ðam hundrede, healf ðam hlaforde—butan mannum; 7 fo se hlaford to ðam mannum.

3. And se man ðe ðis forsitte 7 ðæs hundredes dóm forsace, 7 him mon eft þæt illce gerecce, gesylle man ðam hundrede xxx peninga 7 æt ðam æftran cyrre syxtig penega, half ðam hundrede, half ðam hlaforde.

    § 1. Gyf hit ðriddan siðe dó, sylle healf pund; æt ðam feorðan cyrre ðolie ealles ðæs ðe he age 7 beo útlah[4], buton him se cyng eard alyfe.

4. And we cwǽdon be uncuðum yrfe, þæt nan man næfde, buton hé hæbbe ðæs hundredesmanna gewitnyssa oððe ðæs teoðingmannes, 7 se sy wel getrýwe.

    § 1. 7 buton þara oðer hæbbe, nele him mon nænne team geþafian.

---

[1] þæt h. h. s. Ærest has been omitted in the text and added in the margin in the 12th cent.
[2] m̃.
[3] The rubric is in the margin, in red ink.
[4] utlaht—t struck out later.

I EDGAR[1]

This is the ordinance concerning the administration of the hundred[1].

1. In the first place, they[1] shall assemble without fail every four weeks[2], and every man shall do justice to his fellow.
2[1]. That men go without delay[2] in pursuit of thieves.

    If the need is urgent, the chief official of the hundred[3] shall be informed, and shall forthwith inform the chief officials of the tithings[3], and all shall go forth, as God shall direct them, until they succeed in coming upon the thief[4]. He shall receive his deserts as has already been decreed by Edmund[5].

    § 1. And the value of the livestock[1] shall be paid to its owner, and the remainder [of the thief's property]—all except his men—shall be divided in two, half [being given] to the hundred, and half to his lord who shall also take over his men.

3. And whosoever neglects this[1], and ignores the authority[2] of the hundred—and the charge is established against him subsequently[3]—shall pay 30 pence[4] to the hundred, and on the second occasion 60 pence, half to the hundred and half to his lord.

    § 1. If he does it a third time, he shall pay half a pound[1]. On the fourth occasion he shall suffer the loss of all that he possesses and be outlawed, unless the king allow him to remain in the country.

4[1]. And with regard to strange cattle, we have declared that no-one shall keep any such, except with the cognisance of the men of the hundred[2] or with that of the chief official of the tithing; and he must be a thoroughly trustworthy man.

    § 1. And unless he has the cognisance of one or other of these, he shall not be permitted to vouch to warranty.

5. Eac we cwædon, gyf him hundred bedrife tród on oðer hundred, þæt mon cyðe ðam hundredsmen[1], 7 he ðonne ðær midfare.

§ 1. Gyf he hit forsitte, gesylle ðam cynge ðrittig scill'.

6. Gyf hwá riht forbuge 7 uthleape, forgylde þæt angylde se ðe hine to ðam hearme geheold.

§ 1. And gyf hine man teó, þæt he hine utsceóte, geladige hine swa hit on lande stande.

7. On hundrede swa on oðer gemote we wyllað þæt mon folcriht getæce æt ælcere spǽce, 7 andagie hwænne man þæt gelæste.

§ 1. 7 se ðe ðone andagan brece—buton hit sy ðurh hlafordes geban—gebete mid xxx scill', 7 to gesetton dæge gelæste þæt he ær sceolde.

8. Hryðeres belle[2], hundes hoppe[2], blæshorn—ðissa ðreora ælc bið anes scill' weorð; 7 ælc is melda geteald.

9. Ðæt isen ðe bið to ðrimfealdum ordale, þæt wege III pund[3].

[1] m̃ with *anna* added above in later handwriting; *men* Lieb.
[2] 7 added in later handwriting.
[3] 7 *to anfaldum an pund*, added in the margin in later handwriting.

5. We have further declared, that if one hundred follow up a track into another hundred, notice shall be given to the chief official of the latter[1], and he shall then take part in the search.

§ 1. If he neglects to do so, he shall pay 30 shillings[1] to the king.

6[1]. If anyone evades the law and escapes, he who has supported him in wrongdoing shall pay the damage[2].

§ 1. And if he is accused of abetting him in his escape, he shall clear himself according to the established custom of the district[1].

7. In the hundred, as in other courts[1], it is our will that every case be treated in accordance with the public law and have a date fixed for its decision.

§ 1. And he who fails to appear at the appointed time— unless prevented by a summons[1] from his lord—shall pay 30 shillings[2] as compensation and perform on a fixed date what he should have done before.

8[1]. A cow's bell, a dog's collar[2] and a horn for blowing[3]—each of these three shall be worth a shilling, and each is reckoned as an informer[4].

9[1]. The iron for the triple ordeal shall weigh three pounds.

II EDGAR

Her is Eadgares cynincges gerædnes[1].

Ðis is seo gerædnes þe Eadgar cyngc mid his witena geþeahte gerædde, Gode to lofe 7 him silfum to cynescype 7 [eallum his leodscype][2] to þearfe.

1. Ðæt synd þonne ærest, þæt Godes cirican syn ælces[3] rihtes wyrðe.

    § 1. 7 man agife ælce teoðunga to ðam ealdum mynstrum[4] þe seo hyrnes tohyrð; 7 þæt sy þonne swa gelæst, ægðer ge of ðegnes inlande ge of neatlande[5], swa hit seo sulh gegange[6].

2. [Be cyricsceat.][7]

    Gif hwa þonne þegna sy þe on his boclande circan hæbbe þe legerstow on sy, gesylle þone[8] þriddan dæl his agenra teoðunga into his circan.

    § 1. Gif hwa circan hæbbe þe legerstow on [ne][2] sy, do[9] he of þam nigoðan dæle[10] his preoste þæt þæt he wille.

    § 2. 7 ga ælc ciricsceat into ðam ealdan mynstre be ælcum frigan heorðe[11].

    § 3[12]. Gelæste man sulhælmessan þonne xv niht beon onufan eastran.

3. [Be teoþungum.]

    7 sy ælcere geoguðe teoðinge gelæst be pentecosten 7 ðara eorðwæstma be emnihte 7 ælc ciricsceat to Martinus[13] mæssan, be þam fullan wite þe seo domboc tæcð.

    § 1. Gif[14] hwa þonne ða teoðunge gelæstan nelle, swa we gecweden habbað, þonne[1] fare þæs cyninges gerefa to 7 þæs biscopes 7 þæs mynstres mæssepreost 7 niman unðances þone teoðan dæl to þam mynstre ðe hit toge-

---

[1] Om. G, A. Ld. [2] G, A, Ld; om. D.
[3] Added in late handwriting in G; om. Ld.
[4] þ. ealdan mynstre G, Ld; þ. ealdan mynstrum A.
[5] geneatlande G, A; neatland Ld. [6] swa swa his sulh gega G, Ld.
[7] The rubrics are found in Ld. only. [8] g. he þane (ðonne) G, Ld.
[9] ðonne do G, Ld. [10] þ. nigan (nigon, nygan) dælum G, A, Ld.
[11] eorðe G (h added later above the line), Ld. [12] Om. G, Ld, Q.
[13] c. sy gelæst be M. G, Ld. [14] 7 gyf (gif) G, A, Ld.

II EDGAR

Here is King Edgar's ordinance.

This is the ordinance which King Eadgar has enacted, with the advice of his councillors, for the glory of God, and his own royal dignity[1], and the good of all his people[2].

1. This is the first provision, that God's churches shall be entitled to all their prerogatives[1].

    § 1[1]. And all tithes shall be paid to the old churches[2] to which obedience is due; and payment shall be made both from the thegn's demesne land and the land held by his tenants[3]—all that is under the plough[4].

2[1]. If, however, there is a thegn who, on the land which he holds by title-deed, has a church to which is attached a graveyard, he shall pay the third part of his own tithes to his church.

    § 1. If anyone has a church to which there is no graveyard attached, he shall pay what he will to his priest out of the next tenth part[1].

    § 2. And every church-due for every free household[1] shall go to the old church.

    § 3[1]. Plough-alms shall be rendered 15 days[2] after Easter.

3[1]. And the tithe of all young animals shall be rendered by Pentecost, and that of the fruits of the earth by the Equinox, and every church due shall be rendered by Martinmas, under pain of the full penalty[2] which the written law[3] prescribes.

    § 1[1]. If, however, anyone refuses to render tithes in accordance with what we have decreed, the king's reeve, and the bishop's reeve, and the priest of the church shall go to him, and, without his consent, shall take the tenth part for the church to which it is due, and the next

birige, 7 tæcan¹ him to ðam nigoðan dæle, 7 todæle man ða eahta dælas on twa, 7 fo se landhlaford² to healfum, to healfum se biscop, si hit cyninges man si hit þegnes.

4. [Be þon heorþpeninge.]
7 sy ælc heorðpænig agifen be Petres mæssedæg.

§ 1. 7 se ðe hine³ to ðam andagan gelæst næbbe, læde hine to Rome 7 ðarto eacan þrittig p', 7 bringe þonne⁴ switelunge þæt he þar swa micel betæht hæbbe; 7 þonne he ham cume, gilde þam cyninge hundtwelftig scill'.

§ 2. 7 gif he hine eft sillan nelle, læde hine eft to Rome 7 oðre swilce bote; 7 þonne he ham cume, gilde þam cynge twahund scill'.

§ 3. Æt þam þriddan siðe⁵, gif he þonne git nelle, þolige ealles ðæs þe he age.

5. [Be freolsdægum 7 fæstenum.]
7 healde man ælces Sunnandæges freolsunga⁶ fram Sæternesdæges nontide⁷ oð Monandæges⁸ lihtinge, be þam wite ðe seo⁹ domboc tæce¹⁰, 7 ælcne oðerne mæssedæg swa he beboden sy¹¹.

§ 1. 7 man ælc⁹ bebodon fæsten healde mid ælcere geornfulnesse [7 ælces Frigedæges fæsten, buton hit freols sy]¹².

§ 2¹³. 7 gelæste man sawlsceat æt ælcan Cristenan men to ðam mynstre þe hit togebirige.

§ 3¹³. 7 stande ælc ciricgrið swa swa hit betst stod.

[1] G, A, Ld. Cf. VIII Atr. 8; I Cn. 8, 2; tæce D. [2] hlaford Ld. [3] ðonne G, Ld.
[4] þonne þanon s. G; þænne þonon s. A; ðone ðonon Ld.
[5] cyrre G, Ld. [6] freols G, Ld. [7] f. nontide þæs s. G, Ld.
[8] ðæs M. G, Ld. [9] Om. G, Ld. [10] tæcð G, A, Ld.
[11] beo G, A Ld. [12] A; om. G, D Ld. [13] Om. G, Ld, Q.

CAP. 4–5 23

tenth shall be allotted to him[2], and the eight [remaining] parts shall be divided in two, and the lord of the manor[3] shall take half and the bishop half, whether the man be under the lordship of the king or of a thegn.

4. And every hearth-penny[1] shall be paid by St Peter's Day.

§ 1[1]. And he who has failed to make payment by the appointed time shall take it to Rome, and 30 pence in addition thereto, and shall bring thence evidence that he has there handed over that amount; and when he comes home, he shall pay 120 shillings to the king.

§ 2. And if he again refuses to give it, he shall take it again to Rome, and hand over the same sum as compensation, and when he comes home, he shall pay 200 shillings to the king.

§ 3. And on the third occasion, if he still refuses, he shall suffer the loss of all that he possesses.

5[1]. And every Sunday shall be observed as a festival from noonday on Saturday till dawn on Monday, under pain of the penalty which the written law prescribes; and every other feast-day according to the regulations appointed for it.

§ 1. And every fast which has been appointed shall be rigorously observed, [and the fast every Friday, unless it be a festival].

§ 2[1]. And payment for the souls of the dead shall be rendered to the church to which it is due on behalf of every Christian man.

§ 3. And every right of sanctuary possessed by the church[1] shall be maintained according to the highest standards of the past[2].

III EDGAR

Eadgares cynincges gerædnes[1].

1. [Weoruldcund gerædnysse.][2]
Þis is ðonne seo worldcunde gerædnes þe ic wille þæt man healde.

§ 1. Þæt is þonne ærest[3] þæt ic wille, þæt ælc man sy folcrihtes wurðe, ge earm ge éadig, 7 heom man rihte domas deme.

§ 2. 7 sy on ðare bote swilc forgifnes, swilce[4] hit for Gode gebeorhlic sy 7 for worlde aberendlic.

2. [Be ðone ðe mon cyng gesece 7 be ðæm were.]
7 ne gesece nan man þone cyngc for nanre spræce, buton he æt ham rihtes [wyrðe][5] beon ne mote, oððe riht abiddan ne mæg[6].

§ 1. Gif þæt riht to hefig sy, secan[7] siððan þa lihtinge to ðam cynge.

§ 2. 7 æt nanum botwyrðum gilte ne forwyrce man mare þonne his wer.

3. [Be unrihtum dome.]
7 se dema, þe oðrum woh deme[8], gesille þam cynge hundtwelftig[9] scill' to bote—buton he[10] mid aðe gecyðan durre, þæt he hit na rihtor ne cuðe—7 polige áá his þegenscipes, buton he hine[11] æt ðam cynge gebicge, swa[12] he him geþafian wille; 7 ofmanige[13] scirebiscop[14] þa bote to ðæs cynges handa.

4. [Be ðon ðe mon operne forsecgaþ.]
And se þe oðerne mid woge forseccan wille, þæt he aðor oððe feo oððe freme[15] þe wyrsa sy, gif þonne se oðer þæt[3] geunsoðian mæge þæt him man onsecgan wolde, sy he his tungan scildig, buton he hine mid his were forgilde.

---

[1] Om. G, A, Ld. [2] The rubrics are found in Ld only.
[3] Om. G, Ld. [4] swilce swilce A. [5] G, A; wyrþ Ld; om. D.
[6] mæge G, A, Ld. [7] sece G, A, Ld. [8] onwoh gedeme G, Ld.
[9] ...twelftig. G₂ begins here after torn out pages. [10] buton h. hit G₂.
[11] h. eft G; eft Ld. [12] swa swa A.
[13] D, G₂; amanige G, A, Ld. [14] þære scyre b. G, A, G₂, Ld.
[15] D, G₂; feo oððe feore G, A (vel freme written above feore in A), Ld.

III EDGAR

King Edgar's ordinance.

1. My will is further[1] that the following be observed as a secular ordinance.

    § 1[1]. In the first place, my will is that every man[2], rich or poor[3], obtain the benefit of the public law and be awarded just decisions.

    § 2. And that there be such remission in the case of compensations as shall be justifiable in the sight of God and acceptable in the eyes of men[1].

2[1]. And no-one shall apply to the king about any case, unless he cannot obtain the benefit of the law or fails to command justice at home[2].

    § 1. If the law is too oppressive, he shall apply to the king for mitigation[1].

    § 2. And no man shall forfeit more than his wergeld for any offence for which compensation may be paid[1].

3[1]. And a judge[2] who gives a false judgment against another man shall pay 120 shillings as compensation to the king, unless he is prepared to declare on oath that he did not know how to give a more just decision; and he shall forfeit for ever his rank as a thegn, unless he redeem it from the king on such terms as the king will allow him. And the bishop of the diocese shall exact the compensation on the king's behalf.

4. And if anyone seeks to accuse another man falsely, so that he is injured either in property or in reputation[1], and if the second man can refute the charge which the first has sought to bring against him, the first shall forfeit his tongue, unless he redeem himself with his wergeld.

III EDGAR

5. [Be gemotum.]
7 sece man hundredes gemot¹ swa hit ǽr geset wæs.
§ 1. 7 hæbbæ man þriwa on geare buruhgemot 7 tuwa scirgemot.
§ 2. 7 ðar beo on þare scire biscop² 7 se ealdorman, 7 ðar ægðer tæcan Godes³ riht ge worldriht.

6. [Be borgum.]
7 finde him ælc man þæt he borh habbe; 7 se borh hine⁴ to ælcon rihte gelǽde 7 gehealde.
§ 1. 7 gif hwa ðonne woh wirce 7 utaberste⁵, abere se borh þæt he beran⁶ scolde.
§ 2. Gif hit þonne⁷ þeof⁸ beo, 7 gif he hine þonne⁷ binnan XII monðum gelangian mæge, agife hine to rihte, 7 him man agife þæt he ær geald⁹.

7. [Be tyhtbysigum.]
7 se þe tihtbisig sy 7 folce ungetrywe 7 þas gemot forbuge þrywa¹⁰, þonne scifte¹¹ man of þam gemote ða ðe him toridan, 7 finde þonne¹² git borh, gif he mæge.
§ 1. Gif he þonne ne mæge, gewilde man hine swa hwaðer swa¹³ man mæge, swa cucune swa deadne, 7 niman¹⁴ eal þæt he age, 7 gilde man ðam teondan¹⁵ his ceapgild angildes, 7 fo se hlaford¹⁶ elles¹⁷ to healfum, to healfum þæt hundred.
§ 2. 7 gif aðer oððe mæg oððe fremde ða rade forsace, gilde þam cyninge hundtwelftig scill'.
§ 3. 7 gesece se æbæra þeof þæt þæt he gesece, oððe se þe on hlafordsearwe gemet sy, þæt hi næfre feorh ne gesecan, buton se cyningc him feorhgeneres unne¹⁸.

---

[1] *hundredgemót* G, A; *hundrede gemote* Ld.
[2] *ðær sciregemote bisceop* Ld.   [3] *ge G*. G, A, G₂, Ld.
[4] *h. þonne* G, A, G₂, Ld.   [5] *utoðberste* G, Ld; *utætberste* A, G₂.
[6] *aberan* G, A, Ld.   [7] Om. G, A, G₂, Ld.   [8] *þyfð* G; *ðyfþe* Ld.
[9] *sealde* G, Ld.   [10] Om. G, Ld.
[11] *sceawie (-ige)* G, Ld; *sceapige* A; *scawie* G₂.   [12] *f. him þ.* G, A, Ld.
[13] *hine swaðor (-er) m. m.* G, A, Ld; *hine mon swæðer m. m.* G₂.
[14] *nime man* G, G₂, Ld.   [15] *teonde* G, A, G₂; *ða teonde* Ld.
[16] *landhlaford* G, Ld.   [17] Om. G, Ld.
[18] *buton...unne* om. G, A, G₂, Ld.

5. And the hundred court shall be attended as has been previously ordained[1].

§ 1[1]. And the borough court shall be held three times in the year and the county court twice[2].

§ 2[1]. And the bishop of the diocese and the ealdorman[2] shall be present, and shall direct the observance of[3] both ecclesiastical and secular law.

6. And every man shall see that he has a surety[1], and this surety shall bring and keep him to [the performance of] every lawful duty.

§ 1. And if anyone does wrong and escapes[1], his surety shall incur what the other should have incurred[2].

§ 2. If the case be that of a thief[1] and his surety can lay hold of him within twelve months, he shall deliver him up to justice, and what he has paid shall be returned to him.

7[1]. And if anyone who has a bad reputation and is unworthy of public confidence[2] fails to attend the court-meetings three times, men shall be chosen[3] from the meeting who shall ride to him[4], and he may then still find a surety, if he can.

§ 1[1]. And if he cannot do so, they shall seize him as they can, either alive or dead, and they shall take all that he has, and shall pay to the accuser the unaugmented value of his goods[2]; and the lord of the manor shall take half [of what remains], and the hundred half.

§ 2. And if anyone, either kinsman or stranger[1], refuses to ride [against him], he shall pay the king 120 shillings.

§ 3[1]. And the proved thief[2], or he who has been discovered in treason against his lord[3], whatever refuge he seeks, shall never be able to save his life, unless the king grant that it be spared[4].

8. [Be mynetum 7 gemettum.]
7 gange[1] án mynet ofer ealne þæs cyninges anweald, 7 þone nan man ne forsace.

§ 1. 7 gange án[2] gemet 7 an gewihte[3], swilce man on Lundenbirig 7[4] on Wintaceastre healde.

§ 2. 7 ga seo wæge wulle to cxx p'[5], 7 nan man hig undeoror[6] ne sille.

§ 3[7]. 7 gif hwa hi þonne undeoror sille, oððe eawunga oððe dearnunga, gilde ægðer þam cynge LX[8] scill' ge se þe hi sille ge se þe hi bicge.

IV EDGAR

Her is geswutelod on þisum gewrite, hu Eadgar cyncg wæs smeagende, hwæt to bote mihte æt þam færcwealme þe his leodscype swyðe drehte 7 wanode, wide gynd his anweald.

1. Ðæt is þonne ærest þæt him þuhte 7 his witum, þæt ðus gerad ungelimp mid synnum 7 mid oferhyrnysse Godes beboda geearnod wære, 7 swyðost mid þam oftige þæs neadgafoles þe Cristene men Gode gelæstan scoldon on heora teoðingsceattum. He beþohte 7 asmeade þæt godcunde be woruldgewunan:

§ 1. Gif geneatmanna hwylc forgymeleasað his hlafordes gafol 7 hit him to ðæm rihtandagan ne gelæst, wen is, gyf se hlaford mildheort bið, þæt he ða gymeleaste to forgyfenesse læte 7 to his gafole buton witnunge fó.

§ 2. Gyf he ðonne gelomlice þurh his bydelas his gafoles myngað 7 he ðonne aheardað 7 hit þencð to ætstrengenne, wen is, þæt ðæs hlafordes grama to ðam swyðe weaxe, þæt he him ne unne naðer ne æhta ne lifes:

---

[1] *ga* G, Ld.   [2] *g. a.* om. G, Ld.   [3] 7 *a. g.* om. G, Ld.
[4] *on L.* 7 om. G, Ld.   [5] *ealfan (healf.) punde* G, G₂.
[6] *hie n. m. ná deoror* G, Ld; *n. m. hy na undeoror* A, G₂.
[7] Om. G, Ld.   [8] A, G₂; XL D.

8[1]. And one coinage[2] shall be current throughout all the king's realm, and no-one shall refuse it.

§ 1. And there shall be one system of measurement[1], and one standard of weights[2], such as is in use in London and in Winchester[3].

§ 2. And a wey[1] of wool shall be sold for 120 pence, and no-one shall sell it at a cheaper[2] rate.

§ 3[1]. And if anyone sells it at a cheaper rate, either openly or secretly, both he who sells it and he who buys it shall pay 60 shillings[2] to the king.

IV EDGAR

[1]Notification is hereby given in this order[2], that King Eadgar has been considering what remedy could be found for the plague[3] which has greatly afflicted and reduced his people throughout the length and breadth of his dominion.

1. In the first place, he and his councillors are of opinion that misfortune such as this has been merited because of sin and disregard of God's commands[1], and especially through the withholding of the tribute which Christian people should render to God by their tithes. He has been thinking over and considering the ways of God[2] by an analogy with human actions:

    § 1. If any tenant[1] neglects the payment due to his lord and does not render it to him on the appointed day, it is to be expected that, if the lord is merciful, he will grant forgiveness for the neglect and take his payment without exacting a penalty.

    § 2. If, however, through his bailiffs[1] he repeatedly claims his rent, and the tenant proves obstinate, and thinks to stand out against it[2], it is to be expected that the lord's anger will grow so great that he will grant him neither property nor life[3].

§ 3. Swa is wén þæt ure Drihten dó þurh ða gedyrstignysse þe folces men wiðhæfton þære gelomlican myngunge þe ure lareowas dydon ymbe þæt neadgafol ures Drihtnes —þæt syn ure teoðunga 7 cyricsceattas.

§ 4. Ðonne beode ic 7 se arcebisceop, þæt ge God ne gremian, ne naðer ne geearnian ne þone færlican deað þises andweardan lifes, ne huru þone toweardan écere helle, mid ænigum oftige Godes gerihta; ac ægðer ge earm ge eadig þe ænige teolunga hæbbe, gelæste Gode his teoðunga mid ealre blisse 7 mid eallum unnan, swa seo gerædnys tæce þe mine witan æt Andeferan geræddon 7 nu eft æt Wihtbordesstane mid wedde gefæstnodon.

§ 5. Ðonne beode ic minum gerefan, be minum freondscype 7 be eallum þam ðe hi ágon, þæt hi styran ælcum þara ðe þis ne gelæste 7 minra witena wed abrecan mid ænegum wacscype wille, swa swa him seo foresæde geradnes tæce; 7 on ðære steore ne sy nan forgyfnes.

§ 5a. Gyf he swa earm bið þæt he aþer deð oððe þa Godes wanað, his sawla to forwyrde, oððe waccor mid modes graman hy behwyrfð þonne þæt he him to agenum teleð, þonne him micele agenre is þæt him æfre on écnysse gelæst, gyf he hit mid unnan 7 mid fulre blisse dón wolde.

§ 6. Ðonne wille ic, þæt ðas Godes gerihta standan æghwær[1] gelice on minum anwealde;

§ 7. 7 ða Godes þeowas þe ða sceattas underfoð, þe we Gode syllað, libban clænan life, þæt hy ðurh ða clænnysse ús to Gode þingian mægen;

[1] F; ægðer C.

§ 3. It is to be expected that our Lord will act in like manner, because of the audacity with which laymen have withstood the repeated admonitions given [us] by our teachers with regard to the payments which we are in duty bound to render to our Lord, namely, our tithes and church-dues.

§ 4. I and the archbishop[1] enjoin, therefore, that you do not, by withholding any of God's dues, provoke Him to wrath, and incur either the sudden death[2] [which is befalling you] in this present life or, still worse, the death to come in everlasting hell[3]; but everyone, both rich and poor, whose property has yielded him anything[4], shall, with all gladness and with all willingness, render his tithes to God, as is prescribed by the ordinance which my councillors enacted at Andover[5], and have now confirmed by solemn declaration[6] at Wihtbordestan.

§ 5. Further, I enjoin upon my reeves, on pain of forfeiting my friendship and all they possess, to deal in the manner prescribed by the aforesaid ordinance with everyone who fails to perform this and, by any remissness on his part, consents to violate the solemn declaration of my councillors. And there shall be no remission of the [prescribed] punishment.

§ 5a. If he is so debased[1] as either to curtail what is due to God[2], to the ruin of his soul, or, with angry heart, to attend to it less diligently than to what he accounts his own, [he ought to realise that][3] what endures for him to all eternity will be much more his own, if he has been willing to give his tribute with gladness and with all willingness.

§ 6. Further, it is my will that these ecclesiastical dues be everywhere[1] alike throughout my dominion.

§ 7[1]. And that the servants of God who receive the dues which we render to Him shall live a pure life, so that, by virtue of their purity, they may intercede for us with God.

§ 8. 7 ic 7 mine þegnas wyldan ure preostas to ðan þe ure saula hyrdas us tæcað, þæt syndon ure bisceopas, þe we næfre mishyran ne sceolon on nan þara ðinga þe hi us for Gode tæcað, þæt we ðurh þa hyrsumnysse, þe we heom for Gode hyrsumiað, þæt ece líf geearnian, þe hy us towemað mid lare 7 mid bysene godra weorca.

2. Woruldgerihta ic wille þæt standen on ælcum leodscype swa gode swa hi mon betste aredian mæge, Gode to gecwemnysse 7 me to fullum cynescype 7 earmum 7 eadegum to ðearfe 7 to friðe.

2a. 7 to ælcere byrig 7 on ælcere scyre hæbbe ic mines cynescypes gerihta swa min fæder hæfde, 7 mine þegnas hæbben heora scipe on minum timan swa hi hæfdon on mines fæder.

§ 1. 7 ic wille þæt woruldgerihta mid Denum standan be swa godum lagum, swa hy betste geceosan mægen.

§ 1a. Stande þonne mid Englum þæt ic 7 mine witan to minra yldrena domum geyhton, eallum leodscype to ðearfe.

§ 2. Sy þeahhwæðere þes ræd gemæne eallum leodscype, ægðer ge Englum ge Denum ge Bryttum, on ælcum ende mines anwealdes, to ðy þæt earm 7 eadig mote agan þæt hi mid rihte gestrynað, 7 þeof nyte hwær he þeofte[1] befæste ðeah he hwæt stele, 7 him swa geborgen sy, heora unwilles, þæt heora to feola ne losien.

3. Ðæt þonne his[2] þæt ic wille, þæt ælc mann sy under borge ge binnan burgum ge buton burgum.

§ 1. 7 gewitnes[3] sý geset to ælcere byrig 7 to ælcum hundrode:

[1] þyfþe F. [2] Ð. is þ. F. [3] F; gehitnæs C.

§ 8. And that I and my thegns shall enforce upon our priests[1] the duties prescribed for us by the guardians of our souls, namely our bishops, whom we ought never to disobey in any of those matters which they, as representatives of God, prescribe for us, so that we, through the obedience which we show them as representatives of God, may inherit the eternal life to which they draw us by their teaching and by the example of good works.

2[1]. My will is that the rights of the laity[2] be maintained in every province[3] at the best standard which can be devised, in accordance with what will be acceptable to God[4], and will preserve my royal dignity unimpaired, and tend to the advantage and security of rich and poor.

2a. And that in every borough and in every county I possess my royal prerogatives as my father[1] did, and that my thegns keep their rank[2] in my lifetime[3] as they did in my father's.

§ 1. And it is my will that the rights of the laity be maintained among the Danes in accordance with the best constitution[1] which they can determine upon.

§ 1a. Among the English, however, the additions which I and my councillors have made to the laws of my ancestors[1] shall be observed, for the benefit of the whole nation[2].

§ 2. The following measure, however, shall apply generally to the whole nation—to the English, Danes[1] and Britons[2] in every part of my dominion—to the end that rich and poor may possess what they have lawfully acquired; and that thieves, even if they steal anything, may not know where to deposit their stolen goods; and that, little as they may like it, such precautions be taken against them that very few of them may escape.

3. My will is, further, that every man be under surety[1], whether he live within a borough or in the country[2].

§ 1. And a body of standing witnesses shall be appointed for every borough and for every hundred.

IV EDGAR

4. To ælcere byrig XXXVI[1] syn gecorene to gewytnesse.

5. To smalum burgum 7 to ælcum hundrode XII, buton ge má wyllan.

6. 7 ælc mon mid heora gewytnysse bigcge 7 sylle ælc þeora ceapa þe he bicgcge oððe sylle aþer oððe burge oððe wæpengetace[2].

§ 1. 7 heora ælc, þonne hine man ærest to wytnesse[3] gecysð, sylle þone að, þæt he næfre, ne for feo ne for lufe ne for ege, ne ætsace nanes þara þinga þe he to gewytnesse wæs, 7 nan oðer þingc on gewytnesse ne cyðe butan þæt án þæt he geseah oððe gehyrde.

§ 2. 7 swa geæðedra[4] manna syn on ælcum ceape twegen oððe þry to gewitnysse.

7. 7 se ðe æfter ænegum[5] ceape ride, cyðe his neahgeburum ymbe hwæt he ride; 7 ðonne he ham cume, cyðe eác on hwæs[6] gewitnysse he ðone ceap gebohte.

8. Gif he þonne unmyndlunge ceap áredige ut on hwylcere fare, buton he hit ær cydde þa he útrád, cyðe hit þonne he ham cyme; 7 gyf hit cuce orf bið, mid his tunscipes gewitnysse on gemænre læse gebringe.

§ 1. Gif he swa ne deð ær fif nihtum, cyðan hit þæs tunes men þam hundrodes ealdre, 7 beon buton wite ægðer ge hy sylfe ge heora hyrdas; 7 ðolige þæs orfes ðe hit þider brohte, for ði þe he hit his neahgeburum cyðan nolde, 7 fó se landrica to healfon 7 to healfan þæt hundred.

9. Gif hit þonne ofer v niht ungecyd on gemænre læse wunað, þolige þæs orfes swa we ær cwædon, 7 ðara hyrda ælc ðolige ðære hyde, 7 ðæs ne sy nan forgyfnes, gesecan[7] þæt hi gesecan[7]; 7 he ðeahhwæðere cyðe on hwæs gewitnysse he þæt orf bohte.

---

[1] F; *XXXIII.* C. [2] *on w.* F. [3] *gewitnysse* F.
[4] *geæþdera* F. [5] F; *agenum* C. [6] F; *ðæs* C. [7] *-en* F.

4. 36[1] persons shall be chosen as witnesses for every borough.
5. 12 [shall be chosen] for small boroughs and for every hundred, unless you desire more.
6. And every man shall buy or sell in the presence of these witnesses all the goods which he buys or sells either in a borough or in a wapentake[1].
   § 1. And each of them, when he is first chosen as a witness, shall swear an oath that he will never, for money[1] or favour or fear[2], deny any of the things of which he has been witness, or declare in his testimony anything except only what he has seen or heard.
   § 2. And two or three men who have taken the oath in this manner shall be present as witnesses at every transaction.
7. And he who sets out[1] to make any purchase shall inform his neighbours of the object of his journey; and when he comes home, he shall also declare who was present as witness when he bought the goods.
8. If, however, he makes a purchase unexpectedly, when he is away on some journey or other, and he had not given notice of it when he set out, he shall do so when he comes home; and, if it is livestock, he shall bring it to the common pasture with the cognisance of the village to which he belongs.
   § 1. If he does not do so within 5 days, the villagers shall inform the head of the hundred[1], and neither they nor their herdsmen shall be fined; and he who brought the livestock there shall forfeit it, because he has failed to give notice of it to his neighbours, and the lord of the manor shall take half and the hundred half.
9. If, however, it remains unnotified on the common pasture for more than 5 days, he shall forfeit the livestock as we have stated, and each of the herdsmen shall undergo the lash[1], and there shall be no remission of that punishment, whatever refuge they seek; and the man himself shall declare none the less who was present as witness when he bought the livestock.

10. Gif he ðonne cenð þæt he hit mid gewitnysse bohte þara manna þe to gewitnysse genamode synt, aðer oððe on byrig oððe on hundrode, 7 se hundrodes¹ ealdor þæt geacsoð þæt hit soð is, þolige þeah þæs orfes, for ði þe he hit his neahgeburum cyðan nolde ne his hundrodes ealdre, 7 næbbe his na maran hearm.

11. Gyf he þonne cænne þæt he hit mid gewitnysse bohte, 7 þæt leas bið, sy he þeof 7 ðolige heafdes 7 ealles ðæs þe he age; 7 healde se landhlaford þæt forstolene orf 7 ðæs orfes ceapgyld, oð þæt se agenfrigea þæt² geacsige 7 mid gewitnesse him þæt orf geahnige.

12. Þonne wille ic þæt stande mid Denum swa gode laga swa hy betste geceosen; 7 ic heom á geþafode 7 geðafian wille, swa lange swa me lif gelæst, for eowrum hyldum þe ge me symble cyddon.

§ 1. 7 ðæs wilnige þæt ðes án dom on swylcere smeagunge sy ús eallon gemæne, to gebeorge 7 to friðe eallum leodscype.

13. 7 ic wille þæt tunesmen 7 heora hyrdas habban þas ylcan smeagunge on minum cucum orfe 7 on minra þegena, ealswa hy habbað on heora agenum.

§ 1. Gif hit þonne min gerefa oððe ænig oðer man, riccre oððe unriccre, onscunað 7 ungerysena gebyt aðer oððe tunesmannum oððe heora hyrdon, ceose Dene be lagum hwylce steore hy be ðan healdan willað.

14. Mid Anglum ic hæbbe gecoren 7 mine witan, hwæt seo steor beon mæge, gif ænig man mid ánbyrdnysse beginð oððe mid ealle ofslyhð ænigne þara þe ymbe þas smeagunge bið 7 þæt dyrne orf ameldað, oððe þara ænigne þe on soðre gewitnesse bið [7]³ mid his soðe þæne unscyldigan ahret 7 ðæne scyldigan rihtlice fordeð.

[1] *hundrodest* C; *hundredes* F.   [2] F; *agenfrige að* C.
[3] F; om. C.

10. If, however, he makes it known that he has bought it with the cognisance of the men who have been nominated as witnesses, either in a borough or in a hundred[1], and the head of the hundred learns that his statement is true, he shall none the less forfeit the livestock, because he has failed to give notice of it to his neighbours or to the head of his hundred, but he shall suffer no greater loss[2].

11. If, however, he makes it known that he has bought it in the presence of witnesses, and that statement proves false, he shall be regarded as a thief, and shall forfeit his head and all that he possesses; and the lord of the manor shall keep the stolen livestock, or[1] its equivalent value, till the owner hears of it, and proves his claim to the livestock with the help of witnesses.

12. Further, it is my will that the Danes continue to observe the best constitution which they can determine upon[1]. I[2] have always granted you such a concession and will continue to do so, as long as my life lasts, because of the loyalty[3] which you have constantly professed to me.

    § 1. But I desire that this one decree relating to investigations such as these[1] shall apply equally to us all[2], for the protection and security of the whole population.

13. And it is my will that villagers and their herdsmen shall have the same right of investigation with regard to my livestock and that of my thegns as they have with regard to their own.

    § 1. If, however, any reeve of mine or any other man[i], whether of high or low position, refuses this, and offers any indignity to either the villagers or their herdsmen, the Danes shall determine, according to their constitution, what penalty they will fix for this offence.

14. I and my councillors have determined what the penalty[1] shall be among the English, if any man ventures[2] to offer resistance or slays outright anyone who is engaged in this investigation and who gives notice of the concealed cattle, or anyone who is giving true witness and, by his veracity, saves the innocent and brings just doom upon the guilty.

§ 1. Þonne wille ic þæt symble mid eow gehealden sý þæt ge to friðes bote gecoren hæfdon mid micclum wisdome 7 me swyðe gecwemlice.

§ 2. 7 ðas eaca sy ús eallum gemæne þe on ðissum iglandum wuniað.

15. Þonne fyrðrige Oslác eorl 7 eall here þe on his[1] ealdordome wunað, þæt ðis stande, Gode to lofe 7 ure ealra saula to ðearfe 7 eallum folce to friðe.

§ 1. 7 write man manega gewrita be ðisum 7 sende ægðer ge to Ælfere ealdormen ge to Æþelwine[2] ealdormen, 7 hi gehwyder, þæt ðes ræd cuð sy ægðer ge earmum ge eadigum.

16. Ic beo eow swyðe hold hlaford þa hwyle þe me lif gelæst, 7 eow eallum swyðe bliðe eom, for ði þe ge swa georne ymbe frið syndon.

[1] F; ðis C.   [2] F; Ægelwine C.

§ 1. Further, it is my will that the provisions which you have made, with great wisdom and very acceptably to me, for the improvement of public security, be continually observed among you.

§ 2. But this addition shall apply generally to all of us[1] who dwell in these islands.

15. Further, Earl Oslac[1] and all the population[2] dwelling in his earldom shall promote the observance of this, to the praise of God, and for the good of the souls of all of us, and the security of the whole nation.

§ 1. And many copies of this order shall be made and sent to both the ealdormen, Aelfhere[1] and Aethelwine[2], and they shall distribute them in all directions, so that this measure shall be known both to rich and poor.

16. I will be a very gracious lord to you as long as my life lasts. I am very well pleased with you all[1], because you are so zealous for the preservation of the public peace.

PROMISSIO REGIS

The Anglo-Saxon version of the Coronation oath given here is taken from the eleventh century MS Cotton Cleopatra B XIII (Cp). It is contained also in the sixteenth century MS Oxford Bodley Junius 60 into which it was copied from the eleventh century MS Cotton Vitellius A VII (Cv) now destroyed (see Liebermann, I. p. 214). It is evidently a translation of the oath included in the Latin coronation ritual of which four recensions, dating from the tenth to the fourteenth centuries, are extant (see Legg, *English Coronation Records*). The consecration of English kings is recorded as early as the eighth century (see *Sax. Chr.* ann. 785), and Liebermann suggests that the liturgy and oath may date from the ninth century at least. None of the three MSS representing the earliest recension, however, is earlier than the tenth century (see Liebermann, III. p. 144). One of them is traditionally connected with Egbert, Archbishop of York (d. 766, see Stubbs, *Registr. Sacr. Anglic.* p. 10), and may be a copy of a Pontifical of his, though there is no real evidence in favour of this ascription. The second recension falls before 973 and may have been employed at the coronation of Edgar (see Ramsay, *Athenæum*, 29 March 1902, p. 401). It spread to the Continent where it was used at coronations both in France and Italy (see Legg, *op. cit.* p. 14). The A.S. version has points in common with both these forms. The third recension is found in MSS of the twelfth century, while the fourth, which dates from the fourteenth century, is contained in the *Liber regalis* (see Legg, *op. cit.* p. 81).

The preamble of the Anglo-Saxon version names Dunstan as the archbishop officiating at the ceremony, and gives the place as Kingston. Dunstan consecrated Edgar (973), Edward (975) and Æthelred (978 or 979), but the coronation of Edgar took place at Bath (see *Sax. Chr.* A) and it is not certain where Edward was crowned. Æthelred, however, was crowned at Kingston (see *Sax. Chr.*; Florence of Worc., ed. Thorpe, I.

p. 146; Henry of Hunt., Rolls Series, p. 167), so that this document is generally taken to refer to him. Liebermann, however, does not preclude the possibility of its referring to Edward, and consequently leaves it in doubt as to whether the event mentioned belongs to 975 or 978. The coronation oath is followed both in Cp and Ju by a commentary detailing the duties of a Christian king (see Wright and Halliwell, *Reliquiae Antiquae* II. p. 194; Stubbs, *Mem. of St Dunstan*, p. 356). Liebermann directs attention to the general resemblance between this passage and the section entitled *Be eorðlicum cyninge* in the Institutes of Polity (ed. Thorpe, *Anc. Laws*, II. p. 304) as well as Wulfstan's Homilies (ed. Napier, p. 266 f.). In tone and phraseology also it suggests comparison with V and VI Æthelred. He is of opinion that this addition may have been due to the Anglo-Saxon translator.

PROMISSIO REGIS[1]

Ðis gewrit is gewriten stæf be stæfe be þam gewrite þe Dunstan arcebisceop sealde urum hlaforde æt Cingestune, þa on dæg þa hine man halgode to cinge, 7 forbead him ælc wedd to syllanne butan þysan wedde þe he up on Cristes weofod léde, swa se bisceop him dihte:

1. On þære halgan þrinnesse naman! Ic þreo þing beháte Cristenum folce 7 me underðeoddum:

   § 1. án ærest, þæt Godes cyrice 7 eall Cristen folc minra gewealda soðe sibbe healde;

   § 2. oðer is, þæt ic reaflac 7 ealle unrihte þing eallum hádum forbeode;

   § 3. þridde, þæt ic beháte 7 bebeode on eallum dómum riht 7 mildheortnisse, þæt us eallum arfæst 7 mildheort God þurh þæt his ecean miltse forgife, se lifað 7 rixað.

Finit.

[1] *Sacramentum vel Pr. r. in consecratione* Ju.

PROMISSIO REGIS

This document has been copied, letter by letter, from that which Archbishop Dunstan[1] gave to our lord at Kingston[2], on the day when he was consecrated as king, forbidding him to give any pledge[3] except this one which he laid upon Christ's altar, as the bishop directed him:

1. In the name of the Holy Trinity![1] I promise three things to the Christian people who are under my authority[2]:

    § 1[1]. Firstly, that true peace shall be assured to[2] the church of God and to all Christian people in my dominions.

    § 2[1]. Secondly, I forbid robbery and all unrighteous deeds by all classes of society.

    § 3[1]. Thirdly, I promise and enjoin justice and mercy in the decision of all cases, in order that God, who liveth and reigneth, may in his grace and mercy be brought thereby to grant us all his eternal compassion.

THE LAWS OF ÆTHELRED

THE LAWS OF ÆTHELRED

Eight series of laws issued by Æthelred are extant, together with short fragments of two other series. They fall naturally into two groups, I–IV being concerned with secular affairs while V–X are almost entirely ecclesiastical in content. Of the first four codes the only one which can be dated with any certainty is II. It contains the terms of peace made between Æthelred and his councillors and a force of so-called 'Danes,' of which one of the leaders was Olaf Tryggvason (see Notes). It would seem that money was paid to invading forces both in 991 and 994—on the first occasion after the battle of Maldon in which Byrhtnoth, Ealdorman of Essex, was defeated and killed (see *Sax. Chr.* ann. 991 E, F, where, however, none of the Danish leaders is mentioned by name); on the second occasion after a considerable part of the country had been ravaged by Olaf (*ib.* ann. 994 E, F). Archbishop Sigeric is mentioned in the Chronicle only in connection with the former transaction and he died in the autumn of 994 before terms could have been arranged with the invaders. Liebermann therefore, for this and other reasons (see III. p. 149 f.), concludes that the treaty given here accompanied the former transaction[1]. On the latter occasion Olaf was baptised—and we know that after his return to Norway he was a most zealous Christian—but there is no reference to this here.

The treaty, as distinguished from that between Alfred and Guthrum, is entirely concerned with the personal relations between the two parties. The invading army obviously had no intention of permanently settling in the country. Clauses 8 and 9 have no intrinsic connection with what precedes, and are regarded by Liebermann as an independent piece of legislation. He attributes them to a date about 1000 in view both of their style and of their contents (cf. III Atr. 6, 1 and II Cn. 24, 2, which apparently mark later developments in the system of vouching to warranty).

---

[1] See also Schmid, p. li; Freeman, *Norman Conq.* I. p. 278; Steenstrup, *Normannerne*, III. p. 238, IV. p. 56 f.; Stevenson, *Crawford Ch.* p. 120; Plummer, *Sax. Chr.* II. p. 173; Hodgkin, *Hist. of Engl.* p. 381; Oman. *Engl. bef. Conq.* p. 558.

I and III have points in common and may have been issued about the same time. Both refer to an earlier assembly at Bromdun, and clauses found in I are repeated in III (see Notes). I is particularly concerned with the districts under English Law (see Preamble), whereas III, with its regulations for the Five Boroughs, its Scandinavian money-system and its Northern terms, seems specially intended for the Danelaw. I was enacted at Woodstock in Mercia (cf. IX), III at Wantage in Wessex. At the latter place a notable assembly met in 997 (cf. Kemble, No. 698), and hence III is attributed to that year by Kemble (*Saxons in England*, II. p. 257), Schmid (p. li) and Freeman (*Norman Conquest*, I. p. 295). Liebermann, however, does not consider this conclusion justified, although he attributes both codes to the period preceding Æthelred's exile in 1013. He notes that the laws issued after his return lay particular stress on the necessity for loyalty to one royal lord—an injunction which does not appear in either of these. Both codes contain definite regulations with regard to legal procedure and stand in line with the laws of Æthelstan and Edgar.

In IV no king's name is mentioned but it almost certainly belongs to the reign of Æthelred. The order observed in referring to both sections of the people (i.e. *Dani et Angli*, cap. 8), and the insistence upon the fixed relationship of 15 ores to a pound (cap. 9, 2), point to a period when Danish influence was particularly strong. That it was not issued during the reign of Canute, however, seems evident from the fact that the Danes are not mentioned among those enjoying special trade privileges. Liebermann points out, in addition to these considerations, that Normandy appears in peaceful intercourse with England (cap. 2, 5 f.), and that relations between the Danes and English inhabitants of the country are apparently amicable. He consequently attributes the code to a date between 991—the year of the treaty between Æthelred and Richard, Duke of Normandy (see Notes)—and 1002, when the violent outbreak of hatred against the Danes was followed by the ravages and final conquest of Sweyn, 1003–1014. The code combines an account of the special regulations in force at London (chiefly with regard to the payment of toll and the trading rights of foreigners) with general decrees (mainly with regard to the coinage), applicable apparently to the whole country. The first part is particularly interesting for the light it sheds not only on the topography of London about the year 1000, but also on the trade of N.W. Europe at the time. As a document relating particularly to London it stands beside VI Æthelstan, the Charter of Henry I (Hn Lond) and the *Libertas Londoniensis* (see Liebermann, I. p. 673).

The last codes of Æthelred's reign are thoroughly ecclesiastical in tone and homiletic in style, full of tiresome repetitions and injunctions, but giving small sign of any practical policy with regard to the difficulties of the time. They bear witness to the strong influence exercised by Archbishop Wulfstan of York, to whose sermons whole passages afford close parallels (see Notes).

Codes V and VI are alike in substance, though individual differences justify their being regarded as independent. Certain clauses in VI (e.g. caps. 5, 2; 12 ff.; 32 ff.; 34) are not found in V, while additional passages, probably due to scribes, are peculiar to certain MSS (e.g. V D, caps. 32, 1–5; VI D and K, caps. 41–49; VI K, caps. 50–53). Liebermann supports Schmid's suggestion that both codes are descended from the same ordinance issued at King's Enham in 1008 (cf. X Preamble, cap. 3 ff.; VI Preamble and Note; V Heading G). The arrangement of both is practically the same, and both deal with the duties of Christian men in general, also the duties of clerics and the rights and revenues of the Church. The promotion of public security is enjoined, also attention to the repair of bridges and fortifications, to military service and to the fitting out of ships. A Latin paraphrase of VI, written in a very inflated style, is valuable for the additional information which it supplies in the preamble and in the concluding paragraph (see Notes).

Code VII is preserved in the Quadripartitus and in an Anglo-Saxon copy. In spite of differences in arrangement these point back to a common ancestor—an edict issued at Bath in a year of invasion when Michaelmas fell sometime between Thursday and Sunday (cf. VII, cap. 2, 3*a*; VII (A.S.), cap. 1). The years possible, as Liebermann points out, are 992–5, 998–1000, 1004–6, 1009–11 and 1015. The absence of reference to the approaching end of the world dreaded in the year 1000 (cf. Ælfric, *Homilies*,

I. pp. 578, 608; II. p. 370) suggests that the edict belongs to a later date, while the heading of the Anglo-Saxon version recalls *se ungemetlica unfriðhere* which began its ravages on the south and east of England in August 1009 (see *Sax. Chr.*). There is no clue however to the exact date. The occasion obviously was one of great national stress owing to the attacks of the Danes, and the purpose of the edict was to enforce the observance of Christian duties and to appoint certain special days in that year for fasting and prayer. It is particularly interesting for the light it sheds on the terror inspired by the invaders, and also notable for its entire lack of reference to practical measures of defence. Other traces of this edict of penitence are to be found in Wulfstan's Homilies (ed. Napier, pp. 169–175).

The heading of VIII in MS D ascribes it to the year 1014. No king's name is mentioned in the preamble, but resemblances both in content and phraseology to V and VI, and more particularly to Wulfstan's sermon of 1014, are in favour of accepting that date as correct. The arrangement in this code is more logical than in those preceding, and several new and important regulations appear with regard to the grading of churches, the division of tithes and the trial of members of the clergy. The expression of a desire to revive the better conditions of former days, as established by Æthelstan, Edmund and Edgar (cap. 43), is noteworthy, even though the point of view is purely ecclesiastical.

The fragments IX and X were first included by Liebermann in his edition of the Laws. The preamble and two clauses of IX are preserved in Hickes' *Thesaurus Linguarum Septentrionalium* II. p. 232, the MS having been burnt. In the preamble the place of assembly is named as Woodstock (cf. I), while the two extant clauses are repetitions from V and VI. For the text of X (preserved in MS Christina 946 in the Vatican at Rome) I am indebted to Liebermann's edition. The preamble, which has echoes of Edmund and Edgar, explains the aim of law-giving, while the only two extant clauses are quotations from V.

As regards the MSS of the other codes—I and II are preserved in B (from which the present text is taken), in Lambarde's edition (drawn from B and a lost MS) and in Q, while I is also found in H; III is found in H and Q; IV only in Q; V is preserved in D (from which the present text is taken), G and G_2 (the two latter in the same codex but in different handwriting); VI is found in K (from which the present text is taken) and partly in D; VII in Q and D; VIII in D, while the first section entitled *Be Cyricgriðe* is also found in G among a series of pieces of the same type. A few clauses appear likewise in the *Consiliatio Cnuti*. For the relationship of the various MSS see Liebermann, III. pp. 146, 149, 156, 169, 178, 182.

I ÆTHELRED

Æðelredes lage[1].

Ðis is seo gerædnys[2] þe Æþelred cining 7 his witan geræddon, eallon folce to friðes bote, æt Wudestoce on Myrcena lande, æfter Engla lage.

1. [Be borgum.][3]
Þæt is, ðǽt ælc freoman getreowne borh hæbbe, þæt se borh hine to ælcon rihte gehealde, gyf he betyhtlad wurðe.

§ 1. Gyf he ðonne tyhtbysig sy, gange to ðam ðreofealdan ordale.

§ 2. Gyf se hlaford sæcge þæt him naðor ne burste ne að ne ordal syððan þæt gemot wæs æt Bromdune, nime se hlaford him twegen getreowa ðegenas innan ðam hundrede 7 swerian þæt him næfre að ne burste ne he[4] ðeofgyld ne gulde—buton he ðone gerefan hæbbe ðe ðæs wyrðe sy þe þæt don mæge.

§ 3. Gyf se að ðonne forðcume, ceose se man ðonne, ðe ðær betyhtlad sy, swa hweðer swa he wylle, swa anfeald ordal swa pundes wurðne að, innan ðam ðrim[5] hundredan, ofer ðrittig penega.

§ 4. Gyf hi ðonne að syllan ne durron, gange to ðam ðrifealdan ordale.

§ 5. Gyf he ðonne ful wurðe, æt ðam forman cyrre bete ðam teonde twygylde 7 ðam hlaforde his were 7 sette getreowe borgas þæt he ælces yfel[es][6] eft geswice.

§ 6. And æt ðam oðran cyrre ne sy ðær nan oðer bot buton þæt heafod.

§ 7. Gyf he ðonne uthleape 7 þæt ordal forbuge, gylde se borh ðam teonde his ceapgyld 7 ðam hlaforde his were ðe his wites wyrðe sy.

§ 8. And gyf mon ðone hlaford teo, þæt he be his ræde[7] uthleope 7 ær unriht worhte, nime him fif ðegnas to 7 beo him sylf syxta 7 ladie hine ðæs.

---

[1] Om. Ld; Æþelredes cyninges gerædnisse H.   [2] H; þa gerædnysse B.
[3] The rubrics are found only in Ld.   [4] Om. Ld.   [5] H, Ld; drim B.
[6] yfeles H; yfel B; yfle Ld.   [7] H, Ld; hræde B.

I ÆTHELRED

Æthelred's laws[1].

This is the ordinance[1] which King Æthelred and his councillors have enacted, at Woodstock in Mercia[2], for the promotion of public security[3], wherever English law prevails[4].

1. Namely, that every freeman shall have a trustworthy surety[1] who shall hold him to the performance of every legal duty, if he has been accused.

    § 1[1]. If, however, he is of bad reputation, he shall go to the triple ordeal.

    § 2. If his lord asserts that he (the accused) has failed neither in oath nor in ordeal since the assembly was held at Bromdun[1], he (the lord) shall choose two trustworthy thegns within the hundred, and they shall swear that neither has his oath ever failed nor has he been convicted of stealing—unless the lord have a reeve[2] who is qualified to discharge this duty.

    § 3. If the oath is forthcoming, the man who is accused there shall choose whichever he will, either the simple ordeal or an oath equivalent to a pound in value, [supported by compurgators found] within the three hundreds[1], [in the case of any object] over 30 pence [in value][2].

    § 4. If they dare not give the oath, he (the accused) shall go to the triple ordeal[1].

    § 5. If he is found guilty, on the first occasion he shall pay the accuser double value and his wergeld[1] to his lord[2], and shall appoint trustworthy sureties[3] that henceforth he will desist from every kind of misdeed.

    § 6. And on the second occasion he shall not be able to make any amends except by his head[1].

    § 7[1]. If he escapes and avoids the ordeal, his surety shall pay the value of his goods to the accuser and the wergeld of the accused to the lord who is entitled to the fines incurred by him.

    § 8[1]. And if the lord is accused of advising the man who had done wrong to escape, he shall choose five thegns, and shall himself make a sixth, and shall clear himself of the accusation.

§ 9. 7 gyf seo lad forðcume, beo he ðes weres wyrðe.
§ 9a. 7 gyf héo forð ne cume, fo se cyng to ðam were 7 beo se ðeof utlah wið eal folc.
§ 10. 7 hæbbe ælc hlaford his[1] hiredmen on his agenon borge.
§ 11. Gyf he ðonne betyhtlad wurðe 7 he ut oðhleape[2], gylde se hlaford ðæs mannes were ðam cynge.
§ 12. 7 gyf mon ðone hlaford téo, þæt he be[1] his ræde utleope, ladie hine mid fif ðegnum 7 beo him sylf sixta.
§ 13. Gyf him seo lad byrste, gylde ðam cynge his were 7 si se man utlah.
§ 14. 7 beo se cyng ælces ðara wita wyrðe ðe ða men gewyrcean þe boclond hæbben, 7 ne bete nan man for nanre tihtlan, buton hit sy ðæs cynges gerefan gewitnysse.

2. [Be ðeowmen ðe ful wyrþe.]
And gyf ðeowman ful wurðe æt þam ordale, mearcie man hine æt[3] ðam forman cyrran.
§ 1. 7 æt ðam oðran cyrre ne sy ðær nan bót buton þæt heafod.

3. [Be ðon ðe mon ne ceapige buton gewitnysse.]
7 þæt[4] nan man ne dó naðor: ne ne bycgge ne ne hwyrfe, buton he borh hæbbe 7 gewitnysse.
§ 1. And gyf hit hwa do, fo se landhlaford to 7 healde þæt órf, oð þæt mon wite hwa hit mid rihte áge.

4. [Be ðæm men ðe eallum folc ungetrywe sy.]
7 gyf hwylc man sy ðe eallon folce ungetrywe sy, fare ðæs cynges gerefa to 7 gebringe hine under borge þæt hine man to rihte gelæde ðam ðe him onspæcon.
§ 1. Gyf he ðonne borh næbbe, slea man hine 7 hine[5] on ful lecge.
§ 2. 7 gyf hwá hine forne forstande, beon hi begen anes rihtes wyrðe.
§ 3. 7 se ðe þis forsitte 7 hit geforðian nylle, swa ure ealra cwide is, sylle ðam cynge hundtwelftig scill'.

[1] Added above in later handwriting in B.
[2] uthleape Ld.
[3] þam ordale...æt. Added in margin in later handwriting in B.
[4] Om. Ld.   [5] Om. H.

§ 9[1]. And if he succeeds in clearing himself, he shall be entitled to the wergeld.

§ 9a. And if he fails, the king shall take the wergeld, and the thief shall be treated as an outlaw[1] by all the nation.

§ 10[1]. And every lord shall be personally [responsible as] surety for the men of his own household.

§ 11. And if a man is accused and escapes, the lord shall pay his wergeld to the king.

§ 12[1]. And if the lord is accused of advising him to escape, he shall clear himself with [the help of] five thegns, himself making a sixth.

§ 13. If he fail to clear himself, he shall pay his (own)[1] wergeld to the king, and the man shall be an outlaw.

§ 14. And the king shall be entitled to all the fines which are incurred by men who hold land by title deed, and no-one [of these] shall pay the compensation following upon any charge, unless in the presence of the king's reeve.

2. And if a slave is found guilty at the ordeal, he shall be branded[1] on the first occasion[2].

§ 1[1]. And on the second occasion he shall not be able to make any amends except by his head.

3[1]. And no-one shall either buy or exchange anything, unless he have a surety and witnesses.

§ 1. And if anyone do so, the lord of the manor[1] shall seize and keep the stock, until it is known who is the rightful owner.

4[1]. And if there is anyone who is regarded with suspicion by the general public, the king's reeve shall go and place him under surety so that he may be brought to do justice to those who have made charges against him.

§ 1. If he has no surety, he shall be slain and buried in unconsecrated ground[1].

§ 2[1]. And if anyone interposes in his defence[2], they shall both incur the same punishment.

§ 3[1]. And he who ignores this, and will not further what we have all decreed, shall pay 120 shillings to the king.

II ÆTHELRED

Ðis synd ða friðmal 7 ða forword ðe Æthelred cyng 7 ealle his witan wið ðone here gedon habbað, ðe Anlaf 7 Iustin 7 Guðmund Stegitan sunu mid wæron.

1. Ðæt ærost, þæt woroldfrið stande betweox Æthelrede cynge 7 eallum his leodscipe 7 eallum ðam here ðe se cyng þæt feoh sealde æfter ðam formalan ðe Sigeric arcebiscop 7 Æðelwerd ealdormann 7 Ælfric ealdorman worhton, ða h[i][1] abædon æt ðam cynge, þæt hy mostan ðam læppan frið gebicgean, ðe hy under cynge[2] hand ofer hæfdon.

   § 1. 7 gif ænig sciphere on Englaland hergie, þæt we habban heora ealra fultum; 7 we him sculon mete findon, ða hwile ðe hy mid us beoð.

   § 2. 7 ælc ðæra landa ðe ænigne friðige ðæra ðe Ænglaland hergie, beo hit utlah wið us 7 wið ealne here.

2. [Be ceapscypum.][3]
   7 ælc ceapscip frið hæbbe ðe binnan muðan cuman, ðeh hit unfriðscyp sy, gyf hit undrifen bið.

   § 1. 7 ðeh hit gedriuen beo 7 hit ætfleo to hwilcre friðbyrig, 7 ða menn up ætberstan into ðære byrig, ðonne habban ða men frið 7 þæt hy him mid bringað.

3. [Be ðæs cyninges fryþmannum.]
   7 ælc agenra friðmanna frið hæbbe, ge on lande ge on wætere, ge binnan muðan ge butan.

   § 1. Gyf Æðelredes cynges friðman cume on unfriðland 7 se here ðærto cume, hæbbe frið his scip 7 ealle his æhta.

   § 2. Gyf he his scip upp getogen hæbbe oððon hulc geworhtne oððon[4] geteld geslagen—þæt he ðær frið hæbbe 7 ealle his æhta.

---

[1] Ld: *hu* B. [2] *cynges* Ld. [3] The rubrics are found only in Ld.
[4] *oððe on* Ld.

II ÆTHELRED

These are the terms of the truce and the agreement which King Æthelred and all his councillors have made with the (Viking) fleet led by Olaf[1] and Justin[2] and Guðmund[3], the son of Stegita.

1. In the first place, a general truce[1] shall be established between King Æthelred and all his subjects and the whole (Viking) fleet to which the king has paid tribute, in accordance with[2] the terms which Archbishop Sigeric[3] and Ealdorman Æthelweard and Ealdorman Ælfric[4] made, when they obtained the king's permission to purchase peace for the districts[5] which, subject to him, they ruled over[6].
   § 1. And if any hostile fleet harry in England[1], we shall have the help of all of them; and we shall be under the obligation of finding provisions[2] for them, as long as they remain with us[3].
   § 2. And every region[1] which affords protection to any of those who harry England shall be treated as an enemy [country] by us and all the aforesaid fleet[2].
2. And every merchant ship which enters an estuary, even if it belong to a region not included in the truce[1], shall be afforded protection, provided it is not pursued[2].
   § 1. And even if it is pursued and reach any town included in the truce[1] and the men escape into the town, protection is to be afforded to them and to what they bring with them.
3. But all of those who are specially included in the truce[1] are to enjoy the protection of the truce, whether on land or on water, whether within an estuary or not.
   § 1. If a subject of King Æthelred's who is included in the truce comes to a region to which it does not apply[1], and the aforesaid fleet arrives there, protection shall be afforded to his ship and all his goods.
   § 2. If he has drawn his ship ashore or built a hut or pitched a tent, protection shall be afforded to himself and to all his goods.

§ 3. Gyf he his æhta bere geman ðara unfriðmanna æhta into huse, ðolie his æhta, 7 æbbe sylf frið 7 feorh, gif he hine cyðe.

§ 4. Gyf se friðman fleo oððon feohte 7 nelle hine cyðan, gif hine man ofslea, licge ungylde[1].

4. [Be ðon ðe mon on scipe bereafod sy.]
Gyf man beo æt his æhtan bereafod, 7 he wite of hwilcum scipe, agyfe steoresman ða æhta oððon gange feowra sum tó 7 oðsace—7 beo him sylf fifta—þæt he hit ariht name, swa hit ær geforword wæs.

5. [Be monslege.]
Gyf Ænglisc man Deniscne ofsleo, frigman frigne, gylde hine mid xxv pundum, oððon man ðone handdædan agyfe; 7 do se Denisca ðone Engliscan ealswa, gif hine[2] ofslea.

§ 1. Gyf Englisc man Deniscne ðræl ofslea, gylde hine mid punde, 7 se Denisca Engliscne ealswa, gif he hine ofslea.

§ 2. Gyf eahta men beon ofslagene, ðonne is þæt friðbrec, binnan byrig oððon buto[n][3]. Binnan eahta mannum bete man þæt fullum were.

6. [Be friþbrec binnan byrig.]
Gyf hit binnan byrig gedon bið, seo friðbræc, fare seo buruhwaru sylf to 7 begyte ða[4] banan, cuce[5] oððe deade, heora nyh[s]tan[6] magas heafod wið heafde. Gyf hy nellan, fare se ealdorman to; gif he nelle, fare se cyning to; gif he nelle, licge se ealdordóm on unfriðe.

§ 1. Æt eallum slyht 7 æt ealre ðære hergunge 7 æt eallum ðam hearmum ðe ær ðam gedon wære, ær ðæt frið geset wære, man eall onweig[7] læte, 7 nan man þæt ne rece[8] ne bote ne bidde.

§ 2. 7 þæt naðor ne hy[9] ne we ne underfon oðres wealh ne oðres ðeof ne oðres gefan.

---

[1] *orgylde* Ld.   [2] *g. he h.* Ld.   [3] Ld; *buto* B.   [4] *ðe* Ld.
[5] *cute* B; *cucne o. deadne* Ld.   [6] *nyhtan* B, Ld.   [7] *on wege* Ld.
[8] *wræce* Ld.   [9] *hine* Ld.

§ 3. If he bears his goods into a house in common with those of the men not included in the truce[1], he shall forfeit his goods, but he himself shall have protection and his life [shall be spared], if he makes himself known.

§ 4. If a man included in the truce flees or fights and fails to make himself known, no compensation shall be paid for him[1], if he is slain.

4. If anyone has been robbed of his goods and he knows the ship by[1] which it has been done, the captain[2] shall restore the goods or shall go with four compurgators[3]—himself making a fifth—and deny [the charge, proving] that he was justified in taking them, according to the terms laid down above[4].

5. If an Englishman slays a Dane, both being free men, he shall pay 25 pounds[1] for him, or the actual delinquent shall be delivered up. And likewise in the case of a Dane who slays an Englishman.

§ 1. If an Englishman slays a Danish slave[1], he shall pay one pound[2] for him, and the Dane likewise for the English slave whom he slays.

§ 2. If eight men are slain, that constitutes a breach of the truce[1], whether in a town or in the open country. For less than eight men the full wergeld shall be paid as compensation.

6. If the breach of the truce takes place inside a town, the burghers themselves shall go and take the slayers alive or dead[1]—the nearest relatives[2] [of the slain men] shall take head for head[3]. If they fail to do so[4], the ealdorman[5] shall act; if he fails to do so, the king[5] shall act; if he fails, that earldom shall be excluded from the provisions of this truce[6].

§ 1. As regards all the slaughter and all the harrying and all the injuries[1] which were done[2] before the truce was made—all of them shall be forgotten, and no-one shall avenge them or demand compensation for them.

§ 2[1]. And neither of the two parties to the truce—neither they nor we—shall harbour a slave[2] belonging to the other party, or a thief pursued by them, or anyone who is involved in vendetta with them.

II ÆTHELRED

7. [Be landesmannes tyhte.]

7 gif man secge on landesmann þæt he orf stæle[1] oððon man sloge, 7 hit secge an sceiðman 7 an landesman, ðonne ne beo he nane[s][2] andsæces wyrðe.

§ 1. 7 gif heora menn slean ure eahta, ðonne beoð hy utlage ge wið hy ge wið us, 7 ne beo nanre bote weorðe.

§ 2. Twa and twentig ðusend[3] punda goldes 7 seolfres man gesealde ðam here of Ænglalande wið friðe.

8. [Be ðon ðe mon gefô ðe him losod wæs.]

Gyf hwa befo þæt him losod wæs, cenne se ðe he hit æt befo, hwanon hit him come; sylle[4] on hand 7 sette borh, þæt he bringe his geteaman in ðær hit besprecen bið.

§ 1. Gif he liuiendre handa team gecenne 7 sy on oðere scire se ðe he to tymð, hæbbe swa la[n]gne[5] fyrst swa ðærto gebyrige. Sette on ða hand ðe hit him sealde 7 bidde þæt he clænsie, gif he mæge.

§ 2. Gif he tofeóht, ðonne clænsnoð he ðene ðe hit ær æt befangen wæs. Cenne he syððan hwanan hit him[4] come.

§ 3. Gif he cenne ofer I scira, hæbbe I wucena fyrst; gif he cenne ofer II scira, hæbbe II wucena fyrst; gyf he cenna[6] ofer III scira, hæbbe III wucena fyrst; ofor eallswa fela scira swa he cenne, hæbbe swa fela wycena fyrst.

§ 4. 7 tyme[7] hit mon æure ðær hit ærost befangen beo[8].

9. [Be teamum.]

Hwilon stod þæt man sceolde ðrywa tyman ðær hit ærest befangen wære, 7 syððan fylgean teame, swa hwær swa man

---
[1] Ld; scæle B. [2] Ld; nan ei B.
[3] n added in later handwriting, B. [4] Om. Ld. [5] Ld; lagne B.
[6] cenne Ld. [7] cume B, Ld; tyme Lieb. [8] wære Ld.

7. And if a man of our country[1] is charged with having stolen cattle or with having slain anyone, and the charge is brought by one Viking[2] and one man belonging to this country, he shall not be entitled to make any denial.
   § 1[1]. And if their men slay eight of us, they shall be treated as outlaws both by them and by us, and shall not be allowed to settle the matter by any payment of compensation.
   § 2[1]. 22,000 pounds in gold and silver[2] have been paid out of England to the (Viking) fleet as the price of the truce.

[II Æthelred, Appendix.]

8. If anyone attaches what he has lost, the man in whose possession it is attached shall declare how it came to him. He shall give pledges and furnish surety that he will produce his warrantor, when the case shall be brought into court.
   § 1. If he vouches a living person to warranty and the man whom he vouches is in another county, he shall be granted as long adjournment as is necessary for the purpose[1]. He shall lay it to the charge of the man who sold it to him, and request him to justify the transaction, if he can.
   § 2. If the latter accepts the charge, he [thereby] clears the man in whose possession it has been attached. He himself shall afterwards declare how it came to him.
   § 3[1]. If he can specify the county in which the man whom he vouches to warranty lives, he shall have a week's adjournment; if he can locate him within two counties, he shall have two weeks; if within three, he shall have three weeks—the number of weeks' adjournment granted him shall correspond to the number of counties which he names.
   § 4. And vouching to warranty shall always[1] take place where the property has first been attached.

9. Formerly it was the rule that vouching to warranty for the first three times should take place where the goods were first attached, and afterwards[1] the process should be trans-

to cende. Ða geræddan[1] witan, þæt hit betere wære, þæt man æure tymde ðær hit ærest befangen wære, swa longe þæt man wiste hwær hit ætstandan wolde, ðy læs ðe mon unmihtigne man to feor 7 to lange for his agenan swencte. Swunce mare se ðe þæt unriht gestreon on his handa stode 7 læsse se ðe ðær ariht onspræce.

§ 1. Warige eac hine se ðe his agen[2] befoð: he to ælcan teame hæbbe getrywne borh 7 beorge þæt he awoh ne befo, ðy les ðe hine mon swence, swa he oðerne man ðohte.

§ 2. Gyf hwa to deadan tyme—buton he yruenoman hæbbe ðe hit clænsie—geswutelie mid gewitnysse, gif he mæge, þæt he riht cenne se ðe hit tyme 7 clænsnige hine sylfne mid ðam. Ðonne bið se deada besmiten, buton he frind hæbbe ðe hine mid rihte clænsnian, swa he sylf scolde, gif he mehte oðð liues wære.

§ 3. Gif he ðonne ðære freonda hæfð ðe þæt don durron, ðonne berst se team, swa wel swa he liues wære 7 sylf andsæc[3] worhte; stent ðonne ðeofscyldig se ðe hit on handa hæfð, forðam a bið andsæc swiðere ðonne onsagu.

§ 4. Eac betweox teame, gif hwa tofehð 7 na furðor team ne cenð ac agnian wille, ne mæg mon ðæs wyrnan, gif getrywe gewitnes him to agenunge rymð, forðam agnung bið ner ðam ðe hæfð ðonne ðam ðe æftersprecð.

[1] *-don* Ld.   [2] Ld; *hagen* B.   [3] Ld; *and sæt* B.

ferred to the locality indicated (by the evidence of the third person). Then the authorities decided that it would be better for the vouching to warranty always to take place where the property was first attached, until it should appear where the process would end, lest a man of small means should be burdened by long and distant journeys in order to recover his property. The burden should rather be borne by him who has in his possession property to which he is not entitled, than by him who is putting forward a just claim to it.

§ 1. Likewise, he who attaches his goods shall see to it that he has trustworthy security[1] in every case of vouching to warranty, and shall beware of attaching wrongly, lest the burden which he had thought should be borne by the other man should be laid upon him.

§ 2. If anyone vouches a dead person[1] to warranty—unless he have an heir who can answer the charge—he who vouches him to warranty shall show by means of witnesses, if he can, that he is acting justly, and by means of them shall clear himself. Then the dead man will be held guilty, unless he have friends who will clear him according to the law, as he himself would have been obliged to do, had he been able or had he been alive.

§ 3. If, however, he has friends[1] who are prepared to do so, the vouching to warranty shall fail as completely as if he had himself been alive and had proved his denial. Then he, in whose possession the goods are, will be held guilty of theft[2], because denial is always stronger than accusation.

§ 4. Further, in the course of vouching to warranty, if anyone accepts and does not carry the process any farther but desires to declare himself the owner [of the goods][1], no-one can deny his claim, if trustworthy witnesses establish his ownership of the goods, for a priori the actual possessor must be regarded as having more right than the claimant[2].

III ÆTHELRED

Ðis syndon þa lága þe Æðelred cyng 7 his witan gerædd habbað æt Wánetingc to friðes bóte.

1. Ðæt is: þæt his grið stande swa forð swa hit fyrmest stód on his yldrena dagum, þæt þæt sy bótléas þæt he mid his agenre hánd sylð.

    § 1. 7 þæt grið, þæt se ealdormann 7 kinges geréfa on Fif burga geþincða sylle, bete man þæt mid XII hund'.

    § 2. And þæt grið þæt man sylleð on I burhgaþinðe[1], bete man þæt mid VI hundī; and þæ[t][2] man sylle on wǽpentáke, bete man þæt mid hundī, gif hit man brecð; and þæt man sylle on éalahuse, bete man þæt æt deadum menn mid VI healfmarce 7 æt cwicon mid XII óran.

2. And þæt þæt man cyðe mid gewitnesse, þæt nan man þæt ne awende æt cwícon þe ma þe æt déadon.

    § 1. 7 gange ælc man þæs to gewitnesse þe he durre on þam haligdóme swerian þe him man on hand sylð.

3. And lándcóp 7 hlafordes gifu þe he on riht age to gifanne 7 lahcóp 7 witword 7 gewítnes, þæt þæt stande þæt hit nan man ne awénde.

    § 1. 7 þæt man habbe gemót on ælcum wæpen[t]ace[3]; 7 gán út þa yldestan XII þegnas 7 se gerefa mid 7 swerian on þam haligdome þe heom man on hand sylle, þæt hig nellan nǽnne sacleasan man forsecgean ne nǽnne sacne forhélan.

---

[1] *burhga* (I) *þinðe* (I written above the line) H; *unius burgi þincþa* Q.
[2] *þær* H.   [3] *-kace* H.

III ÆTHELRED

These are the constitutions[1] which King Æthelred and his councillors have enacted at Wantage[2] for the promotion of public security[3].

1. Namely, that the king's peace[1] shall continue to be maintained in accordance with the highest standards[2] observed in the days of his ancestors, so that breach of the peace which he establishes in person shall not be atoned for by any payment of compensation[3].
    § 1. But for breach of the peace which the ealdorman or[1] the king's reeve establishes in the Court of the Five Boroughs[2], 1200 of silver shall be paid as compensation.
    § 2. And for breach of the peace established in the court of one borough[1] 600 [of silver] shall be paid as compensation, and 100 for that established in a wapentake. In the case of breach of the peace in an ale-house, 6 half marks[2] shall be paid as compensation if a man is slain, and 12 ores if no-one is slain[3].
2. Secondly, declarations made with the support of witnesses shall be incontrovertible, whether the persons concerned be alive or dead[1].
    § 1. And a man shall appear as witness to such things[1] [only] as he is prepared to swear to on the relics[2] which are given into his hand.
3. And there shall be no interference with purchases of land[1], or gifts by a lord of what he has a legal right to bestow, or purchases of legal rights[2], or asseverations (which have been duly made) or testimonies[3] (which have been duly given).
    § 1. And a court shall be held in every wapentake, and the twelve leading thegns[1] along with the reeve shall go out and swear on the relics[2] which are given into their hands, that they will not accuse any innocent[3] man or shield any guilty[4] one.

§ 2. 7 niman þonne þa tihtbysian men þe mid þam gerefan [sace]¹ habbað, 7 heora ælc sylle vi healfmarc wedd, healf landrícan 7 healf wǽpentake.

§ 3. 7 ælc bicge him lage mid xii óran, healf landrican, healf wæpentake.

§ 4. 7 ælc tihtbysig man gange to þryfeldan órdale oððe gilde feowergilde.

4. Gif se hlaford þonne hine ladian wylle mid twam godum þegenum, þæt he næfre þeofgild né gúlde, siððan þæt gemót wæs on Brómdune, ne he betihlod nære, gange tó anfealdum órdale oððe gilde iiigilde.

§ 1. Gif he þonne ful beo, slea man hine, þæt him forberste se swéora; 7 gif he þæt ordal forbuge, gilde angylde þam agenan frian 7 landrícan xx óran 7 gá eft to þam órdale.

§ 2. And gif se ágena frígia nelle þæt ordal gesecean, gilde xx óran 7 sy his spæce forlóren; 7 he þeah gange þam landrícan to ordale oððe agife twygilde.

5. And gif hwa borhleas órf habbe 7 landrícan hit befón, agife þæt órf 7 gilde xx oran.

6. 7 ælc tíond áge geweald, swa hwæðer he wille, swa wæter swa ísen.

§ 1. 7 ælc téam 7 ælc ordal beo on þæs kyninges byrig.

§ 2. 7 gif he þæt ordal forfleo, gilde se borh hine be his were.

[1] Not in MS.; cf. *causam* Q.

§ 2. And then they shall arrest those men of bad repute against whom the reeve is taking proceedings[1], and each of them shall pay six half marks[2] as security, half to the lord of the manor and half to the wapentake[3].

§ 3. And each of them shall pay 12 ores[1], half to the lord of the manor and half to the wapentake. in order to obtain the benefit of the law.

§ 4[1]. And every man of bad repute shall go to the triple ordeal or pay fourfold [the value of the goods involved].

4[1]. If, however, his lord is willing to clear him, [swearing], along with two good thegns, that he has neither been convicted of theft nor been accused since the assembly was held at Bromdun, he shall go to the simple ordeal[2] or pay threefold [the value of the goods involved].

§ 1[1]. If then he is proved guilty, he shall be struck such a blow as shall break his neck. But if he evades the ordeal, he shall pay the value [of the goods] to their owner, and 20 ores[2] to the lord of the manor, and shall thereafter go to the ordeal.

§ 2. But if the owner [of the goods] shall fail to appear at the ordeal, he shall pay 20 ores and shall lose his case. But nevertheless the lord of the manor shall cause him (the thief) to go to the ordeal[1] or to pay double the value of the goods[2].

5. And if anyone has livestock acquired without surety[1], and manorial lords attach it[2], he shall give up the livestock[3] and pay 20 ores.

6[1]. And every accuser shall have the choice of whichever ordeal he desires [for the accused]—either ordeal by water or by iron.

§ 1. And every vouching to warranty[1] and every ordeal shall take place in a royal manor[2].

§ 2[1]. And if he (the accused) flees from the ordeal, his surety shall pay for him to the amount of his (the fugitive's) wergeld.

7. And gif hwa þeof clænsian wylle, lecge an c to wedde, healf landrican 7 healf cinges gerefan binnan port, 7 gange to þrimfealdan ordale.

§ 1. Gif he clæne beo æt þam ordale, nime úpp his mǽg; gif he þonne ful beo, licge þar he lǽg, 7 gilde an c.

8. And ælc mynetére þe man tihð þæt fals feoh sloge, syððan hit forboden wæs, gange to þrimfealdan ordale; gif he ful beo, slea hine man.

§ 1. And nan mann ne áge nænne mynetere buton cyng.

§ 2. 7 ælc mynetere þe betihtlad sí, bicge him láh mid XII oran.

9. 7 nan mann hryðer ne sléa, buton he habbe twégra trywra manna gewitnesse, 7 he healde III niht hyde 7 heafod; 7 sceapes eallswa.

§ 1. 7 gif he þa hyde ǽr þam awég sylle, gilde XX oran.

10. 7 ælc flyma beo flyma on ælcum lande þe on ánum sy.

11. 7 nan man náge náne socne ofer cynges þegen buton cyng sylf.

12. And æt cynges spǽce lecge man VI healfmarc wedd 7 æt eorles 7 biscopes XII óran wedd 7 æt ælcum þegene VI óran wedd.

13. 7 gif man hwilcne man téo, þæt he þone man féde þe ures hlafordes grið tóbrocen habbe, ladige hine mid þrinna XII, 7 se geréfa namige þa lade.

§ 1. And gif hine man mid him befare, béon hig begen ánes rihtes weorðe.

§ 2. 7 þæt dóm stande þar þegenas sámmǽle beon; gif hig sacan, stande þæt hig VIII secgað; 7 þa þe ðær oferdrífene beoð, gilde heora ælc VI healfmarc.

7[1]. And if anyone seeks to clear a thief, he shall deposit 100 [of silver] as security[2], half with the lord of the manor[3] and half with the king's town-reeve[4] and he shall go to the triple ordeal.
- § 1. And if he prove innocent at the ordeal, he shall remove his kinsman [from his grave in unconsecrated ground][1]. If, however, he be guilty, the thief shall lie where he is, and he himself shall pay 100 [of silver][2].

8. And every moneyer who is accused of striking false coins, after it was forbidden[1], shall go to the triple ordeal; if he is guilty, he shall be slain.
- § 1. And no-one except the king[1] shall have a moneyer.
- § 2[1]. And every moneyer who is accused shall pay 12 ores in order to obtain the benefit of the law.

9. And no-one shall kill a cow unless he has two trustworthy men as witnesses, and he shall keep the hide and the head[1] for three days; and those of a sheep likewise.
- § 1. And if he disposes of the hide before that, he shall pay 20 ores[1].

10. And everyone who is an outlaw in one district shall be an outlaw everywhere.

11[1]. And no-one shall have jurisdiction over a thegn of the king except the king himself.

12. And in the case of an action brought by[1] the king, 6 half-marks shall be deposited as security, and in the case of one brought by an earl or a bishop, 12 ores, and of one brought by a thegn, 6 ores as security.

13. And if anyone is accused of furnishing with food a man who has broken our lord's peace, he shall clear himself with three times twelve[1] compurgators who shall be nominated by the reeve.
- § 1. And if he (the accused) is found in his company, they shall both incur the same penalty[1].
- § 2. And a verdict in which the thegns are unanimous[1] shall be held valid; if they disagree, the verdict of eight[2] of them shall be valid, and those who are outvoted[3] in such a case shall each pay 6 half-marks[4].

§ 3. 7 þar þegen áge twegen costas, lufe oððe lage, 7 he
þonne lufe geceose, stande þæt swa fæst swa sé dom.

§ 4. 7 se ðe ofer ðæt láde geþafie oððe se þe hy sylle, gilde
VI healfmarc.

14. And se þe sitte úncwydd 7 uncrafod on his áre on life, þæt
nan mann on his yrfenuman ne spéce æfter his dǽge.

15. And se þe reafað man leohtan dǽge 7 he hit kyþe to þrim
túnan, þæt he ne beo nanes fryðes weorðe.

16. 7 þa myneteras þe inne wuda wyrceð oððe elles hwær, þæt
þa bion heora feores scyldig, buton se cyning heom arian
wille.

IV ÆTHELRED

[Item rex Lundoniae.][1]

[2][De institutis Lundoniae; et primum: quae[3] portae observabantur[4]. [2.] De teloneo dando ad Bilingesgate. [3.] De teloneo retento. [4.] De hamsocna vel in porto[5] vel in via regia[6]. [5.] De falsariis et eis consentientibus. Et de cum falsa moneta deprensis[7]. [6.] Et de monetariis[8].]

1. Ealdredesgate[9] et Cripelesgate[10] (id est portas illas) observabant[11] custodes.

2. Ad Billingesgate si advenisset una navicula—I obolus tolonei[12] dabatur; si maior et haberet[13] siglas[14]—unum den.

§ 1. Si adveniat ceol vel hulcus, et ibi iaceat—quatuor d. ad teloneum[15].

§ 2. De navi plena lignorum—unum lignum ad tol'[16].

§ 3. In ebdomada pañ'[17] teloñ[18] III diebus: die Dominica et[19] die Martis et[19] die Iovis.

[1] R.   [2] This table of contents is found in M, Hk, Br.   [3] quod Br.
[4] -buntur Br.   [5] -tu Br.   [6] -gis Br.
[7] Instead of Et...depr. Br has: [6.] De sonantibus pecuniam puram. [7.] De mercatoribus qui falsum et lactum afferunt ad portum. [8.] De suasione regis contra falsum operantes.
[8] [9]...m. et ubi erunt Br.   [9] T; Aaldretes R; Aldretes M, Hk; Aldredes Br.
[10] Crypeleg. T; Cyrpnleg. M, Hk; Ciryclegate Br.   [11] -bunt Br.
[12] thel. T, Br.   [13] habet T, M, Hk, Br.   [14] gulas R, T.
[15] a. t. dentur Br.   [16] a. t. detur Br.   [17] R, T; panū M; panum Br.
[18] thelonium detur Br.   [19] Om. M, Hk, Br.

§ 3. And where a thegn has two alternatives[1] before him—amicable agreement or legal proceedings—and he decides upon the former, it shall be as binding as a legal decision.

§ 4. And he who subsequently[1] permits a man to clear himself [of a transaction], and [likewise] he who offers to clear himself shall pay 6 half-marks.

14. And if a man dwells on his property free from claims and charges[1] during his lifetime, no-one shall bring an action against his heirs[2] after his death.

15. And if a man robs another in daylight[1], and the latter makes the deed known in three villages[2], he shall not be entitled to protection[3] of any kind.

16[1]. And moneyers who work in a wood[2] or elsewhere[3] shall forfeit their lives, unless the king is willing to pardon them.

IV ÆTHELRED

1. The gates called Aldersgate[1] and Cripplegate[1] (i.e. the actual gates) were in the charge of guards.

2. If a small ship came to Billingsgate[1], 1 half-penny was paid as toll; if a larger ship with sails, 1 penny was paid.

§ 1. If a barque or a merchantman[1] arrives and lies there, 4 pence is paid as toll.

§ 2. From a ship with a cargo of planks, one plank is given as toll.

§ 3. On three days of the week toll for cloth[1] [is paid]—on Sunday and Tuesday and Thursday[2].

§ 4. Qui ad pontem venisset[1] cum uno[2] bato ubi piscis inesset[3], ipse mango[4] unum obolum dabat[5] in telon., et de una[2] maiori nave unum d.

§ 5. Homines de Rotomago qui veniebant cum vino vel craspisce[6] dabant[7] rectitudinem sex sol. de magna navi et viginti frustum de ipso craspisce[6].

§ 6. Flandrenses et Ponteienses et Normannia et Francia monstrabant res suas et extolneabant.

§ 7. Hogge et Leodium et Nivella qui pertransibant[8] ostensionem dabant et telon.

§ 8. Et homines imperatoris qui veniebant in[9] navibus suis bonarum legum digni tenebantur sicut et nos.

§ 9. Praeter[10] discarcatam[11] lanam et dissutum unctum, et tres porcos vivos licebat eis emere in naves suas.

§ 10. Et non licebat eis aliquod forceapum facere burhmannis, et dare toll' suum et in sancto natali Domini duos grisengos pannos et unum brunum et decem libras piperis et cirotecas quinque hominum et duos caballinos tonellos[12] aceto plenos; et totidem in pascha.

§ 11. De dosseris cum gallinis I gallina telonei, et de[13] uno dossero cum ovis v ova telonei, si veniant ad mercatum.

§ 12. Smeremangestrae (quae mangonant in caseo et butiro) XIIII diebus ante natale Domini unum den., et septem diebus ante[14] natale Domini[15] unum alium[16].

3. Si portireva vel tungravio compellet[17] aliquem vel alius praepositus quod teloneum supertenuerit, et homo respondeat quod nullum tolneum[18] concelaverit quod iuste dare[2] debuisset[19], iuret hoc se VII°[20] et sit quietus.

§ 1. Si appellet quod tolneum[21] dedit[22], inveniat cui dedit et sit quietus.

---

[1] *veniat* Br. [2] Om. M, Hk, Br. [3] *inest, unus ob. dabatur* Br.
[4] *magno* M, Hk. [5] *dabit* R. [6] *craspice* R.
[7] *dabant...craspisce* om. M, Hk, Br. [8] *per terras ibant* T, M, Hk, Br.
[9] *cum* M, Hk, Br. [10] *Praeter...v. l. eis* om. M, Hk, Br. [11] *discartatam* T.
[12] *tolennos* M; *collennos* Hk; *colennos* Br. [13] Om. M, Hk. [14] *post* Br.
[15] M, Hk, Br. [16] *u. a. denarium ad theloneum* Br.
[17] *v. alius p. compellat aliquem* Br. [18] R; *teloneum* T, M, Hk, Br.
[19] *debuit* Br. [20] VI° M, Hk, Br. [21] R, T; *telon.* M, Hk; *thel.* Br.
[22] *dederit* Br.

§ 4. A merchant who came to the bridge[1] with a boat containing fish paid 1 half-penny as toll, and for a larger ship 1 penny.

§ 5. Men of Rouen[1], who came with wine or blubber-fish[2], paid a duty[3] of 6 shillings for a large ship and 5 %[4] of the fish.

§ 6. Men from Flanders[1] and Ponthieu and Normandy and the Isle of France exhibited their goods and paid toll[2].

§ 7. Men from Huy[1] and Liège and Nivelles who were passing through (London)[2] paid a sum for exhibition[3] and toll.

§ 8. And subjects of the Emperor[1] who came in their ships[2] were entitled to the same privileges[3] as ourselves.

§ 9. Besides wool, which had been unloaded[1], and melted fat[2], they were also permitted to buy three live pigs[3] for their ships.

§ 10. But they were not allowed any right of pre-emption[1] over the burgesses, and [they had] to pay their toll[2], and at Christmas[3] two lengths of grey cloth[4] and one length of brown and 10 pounds of pepper[5] and five pairs of gloves and two saddle-kegs[6] of vinegar, and the same at Easter.

§ 11. From hampers[1] with hens, one hen [is given] as toll, and from one hamper of eggs, five eggs as toll, if they come to the market.

§ 12. Women who deal in dairy produce[1] (i.e. cheese and butter) pay 1 penny a fortnight before Christmas, and another penny a week before Christmas.

3. If the town-reeve or the village reeve[1] or any other official[2] accuses[3] anyone of having withheld[4] toll, and the man replies that he has kept back no toll which it was his legal duty to pay, he shall swear to this with 6 others and shall be quit of the charge.

§ 1. If he declares[1] that he has paid toll, he shall produce the man to whom he paid it, and shall be quit of the charge.

§ 2. Si tunc hominem invenire non possit cui dederit[1], reddat ipsum tolneum et persolvat et[2] quinque libras regi.

§ 3. Si cacepollum advocet quod ei teloneum dedit, et ille neget, perneget ad Dei iudicium et in nulla alia lada[3].

4. Et diximus: homo qui hamsocnam faciet intra[4] portum sine licentia et summam infracturam aget[5] de placito ungebendeo[6], vel qui aliquem innocentem affliget[7] in via regia, si iaceat[8], iaceat in ungildan ækere.

§ 1. Si pugnet antequam sibi[9] rectum postulet ac vivat, emendet regis[10] burhbrece quinque libris.

§ 2. Si curet[11] amicitiam ipsius porti, reddat nobis triginta sol. emendationis, si rex hoc concedat nobis.

5. Etiam dixerunt quod nichil eis interesse videbatur inter falsarios et mercatores qui bonam pecuniam portant ad falsarios et ab ipsis emunt ut inpurum et minus appendens operentur, et inde mangonant[12] et barganiant, et eos etiam qui conos faciunt in occultis et vendunt falsariis pro pecunia et incidunt alterius monetarii nomen[13] in eo et non ipsius immundi.

§ 1. Unde visum est sapientibus omnibus, quod isti tres homines unius rectitudinis essent digni.

§ 2. Et si aliquis eorum accusetur, sit[14] Anglicus sit transmarinus, ladiet se pleno ordalio.

§ 3. Et constituerunt, monetarii cur[15] manum perdant et ponatur super ipsius monetae fabricam.

§ 4. Et monetarii[16], qui in nemoribus operantur[16] vel alicubi[17] similibus fabricant, vitae suae culpabiles sint, nisi rex velit eorum misereri.

---

[1] *dedit* Br. [2] R; om. T, M, Hk, Br. [3] *laga* T. [4] *faciat inter* R.
[5] *age* Hk; *agat* Br. [6] R; *-dro* T, M, Hk, Br. [7] *-gat* Br.
[8] *s. i.* om. Br. [9] Om. M, Hk, Br. [10] Om. T. [11] *-at* M, Hk.
[12] *mag.* M, Hk. [13] *monctam mundam et n. ipsam immundam* Br.
[14] *si* R. [15] *cur mon.* M, Hk; *quod mon.* Br. [16] Om. Br.
[17] *alibi* T, M, Hk, Br.

§ 2. If, however, he cannot produce the man to whom he paid it, he shall pay the actual toll and as much again[1] and 5 pounds to the king[2].

§ 3. If he vouches the tax-gatherer[1] to warranty[2] [asserting] that he paid toll to him, and the latter denies it, he shall clear himself by the ordeal and by no other means of proof.

4. And we[1] have decreed that a man who, within the town, makes forcible entry into another man's house without permission and commits a breach of the peace[2] of the worst kind...[3] and he who assaults an innocent person on the king's highway[4], if he is slain, shall lie in an unhonoured grave[5].

§ 1[1]. If, before demanding justice, he has recourse to violence, but does not lose his life thereby[2], he shall pay 5 pounds for breach of the king's peace[3].

§ 2. If he values the good-will[1] of the town itself, he shall pay us[2] 30 shillings[3] as compensation, if the king will grant us this concession.

5. Further, they[1] have decided that no distinction is to be drawn between those who issue base coin, and traders who take good money to such men and bribe[2] them to produce [from it] coin which is defective in quality and weight[3] with which they trade and buy, and, thirdly, those who make dies in secret and sell them to coiners for money, engraving upon them a name which is that of another moneyer and not that of the guilty one.

§ 1. It has therefore been determined by the whole council that these three [classes of] men shall incur the same punishment[1].

§ 2. And if one of them is accused, whether he be an Englishman or a foreigner, he shall clear himself by the full ordeal[1].

§ 3[1]. And they have decreed that[2] coiners shall lose a hand, and that it shall be fastened up over the mint.

§ 4[1]. And moneyers who carry on their business in woods or work in other such places shall forfeit their lives, unless the king is willing to pardon them.

6. Et praecipimus ne quis pecuniam puram et recte appendentem sonet, monetetur in quocumque portu monetetur[1] in regno meo, super overhirnessam meam.

7. Et diximus de mercatoribus qui falsum et lacum[2] afferunt ad portum, ut advocent si possint.

   § 1. Si non possint[3], werae suae culpa sit[4] vel vitae suae, sicut rex volet[5], vel eadem lada se innoxient quam praediximus, quod in ipsa pecunia nil immundum sciebant unde suam negotiationem exercuerunt.

   § 2. Et habeat postea dampnum illud ex incuria sua, ut cambiat[6] ab institutis monetariis purum et recte[7] appendens.

   § 3. Et portirevae qui falsi huius consentanei[8] fuerint, eiusdem censurae digni sint[9] cum falsis monetariis, nisi rex indulgeat eis vel se possint[10] adlegiare eodem cyrað[11] vel ordalio praedicto.

8. Et rex suadet et mandat episcopis suis et comitibus et aldremannis et praepositis omnibus, ut curam adhibeant[12] de illis qui tale falsum operantur et portant per patriam, sicut praemissum[13] est, utrobique cum Danis et Anglis.

9. Et ut monetarii pauciores sint quam antea fuerint[14]: in omni summo portu III[15], et in omni alio portu sit unus monetarius.

   § 1. Et illi habeant suboperarios suos in suo crimine, quod purum faciant et recti ponderis, per eandem witam quam praediximus.

---

[1] *monetur* M, Hk, Br; *in q. p. m.* om. R.   [2] *laccum* M, Hk; *lactum* Br.
[3] *s. n. p.* om. R.   [4] *culpabiles sint* Br.   [5] *velit* Br.   [6] Om. M, Hk, Br.
[7] *rectum* Br.   [8] *falso cons.* Br.   [9] *sunt* R, T.   [10] *possit* R, T.
[11] *cir.* R; *syrað* M, Hk; *sirath* Br.   [12] *-eat* R.   [13] *prom.* R, T.
[14] *-runt* Br.   [15] *sint tres monetarii* Br.

6. And we enjoin that no-one shall refuse pure money of the proper weight, in whatever town[1] in my kingdom it be coined, under pain of incurring the fine for insubordination to me.

7. And we have decreed with regard to traders who bring money which is defective in quality and weight to the town, that they shall name a warrantor if they can.
    § 1. If they cannot do so, they shall forfeit their wergeld or their life, as the king shall decide[1], or they shall clear themselves by the same method[2] as we have specified above, [asserting] that they were unaware that there was anything counterfeit about the money with which they were carrying on their business.
    § 2. And afterwards such a trader shall pay the penalty of his carelessness by having to change [his base money] for pure money of the proper weight obtained from the authorised moneyers[1].
    § 3[1]. And town-reeves who have been accessories to such a fraud shall be liable to the same punishment as coiners, unless the king pardon them, or they can clear themselves by a similar oath of nominated jurors[2], or by the ordeal specified above[3].

8. And the king advises and commands his bishops and earls and ealdormen[1] and all his reeves that, both[2] among the Danes and the English[3], they be on the watch for those who coin such base money and spread it abroad through the country, as has been stated above.

9. And moneyers shall be fewer in number than they have been in the past. In every principal town[1] [there shall be] three, and in every other town [there shall be] one.
    § 1. And they shall be responsible for the production by their employees of pure money of the proper weight, under pain of incurring the same fine[1] as we have fixed above.

§ 2. Et ipsi qui portos[1] custodiunt, efficiant per overhernessam meam, ut omne pondus sit marcatum ad pondus quo pecunia mea recipitur; et eorum singulum signetur ita, cur[2] xv[3] orae libram[4] faciant.

§ 3. Et custodiant omnes monetam, sicut vos docere praecipio et omnes elegimus.

V ÆTHELRED

In nomine Domini[5].

Ðis is seo gerædnes, þe Engla cyningc [7][6] ægðer [ge][6] gehadode ge læwede witan gecuron 7 geræddon.

1. Þis[7] þonne ærest, þæt we ealle[8] ænne God lufian 7 wurðian 7 ænne Cristendom georne healdan 7 ælcne hæðendom mid ealle awurpan[9]; 7 þæt we habbað ealle ægðer ge mid worde ge mid wedde gefæstnod, þæt we under anum cynedome ænne Cristendom healdan willað.

§ 1. 7 ure[s][10] hlafordes gerædnes 7 his witena is[11], þæt man rihte lage[12] up arære 7 ælce unlage georne afille, 7 þæt man læte æghwilcne man beon rihtes wurðe, 7 [þæt][6] man frið 7 freondscipe rihtlice healde [innan þysan earde for Gode 7 for worolde][6].

2. 7 ures hlafordes gerædnes 7 his witena is, þæt man Cristene men 7 unforworhte of earde ne sylle, ne huru on hæðene þeode[13], ac beorge[14] georne þæt man þa sawla ne forfare þe Crist mid his agenum life gebohte.

---

[1] *porcos* R, T.   [2] *quod* Hk.
[3] Om. Br.   [4] *bilibram* inst. of *o. l.* T.
[5] *I. n. D.*, *anno dominicae incarnationis* MVIII G; *Be Angolwitena gerednesse* G$_2$.
[6] G, G$_2$; om. D.   [7] *Ðæt is* G; *Ðæt* G$_2$.
[8] *w. e. fram synnan georne gecyrran* 7 *ure misdæda geornlice betan* 7 *æ. G.* G$_2$.
[9] The rest of the sent. is omitted in G$_2$.   [10] *ures* G; *ure* D.
[11] 7 *witena gerædnes is* G$_2$ (throughout).   [12] *laga* G, G$_2$.
[13] *leode* G, G$_2$.   [14] *b. man* G, G$_2$.

§ 2. And those who have the charge of towns shall see to it, under pain of incurring the fine for insubordination to me, that every weight is stamped according to the standard employed in my mint[1]; and the stamp used for each of them shall show that the pound contains 15 ores[2].

§ 3. And the coinage is to be maintained by all at the standard which I lay down in your instructions, in accordance with the decision at which we have all arrived.

V ÆTHELRED

In the name of the Lord[1].

This is the ordinance which has been determined upon and enacted by the king of England[1] and his councillors, both ecclesiastic and lay[2].

1. The first provision is: that we all[1] love and honour one God[2], and zealously observe one Christian faith[3], and wholly renounce all heathen practices[4]. We have confirmed, both by word and by pledge, our firm intention of observing one Christian faith under the authority of one king[5].

    § 1[1]. And the decree of our lord and of his councillors is, that justice shall be promoted and all injustice zealously suppressed, and that every man shall be allowed the benefit of the law[2], and that peace and good-will[3] shall be duly maintained [within this land in matters both religious and secular[4]].

2[1]. And it is the decree of our lord and his councillors, that Christian men who are innocent of crime shall not be sold out of the land[2], least of all to the heathen[3], but care shall diligently be taken that the souls which Christ bought with his own life[4] be not destroyed.

3. 7 ures hlafordes gerædnes 7 his witena is, þæt man Cristene men for ealles to litlum to deaðe ne fordeme[1]; ac elles geræde man friðlice steora folce to þearfe, 7 ne forspille for litlum Godes handgeweorc 7 his agenne ceap þe he deore gebohte.

4. 7 ures hlafordes gerædnes 7 his witena is, þæt ælces hades men georne gebugan, for Gode 7 for worlde, ælc to ðam rihte þe him to gebirige. And huruþinga Godes þeowas— biscopas 7 abbodas, munecas 7 minicena, preostas 7 nunnan —to rihte gebugan 7 regollice libban 7 for eal Cristen folc geornlice þingian.

5. And ures hlafordes gerædnes 7 his witena is, þæt muneca gehwilc þe ute sy of mynstre 7 regoles ne gime, do swa him þearf is: gebuge georne into mynstre mid eallum eadmettum, 7 misdæda geswice 7 bete swiðe georne þæt he abrocen hæbbe; geþence word 7 wed þe[2] he Gode betæhte.

6. And se munuc, þe mynster næbbe, cume [him][3] to[4] scirebiscope 7 trywsige hine sylfne wið God 7 wið men, þæt he huru þreo þingc þananforð behealdan[5] wille, þæt is his clænnesse 7 munuclice scrudware 7 þeowian his Drihtene swa wel swa he betst mæge; 7 gif he þæt gelæste, þonne bið he wyrðe þæt hine man þe bet healde, wunige þar he wunige.

7. And canonicas þar seo ár sý þæt hi beoddern 7 slæpern habban magan, healdan heora mynster mid rihte 7 mid clænnisse, swa heora regol tæce; oððe riht is þæt he[6] þolige þare are se ðe þæt nelle.

8. And ealle mæssepreostas we biddað 7 læraðþæt hi beorgan heom silfum wið Godes irre.

---

[1] G, G₂; -demde D.   [2] þæt G₂.
[3] Written in the margin in a handwriting of the same period.
[4] Om. G.   [5] healdan G, G₂.   [6] Om. G, G₂.

3[1]. And it is the decree of our lord and his councillors, that Christian men shall not be condemned to death for too trivial offences, but, on the contrary, merciful punishments[2] shall be determined upon for the public good, that the handiwork of God, and what he purchased for himself at a great price, be not destroyed for trivial offences.

4[1]. And it is the decree of our lord and his councillors, that men of every estate shall readily submit, in matters both religious and secular, to the duty which befits them; and most of all the servants of God, bishops and abbots, monks and nuns[2], priests and women under religious vows[2], shall submit to their duty, and live according to their rule, and zealously intercede[3] for all Christian people.

5[1]. And it is the decree of our lord and his councillors, that every monk, who is out of a monastery[2] and who is not observing a rule, shall do what is his duty, namely, he shall readily return into the monastery with all humility, and desist from his misdeeds, and zealously make amends for the transgressions he has committed. Let him remember the vows[3] which he rendered to God.

6. And the monk who has no monastery[1] shall come to the bishop of the diocese, and shall vow to God and to men henceforth to observe three things at least, namely, celibacy, and the wearing of the monastic habit, and the service of his Lord to the best of his ability. And if he carries out this vow, he shall be entitled to be treated with greater consideration[2], wherever he may dwell.

7[1]. And canons[2], wherever their property admits of their having a refectory and a dormitory, shall maintain regularity and celibacy in their foundation, as their rule prescribes; otherwise it is right that he who refuses to do so should forfeit his endowment[3].

8[1]. And we pray and admonish all priests to guard against incurring the wrath of God.

9. Fulgeorne hi wi[t]an¹ þæt hi nagan mid rihte þurh hæmed-þingc wifes gemanan.

§ 1. 7 se þe þæs geswican wille 7 clænnesse healdan, habbe he Godes mildse, 7 þar to eacan to worldwurðscipe þæt he sy þegenweres 7 þegenrihtes wurðe, ge on life ge on legere.

§ 2. 7 se þe þæt nelle, [þæt his hade gebyrige]², wanige his wurðscipe ge for Gode ge for worlde.

10. And æghwilc Cristen man³ unriht hæmed georne forbuge 7 godcunde laga rihtlice healde.

§ 1. 7 sy ælc cirice on Godes griðe 7 on ðæs cynges 7 on ealles Cristenes folces.

§ 2. And æni man heonan forð cirican ne ðeowige, ne ciric-mangunge mid unrihte ne macyge, ne ciricðen ne utige buton biscopes geþeahte.

11. 7 gelæste man Godes gerihta georne⁴ æghwilce geare.

§ 1. Þæt is sulhælmessan⁵ xv niht onufan eastron 7 geoguðe teoðunge be pentecosten 7 eorðwæstma be ealra halgena mæssan [7 Romfeoh be Petres mæssan]² 7 leohtgescot þriwa on geare.

12. 7 sawlsceat is rihtast þæt man symle gelæste æt openum græfe.

§ 1. 7 gif man ænig lic of rihtscriftscire elles hwar lecge, gelæste man sawlsceat swa ðeah into ðam mynstre þe hit to hirde.

§ 2. 7 ealle Godes rihta friðige⁶ man georne, ealswa hit þearf is.

§ 3. 7 freolsa 7 fæstena rihtlice healde⁷.

13. Sunnandæges freols healde man georne swa ðarto gebirige.

§ 1. 7 cipinga 7 folcgemota on ðam halgan dæge geswice man georne.

---

¹ G, G₂; *wican* D.   ² G, G₂; om. D.   ³ *m. eac* G, G₂.
⁴ Om. G₂.   ⁵ *s. huru* G₂.   ⁶ *gerihta fyrðrige* G, G₂.
⁷ *h. man r.* G, G₂.

9 § 1. They know full well[2] that they have no right to marry.
  § 1[1]. But he who will turn from marriage and observe celibacy shall obtain the favour of God, and in addition, as worldly honour, he shall enjoy the wergeld and the privileges of a thegn, both during his life and after his death[2].
  § 2[1]. And he who will not do [what befits his order] shall impair both his ecclesiastical and his civil status.

10[1]. And all Christian men shall carefully avoid illicit unions, and duly observe the laws of the church.
  § 1[1]. And all churches shall be under the special protection of God and of the king and of all Christian people.
  § 2[1]. And no-one henceforth shall oppress[2] the church, or make it an object of improper traffic[3], or turn out a minister of the church without the bishop's consent.

11[1]. And ecclesiastical dues shall be promptly rendered every year.
  § 1. Namely, plough-alms fifteen days[1] after Easter, and the tithe of young livestock at Pentecost, and [the tithe] of the fruits of the earth at the feast of All Saints[2], [and Peter's Pence by St Peter's Day], and light dues three times in the year[3].

12[1]. And it is best that payment for the souls of the dead should always be rendered before the grave is closed.
  § 1[1]. And if any body is buried elsewhere than in the parish to which it properly belongs, the payment shall nevertheless be made to the church to which the deceased belonged.
  § 2[1]. And all God's dues shall be promptly rendered[2], as the occasion requires.
  § 3[1]. And festivals and fasts shall be duly observed.

13[1]. The festival of Sunday shall be diligently observed in a fitting manner.
  § 1. And marketings[1] and meetings shall be strictly abstained from on the holy day.

14. And sancta Marian freolstide ealle wurðian[1] man georne, ærest mid fæstene 7 siððan mid freolse.

§ 1. 7 to æghwilces apostoles heahtida[2] fæste man[3] 7 freolsige; butan to Philippus 7 Iacobus freolse ne beode we nan fæsten [for þam eastorlican freolse][4].

15. Elles oðre freolsa 7 fæstena healde man georne, swa swa þe heoldon þa ðe betst heoldon.

16. 7 sancte Eadwardes mæssedæg witan habbað gecoran[5] þæt man freolsian sceal ofer eal Englaland on xv kl. Apr'.

17. 7 fæstan ælce Frigedæg, buton hit freols sy.

18. 7 ordol 7 aðas sindon tocweðen[6] freolsdagum 7 ymbrendagum[7] 7 ab[8] Adventum Domini oð xiiii niht ofer middewintres tid[9] 7 fram Septuagesima oð xiiii[10] niht ofer eastron.

19. 7 beo ðam halgum tidan, ealswa hit riht is, eallum Cristenum mannum sóm 7 sib gemæne, 7 ælc sacu getwæmed.

20. 7 gif hwa oðrum scule borh oððe bote æt worldlican þingan, gelæste hit georne ær oððe æfter.

21. 7 si ælc wuduwe þe hi silfe mid rihte healde[11] on Godes griðe 7 on ðæs cynges.

§ 1. 7 sitte ælc xii monað werleas; ceose siððan þæt heo sylf wille.

22. 7 æghwilc Cristen man do swa him ðearf is—gime his Cristendomes georne 7 gewunige gelomlice to scrifte[12] 7 unforwandodlice his synna gecyðe 7 geornlice bete swa swa him man tæce.

§ 1. 7 gearwige eac to huselgange oft 7 gelome gehwa hine silfne.

§ 2. 7 word 7 weorc fadige mid rihte 7 að 7 wed wærlice healde.

---

[1] weorðie G; weorðige G₂.   [2] -tide G, G₂.   [3] f. m. georne G₂.
[4] G, G₂; om. D.   [5] -en G, G₂.   [6] D, G; tocwedene G₂.
[7] rihtymb. G, G₂.   [8] fram G, G₂.
[9] oð octabas Epiphanię (-ige) G, G₂.   [10] xv G, G₂.
[11] gehealde G, G₂.   [12] G, G₂; Criste D.

14 1. And all St Mary's festivals[2] shall be zealously honoured, first with fasting and afterwards with festivity.

§ 1[1]. And at the festival of every apostle there shall be fasting and festivity, except that at the festival of Philip and James[2] we enjoin no fast [because of the Easter festival][3].

15 1. Otherwise, festivals and fasts shall be strictly observed in accordance with the highest standards of the past[2].

16 1. And the authorities have decided that St Edward's[2] festival shall be celebrated throughout England on the 18th of March.

17 1. And a fast [shall be observed] every Friday, unless it be a festival.

18 1. And trial by ordeal and [the rendering of] oaths are forbidden during festivals and on Ember days, and from the Advent[2] till a fortnight after Christmas[3], and from the Septuagesima[4] till a fortnight after Easter.

19 1. And at the holy festivals, as is fitting, there shall be peace and concord among all Christian men, and every dispute shall be laid aside.

20 1. And if anyone owes another a debt or compensation in connection with secular matters, he shall render it readily either before or after [the festival].

21 1. And all widows who lead a respectable life shall enjoy the special protection of God and of the king.

§ 1[1]. And each of them shall remain without a husband for a year, after which she may decide as she herself desires.

22 1. And every Christian man shall do what is his duty: he shall pay zealous regard to his Christian profession, and shall frequently go to confession, and freely confess his sins, and readily make amends as is prescribed for him.

§ 1[1]. And everyone shall also prepare himself frequently and often for receiving the sacrament.

§ 2[1]. And he shall order his words and deeds aright and carefully abide by his oath and his pledge.

23. 7 æghwilc unriht awurpe man georne of þisum earde þæs[1] man don[2] mæge.

24. 7 swicollice dæda 7 laðlice unlaga ascunige man swiðe, þæt is: falsa gewihta 7 woge gemeta 7 lease gewitnessa [7 fracodlice ficunga][3];

25. 7 egeslice manswara 7 deofollice dæda on morðweorcan 7 on manslihtan, on stalan 7 on strudungan[4], on gitsungan 7 on gifernessan, on ofermettan 7 on oferfillan, on swiccræftan 7 on mistlican lagbrycan, on hadbrican 7 on æwbrican [7 on freolsbrycan, on fæstenbrycan][5] 7 on mæniges cynnes misdædan.

26. Ac lufige man Godes riht heonan forð georne wordes 7 dæda; þonne wurð þisse þeode sona God milde.

§ 1. 7 beo man georne ymban friðes bote 7 ymbe feos bote æghwar on earde, 7 ymbe burhbote 7 ymbe bricbote[6] æghwar on earde[7] on æghwilcum ende, 7 ymbe firdunga[8], áá þonne neod sy, be þam þe man geræde.

27. 7 ymbe scipfirðrunga, swa man geornost mæge[9], þæt æghwilc geset sy sona ofer eastron æghwilce geare.

28. And gif hwa buton leafe of firde gewænde þe se cyningc silf on sy, plihte him silfum oððe wergilde[10].
[§ 1[11]. 7 se þe elles (ham)[12] of fyrde gewende, beo se cxx scill' scyldig.]

29. 7 gif ænig amánsumad man, buton hit friðbena sy, on ðæs cynincges neawiste ahwar gewunige, ær ðam þe he hæbbe godcunde bote georne gebogene, þonne plihte he to[13] him silfum oððe to[14] his æhtan.

30. 7 gif hwa ymbe cyninc[15] sirewe, beo[16] his feores scildig, buton[17] he hine ladige be þam deopestan þe witan geræcdan.

---

[1] þæsþe G, G₂.   [2] gedon G, G₂.   [3] G, G₂.
[4] G, G₂; scrutungan D.   [5] G₂.   [6] 7 y. bricb. om. G.
[7] æ. on e. om. G, G₂.   [8] f. eac G, G₂.
[9] gif man þæt geræde, added above in the twelfth cent. in G₂.
[10] h. s. 7 ealre his are G.   [11] G, G₂; om. D.   [12] G₂.
[13] Om. G; added above later in G₂.   [14] h. s. 7 eallan G, G₂.
[15] y. cyninges feorh G, G₂.   [16] sy he G, G₂.
[17] 7 gif he ladian wille do þæt be ðæs cynges wergylde oððe mid þryfealdan ordale on Engla lage inst. of buton...geræcdan G, G₂.

23[1]. And every injustice shall be zealously cast out from this land as far as is possible.

24[1]. And deceitful deeds and hateful injustices shall be strictly avoided, namely, untrue weights[2] and false measures[2] and lying testimonies[3] [and shameful frauds[4]];

25[1]. and horrible perjuries and devilish deeds, such as murders and homicides, thefts and robberies[2], covetousness and greed, gluttony and intemperance[3], frauds and various breaches of the law, violations of holy orders[4] and of marriage, [breaches of festivals and of fasts], and misdeeds of many kinds.

26[1]. But the law of God shall henceforth be zealously cherished both in word and in deed; then forthwith God will have mercy upon this nation.

§ 1[1]. And the promotion of public security and the improvement of the coinage[2] in every part of the country, and the repairing of fortresses[3] and of bridges[3] throughout the country on every side, and also the duties of military service[3] shall always be diligently attended to, whenever the need arises, in accordance with the orders given.

27[1]. And the fitting out of ships[2] as diligently as possible, so that in every year they may all be equipped soon[3] after Easter.

28[1]. And if anyone deserts an army which is under the personal command of the king[2], it shall be at the risk of [losing] his life or his wergeld[3].

[§ 1. And he who deserts any other army shall forfeit 120 shillings[1].]

29[1]. And if any excommunicated man, unless it be one who is a suppliant for protection, remains anywhere near the king, before he has readily submitted to the amends required by the church, it shall be at the risk of [losing] his life or[2] his possessions.

30[1]. And if anyone plots against the king, he shall forfeit his life, unless he clears himself by the most solemn oath[2] determined upon by the authorities[3].

V ÆTHELRED

31. 7 gif hwa forsteal oððe openne wiðercwide ongean lahriht Cristes oððe cyninges ahwar gewyrce, gilde swa wer swa wite swa lahslite, a be þam þe seo dæd sy.

§ 1. 7 gif he ongean riht geonbyrde oððe æhlip gewirce, 7[1] hine man þonne þurh þæt[2] afille, licge ægilde eallum his freondum.

32. 7 æfre alecgan[3] heonan forð þa unlaga þe ure[4] hlaford oft 7 gelome silf het alecgan.

§ 1[5]. Ðæt is þonne án ærest æt ðam ætfengan þe swicigende manswican lufedan be westan, þe mænigne man geswænctan 7 on unriht gedrehtan.

§ 2. 7 oðer is, þæt gewitnessa ne moston standan, þeah hi fulgetreowe wæron 7 hi swa sædan swa hi to woldon swerian.

§ 3. Ðridde is æt swigean, þæt man wolde sweogian 7 on æftergængan eft siððan sprecan þæt man on forgængan næfre becliopode.

§ 4. 7 be norðan stod seo unlagu, þæt man moste banweorc on unsacne secgan, 7 þæt scolde standan, gif hit wurde swa gecyðed ydæges sona.

§ 5. Ac þæt unriht alegde ure hlaford; þæt he ma mote.

[33[6]. 7 æghwylce unlaga alecge man georne.]

§ 1. Forðam þurh þæt hit sceal on earde godian to ahte, þæt[7] man unriht alecge 7 rihtwisnesse lufige for Gode 7 for worlde[8].

34. Ealle we sculon ænne God lufian 7 wurðian 7 ænne Cristendom georne healdan[9] 7 ælcne hæðendom mid ealle awurpan.

---

[1] o. r. þurh æhlyp geonbyrde 7 swa gewyrce þæt G, G₂.
[2] þ. þ. þ. om. G, G₂. [3] alicgan G, G₂.
[4] þe ær þysan wæran to gewunelice wide G, G₂.
[5] §§ 1–5 are found only in D.   [6] G, G₂.   [7] þe G, G₂.
[8] f. w. Amen G₂.   [9] 7 æ. C. g. h. om. G.

31[1]. And if anyone is guilty of offering obstruction or open opposition anywhere to the law of Christ or of the king, he shall pay either wergeld[2] or fine[3] or *lahslit* according to the nature of the offence.

§ 1. And if he offers resistance to the course of justice or commits a breach of the law[1], and through that brings about his own death, no compensation shall be paid for him to any of his friends.

32. And there shall henceforth be an end to the unjust practices which our lord himself has frequently and often commanded us to stop[1].

§ 1[1]. Firstly, with regard to the process of attaching property, to which crafty rogues in the west[2] have been much addicted and by which many people have been harassed and unjustly oppressed.

§ 2. Secondly, that the testimony of witnesses was not allowed to be valid, although they were thoroughly trustworthy and were willing to swear to [the truth of] their statements.

§ 3[1]. Thirdly, with regard to the practice of bringing forward, after long silence, claims against an heir which had never been made against his predecessor.

§ 4. And in the north there has prevailed the unjust practice of bringing accusations of homicide against a guiltless[1] man, and such an accusation was held to be valid, if it was made at once on the very day [of the homicide].

§ 5. But this practice has been stopped by our lord. May he succeed in stopping more!

[33[1]. And injustice of every kind shall be zealously suppressed.]

§ 1[1]. For it is only by the suppression of injustice and the love of righteousness, in matters both religious and secular, that any improvement shall be obtained in the condition of our country.

34. It is the duty of us all to love and honour one God, and zealously uphold one Christian faith, and wholly renounce all heathen practices.

35. 7 uton ænne cynehlaford holdlice healdan 7 lif 7 land samod ealle werian, swa wel swa we betst magon, 7 God ælmihtigne inweardre heortan fultumes biddan.

§ 1[1]. Sit nomen Domini benedictum.

VI ÆTHELRED

Be witena gerædnessan.

Þis syndan þa gerædnessa þe Engla rædgifan gecuran 7 gecwædan 7 geornlice lærdan þæt man scolde healdan.

1. 7 þæt is þonne ærest þæra biscpa frumræd, þæt we ealle fram synnum georne gecyrran, þæs þe we don magan, 7 ure misdæda andettan georne 7 geornlice betan 7 ænne God rihtlice lufian 7 weorðian 7 ænne Christendom anrædlice healdan 7 ælcne hæþendom georne forbugan 7 gebedrædene aræran georne us betweonan 7 sibbe 7 some lufian georne 7 anum cynehlaforde holdlice hyran 7 georne hine healdan mid rihtan getrywðan.

2. 7 witena gerædnes is, þæt abbodas 7 abbodissan heora agen lif rihtlice fadian 7 eac heora heorda wislice healdan 7 þæt ælces hades men georne gebugan for Gode 7 for worolde, ælc to þam rihte þe him to gebyrige, 7 huruþinga Godes þeowas—biscpas 7 abbodas, munecas 7 mynecena, canonicas 7 nunnan—to rihte gecyrran 7 regollice libban 7 for eall Cristen folc þingian georne.

3. 7 witena gerædnes is, þæt muneca gehwilc þe ute of mynstre sy 7 regoles ne gyme, do swa him þearf is: gebuge georne into mynstre mid eallum eaðmettum 7 misdæda geswice 7 bete swyþe georne þæt he abrocen hæbbe; geþence word 7 wedd þe he Gode betæhte.

---

[1] Om. G; *s. n. D. b. et rel.* G₂.

35[1]. And let us loyally support one royal lord, and all of us together defend our lives and our country, to the best of our ability, and from our inmost heart pray to God Almighty for help.

§ 1[1]. Blessed be the name of the Lord.

VI ÆTHELRED

Concerning the ordinances of the councillors.

These are the ordinances[1] which the councillors[2] of England have decided and agreed upon, earnestly enjoining that they should be observed[3].

1[1]. And first of all, the primary ordinance[2] of the bishops is, that we all zealously turn from sins, as far as we can, and readily confess our misdeeds, and zealously make amends, and duly love and honour one God, and unanimously uphold one Christian faith, and zealously renounce all heathen practices, and earnestly promote among us the habit of prayer, and zealously cherish peace and concord[3], and loyally obey one royal lord, and readily support him with due fidelity[4].

2[1]. And the decree of the councillors is[2], that abbots and abbesses shall order their own lives aright, and also keep their flocks with wisdom, and that men of every estate shall readily submit in matters both religious and secular to the duty which befits them, and most of all the servants of God—bishops and abbots, monks and nuns, canons and women under religious vows—shall revert to a proper discharge of their duties and live according to their rule[3], and earnestly intercede for all Christian people.

3[1]. And the decree of the councillors is, that every monk who is out of a monastery[2] and who is not observing a rule, shall do what is his duty, namely, he shall readily return into the monastery with all humility, and desist from his evil ways, and zealously make amends for the transgressions he has committed. Let him remember the vows which he rendered to God.

VI ÆTHELRED

§ 1. 7 se munuc, þe mynster næbbe, cume to scirebiscop 7 trywsige hine sylfne wið God 7 wið men, þæt he huru þreo þing þanon forð healdan wille, þæt is his clænnesse 7 munuclice scrudware 7 þeowian his Drihtne swa wel swa he betst mæge; 7 gif he þæt gelæste, þonne bið he weorðe þæt hine man þe bet healde, wunige þær he wunige.

4. 7 canonicas þær seo ar sy þæt he beodern 7 slæpern habban magan, healdan heora mynster mid clænnesse, swa heora regol tæce, oððon riht is þæt þolige þære are se þe þæt nelle.

5. 7 ealle Godes þeowas, 7 huruþinga sacerdas, we biddað 7 lærað, þæt hy Gode hyran 7 clænnesse lufian 7 beorhgan him sylfum wið Godes yrre.

§ 1. Fulgeorne hi witan þæt hy nagon mid rihte þurh ænig hæmedþing wifes gemanan.

§ 2. Ac hit is þe wyrse þe sume habbað twa oððe ma, 7 sum, þeh he forlæte þa he ær hæfde, he be lifiendre þære eft oþere nimð, swa ænigan Cristenan man ne gedafenað to donne.

§ 3. 7 se ðe þæs geswican wille 7 clænnesse healdan, hæbbe he Godes miltse 7 þær to eacan, to woroldweorðscipe, þæt he sy þegenweres 7 þegenrihtes wyrþe, ge on life ge on legere.

§ 4. 7 se þe þæt nelle, þæt his hade gebyrige, wanige his weorðscipe ægðer ge for Gode ge for worolde.

6. 7 la gyt we willað biddan freonda gehwylcne 7 eal folc eac læran georne, þæt hy inwerdre heortan ænne God lufian 7 ælcne hæþendom georne ascunian.

7. 7 gif wiccan oððe wigeleras, scincræftcan oððe horcwenan, morðwyrhtan oððe mánsworan ahwar on earde wurðan agytene, fyse hy man georne ut of þysan earde 7 clæ[n]sige[1] þas þeode, oþþe on earde forfare hy mid ealle, butan hy geswican 7 þe deoppor gebetan.

[1] clæs. K.

§ 1[1]. And the monk who has no monastery[2] shall come to the bishop of the diocese, and shall vow to God and to men henceforth to observe three things at least, namely, celibacy, and the wearing of the monastic habit, and the service of his Lord to the best of his ability. And if he carries out this vow, he shall be entitled to be treated with greater consideration, wherever he may dwell.

4[1]. And canons, wherever their property admits of their having a refectory and a dormitory, shall maintain celibacy in their foundation, as their rule prescribes; otherwise it is right that he who refuses to do so should forfeit his endowment[2].

5[1]. And we pray and enjoin all the servants of God, and priests above all, to obey God and practise celibacy and guard against incurring the wrath of God.

§ 1[1]. They know full well that they have no right to marry.

§ 2[1]. But some are guilty of a worse practice in having two or more [wives], and others, although they forsake their former wives, afterwards take others while these are still alive—a thing which is unfitting for any Christian man to do.

§ 3[1]. But he who will turn from marriage and observe celibacy shall obtain the favour of God, and in addition, as worldly honour, he shall enjoy the wergeld and the privileges of a thegn, both during his life and after his death.

§ 4. And he who will not do what befits his order shall impair both his ecclesiastical and his civil status.

6[1]. And now behold, we will beseech all our friends[2] and likewise earnestly enjoin upon the whole nation, to love one God from their inmost heart, and zealously shun all heathen practices.

7[1]. And if wizards or sorcerers, magicians[2] or prostitutes, those who secretly compass death or perjurers be met with anywhere in the land, they shall be zealously driven from this land and the nation shall be purified; otherwise they shall be utterly destroyed in the land, unless they cease from their wickedness and make amends to the utmost of their ability.

8. 7 witena gerædnes is, þæt man rihte laga up arære for Gode 7 for worolde 7 æghwilce unlaga georne afylle;

§ 1. 7 þæt man heonan forð læte manna gehwylcne, ge earmne ge eadigne, folcrihtes wyrðe;

§ 2. 7 þæt man frið 7 freondscipe rihtlice healde innan þysan earde for Gode 7 for worolde.

9. 7 witena gerædnes is, þæt man Christene men 7 unforworhte of earde ne sylle, ne huru on hæþene þeode; ac beorge man georne þæt man þa sawla ne forfare þe Crist mid his agenum life gebohte.

10. 7 witena gerædnes is, þæt man Christene men for ealles to lytlan to deaðe ne forræde. Ac elles geræde man friðlice steora, folce to þearfe, 7 ne forspille for lytlum Godes agen handgeweorc 7 his agenne ceap þe he deore gebohte.

§ 1. Ac æghwilce dæde toscade man wærlice 7 dom æfter dæde medemige be mæþe, swa for Gode sy gebeorhlic 7 for worolde aberendlic.

§ 2. 7 geþence swyþe georne se þe oþrum deme, hwæs he sylf gyrne, þonne he þus cweðe: "Et dimitte nobis debita nostra" et reliqua.

11. 7 we læraö swyþe geornlice þæt æghwilc Christen man unriht hæmed georne forbuge 7 Christene lage rihtlice healde.

12. 7 æfre ne geweorðe þæt Christen man gewifige in VI manna sibfæce on his agenum cynne, þæt is binnan þam feorþan cneowe, ne on þæs lafe þe swa neah wære on woroldcundre sibbe, ne on þæs wifes nydmagan þe he ær hæfde.

§ 1. Ne on gehalgodre ænigre nunnan, ne on his gefæderan, ne on ælætan ænig Cristen man ne gewifige æfre; ne na ma wifa þonne an hæbbe, ac beo be þære anre, þa hwile þe heo libbe, se þe wille Godes lage gyman mid rihte 7 wiþ hellebryne beorgan his sawle.

8[1]. And the decree of the councillors is, that justice shall be promoted in matters both religious and secular, and all injustice zealously suppressed;
> § 1[1]. and that henceforth all men, both rich and poor, shall be allowed the benefit of the law;
> § 2[1]. and that peace and goodwill shall be duly maintained within this land in matters both religious and secular.

9[1]. And it is the decree of the councillors that Christian men who are innocent of crime shall not be sold out of the land, least of all to the heathen, but care shall diligently be taken that the souls which Christ bought with his own life be not destroyed[2].

10[1]. And the decree of the councillors is, that Christian men shall not be condemned to death for too trivial offences, but, on the contrary, merciful punishments shall be determined upon, for the public good, that the handiwork of God and what he purchased for himself at a great price be not destroyed for trivial offences.
> § 1[1]. But every deed shall be carefully distinguished and judgment meted out in proportion to the offence, as shall be justifiable in the sight of God and acceptable in the eyes of men[2].
> § 2[1]. And he who judges another shall earnestly consider what he himself desires when he says: "Forgive us our trespasses" etc.

11[1]. And we very earnestly enjoin upon every Christian man carefully to avoid illicit unions and duly to observe the laws of the church.

12[1]. And it must never happen that a Christian man marries among his own kin within six degrees of relationship[2], that is, within the fourth generation[3], or with the widow of a man as nearly related to him[4] as this, or with a near relative of his first wife's.
> § 1. And a Christian man must never marry a professed nun or his godmother[1] or a divorced woman, and he shall never have more wives than one, but he who seeks to observe God's law aright and to save his soul from hell-fire[2] shall remain with the one as long as she lives.

VI ÆTHELRED

13. 7 sy ælc cyrice on Godes griþe 7 on þæs cynges 7 on ealles Cristenes folces.
14. 7 sy ælc cyricgrið binnan wagum 7 cyninges handgrið efen unwemme.
15. 7 ænig man heonan forð cyrican ne þ[e]owige[1] ne cyricmangunge mid unrihte ne macige, ne cyricþén ne utige butan biscopes geþehte.
16[2]. 7 gelæste man Godes gerihta æghwilce geare rihtlice georne, þæt is sulhælmessan huru xv niht ofer eastron.
17. 7 geogoðe teoþunge be pentecosten 7 eorðwæstma be ealra halgena mæssan.
18. 7 Romfeoh be Petres mæssan.
    § 1[3]. 7 cyricsceat to Martinus mæssan.
19. 7 leohtgescot þriwa on geare.
20. 7 saulsceat is rihtast þæt man symble[3] gelæste aa[3] æt openum[4] græfe.
21. 7 gif man ænig lic of riht[scrift]scire[5] elles hwar lecge, gelæste man þone saulsceat swa þeh into þam mynstre þe hit to hyrde.
    § 1. 7 ealle Godes gerihta fyrþrige[6] man georne, ealswa hit þearf is.
22. 7 freolsa 7 fæstena healde man rihtlice.
    § 1. Sunnandæges freols healde man georne swa þærto gebyrige; 7 cypinga 7 folcgemota 7 huntaðfara 7 worldlicra weorca on þam halgan dæge geswice man georne.
    § 2. 7 sancta Marian heahfreolstida[7] ealle[3] weorðige man georne, ærest mid fæstene 7 syþþan mid freolse.
    § 3. 7 to æghwilces apostoles heahtide fæste man georne, butan to[3] Philippus 7 Iacobus freolse ne beode we nan fæsten for þam easterlican[8] freolse, butan hwa wille[9].
    § 4. Elles oðre freolsa 7 fæstena healde man georne, swa swa þa heoldan þa þe betst heoldan.

---

[1] þow. K. [2] At this point MS D begins. [3] Om. D.
[4] ðam op. D. [5] rihtscire K; rihtre scriftscire D. [6] friðige D.
[7] freolst. D. [8] eastran dæges fr. D. [9] b. hw. w. om. D.

13[1]. And every church shall be under the special protection of God and of the king and of all Christian people.
14[1]. And every right of sanctuary within the walls of a church, and the protection granted by the king in person shall remain equally inviolate.
15[1]. And no-one henceforth shall oppress the church, or make it an object of improper traffic, or turn out a minister of the church without the bishop's consent.
16[1]. And ecclesiastical dues shall be promptly and duly rendered every year, namely, plough-alms at the latest fifteen days after Easter.
17. And the tithe of young livestock at Pentecost, and that of the fruits of the earth at All Hallows.
18. And Peter's Pence by St Peter's Day.
§ 1[1]. And church dues at Martinmas.
19[1]. And light dues three times in the year.
20[1]. And it is best that payment for the souls of the dead should always be rendered before the grave is closed.
21[1]. And if any body is buried elsewhere than in the parish to which it properly belongs, the payment shall nevertheless be made to the church to which the deceased belonged.
§ 1[1]. And all God's dues shall be promptly rendered, as the occasion requires.
22[1]. And festivals and fasts shall be duly observed.
§ 1[1]. And the festival of Sunday shall be diligently observed in a fitting manner; and marketings and meetings and hunting expeditions[2] and secular employments shall be strictly abstained from on the holy day.
§ 2[1]. And all St Mary's high-festivals shall be zealously honoured, first with fasting and afterwards with festivity.
§ 3. And at the festival of every apostle fasting shall be strictly observed, except that at the festival of Philip and James we enjoin no fast, because of the Easter festival, unless anyone desires to fast.
§ 4. Festivals and fasts otherwise shall be strictly observed in accordance with the highest standards of the past.

VI ÆTHELRED

23. 7 ymbren fæstena[1] swa swa sanctus Gregorius Angelcynne sylf hit[2] gedihte.

[§ 1[3]. And sancte Eadwardes mæssedæg witan habbað gecoran þæt man freolsian sceal ofer eall Englaland on xv kl. Aprilis.]

24. 7 fæste man ælce Frigedæg, butan hit freols sy.

25. 7 ordal 7 aþas 7 wifunga æfre[4] syndan tocwedene heahfreolsdagum[5] 7 rihtymbrenum[6] 7 fram Adventum Domini oð octabas Epiphanige 7 fram Septuagessima oð xv niht ofer eastran.

§ 1. And beo þam halgan tidan, ealswa hit riht is, eallum Cristenum mannum sibb 7 som gemæne 7 ælc sacu totwæmed.

§ 2. 7 gif hwa oðrum scyle borh oððe bote æt woroldlican þingan, gelæste hit him georne ær oððon æfter.

26. 7 sy ælc wydewe, þe hy sylfe mid rihte gehealde, on Godes griðe 7 on þæs cynges.

§ 1. 7 sitte ælc xii monað werleas; ceose syþþan þæt heo sylf wille.

27. 7 æghwilc Christen man do swa him þearf is: gyme his Christendomes georne 7 gewunige gelomlice to scrifte[7] 7 unforwandodlice his synna gecyðe 7 geornlice bete, swa swa him man tæce.

§ 1. 7 gearwige eac to huslgange huru þriwa on geare gehwa hine sylfne þe his agene þearfe wille understandan[8], swa swa him þearf is.

28. 7 word 7 weorc freonda gehwilc fadige mid rihte 7 að 7 wedd wærlice healde.

§ 1. 7 æghwilc unriht aweorpe man georne of þysan earde þæs þe man don mæge.

---

[1] D; *ymbren 7 fæstena* K.   [2] Om. D.   [3] D; om. K.   [4] 7 *w. æ.* om. D.
[5] *heah* superscribed in later hand.   [6] *rihtymbrendagum* D.
[7] *to his scr.* D.   [8] *und. cunne* D.

23 §1. And the fasts of the Ember Days [shall be observed] as St Gregory himself prescribed for the English nation.

[§ 1¹. And the authorities have decided that St Edward's festival shall be celebrated throughout England on the 18th of March.]

24 §1. And a fast [shall be observed] every Friday, unless it be a festival.

25 §1. And trial by ordeal, and [the rendering of] oaths, and marriages[2] are always forbidden during festivals, and on legally appointed Ember days, and from the Advent till the Octave of Epiphany, and from the Septuagesima till fifteen days after Easter.

§ 1¹. And at the holy festivals, as is fitting, there shall be peace and concord among all Christian men, and every dispute shall be laid aside.

§ 2. And if anyone owes another a debt or compensation in connection with secular matters, he shall render it to him readily either before or after [the festival].

26 §1. And all widows who lead a respectable life shall enjoy the special protection of God and of the king.

§ 1. And each of them shall remain without a husband for a year, after which she may decide as she herself desires.

27 §1. And every Christian man shall do what is his duty: he shall pay zealous regard to his Christian profession, and shall frequently go to confession, and freely confess his sins, and readily make amends, as is prescribed for him.

§ 1. And everyone who seeks to understand what is for his own good shall also prepare himself for sacrament at least three times in the year, as is his duty.

28 §1. And everyone of our friends[2] shall order his words and deeds aright, and strictly abide by his oath and pledge.

§ 1¹. And every injustice shall be zealously cast out from this land, as far as it is possible to do so.

§ 2[1]. 7 swicollice dæda 7 laðlice unlaga ascunige man swyðc, þæt is false gewihta 7 woge gemeta 7 lease gewitnessa 7 fracodlice ficunga 7 fule forligra 7 egeslice mánswara 7 deoflice dæda on morðweorcum 7 on manslihtan, on stalan 7 on strudungan, on gitsungan 7 on gifernessan, on ofermettan 7 on oferfyllan, on swiccræftan 7 on mistlican lahbrican, on æwbrican 7 on hadbrican, on freolsbricon 7 on fæstenbricon, on cyricrénan 7 on mæniges cynnes misdædan.

29. 7 la understande man georne þæt eal swylc is to leanne 7 næfre to lufianne.

30. Ac[2] lufige man Godes riht heonan forþ georne wordes 7 weorces[3]; þonne[4] wyrð þysse þeode sona God milde.

31. Wutan eac ealle ymbe friþes bote 7 ymbe feos bote smeagean swyðe georne.

32. Swa ymbe friþes bote swa þam bondan sy selost 7 þam þeofan sy laþost;

    § 1. 7 swa ymbe feos bote þæt an mynet gange ofer ealle þas þeode butan ælcon false.

    § 2. 7 gemeta 7 gewihta rihte man georne, 7 ælces unrihtes heonan forð geswice.

    § 3. 7 burhbota 7 bricbota aginne man georne on æghwilcon ende[5] 7 fyrdunga eac 7 scipfyrdunga ealswa, a þonne neod[6] sy, swa swa man geræde[7] for gemænelicre neode.

33[8]. 7 wærlic bið þæt man æghwilce geare sona æfter eastron fyrdscipa gearwige.

34. 7 gyf hwa folces fyrdscip awyrde, gebete þæt georne 7 cyninge þa munde; 7 gif hit man amyrre þæt hit ænote weorðe, forgylde hit fullice 7 cyninge þone mundbrice.

---

[1] Caps. 28 § 2–29 (end) om. D.   [2] 7 D.   [3] *dæda* D.
[4] *þ. wurð us Godes miltse þe gearuwre* D.   [5] *on æg. e.* om. D.
[6] *fyrd. eac swa, á þ. þearf* D.   [7] *s. s. m. ger.* om. D.
[8] Caps. 33–39 (end) om. D.

§ 2[1]. And deceitful deeds and hateful injustices shall be strictly avoided, namely, untrue weights, and false measures, and lying testimonies, and shameful frauds, and foul adulteries, and horrible perjuries, and devilish deeds such as murders and homicides, thefts and robberies, covetousness and greed, gluttony and intemperance, frauds and various breaches of the law, violations of marriage and of holy orders, breaches of festivals and of fasts[2], sacrilege[3], and misdeeds of many kinds[4].

29[1]. And now behold it must be clearly understood[2] that all such are to be censured and not to be indulged in.

30[1]. But God's law shall henceforth be zealously cherished in word and in deed; then God will forthwith be gracious towards this people.

31[1]. Further, let us all earnestly take thought for the promotion of public security and the improvement of the coinage.

32[1]. Public security shall be promoted in such a way as shall be best for the householder[2] and worst for the thief.

§ 1[1]. And the coinage shall be improved by having one currency, free from all adulteration, throughout all the country.

§ 2[1]. And weights and measures shall be corrected with all diligence, and an end put to all unjust practices.

§ 3[1]. And the repairing of fortifications and of bridges shall be diligently undertaken on every side, and also the provision of military and naval forces, whenever the occasion demands, as may be ordered for our common need.

33[1]. And it is a wise precaution to have warships made ready every year soon after Easter.

34[1]. And if anyone damages a national warship, he shall with all diligence make compensation for it, and shall pay to the king the fine due for breach of his "mund"[2]; and if it be destroyed[3] so as to be useless, he shall pay for it in full, and shall give the king the fine due for breach of his "mund."

35. 7 gif hwa of fyrde butan leafe gewende þe cyning sylf on sy, plihte his are.

36. 7 gif morðwyrhtan oððe mansworan oððe æbære manslagan to þam geþristian þæt hy on þæs cyninges neaweste gewunian, ær þam þe hy habban bote agunnen for Gode 7 for worolde, þonne plihton hy heora are 7 eallon heora æhten, butan hit friðbenan syndan.

37. 7 gyf hwa ymbe cyninges feorh syrwe, sy he his feores scyldig 7 ealles þæs þe he age, gif hit him ongesoþod weorðe; 7 gif he hine ladian wille 7 mage, do þæt be þam deopestan aðe oþþe mid þryfealdan ordale on Ængla lage, 7 on Dena lage be þam þe heora lagu sy.

38. 7 gif hwa forsteal ongean lahriht Cristes oþþe cyninges ahwar gewyrce, gylde wer oþþe wite be þam þe seo dæd sy; 7 gif he geonbyrde 7 sylf gewyrce þæt hine man afylle, licge ægylde.

39. 7 gif hwa nunnan gewemme oþþe wydewan nydnæme, gebete þæt deope for Gode 7 for worolde.

40. 7 smeage man symle on æghwilce[1] wisan hu man fyrmest mæge ræd aredian, þeode to þearfe and rihtne Christendom swyþost aræran 7 æghwilce unlaga geornost afyllan.

§ 1. Forþam þurh þæt hit sceal on earde godian to ahte, þe man unriht alecge 7 rihtwisnesse lufige for Gode 7 for worlde.

41[2]. Nu wille we eac læran Godes þeowas georne, þæt hy huru hy sylfe wærlice beþencan 7 þurh Godes fultum clænnesse lufian 7 georne heora bocum 7 gebedum fylgean 7 dæges 7 nihtes oft 7 gelome clypian to Christe 7 for eal Christen folc þingian georne.

[1] ælce D.   [2] Om D.

CAP. 35–41

35¹. And if anyone deserts an army which is under the personal command of the king, it shall be at the risk of losing his property².

36¹. And if those who secretly compass death², or perjurers, or proved homicides presume so far as to remain anywhere near the king³, before they have undertaken to make amends both towards church and state, they shall be in danger of losing their (landed) property and all their personal possessions⁴, unless they are suppliants for protection.

37¹. And if anyone plots against the king's life, he shall forfeit his life and all that he possesses, if it is proved against him²; and if he seeks and is able to clear himself, he shall do so by means of the most solemn oath³ or by the triple ordeal in districts under English law, and in those under Danish law in accordance with their constitution⁴.

38¹. And if anyone is guilty of offering obstruction anywhere to the law of Christ or the king, he shall pay either wergeld or fine² according to the nature of the offence, and if he offers resistance and so acts as to bring about his own death, no compensation shall be paid for him.

39¹. And if anyone injures a nun or does violence to a widow, he shall make amends to the utmost of his ability both towards church and state.

40¹. And constant thought shall be taken in every way how best to determine what is advisable for the public good, and how best to promote true Christianity, and to suppress with all diligence every injustice.

§ 1¹. For it is only by the suppression of injustice and the love of righteousness in matters both religious and secular that any improvement shall be obtained in the condition of the country.

41¹. Now we desire likewise earnestly to enjoin upon the servants of God, that above all they carefully take thought for themselves, and by God's help practise celibacy², and diligently apply themselves to their books and prayers, and day and night frequently and often call upon Christ, and zealously intercede for all Christian people.

42. Eac we[1] gyt willað myngian georne[2] freonda gehwilcne, ealswa us neod is gelome to donne, þæt gehwa hine sylfne georne beþence, 7 þæt he fram synnan georne gecyrre 7 oþrum mannum unrihtes styre[3], 7 þæt he oft 7 gelome hæbbe on gemynde þæt mannum is mæst þearf oftost to gemunene, þæt is, þæt hy rihtne geleafan anrædlice[2] habban on þone soþan God, þe is wealdend 7 wyrhta ealra gesceafta, 7 þæt hy rihtne Christendom rihtlice healdan, 7 þæt hy godcundan lareawan geornlice hyran 7 Godes larum 7 lagum geornlice[4] fylgean, 7 þæt hy Godes cyrican æghwar georne griðian 7 friþian 7 mid leohte 7 lacum hi gelome gegretan 7 hy sylfe þær georne to Christe[5] gebiddan.

43. 7 þæt hy Godes gerihta æghwylce geare mid rihte gelæstan, 7 freolsa 7 fæstena rihtlice healdan.

44. 7 þæt hy Sunnandaga[6] cypinga 7 folciscra gemota georne geswican.

45. 7 þæt hy Godes þeowas symle werian 7 weorðian.

46. 7 þæt hy Godes þearfan frefrian 7 fedan.

47. 7 þæt hy wydewan 7 steopcild to oft ne ahwænan ac georne hi gladian.

48. And þæt hi ælþeodige men 7 feorran cumene ne tyrian ne tynan.

49. 7 þæt hy oþrum mannum unriht ne beodan ealles to swyþe, ac manna gehwylc oþrum beode þæt riht þæt he wille þæt man him beode, be þam þe hit mæð sy[7]; 7 þæt is swyþe riht lagu.

50. 7 se þe ahwar heonan forð rihte laga wyrde, Godes oþþon manna, gebete hit georne swa hwæþer swa hit gebyrige, swa mid godcundre bote, swa mid woroldcundre steore.

51. 7 gif for godbotan feohbot ariseð, swa swa wise woroldwitan to steore gesettan, þæt gebyreð rihtlice, be biscpa dihte, to

---

[1] *And git we* D. [2] Om. D.
[3] *stire 7 þæt he (he þæt* MS.) *ofer ealle oðre þingc lufige his Drihten* D.
[4] *rihtlice* D. [5] *to Ch.* om. D. [6] *Sunnandæges* D.
[7] At this point the extract in D ends.

42. And likewise we desire earnestly to exhort all our friends[1], as there is need for us to do frequently, to take thought diligently for themselves, and eagerly to turn from sins, and to restrain other men from wrong-doing, and frequently and often to have in mind what is of supreme importance for men to remember, namely, that they should have a right belief in the true God, who is the ruler and maker of all created things, and that they should duly keep the true Christian faith, and diligently obey their spiritual teachers, and zealously follow the precepts and ordinances of God, and that they should diligently maintain the security and sanctity of the churches of God[2] everywhere, and frequently visit them with candles[3] and offerings, and themselves there earnestly pray to Christ.

43[1]. And that every year they should duly render their ecclesiastical dues, and duly observe festivals and fasts.

44[1]. And that they should diligently abstain from marketings and public assemblies on Sundays.

45[1]. And that they should always protect and honour the servants of God.

46[1]. And that they should comfort and feed the poor of God.

47[1]. And that they should not be constantly oppressing the widow and the orphan, but that they should diligently cheer them.

48[1]. And that they should not vex[2] or oppress strangers and men come from afar.

49[1]. And that they should not excel in offering injustice to other men, but that every man should, to the best of his ability, show the justice to others that he desires should be shown to him[2]—which is a very just rule[3].

50[1]. And he who henceforth anywhere violates the just[2] decrees of God or of men shall render full compensation in whatever way is fitting, whether by making the amends required by the ecclesiastical authority or by paying the penalty demanded by the secular law.

51. And if monetary compensation is paid as amends for religious offences, in accordance with the penalties fixed by

gebedbigene 7 to þearfena hyþþe 7 to cyricbote 7 to lardome 7 to wæde 7 to wiste þam þe Gode þeowian 7 to bocan 7 to bellan 7 to cyricwædan, 7 næfre to woroldlican idelan glengan, ac for woroldsteoran to godcundan neodan, hwilum be wite, hwilum be wergylde, hwilum be halsfange, hwilum be lahslite, hwilum be are, hwilum be æhte, 7 hwilum be maran, hwilum be læssan.

52. 7 á swa man bið mihtigra her nu for worulde oþþon þurh geþingða hearra on hade, swa sceal he deoppor synna gebetan 7 ælce misdæda deoror agyldan, for þam þe se maga 7 se unmaga ne beoð na gelice, ne ne magon na gelice byrþene ahebban, ne se unhala þe ma þam halum gelice; 7 þy man sceal medmian 7 gescadlice toscadan, ge on godcundan scriftan ge on woroldcundan steoran, ylde 7 geogoþe, welan 7 wædle, hæle 7 unhæle, 7 hada gehwilcne.

§ 1. 7 gif hit geweorþeð, þæt man unwilles oþþe ungewealdes ænig þing misdeð, na bið þæt na gelic þam þe willes 7 gewealdes sylfwilles misdeð; 7 eac se þe nydwyrhta bið þæs þe he misdeð, se bið gebeorhges 7 þy beteran domes symle wyrðe, þe he nydwyrhta wæs þæs þe he worhte.

53. Ælce dæde toscade man wærlice 7 a dom be dæde fadige mid rihte 7 medemige be mæþe for Gode 7 for worolde; 7 miltsige man for Godes ege 7 liþige man georne 7 beorge be dæle þam þe þæs þearf sy; forþam ealle we beþurfan þæt us ure Drihten oft 7 gelome his miltse geunne. Amen.

wise secular authorities[1], it is proper that this should be applied, in accordance with the direction of the bishops, to paying for prayers, and to the maintenance of the indigent, and to the repair of churches, and to education, and to clothing and feeding those who serve God, and to the purchase of books and bells and ecclesiastical vestments[2]. It shall never be applied to the pomps and vanities of the world[3], but payments for the needs of religion shall take the place of payments to the secular authorities—whether [they arise from] fines or wergeld or *healsfang* or *lahslit*, whether they affect landed or personal property, and whether the amounts involved are large or small[4].

52[1]. And always the greater a man's position in this present life or the higher the privileges of his rank, the more fully shall he make amends for his sins, and the more dearly shall he pay for all misdeeds; for the strong and the weak are not alike nor can they bear a like burden, any more than the sick can be treated like the sound. And therefore, in forming a judgment, careful discrimination must be made between age and youth, wealth and poverty, health and sickness, and the various ranks of life, both in the amends imposed by the ecclesiastical authority and in the penalties inflicted by the secular law.

§ 1[1]. And if it happens that a man commits a misdeed, involuntarily or unintentionally, the case is different from that of one who offends of his own freewill, voluntarily and intentionally[2]; and likewise he who is an involuntary agent in his misdeeds should always be entitled to clemency and to better terms, owing to the fact that he acted as an involuntary agent.

53[1]. Careful discrimination shall be made in judging every deed, and the judgment shall always be ordered with justice, according to the nature of the deed, and meted out in proportion, in affairs both religious and secular; and, through the fear of God, mercy and leniency and some measure of forbearance shall be shown towards those who have need of them. For all of us have need that our Lord grant us his mercy frequently and often. Amen.

VII ÆTHELRED

[1][I. Ut de omni caruca detur denarius sanctae Dei ecclesiae, et tainus decimet quicquid habet[2]. II. De ieiunio et feriatione III dierum ante festum sancti Michaelis. III. Quid pro rege et populo omni die sit cantandum. IIII. De reddendis omnibus consuetudinibus sanctae Dei ecclesiae. V. Ne quis vendatur extra patriam. VI. De robaria. VII. De elemosinis et rectitudinibus ecclesiae.]

Hoc[3] instituerunt Æþelredus rex et sapientes eius apud Badam[4].

1. Inprimis, ut unus Deus super omnia diligatur et honoretur, et ut omnes regi suo pareant, sicut antecessores sui melius fecerunt, et cum eo pariter defendant regnum suum.

    § 1. Et constituerunt inprimis Dei misericordiam et auxilium invocare ieiuniis, elemosinis, confessione et abstinentia á malefactis et iniustitia[5].

    § 2. Hoc est ut[6] detur de omni carruca denarius vel denarii valens.

    § 3. Et omnis qui familiam habet efficiat, ut omnis hyremannus suus det unum denarium. Qui[7] si non habeat[8], det dominus eius pro eo; et omnis tainus decimet totum quicquid habet.

2. Et instituimus, ut omnis Christianus qui aetatem habet ieiunet tribus diebus in pane et aqua et herbis crudis[9].

    § 1. Et omnis homo ad confessionem vadat et nudis pedibus ad ecclesiam et peccatis omnibus abrenuntiet emendando, cessando.

    § 2. Et eat omnis presbiter cum populo suo ad processionem tribus diebus nudis pedibus.

    § 2a. Et super hoc cantet omnis presbiter XXX missas et omnis diaconus et clericus XXX psalmos.

---

[1] The table of contents is found in M, Hk, Br but not in T.
[2] *De denario s. e. dando et decimatione thaynorum* Br.
[3] *haec* Br.   [4] *Habam* M, Hk, Br.   [5] *et m. et i. abstinere* Br.
[6] *Et ut* Br; *hoc ut* Hk.   [7] *Quod* Br.   [8] *habet* T.
[9] *bis crudis* M, Br; *erudis* Hk; Br adds *ante festum S. Michaelis.*

VII ÆTHELRED

This is the edict which was drawn up by King Æthelred and his councillors at Bath[1].

1[1]. In the first place, one God shall be loved and honoured above all, and all men shall show obedience to their king in accordance with the best traditions of their ancestors[2], and co-operate with him in defending his kingdom.

§ 1[1]. And they agreed first of all to invoke the mercy and help of God by fasts and almsgiving, by confession, and by abstaining from misdeeds and injustice.

§ 2[1]. From every plough-land[2] a penny or the value of a penny[3] shall be given.

§ 3[1]. And everyone who has a household[2] shall see to it that each of his dependents[3] gives a penny. If anyone is without money, his lord shall give it for him; and every thegn shall render a tithe of all that he has.

2[1]. And we have decreed that every adult Christian shall fast on bread and water and raw herbs[2] for three days[3].

§ 1[1]. And everyone shall go to confession and with bare feet to church, and by making amends and ceasing [from evil] shall renounce all [his] sins.

§ 2[1]. And every priest shall go barefoot in the Procession with his people on the three days.

§ 2a[1]. And in addition every priest shall sing 30 masses, and every deacon and cleric 30 psalms.

§ 2*b*. Et apparetur III diebus corredium uniuscuiusque sine carne; in cibo et potu, sicut idem comedere deberet, (et) dividatur hoc totum pauperibus.

§ 3. Et sit omnis servus liber ab opere illis tribus diebus, quo melius ieiunare possit, et operetur sibimet quod vult.

§ 3*a*. Hii sunt illi tres dies—dies Lunae, dies Martis et dies Mercurii proximi ante festum sancti Michaelis.

§ 4. Si quis ieiunium suum infringat, servus corio suo componat, liber pauper reddat xxx denarios et tainus regis cxx sol.; et dividatur haec pecunia pauperibus.

§ 5. Et sciat omnis presbiter et tungravius et decimales homines, ut haec elemosina et ieiunium proveniat[1], sicut in sanctis iurare poterunt.

3. Et praecipimus, ut in omni congregatione cantetur cotidie communiter pro rege et omni populo suo una missa ad matutinalem missam quae inscripta est 'contra paganos.'

§ 1. Et ad singulas horas decantet totus conventus extensis membris in terra psalmum illum: "Domine, quid[2] multiplicati sunt," et collectam contra paganos; et hoc fiat quamdiu necessitas ista nobis est in manibus.

§ 2. Et in omni cenobio et[3] conventu monachorum celebret omnis presbiter singulatim xxx missas pro rege et omni populo, et omnis monacus xxx psalteria.

4. Et praecipimus, ut omnis homo super dileccionem Dei et omnium sanctorum det cyricsceattum[4] et rectam decimam suam, sicut in diebus antecessorum nostrorum stetit[5], quando melius stetit[5]—hoc est sicut aratrum peragrabit per[6] decimam acram.

[1] *perv.* H, Hk, Br.   [2] *qui* Br.   [3] *vel* M, Hk, Br.
[4] *scy.* T; *cyris.* M; *syris.* Hk; *cyrisc.* Br.   [5] *fecit* Br.   [6] Om. M, Hk, Br.

§ 2b¹. And everyone shall have his food served during the three days without meat, and whatever he would have consumed in food and drink shall be distributed among the poor.

§ 3¹. And all slaves shall be exempt from work on those three days, so that they can fast the better and may make² what they want for themselves.

§ 3a¹. These are the three days—the Monday, Tuesday and Wednesday immediately preceding the feast of St Michael².

§ 4¹. In the case of the fast being broken—if it is a slave [who does so], he shall undergo the lash², if it is a poor freeman³, he shall pay 30 pence, and a thegn of the king's [shall pay] 120 shillings⁴. And this money shall be divided among the poor⁵.

§ 5¹. And every priest and the reeve of every village² and the heads of the tithings³ shall be witnesses that this alms-giving and fasting is carried out, and shall be able to swear to it on the holy relics⁴.

3¹. And we decree that in every religious foundation² a mass entitled "Against the heathen" shall be sung daily at matins, by the whole community, on behalf of the king and all his people³.

§ 1. And at the various Hours all the members of the foundation, prostrate on the ground, shall chant the psalm: "O Lord, how are they multiplied," and the Collect against the heathen, and this shall be done as long as the present need continues.

§ 2. And in every foundation and college of monks every priest severally¹ shall celebrate 30 masses for the king and the whole nation, and every monk shall repeat [the psalms from] his psalter 30 times.

4¹. And we decree that all men, for love of God and all the saints, shall give their church-dues and their rightful tithes in accordance with the best rules observed in the days of our ancestors, namely, [the produce of] every tenth acre traversed by the plough².

§ 1. Et omnis consuetudo reddatur super amicitiam Dei ad matrem ecclesiam cui adiacet.

§ 2. Et nemo auferat Deo quod ad eum[1] pertinet et praedecessores[2] nostri concesserunt ei[3].

5. Et prohibemus ne aliquis[4] extra[5] vendatur. Si quis hoc praesumat, sit praeter benedictionem Dei et omnium sanctorum et praeter omnem Christianitatem, nisi peniteat et emendet, sicut episcopus suus edocebit.

6. Et prohibemus omnem robariam omni homini.

§ 1. Et sit omnis homo dignus iure publico, pauper et dives.

§ 2. Et reddatur omnis robaria, si quis aliquam fecerit, et emendet, sicut prius et postea stetit[6].

§ 3. Et si quis praepositus eam fecerit, duppliciter emendet quod alii iudicaretur.

7. Et reddatur pecunia elemosinae hinc[7] ad festum sancti Michaelis, si alicubi retro[8] sit, per plenam witam.

§ 1. Et omnibus annis deinceps reddantur Dei rectitudines in omnibus rebus quae supradictae sunt per amiciciam Dei et sanctorum omnium, ut Deus omnipotens misericordiam nobis faciat et de hostibus triumphum nobis et pacem indulgeat, quem sedulo deprecemur ut misericordiam eius consequamur et gratiam[9] hic et in futuro[10] requiem sine fine. Amen[11].

---

[1] *Deum* M, Hk, Br.   [2] *praec.* Br.   [3] Om. Br.
[4] *quis* M, Hk, Br.   [5] *ex. patriam* Br.   [6] *stet* Hk; *fecit* Br.
[7] *hic* Br.   [8] *rectus* T.   [9] *et gr.* om. Br.   [10] *-ram* T.   [11] Om. Br.

§ 1[1]. And all church dues shall be rendered, for love of God, to the mother-church to which they belong.

§ 2. And no-one shall deprive God of what belongs to him and of what our ancestors[1] granted him.

5[1]. And we forbid that anyone be sold out of the country. If anyone dares to do so, he shall be shut out from the blessing of God and of all the Saints, and from all share in the Christian religion, unless he repents and makes amends as his bishop shall direct.

6[1]. And we forbid anyone to commit theft.

§ 1[1]. And all men, whether poor or rich, shall be entitled to the benefit of the law.

§ 2[1]. And if anyone has committed theft, he shall restore all that he has stolen and make amends, as has always[2] been the rule.

§ 3. And if any reeve has committed theft, the compensation paid by him shall be double[1] that prescribed to any other person.

7. And alms-money[1], if it is in arrears, shall be paid between now and Michaelmas[2], under pain of incurring the full penalty[3].

§ 1[1]. And every year in future God's dues shall be rendered in all cases specified above[2], for love of God[3] and all the saints, so that[4] God omnipotent may show mercy towards us and grant us victory over our foes, and peace. Let us zealously entreat Him, that we may obtain His mercy and grace here, and, in the life to come, rest without end. Amen.

VII ÆTHELRED (ANGLO-SAXON)

Ðis man gerædde ða se micele here com to lande.

Ealle we beþurfan þæt we geornlice earnian þæt we Godes miltse 7 his mildheortnesse habban moton 7 þæt we þurh his fultum magon feondum wiðstandan.

1. Nu wille we þæt eal folc to gemænelicre dædbote þrig dagas be hlafe 7 wirtum 7 wætere, þæt is on Monandæg 7 on Tiwesdæg 7 on Wodnesdæg ær Michaeles mæssan.

2. 7 cume manna gehwilc bærefot to circan buton golde 7 glæncgum 7 ga man to scrifte.
   § 1. 7 gan ealle út mid haligdome 7 clipian inweardre heortan georne to Criste.
   § 2. 7 sceote man æghwilce hide pænig oððe pæniges weorð.
   § 3. 7 bringe man þæt to cirican 7 siððan on þreo dæle be scriftes 7 be tunesgerefan gewitnesse.

3. 7 gif hwa þis ne gelæste, ðonne gebete he þæt, swa swa hit gelagod is: bunda mid xxx p̄, þræl mid his hide, þegn mid xxx scill'.

4. 7 swa hwar swa þæt feoh up arise, dæle man on Godes est æghwilcne pænig.
   § 1. 7 ealswa þone mete þe gehwa brucan wolde, gif him þæt fæsten swa geboden nære, dæle man on Godes est georne æfter þam fæstene eal þearfigendum mannum 7 bedridan 7 swa gebrocedum mannum þe swa fæstan ne magon.

5. 7 hiredmanna gehwilc sille pænig to ælmessan oððe his hlaford sille for hine, buton he silf hæbbe, 7 heafodmen teoðian.
   § 1. 7 þeowemen þa ðrig dagas beon weorces gefréode wið ciricsocne 7 wið ðam þe hi þæt fæsten þe lustlicor gefæstan.

VII ÆTHELRED (ANGLO-SAXON)

This edict was drawn up when the great army came to the country.

All of us have need to strive earnestly that we may obtain the mercy and compassion of God and through his help withstand our foes[1].

1[1]. It is our desire that the whole people, as a national penalty, [fast] on bread and herbs and water for three days, namely, on the Monday, Tuesday and Wednesday before Michaelmas.

2[1]. And everyone shall come barefoot to church without gold or ornaments and shall go to confession.

§ 1[1]. And all shall go out with the relics, and from their inmost heart call earnestly upon Christ.

§ 2[1]. And from every hide a penny or the value of a penny shall be given as dues.

§ 3[1]. And it shall be brought to church and afterwards divided in three[2] in the presence of the confessor and the reeve of the village as witnesses.

3[1]. And if anyone does not render this, he shall make amends as has been established by law: a householder shall pay 30 pence, a slave shall undergo the lash, and a thegn shall pay 30 shillings[2].

4. And wherever such payment has to be made[1], every penny shall be distributed[2] for love of God[3].

§ 1[1]. And likewise all the food which each would enjoy, if this fast were not prescribed for him, shall be zealously distributed after the fast, for love of God[2], among the needy and the bed-ridden and the afflicted who cannot fast in this way.

5[1]. And every member of a household shall give a penny as alms, or his lord shall give it for him, if he has nothing himself, and men of position[2] shall pay tithes.

§ 1[1]. And on these three days slaves shall be exempt from work, in order to attend church and keep the fast more willingly.

6. 7 on æghwilcan mynstre singe eal geferræden ætgædere heora saltere þa ðry dagas.

§ 1. 7 ælc mæssepreost mæssige for urne hlaford 7 for ealle his þeode.

§ 2. 7 þar to eacan mæssige man æghwilce dæge on ælcan minstre ane mæssan sinderlice for ðare neode þe us nu on handa stent, oð þæt hit betere wurðe.

§ 3. 7 æt ælcan tídsange eal hired aþenedum limum ætforan Godes weofode singe þone sealm: "Domine, quid multiplicati sunt" 7 preces 7 col'.

7. 7 ealle gemænelice, gehadode 7 læwede, bugan to Gode georne 7 geearnian his mildse.

8. 7 æghwilce geare heonon forð gelæste man Godes gerihta huru rihtlice, wið ðam þe us God ælmihtig gemiltsige 7 us geunne þæt we ure fynd ofercuman motan.
God ure helpe. Amen.

VIII ÆTHELRED

Anno MXIIII. ab incarnatione Domini nostri Iesu Christi[1].

Þis is an ðara gerædnessa þe Engla cyningc gedihte mid his witena geþeahte.

1. Þæt is ærest, þæt he wile þæt ealle Godes circan beon fulles griðes wurðe.

§ 1. And gif æfre ænig man heonan forð Godes ciricgrið swa abrece þæt he binnon ciricwagum mansleaga wurðe, þonne sy þæt botleas, 7 ehte his ælc þara þe Godes freond sy, buton þæt gewurðe þæt he þanon ætberste 7 swa deope friðsocne gesece þæt se cyningc him þurh þæt feores geunne, wið fulre bote ge wið God ge wið men.

[1] Be cyricgriðe. In nomine Domini G.

6[1]. And in every religious foundation, on these three days, all the brotherhood in common shall chant [the psalms from] their psalters[2].
§ 1[1]. And every priest shall say mass for our lord and for all his people.
§ 2[1]. And in addition, in every religious foundation, one mass shall be said daily with special reference[2] to the distress with which we are now afflicted[3], until an improvement takes place.
§ 3[1]. And at every service all the brotherhood, prostrate before the altar of God, shall chant the psalm: "O Lord, how are they multiplied" and the Prayers and Collect.
7[1]. And all men with one accord, both clerics and laymen, shall zealously turn to God and obtain his mercy.
8[1]. And every year henceforth the most scrupulous care shall be taken in the payment of God's dues, in order that God Almighty may have mercy upon us and grant us victory over our enemies.
God help us. Amen.

VIII ÆTHELRED

In the year 1014 after the incarnation of our Lord Jesus Christ[1].

This is one of the ordinances[1] which the English king drew up with the advice of his councillors.

1[1]. In the first place, it is his will that all the churches of God be entitled to exercise their right of protection to the full.
§ 1. And if ever anyone henceforth violates the protection of the church[1] of God by committing homicide within its walls, the crime shall not be atoned for by any payment of compensation[2], and everyone who is the friend of God shall pursue[3] the miscreant, unless it happen that he escapes from there and reaches so inviolable a sanctuary[4] that the king[5], because of that, grant him his life, upon condition that he makes full amends both towards God and men.

2. And þæt is þonne ærest, þæt he his agenne wer gesille þam cyninge 7 Christe 7 mid þam hine silfne inlagige to bote.

§ 1. Forðam Cristen cyning is Cristes gespelia[1] on Cristenre þeode, and he sceal Cristes abilgðe wrecan swiðe georne.

3. And gif hit þonne to bote gega 7 se cyngc þæt geþafige, þonne bete man þæt ciricgrið into ðare circan, be þæs[2] cyninges fullan mundbryce, 7 þa mynsterclænsunge begite, swa þarto gebirige, [7 ægþer ge mægbote ge manbote fullice gebete][3], 7 wið God huru þingian[4] georne.

4. And gif [elles][3] be cwicum mannum ciricgrið abrocen beo, betan[5] man georne be þam þe seo dæd sy, sy hit þurh feohtlac, si hit þurh reaflac, si hit þurh unriht hæmed[6], si þurh þæt þæt hit sy.

§ 1. Bete[7] man æfre[2] ærest þone griðbryce into ðare circan be þam þe seo dæd sy 7 be þam þe þare circan mæð sy.

5. Ne syn ealle cyrcan na gelicre mæðe worldlice wirðe, þeah hi godcundlice habban halgunge gelice.

§ 1. Heafodmynstres griðbryce æt botwurðan þingan bete man be cyninges munde, þæt is mid v pundum on Engla lage, and medemran mynstres mid hundtwelftigan scill', þæt is be cyninges wite, and þonne git læssan [þær legerstow þeh sy][3] mid sixtigan scill', and æt feldcircan mid xxx scill'.

---

[1] g. geteald G. [2] Om. G. [3] G; om. D. [4] -ie G.
[5] bete G. [6] si hit þ. u. h. om. G. [7] gebete G.

2. And the first condition is, that he shall give his own wergeld[1] to the king and to Christ[2], and by that means obtain the legal right[3] to offer compensation.

§ 1. For a Christian king is Christ's deputy[1] among Christian people, and he must avenge with the utmost diligence offences against Christ.

3. And if it comes to the payment of compensation and the king allows this course, amends for the violation of the protection of the church shall be made by the payment to the church in question of the full fine for breach of the king's "mund,"[1] and the purification of the church shall be carried out as is fitting, [and compensation both to the kin[2] and to the lord[3] of the slain man shall be fully paid], and, above all, supplication shall earnestly be made[4] to God.

4[1]. And if the protection of the church is broken in some other respect, without the taking of life[2], amends shall diligently be made in accordance with the nature of the offence, whether it be fighting or robbery or illicit intercourse[3] or whatever it may be.

§ 1[1]. And in the first instance, amends for breach of its protection shall always be made to the church, in accordance with the nature of the offence and also in proportion to the status[2] of the church.

5[1]. Not all churches are to be regarded as possessing the same status in civil law, though from the side of religion they all possess the same sanctity.

§ 1. Amends for violation of the protection of a principal church[1], in cases in which compensation can be paid[2], shall be made by payment of the fine for breach of the king's "mund," *i.e.* £5 in districts under English law, and in the case of a church of medium rank, by the payment of 120 shillings[3], *i.e.* by the fine due to the king (for insubordination)[4], and in the case of one still smaller [where however there is a graveyard][5], by the payment of 60 shillings, and in the case of a country chapel, by the payment of 30 shillings[6].

§ 2. A sceal mid rihte dom æfter dæde 7 medmung be mǽþe[1].

6. And be teoðunge se cyng 7 his witan habbað gecoren 7 gecweden, ealswa hit riht is, þæt ðriddan dæl þare teoðunge þe to circan gebyrge ga to ciricbote 7 oðer dæl þam Godes þeowum, þridde Godes þearfum 7 earman þeowetlingan.

7. And wite Cristenra manna gehwilc, þæt he his Drihtene his teoþunge, a swa seo sulh þone teoðan æcer gegá, rihtlice gelæste be Godes miltse 7 be þam fullan wite þe Eadgar cyningc gelagode.

8. Ðæt is: Gif hwa teoþunge rihtlice gelæstan nelle, þonne fare tó þæs cyninges gerefa 7 þæs mynstres mæssepreost— oððe þæs landrican 7 þæs biscopes gerefa—7 niman unþances ðone teoðan dæl to ðam mynstre þe hit to gebirige, 7 tæcan him to ðam nigoðan dæle, 7 todæle man ða eahta dælas on twá, 7 fó se landhlaford to healfum, to healfum se biscop, si hit cyninges man, sy hit þegnes.

9. And sy ælc geoguðe teoðung gelæst be pentecosten be wite, and eorðwestma be emnihte, oððe huru be ealra halgena mæssan.

10. And Romfeoh gelæste man æghwilce geare be Petres mæssan.

§ 1. 7 se þe þæt nelle gelæstan, sille þar to eacan xxx p' 7 gilde þam cyninge cxx scill'.

11. And ciricsceat gelæste man be Martinus mæssan.

§ 1. 7 se þe ðæt ne gelæste, forgilde hine mid twelffealdan 7 þam cyninge cxx scill'.

---

[1] At this point the extract in G ends.

§ 2[1]. Judgment, following the principles of justice, shall always be in accordance with the nature of the deed, and the penalty shall be proportionate to the offence.

6[1]. And with regard to tithes, the king and his councillors have decided and agreed, in accordance with the principles of justice, that a third part of the tithes which belong to the church shall be assigned to the repair of churches, the second portion to the servants of God, and the third portion to God's poor[2] and to poverty-stricken slaves[3].

7[1]. And every Christian man, in order to obtain the mercy of God, shall see to it that he duly renders his tithes to his Lord, namely, in every case, the produce of every tenth acre traversed by the plough, or else he shall incur the full penalty[2] which King Edgar[3] instituted by law.

8[1]. Namely: if anyone refuses to make due rendering of his tithes, the king's reeve and the priest of the church—or the reeve of the lord of the manor[2] and the bishop's reeve—shall go to him and, without his consent, shall take the tenth part for the church to which it belongs, and the next tenth shall be allotted to him, and the eight [remaining] parts shall be divided in two, and the lord of the manor shall take half and the bishop half, whether the man be under the lordship of the king or of a thegn.

9[1]. And every tithe of young livestock shall be rendered by Pentecost, under pain of incurring the fine, and the tithe of the fruits of the earth by the equinox, or at least by the feast of All Saints.

10[1]. And Peter's Pence shall be rendered every year by St Peter's Day.

§ 1[1]. And he who refuses to render it shall give in addition 30 pence, and shall pay 120 shillings to the king.

11[1]. And church dues shall be rendered by Martinmas.

§ 1[1]. And he who fails to do so shall pay them twelve-fold and [give] 120 shillings to the king.

12. Sulhælmessan gebireð þæt man gelæste be wite æghwilce geare, þonne xv niht beoð agan ofer eastertid.

§ 1. 7 leohtgescot gelæste man to candelmæssan; dó oftor se ðe wille.

13. And sawlsceat is rihtast þæt man symle gelæste a æt openum græfe.

14. And ealle Godes gerihta firðrige man georne, ealswa hit þearf is.

15. And gif hwa þæt nelle, gewilde man hine to rihte mid worldlicre steore, 7 þæt si gemæne Criste 7 cyninge, ealswa hit iu wæs.

16. And freolsa 7 fæstena be wite healde man rihtlice.

17. And Sunnondaga cypinga forbeode man georne be fullan worldwite.

18. And weofodþéna mæðe medemige man for Godes ege.

19. Gif man mæssepreost tihtlige þe regollice libbe andfealdre spræce, mæssige, gif he durre, 7 ladige hine on ðam husle silf hine silfne.

§ 1. And æt þrifealdre spræce ladige, gif he durre, eac on ðam husle mid twam his gehádan.

20. Gif man diacon tihtlige þe regollice libbe andfealdre spræce, nime twegen his gehádan 7 ladige hine mid þam.

§ 1. And gif man hine tihtlige þryfealdre spræce, nime six his gehádan 7 ladige mid þam 7 beo he silf seofoða.

21. Gif man folciscne mæssepreost mid tihtlan belecge þe regollif næbbe, ladige hine swa swa diacon þe regollife libbe.

12¹. Plough-alms ought to be rendered every year 15 days after Easter, under pain of incurring the fine.

§ 1¹. And light-dues shall be rendered at Candlemas; he who so desires may give them more frequently.

13¹. And it is best that payment for the souls of the dead should always be rendered before the grave is closed.

14¹. And all God's dues shall be promptly rendered, as the occasion requires.

15¹. And if anyone refuses to do so, he shall be brought to justice by a civil penalty, and this shall be divided between Christ and the king, in accordance with former custom.

16¹. And festivals and fasts shall be duly observed, under pain of incurring the fine².

17¹. And Sunday marketings shall be strictly forbidden, under pain of incurring the full civil penalty.

18¹. And the status of the priesthood² shall be respected through the fear of God.

19¹. If a simple accusation is brought against a priest who lives according to a rule, he shall say mass, if he dares, and by his own asseveration clear himself by the Holy Communion².

§ 1. And in the case of a triple accusation he shall also clear himself, if he dares, by the Holy Communion, with two supporters of the same ecclesiastical rank as himself.

20. If a simple accusation is brought against a deacon who lives according to a rule, he shall take two supporters of the same ecclesiastical rank and clear himself with their help.

§ 1. And if a triple accusation is brought against him, he shall take six supporters of the same ecclesiastical rank —himself making a seventh—and clear himself with their help.

21. If an accusation is brought against a secular priest who does not live according to a rule, he shall clear himself in the same way as a deacon who lives according to a rule.

22. Gif man freondleasne weofodþén mid tihtlan belecge, þe adfultum næbbe, gá to corsnǽde 7 þar þonne æt gefare þæt þæt God wille, buton he on husle ladian mote.

23. And gif man gehadodne mid fæhðe belecge 7 secge þæt he wære dǽdbana oððe rædbana, ladige mid his magan þe fæhðe moton mid beran oððe forebetan.

24. And gif he sý mægleas, ladige mid geferan, oððe fæste to corsnǽde 7 þaræt gefare þæt þæt God ræde.

25. And ne þearf ænig mynstermunuc ahwar mid rihte fæhðbote biddan ne fæhðbote betan; he gæð of his mæglage þonne he gebihð to regollage.

26. Gif mæssepreost manslaga wurðe oððe elles mánweorc to swiðe gewurce, þonne þolige he ægðres ge hádes gé éardes 7 wræcnige swa wíde swa papa him scrife 7 dædbete georne.

27. Gif mæssepreost ahwar stande on leasre gewitnesse oððe on mǽnan aðe, oððe þeofa gewita 7 geweorhta beo, þonne sy he aworpen of gehadodra gemanan 7 þolige ægðer ge geferscipes ge freondscipes ge æghwilces wurðscipes, buton he wið God 7 wið men þe deoplicor gebete, fullice swa biscop him tæce, 7 him borh finde þæt he þanan forð æfre swilces geswice.

§ 1. And gif he ladian wille, geladige be dæde mæðe, swa mid þryfealdre, [swa mid anfealdre][1], be þam þe seo dǽd sy.

28. Gif weofodþen be boca tæcincge his agen lif rihtlice fadige, þonne sy he fulles þegnweres 7 weorðscipes wurðe, ge on life ge on legere.

[1] Following Thorpe, cf. I Cn. 5, 4.

CAP. 22–28   125

22. If an accusation is brought against a minister of the altar who has no friends and no-one to support his oath, he shall go to the ordeal of consecrated bread[1], and shall experience there what is the will of God, unless he is allowed to clear himself by the Holy Communion.
23. And if a man in holy orders is charged with vendetta, and accused of having committed or instigated homicide, he shall clear himself with the help of his kin[1], who must share the vendetta[2] with him or pay compensation for it.
24. And if he has no kin, he shall clear himself with the help of his fellow-ecclesiastics[1], or fast in preparation for the ordeal of consecrated bread, and experience there what God shall decree.
25[1]. And no monk who belongs to a monastery anywhere may lawfully either demand or pay any compensation incurred by vendetta. He leaves the law of his kindred behind when he accepts monastic rule.
26[1]. If a priest commits homicide or perpetrates any other great crime, he shall be deprived of his ecclesiastical office and likewise banished, and shall travel as a pilgrim as far as the Pope appoints for him, and zealously make amends.
27[1]. If a priest anywhere be concerned in false witness or perjury[2], or be the accessory and accomplice of thieves, he shall be cast out from the fellowship of those in holy orders, and shall forfeit both their society and their friendship and every kind of privilege[3], unless he make full amends, both towards God and towards men, to the utmost of his ability, as the bishop shall prescribe for him, and find surety that henceforth he will cease for ever from all such [wrong-doing].
§ 1. And if he seeks to clear himself, he shall do so in proportion to the deed, either by the triple mode of proof, [or by the simple][1], in accordance with the nature of the deed.
28[1]. If a member of the priesthood orders his own life aright, according to the teaching of the canon law[2], he shall be entitled to the full wergeld and privileges of a thegn, both during his life and after his death.

29. And gif he his lif misfadige, wanige his weorðscipe be þam þe seo dæd sy.

30. Wite, gif he wille, ne gebirað him nan þingc ne to wife ne to worldwige, gif he Gode wile rihtlice hyran 7 Godes laga healdan, swa swa his hade gedafenað mid rihte.

31. Ac we læraþ georne 7 luflice biddað, þæt ælces hades men þam life libban þe heom to gebirige.

    § 1. 7 heonan forð we willað þæt abbodas 7 munecas regollicor libban þonne hi nu ær ðisan on gewunan hæfdon.

32. And se cyngc beodeð eallum his gerefan on æghwilcere stowe, þæt ge þam abbodan æt eallum worldneodum beorgan swa ge betst magon, 7 be þam þe ge willan Godes oððe minne freondscipe habban, filstan heora wícneran æghwar to rihte, þæt heo sylfe magan þe oftor on mynstrum fæste gewunian 7 regollice libban.

33. And gif man gehadodne oððe ælþeodigne man þurh ænig þinc forræde æt feo oððe æt feore, oððe hine bænde oððe hine beate oððe gebismrige on ænige wisan, þonne sceal him cyngc beon for mæg 7 for mundboran, buton he elles oðerne hæbbe.

34. And bete man ægðer ge him ge þam cynge, swa swa hit gebirige, be þam þe séo dæd sy, oððe he ða dæde wrece swiðe deope.

35. Cristenum mannan[1] gebirað swiðe rihte þæt he Godes abilgðe wrece swiðe georne.

36. And wise wæran worldwitan þe to godcundan rihtlagan woroldlaga settan, folce to steore, 7 Criste 7 cyninge gerehtan[2] þa bote þar man swa scolde manega for neode gewildan to rihte.

37. Ac on þam gemotan, þeah rædlice wurðan on namcuðan stowan, æfter Eadgares lifdagum, Cristes lage wanodan 7 cyninges laga litledon.

---

[1] -um D.   [2] -rihtan D.

29. And if he misdirects his life, his privileges shall be reduced, according to the nature of the offence.
30. Let him understand, if he will, that it is not seemly for him to have anything to do either with marriage or with worldly strife, if he will duly obey God and observe his laws, as properly befits his estate.
31[1]. But we earnestly enjoin and, with all good-will, beg men of every estate to live such a life as befits them.
   § 1. And henceforth we desire abbots and monks to live more according to a rule than they have been accustomed to do until now.
32. And the king enjoins upon all his reeves in every locality: you shall support the abbots in all their temporal needs as you best can, and if you desire to have God's favour and mine[1], help their stewards everywhere to obtain their rights, so that they themselves may constantly remain secure in their monasteries and live according to their rule.
33[1]. And if an attempt is made to deprive in any way a man in orders or a stranger of either his goods or his life, or if he is bound[2] or beaten or insulted in any way, the king shall act as his kinsman and protector, if he has no other.
34. And compensation according to the nature of the deed shall be paid both to him and to the king, as is fitting, or he (the king) shall avenge the deed to the uttermost.
35[1]. It is the duty most incumbent upon a Christian man that he should avenge offences against God with the utmost diligence.
36[1]. And secular councillors showed wisdom in appointing civil laws to uphold the privileges of religion, for the governance of the people, and in assigning the compensation to Christ and the king, so that[2] thereby many are forced of necessity to submit to justice.
37. But in the assemblies since the days of Edgar, though advisedly they have been held in places of note[1], the laws of Christ have been neglected and the laws of the king disregarded[2].

38. And þa man getwæmde þæt ær wæs gemæne Criste 7 cynincge on worldlicre steore, 7 a hit wearð þe wirse for Gode 7 for worlde; cume nu to bote, gif hit God wille.

39. And git mæg ðeah bot cuman, wille hit man georne on eornost aginnan.

40. And gif man eard wille rihtlice clænsian, þonne mot man smeagan 7 geornlice spirian, hwar ða manfullan wununge habban þe nellað geswican ne for Gode betan, ac swa hwar swa hi man finde, gewilde hi to rihte, þances oððe unðances, oððe hi afirsige mid ealle of earde, buton hi gebugan 7 to rihte gewændan.

41. Gif munuc oððe mæssepreost wiðersaca wurðe mid ealle, he sy amansumod æfre, buton he þe rædlicor gebuge to his þearfe.

42. And se þe Godes utlagan ofer þone andagan, þe se cyngc sette, hæbbe on gewealde, plihte to him sylfum 7 ealre his are wið Cristes gespelian þe Cristendom 7 cynedom healdað 7 wealdað, þa hwile þe þæs God geann.

43. Ac uton don swa us þea[r]f[1] is: uton niman us to bisnan þæt ærran worldwitan to ræde geræddon, Æþelstan 7 Eadmund 7 Eadgar þe nihst wæs, hu hi God weorðodon 7 Godes lage heoldon 7 Godes gafel læstan, þa hwile þe hi leofodon.

§ 1. 7 utan God lufian innewerdre heortan 7 Godes laga gíman, swa wel swa we betst magon.

44. And uton rihtne Cristendom geornlice wurðian 7 ælcne hæðendom mid ealle oferhogian.

§ 1. And uton ænne cynehlaford holdlice healdan, 7 freonda gehwilc mid rihtan getriwðan oðerne lufige 7 healde mid rihte.

[1] þeaf D.

38. And then the [dues from] civil penalties which had previously been shared between[1] Christ and the king were separated, and things have continually gone from bad to worse both in religious and in secular affairs. God grant that there may now be improvement![2]

39[1]. And yet nevertheless improvement can come, if there is the zealous desire to begin it in earnest.

40[1]. And if the land is to be thoroughly purified, inquiry and search must be diligently made for the dwelling-places of the wicked who will not abstain [from evil] or make amends in the sight of God, and wherever they are found they shall be brought to justice, willingly or unwillingly, or they shall be utterly driven from the land, unless they submit and amend their ways.

41[1]. If a monk or a priest becomes an utter apostate, he shall be excommunicated for ever, unless he is wise enough to return to his duty.

42[1]. And he who keeps under his protection an excommunicated man[2], beyond the term fixed by the king, shall be in danger of forfeiting his life and all his property to the deputies of Christ[3], who shall be the defenders and upholders of the Christian religion and the royal authority[4], as long as God shall permit.

43. But let us do what is our duty, let us take as our example what the secular authorities of old wisely decreed—Æthelstan and Edmund[1] and Edgar[2], who came last—how they honoured God and kept his law[3] and rendered tribute to him, as long as they lived.

§ 1[1]. And let us love God from our inmost heart and observe his laws to the best of our ability.

44[1]. And let us zealously honour the true Christian religion and utterly despise all heathen practices.

§ 1[1]. And let us loyally support one royal lord, and let each of our friends[2] love the other with true fidelity and treat him justly.

IX ÆTHELRED

(*Incip.*)[1] Ðis is sio gerædnes þe Æþelred cyning and ealle his witan æt Wudustoce geræddan.

1. An ærest, þæt we ealle to Gode ælmihtigan georne gebugan 7 his bebodu healdan 7 unrihtes ealle geswican.

(*Expl.*)[1] An[d][2] uton ænne God lufian and weorðian and ænne Cristendom ealle heald[an][3] 7 ælcne hæþendom mid ealle aweorpan. Uton ænne cynehlaford holdliche...(*desunt reliqua*.)[1]

X ÆTHELRED

An is ece Godd wealdend 7 wyrhta ealra gesceafta; 7 on þæs naman weorðunge ic, Æðelred cyning, ærest smeade, hu ic Cristendom æfre mihte 7 rihtne cynedom fyrmest aræran, 7 hu ic mihte þearflicast me sylfum gerædan for Gode 7 for worolde 7 eallum minum leodscype rihtlicast lagian þa þing to þearfe þe we scýlan healdan.

§ 1. Mearn to gemynde oft 7 gelome þe godcunde lara 7 wislice woroldlaga Cristendom fyrðriað 7 cynedom micliað, folce gefremiað 7 weorðscypes wealdað, sibbiað 7 sehtað 7 sace twæmað 7 þeode þeawas ealle gebetað.

§ 2. Nu wille ic georne æfter þam spyrian, hu we lara 7 laga betst magan healdan 7 æghwylce unlaga swyþost aweorpan.

§ 3. 7 þis is seo gerædnes þe we willað healdan, swa swa we æt Eanham fæste gecwædon.

[1] Wanley.   [2] *An.*   [3] *-e.*

IX ÆTHELRED

This is the ordinance which King Æthelred and all his councillors have determined upon at Woodstock[1].

1[1]. In the first place, we shall all zealously turn to God Almighty and keep his commandments and all cease from evil....

And let us love and honour one God and all uphold[1] one Christian faith and utterly renounce all heathen practices. Let us loyally[1] [support] one royal lord[2]....

X ÆTHELRED

The eternal God alone is the ruler and maker of all created things[1], and in honour of his name I, King Æthelred, have been considering first of all how I could best promote Christianity[2] and the just interests of the royal authority, and how, in affairs both religious and secular, I could determine with the greatest profit to myself[3], and ordain most justly[4], for the advantage of all my subjects, the conditions which we ought to observe.

- § 1[1]. Frequently and often it has come into my mind that sacred precepts and wise secular decrees promote Christianity and strengthen royal authority, further public interests and are the source of honour, bring about peace and reconciliation, put an end to strife and improve the whole character of the nation.
- § 2. Now I desire zealously to search out how we may best uphold precepts and laws and most fully renounce all unjust practices[1].
- § 3. And this is the ordinance which we desire to observe in accordance with what we have firmly decreed at Enham[1].

1. Ðæt is þonne ærest, þæt we ealle fram synnan georne gecyrran 7 ure misdæda geornlice betan 7 ænne God æfre lufian 7 weorðian 7 ænne Christendom georne healdan 7 ælcne hæðendom mid ealle aweorpan.

2. 7 witena gerædnes is, þæt man rihte laga upp arære 7 ælce unlaga georne afylle, 7 þæt man læte beon æghwylcne man rihtes wyrðe.

§ 1. 7 þæt man frið 7 freondscype rihtlice healde for Gode 7 for worolde.

1[1]. The first provision is, that all of us zealously turn from sins and zealously make amends for our misdeeds, and love and honour for all time one God, and zealously uphold one Christian faith, and utterly renounce all heathen practices.

2[1]. And the decree of the councillors is, that justice be promoted and every injustice zealously suppressed, and that every man be allowed the benefit of the law.

§ 1. And that peace and goodwill be duly maintained in matters both religious and secular.

THE LAWS OF CANUTE

THE LAWS OF CANUTE

Two proclamations and one long code of laws issued by Canute have been preserved. The latter falls into two parts, generally distinguished as I and II Canute, the first of which deals with ecclesiastical affairs, the second with secular (cf. II, III Edgar).

The first Proclamation seems to have been issued early in 1020 (see Notes), and is addressed to all his subjects in England. It contains interesting references to recent events, *e.g.* the receipt of letters and injunctions from the Pope (cap. 3), the removal of the menace of hostility from Denmark, for which Canute takes full credit to himself (cap. 5), and the general acceptance of the laws of Edgar at Oxford (cap. 13). It marks therefore an important stage in the history of the country. The wars, discord and unrest of the preceding years are at an end, and just government is assured for the future. The homiletic tone of the whole proclamation recalls the Laws of Æthelred, and may be due to the influence of Wulfstan of York (see Notes).

The second Proclamation, prepared by Canute on his way from Rome to Denmark, belongs to the year 1027 (see cap. 3 and Note). Historically it is of great importance for the information it supplies regarding Canute's movements in 1027 (see caps. 13, 14), his position in relation to the Pope and the princes of Western Europe (cap. 5), and his diplomatic successes abroad (caps. 6, 7). His instructions to his officials to maintain justice and to secure full payment of church dues contain nothing new. In both Proclamations the statement of his resolution to rule justly rings sincere (1020, cap. 2; 1027, cap. 10).

Canute's Code of laws was issued one Christmas at Winchester (see Preamble). The year is not stated and cannot be exactly determined, but a date later than 1018, when the assembly met at Oxford and swore to uphold the laws of Edgar, seems most likely. The fact that Canute calls himself King of Denmark further supports this supposition (see 1020, cap. 5 and Note). The years 1019, 1026 and 1028 are definitely excluded, because in each of these Canute was absent from England at Christmas (see Steenstrup, *Normannerne*, III. 312, 409). This leaves as possible the years 1020–1025, 1027, 1029–1034. The statement in the heading of MS D, that the code was drawn up immediately after the establishment of peace between Danes and English, would indicate an early date, but, as it does not appear in any of the other MSS, and as D otherwise is fragmentary and untrustworthy, it is probably not authentic (see Liebermann, III. p. 194). In one MS class (A, *Consiliatio Cnuti*) the title "King of Norway" is also found but may have been added by a scribe (see 1027, Preamble and Note). From the statement of Wm. of Malmesbury (*Gesta Regum*, § 183, Rolls Series, p. 224) it would seem that the laws were not promulgated till after Canute's return from Rome. The fact that no reference occurs in either of his proclamations to earlier enactments of his own, and that certain points brought forward there are dealt with more fully in the Laws (cf. 1027, cap. 16 and I Cn. 8–14) seems to confirm this statement. The years most likely therefore are 1027, 1029–34 (see Liebermann, III. p. 194).

Canute's Code of laws is notably comprehensive. It shows no marked originality, however, as a large proportion of its injunctions and regulations are drawn from homilies and penitentials and from earlier laws (especially those of Edgar and Æthelred). In arrangement the Code shows little advance on those of Canute's predecessors. Repetitions are frequent, but in general the style is clear and straightforward. Especially interesting are the sections giving detailed accounts of the dues to which the king was entitled in Wessex, Mercia and the Danelaw (II Cn. caps. 12–15), and of the grading of heriots (II Cn. caps. 70–72, 1). In both cases probably, to judge from the evidence of earlier and contemporary documents, the regulations here definitely expressed for the first time in a code of laws had long been observed in practice.

The only MS copy of the Proclamation of 1020 dates from about 1050 and is preserved in the Minster Library at York. The Proclamation of 1027 has been preserved only in a Latin translation and is found in Florence of Worcester, ed. Thorpe, I. p. 185 ff. (which I have collated with MS Oxford Corpus 157, p. 329), and Wm. of Malmesbury, *Gesta Reg.* Lib. II. § 183.

THE LAWS OF CANUTE

I, II Canute is found complete in MSS G and A and in Lambarde's edition. Some leaves of MS B containing caps. 1–14, 2 have been lost but from that point the code is complete. Fragments appear in MS D (see Notes). Three Latin translations are also extant, namely, in the Quadripartitus, the Instituta Cnuti and the Consiliatio Cnuti. For an account of the various MSS and their relationship see Liebermann, III. p. 192 f. The following text of I and II Canute has been taken from B, the missing clauses of I being supplied from G.

CANUTE'S PROCLAMATION OF 1020

1. Cnut cyning gret his arcebiscopas 7 his leodbiscopas 7 Þurcyl eorl 7 ealle his eorlas 7 ealne his þeodscype, twelfhynde 7 twyhynde, gehadode 7 læwede, on Englalande freondlice.

2. 7 ic cyðe eow þæt ic wylle beon hold hlaford 7 unswicende to Godes gerihtum 7 to rihtre woroldlage.

3. Ic nam me to gemynde þa gewritu 7 þa word þe se arcebiscop Lyfing me fram þam papan brohte of Rome, þæt ic scolde æghwær Godes lof upp aræran 7 unriht alecgan 7 full frið wyrcean be ðære mihte þe me God syllan wolde.

4. Nu ne wandode ic na minum sceattum, þa hwile þe eow unfrið on handa stod; nu ic mid Godes fultume þæt totwæmde mid minum scattum.

5. Þa cydde man me þæt us mara hearm to fundode þonne us wel licode; 7 þa for ic me sylf, mid þam mannum þe me mid foron, into Denmearcon þe eow mæst hearm of com; 7 þæt hæbbe [ic][1] mid Godes fultume forene forfangen, þæt eow næfre heonon forð þanon nan unfrið to ne cymð, þa hwile þe ge mé rihtlice healdað 7 min lif byð.

6. Nu ðancige ic Gode ælmihtigum his fultumes 7 his mildheortnesse, þæt ic þa myclan hearmas þe us to fundedon swa gelogod hæbbe, þæt we ne þurfon þanon nenes hearmes us asittan, ac us to fullan fultume 7 to ahreddingge, gyf us neod byð.

7. Nu wylle ic þæt we ealle eadmodlice Gode ælmihtigum þancian þære mildheortnesse þe he us to fultume gedon hæfð.

[1] Not in MS.

CANUTE'S PROCLAMATION OF 1020

1. King Canute[1] sends friendly greetings[2] to his archbishops[3] and his diocesan bishops and Earl Thurkil[4] and all his earls[5] and all his subjects in England, nobles and commoners, ecclesiastics and laymen.

2. And I declare to you that I will be a gracious lord[1], and will not fail to support the rights of the church[2] and just secular law.

3. I have taken cognisance of the written[1] and verbal injunctions which Archbishop Lyfing brought me from Rome from the Pope[2], namely, that I should everywhere magnify the glory of God and suppress injustice and establish perfect security through the power which God has been pleased to grant me.

4. Recently I did not spare my money when hostility[1] was threatening you, and now, with the help of God, I have averted[2] it with my money.

5. When I was informed that we were threatened with danger greater than we could regard with equanimity, I went[1] in person, with those who accompanied me, to Denmark[2], which was the chief source of danger to you, and, with the help of God, I have taken measures to prevent hostility ever from this time forth coming upon you from that quarter, as long as you support me loyally and my life lasts[3].

6. Now I thank God Almighty for his help and his mercy, that I have disposed of the great dangers which threatened us, with the result that we need not expect any danger from that quarter, but rather [that they will grant] us abundant help and deliverance, if we need it.

7. Now it is my desire that we all humbly thank God Almighty for the mercy which he has shown in aiding us[1].

8. Nu bidde ic mine arcebiscopas 7 ealle mine leodbiscopas, þæt hy ealle neodfulle beon ymbe Godes gerihta, ælc on his ende þe heom betæht is; 7 eac minum ealdormannum ic beode, þæt hy fylstan þam biscopum to Godes gerihtum 7 to minum kynescype 7 to ealles folces þearfe.

9. Gif hwa swa dyrstig sy, gehadod oððe læwede, Denisc oððe Englisc, þæt ongean Godes lage ga 7 ongean minne cynescype oððe ongean woroldriht, 7 nelle betan 7 geswican æfter minra biscopa tæcinge, þonne bidde ic Þurcyl eorl 7 eac beode, þæt he ðæne unrihtwisan to rihte gebige, gyf he mæge.

10. Gyf he ne mæge, þonne wille ic mid uncer begra cræfte þæt he hine on earde adwæsce oððe ut of earde adræfe, sy he betera sy he wyrsa.

11. 7 eac ic beode eallum minum gerefum, be minum freondscype 7 be eallum þam þe hi agon 7 be heora agenum life, þæt hy æghwær min folc rihtlice healdan 7 rihte domas deman be ðære scira biscopa gewitnesse, 7 swylce mildheortnesse þæron don swylce þære scire biscope riht þince 7 se man acuman mæge.

12. 7 gyf hwa þeof friðige oððe forena forlicge, sy he emscyldig wið me þam ðe þeof scolde, buton he hine mid fulre lade wið me geclænsian mæge.

13. 7 ic wylle þæt eal þeodscype, gehadode 7 læwede, fæstlice Eadgares lage healde þe ealle men habbað gecoren 7 to gesworen on Oxenaforda.

14. For ðam þe ealle biscopas secgað þæt hit swyþe deop wið God to betanne þæt man aðas oððe wedd tobrece.

8. Now I pray my archbishops and all my diocesan bishops to be zealous with regard to the rights of the church[1]—each one in the district which is entrusted to him[2]; and likewise I enjoin upon my ealdormen[3] to support the bishops in furthering the rights of the church[1] and my royal authority and the well-being of the whole nation.

9. If anyone, whether a man in orders or a layman, a Dane or an Englishman[1], is so presumptuous as to defy the law of God and my royal authority or secular law, and will not make amends and desist from so doing, according to the instruction given by my bishops[2], then I pray and likewise enjoin upon Earl Thurkil to bring the evil-doer to justice, if he can.

10. If he cannot, it is my will that he should make use of both his own resources and mine for the purpose of driving him out of the country or crushing him, if he remains in the country, whether he be of high[1] or humble station.

11[1]. And likewise I enjoin upon all my reeves, under pain of forfeiting my friendship and all that they possess and their own lives, to govern my people justly everywhere, and to pronounce just judgments with the cognisance of the bishops of the dioceses[2], and to inflict such mitigated penalties[3] as the bishop may approve and the man himself may be able to bear.

12. And if anyone protects a thief or takes action[1] on his behalf, he shall incur the same penalty at my hands as the thief was liable to, unless he can clear himself to my satisfaction with a full oath of exculpation[2].

13[1]. And it is my will that the whole nation, ecclesiastics and laymen, shall steadfastly keep the law of Edgar to which all have given their adherence under oath at Oxford.

14. For all the bishops declare that very severe amends must be made to God for the violation of oaths or pledges.

15. 7 eac hy us furðor lærað, þæt we sceolon eallan mægene 7 eallon myhton þone ecan mildan God inlice secan, lufian 7 weorðian 7 ælc unriht ascunian—ðæt synd mægslagan 7 morðslagan 7 mansworan 7 wiccean 7 wælcyrian 7 æwbrecan 7 syblegeru.

16. 7 eac we beodað on Godes ælmihtiges naman 7 on ealra his haligra, þæt nan man swa dyrstig ne sy, þæt on gehadodre nunnan oððe on mynecenan gewifige.

17. 7 gyf hit hwa gedon hæbbe, beo he utlah wið God 7 amansumod fram eallum Cristendome 7 wið þone cyning scyldig ealles þæs þe he age, buton he ðe raðor geswice 7 þe deopplicor gebete wið God.

18. 7 gyt we furðor maniað, þæt man Sunnandæges freols mid eallum mægene healde 7 weorðige fram Sæternesdæges none oð Monandæges lyhtinge, 7 nan man swa dyrstig ne sy, þæt he aðor oððe cypinge wyrce oððe ænig mot gesæce [on][1] þam halgan dæge.

19. 7 ealle men, earme 7 eadige, heora cyrcan secean 7 for heora synnum þingian 7 ælc beboden fæstan geornlice healdan 7 þa halgan georne weorðian þe us mæssepreostas beodan sceolan.

20. Þæt we magan 7 moton ealle samod, þurh þæs ecean Godes mildheortnesse 7 his halgena þingrædene, to heofena rices myrhðe becuman 7 mid him wunian þe leofað 7 rihxað a butan ende. Amen.

[1] Not in MS.

15. And likewise they teach us further that, with all our might and with all our strength, we should fervently seek, love and honour the eternal, merciful God, and put away from us every form of unrighteousness, such as [the deeds of] parricides[1], murderers, perjurers, witches, sorceresses[2] and adulterers, and incestuous deeds.

16[1]. And likewise we enjoin, in the name of God Almighty and of all his Saints, that no man be so presumptuous as to take to wife a professed nun or a woman who has taken religious vows.

17. And if anyone has done so, he shall be an outcast before God and cut off from the whole community of Christians, and he shall forfeit to the king all that he has, unless he desists [from the unhallowed wedlock] as quickly as possible, and makes amends towards God to the utmost.

18. And further still we admonish all men to keep and observe the Sunday festival[1] with all their might from noon on Saturday till dawn on Monday, and no man shall be so presumptuous as either to trade[2] or to attend any assembly[2] on the holy day.

19. And all men, both rich and poor, shall attend their churches[1] and make supplication for their sins, and zealously keep every prescribed fast[2], and diligently celebrate the saints-days[3] which the priests enjoin upon us[4].

20. So that, through the mercy of the eternal God and the intercession of his saints, we may all together have power and permission to attain to the joy of the kingdom of Heaven[1] and to dwell with Him who liveth and reigneth for ever without end. Amen.

CANUTE'S PROCLAMATION OF 1027

Canutus[1], rex totius Angliae et Denemarciae[2] et Norreganorum[3] et partis Suanorum[4], Æthelnotho[5] metropolitano et Alfrico Eboracensi archiepiscopo[6] omnibusque episcopis et primatibus et toti genti Anglorum tam nobilibus quam plebeiis, salutem.

1. Notifico vobis me noviter isse Romam, oratum pro redemptione peccaminum meorum et pro salute regnorum quique meo subiacent regimini populorum.

2. Hanc quidem profectionem Deo iam olim devoveram, sed pro negotiis regni et causis impedientibus huc usque perficere non poteram.

3. Nunc autem ipsi Deo meo omnipotenti valde humiliter gratias ago, qui[7] mihi[6] concessit in vita mea sanctos[8] apostolos suos[6] Petrum et Paulum et omne sanctuarium quod intra[9] urbem Romam aut extra addiscere potui expetere, et secundum desiderium meum praesentialiter venerari et adorare.

4. Ob id ergo maxime[10] hoc patravi, quia a sapientibus didici sanctum Petrum apostolum magnam potestatem a Domino[11] accepisse ligandi atque[12] solvendi clavigerumque esse coelestis regni, et ideo specialius[13] eius patrocinium apud Deum[14] diligenter[6] expetere valde utile duxi.

5. Sit autem vobis notum, quia magna congregatio nobilium in ipsa pascali solennitate ibi cum domino papa Iohanne et imperatore Cuonrado[15] erat, scilicet omnes principes gentium a monte Gargano usque ad istud proximum mare, qui omnes me et honorifice suscepere et donis pretiosis honoravere[16]; maxime autem ab imperatore donis variis et muneribus pretiosis honoratus sum, tam in vasis aureis et argenteis quam in palliis et vestibus valde pretiosis.

[1] *Cnuto* Ma.   [2] *-marchiae* Ma.   [3] *-giae* Ma.
[4] *Swavorum* Ma.   [5] *Aiel., Ail., Al.* Ma; *Athel.* Ox.   [6] Om. Ma.
[7] *quod* Ma.   [8] *beatos* Ma.   [9] *infra* Ox.   [10] *Et ideo max.* Ma.
[11] *Deo* Ox.   [12] *et* Ma.   [13] *-liter* Ma.   [14] *Dominum* Th.
[15] *Con.* Ma.   [16] *magnificis d. h.* Ma.

CANUTE'S PROCLAMATION OF 1027

Canute, King of all England and Denmark and of Norway[1] and part of Sweden[2], to Æthelnoth the Metropolitan[3], and to Ælfric, Archbishop of York[4], and to all the bishops and notables and the whole of the English nation, both nobles and commoners[5], greeting.

1. I make known to you that I have lately been to Rome to pray for the redemption of my sins and for the security of the realms and the peoples who are subject to my rule.

2. Long ago I had vowed this journey to God, but, on account of affairs of State and other delays[1], I had not been able to perform it until now.

3. But now very humbly I render thanks to God Almighty, who has permitted me during my life-time to visit his holy apostles, Peter and Paul, and all the sacred places of which I could learn, either within or without the city of Rome, and to worship and adore them in person there in accordance with my desire.

4. My chief reason for doing this was, that I learned from the wise that the holy apostle Peter[1] had received from the Lord great power both to bind and to release, and was the keeper of the keys of the kingdom of Heaven. For this reason, in particular, I thought it exceedingly advantageous to seek diligently to obtain his favour before God.

5. Now be it known to you that there was a great assembly of nobles there at the celebration of Easter with my lord the Pope John and the Emperor Conrad[1], namely, all the princes of the nations from Mount Garganus[2] to the sea which is nearest [to us][3], all of whom received me graciously and honoured me with costly gifts; but chiefly was I honoured by the Emperor[4] with various gifts and costly presents, both vessels of gold and silver and mantles and very costly robes.

6. Locutus sum igitur cum ipso imperatore et domino papa et principibus qui ibi erant de necessitatibus totius populi universi regni[1] mei, tam Anglorum quam Danorum[2], ut eis concederetur lex aequior et pax securior in via Romam adeundi, et ne tot clausuris per viam artentur[3] et propter thelon[4] iniustum fatigentur; annuitque postulatis imperator et Rodulfus[5] rex qui maxime ipsarum clausurarum dominatur, cunctique principes edictis firmaverunt, ut homines mei, tam mercatores quam alii orandi causa[6] viatores, absque omni angaria clausurarum et theloneariorum[7] firma pace et iusta lege securi[8] Romam eant et redeant.

7. Conquestus sum iterum coram domino papa et mihi valde displicere causabar[9], quod mei archiepiscopi in tantum angariabantur immensitate pecuniarum quae ab eis expetebatur[10], dum pro pallio accipiendo secundum[11] morem apostolicam sedem expeterent; decretumque est ne id deinceps fiat.

8. Cuncta enim[12] quae a domino papa et ab ipso imperatore et a rege Rodulfo[13] caeterisque principibus, per quorum terras nobis transitus est ad Romam, pro meae gentis utilitate postulabam, libentissime[14] annuerunt et concessa sacramento etiam firmaverunt sub testimonio quattuor archiepiscoporum et viginti episcoporum et innumerae multitudinis ducum et nobilium qui ibi aderant[15].

9. Quapropter Deo omnipotenti gratias magnificas reddo, quia omnia, quae desideraveram prout mente decreveram, prospere perfeci votisque meis ad velle satisfeci.

10. Nunc itaque notum sit omnibus vobis[16], quia ipsi Deo omnipotenti[17] supplex devovi vitam meam amodo in omnibus iustificare, et regna mihi subdita populosque iuste et pie regere aequumque iudicium per omnia[18] observare; et si quid

---

[1] *u. r.* om. Ma.   [2] *Angli q. Dani* Ma.   [3] *arct.* Ma.
[4] *in. theloneum* Ma.   [5] *Rodbertus* Ox.   [6] *gratia* Ma.
[7] *-neorum cum f.* Ma.   [8] *et i. l. s.* om. Ma.   [9] *dixi* Ma.
[10] *-bantur* Ma.   [11] *-ndo* Ox.   [12] *ea* Th.
[13] *Rodberto* Ox.   [14] *-nter* Ma.   [15] *quae aderat* Ma.
[16] *o. v.* om. Ma.   [17] Om. Ma.   [18] *omnes* Ox. & most MSS of Ma.

6. I therefore spoke with the Emperor himself, and with my lord the Pope, and with the princes who were present, about the needs of the people throughout my kingdom, both English and Danes, that more just regulations should be accorded them and greater security in their journeys to Rome[1], and that they should not be hindered by so many barriers[2] on their way and harassed by unjust tolls. And the Emperor agreed to my demands, and [so did] King Rudolf[3], in whose dominion lie most of these barriers, and all the princes confirmed by edict[4], that my subjects, both merchants and others travelling in the cause of devotion, should go and come to and from Rome in assured peace and under just regulations, free from all the hindrances caused by barriers and tolls.

7. I complained again in the presence of my lord the Pope, and said how greatly it displeased me, that my Archbishops were so much straitened by the vast sums of money exacted from them when, according to usage, they visited the Apostolic See to receive their pall. And it was decreed that henceforth such exactions should not be made.

8. Indeed, to all the demands which I made, for the benefit of my people, to my lord the Pope and the Emperor and King Rudolf and the other princes, through whose territories lies our way to Rome, they readily agreed, and likewise confirmed their concessions by oath, with the witness of four archbishops and twenty bishops and an innumerable multitude of princes and nobles who were present.

9. Therefore, I render supreme thanks to Almighty God, because, in accordance with my intention, I have successfully accomplished all that I had desired, and have fulfilled my vows in accordance with my wish.

10. Now, therefore, be it known to all of you that, as a suppliant to God Almighty, I have vowed henceforth to regulate my life in all things, and to rule the kingdoms and peoples subject to me justly and uprightly, and to maintain equity in all things, and I purpose henceforth, with the help of

per meae iuventutis intemperantiam aut negligentiam hactenus praeter id quod iustum erat actum est, totum Deo auxiliante deinceps[1] dispono emendare.

11. Idcirco obtestor et praecipio meis consiliariis quibus regni consilia credidi, ne ullo modo aut propter meum timorem aut alicuius potentis personae favorem aliquam iniustitiam amodo consentiant vel patiantur[2] pullulare in omni regno meo.

12. Praecipio etiam omnibus vicecomitibus et praepositis universi regni mei, sicut meam amicitiam aut suam salutem habere volunt, ut nulli homini, nec diviti nec pauperi, vim iniustam inferant, sed omnibus, tam nobilibus quam ignobilibus, et divitibus et pauperibus[3] sit fas iusta lege potiundi, a qua nec propter favorem regium aut[4] alicuius potentis personam nec propter mihi congregandam[5] pecuniam ullo modo devietur[6], quia nulla mihi necessitas est ut iniqua exactione mihi pecunia congregetur[7].

13. Ego itaque vobis[8] notum fieri volo, quod eadem via qua exivi regrediens, Danemarciam eo[9], pacem et firmum pactum omnium Danorum consilio cum eis gentibus et populis compositurus qui nos[10] et regno et vita privare, si eis possibile esset, volebant; sed non poterant[11], Deo scilicet virtutem eorum destruente, qui nos sua benigna[12] pietate in regno et honore conservet, omniumque inimicorum nostrorum potentiam et fortitudinem deinceps dissipet et[13] adnichilet!

14. Composita denique pace cum gentibus quae in circuitu nostro sunt, dispositoque et pacato omni regno nostro hic in oriente, ita ut a nulla parte bellum aut inimicitias aliquorum timere habeamus, quam citius hac aestate apparatum navigii procurare[14] potero, Angliam venire dispono.

---

[1] Om. Ma.   [2] *faciant* Ma.   [3] *et d. et p.* om. Ma.   [4] *nec propter al.* Ma.
[5] *congerendam* Ma.   [6] *devient.* Ma.   [7] *congeratur* Ma.
[8] *quod v. n. f. volo, ea.* Fl; *n. v.* Ma.   [9] *vado* Ma.
[10] *comp. cum eis g. quae nos* Ma.   [11] *potuerunt* Ma.
[12] *benignitate* Ma   [13] *et f. d. d. et* om. Ma.   [14] *habere* Ma.

CAP. 11–14   151

God, to amend whatever has hitherto been done contrary to what is right, through the intemperance of youth[1] or through negligence.

11[1]. I therefore entreat and enjoin upon all my counsellors, to whom I have entrusted the administration of the kingdom, that they shall in no way, whether through fear of me or to gain the favour of any powerful person, henceforth countenance or suffer any form of injustice to flourish in any part of my kingdom.

12[1]. I enjoin likewise upon all the sheriffs[2] and reeves throughout my kingdom that, as they desire to retain my friendship[3] and their own security, they employ no unjust force towards any man, either rich or poor[4], but that all, both nobles and commoners, rich and poor, shall have the right of just possession, which shall not be infringed upon in any way, either for the sake of obtaining the favour of the king or of gratifying any powerful person or of collecting money for me[5]; for I have no need that money should be collected for me by any unjust exactions.

13. I therefore wish to make known to you that, returning by the same way as I went, I am going to Denmark, in order, with the counsel of all the Danes, to make firm and lasting peace with those nations and peoples[1] who, had it been in their power, would have deprived us of both our kingdom and our life; but they were not able to do so, since their strength was destroyed by God. May He, in His loving-kindness, preserve us in authority and in honour, and henceforth confound and bring to naught the power and strength of all our enemies.

14[1]. Then, when peace has been established with the nations round about us, and when all our realm here in the east has been regulated and pacified, so that we need have no fear of war or hostilities on any side, I propose to come to England this summer, as soon as I can have a fleet equipped.

15. Hanc autem epistolam idcirco[1] praemisi, ut de mea prosperitate omnis populus regni mei laetificetur, quia, ut vos ipsi scitis, nunquam memet ipsum nec meum laborem abstinui nec adhuc abstinebo impendere pro omnis populi mei necessaria utilitate.

16. Nunc igitur praecipio et[2] obtestor omnes meos episcopos et regni praepositos, per fidem quam Deo et mihi debetis, quatinus faciatis ut, antequam ego[3] Angliam veniam, omnia[4] debita quae Deo[3] secundum legem antiquam debemus, sint persoluta, scilicet elemosinae[5] pro aratris et decimae animalium ipsius anni[6] procreatorum et denarii quos Romae[7] ad Sanctum Petrum debemus[8], sive ex urbibus sive ex villis, et mediante Augusto decimae frugum et in festivitate Sancti Martini primitiae seminum ad ecclesiam sub cuius parrochia quisque deget[9], quae Anglice ciricsceatt nominantur[10].

17. Haec et his similia si, dum venero[11], non erunt persoluta, regia exactio[12] secundum leges in quem culpa cadit, districte absque venia comparabit. Valete[3].

[1] *iam* Ma.   [2] *p. et* om. Ma.   [3] Om. Ma.   [4] *omnium* Ma.
[5] *-na* Ma.   [6] *ipso anno* Ma.   [7] *Romam* Ma.   [8] *debetis* Ma.
[9] *degit* Ma, one MS of Fl.   [10] *-atur* Ma.   [11] *Haec et alia si, cum ven.* Ma.
[12] *-ione* Ox, Ma.

15. But I have sent this letter in advance, that all the people in my kingdom may rejoice in my success, because, as you yourselves know, I have never spared—nor will I in the future spare—to devote myself[1] and my labours to secure what is necessary for the well-being of all my people.

16. Now, therefore, I enjoin upon and beseech all you my bishops and the reeves of the kingdom, by the fealty which you owe to God and to me, to bring it to pass that, before I come to England, full payment has been made of all the debts which, according to old-established law[1], we owe to God, namely, plough-alms, and the tithe of animals born during the year, and the pence which we owe to St Peter at Rome, both from towns and villages, and, in the middle of August[2], the tithe of fruits, and at the feast of St Martin the first-fruits of the crops[3] (called in English "ciricsceatt") which each one owes to the church of the parish in which he lives.

17. If, when I come, these and other similar dues have not been paid, they shall be exacted by the royal officials[1] in accordance with the laws, sternly and without remission[2], from him who is found to be in fault.

I CANUTE

[Ðis is seo geredness, þe Cnut cyning, ealles Englalandes cyningc 7 Dena cyningc 7 Norþrigena cyningc, gerædde, 7 his witan, Gode to lofe 7 him sylfum to cynescipe 7 to þearfe, rade swa hwæðer swa man wille.][1]

[2]Ðis is seo gerædnys þe Cnut ciningc, ealles Englalandes ciningc 7 Dena cining[3], mid his witena geþeahte gerædde, Gode to lofe 7 him sylfum to cynescipe 7 [folce][4] to þearfe; 7 þæt wæs on ðære halgan midewintres tide on Winceastre.

1. Ðæt is þonne ærest[5], þæt hi ofer ealle oþre þingc ænne God æfre woldan lufian 7 wurþian[6] 7 ænne Cristendom anrædlice healdan and Cnut cingc lufian[7] mid rihtan[8] getrywþan.

2. And [uton][9] Godes cyrican griðian 7 friðian 7 gelomlice secean saulum to hæle 7[10] us sylfum to þearfe.

§ 1. Ælc cyrice is mid rihte on Cristes agenan griðe 7 ælc Cristen man ah mycele þearfe þæt he on þam griðe mycele mæðe wite, forðam Godes grið is ealra griða selost to geearnigenne 7 geornost to healdenne, 7 þær nehst cininges.

§ 2. Þonne is swiðe rihtlic, þæt Godes ciricgrið binnon wagum 7 Cristenes ciningces handgrið stande æfre[11] unwemme[12]; 7 se ðe aðor fulbrece þolige landes 7 lifes, butan [him][13] se ciningc gearian wille.

---

[1] A; *In nomine Domini. Ðis is seo gerædnes þe witan geræddon 7 be manegum godum bisnum asmeadon; and þæt wæs geworden sona swa Cnút cyngc mid his witena geþeahte friÐ 7 freondscipe betweox Denum 7 Englum fullice gefæstnode 7 heora ærran saca ealle getwæmde* D.
[2] G; no preamble in D.   [3] *ealles...cining* om. A.
[4] *folc* Ld, om. G, A.   [5] G, A; *þonne is þæt ærest þæt witan geræddan* D.
[6] 7 *w.* om. Ld; æ. *G.* æ. *wurðodon* D.   [7] 7 *wurþian* Ld.
[8] 7 *mid trywðan* 7 *Eadgares lagan geornlice folgian. And hig gecwædan þæt hi furðor on æmtan smeagan woldan þeode þearfe mid Godes filste swa hi betst mihton. Nu wille we swutelian hwæt us mæg to ræde for Gode* 7 *for worlde, gime se þe wille. Uton swiþe georne fram sinnan acirran* 7 *ure misdæda geornlice betan* 7 *ænne God rihtlice lufian* 7 *wurðian* 7 *ænne Cristendom anrædlice healdan* 7 *ælcne hæðendom georne forbugan* D.
[9] D; *witan* A; om. G.   [10] *s. to h.* 7 om. D, A.   [11] *efen* D, A.
[12] II Cn. 1–7 follows in D.   [13] A, Ld, om. G.

I CANUTE

[This is the ordinance[1] which King Canute, King of all England and of the Danes and the Norwegians, determined upon, together with his Councillors, to the praise of God and for the furtherance of his own royal authority and for his own benefit—let each man decide which course he will adopt[2].]

This is the ordinance which King Canute, King of all England and King of the Danes, determined upon with the advice of his Councillors, to the glory of God and for the furtherance of his own royal authority and for his [people's][1] benefit; and that was during the holy Christmas[2] season at Winchester[3].

1. The first provision is, that above all else they would ever love and honour one God, and unanimously uphold one Christian faith[1], and love King Canute[2] with due fidelity.

2[1]. And let us maintain the security and sanctity of the churches of God[2], and frequently attend[3] them for the salvation of our souls and our own benefit[4].

§ 1[1]. Every church is rightly in the protection of Christ himself, and it is the special duty of every Christian man to show great respect for that protection, for the protection of God is of all kinds of protection most especially to be sought after and most zealously to be upheld, and next to that the protection of the king.

§ 2[1]. Therefore it is very right and proper that the protection given by the church of God within its walls, and the protection granted by a Christian king in person should always remain inviolate; and he who violates[2] either of them shall lose both land and life[3], unless the king[4] is willing to pardon him.

§ 3. And gyf æfre ænig mann heonon forð Godes cyricgrið swa abrece þæt he binnon ciricwagum mannslaga weorþe, þonne sig¹ þæt botleas, 7 ehte his ælc þæra þe Godes freond sig, butan þæt geweorðe þæt he þanon ætberste 7 swa deope friðsocne gesece, þæt se cyningc him þurh ðæt feores geunne wiþ fulre bote ge wið God ge wið menn.

§ 4. And þæt is þonne ærest, þæt he his agenne wer Criste 7 þam cyningce gesylle 7 mid þam hine sylfne inlagie to bote.

§ 5. 7 gif hit þonne to bote gegá 7 se cyningc þæt geþafige, þonne bete man þæt cyricgrið into þære cyricean be ciningces fullan mundbryce, 7 þa my[n]sterclænsunge² begyte swa þærto gebyrige, 7 ægþer ge mægbote ge manbote fullice gebete, 7 wið God³ huru þingie georne.

3. And gyf elles be cwicum mannum⁴ ciricgrið abrocen sy, bete man georne be þam þe seo dæd sy, sy hit þurh feohtlac, si hit þurh reaflac, sig þurh þæt he hi[t]⁵ sy.

3a. Bete man ærest þone⁶ griðbryce into þære cyrican be þam þe seo dæd sy 7 be þam þe ðære cyricean mæð sy.

§ 1. Ne synd ealle cyricean na gelicre mæðe woruldlice wurðscipes⁷ wyrðe, þeah hig godcundlice habban hal-[g]unge⁸ gelice.

§ 2. Heafodmynstres⁹ griðbryce is æt botwyrþum þingum be cingces munde, þæt is mid v pundum on Engla lage, (7 on Centlande æt þam mundbryce v pund þam cingce

---
¹ *is* A, Ld.   ² *myst.* G; *þas mynstres clansunge* A, Ld.
³ *Gode* A, Ld.   ⁴ *b. c. m.* om. Ld.   ⁵ *hi* G.   ⁶ *þonne* A, Ld.
⁷ Om. A, Ld.   ⁸ A; *halsunge* G.   ⁹ *heafodcyricum* Ld.

§ 3[1]. And if ever anyone henceforth violates the protection of the church of God by committing homicide within its walls, that crime shall not be atoned for by any payment of compensation, and everyone who is the friend of God shall pursue the miscreant, unless it happen that he escapes from there and reaches so inviolable a sanctuary[2] that the king, because of that, grants him his life, upon condition that he makes full amends both towards God and towards men.

§ 4[1]. And the first condition is, that he shall give his own wergeld to Christ and to the king and by that means obtain the legal right to offer compensation.

§ 5. And if it comes to the payment of compensation, and the king allows this course, amends for the violation of the protection of the church shall be made by the payment to the church in question of the full fine for breach of the king's *mund*, and the purification of the church shall be carried out as is fitting, and compensation both to the kin and to the lord of the slain man shall be fully paid, and above all supplication shall earnestly be made to God.

3[1]. And if the protection of the church is broken in some other respect, without the taking of life, amends shall diligently be made in accordance with the nature of the offence, whether it be fighting or robbery or whatever it may be.

3a. In the first instance, amends for breach of its protection shall be made to the church, in accordance with the nature of the offence and also in proportion to the status of the church.

§ 1[1]. Not all churches are to be regarded as possessing the same status in civil law, though from the side of religion they all possess the same sanctity.

§ 2. Amends for violation of the protection of a principal church[1], in cases in which compensation can be paid, shall be made by payment of the fine for breach of the king's *mund*, *i.e.* £5 in districts under English law, (and in Kent[2] for breach of the *mund*, £5 to the king and

I CANUTE

7 þreo þam arcebiscope)[1], 7 medemran mynstres mid cxx scill', þæt is be cingces wite, 7 þonne gyt læssan þær lytel þeowdom sig 7 legerstow þeah sig, mid LX scill', and feldcyricean þær legerstow ne sig mid xxx scyll'.

4. Eallum Cristenum mannum gebyrað swiþe rihte, þæt hig haligdom 7 hadas 7 gehalgode Godes hus æfre swiþe georne griðian 7 friðian, 7 þæt hi hada gehwylcne weorðian be mæðe.

§ 1. Forþam, understande se ðe[2] cunne, mycel is 7 mære þæt sacerd ah to donne folce to þearfe, gif he his Drihtne gecwemeð mid rihte.

§ 2. Mycel is seo halsung 7 mære is seo halgung þe[3] deofla afyrsað 7 on fleame gebringeð, swa oft swa[4] man fullað oððe husel halgað; 7 halige[5] englas þær abutan[5] hwearfiað 7 þa dæda beweardiað 7 þurh Godes mihta þam sacerdon fylstað, swa oft swa hig Criste ðeniað mid rihte.

§ 3. 7 swa hi doð symle, swa oft swa hig geornlice inweardre heortan clypiað to Criste 7 for folces neode þingiað georne, 7 þi man sceal for Godes ege mæðe on hade gecnawan mid gesceade.

5. And gyf hit geweorðe þæt man mid tyhtlan 7 mid uncræftum sacerd belecge þe regollice libbe, 7 he hine sylfne wite þæs clænne, mæssige, gyf he durre, 7 ladige on þam husle he ana[6] hine sylfne æt anfealdre spæce.

5a. 7 æt þryfealdre spæce ladige he[5], gyf he durre, eac on þam husle mid twam his gehádan.

---

[1] 7 on...arcebiscope only in G. [2] wylle oðð A; wille oððe Ld.
[3] þe he d. afyrseð A, Ld. [4] he man A, Ld. [5] Om. A, Ld.
[6] sylf A; sylfe Ld instead of h. a.

£3[3] to the Archbishop), and in the case of a church of medium rank[4], by the payment of 120 shillings, *i.e.* by the fine due to the king (for insubordination), and in the case of one still smaller where there is little divine service but where, however, there is a graveyard, by the payment of 60 shillings, and in the case of a country chapel where there is no graveyard, by the payment of 30 shillings.

4[1]. It very justly befits all Christian men to maintain very zealously at all times the security and sanctity of holy things[2], and of the members of the clergy, and of the consecrated houses of God, and to honour each member of the clergy according to his rank.

§ 1[1]. Because—let him understand who can—great and wonderful are the things which a priest is able to do for the benefit of the people, if he is duly pleasing to his Lord.

§ 2. Great is the exorcising and wonderful is the hallowing[1] through which he drives away devils and puts them to flight, as often as he baptises anyone or hallows the Eucharist; and holy angels[2] hover round there and protect these acts, and, through the power of God, help the priests as often as they serve Christ as they ought.

§ 3. And that they always do as often as they earnestly call upon Christ from their inmost heart, and zealously make intercession for the needs of the people[1], and therefore the various ranks in holy orders must be recognised and distinguished for the fear of God.

5[1]. And if it happens that an accusation and a charge of evil practices[2] is brought against a priest who lives according to a rule, and he knows himself to be guiltless of the charge, he shall say Mass, if he dares, and by his own asseveration clear himself by the Holy Communion in the case of a simple accusation.

5*a*. And in the case of a triple accusation he shall also clear himself, if he dares, by the Holy Communion with two supporters of the same ecclesiastical rank as himself.

I CANUTE

§ 1. Gif man deacon tihtlige þe regollice libbe anfealdre spæce, nime twegen his gehadan 7 ladige hine mid þam.

§ 1a. 7 gyf man hine tihtlige þryfealdre spæce, nime VI his gehadan 7 ladige hine mid ðam 7 beo he sylf seofeþa.

§ 2. Gif man folciscne mæssepreost mid tihtlan belecge ðe regollif næbbe, ladige hine swa diacon þe regollife libbe.

§ 2a. And gyf man freondleasne weofodþen mid tihtlan belecge, þe aðfultum næbbe, ga to corsnǽde 7 þær þonne æt gefare þæt þæt God wylle, buton he on husle geladian mote.

§ 2b. And gyf man gehadodne mid fæhþe belecge 7 secge þæt he wære dædbana oððe rædbana, ladige mid his magum þe fæhðe moton mid beran oððe forebetan.

§ 2c. 7 gyf he sig[1] mægleas, ladige[2] mid geferan oððe on fæsten fó, gif he þæt þurfe, 7 ga to corsnæde 7 þæræt gefare swa swa God ræde.

§ 2d. And na þearf ænig mynstermunuc ahwær mid rihte fæhðbote biddan ne fæhþbote betan; he gæð of his mægðlage, þonne he gebyhð to regollage.

§ 3. And gyf mæssepreost æfre ahwær stande on leasre gewitnesse oððe on mænan aðe oððe ðeofa gewita oððe gewyrhta beo, þonne sy he aworpen of gehadodra gemanan 7 þolige ægþer ge geferscipes ge freondscipes ge æghwylces weorðscipes, butan he wið God 7 wið menn þe deoplicor gebete, swa bisceop him tæce, 7 him borh finde þæt he þanon forð æfre swylces geswice.

---

[1] *hi is* A, Ld. [2] *l. hine* A, Ld.

CAP. 5

§ 1. If a simple accusation is brought against a deacon who lives according to a rule, he shall take two supporters of the same ecclesiastical rank and clear himself with their help.

§ 1*a*. And if a triple accusation is brought against him, he shall take six supporters of the same ecclesiastical rank —himself being a seventh—and clear himself with their help.

§ 2. If an accusation is brought against a secular priest who does not live according to a rule, he shall clear himself in the same way as a deacon who lives according to a rule.

§ 2*a*. And if an accusation is brought against a member of the priesthood who has no friends and no-one to support his oath, he shall go to the ordeal of consecrated bread, and shall experience there what is the will of God, unless he is allowed to clear himself by the Holy Communion.

§ 2*b*. And if a man in holy orders is charged with vendetta and accused of having committed or instigated homicide, he shall clear himself with the help of his kin, who must share the vendetta with him or pay compensation for it.

§ 2*c*. And if he has no kindred, he shall clear himself with the help of his fellow-ecclesiastics, or have recourse to fasting, if he must, and go to the ordeal of consecrated bread, and experience there what God shall decree.

§ 2*d*. And no monk who belongs to a monastery anywhere may lawfully either demand or pay any compensation incurred by vendetta. He leaves the law of his kindred behind when he accepts monastic rule.

§ 3[1]. And if a priest anywhere be concerned in false witness or perjury, or be the accessory and accomplice of thieves, he shall be cast out from the fellowship of those in holy orders and shall forfeit both their society and their friendship and every kind of privilege, unless he make amends, both towards God and towards men, to the utmost of his ability, as the bishop shall prescribe for him, and find surety that henceforth he will cease for ever from all such [wrong-doing].

§ 4. 7 gyf he ladian¹ wille, geladige þonne be dæde mæðe, swa mid þryfealdre swa mid anfealdre² lade, be ðam þe seo dæd sy.

6. And³ we wyllað þæt ælces hades menn georne gebugan ælc to þam rihte þe him to gebyrige.

6a. 7 huruþinga Godes þeowas—bisceopas 7 abbodas, munecas 7 mynecena, canonicas 7 nunnan—to rihte gebugan 7 regollice libban 7 dæges 7 nihtes oft 7 gelome clypian to Criste 7 for eall Cristen folc þingian georne.

§ 1. 7 ealle Godes þeowas we biddað 7 lærað 7 huruþinga sacerdas, þæt hi Gode hyran 7 clænnesse lufian 7 beorgan heom sylfum wið Godes yrre 7 wið ðone weallendan brýne þe weallað on helle.

§ 2. Fullgeorne hig⁴ witan þæt hig nagon mid rihte þurh hæmedþingc wifes gemanan.

§ 2a. 7 se ðe þæs geswican wille 7 clænnesse healdan, hæbbe he Godes miltse 7 to woruldwurðscipe si he þegenlage wyrðe.

§ 3. And æghwylc Cristen mann eac for his Drihtenes ege unrihthæmed georne forbuge 7 godcunde lage rihtlice healde.

7. And we lærað 7 biddað 7 on Godes naman beodað, þæt ænig Cristen mann binnon VI manna sibfæce⁵ on his agenum cynne æfre ne gewifie⁶, ne on his mæges lafe þe swa neahsib wære, ne on þæs⁷ wifes nedmagon þe he sylf ær hæfde;

§ 1. ne on his gefæderan, ne on gehalgodre nunnan, ne on ælætan ænig Cristen mann æfre ne gewifige⁸;

§ 2. ne ænige forligru ahwar ne begange;

§ 3. ne na má wifa þonne án hæbbe⁹ 7 þæt beo his beweddode wif¹⁰, 7¹¹ beo be þære anre, þa hwile þe heo libbe¹², se ðe wyle Godes lage giman mid rihte 7 wið hellebryne beorhgan his sawle¹³.

[1] *h. hine l.* A, Ld. [2] *s. m. a.* om. A; *þrifeald lade swa be* Ld.
[3] *And witena gerædnes is þæt hi w.* D. [4] *we* D. [5] *sibba fæce* A, Ld.
[6] *wifige* D. [7] *his* A, Ld. [8] *n. wifige afre* A; *n. w. æfre* D, Ld.
[9] *ne...h.* om. A. [10] *7...wif* om. D, A. [11] *ac* D, A.
[12] The scribe of G has added by mistake: *þus scyldon æfre ge.*
[13] Here follows VI Atr. 16 in D.

§ 4. And if he seeks to clear himself, he shall do so in proportion to the deed, either by the triple mode of proof or by the simple, in accordance with the nature of the deed.

6[1]. And we desire that men of every estate[2] readily submit to the duty which befits them.

6a[1]. And most of all the servants of God—bishops and abbots, monks and nuns, canons and women under religious vows—shall submit to their duty and live according to their rule, and day and night frequently and often call upon Christ, and zealously intercede for all Christian people.

§ 1[1]. And we pray and enjoin all the servants of God, and priests above all, to obey God and practice celibacy and guard themselves[2] from the wrath of God and from the raging fire which blazes in hell[3].

§ 2[1]. They know full well that they have no right to marry.

§ 2a. And he who will turn from marriage and observe celibacy shall obtain the favour of God, and as worldly honour he shall enjoy the privileges of a thegn[1].

§ 3[1]. All Christian men likewise through the fear of God[2] shall strictly avoid illicit unions[3] and duly observe the laws of the church.

7[1]. And we instruct and pray and enjoin, in the name of God, that no Christian man shall ever marry among his own kin within six degrees of relationship, or with the widow of a man as nearly related to him as that, or with a near relative of his first wife's.

§ 1. And no Christian man shall ever marry his god-mother[1] or a professed nun or a divorced woman.

§ 2[1]. And he shall never commit adultery anywhere.

§ 3. And he shall have no more wives than one, and that shall be his wedded wife[1], and he who seeks to observe God's law aright and to save his soul from hell-fire shall remain with the one as long as she lives[2].

8. And gelæste mann Godes gerihta æghwylce geare rihtlice georne.
   § 1. Þæt is sulhælmesse xv niht ofer Eastran 7 geoguþe teoðunge be Pentecosten 7 eorðwæstma be Ealra halgena mæssan.
   § 2. 7 gyf hwa þonne þa teoþunge gelæstan nelle swa we gecweden habbað, þæt is se teoða æcer ealswa seo sulh hit gegá[1], þonne fare þæs cingces gerefa to 7 þæs bisceopes 7 þæs landrican 7 þæs mynstres mæssepreost 7 nim[an][2] unþances ðone[3] teoðan dæl to þam mynstre þe hit to gebyrige, 7 tæcan him to þam nigoðan dæle, 7 todæle mann þa eahta dælas on twa, 7 fo se landhlaford to healfum, to healfum se bisceop, si hit ciningces mann, se hit þegnes.
9. And Romfeoh be Petres mæssan.
   § 1. 7 se ðe ofer þæne dæg hit healde, agyfe þam bisceope þæne penig 7 þærto xxx[4] 7 þam cingce cxx[5] scyll'.
10. And cyricsceat to Martines mæssan.
    § 1. 7 se þe hine ofer þæne dæg healde agyfe hine þam bisceope 7 forgylde hine xi siðan 7 ðam cingce cxx[5] scyll'.
11. Gyf hwa þonne þegna[6] sig þe on his boclande cyrican hæbbe þe legerstow on sig, gesylle þone[7] þriddan dæl his agenre teoþunge into his cyrican.
    § 1. And[8] gyf hwa cyricean hæbbe þe legerstow on ne sig, do he of ðam nigon dælum his preoste þæt þæt he wylle.
    § 2. 7 gá ælc cyricsceat into þam ealdan mynstre be ælcon frigan heorðe.
12. And leohtgesceot þriwa on geare: ærest on Easteræfen healfpenigwurð wexes æt ælcere híde 7 eft on[9] Ealra halgena mæssan eallswa mycel [7 eft[10] to þæm (æfene)[11] sanctan Marian clænsunge ealswa].

---

[1] gegað A, Ld. [2] A, Ld; nime G. [3] þonne A, Ld.
[4] penega A; pening Ld. [5] twa hundred 7 twentig scill' A; 220 scill. Ld.
[6] þegen A, Ld. [7] þonne A. [8] Om. A, Ld. [9] to A, Ld.
[10] 7 eft...ealswa Ld and in the margin of G in handwriting of 16th cent.
[11] Following Liebermann.

8¹. And ecclesiastical dues shall be promptly and duly rendered every year.
: § 1. Namely, plough-alms 15 days after Easter, and the tithe of young animals at Pentecost, and [the tithe] of the fruits of the earth at All Saints.
: § 2¹. And if anyone refuses to render his tithes as we have decreed, namely, the produce of every tenth acre traversed by the plough, then the king's reeve and the bishop's and the reeve of the lord of the manor and the priest of the church shall go, and, without his consent, take the tenth part for the church to which it is due, and shall assign the next tenth to him, and the eight [remaining] parts shall be divided in two, and the lord of the manor shall take half and the bishop half, whether the man be under the lordship of the king or of a thegn.

9¹. And Peter's Pence [shall be rendered] by St Peter's Day².
: § 1¹. And he who withholds it beyond that date shall give the bishop the penny and 30 pence in addition, and 120 shillings² to the king.

10. And church dues [shall be rendered] at Martinmas.
: § 1¹. And he who withholds them beyond that date shall give them up to the bishop, and repeat the payment eleven times, and [pay] 120 shillings to the king.

11¹. If, however, there is any thegn who, on the land which he holds by title deed², has a church to which a graveyard is attached, he shall give the third part of his own tithes to his church.
: § 1. If anyone has a church to which no graveyard is attached, he shall give his priest whatever he desires from the nine [remaining] parts.
: § 2. And all the church dues from every free household shall go to the old parish church.

12¹. And light dues [shall be paid] three times a year: first a halfpennyworth of wax from every hide on Easter Eve, and as much afterwards at the feast of All Saints, [and as much afterwards at the Feast of the Purification of St Mary]².

13. And sawlsceat is rihtast þæt man symle gelæste á æt openum græfe.
   § 1. And gyf man ǽnig líc of rihtscriftscire elles hwær lecge, gelæste man þone sawlsceat swa þeah into þam mynstre þe hit to hyrde.
14. And ealle Godes gerihta fyrðrige[1] man georne, ealswa hit þearf is.
   § 1. And freolsa 7 fæstena healde mon rihtlice[2].
   § 2. 7 healde man[2] ælces Sunnandæges freolsunge fram Sæternesdæges none oð Monandæges lihtingce 7 ælcne oðerne mæssedæg[3] swa he beboden beo.
15. 7 Sunnandæges[4] cypinge we forbeodað eac eornostlice 7 ælc folcgemót, buton hit for mycelre nydðearfe sy.
   § 1. And huntaðfara 7 ealra woruldlica weorca on ðam halgan dæge geswican[5] man georne.
16. Be fæstene[6].
   Þæt man ælc beboden fæsten healde, sy hit ymbrenfæsten, sy hit lenctenfæsten, sy elles oðer fæsten, mid ealr[e][7] geor[n]fulnysse[8].
16a. And to Sancta Marian mæssan ælcere 7 to ælces apostoles mæssan fæstan[9], buton Philippi et Jacobi[10] we ne beodað nan fæsten for ðan eastorlicon freolse, 7 ælce[s][11] Frígdæges fæston[12], buton hit freols sy.
   § 1. 7 na ðearf man na fæsten[13] fram Eastron oð Pentecosten, buton hwa gescrifen sy oððe he elles fæsten[13] wylle, 7[14] of middanwintre oð octabas Epiphanie[15].
17. We forbeodað ordal 7 aðas freolsdagum 7 ymbrendagum 7 lenctendagum [7 rihtfæstendagum][16] 7 fram Aduentum Domini oð(ðe)[17] se eahteoða dæg agán sy ofer Twelftadæg[18] 7 fram Septuagessima oþ(þe)[17] fiftyne niht ofer Eastron.

---
[1] friðige A, Ld. [2] r.—man om. A, Ld.
[3] At this point (with the word mæssedæg) B begins and is used here for the remainder of I Cn.
[4] -daga G; -dæga A, Ld. [5] -swícæ G; -swice A, Ld.
[6] The rubrics in this code are found in B only. [7] G, A; -ra B.
[8] georf. B. [9] fæste man G; fæsten A, Ld.
[10] b. to P. et J. mæssan w. G. [11] G, A; ælce B. [12] -en G, A, Ld.
[13] fæstan G. [14] callswa G.
[15] Epiphanige, þæt is seofen niht ofer Twelftan mæssedæge G.
[16] G, A, Ld; om. B. [17] oððe B; oð G, A, Ld. [18] Twelftan mæssedæge G.

13[1]. And it is best that payment for the souls of the dead should always be rendered before the grave is closed.

§ 1. And if a body is buried elsewhere than in the parish to which it properly belongs, the payment shall nevertheless be made to the church to which the deceased belonged.

14. And all God's dues shall be promptly rendered[1], as the occasion requires.

§ 1[1]. And festivals and fasts shall be duly observed.

§ 2[1]. And the festival of every Sunday shall be observed from noon on Saturday till dawn on Monday, and every other feast-day as has been prescribed[2].

15[1]. And likewise we strictly forbid Sunday trade and all public gatherings, unless in cases of great necessity.

§ 1. And hunting and all secular occupations shall be strictly abstained from on the holy day.

16[1]. Concerning fasts.

And every prescribed fast shall be observed with all diligence, whether it be the fast of the Ember Days, or the Lent fast, or any other fast.

16a[1]. And at all the festivals of St Mary and at the festival of every apostle a fast [shall be observed]—except at the festival of St Philip and St James when we do not enjoin a fast because of the Easter festival—and a fast [shall be observed] every Friday, unless it be a festival.

§ 1. And no man need fast from Easter till Pentecost—unless it has been prescribed to him[1] as a penance or he desires to fast for some other reason—or from Christmas to the Octave of Epiphany[2].

17[1]. And we forbid ordeals and oaths during festivals and the Ember Days and days in Lent, and on legally appointed fast days, and from the Advent till the eighth day after Twelfth Night, and from the Septuagesima till fifteen days after Easter.

I CANUTE

§ 1. 7 sancte Eadwardes mæssedæg witan habbað gecoren þæt man freolsian sceal ofer eall Englaland[1] on quintadecima kalendas Aprilis 7 sancte Dunstanes mæssedæg on xiiii kl. Iunii[2].

§ 2. 7 beo ðam halgum tidum eallum Cristenum mannum, ealswa hit riht is, sib 7 sóm gemǽne 7 ælc sacu[3] totwæmed.

§ 3. 7 gyf hwá oðrum scyle borh oððe bote æt woruldlicum ðingum, gelæste hít him georne ǽr oððe æfter.

18. We wyllað[4] 7 we biddað for God[e]s[5] lufan, þæt ælc Cristen man understande georne his agene ðearfe.

18a. Forðam ealle we sceolan ænne timan gebidan, þæt[6] us wære leofra ðonne all[7] þæt on middanearde is, ðæ[t][8] we aworhton[9], ða hwile ðe we mihton, georne Godes willan.

18b. Ac we ðonne sceolon habban anfeald lean ðæs ðe we on life ær geworhton; wa ðam ðonne ðe ær geærnode hellewíte!

§ 1. Be scrifte.

Ac uton swiðe georne fram synnum gecyrran 7 ure ælc his misdǽda urum scriftum geornlice andettan 7 æfre geswican[10] 7 geornlice betan.

§ 2. 7 ure ælc oðrum beode þæt we wyllan þæt man us beode; þæt is[11] rihtlic dóm 7 Gode swiðe gecwéme; 7 se bið swiðe gesæli[12] ðe ðæne dóm gehealt.

§ 3. Forþan Gód ælmihtig us ealle geworhte 7 eft deopum ceape[13] gebohte, þæt is mid his agenum blode[14] ðe hé for us eallum ageat[15].

19. Gehwylc[16] Cristen man dó, swa him ðearf is: gyme his Cristendom[17] georne 7 gearwie hine eac to huselgange huru ðriwa on geare gehwá hine sylfne [s]e[18] ðe his agene ðearfe wille understandan, swa swa heom ðearf si.

---

[1] *Engl. þæt is on þam feowerteoðan dæge on Martige*, xviiii (changed later to xv) *kl. Ap.* G.
[2] *Iun. þæt ys on þam þreolteoðan dæge þe byð on Mæge* G.
[3] *facn* Ld.   [4] *w. w.* only in B.   [5] G, A; *Godas* B.
[6] *þonne* G, A, Ld.   [7] Added in 16th cent. in B.
[8] *ðær* B, G; *þ* A, Ld.   [9] *á worhtan (-ton)* G, Ld.   [10] *swican* A.
[11] *þis* A instead of *þ. is.*   [12] *(ge)sælig* G, A, Ld.   [13] *-þum* A.
[14] *life* G, A, Ld.   [15] *sealde* G, A, Ld.   [16] *ac g.* G; *ac æghwilc* A; 7 *ægh.* Ld.
[17] *-domes* G, Ld ; *-domes á.* A.   [18] *ðe* B; om. G, A, Ld.

§ 1[1]. And the authorities have decided that St Edward's festival shall be celebrated throughout England on the 18th of March, and St Dunstan's festival on the 19th of May.

§ 2[1]. And at the holy festivals, as is fitting, there shall be peace and concord among all Christian men, and every dispute shall be laid aside.

§ 3. And if anyone owes another a debt or compensation in connection with secular matters, he shall render it to him readily either before or after [the festival].

18. We desire and we pray, for the love of God, that every Christian man should readily understand what is for his own good.

18a[1]. For we shall all arrive at a time when we shall wish, above all else in the world, that we had zealously done the will of God, as long as we could.

18b[1]. But we shall then receive simply[2] the reward for what we have done in our lifetime. Woe then to him who has earned the torment of hell![3]

§ 1[1]. Concerning confession.

But let us very zealously turn from sins, and let us all readily confess our misdeeds to our confessors, and altogether cease [from evil], and zealously make amends.

§ 2[1]. And each of us shall treat others as we desire ourselves to be treated; that is a just maxim and very pleasing to God; and he who upholds that maxim shall be greatly blessed.

§ 3. For God Almighty made us all, and afterwards bought us at a great price[1], namely, with his own blood which he shed for us all.

19[1]. Every Christian man shall do as is his duty: he shall pay zealous regard to his Christian profession and shall likewise prepare himself for the sacrament at least three times a year, if he seeks to understand, as he ought, what is for his own good.

170 I CANUTE

§ 1. 7 word 7¹ weorc freonda gehwylc fadige mid rihte 7 að 7 wed wærlice healde.

§ 2. 7 æghwylc unriht aworpe man georne of ðisson earde, ðæs ðe man don mæge.

§ 3. 7 lufie man² Godes riht heonan forð georne wordes 7 dæde; ðonne wurð us eallum Godes miltse ðe gearwre.

20. Uton don eac georne² swá we gyt læran wyllað; uton beon á urum hlaforde holde 7 getréowe 7 æfre eallum mihtum his wurðscipe ræran 7 his willan gewyrcean.

§ 1. Forðam eall þæt we æfre for rihthlafordhylde doð, eall we doð hit us sylfum to mycelre ðéarfe, forðam ðam³ bið witodlice² God hold ðe biþ his hlaforde rihtlice² hold⁴.

§ 2. 7 eac ah laforda gehwylc ðæs formyccle ðearfe þæt he his men rihtlice healde.

21. 7 ealle Cristene men we lǽrað swiðe georne, þæt hí inweardre⁵ heortan æfre God lufian 7 rihtne Cristendóm geornlice healdan 7 godcundan lareowan geornlice hyran 7 Godes lara 7 laga smeagan 7 spyrian oft 7 gelóme, heom sylfum to ðearfe.

22. We lærað þæt ælc Cristen man geleornige þæt he cunne huru rihtne geleafan ariht⁶ understandan 7 Pater noster 7 Credan⁷ geleornian.

§ 1. Forðam mid ðam oðrum [sceal ælc Cristen mann hine to Gode gebiddan 7 mid þam oðrum]⁸ geswytelian rihtne gehleafan.

§ 2. Crist sylf sang Pater noster ærest 7 þæt gebed his leorni[n]gcnihtum⁹ teahte.

§ 3. 7 on þam godcunda[n]¹⁰ gebede syn¹¹ seofen gebedu mid ðam se ðe hit inweardlice gesingð he geærndað to Gode sylfum ymbe æfre ælce neode ðe man beðearf aðor oððe for ðissum life oððe for ðam toweardan.

---
¹ *ac* later changed to 7 B.   ² Om. A.
³ Om. G.   ⁴ *ðe—hold* om. Ld.   ⁵ *inweardlice* A; *-lic* Ld.
⁶ 7 *ariht* B, G.   ⁷ *Credo* A, Ld.
⁸ G, A; om. B and *we ssculan us gebiddan 7 mid þam credan* added in later handwriting in the margin.
⁹ *leornig.* B.   ¹⁰ G, A; *-am* B, Ld.   ¹¹ Changed later to *synd.*

§ 1[1]. And everyone of our friends[2] shall order his words and deeds aright, and strictly abide by his oath and pledge.

§ 2[1]. And every injustice shall be zealously cast out from this land, as far as it is possible to do so.

§ 3[1]. And God's law shall henceforth be zealously cherished in word and in deed; then the mercy of God will be granted the more readily to us all.

20[1]. Let us likewise zealously carry out what we further desire to enjoin: let us ever be faithful and true[2] to our lord, and always, with all our might, promote his honour and carry out his will.

§ 1. For all that we ever do, through just fidelity to our lord, we do to our own great advantage, for truly God shall be gracious to him who is justly faithful to his lord.

§ 2[1]. And likewise it is the great[2] duty of every lord to treat his men justly.

21[1]. And very zealously we enjoin upon all Christian men that ever, from their inmost hearts, they love God and zealously uphold the true Christian faith, and eagerly obey their spiritual teachers, and frequently and often ponder over and inquire into the precepts and laws of God for their own advantage.

22[1]. We enjoin that every Christian man apply himself[2] until he can at least understand aright the true belief, and learn the Pater Noster and the Creed.

§ 1. For with the first every Christian man shall pray to God, and with the second declare the true belief.

§ 2. Christ himself first recited the Pater Noster and taught the prayer to his disciples.

§ 3. And in that sacred prayer there are seven petitions[1], and he who recites it from the depths of his heart inwardly makes supplication thereby to God himself for everything of which a man has need, both for this life and for the life to come.

172   I CANUTE

§ 4. Ac hu mæg ðonne æfre ænig man hine inweardlice to Gode gebiddan, buton he on God hæbbe inwardlice rihtne geleafan?[1]

§ 5. Forðam he nah æfter forðsiðe mid Cristenra[2] gemána[n][3] on gehalgodan restan oððe her on lífe husles beon wyrðe[4].

§ 6. Ne[5] he ne bið wel Cristen ðe þæt geleornian nyle[6], ne he nah mid rihte oðres mannes to onfonne æt fulluhte ne æt bisceopes hánda ðe má, ær he hit geleornige þæt he hit wel cunne.

23. Godlar.

We lærað þæt man wið healice synne 7 wið deoflice dǽda scylde[7] swiðe georne on æghwylcne timan, 7 bete swiðe georne be his scriftes geðeahte se ðe ðurh deofles scyfe on synne befealle.

24. 7 we lærað þæt man wið fulne galscipe 7 wið unrihthǽmed 7 wið æghwylce ǽwbryce warnian georne[8].

25. 7 we lærað eac georne manna gehwylcne, þæt he Godes ege hæbbe symble on his gemynde, 7 dæges 7 nihtes forhtige for synnum, Domesdæg[9] ondrǽde 7 for helle agrise, 7 æfre him gehénde endedæges[10] wene.

26. Bisceopas syndon bydelas 7 Godes larðeowas[11] 7 hy scylan bodian 7 bisnian georne godcunde ðéarfe, gyme se ðe wylle.

§ 1. Forðam wace se hyrde bi[ð][12] funden to hyrde ðe nele ða heorde ðe he healdan scéal mid hréame bewerian, buton he elles[13] mǽge, gyf ðær hwylc ðeodsceaða sceaðian onginneð.

§ 2. Nis nan swa yfel sceaða swa is deofol sylf; he bið a ymbe þæt án, hu he mæge on mannum[14] sawlum mæst gesceaðian.

---

[1] b. he h. inweardlice soðe lufe 7 r. g. to Gode G.
[2] Cristene A; Crisne Ld; Cristenra manna G.   [3] G, A, Ld; -na B.
[4] gemanan ne on gehalgedan lictune to restene ne he nah þæs halgan husles to onfonne her on life G.
[5] þe A.   [6] nolde A, Ld.   [7] Corrected from earlier scyle B.
[8] warnige symle G; wærnige s. A, Ld.   [9] Domdæg G, A, Ld.
[10] endes dæges A, Ld.   [11] Godes lage lareowas (-æs) G, A; laga larewæs Ld.
[12] bid B.   [13] helles B.   [14] manna G.

§ 4¹. But how then can any man ever pray from the depths of his heart to God, unless he have true belief in God in the depths of his heart?

§ 5¹. Verily, after his death he cannot rest in a hallowed grave² among Christians or here in this life be entitled to receive the sacrament.

§ 6. He is not a true Christian who refuses to learn it, nor may he lawfully stand sponsor to another man at baptism, and as little at confirmation, until he learns it and knows it well.

23¹. Divine Precepts.
We enjoin that grievous sins and devilish deeds² be very zealously guarded against at all times. He who, through the instigation of the devil, falls into sin shall very zealously make amends according to his confessor's advice.

24¹. And we enjoin that foul lasciviousness and illicit unions² and every [kind of] adultery be zealously abhorred.

25¹. And likewise we earnestly enjoin all men to have the fear of God constantly in their hearts, and day and night to be in terror of sin, dreading the Day of Judgment and shuddering at the thought of hell, and ever expecting their last day to be close at hand.

26¹. The bishops are God's heralds and teachers², and they shall proclaim and zealously give example of our duty towards God—let him who will take heed.

§ 1¹. For a shepherd² will be considered failing in his trust, if he will not provide for the safety of the flock, which is committed to his keeping, by raising the alarm, if he cannot do anything else, when any spoiler proceeds to harm it.

§ 2. There is no spoiler so evil as is the devil himself; he is ever concerned with one thing only, namely, how he can do most harm to the souls of men.

§ 3. Ðonne moton ða hyrdas beon swiðe wácore 7 geornlice clypiende ðe wið ðone ðeodscaðan folce sceal[1] scyldan: ðæt synda[n][2] bisceopas 7 mæssepreostas ðe godcunde heorda bewarian 7 bewerian sceolan mid wislicum laran, þæt se wodfreca werewulf to swiðe ne slite ne to feola abíte of godcundre heorde.

§ 4. And se ðe ofærhogie þæt he Godes bodan hlyste, hæbbe him gemǽne þæt wið God sylfne.

Á sy Godes nama écelice gebletsod 7 lof him 7 wuldor 7 wurðmynt symble æfre to worulde! Amen[3].

II CANUTE

Ðis is ðonne[4] seo woruldcunde gerædnysse ðe ic wille, mid minan witenan ræde, þæt man healde ofer eall Englaland.

1. Þæt is ðonne æryst, þæt ic wylle[5] þæt man rihte lage up arǽre 7 æghwylce unlage georne afylle, þæt man awéodige 7 awyrtwalie æghwylc unriht, swa man geornost mæge, of [ð]issum[6] earde 7 arǽre up Godes riht.

§ 1. 7 héonon forð lǽte manna gehwylcne, ge earmne ge eadigne, folcrihtes weorðe[7] 7 him man rihte domas deme.

2. 7 we lærað þæt[8], þeah hwa agylte 7 hine sylfne deope forwyrce, ðonne gefadie[9] man ða[4] steore, swa hit for Gode sy gebeorhlic 7 for worulde aberendlic.

2a. 7 geðence swiðe georne se ðe domes geweald áge hwæs he sylf gyrnne[10], ðonne he ðus cweðe: "Et dimitte nobis debita nostra sicut et nos dimittimus[11]."

---

[1] *sceolon* G; *-an* A, Ld.   [2] *syndas* B.
[3] *Á—Amen.* Not in A; written in the margin in later handwriting in G, Ld.
[4] Om. G.   [5] *And witena gerædnes is þæt man* D.   [6] *di.* B.
[7] *f. wurðe beon* D with the rest of the clause omitted.
[8] *And witena gerædnes is þæt* D.   [9] *medemige* D.
[10] *hwæt he æt us sylf gyrne* D.
[11] G adds:—*þæt is on Englisc:* 7 *forgyf us Drihten ure gyltas swa we forgyfað þam ðe wið us agyltað*.

§ 3. Therefore the shepherds whose duty it is to guard the people against this spoiler, namely, the bishops and priests whose duty it is to protect and provide for the safety of the divine flocks with wise precepts, must be very active, and keep earnestly crying out, in order to prevent this ravening wolf[1] from inflicting excessive injury and from making very frequent depredations upon the divine flock.

§ 4[1]. And he who disdains to hearken to the messengers of God shall have to settle his case with God himself.
Ever be the name of God eternally blessed[2], and praise and glory and honour be to Him for ever and ever. Amen.

II CANUTE

This is further the secular ordinance[1] which, by the advice of my councillors[2], I desire should be observed over all England.

1[1]. The first provision is, that I desire that justice be promoted and every injustice zealously suppressed, that every illegality be rooted up and eradicated from this land with the utmost diligence, and the law of God[2] promoted.

§ 1[1]. And henceforth all men, both poor and rich, shall be regarded as entitled to the benefit of the law, and just decisions shall be pronounced on their behalf.

2[1]. And we enjoin that, even if anyone sins and commits grievous crime[2], the punishment shall be ordered as shall be justifiable in the sight of God and acceptable in the eyes of men.

2a[1]. And he who has authority to give judgment shall consider very earnestly what he himself desires when he says thus: "And forgive us our trespasses as we forgive [them that trespass against us]."

§ 1. ⁊ we forbeodað¹ þæt man Cristene men for ealles to lytlum huru to deaðe ne forrǽde, ac elles gerǽde man friðlice steora folce to ðearfe ⁊ ne forspille man² for ıytlum Godes handgeweorc ⁊ his agene ceap ðe he deore³ gebohte.

3. We beodað⁴ þæt man Cristene men ealles to swiðe of eardan ne sylle ne on hæðendóme huru ne bringe, ac beorgan man georne⁵, þæt man ða sawla ne forfáre ðe Crist mid his agenum life gebohte.

4. ⁊ we beodað⁶ þæt man eard georne clǽnsian aginne on æghwylcum énde ⁊ manfulra dǽda æghwár geswíce.

4a. Wiccean⁷.

Gyf wiccan oððe wigeleres⁸, morðwyrhtan oððe horcwéonan ahwar on lande wurðon agytene, fyse hi man georne ut of ðissan earde, oððe on earde forfare hi mid ealle, buton hi geswican ⁊ ðe deoppor gebétan.

§ 1. We beodað⁶ þæt wiðersacan ⁊ útlagan Godes ⁊ manna of earde gewítan, buton hig gebúgan ⁊ ðe geornor gebétan⁹.

§ 2. ⁊ ðeofas ⁊ ðeodsceaðan to tíman forwurðan, buton hi geswican.

5¹⁰. Be hæðenscipe.

We forbeodað eornostlice ælcne hæðenscipe.

§ 1¹⁰. Þæt¹¹ bið þæt man idol¹² weorðige, hæþne¹³ godas ⁊ sunnan oððe monan, fyr oððe flod, wǽterwyllas oððe stanas oððe æniges cynnes wudutréowa, oððe wiccecræft lufie, oððe morðweorc gefremme on ænige wisan, oððe on blote¹⁴ oððe on fyrhte, oððe swylcra gedwímera ænig ðing dreoge.

---

[1] *beodað* G, A; *And witena gerædnes is þ.* D.   [2] Om. G, A, D.
[3] *deope* A, Ld.   [4] *forbeodað* A, Ld; *And witena* &c. D.
[5] *huru—georne* om. A, Ld.   [6] *And witena* &c. D.
[7] The rubrics are found only in B.
[8] *wigel* with *eres* added later on an erasure in B; *wigleras* G, A, D, Ld.
[9] *betan* A, Ld.   [10] Om. D.
[11] Added later in B; *hæðenscipe* G; *hædenscype* A, Ld.
[12] *deofolgyld* G; *idola* A, Ld.   [13] *þæt is þæt man weorðige h.* G, A, Ld.
[14] *hlotæ* A; -*e* Ld; cf. *sorte* Q.

§ 1[1]. And we forbid the practice of condemning Christian people to death for very trivial offences. On the contrary, merciful punishments[2] shall be determined upon for the public good, and the handiwork of God and the purchase which he made at a great price[3] shall not be destroyed for trivial offences.

3[1]. We forbid the all too prevalent practice[2] of selling Christian people out of the country[3], and especially of conveying them into heathen lands, but care shall be zealously taken that the souls which Christ bought with his own life be not destroyed.

4[1]. And we enjoin that the purification of the land in every part shall be diligently undertaken, and that evil deeds shall everywhere be put an end to.

4a[1]. Wizards.

If wizards or sorcerers[2], those who secretly compass death[3], or prostitutes be met with anywhere in the land, they shall be zealously driven out of this land or utterly destroyed in the land, unless they cease from their wickedness and make amends to the utmost of their ability[4].

§ 1[1]. We enjoin that apostates and those who are cast out from the fellowship of God[2] and of men shall depart from the land, unless they submit and make amends to the utmost of their ability.

§ 2. And thieves and robbers[1] shall forthwith be made an end of, unless they desist.

5. Concerning heathen practices.
We earnestly forbid all heathen practices.

§ 1[1]. Namely, the worship of idols, heathen gods[2], and the sun or the moon, fire or water, springs or stones or any kind of forest trees, or indulgence in witchcraft, or the compassing of death in any way, either by sacrifice[3] or by divination[4] or by the practice of any such delusions.

6. Mannslagan 7 mánswaran, hádbrecan 7 ǽwbrecan gebugan 7 gebetan oððe of cyððan mid synnan gewitan.

7. Liceteras[1] 7 leogeras, ryperas 7 hreaferas Godes graman habban, buton hig geswican 7 ðe deoppor gebetan.

§ 1. 7 se ðe eard wylle rihtlice clænsian 7 unriht alecgan 7 rihtwisnysse lufian, ðonne mot he georne ðyllices steoran 7 ðyllic ascunian[2].

8. Feos bote. Uton eac ealle ymbe friðes bote 7 ymbe feos bóte smeagian swiðe georne: swa ymbe friðes bote swa ðam bondan sy selost 7 ðam ðeofan sy laðost, 7 swa ymbe feos bóte, þæt an mynet gange ofer ealle ðas ðéode butan ælcon fal[s]e[3]; 7 þæt nan man ne forsace.

§ 1. 7 se ðe ofer ðis fals wyrce ðolie ðara handa ðe he þæt fals mid worhte, 7 he hí mid nanum ðingum ne bycge, ne mid golde ne mid seolfre.

§ 2. 7 gyf man[4] ðone refan[5] téo, þæt he be his hléafe þæt fals worhte, ladie hine mid ðryfealdre lade, 7 gyf seo lád ðonne byrste, habbe ðone ilcan dóm ðe se ðe þæt fals worhte.

9. Geméta 7 gewihta rihte man georne 7 ælces unrihtes [heonan forð][6] geswíce.

10. 7 burhbota 7 brycgbota[7] 7 scipforðunga[8] aginne man georne 7 fyrdunga eac swá, á ðonne ðearf sy for mænelicre[9] neode.

11. 7 smeage man georne[10] on æghwylce wísan, hu man fyrmæst mǽge rǽd aredian ðeode to ðearfe 7 rihtne Cristendóm swiðast arǽran 7 æghwylce unlage georne[11] afyllen.

---

[1] *licceras* A, Ld.   [2] At this point the extract in D ends.
[3] *falfe* B.   [4] *g. m. þonne* G, A. Ld.   [5] *gerefan* G, A, Ld.
[6] G, A, Ld; om. B, and inserted in cap. 10.
[7] *br. heonan forð* B.   [8] Later altered to *-fyrð*. B.
[9] *gemæn.* G, Ld; *gemen.* A.   [10] *symle* G, A, Ld.
[11] *geornost* G, Ld; *-nnod* A.

6[1]. Murderers and perjurers[2], injurers of the clergy and adulterers[3] shall submit and make amends or depart with their sins from their native land.

7[1]. Hypocrites and liars, robbers and plunderers shall incur the wrath of God, unless they desist and make amends to the utmost.

§ 1. And he who desires to purify the land aright[1] and to suppress injustice and cherish righteousness must zealously prohibit and avoid such crimes.

8[1]. The reform of the coinage.

Let us all likewise very zealously take thought for the promotion of public security and the improvement of the coinage—for the promotion of public security in such a way as shall be best for householders and worst for thieves[2], and for the improvement of the coinage in such a way that there shall be one currency free from all adulteration throughout this land; and no-one shall refuse it.

§ 1. And he who henceforth coins false money shall forfeit the hand[1] with which he made the false money, and he shall not redeem it in any way, either with gold or with silver.

§ 2[1]. And if the reeve is accused of having granted his permission to the man who coined false money[2], he shall clear himself by the triple oath of exculpation[3], and if it fails, he shall have the same sentence as the man who has coined the false money.

9[1]. Measures and weights shall be diligently corrected, and an end put to all unjust practices.

10[1]. And henceforth the repair of fortifications and bridges, and the preparation of ships and the equipment of military forces likewise shall be diligently undertaken for the common need, whenever the occasion arises.

11[1]. And thought shall diligently be taken in every way how best to determine what is advisable for the public good, and how best to promote true Christianity and diligently suppress every injustice.

§ 1. Forðam þurh þæt hit sceal on earde godian to ahte, þæt man unriht alecge 7 rihtwisnysse lufie for Gode 7 for worulde. Amen[1].

12. Ðis syndon ða gerihta ðe se cyning ah ofer ealle men on Wessexan, þæt is mundbryce 7 hamsocne, forstal[2] 7 fyrdwite[3], buton hwǽne he[4] furðor gemæðian[5] wylle[6].

13. Utlaga.
Se ðe útlages weorc gewyrce wealde se cyng ðæs friðes.
§ 1. 7 gyf he bócland habbe, sy þæt forworht ðam cynge to hánde, sy ðæs mannes man ðe he sy.
§ 2. 7 lóchwá ðone fleman féde oððe feormie, gylde fíf pund ðam cýnge, butan he hine geladige þæt he hine flema nyste.

14. 7 on Myrcean he ah, ealswa her beforan gewriten is, ofer ealle men.

15. 7 on Dena lage hé ah fihtwite 7 fyrdwita, griðbryce 7 hamsocne, butan he hwǽne[7] furðor gemæðrian wylle.

15a. 7 gyf hwá ðonne[8] friðleasan man healde oððe feormie[9], bete swa hit[10] lagu wǽs.
§ 1. 7 se ðe unlage rǽre oððe undóm gedeme héonan forð, for lǽððe oððe for feohfange, beo se wið ðone cyng hundtwelftig scill'[11] scyldig on Engla láge, buton he míd aðe cyðan durre, þæt he hít na rihtor ne cuðe, 7 ðolie áá his þegenscipes, butan he híne æt ðam cýng gebycge[12], swa he him geðafian wylle.

---

[1] Om. A, Ld. [2] *forsteal 7 flymena fyrmðe* G.
[3] *fyrdigce* A, for which Liebermann, in view of Q's reading *fyrdunga*, suggests the emendation *fyrdinge*.
[4] *he hwæne ðe* G; *he hw.* A, Ld. [5] *gemæðrian* G, Ld; *mæðrian* A.
[6] G adds: 7 *he him ðæs weorðscipes geunne.* [7] *he hw. ðe* G.
[8] *þæne* G. [9] *o. flyman f.* G. [10] *b. þæt s. h. ær* G, A, Ld.
[11] *w. þonne cyningc his weores sc.* A, Ld. [12] *eft gebicge* G.

§ 1. For it is only by the suppression of injustice and the love of righteousness, in matters both religious and secular, that any improvement shall be obtained in the condition of the country. Amen.

12. These are the dues[1] to which the king is entitled from all men in Wessex, namely, [the payments for] violation of his *mund*[2], and for attacks on people's houses, for assault[3] and for neglecting military service[4], unless he desires to show especial honour to anyone [by granting him these dues][5].

13. Outlawry.
If anyone does the deed of an outlaw[1], the king[2] alone shall have power to grant him security.

§ 1[1]. And if he has land held by title-deed, it shall be forfeited into the hands of the king without regard to the question whose vassal he is.

§ 2[1]. And whoever feeds or harbours the fugitive shall pay £5[2] to the king, unless he clear himself by a declaration that he did not know[3] that he was a fugitive.

14. And in Mercia he is entitled to all the dues described above, from all men.

15[1]. And in the Danelaw he has the receipt of fines for fighting[2], neglect of military service, breach of the peace and attacks upon people's houses, unless he desires specially to honour anyone [by granting him these dues].

15a. And therefore if anyone maintains or harbours an outlawed man[1], he shall make amends in accordance with the established law[2].

§ 1[1]. And he who henceforth promotes injustice or pronounces unjust judgments[2], as the result of malice or bribery, shall forfeit 120 shillings[3] to the king, in districts under English law, unless he is prepared to declare on oath that he did not know how to give a more just verdict[4], and he shall lose for ever his rank as a thegn, unless he redeem it from the king, provided the latter is willing to allow him to do so.

II CANUTE

§ 1*a*. 7 on Dena laga lahslites scyldig, buton he híne¹ geladige, þæt he na bet ne cuðe.

§ 2. 7 se ðe rihte lage 7 riht dóm² forsace, beo se scyldig wið ðone ðe hit age, swa wið cyng hundtwelftig scill', swa wið eorl syxtig scill', swa wið hundred xxx³ scill', swa wið ælc ðára, gyf hit swa geweorðeð, on Engla lage.

§ 3. 7 se ðe on Dena lage rihte lage wyrde, gylde hé lahslíte.

16. 7 se ðe oðerne mid wó forsecgan wille, þæt he aðer oððe feo oððe freoma⁴ ðe wyrse si, gyf ðonne se oðer þæt geunsoðian mæge þæt hím man on secgan wolde, sy he his tungan scyldig, buton he him⁵ mid his wére forgylde.

17. Ne geséce nan man ðonne⁶ cyng, buton he ne mote beon nanes rihtes wurðe innan his hundrede.

§ 1. Sece man his hundred.

Séce man hundredes gemót be wíte, ealswa hit riht¹ is to secanne.

18. 7 habbe man ðreowa⁷ burhgemot 7 twá⁸ scirgemot be wíte, ealswa hit riht is⁹, buton hit oftor neod¹⁰ sy.

§ 1. 7 þær beo on ðære scire bisceop 7 se ealdorman 7 þær ægðer tæcan ge Godes riht ge woruldriht.

19. Be nááme.

7 ne nime nan man nane¹¹ náme ne inne scire ne ut of scire, ær man hæbbe [þriwa on hundrede his]¹² rihtes gebeden.

§ 1. Gyf he æt ðam ðriddan cyrre nan riht næbbe, ðonne fare he feorðan siðe¹³ to scirgemote 7 seo scir him sette ðone feorðan andagan.

§ 2. And gyf se¹⁴ ðonne byrste, nime ðonne leafe ge heonan ge ðeonan þæt he mote hæntan æfter [h]is¹⁵ agan¹⁶.

---

¹ Om. G.
² *rihtne dom* G, A, Ld; Liebermann suggests the reading *rihtdom* in B.
³ G, A, Ld; xx B.   ⁴ *freme* G; *feorme* A; *feorh* Ld.
⁵ *hine* G, A, Ld.   ⁶ *ðone* G, Ld.
⁷ *þriwa on geare* (*-a*) G, A, Ld.   ⁸ *tuwa* G.
⁹ *be w.—riht is.* Only in B and probably carried over from the preceding clause.
¹⁰ Om. G, A, Ld; added in B in 16th cent.   ¹¹ Om. A.
¹² G, A, Ld; om. B.   ¹³ *æt þam f. s.* A, Ld.
¹⁴ *anddaga* added in 16th cent. in B.   ¹⁵ *is* B.
¹⁶ *agenan* G, A, Ld.

CAP. 16–19   183

§ 1a. And in the Danelaw he shall forfeit *lahslit*[1], unless he clear himself, asserting that he did not know any better verdict.

§ 2[1]. And he who refuses [to observe] just laws and just judgments shall forfeit, in districts under English law, [a fine] to the party who is entitled thereto—either 120 shillings to the king, or 60 shillings to the earl, or 30 shillings to the hundred[2], or to all of them, if they are all concerned.

§ 3. And he who violates justice in the Danelaw shall pay *lahslit*.

16[1]. And if a man seeks to accuse another man falsely in such a way as to injure him in property or reputation[2], and if the latter can refute the accusation brought against him, the first shall forfeit his tongue, unless he redeem himself with his wergeld.

17[1]. And no-one shall appeal to the king, unless he fails to obtain justice within his hundred.

§ 1[1]. Everyone shall attend his hundred [court].

Everyone shall attend the hundred court, under pain of fine[2], whenever he is required by law to attend it.

18[1]. And the borough court shall be held three times and the shire court twice, in accordance with the law[2], under pain of fine, unless need arises for more frequent meetings.

§ 1[1]. And the bishop of the diocese and the ealdorman shall attend, and they shall direct the administration of both ecclesiastical and secular law.

19[1]. Concerning distraint of property.

And no-one shall make distraint[2] of property either within the shire[3] or outside it, until he has appealed for justice [three times in the hundred court].

§ 1. If on the third occasion he does not obtain justice, he shall go on the fourth occasion to the shire court, and the shire court shall appoint a day when he shall issue his summons for the fourth time.

§ 2. And if this summons fails, he shall get leave, either from the one court or the other[1], to take his own measures for the recovery of his property.

20. Þæt ælc mon beo on teoðunge.

We wyllað þæt ælc freoman beo on hundrede 7 on teoðunge gebroht, ðe lade wyrðe beon wylle oððe weres wyrðe, gyf hine hwa afylle[1], ofer[2] twelfwintre; oþþe he ne beo[3] æniges freorihtes[4] wyrðe, sy he heorðfæst, sy hé folgere—þæt ælc sy on hundre[d][5] 7 on borh[6] gebroht 7 gehealde se borh híne 7 gelæde to ælcon gerihte[7].

§ 1. Manig stréc man wyle, gyf he mæg 7 mot, werian his man, swa hwæðer swa him ðincð þæt he hine yð[8] awerian mǽge—swá for frigne swá for ðeowne—ac we nyllað geðafian þæt unriht.

21. Be ðeofan.
We[9] wyllað þæt ælc man ofer twelfwintre sylle þone[10] að, þæt he nyle ðeof beon ne ðeofes gewita.

22. 7 sy ælc getreowe man ðe tihtbysi nǽre 7 naðer ne burste ne að ne ordal innan hundrede[11] anfealde lade wyrðe.

§ 1. And ungetreowan men ceose man anfealdne að on þreom hundredan 7 þreofealdne að[12] swa wíde swa hit to ðære byrig hyre, oððe gá to ordale[13].

§ 1a. Ofga mán anfealde láde mid anfealde foraðe 7 ðrifealde lade[14] mid ðrifealdan foraðe.

§ 2. 7 gyf ðegen hæbbe getreowe man to foraðe for híne þæt swa sy; gyf he næbbe, ofga sylf his spæce.

§ 3. 7 ne beo[15] ænig forað forgyfen.

---

[1] *teon wylle* G; *fylle* A.   [2] *o. þæt he byð* G.   [3] *b. syððan* G.
[4] *freo* added in 16th cent. in B.   [5] *hundre* B.
[6] *borge* G, A; *borghe* Ld.   [7] *rihte* G, A, Ld.   [8] Om. A, Ld.
[9] *Ac we* G; 7 *we* A.   [10] *þonne* (ð-) A, Ld.   [11] *i. his h.* A, Ld.
[12] *on þr. h...að.* Added in margin of B in 16th cent.   [13] *þam o.* G, A, Ld.
[14] *mid anf....lade* om. A, Ld.   [15] *ne b. æfre* G, A, Ld.

20[1]. Every man shall be in a tithing.
It is our desire that every freeman, over twelve years of age, who desires to have the right of exculpation and of being atoned for by the payment of his wergeld, if he is slain[2], shall be brought within a hundred and a tithing[3]; otherwise he shall not be entitled to any of the rights of a freeman, whether he has an establishment of his own or is in the service of another—everyone shall be brought within a hundred and under surety, and his surety shall hold and bring him to the performance of every legal duty.
 § 1. Many self-assertive[1] men seek, if they can and may, to protect their men[2] in whichever way it seems to them that they can do so the more easily—namely, by representing them either as freemen or slaves—but we will not permit this injustice.

21. Concerning thieves.
It is our desire that everyone, over twelve years of age, shall take an oath that he will not be a thief or a thief's accomplice.

22. And every trustworthy man, who has never earned a bad reputation[1] and who has never failed[2] either in oath or in ordeal, shall be entitled to clear himself within the hundred[3] by the simple oath of exculpation[4].
 § 1. And for an untrustworthy man compurgators for the simple oath shall be selected[1] within three hundreds, and for the triple oath, throughout the district under the jurisdiction of the borough-court; otherwise he shall go to the ordeal.
 § 1a. In cases where a simple oath of exculpation is involved, the case shall be begun with a simple oath of accusation[1], but where a triple oath of exculpation is involved, it shall be begun with a triple oath of accusation[2].
 § 2. And if a thegn has a trustworthy man to give his oath of accusation for him, he may be allowed to make use of him; if he has not, he must begin his case in person.
 § 3. And there shall be no remission with regard to any oath of accusation[1].

23. Ne beo ænig man æniges teames wyrþe, buton he habbe treowe gewitnysse[1] hwanon him cóme þæt him mon æt befehð.

§ 1. 7 gecyðe seo gewitnysse[2] þæt on Godes helde 7 on his[3] hlafordes, þæt heo him on soðre gewitnysse si, swa heo hít eagum ofersæh 7 earum oferhyrdon, þæt he hit mid rihte begeate.

24. 7 nan man nan ðing ne bycge oter ɪeower peninga weorð, ne libbende ne licgende, buton mon habbe getreowe gewitnysse feower manna, sy hit binnan byrig, sy hit up[4] on lande.

§ 1. 7 gyf hit mon ðonne gefó[5] 7 he ðyllice gewitnysse næbbe, ne beo ðær nan team, ac gyfe man ðam agenfrigean his agen 7 þæt æftergyld 7 þæt wite ðam ðe hit áge.

§ 2. 7 gyf he witnysse[6] habbe, swa we ær cwædon[7], ðonne tyma hit man ðriwa; æt þam feorðam cyrre áhnige hit oððe agyfe ðam ðe hit age.

§ 3. And us ne ðincð na[8] riht þæt ænig man ahnian scule, ðær gewitnysse bið 7 man[9] gec[n]awan[10] cán, þæt þær brygde biþ; þæt nan man hit nah to geahnianne raðost ðinga ær syx monðum ðe[11] hit forstolen wæs.

25. 7 se ðe tyhtbysig sy 7 folce ungetreowe 7 ðas gemot forbuga ðríwa, ðonne sceawie[12] man of ðam feorðan gemote ða ðe him to ridan, 7 finde ðone[13] gyt borh, gyf he mæge.

25a. Gyf he ðonne ne mæge, gewylde man hine swa hwæðer swa man mæge, swa cwicne swa deadne, 7 nimen eall þæt he ah[14].

---

[1] *getrywe witnesse (wittenesse)* G, A, Ld.
[2] *hwanon him come* wrongly repeated in B after *gewit.*
[3] Om. G, A, Ld.
[4] In 16th cent. changed to *upp* in B.
[5] *befo* G, A, Ld.
[6] *gewitnesse* G; *-witnysse* A.
[7] *s. w. her beforan cw.* G; *swa hær b. cw. is* A, Ld.
[8] Changed in 16th cent. to *nan.*
[9] *7 man...biþ.* Added in the margin in 16th cent. in B.
[10] *gecra.* B.   [11] *æfter ðam þe* G, A, Ld.   [12] *scepige* A, Ld.
[13] *þonne* G, Ld.   [14] *ahte* G; *age* A, Ld.

23. And no man shall be entitled to vouch to warranty[1], unless he has trustworthy witnesses [to declare] whence he acquired the stock which is attached in his possession.

  § 1. And the witnesses, as they wish to obtain the favour of God and of their lord, shall declare that, in bearing testimony on his behalf to the effect that he acquired it legally, they are speaking the truth[1], in accordance with what they saw with their eyes and heard with their ears.

24. And no-one shall buy anything over four pence in value, either livestock or other property[1], unless he have four men as trustworthy witnesses, whether [the purchase be made] within a town or in the open country[2].

  § 1. If, however, any property is attached, and he [who is in possession of it] has no such witnesses, no vouching to warranty shall be allowed, but the property shall be given up to its rightful owner and also the supplementary payment[1], and the fine to the party who is entitled thereto.

  § 2. And if he has witnesses in accordance with what we have declared above, vouching to warranty shall take place three times. On the fourth occasion he shall prove his claim[1] to it or give it back to its rightful owner.

  § 3. But we regard it as unjust that anyone should claim ownership in a case where there is evidence by which it can be recognised that fraud is involved; so that no-one ought to claim ownership of it in less than six months at least from the time when it was stolen.

25[1]. And if anyone who is of bad reputation and unworthy of public confidence fails to attend the court-meetings three times, men shall be chosen from the fourth meeting who shall ride to him, and he may then still find a surety, if he can.

25a. If, however, he cannot [do so], they shall seize him as they can, either alive or dead, and they shall take all that he has.

188 II CANUTE

§ 1. 7 gylde man ðam teonde his ceapgyld 7 fó se hlaford elles to healfum 7 to healfum þæt hundred.

§ 2. 7 gyf aðor oððe mæg oððe fremde man[1] ða ráde forsace, gylde ðam cynge hundtwelfti[2] scill'.

26. Be ðeofan.

7 gesece se ebǽra ðeof þæt he sece[3], oððe se ðe on hlafordsearwe gemet sy, þæt hi næfre feorh ne gesecan.

§ 1. 7 se ðe ofer ðis stalie, sece þæt he sece, þæt he næfre þæt feorh ne[4] séce æt openre ðyfðe.

27. 7 se on gemote mid wiðertihtlan hine sylfne oððe his man[5] werie, hæbbe eall þæt forspecen 7 geandwyrde ðam oðrum, swa hundrede riht ðynce.

28. 7 þæt nan man nænne man underfó[6] na leng ðonne III niht, buton híne se befæste ðe[7] he ær folgade.

§ 1. 7 nan man his men fram him ne tǽce, ær hé clǽne sy æt[1] ælcere spǽce ðe he ær beclypad wæs.

29. 7 gyf hwá ðeof gemete 7 hine his ðances aweg lǽte buton réame, gebete be ðæs ðeofes wére oððe hine mid fullum aðe[8] geladige, þæt he him mid nan facn nyste.

§ 1. 7 gyf hwa ream gehyre 7 hine forsitte, gylde ðæs cynges oferhyrnysse oððe hine be fullan geladige.

30. Swyðe ungetreowe.

7 gyf hwylc man sy swa ungetreowe ðam hundrede 7 swa tihtbysig 7 hine[9] ðreo men ætgædere téon, ðonne ne beo ðær nan oðer, buton ðæt hé ga to ðam ðrifealdan ordale.

[1] Om. G, A.
[2] cxx G, Ld; hundtwentig A.
[3] þæt þæt he gesece G, A, Ld.
[4] From gesecan to ne om. A.
[5] Changed in 16th cent. to mann B.
[6] ne u. G, A, Ld.
[7] buton he (se) h. b. se ðe A, Ld.
[8] Beside this in the margin Ld has al. lade.
[9] h. þonne G, A, Ld.

§ 1. And they shall pay to the accuser the value of his goods, and the lord shall take half of what remains and the hundred half.

§ 2. And if anyone, either kinsman or stranger, refuses to ride [against him], he shall pay the king 120 shillings.

26. Concerning thieves.

And the proved thief and he who has been discovered in treason against his lord, whatever sanctuary he seeks, shall never be able to save his life.

§ 1. And he who steals after this—if the case is one of open theft—shall never save his life, whatever sanctuary he seeks.

27. And he who in Court tries to protect either himself or one of his men by bringing a countercharge[1] shall have wasted his words, and shall meet the charge brought by his opponent in such a way as the hundred court shall determine.

28. And no-one shall entertain any man for more than three days, unless he is committed to his charge by the man whom he has been serving[1].

§ 1[1]. And no-one shall dismiss one of his men from his service until he is quit of every accusation which has been brought against him.

29[1]. And if anyone comes upon a thief and of his own accord lets him escape without raising the hue and cry, he shall make compensation by the payment of the thief's wergeld, or clear himself with the full oath[2], [asserting] that he did not know him to be guilty of any crime.

§ 1. And if anyone hears the hue and cry and neglects it, he shall pay the fine for insubordination to the king, or clear himself by the full oath.

30. Thoroughly untrustworthy men.

If anyone has forfeited the confidence of the hundred[1], and has charges brought against him to such an extent that[2] he is accused by three men at once, no other course shall be open to him but to go to the triple ordeal.

§ 1. Gyf se hlaford ðonne secge þæt him naðor ne burste ne að ne ordal syþðan þæt gemot wæs on Winceastre, níme se hlaford him twegen getrywe men to innan ðam hundrede, and swerian þæt him næfre að ne burste ne ordal ne ðeófgyld ne gulde—buton hé ðone[1] gerefan hæbbe þe þæs wurþe si[2] ðe þæt don mæge.

§ 2. Gyf se að ðonne forðcume, ceose se man ðe ðær betyhtlod sy swa hwæðer swa[3] he wylle, swa anfeald ordal swa pundes wurðne að innan ðrim hundrede, ofer xxx peninga.

§ 3. Be ordale.
7 gyf hi ðonne[4] að syllan ne durran, gange he to ðam ðrifealdan ordale.

§ 3a. 7 ofgá man þæt ðryfealde ordal ðus, nime fife 7 beo him[5] sylf syxta.

§ 3b. 7 gyf he ðonne ful wurðe, æt ðam forman cyrre bete ðam teonde twygylde 7 ðam hlaford his wér ðe his wites[6] wyrðe sy 7 sette getreowe borgas, þæt he ælces yfeles geswice[7].

§ 4. And æt ðam oðran cyrre ne sy ðær nan oþer bot, gyf[8] he ful wurðe, buton ðæt man ceorfe him ða handa oððe ða fét óf oððe ægðer, be ðam ðe seo dæd sy.

§ 5. 7 gyf h[e][9] ðonne gyt mare weorc geweorht hæbbe, ðonne do man ut his eagan 7 ceorfan of his nose 7 eáran 7 ða uferan lippan oððe hine hǽttian, swylc ðisra[10] swa man wyle, oððe[11] ðonne geræde ða ðe ðærto rædan sceolon; swa man sceal[12] steoran 7 eac ðære saule beorgan.

§ 6. Gyf he ðonne ut leape 7 þæt ordal forbuge, gylde se borh ðam teonde his ceapgyld 7 ðam cynge his wer oððe ðam ðe his weres[13] wyrðe sy.

---

[1] þonne A.   [2] þe þ. w. si. Added in the margin in 16th cent. in B.
[3] swæðer he G, Ld; swa weðer he A.   [4] þone G, Ld.
[5] he G; om. A, Ld.   [6] þe þæs wyrðe A.   [7] eft g. G, A, Ld.
[8] gif G, A, Ld; buton gyf B.   [9] hit B, Ld.
[10] swa hwylc þyssa (þissa) G, A; -ce ðissa Ld.   [11] w. o. om. G, A.
[12] sceal written above in 16th cent. in B; mæg G, A, Ld.
[13] wites G, A, Ld.

§ 1. If, however, his lord asserts that he has failed neither in oath nor in ordeal since the assembly was held at Winchester[1], he (the lord) shall choose two trustworthy men within the hundred—unless he have a reeve who is qualified to discharge this duty—and they shall swear that he has never failed in oath or in ordeal or been convicted of stealing.

§ 2[1]. If the oath is forthcoming, the man who is accused there shall choose whichever he will—either the simple ordeal or an oath equivalent to a pound in value, [supported by compurgators found] within the three hundreds, [in the case of an object] over 30 pence in value.

§ 3. Concerning the ordeal.
If they dare not give the oath, he (the accused) shall go to the triple ordeal.

§ 3a. And a case which involves the triple ordeal shall be opened as follows: five [compurgators] shall be selected by the accuser and he himself shall make a sixth.

§ 3b[1]. And if then he (the accused) is proved guilty, on the first occasion he shall pay double value to the accuser and his wergeld to the lord who is entitled to receive his fine, and he shall appoint trustworthy sureties, that henceforth he will desist from all wrong-doing.

§ 4[1]. And on the second occasion, if he is proved guilty, there shall be no compensation possible to him but to have his hands or his feet cut off or both, according to the nature of the offence.

§ 5. And if he has wrought still greater crime, he shall have his eyes put out and his nose and ears and upper lip cut off or his scalp removed[1], whichever of these penalties is desired or determined upon by those with whom rests the decision of the case; and thus punishment shall be inflicted, while, at the same time, the soul is preserved from injury.

§ 6[1]. If, however, he escapes and avoids the ordeal, his surety shall pay the value of his goods to the plaintiff and the wergeld of the accused to the king or to the man who is entitled to receive his wergeld.

§ 7. And gyf mon ðone[1] laford teo, þæt he be his ræde ut léope 7 ær unriht worhte, nime him fif getreowe men[2] tó 7 beo him sylf sixta 7 ladige hine ðæs.

§ 8. Gyf seo lád [forðcume, beo he þæs weres wyrðe.

§ 9. 7 gif heo][3] forð ne cume, fo se cyng to þam wére 7 beo seo þeof utlah wið eal folc.

31. Be hiredmonnum.
7 hæbbe ælc laford his hiredmen on his agenum borhge[4].

31a. 7 gyf hine man æniges ðinges téo, andswarie innan ðam hundrede ðær he on beclypod béo, swa hit lagu[5] séo.

§ 1. 7 gyf he betyhtlod weorðe 7 he ut ætleape[6], gylde se hlaford ðæs mannes wér ðam cynge.

§ 1a. 7 gyf hi[7] ðone laford teon[8], þæt he be his ræde ut leope, ladige hine mid fif ðegnum 7 beo him sylf syxta.

§ 2. [Gyf him seo lad berste, gylde þam cingce his were][3] 7 beo se man utlah wið ðone cyng[9].

32. 7 gyf þeo[w]man[10] æt ðam ordale ful wurðe, mearcie [man][3] hine ðonne[2] æt ðam forman cyrre.

§ 1. 7 æt ðam oðran cyrran ne sy ðær nan bot[11] buton þæt heafod.

33. Be ungetreowum mannum.
Gyf hwylc man sy ðe eallum folce ungetrywe sy, fare ðæs cynges geréfa to 7 gebringe hine under borge, þæt hine man to rihte læde ðam ðe him on specan.

§ 1. Gyf he ðonne borh næbbe, slea hine man 7 on fulan lecge.

§ 1a. 7 gyf hine hwá forstande[12], beo hig begen anes rihtes wyrðe.

§ 2. 7 se ðe ðis forsitte 7 hit geforðian nylle, swa ure[13] cwide is, sylle ðam cynge hundtwelftig scill'.

---

[1] þonne A, Ld. [2] Om. G, A, Ld. [3] G, A, Ld; om. B.
[4] Written above in 12th cent. in B. [5] rihtlagu (-a) G, A, Ld.
[6] oðhleape G, Ld; hleape A.
[7] man G, A, Ld; hi written on an erasure in B.
[8] n added later to earlier teo in B. [9] w. ð. c. Not in G, A, Ld.
[10] G, Ld; ðeofman B, A. [11] n. oðer b. G.
[12] forene f. G; fora f. A, Ld. [13] u. ealra (eallre) G, A, Ld.

§ 7. And if the lord is accused of advising the man who had done wrong to escape, he shall choose five trustworthy men, and shall himself make a sixth, and shall clear himself of the accusation.

§ 8. If he succeeds in clearing himself, he shall be entitled to the wergeld.

§ 9. And if he fails, the king shall take the wergeld, and the thief shall be treated as an outlaw by the whole nation.

31. Concerning the men belonging to a household.
And every lord shall be personally responsible as surety for the men of his own household.

31a. And if any accusation is brought against one of them, he shall answer [it], in accordance with the law, within the hundred in which he is accused.

§ 1[1]. And if he is accused and escapes, the lord shall pay his (the man's) wergeld to the king.

§ 1a. And if the lord is accused of advising him to escape, he shall clear himself with [the help of] five thegns, himself making a sixth.

§ 2. [And if he fails to clear himself, he shall pay his (own) wergeld to the king], and the man shall be an outlaw towards the king[1].

32. And if a slave[1] is found guilty at the ordeal, he shall be branded on the first occasion.

§ 1. And on the second occasion he shall not be able to make any amends except by his head.

33[1]. Concerning untrustworthy men.
If there is anyone who is regarded with suspicion by the general public, the king's reeve shall go and place him under surety so that he may be brought to do justice to those who have made charges against him.

§ 1. If he has no surety, he shall be slain and buried in unconsecrated ground.

§1a. And if anyone interposes in his defence, they shall both incur the same punishment.

§ 2. And he who ignores this and will not further what we have all determined upon shall pay 120 shillings to the king.

34. 7 stande betwyx burgum an laga æt ladunge.

35. Be freondleasan.

Gyf freondleas man oððe feorran cuman swa geswencad wurðe ðurh freondlæste þæt he borh næbbe, æt frumtyhtlan ðonne gebugé he hengene 7 ðær gebide, oð þæt he ga to Godes ordale 7 gefáre ðær þæt he mæge.

§ 1. Witodlice, se ðe freondleasan 7 feorran cumenan wyrsan dóm demeð ðonne his geferan, he derað him sylfum.

36. Be mænan aðe.

Gyf hwa mæne að on haligdome swerie 7 he oferstǽled weorðe, ðolie ðara hánda oððe healfes weres, 7 ðæt sy gemæne hlaforde 7 bisceope.

§ 1. 7 ne beo ðanon forþ aðes wyrðe, buton he for God ðe deoppor gebete 7 him borh finde, þæt he æfre eft swylces geswice.

37. Be leasre gewitnesse.

And gyf hwa on leasre gewitnysse openlice stande 7 he oferstæled wurðe, ne stande his gewitnysse syððan for naht[1], ac gylde ðam cynge oððe landrican[2] be halsfange.

38. Nis on ænigne[3] timan unriht alyfad, 7 ðeah man sceal freolstídan[4] 7 on freolsstowan geornlicost bebyrgan[5].

§ 1. 7 a swa man bið mihtigra oððe maran hades, swa sceal hé deoppor for Gode 7 for worulde unriht gebetan.

§ 2. 7 godcunde bote sece man georne[6] 7 symble[7] be boctale[8], 7 woruldbote[9] sece man be woruldlage.

[1] *aht* G.   [2] *l. þe his socne ahe* G.   [3] *nanre* Ld.
[4] *freolst. 7 fæstentidan* G.   [5] *beorgan* G, A, Ld.
[6] *symle g.* G, A, Ld.   [7] *7 s.* om. G, A, Ld.
[8] *boctæcinge* G.   [9] *woruldcunde bote* G; *for w. b.* A, Ld.

34. And the various boroughs shall have one common law with regard to exculpation.

35. Concerning the friendless.

If a friendless man or one come from afar is so utterly destitute of friends as not to be able to produce a surety, on the first occasion that he is accused he shall go to prison, and wait there until he goes to God's ordeal where he shall experience whatever he can.

§ 1. Verily, he who pronounces a more severe judgment upon one who is friendless or come from afar than upon one of his own acquaintances injures himself.

36[1]. Concerning perjury.

If anyone swears a false oath on the relics and is convicted, he shall lose his hand[2] or half his wergeld which shall be divided between the lord and the bishop.

§ 1. And henceforth[1] he shall not be entitled to swear an oath, unless he makes amends to the best of his ability before God, and finds surety that ever afterwards he will desist from such [perjury].

37[1]. Concerning false witness.

And if anyone has given testimony which is manifestly false, and is convicted thereof, his testimony henceforth shall be valueless, and he shall pay to the king or to the lord of the manor a sum equivalent to his *healsfang*[2].

38[1]. Lawlessness is not permitted at any time, yet at sacred seasons and in sacred places special care must be taken to prevent it.

§ 1[1]. And in all cases, the greater a man is and the higher his rank, the more stringent shall be the amends which he shall be required to make to God and to men for lawless behaviour.

§ 2[1]. And ecclesiastical amends shall always be diligently exacted in accordance with the directions contained in the canon law, and secular amends in accordance with secular law.

39. Gif hwa preost ofslea.
Gyf hwa weofoððegen afylle, sy he utlaga wið God 7 wið men, buton he ðurh wrecsið ðe deoppor gebete 7 eac wið ða mægða, oððe ladige[1] mid werlade.

§ 1. 7 binnon xxx nihta aginne þa[2] bote ægðer ge wið God ge wið men be eallum ðam ðe he age.

40. Gyf man gehadodne man[2] oððe ælðeodigne man[2] ðurh ænig ðingc forræde æt feo oððe æt feore, ðonne sceal him se[2] kingc beon for mæg 7 for mundboran, buton he elles oðerne[3] hæbbe.

§ 1. 7 beton[4] ðam kyninge swa hit gebyrige, oððe he ða dæde wrece swyðe deope.

§ 2. Cristenum kyninge gebyrað swyðe rihte þæt he Godes æbylðe wrece swyðe deope, be ðam ðe seo dǽd sy.

41. Be gehadedum mannum.
Gyf weofodðegen manslaga wyrðe oððon[5] elles to swiðe mánweorc gewyrce, ðonne ðolie he ægðer ge hades ge éðles, 7 wrécnige swa wíde swa se[2] papa him scrife 7 dædbete georne.

§ 1. 7 gyf he ladian wylle, ladie hine[6] mid ðryfealdan.

§ 2. 7 buton he binnon xxx nihta bote agynne wið God 7 wið men, ðonne sy he utlaga.

42. Ðæt man gehadodne man [ne][7] bende ne beate.
Gyf hwa gehadodne man bende oððan[5] beate oððon[5] swyðe bismærige[8], bete wið hine swa[9] hit riht sy, 7 ðam[2] bisceope weofodbote be ðæs[2] hades mæðe, 7 ðam[2] laforde oððe þam[2] kynincge be fullan mundbryce, oððe geladige hine sylfne[10] mid fulre lade.

---
[1] *geladige hine* G, A, Ld. [2] Om. G, A. [3] *o. hlaford* G.
[4] *bete man* G, A, Ld. [5] Altered in 16th cent. to *oððe*.
[6] *.N. ladige* A; *hine* in B added later on an erasure; om. G.
[7] Om. in B. [8] *gebysmrige* G, A, Ld. [9] *swa swa* G, A, Ld.
[10] *h. s.* written in the margin in 16th cent. in B; *sylfne* om. G, A.

39. If anyone slay a priest.

If anyone slays a minister of the altar, he shall be both excommunicated and outlawed, unless he make amends to the best of his ability by pilgrimage[1], and likewise by [the payment of compensation] to the kin [of the slain man], or else he shall clear himself by an oath equal in value to his wergeld.

§ 1. And he shall begin to make amends both to God and men within 30 days[1], under pain of forfeiting all that he possesses.

40[1]. If an attempt is made to deprive in any wise a man in orders or a stranger of either his goods or his life, the king shall act as his kinsman and protector, unless he has some other.

§ 1[1]. And such compensation as is fitting shall be paid to the king, or he shall avenge the deed to the uttermost.

§ 2[1]. It is the duty most incumbent upon a Christian king that he should avenge to the uttermost offences against God, in accordance with the nature of the deed.

41[1]. Concerning men in holy orders.

If a minister of the altar[2] commits homicide or perpetrates any other great crime, he shall be deprived of his ecclesiastical office and banished, and shall travel as a pilgrim as far as the Pope appoints for him, and zealously make amends.

§ 1. And if he seeks to clear himself, he shall do so by the triple mode of proof.

§ 2. And unless he begins to make amends both to God and men within 30 days, he shall be outlawed.

42[1]. A man in holy orders shall not be bound or beaten.

If anyone binds or beats or deeply insults a man in holy orders, he shall make amends towards him in accordance with the law, and shall pay the fine due to the bishop for sacrilege[2], in accordance with the rank [of the injured man], and to his lord or to the king the full fine for breach of his *mund*, or he shall clear himself by the full process of exculpation.

43. Gyf gehadod man hine forwyrce mid deaðscylde, gewylde man hine 7 healde to ðæs¹ bisceopes dome, be ðam ðe seo dæd sy.

44. Gyf deaðscyldig man scriftspréce gyrne, ne wyrne him nan¹ man næfre².

§ 1. 7 gyf him man³ wyrne, gebete þæt wið ðone⁴ kyningc mid hundtwentig scyllinga oððe geladige hine—nime v men⁵ 7 beo him⁶ sylf vɪ-ta.

45. Gyf man wealdan mæge, ne dyde man næfre⁷ on Sunnandæges freolse ǽnigne forworhtne man, buton he fleo oððe feohte, ac wylde man hine⁸ 7 healde þæt se freolsdæg agan sy.

§ 1. Be haligdæiges freolse.
Gyf frigman freolsdæge wyrce, ðonne gebete he¹ þæt mid his healsfange, 7 huru wið God bete hit georne, swa swa him man tæce.

§ 2. Ðeowman, gyf he⁹ wyrce, ðolie his hyde oððon hydgyldes, be ðam ðe seo dæd sy.

§ 3. Gyf laford his ðeowan freolsdæge nyde to weorce, ðolie ðæs ðeowan 7 beo he syððan folcfrig; 7 gylde lahslit se laford mid Denum, wite mid Englum, bi ðam þe seo dæd sy; oððe geladie hine.

46. Be festene.
Gyf friman riht¹⁰ fæsten abrece, gylde lahslit mid Denum, wite mid Englum, be ðam ðe¹⁰ seo deed sy.

§ 1. Yfel bið hit¹ þæt man fæstentide¹¹ ær mæle éte, 7 gyt hit¹ bið¹ wyrse þæt man mid flæscmete hine sylfne¹⁰ gefyle.

§ 2. Gyf hit ðeowman gedó, ðolie his hyde oððe hydgyldes¹², be ðam ðe seo dæd sy.

---

¹ Om. G, A, Ld.   ² æfre G, A, Ld.   ³ hwa G, A, Ld.
⁴ Om. A, Ld.   ⁵ Om. G, A.   ⁶ Om. G, A; he Ld.
⁷ æfre G, A.   ⁸ m. h. om. G, A.   ⁹ Om. G.
¹⁰ Written above in 16th cent. in B.   ¹¹ rihtf. G.
¹² o. h. om. A, Ld.

43¹. If a man in holy orders places his life in jeopardy by committing a capital crime, he shall be arrested, and his case shall be reserved for the bishop's decision, according to the nature of the deed.

44¹. If a condemned man desires confession, it shall never be refused him.

§ 1. And if anyone refuses it to him, he shall make amends for it to the king by the payment of 120 shillings, or he shall clear himself. He shall select five men and be himself a sixth.

45¹. If it can be so contrived, no condemned man shall ever be put to death during the Sunday festival, unless he flees or fights, but he shall be arrested and kept in custody until the festival is over.

§ 1¹. Concerning the Sunday festival.

If a freeman works during a church festival, he shall make amends for doing so by the payment of his *healsfang*, and especially he shall zealously make amends to God, according to the directions given him.

§ 2¹. If a slave works, he shall undergo the lash or pay the fine in lieu thereof, according to the nature of the offence.

§ 3¹. If a lord compels his slave to work during a church festival, he shall lose the slave, who shall henceforth obtain the rights of a freeman, and the lord shall pay *lahslit* in a Danish district and a fine in an English one, according to the nature of the offence, or else he shall clear himself.

46¹. Concerning fasts.

If a freeman breaks a legally ordained fast, he shall pay *lahslit* in a Danish district, a fine in an English one, according to the nature of the offence.

§ 1. It is wrong for anyone during a fast to eat before the appointed time, and it is still worse for anyone to defile himself with flesh.

§ 2¹. If a slave does so, he shall undergo the lash or pay the fine in lieu thereof, in accordance with the nature of the deed.

47. Gyf hwa opendlice lencgtenbryce gewyrce ðurh feohtlac oððe ðurh wiflac oððe ðurh reaflac oððe ðurh ænige healice misdæde, sy þæt twibote[1], swa eac[2] on heahfreolse, be ðam ðe seo dæd sy.

§ 1. And gyf man ætsace, ladige hine[3] mid ðryfealdre lade.

48. Gif hwa forwyrne godcunde gerihte.

Gyf hwa godcundra rihta[4] mid wige forwyrne, gylde lahslit mid Denum 7[5] fulwite mid Englum, oððe geladige hine— nime XI men[5] 7 beo him[5] seolf twelfta.

§ 1. Gyf he man wundige, gebete þæt 7 gylde fulwite ðam hlaforde 7 æt ðam[5] bisceope þa handa alyse oððon híg forlete[6].

§ 2. Gyf he man afylle, beo he utlage 7 his hænte mid hearme ælc ðara ðe riht wylle.

§ 3. Gyf he gewyrce þæt man hine afylle ðurh þæt ðe he ongean riht geanbyrde, gif mann þæt gesoðian mage[7], licge he[5] ǽgylde.

49. Gif hwá hadbryce gewyrce, gebete þæt be ðæs[3] hades mæðe, swa be were swa be wite swa be lahslite swa be ealre are.

50. Be æwbryce.

Gif hwa æwbryce gewyrce, gebete þæt be ðam þe seo dæd sy.

§ 1. Yfel æwbryce bið þæt eawfeste m[a]n[8] wið emtige [hine][9] forlicge, 7 mycele wyrse wið oðres æwe oððe wið gehadode.

51. Be siblegere.

Gyf hwa sibleger gewyrce, gebete þæt be sibbe mæðe, swa be were swa be wite swa be ealra æhta.

---

[1] *twybete* G, A, Ld.   [2] Om. G, A; written above the line in B.
[3] Om. G, A.   [4] *gerihta* G, A, Ld.   [5] Om. G, A, Ld.
[6] *alæte* G, A, Ld.   [7] *þ. gesoðige* G, A, Ld.   [8] G, A, Ld; *men* B.
[9] Om. G, A, Ld; written above the line in 16th cent. in B.

47[1]. If anyone openly causes a breach of the fast of Lent by fighting or by intercourse with women or by robbery or by any great misdeed, he shall pay double compensation[2], in accordance with the nature of the offence, just as he must do during a high festival.
> § 1. And if anyone denies [the charge], he shall clear himself by the triple process of exculpation.

48[1]. If anyone refuses to render ecclesiastical dues.
If anyone resists by force the payment of ecclesiastical dues, he shall pay *lahslit* in a Danish district, and the full fine[2] in an English one, or he shall clear himself: he shall select 11 men and shall himself make a twelfth.
> § 1[1]. If he wounds anyone, he shall make amends for doing so, and shall pay the full fine to the lord and redeem his hands[2] from the bishop or lose them.
> § 2[1]. If he kills a man, he shall be outlawed, and he shall be pursued with hostility[2] by all those who wish to promote law and order.
> § 3[1]. If he so acts as to bring about his own death by setting himself against the law, no compensation shall be paid for him, if this can be proved.

49. If anyone injures one of the clergy[1], he shall make amends according to the rank of the person injured, either by the payment of [his] wergeld or a fine or *lahslit*, or by the forfeiture of all his property.

50. Concerning adultery.
If anyone commits adultery[1], he shall make amends according to the nature of the offence.
> § 1. It is wicked adultery for a pious man to commit fornication with an unmarried woman, and much worse [for him to do so] with the wife of another man or with any woman who has taken religious vows.

51[1]. Concerning incest.
If anyone commits incest, he shall make amends according to the degree of relationship [between them], either by the payment of wergeld or of a fine, or by the forfeiture of all his possessions.

§ 1. Ne byð na gelic þæt man wið swustor gehæme 7 þes þe[1] hit bið[2] feor sibbe.

52. Be wydewan.
Gyf hwa wuduwan nydnæme, gebete þæt be his[3] were.
§ 1. Mæden.
Gyf hwa mæden nydnæme, gebete þæt be his[3] were.

53. Ðæt nan wif heo ne forlicgge.
Gyf be cwicum ceorle wif hig be oðrum were forlicge, 7 hit open wyrðe, gewyrðe heo to woruldsceame syððan hyre sylfre, 7 hæbbe se rihtwere eall þæt heo age[4], 7 heo ðonne[3] ðolie ægðer ge nosu ge ða earan[5].
§ 1. And gyf hit tihtla beo 7 lad forbersta, ðonne wealde se[3] bisceop 7 stiðlice deme.

54. Gyf wiffæst wer[6] hine forlicge be his agenre wylne, ðolie ðære 7 bete for hine sylfne wiþ Godd[7] [7][8] wið men.
§ 1. And se ðe habbe rihtwif 7 eac cefese, ne do him nan preost nan ðære rihte[9] ðe man Cristenum men don sceal, ær he geswice 7 swa deope gebete swa him se[3] bisceop tæce, 7 æfre swilces geswice.

55. Ælðeodige men, gif hig heora hemed rihtan nellað, [driue hi man of][10] lande mid heora æhtan 7 on[3] synnan gewitan.

56. Open morð.
Gif open morð weorðe ðæt man amyrred[11] sy, agyue man magum[12] [þone banan][10].
§ 1. 7 gif hit tihtle sy 7 æt lade mistide, deme se bisceop.

---

[1] þ. þ. om. G, A, Ld.   [2] wære G, A, Ld.   [3] Om. G, A, Ld.
[4] ahte G, A, Ld.   [5] þolige nasa (-e) 7 earena G, A.
[6] G, A, Ld; were B.
[7] w. G. G, A, Ld; added in the margin in 16th cent. in B.
[8] G, A, Ld; om. B.   [9] þæra (þara, ðara) gerihta G, A, Ld.
[10] Written in the margin in 16th cent. in B; om. G, A, Ld.
[11] amyrdred (-drede) A, Ld.   [12] þam (þara, ðara), m. G, A, Ld.

§ 1. The cases are not alike if incest is committed with a sister or with a distant relation.

52[1]. Concerning widows.

If anyone does violence to a widow, he shall make amends by the payment of his wergeld.

§ 1. Maidens.

If anyone does violence to a maiden he shall make amends by the payment of his wergeld.

53. No woman shall commit adultery.

If, while her husband is still alive, a woman commits adultery with another man and it is discovered, she shall bring disgrace upon herself, and her lawful husband shall have all that she possesses, and she shall then lose both her nose and her ears.

§ 1. And if a charge is brought and the attempt to refute it fails, the decision shall then rest with the bishop[1], and his judgment shall be strict.

54[1]. If a married man commits adultery with his own slave, he shall lose her and make amends for himself both to God and to men.

§ 1[1]. And if anyone has a lawful wife and also a concubine, no priest shall perform for him any of the offices which must be performed for a Christian man, until he desists and makes amends as thoroughly as the bishop shall direct him, and ever afterwards desists from such [evil-doing].

55[1]. Foreigners, if they will not regularise their unions, shall be driven from the land with their possessions, and shall depart in sin.

56. Murder which is discovered.

If anyone dies by violence and it becomes evident that it is a case of murder[1], the murderer shall be given up to the kinsmen [of the slain man].

§ 1. And if the accusation[1] is brought and the attempt [of the accused] to clear himself fails, the bishop[2] shall pronounce judgment.

57. Lafordes syrwunge.

Gyf hwa embe kinincg syrwe oððe ymbe[1] his[1] hlaford, sy he his feores scyldig 7 ealles ðæs ðe he age, buton he ga to ðryfealdan ordale [7 þær clæne wyrþ][2].

58. Be borhbryce.

Gif hwa kynincges borh abrece, gebete þæt mid v pundum.

§ 1. Gyf hwa arcebisceopes borh brece oððe æðelinges, gebete þæt mid ðrym pundum.

§ 2. Gyf hwa leodbisceopes oððe ealdormannes borh[3] abrece, gebete[4] mid twam pundum.

59. Be ðam þe on cynincges hirde feohteð.

Gyf hwa on kynincges hirede gefeohte, ðolie ðæs liues, buton him se kynincg geárian wylle.

60. Be ðam þæt man oðerne bewepnað.

Gyf man æt unlagum man bewepnie, forgylde hine be his[1] healsfange, 7 gyf man hine gebinde, forgildon hine[5] be healfan were.

61. Griðbryce.

Gyf hwa on fyrde griðbryce fulwyrce, ðolie liues oððon weregyldes.

§ 1. Gyf he samwyrce[6], bete be ðam ðe seo dæd sy[7].

62. Hamsocne.

Gyf hwa hamsocne gewyrce, gebete ðæt mid v pundum ðam kynincge on Engla lage[8], [7 on Dena][9] lage swa hit ær stod.

§ 1. 7 gyf hine man ðær afylle[10], licge ægylde.

63. Reaflac.

Gyf hwa reaflac gewyrce, agyue 7 forgylde 7 beo his weres scyldig wið ðone kinincg[11].

---

[1] Om. G, A, Ld.   [2] Written in the margin in 16th cent. in B; om. G, A, Ld.   [3] burg A.   [4] g. þæt G, A, Ld.
[5] forgilde be G, A, Ld.   [6] ran wyrce Ld.   [7] G adds ·N·.
[8] 7 on Cent æt hamsocne v þam cingce 7 þreo þam arcebisceope G.
[9] Written above the line in 16th cent. in B.   [10] alecge A, Ld.
[11] oððe wið þone þe his socne age G.

57[1]. Of plotting against a lord.
> If anyone plots against the king or against his own lord, he shall forfeit his life and all that he possesses, unless he goes to the triple ordeal and there proves himself innocent.

58[1]. Concerning the violation of protection.
> If anyone violates the king's protection, he shall pay £5 as compensation.
>> § 1. If anyone violates the protection of an archbishop or of a member of the royal family[1], he shall pay £3 as compensation.
>> § 2. If anyone violates the protection of the bishop of a diocese or of an ealdorman, he shall pay £2 as compensation.

59[1]. Concerning those who fight at the king's Court.
> If anyone fights at the king's Court[2], he shall lose his life, unless the king is willing to pardon him.

60. Concerning the case of one man disarming another.
> If one man unjustly disarms another, he shall compensate him[1] by the payment of a sum equivalent to his *healsfang*, and if he binds him[2], he shall compensate him by the payment of a sum equivalent to half his wergeld.

61. Breach of the peace.
> If anyone is guilty of a capital deed of violence[1] while serving in the army, he shall lose his life or his wergeld.
>> § 1. If he is guilty of a minor deed of violence[1], he shall make amends according to the nature of the deed.

62[1]. Attacks upon men's houses.
> If a man makes forcible entry into another man's house, he shall pay £5 to the king as compensation for so doing in districts under English law[2], and in the Danelaw the amount fixed by existing regulations.
>> § 1[1]. And if he is slain in such a case, no compensation shall be paid for his death.

63. Robbery.
> If anyone is guilty of robbery, he shall restore [the stolen goods], and pay the injured man as much again[1], and forfeit his wergeld to the king[2].

64. **Husbryce.**

Husbryce 7 bærnet 7 open ðyfð 7 æbere morþ 7 hlafordswice æfter woroldlage is botleas.

65. **Burhbote.**

Gyf hwa buruhbote oððe brygcebote[1] oððe fyrdfare forsitte, gebete mid hundtwentigum[2] scill' ðam kyncge on Engle lage, 7 on Dena lage swa hit ær stod, oððe geladige hine, (7)[3] namige man him xiiii 7 begyte xi[4].

§ 1. To cyricbote sceal eall[5] folc fylstan mid rihte.

66. **Be Godes flyman.**

Gyf hwa Godes flyman hæbbe on unriht, agyfe hine mid[6] rihte 7 forgylde ðam ðe hit gebyrige, 7 gylde ðam kynincge[7] be[8] wergilde.

§ 1. Gyf hwa amansodne[9] man oððon utlagene hæbbe 7 healde, plihte him sylfum 7 ealre his are.

67. Gyf hwa wille georne fram unrihte to rihte gecyrran[10], mildsige man him[11] for Godes ege, swa man betst mæge[12], ðam men swyðe georne.

68. And uton don, swa us ðearf is, helpan æfre[13] ðam raðost ðe helpes behofoð[14]; [þonne nime[15] we þæs lean þær us leofast byð][16].

§ 1. **Be unstrangan.**

Forðam a man sceal ðam unstrangan men for Godes lufan 7 for[11] his[3] ege liðelicor deman 7 scrifan ðonne ðam strangan;

§ 1*a*. forðamðe we magon witan fulgeorne, þæt se unmaga 7 se mage ne mæg[17] gelice[18] mycele[19] byrðene aberan[20], ne se unhala ðam halan gelice.

---

[1] The earlier reading *bryceb.* has been altered later to *brygceb.* in B.
[2] cxx G; *hundtwe*(*l*)*ftigum* A, Ld. [3] Om. G, A.
[4] *þærto* added in the margin in 16th cent. in B; om. G, A, Ld.
[5] G, A, Ld; written in the margin in 16th cent. in B. [6] *to* G, A, Ld.
[7] *cyninge ·N·* A. [8] *be his w.* G.
[9] Altered later to *amansumodne* in B.
[10] *gecirran* (-*y*-) *eft to r.* G, A, Ld. [11] Om. G, A, Ld.
[12] *m. ðam men* B, with *ð. m.* crossed out. [13] *áá* G, A, Ld.
[14] *h. betst* (*best*) *behofað* (*be ofað* A) G A Ld. [15] *lese* A, Ld.
[16] G, A, Ld; om. B.
[17] *Forþamþe ne mæg se unmaga þam magan, w. witon fullgeorne, gelice* G; *f. n. m., we witan f., se u. þ. m.* A, Ld.
[18] The rest of the sentence is missing in both A, Ld. [19] Om. G.
[20] *ahebban* G.

64[1]. Assaults upon houses.
According to secular law assaults upon houses[2], arson[3], theft which cannot be disproved, murder which cannot be denied and treachery towards a man's lord[4] are crimes for which no compensation can be paid[5].

65. The repair of fortifications.
If anyone neglects the repair of fortifications or of bridges or military service[1], he shall pay 120 shillings as compensation to the king in districts under English law, and in the Danelaw the amount fixed by existing regulations; or he shall clear himself—[the court] shall nominate 14 compurgators for him and he shall obtain the support of 11 of them.
§ 1. The whole nation, in accordance with the law, shall assist in the repair of churches[1].

66. Concerning excommunicated persons.
If anyone unlawfully maintains an excommunicated person, he shall deliver him up in accordance with the law, and pay compensation to him to whom it belongs, and to the king a sum equivalent to his wergeld.
§ 1[1]. If anyone keeps and maintains an excommunicated man or an outlaw, it shall be at the risk of losing his life and all his property.

67. If anyone zealously desires to turn from lawlessness to observance of the law, as great mercy as possible shall be shown to him, with the utmost readiness, through the fear of God.

68[1]. And let us, as our duty is, ever render help with the utmost speed to those who require help; [then shall we receive the reward for so doing where we most desire it].
§ 1[1]. Concerning the weak.
For the fear of God and out of reverence to him, greater leniency shall always be shown in passing judgment and in imposing penance upon the weak than [in doing so] upon the strong.
§ 1a. Because we may know full well that the weak and the strong cannot bear an equally heavy burden, nor can the sick man bear one equal to that borne by him who is sound.

§ 1*b*. 7 þi we sculon medemian 7 gescadelice todælan ylde 7 geogoðe, [welige 7 wædle, frige 7 þeowe][1], hale 7 unhale.

§ 1*c*. And æðer man sceal, ge on godcundan scriftum ge on woruldcundan dome, ðas ðincg tosceadan.

§ 2. Eac on gemeanre[2] dæde ðonne man bið nydwyrhta, ðonne bið se man[3] ðe bet wyrðe gebeorges, ðe he for neode dyde þæt þæt he dyde.

§ 3. And gyf hwa ungewealdes hwæt[4] gedeð, ne byð þæt eallunga[5] gelíc ðam[6] ðe hit gewealdes deð[7].

69. Ðis is ðonne se lihtingc ðe ic wylle eallon folce gebeorgan, ðe hig ær ðyson mid gedrehte wæron ealles to swyðe.

§ 1. Ðæt is ðonne ærost, þæt ic bebeode eallum minan gerefan þæt hig on minon agenan rihtlice[8] tilian 7 me mid ðam feormian, 7 þæt him nan man ne ðearf to feormfultume nan ðingc syllan, butan he sylf wille.

§ 2. And gyf hwá æfter ðam[4] wite crauian [wille][9], beo he his weres scyldig wið ðone cyningc.

70. Be hergeate.

Gyf of ðysum life man[10] gewíte cwydeleas, sy hit ðurh his gymelyste, sy hyt ðurh færlicne deaþ, ðonne ne teo se laford nan mare on his æhte butan his rihtan heregeate.

§ 1. Ac beo be his dihte seo æht gescyft swyðe rihte wife 7 cildan 7 neahmagon, ælcon be ðære mæðe ðe him to gebyrige.

71. And beon ða herigeata swa gefundene[11] swa hit mæðlic sy.

71*a*. Eorles.

Eorles swa ðærto byrie, þæt syndon eahta hors, IIII gesadelode 7 IIII unsadolede, 7 IIII helmas 7 IIII byrnan 7 VIII spera 7 swa[12] fela scylda 7 IIII swyrd 7 twa hund mancus goldes.

---

[1] *w.* 7 *w. f.* 7 *þ.* written in 16th cent. on an erasure in B; *welan* 7 *w. freot* 7 *þeowet* (*-æt*) G, A, Ld.
[2] *mænigre* (*man.*) G, A; *manige* Ld.   [3] Om. G, A.   [4] Om. A, Ld.
[5] *eallumga* B; *-unga na* G; *eallum na* A, Ld.   [6] Om. G, A, Ld.
[7] *gewurþe* G; *gedeð* A, Ld.   [8] *a. me r.* G.
[9] Om. B; *crafige* G, A, Ld.   [10] *And gif hwa cw.* &c. G, A, Ld.
[11] *swa fundene* G; om. A, Ld.   [12] *eallswa* G, A, Ld.

§ 1*b*. And therefore we must make due allowance and carefully distinguish between age and youth, wealth and poverty, freemen and slaves, the sound and the sick.

§ 1*c*. And discrimination with regard to these circumstances must be shown both in [imposing] ecclesiastical amends and in [passing] secular judgment.

§ 2. Likewise, in many cases of evil-doing, when a man is an involuntary agent, he is more entitled to clemency because he acted as he did from compulsion.

§ 3. And if anyone does anything unintentionally, the case is entirely different from that of one who acts deliberately.

69. Now this is the mitigation by means of which I desire to protect the general public in cases where, until now, they have been far too greatly oppressed.

§ 1[1]. The first provision is: I command all my reeves to provide for me in accordance with the law from my own property and support me thereby, and [declare] that no man need give them anything as purveyance, unless he himself is willing to do so.

§ 2[1]. And if anyone [of my reeves] shall demand[2] a fine [in such a case], he shall forfeit his wergeld to the king.

70. Concerning heriots[1].

If a man departs from this life intestate, whether through negligence or through sudden death, his lord shall take no more from his property than his legal heriot.

§ 1. But, according to his direction, the property shall be very strictly divided among his wife and children and near kinsmen, each according to the share which belongs to him.

71. Heriots shall be fixed with due regard to the rank of the person for whom they are paid.

71*a*. An earl's heriot.

The heriot of an earl, as is fitting, shall be eight horses, four saddled and four unsaddled, and four helmets and four byrnies and eight spears and as many shields and four swords and 200 mancuses of gold.

§ 1. Kyncges ðeines.

And syððan kyncges ðægnes¹ heregeata² ðe him nyxste syndon—IIII hors, II gesadelode 7 twa ungesadelode, 7 II swyrd 7 IIII spera 7 ealswa³ feola scylda 7 helm 7 byrnan 7 fiftig mancus goldes.

§ 2. Oðres ðeines.

And medemra ðegen—hors 7 his gerædan 7 his wepna oððe his healsfang on Westsæxan, 7 on Myrcen II pund, 7 on Eastengle II pund.

§ 3. And kyncges ðegnes heregeata inne mid Denum ðe his socne hæbbe—IIII pund.

§ 4. 7 gyf he to ðam kyncge furðor cyððe hæbbe—II hors, an gesadelod 7 oðer ungesadolod, 7 an swyrd 7 II spera 7 twegen scyldas 7 fiftig mancus goldes.

§ 5. 7 se ðe læsse habbe 7⁴ læsse maga sy—II pund.

72. And ðær se bunda sæt uncwyd [his deig]⁵ 7 unbecrafod, sitte þæt wif 7 ða cild [on þam ylcan]⁶ unbesacen.

§ 1. And gyf se bunda, ær he dead wære, wære beclypad, ðonne andwyrde ða yrfnumen swa he sylf sceolde, ðeah he lif hæfde.

73. Be wydewan, þæt heo sitte XII monðas ceorlæs.

And sitte ælc wuduwe werleas twelf monað 7⁷ ceose heo⁷ syððan þæt heo sylf wille.

73a. 7 gyf heo ðonne⁷ binnon ðæs⁷ geares fæce wer geceose, ðonne ðolie heo ðære morgengeafe 7 ealre [þære]⁸ æhtan ðe he[o⁹ þurh þone⁷ ærran were heafde, 7 fon þa nyxtan frynd to þam lande¹⁰ 7 to þam æhte¹¹ þæt heo ær hæfde.

§ 1. 7 si he his] weres scyldig wið ðone kyning oððe wið ðone ðe he hit¹² geunnen hæbbe.

---

¹ þegnas G; þegenas A. ² Om. G, A. ³ swa G, A, Ld.
⁴ l. h. 7 om. G, A.
⁵ Om. G, A, Ld; written in the margin in 16th cent. in B.
⁶ G, A, Ld; om. B. ⁷ Om. G, A, Ld.
⁸ Written above in 16th cent. in B.
⁹ o þurh...he his. Written in the margin in 16th cent. in B.
¹⁰ landan G. ¹¹ þan æhtan (eh.) G, A, Ld. ¹² his socne G.

§ 1. The heriot of a king's thegn.

And further, the heriots of king's thegns who stand in immediate relation to him[1] shall be four horses, two saddled and two unsaddled, and two swords and four spears and as many shields and helmets and byrnies and 50 mancuses of gold.

§ 2. The heriot of another thegn.

And the heriot of ordinary[1] thegns shall be a horse and its trappings and his weapons or his *healsfang* in Wessex, and in Mercia £2, and in East Anglia £2.

§ 3. And among the Danes the heriot of a king's thegn who possesses rights of jurisdiction shall be £4.

§ 4. And if he stands in a more intimate relationship to the king[1], it shall be two horses, one saddled and the other unsaddled, and one sword and two spears and two shields and 50 mancuses of gold.

§ 5. And for the man who is inferior in wealth[1] and position the heriot shall be £2.

72[1]. And when a householder has dwelt all his time free from claims and charges, his wife and children shall dwell [on the same property] unmolested by litigation.

§ 1. And if the householder had been cited before his death, then his heirs shall answer the charge, as he himself would have done, had he been alive.

73[1]. Concerning widows, that they remain for a year without a husband.

And every widow shall remain twelve months without a husband, and she shall afterwards choose what she herself desires.

73a[1]. And if then, within the space of the year, she chooses a husband, she shall lose her morning-gift and all the property which she had from her first husband, and his nearest relatives shall take the land and the property which she had held.

§ 1. And he (the second husband) shall forfeit his wergeld to the king or to the lord to whom it has been granted.

§ 2. 7 ðeah heo neadnumen wyrðe, ðolie ðæra æhta, buton heo fram ðam ceorle wille eft ham ongean 7 næfre eft his [no][1] wyrðe.

§ 3. And ne hadige man næfre[2] wuduwan to hrædlice.

§ 4. 7 gelæste ælc wuduwe ða heregeata binnon twelf monðum, buton hyre ær to onhagie, witeleas.

74. And ne nyde[3] man næfre[4] naðor ne wif ne mæden to ðam þe hire sylfre mislicige, ne wið sceatte ne sylle, buton he hwæt agenes ðances gyfan wylle.

75. Be ðam þæt man his spere to oðres mannes dure sette.

And ic læte riht[5], ðeah hwá his agen[4] spere sette to oðres mannes huses duru 7 he ðiderin ærende hæbbe, oððon gyf mon oðer wépn gedreohlice lecge ðær [hi][6] stille mihton beon, gyf hi moston, 7 hwilc man ðonne þæt wepn gelæcce 7 he[4] hwylcne hearm ðærmid gewyrce, ðonne is[7] þæt riht, þæt se ðe ðonne[8] hearm geworhte, þæt se ðone hearm eac[9] gebete.

§ 1. And se ðe þæt wepn age, hine geladige, gyf he durre, ðæt hit næfre næs naðer ne his gewill ne his geweald ne his ræd ne his gewitnes; ðonne is þæt Godes riht, þæt he[10] beo clæne.

§ 2. And wite se oðer þe þæt weorc geweorhte, þæt he hit bete, swa swa lagu tæce[11].

76. Be forstolene æhta.

Gyf hwa[12] forstolen ðingc ham to his coton bringe 7 he arefned[13] wyrðe, riht is[7] þæt he hæbbe þæt he æftereode.

§ 1. 7 buton hit under ðæs wifes cæglocan gebroht wære, sy heo clæne.

---

[1] Written above in 16th cent. in B; *ne* G, A, Ld. [2] *æfre* G, A.
[3] *nime* A.   [4] Om. G, A, Ld.
[5] *nelle* B, with *l. r.* written above it in 16th cent.; *ic l. r.* G; *ic wille* A, Ld.
[6] Written in the margin in 16th cent. B.   [7] *his* B.   [8] *þone* G, Ld.
[9] Om. G.   [10] *heo* B.   [11] *lagan* (later changed to *laga*) *tæcean* G.
[12] *hwylc* (*hwilc*) *man* G, A, Ld.
[13] *arasod* G, A, Ld; Liebermann suggests the emendation *arefsed* for B.

§ 2[1]. And although she has been married by force, she shall lose her possessions, unless she is willing to leave the man and return home and never afterwards be his.

§ 3. And no widow shall be too hastily consecrated as a nun.

§ 4. And every widow shall pay the heriots within twelve months without incurring a fine, if it has not been convenient for her to pay earlier.

74[1]. And no woman or maiden shall ever be forced to marry a man whom she dislikes, nor shall she be given for money, except the suitor desires of his own freewill to give something.

75. Concerning the case of a man setting his spear at another man's door.

And I hold it right that if anyone sets his spear at the door of another man's house, he himself having an errand inside, or if anyone carefully lays any other weapons in a place where they might remain quietly, if they were allowed to, and if anyone then seizes the weapon and works mischief with it, the law shall be, that he who wrought the mischief shall likewise pay compensation for it.

§ 1. And he who owns the weapon shall clear himself, if he dare, asserting that the mischief was done without his desire or authority or advice or cognisance; then according to the law of God he shall be clear [of any charge of complicity].

§ 2. And the other who wrought the mischief shall see to it that he pays compensation for it, according as the law directs.

76[1]. Concerning stolen goods.

If anyone carries stolen goods home to his cottage and is detected[2], the law is that he (the owner) shall have what he has tracked.

§ 1[1]. And unless the goods had been put under the wife's lock and key, she shall be clear [of any charge of complicity].

§ 1a. Ac ðara cægan heo sceal weardian, þæt is hire heddernes cæge[1] 7 hyre cyste cæge[2] [7 hire tægan][3]; gyf hit under ðyssa ænigum gebroht byð, ðone[4] bið heo scyldig.

§ 1b. And ne mæg nan wif hire bundan forbeodan þæt he ne mote into his cotan gelegian[5] þæt þæt he wille.

§ 2. Hit wæs ær ðysson þæt þæt cild ðe læg on ðam[6] cradole, þeah hit næfre metes ne abite, þæt ða gytseras lætan ealswa[7] scyldigne 7 hit gewittig wære.

§ 3. Ac ic hit forbeode heonon forð eornostlice 7 eac swyðe manega[8] ðincg[2] ðe Gode syndon swyðe[9] laðe.

77. Be ðam þe flihð fram his laforde.

And ðe man ðe fleo[10] fram his hlaforde oððe fram his geferan for his yrhðe, sy hit on scypfyrde, sy hit on landfyrde, ðolie he[2] ealles ðæs ðe he age 7 his agenes feores, 7 fo se hlaford to ðam æhton 7 to his lande ðe he him ær sealde.

[§ 1. 7 gyf he bocland hæbbe, ga þæt þam cingce to handa.][11]

78. Be ðam ðe toforan his laforde fealleð.

And se man ðe on fyrdunge[12] ætforan his hlaforde fealle, sy hit innon lande, sy hit ut[2] of lande, beon ða heregeata forgyfene, 7 fon ða yrfenuman to lande 7 to æhte 7 scyften hit swiðe rihte.

79. And se ðe land gewerod hæbbe on scypfyrde 7 on landfyrde[13] be[14] scire gewitnysse[15], habbe he unbesaken on dæge 7 æfter dæge to syllanne 7 to gyfane ðam ðe him leofost sy.

80. Be huntnaðe.

And ic wylle þæt ælc man sy his huntnoðes wyrðe on wuda 7 on felda on his agenan.

§ 1. 7 forgá ælc man minne huntnoð lochwar ic hit gefriðod wille habban [on minon agenan][16], be fullan wite.

---

[1] h. hordern 7 G, A, Ld. [2] Om. G, A, Ld.
[3] Written in the margin in 16th cent. in B; 7 hyre tege (tyge) G, A; tyge Ld, with in the margin al. teah.
[4] Cf. cap. 25; þonne G, A, Ld.
[5] Altered later to gelogian which is also G's reading; gelaðyan A.
[6] Om. G, A. [7] efen G, A, Ld.
[8] 7 swylce (swilce) manege (manage, manige) G, A, Ld.
[9] Om. A, Ld. [10] ætfleo G, A; -flea Ld.
[11] G, A, Ld; om. B. [12] on þam f. G, A; æt ð. f. Ld.
[13] o. sc. 7 on l. Only in B. [14] on G.
[15] G adds: 7 se nolde oððe ne mihte þe hit ær ahte.
[16] on m. ag. written above in 16th cent. in B; om. G, A, Ld.

CAP. 77–80

§ 1*a*. But it is her duty to guard the keys of the following—her storeroom and her chest and her cupboard[1]. If the goods have been put in any of these, she shall be held guilty.

§ 1*b*[1]. But no wife can forbid her husband to deposit anything that he desires in his cottage.

§ 2[1]. It has been the custom up till now for grasping persons to treat a child which lay in the cradle, even though it had never tasted food, as being as guilty as though it were fully intelligent.

§ 3. But I strictly forbid such a thing henceforth, and likewise very many things which are hateful to God.

77[1]. Concerning the man who deserts his lord.

And the man who, through cowardice, deserts his lord or his comrades on an expedition, either by sea or by land[2], shall lose all that he possesses and his own life, and the lord shall take back the property and the land which he had given him.

[§ 1[1]. And if he has land held by title-deed it shall pass into the king's hands.]

78. Concerning the man who falls before his lord.

And the heriots of the man who falls before his lord during a campaign, whether within the country or abroad[1], shall be remitted, and the heirs shall succeed to his land and his property and make a very just division of the same.

79. And he who, with the cognisance of the shire, has performed the services demanded from a landowner[1] on expeditions either by sea or by land shall hold [his land] unmolested by litigation during his life, and at his death shall have the right of disposing of it or giving it to whomsoever he prefers.

80. Concerning hunting.

And it is my will that every man shall be entitled to hunt in the woods and fields on his own property.

§ 1. But everyone, under pain of incurring the full penalty, shall avoid hunting on my preserves, wherever they may be[1].

81. 7 dryncelean 7 hlafordes rihtgyfu stande æfre unawended.
82. And ic wille þæt ælc man beo griðes wyrðe to gemote 7 fram gemote, buton he æbere ðeof beo.
83. Se ðe ðas lage wyrde ðe se kyningc hæfð nu ða[1] eallum mannum forgyfen, seo he Denisc sy he[2] Engli[s]c[3], beo he his weres scyldig wið ðone kyningc.
    § 1. And gyf he hit eft wyrde, gylde twywa his were.
    § 2. And gyf he ðonne swa dyrstig sy þæt he hi[4] ðridde siðe abrece[5], ðolige ealles ðæs ðe he age.
84. Nu bidde ic georne 7 on Godes naman beode manna gehwylcne, þæt he inweardre[6] heortan gebuga to his Drihtene, 7 oft 7 gelome smeage[7] hwæt him sy to donne 7 hwæt to forganne.
    § 1. Eallum us is mycel ðearf þæt we God lufian 7 Godes lage fylian[8] 7 godcundan lareowan[9] geor[n]lice[10] hyran[11].
    § 1a. Forðam hig us sceolan lædan forð æt ðam dome, ðonne God demeð manna gewilcum be ærran gehwyrhtum.
    § 2. And geselig byð se hyrde ðe ðonne ða heorde into Godes rice 7 to heofenlicre myrðe bliðe mot lædan for ærran[12] gewyrhtan.
    § 2a. And wel ðære heorde ðe gefolgað ðam hyrde ðe hig deoflum ætwenað 7 Gode hig gestreonað.
    § 3. Uton ðonne ealle anmodre heortan georne urum Drihtene cweman mid rihte 7 heononforð mid rihte[13] symble scyldan us georne wið ðone hatan bryne ðe weallað on helle.
    § 4. And do nu eac lareowas 7 godcunde bydelas swa swa riht is 7 ealra manna ðearf is: bodian gelome godcunde ðearfe.
    § 4a. And ælc ðe gescead wite, hlyste him georne 7 godcunde lare gewha on geðance healde swyðe fæste him sylfum to ðearfe.

---

[1] Om. A, Ld.   [2] D. oððe E. G.   [3] Englic B.
[4] hit G; om. A, Ld.   [5] wyrde G, A, Ld.   [6] inweardlice A, Ld.
[7] sm. swyðc (swiðe) georne G, A, Ld.   [8] fylgean G, A, Ld.
[9] lar. 7 g. B.   [10] georl. B.   [11] A repeats: 7 Godes lage fylgean.
[12] G, A; his ærran B.   [13] m. r. om. G, A, Ld.

81 [1]. And there shall never be any interference with bargains successfully concluded[2] or with the legal gifts made by a lord.

82. And it is my will that every man shall be entitled to protection in going to and from assemblies, unless he be a notorious thief.

83 [1]. He who violates the law which the king has now granted to all men, whether he be a Dane or an Englishman, shall forfeit his wergeld to the king.
 § 1. And if he violates it again, he shall pay his wergeld twice over.
 § 2. And if he is so presumptuous as to break it a third time, he shall lose all that he possesses.

84 [1]. Now I earnestly entreat all men and command them, in the name of God, to submit in their inmost hearts to their lord, and often and frequently consider what they ought to do and what they ought to forgo.
 § 1. There is great need for us all to love God and to follow God's law, and zealously to obey our spiritual teachers.
 § 1a. For it is their duty to lead us forth to the judgment where God shall judge each man according to the works which he has wrought.
 § 2 [1]. And blessed is the shepherd who then may gladly lead his flock into the kingdom of God and to the joy of Heaven, because of the works which they have wrought.
 § 2a. And well is it for the flock which follows the shepherd who delivers them from devils and wins them for God.
 § 3 [1]. Let us all then, with humble heart, be zealous in pleasing our Lord aright, and henceforth, by doing what is right, always zealously guard ourselves from the hot fire which surges in hell.
 § 4 [1]. And likewise teachers and spiritual messengers shall do what is right and for the well-being of all men: they shall frequently inculcate spiritual duties.
 § 4a. And everyone who has discernment shall earnestly give heed to them, and everyone for his own well-being shall keep fast in his mind their spiritual instruction.

§ 4b. And[1] manna gehwylc to weorðunga his Drihtene do to gode þæt[2] he mæge wordes 7 weorces[3] 7 dæde[4] glædlice æfre; ðonne byð us eallum God[5] þe gearwera.

§ 5. A[a][6] sy Godes nama ecelice gebletsod, 7 lof him 7 wuldor 7 wyrðmynt æfre[7] to worulde. Amen[8].

§ 6. God ælmihtig us eallum gemiltsie swa his willa sy[9]. Amen.

[1] 7 á G; and ha A.
[2] þæs þe A, Ld.
[3] 7 w. om. G, A, Ld.
[4] 7 d. 7 B.
[5] Godes milts (miltsa) G, A, Ld.
[6] á G, A; aá Ld; ac B.
[7] symle (symble) æ. G, A, Ld.
[8] Om. G, A, Ld.
[9] s. his milda w. sig 7 gehealde us æfre on ecnesse! Si hit swa! G.

§ 4*b*. And every man, for the honour of his Lord, shall always gladly do his utmost by word and by work and by deed[1] for the furtherance of what is good; then shall God be the more ready [to help us].

§ 5[1]. May the name of God be eternally blessed, and to Him be praise and glory and honour for ever and ever. Amen.

§ 6. God Almighty have mercy upon us all, as His will may be. Amen.

THE LAWS OF WILLIAM I
AND OF HENRY I

THE LAWS OF WILLIAM I
AND OF HENRY I

Only three short pieces of legislation have been preserved in the form in which they were issued by William I. These are (1) a short document addressed to the bishop, the reeve and all the citizens of London, assuring them of the continuance of the privileges which they enjoyed in the days of King Edward (Wl Lond); (2) a decree establishing the procedure in the case of an accusation brought by an Englishman against a Frenchman and vice versa (Wl lad); and (3) a decree forbidding bishops and archdeacons to hold pleas involving matters of ecclesiastical discipline in the hundred courts (Wl ep).

The original text of the first of these documents is preserved in the Town Clerk's Office, London. It is written on a small strip of parchment to which a single seal (now lost) had been attached. A facsimile, from which the present text has been taken, is given by Sharpe, *London and the Kingdom*, I. frontispiece. A Latin translation, dated by Liebermann about 1075–1300, is preserved in the Liber Custumarum, f. 187 (ed. Riley, *Munim. Gildhal.* II. p. 247), in the Liber Horn f. 205 b, 362, and in the Liber Memorandorum f. 110 b. Both the contents and the style of the document point to its issue soon after William was crowned King of England (Dec. 25th, 1066). It is an explicit statement of his intention to continue the privileges enjoyed under his predecessor, to pay due regard to the laws of inheritance, and to protect the citizens from injury. It seems most likely that such an assurance of goodwill would be issued at a time when there was considerable doubt and uneasiness as to the course of action which the new ruler would adopt. The latest possible date for its issue is 1075, the year of the death of William, Bishop of London, who is named in the preamble.

Noteworthy points with regard to the language are the form *portirefan* and the dual of the 2nd pers. pronoun which occurs twice (cap. 2).

Of the second document a copy, in English, is found in the

Textus Roffensis f. 47 (H) and a Latin translation in the Quadripartitus. Liebermann is of opinion that the original had probably been issued in both languages, but regards the version in Q as a translation in view of the use of the word *untrum*, glossed *id est invalidus*, in cap. 2, 1. Consideration of the contents of the decree and of the language leads him to suggest a date between 1068 and 1077 as most probable for its issue. The possibility of choice between trial by ordeal and trial by combat in the case of an Englishman, he argues, points to a time when the Norman mode of proof was familiar but not yet established as that most regularly employed. It is to be noted, however, that the ordeal was frequently used throughout the Norman period and that instances of it are numerous in Domesday Book (see Bigelow, *Placita Anglo-Normannica*, 1879, pp. xii f., 38, 40 ff.). Noteworthy points with regard to the language are the occasional use of *y* for *i*, the occurrence of dative plural forms in *-an*, of an inflected infinitive in *-enne* (Pre.) and of a past participle in *-an* (cap. 2, 2).

Only the Latin text of the third decree has survived, although, according to the statement of one MS, it was issued also in English (see last line of text). Copies of this decree seem to have been sent throughout the country, two of them being represented by later transcripts, namely, that sent to Essex, Hertfordshire and Middlesex preserved in the Liber pilosus S. Pauli London., f. 1 (Lp), from which the following text is taken, and that sent to the diocese of Lincoln, preserved in the Registrum Antiquissimum Remigii A I 5, f. 1 and 9 (Lc), in Rymer's *Foedera* (1816), I. p. 3 (Ry), the source of which is unknown (see Liebermann, I. p. 485[3]), and in the Rot. Inspeximus Chartarum, a. 2 Rich. II, mb. 13 (Insp) in the Public Record Office.

The original decree seems to have been issued sometime between 1070 and 1076. In 1067 Remigius was consecrated Bishop of Lincoln. In August 1070 Lanfranc was consecrated Archbishop of Canterbury, and it seems natural to trace his influence in the reforms which the decree enjoins A date earlier than Easter 1076 must be assumed in view of the use made of cap. 3, 2 at a synod held by Lanfranc then (see Liebermann, I. p. 485 f.). Liebermann suggests April 1072 as a possible date.

Lanfranc's first synod after his return from receiving the pallium at Rome was held at Winchester then and, according to the Acta Lanfranci, *multa de Christianae religionis cultu seruanda instituit* (ed. Plummer *Sax. Chr.* I. p. 288). It is to be noted that the agreement between Lanfranc and Thomas of York regarding the primacy of the See of Canterbury, the discussion of which was begun at Winchester, was concluded in the following month at Windsor in the presence of the King and Queen, 13 bishops (including Remigius) and 12 abbots (see Davis, *Regesta Regum A.N.* n. 64 f.). It seems possible that Wl ep may have been issued then.

In addition to these three pieces of legislation there are several collections of laws attributed to William I. One of these beginning "Hic intimatur" (Wl art) appears in three forms (1) in Latin, (2) in a French translation, (3) in a later Latin form with several additions and variations (Wl art retr). The first version is preserved in about 30 MSS including H (the earliest, from which the present text is taken), Rl (Oxford Bodley Rawlinson C 641, f. 44)—both of which are derived from a lost predecessor (see Liebermann, III. p. 277)— and one MS (T) of the Quadripartitus. Elsewhere it appears as the first part of the Tripartita—a collection of three pieces of which the other two are ECf retractatus and Genealogia Normannica (see Liebermann, I. p. xli). The French version is found in one MS of the Tripartita, namely, Cu (Cambridge Univ. Ee 1, 1 f. 3), and seems to belong to the year 1192 or 1193 (see Notes). It keeps to the 3rd pers. throughout and occasionally makes slight additions to the earlier (Latin) version. The text (see Liebermann, I. p. 488 f.) is not reproduced in full here, but variations as compared with Wl art are given in the Notes. Wl art retr represents a revision of Wl art made about 90 years later. It forms part of the Leges Anglorum Londoniis s. XIII in. collectae (see Liebermann, I. p. xxxiv *s.v. Lond.*), the MSS in which it is found being Rs f. 51[1], Co (C.C.C. 70, p. 53), Or (Oxford, Oriel College, 46 f. 27), and K 2 (Cotton Claudius D. II. f. 31, where only the clauses from 14, 2 to the end are extant, the preceding leaf having been lost). It appears also in

[1] John Rylands Library, Manchester, Codex n. 155, see *E.H.R.* 1913, p. 737.

Sc (Scaccarii Liber rubeus f. 162 b in the Public Record Office) with its later copies Hg (British Museum, Hargrave, 313 f. 99) and K 3 (Cotton Claudius D II. f. 41), and is included in Lambarde's edition. Only the clauses which differ from, or have been added to Wl art are reproduced here, the MS followed being Rs.

Certain clauses in Wl art closely resemble, not only in content but also in phraseology, clauses in the *Instituta Cnuti* (see Notes and Liebermann, III. p. 278). In caps. 6–6, 3 Wl lad has been used although it is not fully reproduced. Elsewhere, Liebermann is of opinion, genuine decrees and regulations of the Conqueror's may have been followed, *e.g.* in caps. 3 and 4, where a distinction is drawn between the Frenchmen who had settled in England before 1066 and those who came as followers of the Conqueror. The procedure in the case of non-appearance before a court (cap. 8, 2 f.) probably also represents the actual practice of the time. For a full discussion of the contents of Wl art see Liebermann, III. p. 278. There seems no reason to doubt the generally accepted view that it was compiled in the early years of the twelfth century. In view of the use made of the *Instituta Cnuti* it must certainly be later than 1095. Liebermann assigns it to a date between 1110 and 1135.

The longest collection of laws attributed to William I is that generally referred to as the *Leis Willelme*. The French text of this compilation is found in Hk (Holkham n. 228, f. 141) and in three seventeenth century prints, namely, Im (*Rer. Angl. Script. vet.* I. p. 88), Io (Selden, Eadmer, *Hist. Nov.* p. 173) and Isp (Spelman, *Concilia M. Brit.* I. p. 624) which represent a lost predecessor I (Pseudo-Ingulf, *Historia Croylandensis*). A Latin translation (L) which is not derived from either Hk or I is found in S (Harley, 746 f. 55). In Hk the text of the Leis Wl ends at cap. 28, 2, while only five clauses are given in Isp. It is evident from differences in the text that Hk and I are independent, and it is also evident from the instances where I and L agree as against Hk that these two are derived from a common ancestor (il). For a full discussion of the MSS and their relationship see Liebermann, III. p. 283 f. The compilation falls into three parts, namely (1) a section ending with cap. 28, 2 which contains many regulations undoubtedly in force under the Conqueror and later, (2) a section extending from cap. 29 to cap. 38 which strongly betrays the influence of Roman law, and (3) a section from cap. 39 to the end, translated almost word for word from II Canute.

The first section is the most valuable. Many of its clauses are simply re-statements of older laws and customs (see Notes), while others apparently represent Norman innovations and may probably rest on actual decrees issued by the Conqueror. The view that he was the author of several reforms is supported by the statement of Henry I (Hn Cor cap. 13), but the assumption that he issued any long code of laws is disproved by the absence of reference to any such by Henry. The precedence given to Mercian Law and the reckoning of the English shilling as four-pence in value point to Mercia as the place where the Leis were compiled. Matzke[1], as the result of a detailed study of the language of Hk, assigns the original text to a date between 1150 and 1170. This, in Liebermann's opinion, is too late in view of the archaisms traceable in I (see *Arch. Stud. Neu. Spra.* cvi. pp. 113 ff.). He assigns it to a date not later than 1135 and conceivably as early as 1090.

The legislative measures of Henry I are represented by four Latin documents all of which open with a clause of salutation and end with a list of witnesses.

The earliest of these (Hn Cor) was issued at Westminster at his coronation (5 August 1100), and consists chiefly of a list of the evil practices of the preceding reigns which he has thought fit to abolish. Cap. 13 contains the assurance that he will uphold the law of Edward together with the reforms introduced by his father. Copies of this charter seem to have been sent throughout the country (see Eadmer, *Nov. Lib.* III. ed. Rule, Rolls Series, p. 119; Wm. of Malm. *Gesta Reg.* v. § 393, Rolls Series, II. p. 470), but none of the originals of these has survived. Later transcripts of three of them are found in Chronicles and compilations of the twelfth and thirteenth centuries, namely, a Worcestershire copy in Sc 2 (Liber rub. Sc. f. 163 b, copied by Hg f. 99 b), a Hertfordshire copy in Alb (Chr. of St Albans in

[1] J. E. Matzke, *Les Lois de Guillaume le Conquérant en français et en latin*, 1899.

Roger Wendover's *Flores hist.* ann. 1100, 1213, copied by Matth. Paris, *Chron.* ed. Luard, II. pp. 115, 552, ann. 1100, 1213, and *Hist. Angl.* ed. Madden, I. p. 177, ann. 1100), and a copy with a general address found in H f. 96 (from which the present text is taken), Rl f. 43, Haug (Ricard. Haugustald. *Hist. Stephani*[1], ann. 1135), Dm (Cotton Domitian, VIII. f. 118), Q (copied in Sc f. 16), and in a Westminster revision represented by Gl (Regist. episc. Glasgu. f. 25), Lond, Hl (Harley, 458 f. 1), Cust (f. 13 b) and S (f. 59).

Two short charters deal with matters concerning the coinage and the holding of the hundred and county courts respectively. It is probable that copies of these were sent to the various counties (cf. Hn Cor), but only one is represented in each case, namely, that intended for Worcestershire. The earlier (Hn mon) is preserved in Sc (f. 163 b) from which copies were taken by K 3 (Cotton Claudius D. II. f. 41) and Hg (f. 100). It is dated Christmas and the place of issue is named as Westminster. The year is practically established as 1100 by the fact that William, who signs as Chancellor, was succeeded in office by Roger le Poor before 3 September 1101 (see *E.H.R.* 1913, p. 426).

The second (Hn Com) is likewise preserved in Sc (f. 164), Hg (f. 100) and K 3 (f. 41 b); also in the Quadripartitus. A copy in Co (C.C.C. 70, p. 76) seems to have been taken from MS T (see Liebermann, I. p. 524 a). It enjoins that the county and hundred courts shall be held as they were in the time of King Edward, and shall not be arbitrarily summoned by the sheriff. The King himself reserves the right of calling an extraordinary meeting of either court. Regulations follow with regard to the courts in which cases between parties of various ranks are to be held. It is noteworthy that no distinction is drawn between Normans and Englishmen, and likewise that trial by combat is regarded as the regular mode of proof.

The date is fixed by Liebermann between May 1109 and August 1111—that being the only time spent by Henry in England between the consecration of Richard as Bishop of London (26 July 1108) and the death of Samson, Bishop of Worcester (5 May 1112). Of these the former signs as a witness, while the latter is named in the Preamble. In the case of both of these documents the text given here follows Sc.

---

[1] Ed. Howlett, *Chronicle of Stephen*, III. p. 142.

THE LAWS OF WILLIAM I AND OF HENRY I

The remaining document, which announces the rights and privileges granted to the citizens of London (Hn Lond), is preserved in various MSS, namely, Lond., Cc (C.C.C. 476, f. 160), Liber Horn, Liber Custumarum, f. 14 (Cus) and f. 187 (Cust), El (Excerptum Lond. in Liber Albus ed. Riley, *Mun. Gildhal. Lond.* I. p. 128), E IV (Patent roll of a. 2 Edward IV, pt. 5, quoted by Brady, *Hist. Treatise of Cities*, App. p. 25 and Rymer, *Foedera*, I. p. 11), Po (Posteriores Chartae London., ann. 1155 and 1199). The present text follows Rs (f. 77). The original text of this document was lost before 1206 (see Round, *Commune of London*, p. 256; Liebermann, *Leges Angl. Lond.* p. 71; Bateson, *E.H.R.* 1902, p. 505). A London Yearbook of about 1250 states (ann. 1209) that it was burned by King John (see *Chr. of Ed. I*, ed. Stubbs, I. p. 14), a statement which is repeated in the fourteenth century Liber memorandorum, f. 121 b.

Liebermann suggests a date between 1115 and 1133 for the issue of the Charter, the probability being in favour of the year 1131. The complaint with regard to "miskenning" made by the compiler of the Leges Henrici, working sometime between 1114 and 1118, suggests that the removal of this abuse came later (cf. Hn 22 and Hn Lond 8). The statement of the Pipe Roll of 1130 that the men of London paid "*C marc ut habeant vicecomitem ad electionem suam*" is also quoted by Liebermann, but is not regarded by him as a convincing proof that the payment fixed by Hn Lond cap. 1 is of later date. He points out, however, that the list of witnesses supports the theory that it belongs to the last years of Henry's reign. Some of them appear later at Stephen's court and all of them seem to have been alive in 1135. Henry was absent from England from the Autumn of 1130 until August 1131 and left again in 1133.

Much that is contained in this charter is without doubt in the nature of a written confirmation of rights and privileges already enjoyed in practice. The most important clause is the first, which confers on the citizens the right of appointing their own sheriff and justiciar and gives them control of the revenues of London and Middlesex in return for the yearly payment of £300 to the King.

WILLIAM I: LONDON CHARTER

1. Willelm kyng gret Willelm bisceop 7 Gosfregð portirefan 7 ealle þa burhwaru binnan Londone, Frencisce 7 Englisce, freondlice.

2. 7 ic kyðe eow þæt ic wylle þæt get beon eallra þæra laga weorðe þe gyt wæran on Eadwurdes dæge kynges.

3. 7 ic wylle þæt ælc cyld beo his fæder yrfnume æfter his fæder dæge.

4. 7 ic nelle geþolian þæt ænig man eow ænig wrang beode.

5. God eow gehealde.

WILLIAM I: LONDON CHARTER

1. King William sends friendly greetings[1] to Bishop William[2] and Geoffrey[3] the mayor[4], and all the burgesses within London, both French and English.
2. I declare to you that it is my will that both of you[1] shall be entitled to all the rights which you had in the time of King Edward.
3[1]. And it is my will that every child shall be his father's heir after his father's death.
4. And I will not suffer any man to offer you any wrong.
5. God keep you!

WILLIAM I: REGULATIONS REGARDING EXCULPATION

Willelmes cyninges asetnysse.

Wilhelm cyng gret ealla[1] þa þe ðys gewrit to cymð ofer eall Englaland freondlice, 7 beot 7 eac cyð eallum mannum ofer eall Angelcynn to healdenne, þæt is:

1. Gif Englisc man beclypað ænigne Frænciscne mann to orneste for þeofte oððe for manslihte oððe for ænigan þingan þe gebyrige ornest fore to beonne oððe dóm betweox twam mannum, habbe he tulle leafe swa to donne.

   § 1. 7 gif se Englisca forsæcð þæt ornest, þe Frencisca þe se Englisca beclypað ladige hine mid aðe ongean hine mid his gewitnesse æfter Norðmandiscere lage.

2. Eft: Gif Frencisc man beclypað Engliscne man to orneste for ðam ylcan þingan, se Englisca be fulre leafe hine werige mid orneste oððe mid irene, gif him þæt gecwemre byð.

   § 1. 7 gif he untrum byð 7 nelle þæt ornest oððe ne mage, begyte him lahlicne spalan.

   § 2. 7 gif se Fræncisca byð ofercuman, he gyfe þam cynge iii pund.

   § 3. 7 gif se Englisca nele hine werian mid orneste oððe mid gewitnesse, he ladige hine mid irene.

3. Æt eallan utlaga þingan se cyng gesette þæt se Englisca ladige hine mid irene.

   § 1. 7 gif se Englisca beclypað Frencisne mid utlagan þingan 7 wille hit þonne on him gesoðian, se Fræncisca bewerie hine mid orneste.

   § 2. 7 gif se Englisca ne durre hine to orneste beclypian, werige hine se Fræncisca mid unforedan aðe.

[1] MS reading.

WILLIAM I: REGULATIONS REGARDING EXCULPATION

King William's ordinances[1].

King William sends friendly greetings to all those throughout England to whom this document comes, and enjoins and instructs all men throughout all England to observe what follows:

1. If an Englishman summons a Frenchman to trial by combat[1] for theft or homicide or for anything for which it is fitting that there should be trial by combat or judicial suit[2] between two men, he shall have full permission to do so.
   § 1. If the Englishman declines trial by combat, the Frenchman, who is accused by the Englishman, shall clear himself against him with an oath supported by those who are qualified by Norman law to be his compurgators[1].
2. Further, if a Frenchman challenges an Englishman to trial by combat for the same things, the Englishman shall have full permission to defend himself by combat or by the ordeal of iron, if he prefers it.
   § 1. And if he is infirm and will not or cannot undertake trial by combat, he shall procure a lawful substitute[1].
   § 2. And if the Frenchman is defeated, he shall give the king £3[1].
   § 3. And if the Englishman will not defend himself by combat or by compurgation[1], he shall clear himself by the ordeal of iron.
3. And in all charges involving outlawry[1] the king has decreed that the Englishman shall clear himself by the ordeal of iron.
   § 1. And if the Englishman brings a charge involving outlawry against a Frenchman, and desires further to prove it against him, the Frenchman shall defend himself by combat.
   § 2. And if the Englishman dare not summon him to trial by combat, the Frenchman shall defend himself by a comprehensive oath[1].

WILLIAM I: EPISCOPAL LAWS

De libertatibus restitutis ecclesiis et ecclesiasticis personis[1].

W[illelmus], Dei gratia rex Anglorum, R[adulfo] Bainardo et G[osfrido] de Magnavilla, P[etro] de Valoines ceterisque meis fidelibus de Essex et de Hertfordschire et de Middelsexe— salutem[2].

1. Sciatis vos omnes et ceteri mei fideles qui in Anglia manent, quod episcopales leges, quae non bene nec secundum sanctorum canonum praecepta usque ad mea tempora in regno Anglorum fuerunt, communi concilio et consilio archiepiscoporum et episcoporum[3] et abbatum et omnium principum regni mei, emendandas iudicavi.

2. Propterea, mando et regia auctoritate praecipio, ut nullus episcopus vel archidiaconus de legibus episcopalibus amplius in hundret placita teneant[4], nec causam quae ad regimen animarum pertinet ad iudicium saecularium hominum adducant[4], sed quicumque secundum episcopales leges de quacumque causa vel culpa interpellatus fuerit, ad locum, quem ad hoc episcopus elegerit et nominaverit, veniat ibique de causa vel culpa[5] sua respondeat, et non secundum hundret sed secundum canones et episcopales leges rectum Deo et episcopo suo faciat.

3. Si vero aliquis, per superbiam elatus, ad iusticiam episcopalem venire contempserit vel[6] noluerit, vocetur semel et[7] secundo et tertio.

   § 1. Quodsi nec sic ad emendationem venerit, excommunicetur; et si opus fuerit ad hoc vindicandum, fortitudo et iusticia regis vel[8] vicecomitis adhibeatur.

---

[1] The heading is found only in Lp.
[2] *W. gr. D. rex Angl' comitibus (et* Ry) *vicecomitibus et omnibus Francigenis et Anglis qui in episcopatu Remigii episcopi terras habent, salutem* Lc, Ry, Insp.
[3] *arch. meorum et ceterorum ep.* Lc, Insp.   [4] *-at* Ry.
[5] *v. c. om.* Lc, Insp.   [6] *c. v. om.* Lc, Insp; *c et* Ry.
[7] Om. Ry.   [8] *sive* Lc.

WILLIAM I: EPISCOPAL LAWS

Concerning the liberties restored to churches and ecclesiastics.

William, by the grace of God King of England, to Ralph Bainard[1] and Geoffrey de Maundeville[2] and Peter de Valognes[3] and the rest of my loyal subjects in Essex, Hertfordshire and Middlesex[4]—greeting[5].

1. Be it known to all of you and the rest of my loyal subjects who dwell in England, that I have decided, in full council and with the advice of my archbishops[1], bishops, abbots and all the magnates of my kingdom, upon the improvement of the conditions of episcopal jurisdiction which, up to my time, has not been of a proper character in England, or in accordance with the precepts of the holy Canon Law.

2. I therefore command and enjoin, by my royal authority, that no bishop or archdeacon shall henceforth hold pleas affecting episcopal jurisdiction[1] in the hundred court[2], nor shall they bring forward any case which concerns spiritual jurisdiction for the judgment of laymen; but whoever has been summoned for some suit or offence which falls within the province of episcopal jurisdiction[1] shall appear at the place appointed and named by the bishop for the purpose, and shall there make answer concerning his suit or offence, and he shall make amends to God and his bishop, not according to the [decree of the] hundred court, but in accordance with the Canon Law and the laws established by the authority of the bishops.

3. If indeed anyone, puffed up with pride, disdains or refuses to appear before the bishop's court, he shall be summoned once, twice and three times.

    § 1. But if even then he will not come to make amends, he shall be excommunicated. And if there is need to enforce this[1], the power and authority of the king or the sheriff shall be employed.

§ 2. Ille autem qui vocatus ad iusticiam episcopi venire noluerit, pro unaquaque vocatione legem episcopalem emendabit.

4. Hoc etiam defendo et mea auctoritate interdico, ne ullus vicecomes aut praepositus seu[1] minister regis nec[2] aliquis laicus homo de legibus quae ad episcopum pertinent se intromittat.

§ 1. Nec aliquis laicus homo alium hominem sine iusticia episcopi ad iudicium adducat.

§ 2. Iudicium vero in nullo loco portetur nisi in episcopali sede aut in illo[3] loco quem episcopus ad hoc constituerit.

In hac eadem carta ponuntur eadem verba Anglico sermone verbo ad verbum[4].

[1] *aut* Lc, Insp.   [2] *nec...intromittat* om. Lc.   [3] Om. Ry.
[4] *In...verbum* Lp.

§ 2. But he who, when summoned, refuses to appear before the bishop's court shall pay the (proper) fine for contempt of the bishop's authority[1] for each time of summoning.

4. I likewise forbid and, by my authority, prohibit any sheriff or reeve[1] or baron[2] or any layman from interfering with the jurisdiction which belongs to the bishop.

§ 1. And no layman shall make a man undergo trial by ordeal without the authority of the bishop[1].

§ 2. Trial by ordeal, likewise, shall not take place anywhere except at the bishop's see or at the place appointed for the purpose by the bishop.

In this same document the same words are put in the English tongue, word for word.

THE TEN ARTICLES OF WILLIAM I

[1]Hic intimatur quid Willelmus rex Anglorum cum principibus suis constituit post conquisitionem Angliae[2].

1. Inprimis, quod super omnia unum vellet Deum per totum regnum suum venerari, unam fidem Christi semper inviolatam custodiri, pacem et securitatem inter Anglos et Normannos servari.

2. Statuimus etiam, ut omnis liber homo foedere et sacramento affirmet, quod infra[3] et extra Angliam Willelmo regi fideles esse volunt, terras et honorem illius omni fidelitate cum eo servare et ante eum contra inimicos defendere.

3. Volo autem, ut omnes homines quos mecum adduxi aut post me venerunt sint in pace mea et quiete.

   § 1. Et si quis de illis occisus fuerit, dominus eius habeat infra quinque[4] dies homicidam eius, si potuerit; sin autem, incipiat persolvere mihi quadraginta sex marcas argenti, quamdiu substantia illius domini[5] perduraverit.

   § 2. Ubi vero substantia domini[6] defecerit, totus hundredus in quo occisio facta est, communiter persolvat quod remanet.

4. Et omnis Francigena qui, tempore regis Eadwardi propinqui mei, fuit in Anglia particeps consuetudinum Anglorum, quod ipsi dicunt on hlóte et an scóte, persolvatur[7] secundum legem Anglorum.
   Hoc decretum sancitum est in Civitate Claudia.

5. Interdicimus etiam ut nulla viva pecunia vendatur aut ematur nisi infra[8] civitates et hoc ante tres fideles testes,

---

[1] Various headings are found preceding *Hic* etc. in the Tripartita, e.g. *Emendationes legis quas Willelmus fecit in Anglia; Decreta (domini regis) W. bastardi et emend. q. posuit in A.; (Incipiunt) decreta W. regis qui Angliam conquisivit, legum mutationes et emendationes, quas in Anglia posuit.*
[2] *Hic...Angliae* om. Rl.   [3] *intra* T and some MSS of Trip.
[4] *quindecim* Hv.   [5] Om. T.   [6] Om. Rl.
[7] Several MSS of the Trip. have *persolvat*.   [8] *intra* T, Hv.

THE TEN ARTICLES OF WILLIAM I

Intimation is hereby given[1] of the enactments made by William, King of England, and his magnates after he had obtained possession[2] of England.

1[1]. In the first place, he desires above all that one God should be honoured throughout the whole of his kingdom, and that one Christian faith should be kept inviolate, and that peace and security should be maintained among the English and Normans[2].

2[1]. Further, we have decreed that all freemen shall affirm by covenant and oath[2], that, both in and out of England[3], they will be loyal to King William, and along with him uphold his lands and honour with the utmost loyalty, and defend them before him against his enemies.

3. I desire likewise that all the men whom I brought with me or who have come after me shall enjoy the benefit of my protection.

    § 1. And if any of them is slain, his lord[1] shall arrest the slayer within five days[2], if he can. If not, however, he shall begin to pay me 46 marks of silver[3] from the property of that lord as long as it lasts out.

    § 2[1]. When, however, the property of the lord fails, the whole hundred in which the murder was committed shall pay in common what remains.

4. But every Frenchman who, in the time of King Edward, my kinsman, was admitted to the status of an Englishman[1], which they call being "in lot and in scot," shall be paid for[2] according to English law.
This decree was enacted at Gloucester[3].

5[1]. Further, we forbid the buying or selling of any livestock except within towns and before three trustworthy witnesses, likewise that of any second-hand goods[2] without a surety

nec aliquam rem vetustam[1] sine fideiussore et waránto. Quodsi aliter fecerit solvat et persolvat et postea forisfacturam.

6. Decretum est etiam ibi, ut, si Francigena appellaverit Anglum de periurio aut mordro, furto, homicidio, rán, quod Angli dicunt apertam rapinam quae negari non potest, Anglus se defendat per quod melius voluerit, aut iudicio ferri aut duello.

§ 1. Si autem Anglus[2] infirmus fuerit, inveniat alium qui pro eo faciat.

§ 2. Si quis eorum victus fuerit, emendet XL[3] solidos regi.

§ 3. Si [autem][4] Anglus Francigen[a]m[5] appellaverit et probare noluerit iudicio aut duello, volo tamen Francigenam purgare se sacramento non fracto.

7. Hoc quoque praecipio et volo, ut omnes habeant et teneant legem Eadwardi regis in terris et in omnibus rebus, adauctis iis quae constitui ad utilitatem populi Anglorum.

8. Omnis homo, qui voluerit se teneri[6] pro libero, sit in plegio, ut plegius teneat et habeat illum ad iusticiam si quid offenderit;

8 a. et si quisquam talium evaserit, videant plegii ut simpliciter solvant quod calumniatum est, et purgent se, quia in evaso nullam fraudem noverunt.

§ 1. Requiratur hundred et comitatus, sicut antecessores nostri statuerunt.

§ 2. Et qui iuste venire deberent et venire noluerint, semel summo[n]eantur[7]; et si secundo venire noluerint, accipiatur unus bos et summo[n]eantur[7] tertio; et si non tertio venerint, accipiatur alius bos.

---

[1] H, Rl, T; readings in other MSS are: *vectam, aportee, nettam* or *veccam, vetitam.*
[2] Om. T, Cb.   [3] LX Cb.   [4] T and Trip; om. H, Rl.   [5] *-nem* H, Rl.
[6] H, Rl; *-ere* T and most MSS of Trip.   [7] *summoue.* H.

and warrantor. If anyone does otherwise, he shall pay the value of the goods twice over and in addition the fine for insubordination.

6[1]. It has likewise been decreed that, if a Frenchman summon an Englishman for perjury or murder, theft, homicide or "ran,"[2] by which the English mean open robbery which cannot be denied, the Englishman shall defend himself by whichever method he prefers, either the ordeal of iron[3] or trial by combat.

§ 1[1]. If, however, the Englishman is infirm, he shall find a substitute to act for him.

§ 2[1]. If either of them is defeated, he shall pay 40 shillings[2] to the King.

§ 3[1]. If, however, an Englishman summons a Frenchman and declines to prove [the charge] by ordeal[2] or by combat, it is my will that the Frenchman shall clear himself by a comprehensive oath[3].

7[1]. I likewise enjoin and desire that all men shall keep and observe the law of King Edward relating to the tenure of estates and all [other] matters, with the additions which I have decreed for the benefit of the English nation.

8. Everyone who desires to keep the status of a freeman shall be in a frankpledge[1], so that the frankpledge may bring him to justice, if he has committed an offence.

8a. And if any such escapes, the members of the frankpledge[1] shall be responsible for the simple payment of what is claimed, and shall clear themselves from [the charge of] any knowledge of fraud on the part of the runaway.

§ 1[1]. The hundred and county courts shall be attended in accordance with the decrees of our predecessors.

§ 2[1]. And those who are legally required to appear before them, and refuse to do so, shall be summoned once; and if they refuse to appear on the second summons, an ox[2] shall be confiscated and they shall be summoned a third time; and if they do not come on the third summons, another ox shall be confiscated.

§ 3. Quarta autem vice si non venerint, reddatur de rebus hominis illius qui venire noluerit quod calumniatum est, quod dicitur ceapgeld, et insuper forisfactura regis.

9. Ego[1] prohibeo ut nullus vendat hominem extra patriam super plenam forisfacturam meam.

10. Interdico etiam ne quis occidatur aut suspendatur pro aliqua culpa, sed eruantur oculi et testiculi abscidantur; et hoc praeceptum non sit violatum super forisfacturam meam plenam.

[1] Several MSS of Trip. read *et*.

§ 3. But if they do not come on the fourth summons, the amount claimed, called the "ceapgeld,"[1] shall be paid from the property of the man who has refused to appear, and in addition the fine for insubordination to the King[2].

9[1]. I forbid anyone to sell a man out of the country[2], under pain of incurring the full fine for insubordination to me.

10[1]. I likewise prohibit the slaying or hanging of anyone for any offence, but his eyes shall be put out and he shall suffer castration; and this decree shall not be violated under pain of incurring the full fine for insubordination to me.

WILLELMI ARTICULI RETRACTATI

Decreta domini regis Willelmi bastardi et emendaciones quas posuit in Anglia quae olim vocabatur Britannia[1].

Hic eciam intimatur &c.[2]

1. Imprimis[3], quidem super omnia unum Deum vellet[4] p. t. r. s. venerari...pacem et securitatem et concordiam, iudicium et iusticiam, inter Anglos et Normannos, similiter inter[5] Francigenos[6] et Britones Walliae et Cornubiae, et[4] Pictos et Scottos Albaniae, similiter inter Francos et insulicolas[7] omnium insularum et[8] provinciarum et patriarum[9] quae pertinent ad coronam et ad[4] dignitatem et ad[10] defensionem et ad[4] observationem et ad[4] honorem regni[11], et[12] inter omnes sibi[13] subiectos per universam monarchiam regni Britanniae firmiter et inviolabiliter modis omnibus[14] observari, ita quod nullus alii forisfaciat in ullo[15] super forisfacturam nostram plenam.

2. Statuimus eciam, ut omnes liberi homines...affirment quod intra et extra universum regnum Angliae[12], quod olim vocabatur regnum Britanniae, Willelmo regi[16] domino suo fideles esse volunt, terras et honores illius[17]...ubique servare cum eo et contra inimicos et alienigenas defendere.

3. Volumus autem et firmiter praecipimus, ut omnes homines quos nobiscum adduximus aut post nos venerint sint sub protectione et in pace nostra per universum regnum praedictum.

§ 1[18]–Cap. 4. Cf. Wl. art. 3 § 1–Cap. 4 (ending with "legem Anglorum").

[1] *Carta regis Willelmi conquisitoris de quibusdam statutis etc.* Sc.
[2] *Willelmus (Dei gratia* K 3) *rex Anglorum dux Normannorum omnibus hominibus suis Francis et Anglis* (*-icis* K 3) *salutem* Sc, Hg, K 3.
[3] *Statuimus* imp. Sc, Hg, K 3.   [4] Om. Sc, Hg, K 3.   [5] *s. i.* om. Sc, K 3.
[6] *Francos* Sc, K 3; *Scancig.* Co, Or.   [7] *insulanos* Sc, Hg, K 3.
[8] *o. ins. et* om. Sc, Hg, K 3.   [9] *provincias et patrias* Sc, Hg, K 3.
[10] *et ad* om. Sc, Hg, K 3.   [11] *r. nostri* Sc, Hg, K 3.   [12] Om. Co, Or.
[13] *nobis* Sc, Hg, K 3.   [14] *m. o.* om. Sc, Hg, K 3.
[15] *nullo* Co, Or, K 3.   [16] Om. K 3.
[17] *suos* Co, Or.   [18] *De Englecherie* is written in the margin of Co, Or.

WILLELMI ARTICULI RETRACTATI

The decrees and legal reforms of our lord King William the Bastard, which he established in England, formerly called Britain.

Notice is hereby given &c.

1. In the first place he desires above all that one God should be honoured throughout the whole of his kingdom,...and that peace, security and concord, law and justice should be observed by all means, firmly and inviolably, among English and Normans, likewise among those of French birth and the Britons of Wales and Cornwall, and the Picts and Scots of Albania, and likewise among the French and the inhabitants of all the islands[1], provinces and countries which appertain to the Crown and to the dignity, defence, maintenance and honour of the realm, and among all his subjects throughout the whole realm of Britain, so that no-one shall do any injury to another in any respect, under pain of incurring the full fine for insubordination to us.

2. We have likewise decreed that all free men...shall affirm that in and out of the whole kingdom of England, which was formerly called the kingdom of Britain, they will be loyal to King William their lord, and everywhere along with him uphold his lands and honours...and defend them against enemies and aliens.

3. We desire likewise and firmly enjoin, that all the men, whom we brought with us or who have come after us, shall enjoy the benefits of protection[1] throughout the whole of the aforesaid realm.

§ 1[1]–Cap. 4. Cf. Wl. art.

5. Volumus eciam et firmiter[1] praecipimus et concedimus, ut omnes liberi homines totius monarchiae regni nostri praedicti, habeant et teneant terras suas et possessiones suas bene et in pace, liberae ab omni exactione iniusta et ab omni tallagio, ita quod nichil ab eis exigatur vel capiatur nisi servicium suum liberum, quod de iure nobis facere debent et facere tenentur, et prout statutum est eis et illis a nobis datum et concessum iure hereditario in perpetuum per commune consilium totius regni nostri praedicti.

6. Statuimus eciam et firmiter[2] praecipimus, ut omnes civitates et burgi et castella et hundreda[3] et wapentagia[4] totius regni nostri praedicti, singulis noctibus vigilentur et custodiantur in girum pro maleficis[5] et inimicis, prout vicecomites et aldermani et praepositi et ceteri[6] ballivi et ministri nostri melius per commune consilium ad utilitatem regni providebunt.

7[7]. Et quod habeant per universum regnum mensuras fidelissimas et signatas, et pondera fidelissima et signata sicut boni praedecessores statuerunt.

8. Statuimus eciam et firmiter praecipimus, ut omnes comites et barones et milites et servientes et universi liberi homines tocius regni nostri praedicti habeant et teneant se semper bene in armis et in equis, ut decet et oportet, et quod sint semper prompti et bene parati ad servicium suum integrum nobis explendum et peragendum, cum semper opus adfuerit, secundum quod nobis debent de feodis et de[8] tenementis suis de iure facere, et sicut illis statuimus per commune consilium tocius regni nostri praedicti, et illis dedimus et concessimus in feodis iure hereditario. Hoc praeceptum[9] non sit violatum ullo modo super forisfacturam nostram[6] plenam.

---

[1] *vol. et h'* (*hoc* Ld) *f.* Co, Or, Ld.
[2] *similiter* Ld.
[3] *-da* Rs, Co, Or; *-di* elsewhere.
[4] *-cha* Co, Or; *-chia* Sc, Hg, K 3.
[5] *-ciis* Co, Or, K 3.
[6] Om. Co, Or.
[7] *De ponderibus et mensuris* has been added in the margin of Sc in the 14th cent.
[8] Om. Sc, Hg, K 3.
[9] *pr. nostrum* Sc.

5. We desire likewise and firmly enjoin and grant, that all free men throughout the whole of our realm aforesaid shall have and hold their lands and possessions properly and peacefully, free from all unjust exaction[1] and from all tallage, so that nothing shall be demanded or taken from them except the free service which they legally owe and are bound to perform for us, in accordance with what we have ordained for them and granted and conceded to them as a hereditary right for all time, with the full consent of our whole realm aforesaid.

6. We likewise decree and firmly enjoin, that all cities, boroughs, castles, hundreds and wapentakes throughout the whole of our realm aforesaid shall be watched and guarded every night on all sides against malefactors and enemies, as our sheriffs, ealdormen, reeves and our other officials and servants shall, with the general approval, best provide for the benefit of the realm.

7[1]. And throughout the whole of the realm they shall have weights and measures which are stamped and thoroughly reliable, in accordance with the decrees of our worthy predecessors.

8. We decree likewise and firmly enjoin, that all earls, barons, knights, tenants by serjeanty[1] and all free men throughout the whole of our realm aforesaid shall always keep themselves well supplied with arms and horses[2], as is fitting and right, and that they shall always be ready and well prepared to perform and fulfil the whole of their service to us, whenever the need shall arise, in accordance with their legal duty to us, by virtue of their fiefs and holdings, and in accordance with what we have ordained for them, with the general approval of our whole realm aforesaid, and have granted and conceded to them [to be held] as fiefs by hereditary right. This decree shall not be violated in any way, under pain of incurring the full fine for insubordination to us.

9[1]. Statuimus etiam et firmiter praecipimus, ut omnes liberi homines totius regni nostri praedicti sint fratres coniurati ad monarchiam nostram et ad regnum nostrum pro viribus suis et facultatibus contra inimicos pro posse suo defendendum et viriliter servandum, et pacem et dignitatem coronae nostrae integram observandam, et ad iudicium rectum et iusticiam constanter modis omnibus pro posse suo sine dolo et sine dilatione faciendam. Hoc decretum sanctitum[2] est in civitate [C]laudia[3].

10. Cf. Wl. art. 5....aliq. rem vetitam[4]....

11. Item nullum mercatum vel forum sit nec fieri permittatur nisi in civitatibus regni nostri, et in burgis clausis[5] et muro vallatis, et in castellis, et in locis tutissimis ubi consuetudines regni nostri et ius nostrum commune et dignitates coronae nostrae quae constitutae sunt a bonis praedecessoribus nostris deperiri[6] non possunt nec defraudari nec violari, sed omnia rite et in aperto et per iudicium et iusticiam fieri debent.

§ 1. Et ideo castella et burgi et civitates sitae[7] sunt et fundatae et aedificatae, scilicet ad tuitionem gentium et populorum regni et ad defensionem regni, et idcirco observari debent cum omni libertate et integritate et ratione.

12-15. Cf. Wl. art. 6-9 (ending with "patriam").

15. § 1[8]. Si quis vero[9] velit servum suum liberum facere, tradet eum vicecomiti per manum dextram in pleno comitatu; quietum illum clamare debet a iugo servitutis suae per manumissionem, et ostendat ei liberas vias et portas, et tradat illi libera arma, scilicet lanceam et gladium, deinde liber homo efficitur.

---

[1] *Quod liberi homines sint coniurati ad dignitates coronae servandas et faciendum rectum iudicium.* In the margin in 14th cent. handwriting in Sc.
[2] *factum* Co.
[3] *London* Sc, Hg; *London* K 3; *Londra* Ld, with *Claudia* in the margin.
[4] *veitam* Rs; *venditam* Co, Or; *aliqua res vendita* Ld.
[5] Om. Sc, Hg, K 3.   [6] *-re* Or, Hg, K 3.   [7] Om. Co, Or, Hg.
[8] *De modo manumittendi servum.* In 14th cent. handwriting in Sc.
[9] *enim* Co, K 2.

9[1]. We decree likewise and firmly enjoin, that all free men throughout the whole of our realm aforesaid shall be brothers sworn to defend to the utmost of their power and strenuously uphold our monarchy and our realm, with all their strength and might, against our enemies, and to maintain inviolate the peace and dignity of our crown, and to execute justice and right judgments constantly by all the means in their power, without guile and without delay. This decree was enacted in the city of Gloucester.

10[1]. Cf. Wl. art. 5.

11. Likewise, no market or fair[1] shall be held or permitted to take place except in the cities of our realm, and in boroughs which are enclosed and walled, and in castles, and in well-guarded places, where the customs of our realm and our common law and the dignities of our crown, which were established by our worthy predecessors, cannot lapse or be defrauded or violated, but where all things must be done duly, openly and in accordance with law and justice.

> § 1. And for this purpose castles, boroughs and cities have been founded and established, namely, for the protection of the races and peoples of the realm and for the defence of the realm, and therefore they should be maintained in full liberty and independence and with the best possible organisation.

12–15. Cf. Wl. art. 6–9.

15. § 1[1]. If anyone, however, desires to set free one of his slaves, he shall present him to the sheriff by the right hand in a full meeting of the county court. He shall declare him free by manumission from the yoke of slavery, and show him that all ways and doors lie open to him, and give him the arms of a freeman, namely, a lance and a sword. Then he shall become a freeman.

16[1]. Item si servi permanserint sine callumpnia per annum et diem in civitatibus nostris vel in burgis nostris[2] muro vallatis vel in castellis[3] nostris, a die illa liberi homines[4] efficiuntur, et liberi a iugo servitutis suae sint in perpetuum.

17. Interdicimus eciam ne quis occidatur vel suspendatur pro aliqua culpa, sed eruantur occuli et abscidantur pedes vel testiculi vel manus, ita quod truncus vivus remaneat in signum prodicionis et nequiciae suae, secundum enim quantitatem delicti debet pena maleficis infligi.

Et ista praecepta et statuta[5] non sint violata super forisfacturam nostram plenam[6].

---

[1] Om. Trip., Ld; *Quod servi fiunt liberi per moram in burgis muro vallatis.* In 14th cent. handwriting in Sc.
[2] .*n.* Sc.   [3] *castris* Sc, Hg.   [4] Om. Sc, Hg.   [5] *et st.* om. Sc, Hg.
[6] Sc, Hg add: *Testibus etc.*; *n. pl. weram* Co, Or; *war.* K 2.

16[1]. Likewise, if slaves have remained for a year and a day, without being claimed[2], in our cities or in our walled boroughs or in our castles, from that day they shall become free men and shall remain for ever free from the yoke of slavery.

17[1]. We likewise forbid that anyone be slain or hanged for any offence, but his eyes shall be put out and his feet or his hands cut off, or he shall suffer castration, so that the trunk remains alive as a sign of his treachery and wickedness; for the penalty inflicted on malefactors should be in proportion to the crime committed.

And these ordinances and statutes shall not be violated, under pain of incurring the full fine for insubordination to us.

THE (SO-CALLED) LAWS OF WILLIAM I

Cez sunt les leis e les custumes que li reis Will. grantad al pople[1] de Engleterre aprés le cunquest de la terre, iceles meimes que li reis Edward sun cusin tint devant lui.

1. Ceo est a saver, pais a seinte iglise. De quel forfeit que hom fet oust[2] e il poust venir a seinte iglise, oust pais de vie e de menbre.

    § 1. E si aucuns meist main en celui ki la mere iglise requereit, si ceo fust u evesqué[3] u abeie u iglise de religiun, rendist ceo qu'il avreit pris[4] e cent souz le[5] forfeit, e de mere iglise de parosse xx souz, e de chapele x souz.

2. E ki enfrei[n]t[6] pais[7] le rei, en Merchenelahe cent souz les amendes. Autresi de hemfare et de agwait purpensé. Ice[z] plai[z] afierent[8] a la curune le rei.

    § 1. E si aucuns vescunte[9] u provost mesfait as humes [de sa baillie][10], e de ceo seit[11] ateint devant[12] justise le [rei][13], forfeit est[14] a duble de ceo que auter fust forfeit.

    § 2. Et ki en Denelahe enfreint[15] la pais le rei, set vint livres e quatre les amendes.

    § 2 a. E les forfez le rei[16] ki aferent al vescunte, xl[17] souz en Merchenelahe e l[18] souz en Westsexenelahe.

    § 3. E cil francs hom ki ad[19] e sache e soche e toll e tem e infangentheof, se il est enplaidé e il seit mis en forfeit el cunté, afert a l'os le vescunte[20] en Denelahe xl ores, et de cel[21] hume ki ceste franchise nen ad xxxii ores.

---

[1] *a tut le puple (peuple* Io) I.   [2] *en (on* Isp) *cel tens* added by I.
[3] *u ev.* om. Io.   [4] *i av. p.* I.   [5] *de* I.
[6] *enfreit* Hk; *enfraint* Im; *enfraiant* Isp; *ensyaint* Io.   [7] *la p.* I.
[8] *Icel plait afert* Hk. The section from the beginning of this clause to cap. 15 is omitted in Isp.
[9] *u quens* I.   [10] I; om. Hk.   [11] *fuist (suist* Io) I.
[12] *de la* I.   [13] *roi* I; om. Hk.   [14] *fust (sust* Io) I.
[15] *fruisse* I.   [16] *le rei* om. Im.   [17] I; L Hk.
[18] I; xl *s. e en.* Hk.   [19] *aveit* I.
[20] *afiert (as-* Io) *al (il* Io) *forfait (-fat* Io) *a oes le v.* I.   [21] *altre* I.

THE (SO-CALLED) LAWS OF WILLIAM I

These are the laws and the rights[1] which King William assured[2] to the people of England after he had obtained possession of the land[3]. They are the same as King Edward his cousin observed before him.

1. [1]. Namely, the protection of holy church shall be inviolable[2]. Whatever crime a man has committed, if he can make his way to a holy church, he shall have protection for life and limb.

    § 1[1]. And if anyone has laid hands on a man who has sought a mother church, whether it be a bishop's church or an abbey or a monastic church, he shall pay for anything he has taken away and a fine of 100 shillings[2], and in the case of the mother church of a parish he shall pay 20 shillings[3], and of a chapel 10 shillings[3].

2. And he who violates the king's peace shall pay 100 shillings[1] as compensation in the province of Mercia. And similarly for attacks on people's houses[2] and for premeditated waylaying[3]. These pleas belong to the King's Crown[4].

    § 1. And if any sheriff or mayor does injury to the men in his jurisdiction and is convicted of this in the King's Court, he shall pay double[1] the fine payable by any other person.

    § 2. And he who, in the Danelaw, violates the King's Peace[1] shall pay £144[2] as compensation.

    § 2a. And [he who violates it in Mercia or Wessex shall pay] the king's fines which belong to the sheriff— 40 shillings in the province of Mercia and 50 shillings[1] in the province of Wessex.

    § 3. And if an accusation is brought against a baron[1] who possesses rights of jurisdiction[2], toll[3], vouching to warranty[4] and the exercise of summary justice upon a thief caught in the act[5], and he has to pay a fine in the county court, 40 ores in the Danelaw shall fall to the sheriff; and 32 ores in the case of a man who does not possess these privileges.

§ 4. De cez XXXII [ores][1] averad le vescunte a l'os le rei x ores, e cil ki le plait averad deredné[2] vers lui XII ores, e le seinur, en ki fiu[3] il meindra, les x ores. Ceo est en Denelahe.

3. La custume en Merchenelahe est[4]: si aucuns est apelé de larrecin u de roberie, e il seit plevi a venir devant[5] justise e il s'en[6] fuie dedenz sun plege, il[7] averad terme[8] un[9] meis e un jur de querre le; e s'il le pot truver[10] dedenz le terme, s'il merra a la justise; e s'il nel pot truver, si jurra sei duzime main que, a l'hure qu'il le plevi, larrun nel sout, ne par lui s'en[11] est fuid, ne aver nel pot.

§ 1. Dunc rendrad le chatel dunt il est retez[12], e XX souz pur la teste, e IIII den. [al][13] ceper, e une maille pur la besche, e XL[14] sol. al rei.

§ 2. E en Westsexenelahe C sol., XX sol.[15] al clamif[16] pur la teste, e IIII lib. al rei.

§ 3. En Denelahe, VIII lib. le forfeit, les XX sol. pur la teste, les[17] VII lib. al rei.

§ 4. E s'il pot, dedenz un an e un[18] jur, truver le larrun e amener a justise[19], si lui rendra cil les XX sol., kis averad oud, e si'n ert[20] feite la justise del larrun.

4. Cil ki prendra larrun senz siwte e senz cri, que cil en lest[21] a ki il avera le damage fait, e il vienge aprés[22], si est resun qu'il duinse x sol. de hengwite, e si[23] face la justise a la primere[24] devise.

§ 1. E s'il passe la devise[25] senz le cunged a la justise, si est forfeit de XL sol.

---

[1] I; om. Hk. [2] *de remied* Io; *de remued* Im, for *dereinied*.
[3] *fin* I. [4] *Cost est l. c.* I. [5] *pl. de v. a* I. [6] *seit* I.
[7] *si* I. [8] Om. I. [9] *de* IIII *m.* I, a corrupt reading for *un*.
[10] What follows from *dedenz…truver* om. I. [11] *ne seu* Im; *ne seut* Io.
[12] *dunt…retez* om. I. [13] I; om. Hk. [14] XX Im.
[15] XX *s.* om. I. [16] *clamur* I. [17] *e les* I. [18] IIII *jurs* I (for *un*).
[19] *a la j.* I. [20] *sinert* Im; *smert* Io; *si n'ert* Hk. [21] *leist* I.
[22] *v. pois ap.* I. [23] *fin* I; emended to (*s*)*i'n* by Liebermann.
[24] *primer'me* Im; *-merme* Io; for *primer[ein]e* Liebermann.
[25] *E…devise* om. Io.

§ 4. Of these 32 ores the sheriff shall reserve 10 for the King and 12[1] for the man who proves the charge against him, and the [remaining] 10 for the lord of the manor to which he (the accused) belongs. That applies to the Danelaw.

3. It is the custom in the province of Mercia, that if anyone, who is accused of larceny or robbery and is under surety to appear before the Court, escapes in the meantime[1], then his surety shall have respite for a month and a day[2] to seek him, and if he can find him within the set time, he shall bring him before the Court, and if he cannot find him he shall swear along with 11 compurgators that, at the time when he took him under surety, he did not know[3] him to be a thief, and that he was not an accessory to his flight, and that he cannot find him.

§ 1. Then he shall pay for the goods[1] on account of which the thief is accused, and 20 shillings[2] in lieu of his head, and 4 pence[3] to the jailer, and a farthing[4] for the spade[5], and 40 shillings[6] to the King.

§ 2. And in the province of Wessex 100 shillings[1] shall be paid—20 shillings to the plaintiff in lieu of the head [of the accused man] and £4 to the King.

§ 3[1]. In the Danelaw a fine of £8 [shall be paid]—20 shillings in lieu of the head [of the accused man] and £7 to the King.

§ 4. And if he can find the thief within a year and a day[1] and bring him to Court, the plaintiff shall restore to him the 20 shillings which he received (as compensation), and justice shall be executed upon the thief.

4. If a man captures a thief against whom no hue and cry has been raised by the injured man, who afterwards comes forward, then it is right that the latter should pay 10 shillings as a fine for neglecting to arrest the thief[1], and satisfy the law in this way[2] at the first meeting of the Court.

§ 1. And if he lets this meeting pass without the permission of the Court, he shall pay a fine of 40 shillings.

256   THE (SO-CALLED) LAWS OF WILLIAM I

5. Cil ki aveir rescut[1], u chevals u bos u vaches u berbiz u pors, que est forfeng apelé en Engleis, cil kis[2] claimed durrad[3] pur la rescussiun[4] VIII den., ja tant n'i ait, mes qu'il i oust cent almaille ne durrad que VIII den.[5];

§ 1. e pur [un][6] por[c] I[7] den., e pur I berbiz I den., e issi tresque a VIII, pur chascune I[7] den., ne ja tant n'i averad ne durrad que VIII den.;

§ 2. e durrad gwage e truverad plege que, si autre vienge aprof dedenz l'an e le[8] jur pur l'aveir demander, qu'il [l'][9]ait a dreit en la curt celui ki l'aveit rescus[10].

6. Autersi de aveir adiré[11], e autersi de[12] truveure—seit mustred de treis parz del visned qu'il ait testimonie de la truveure.

§ 1. E si aucuns vienged avant[13] pur clamer la chose[14], duinst gwage e truist plege[15] que, si auter le cleimt[16] dedenz l'an e un jur, qu'il l'ait a dreit en la curt celui ki l'avera truved.

7. Si hom ocist auter e il seit cunuissant e il deive faire les amendes, durrad de sa manbote al seinur pur le franch hume x sol. e pur le serf xx sol.

8. La were del thein—xx lib. en Merchenelahe, xxv lib.[17] en Westsexenelahe.

§ 1[18]. E la were del vilain—c sol. en Merchenelahe e ensement en Westsexene[19].

9. De la were primereinement rendrad l'om de l'[halsfang][20] a la vedve e as orfenins x sol., e le surplus les parenz e les orfenins partent[21] entre eus.

§ 1. En la were purra il rendre cheval ki ad la coille pur xx sol., e tor pur x sol., e ver[22] pur v sol.

[1] *escut* I.   [2] *qil* I.
[3] *d. al gros. (grefe?* Lieb.) *s. (sive?* Lieb.) *al provost aveir* I.
[4] *l'escussum (-iun* Lieb.) I.   [5] *ja...*VIII *den.* om. Im.
[6] I; *pro porco* L; IIII *pors* Hk.   [7] IIII I.   [8] *un* I.
[9] Lieb.; *i* I.   [10] *celui de que il aveit escus* I.   [11] *endirez* I.
[12] *e de altre* I.   [13] *apref* I.   [14] *jose* I.   [15] *pleges* I.
[16] *si alter claimid (se altre clamud* Io) *l'aveir* I.   [17] xxv *l.* om. Io.
[18] Om. Im.   [19] *-enelae* I.
[20] *hamsochne* Hk; *halt sanc (sainc* Io) I, emended to *hal[sf]anc* by Liebermann.
[21] *departent* I.   [22] *iter* I.

5. If anyone[1] has taken livestock into his care, whether horses or oxen or cows or sheep or pigs[2]—in English called "forfang"—the man who claims them shall pay[3] 8 pence[4] in return for the care taken of them; however many there are up to a hundred head of cattle, he shall not give more than 8 pence.
   § 1. And for a pig, 1 penny, and for a sheep, 1 penny, and so on up to 8, for each 1 penny; however many there are, he shall not give more than 8 pence.
   § 2. And he shall give pledge and find surety, that, if another man comes forward within a year and a day to claim the livestock, he will bring it for decision to the court of the man who had taken it into his care[1].
6. Similarly in the case of strayed livestock, and also in the case of found property; it shall be exhibited in three (different) parts of the neighbourhood[1] so that he may have witness that it was found property.
   § 1. And if anyone comes forward to claim the thing, he shall give pledge and find surety, that, if another claims it within a year and a day, he will bring it for decision to the court of the man who found it.
7. If a man slays another and confesses it and has to make amends, he shall pay *manbot* to the lord of the slain man—10 shillings[1] for a free man, and 20 shillings[2] for a slave.
8. The wergeld of a thegn is £20[1] in the province of Mercia, £25[1] in the province of Wessex.
   § 1. And the wergeld of a villein is 100 shillings[1] in the province of Mercia, and the same in the province of Wessex.
9. As the first instalment of the wergeld 10 shillings[1] shall be paid as *healsfang*[2] to the widow and orphans, and the relatives and the orphans shall divide what remains among themselves.
   § 1. In payment of the wergeld he can give a stallion as the equivalent of 20 shillings, a bull as the equivalent of 10 shillings, and a boar as the equivalent of 5 shillings[1].

10. Si hom fait plaie [a][1] auter e il deive[2] faire les amendes, primereinement lui rende sien leche[feo][3]. E li plaez jurra sur seinz que pur meins[4] nel pot feire ne pur haur si cher nel fist.

§ 1. De sa[r]bote[5], ceo est de la dulur:—Si la plaie lui vient el[6] vis en descuvert, al pouz tuteveies VIII den.[7], u en la teste u en auter liu u ele seit cuverte, al puoz tuteveies IIII den. E de tanz os cum l'om trait[8] de la plaie al os tuteveies IIII den.

§ 2. Puis a[9] l'acordement si lui metera avant honurs e jurra[10] que, s'il lui oust fai[t][11] ceo qu'il lui ad fet[12], e[13] se sun quor lui purportast e s'un[14] cunseil lui dunast, prendreit de lui ceo que offert[15] ad a lui.

11. Si ceo avient que aucuns coupe le puing a l'auter u le pié, si lui rendrad demi were sulunc ceo qu'il est nez.

§ 1. Del poucer lui rendra la meité de la main. Del dei aprés le poucer, XV sol. de sol. Engleis que est apelé quaer[16] denier. Del lung dei, XVI sol. De l'autre ki porte l'anel, XVII sol. Del petit dei, V sol.

§ 2. De l'ungle, s'il le couped de la charn[17], V sol. de souz Engleis. A l'ungle del petit dei, IIII den.

12. Cil ki autrui femme[18] purgist, si forfeit sun[19] were vers sun seinur.

13. Autersi ki faus jugement fait, pert sa were s'il ne pot jurer[20] sur seinz que mieuz nel sout juger.

14. Si hom apeled auter de larrecin e il seit franchs hom[21] e puissed aver testimonie de lealted, se[22] escundirad par plein serment.

---

[1] I; *en* Hk. [2] *denie* (sim. in cap. 7) *otrei f.* I.
[3] Lieb.; *lecheof* Hk; *-fe* I. [4] *mes* I. [5] I; *saib.* Hk.
[6] *a* I. [7] VIII d....*tuteveies* om. I. [8] *trarad* I.
[9] *a l'* om. I. [10] *e. j.* om. I. [11] *fai* Hk.
[12] *qu'il (qil* Im) *ad f. a lui* I [13] Om. I. [14] *soun* Im; *son* Io.
[15] *ce qu'il offre a lui* I. [16] *ço est quer* I. [17] *si il colpe de cascun* I.
[18] *espouse* I. [19] *la* I. [20] *prover* I; *probare* L.
[21] *home e il ait o[u]d (ond* Io, om. Im) *ça'n crere (cauerere* Im; *cauerre* Io) *testimonie* I (Lieb.). [22] *s'en* I.

10[1]. If a man wounds another and has to pay compensation, he shall, in the first instance, pay the cost of his medical attendance[2]. And the wounded man shall swear on the holy relics that he could not do it for less, and that he has not increased the amount out of malice[3].

§ 1[1]. With regard to *sarbot*[2], that is [compensation] for a wound[3]:—If he is wounded on the face, on a part which is visible, for every inch 8 pence[4] shall be paid in every case; if on the head or in any other place where it is hidden, for every inch 4 pence[4] shall be paid in every case. And for every piece of bone drawn out of the wound 4 pence shall be paid in every case.

§ 2[1]. Then at their reconciliation the attacker shall, in the first place, show honour to the wounded man and shall swear that, if the positions had been reversed, and if his heart prompted him and (similar) advice were given him[2], he would accept the compensation offered.

11. If it happens that a man cuts off the hand or foot of another, he shall pay him (as compensation) half his wergeld[1] according to his inherited rank.

§ 1. For the thumb[1] he shall pay him half the value of his hand; for the finger next the thumb[2] 15 shillings according to the English reckoning, that is 4 pence to the shilling; for the middle finger 16 shillings; for the ring-finger 17 shillings; for the little finger 5 shillings.

§ 2[1]. For the nail if it is cut away from the flesh, 5 English shillings [shall be paid], and for the nail of the little finger 4 pence.

12. He who assaults the wife of another man shall forfeit his wergeld to his lord.

13. Likewise, he who gives a false judgment shall forfeit his wergeld, unless he can swear on the holy relics that he did not know how to give a better decision[1].

14. If a man accuses another of theft and the latter is a free man and can produce witnesses to prove that he is entitled to the benefit of the law, he shall clear himself by the simple[1] oath (of exculpation).

§ 1. E ki blasmé unt esté[1] se escundirunt[2] par serment numé, ceo est a saver par XIIII humes leals par num; s'il les pot aver si s'en escundira sei duzime main.

§ 2. E si il aver nes pot, si s'en defende par juise.

§ 3. E li apelur jurra sur lui par[3] VII humes numez sei siste main[4], que pur haur nel fait[5] ne pur auter chose se pur sun dreit nun purchacer.

15. E si aucuns est apeled de mustier fruissir[6] u de chambre, e il n'ait esté en ariere blasmé, s'en escundisse par XIIII[7] humes leals numez sei duzime main.

§ 1. E s'il ait auter fiede esté blasmé, s'en escundisse a treis duble, ceo est[8] a saveir par XLII[9] leals humes numez sei trente-siste main.

§ 2. E s'il aver nes pot, aut a la juise a treis duble, si cum il deust a treis duble[10] serment.

§ 3. E s'il ad larrecin ça en ariere amendé, aut a l'ewe.

16. Li ercevesque averad de forfeiture XL sol. en Merchenelahe, e li eveske XX sol., e li queons XX sol., e li barun X sol., e li socheman[11] XL den.

17. Cil ki[12] ad aveir champestre XXX den. vaillant deit duner le den. Sein Piere.

[17a[13]. Le seignur pur un[14] den. que il dourad si erunt quites ses bordiers e ses boverz e ses serjanz.

17b. Li burgeis qui ad en soun propre chatel demi marc vailant deit doner le dener Seint Pere.]

§ 1. Ki en Denelahe franch hume est, s'il ad[15] demi marc[16] vaillant d'aveir champestre, si duinst[17] le den. Seint Piere[18], e par le den. que li sire[19] durrad si erent quite cil ki meindrunt[20] en sun demeine.

---

[1] altre qui blasmed ait (an Im) ested I.   [2] se esc. om. I.   [3] iur I.
[4] s. s. m. om. I.   [5] fist I.   [6] fruisser I.
[7] XLII al. XLIIII Io; XII Im, Isp.   [8] Om. I.   [9] XLVIII I, L.
[10] dublein I.   [11] vilain I; villanus L.
[12] Franc home qui (qi Im) I; Liber homo qui L.
[13] 17 a and b are from I; om. Hk.   [14] IIII I; pro uno denario L.
[15] e il averad I.   [16] marc en argent I.   [17] devrad duner (dinier Io) I.
[18] s'. P. Hk.   [19] seignur I.   [20] meinent I.

§ 1. And those who have been (previously) accused shall clear themselves by the oath with selected compurgators, that is by means of 14 qualified men nominated [by the court], of whom 11 must act as the accused man's compurgators to clear him of the charge, if he can find as many to do so[1].

§ 2. And if he cannot find them, he shall defend himself against the charge by the ordeal.

§ 3. And the plaintiff shall swear by means of 7 men nominated [by the court], of whom 5 must act as his compurgators, that he does nothing through malice[1] or for any other reason[2] than to obtain his legal right.

15. And if anyone is accused of breaking into a church[1] or a treasury[2], and has no previous convictions against him, he shall clear himself of the charge with 11 compurgators found among 14 qualified men nominated [by the court].

§ 1. And if he has been previously accused, he shall clear himself with three times as many, namely with 35 compurgators found among 42 qualified men nominated [by the court].

§ 2. And if he cannot find them, he shall go to the triple ordeal, just as he had [to produce] a triple oath.

§ 3. And if he has previously paid compensation for theft, he shall go to the water ordeal[1].

16. The archbishop shall have as compensation [for breach of his protection] 40 shillings in the province of Mercia, a bishop 20 shillings, an earl 20 shillings, a baron 10 shillings, and a sokeman[1] 40 pence.

17[1]. He who possesses livestock[2] of the value of 30 pence shall pay Peter's Pence.

[17a. By the payment of one penny on the part of a lord his labourers[1], herdsmen[2] and servants shall be exempt.

17b[1]. A burgess who possesses property of his own of the value of half a mark shall pay Peter's Pence.]

§ 1. A free man in the Danelaw who has livestock worth half a mark shall pay Peter's Pence. And by the payment of a penny on the part of a lord, those who live on his demesne land shall be exempt.

[§ 2[1]. Ki retient le dener Seint Pere, le dener rendra per la justice de seinte eglise e xxx den. forfait.

§ 3. E si il en est plaidé de la justise le rei, le forfait al evesque xxx den. e al rei xl solz.]

18. Cil ki purgist femme a[2] force forfeit ad les menbres.

§ 1. Ki abat femme a terre pur fere lui force, la munte[3] al seinur x sol.

[§ 2[4]. S'il la purgist, forfait est de membres.

19. Si alquns crieve l'oil a l'altre per aventure, quel que seit, si amendrad lxx solz de[5] solz Engleis.

§ 1. E si la pur[n]ele[6] i est remis, si ne rendra lui que la meité.]

20[7]. De relief a[8] cunte ki al rei afert: viii chevals, enfrenez e enseelez [les iiii][9], e iiii[10] haubercs e iiii haumes e iiii escuz e iiii lances e iiii espees. Les autres [iiii][9]: ii[11] chaceurs e ii[11] palefreis a freins e a chevestres.

§ 1. De relief a barun: iiii chevals, les ii[12] enfrenez e enseelez, e ii haubercs e ii haumes e ii escuz e ii espees e ii lances. E les autres ii chevals[11]: un chaceur e un palefrei a freins e a chevestres.

§ 2. De relief a vavassur a sun lige seinur: deit estre quite par le cheval sun pere[13] tel cum il out le jur[14] de sa mort, e par sun haume e par sun escu e par sun hauberc e par sa lance e par s'espee.

§ 2a. E s'il fust desaparaillé qu'il n'oust cheval ne[15] armes, fust quite[16] par c sol.

§ 3[17]. Del relief al vilain: le meillur aveir qu'il averad, u cheval u bof u vache, durrad a sun seinur[18].

§ 3a[19]. E puis seient tuz[20] les vilains en franc plege.

[§ 4[21]. Cil qui tenent lur terre a cense, so[i]t[22] lur dreit relief a tant cum la cense est de un an.]

---

[1] 17, 2 and 3 are from I; om. Hk.   [2] per I.   [3] multe I.
[4] 18, 2–19, 1 from I; om. Hk.   [5] del I.   [6] Lieb.; purvele I.
[7] 20–20, 3 a come after 28, 2 in Hk; this arrangement, adopted by other editors, follows I, L.   [8] al I.   [9] I; om. Hk.
[10] e iiii om. Io.   [11] Om. I.   [12] les ii om. I.
[13] pe[dr]e I (Lieb.); pethe Im; peipe Io.
[14] tel qu'il aveit a jour (jaur Im) I.   [15] ne les a. I.   [16] f. q. om. I.
[17] 20, 3 and 3 a come after 24 in I.   [18] a s. s. de relief (-eif Io) I.
[19] Om. L.   [20] si serait cuz 1, emended to si ser[on]t [t]uz by Liebermann.
[21] I, where it comes after cap. 38; om. Hk; this arrangement follows L.
[22] sort I.

[§ 2¹. He who withholds Peter's Pence shall pay the penny through the court of Holy Church, and 30 pence as a fine.

§ 3. And if he is arraigned in the King's Court, [he shall pay] a fine of 30 pence to the bishop and of 40 shillings[1] to the King.]

18. If anyone assaults a woman he shall suffer castration as a penalty.

§ 1. If anyone throws a woman to the ground in order to offer violence to her, the compensation to her lord for breach of his *mund* shall be 10 shillings.

[§ 2. If he assaults her, he shall suffer castration.

19. If anyone knocks out a man's eye by any kind of accident, he shall pay 70 English shillings[1] as compensation.

§ 1. And if [he destroys the sight] without displacing the pupil[1], he shall pay only half that sum.]

20[1]. The heriot of an earl, which falls to the King, is 8 horses— 4 of them bridled and saddled—4 coats of mail, 4 helmets, 4 shields, 4 lances[2] and 4 swords. Of the other 4 horses, 2 shall be hunters and 2 riding horses with bridles and halters.

§ 1. The heriot of a baron is 4 horses—2 bridled and saddled—2 coats of mail, 2 helmets, 2 shields, 2 swords and 2 lances. And of the other two horses, 1 shall be a hunter and 1 a riding horse with bridles and halters.

§ 2. The heriot of a thegn of lower rank[1] to his liege lord shall be discharged by [delivering up] his father's horse, as it was on the day of his death, his helmet, his shield, his coat of mail, his lance and his sword.

§ 2a. And if he was without equipment, having neither horse nor arms, it shall be discharged by the payment of 100 shillings.

§ 3[1]. The heriot of a villein: he shall give to his lord the best animal that he has, either a horse, an ox or a cow.

§ 3a[1]. And further all villeins shall be in frankpledge.

[§ 4[1]. For those who hold their land by the payment of rent the legal heriot shall be the equivalent of a year's rent.]

21. De entercement de vif[1] aveir: kil voldra clamer pur[2] embled e voldrad[3] duner gwage e truver plege a parsivre[4] sun apel, dunc estuvera celui[5] ki l'avera entre mains numer sun guarant s'il l'ad.

§ 1. E s'il ne l'ad dunc numerad il sun heimelborch [e ses testimonies][6], e ait les a jur e a terme, s'il les ad[7], e li enterceur le mettrad[8] en guage sei siste main, e li auter le mettrad en la main sun guarant u a sun heimelborch, le quel[9] qu'il averad.

§ 1a. E s'il n'ad guarant ne haimelborch e il ait les testimonies qu'il le achatad al marché le rei e qu'il ne set sun guarant ne sun[10] plege vif ne mort, ceo jurrad od ses testimonies od[11] plein serment; si perdera sun chatel, s'il testimonient qu'il heimelborch en prist.

§ 2. E s'il ne pot guarant ne testimonie aveir, si perderad e parsoudrad e pert [sa were][12] vers sun seinur. Ceo est en Merchenelahe e en Denelahge.

§ 3. En Westsexenelahge ne vocherad il mie sun guarant[13] devant[2] iceo qu'il seit mis en guage.

§ 4. En Denelahe mettrad[14] l'om[2] l'aveir[2] en uele main[2] de ici[15] qu'il seit derehdned.

§ 5. Et s'il pot prover que ceo seit de sa nureture, par de[2] treis parz de[2] sun visned, si l'averad derehdné, kar, puis que le serment lui est juged, ne l'en pot l'om[16] puis lever par le jugement de Engleterre.

22[17]. Ki Franceis ocist, e les humes del hundred nel prengent e meinent a la justise dedenz les VIII jurs pur mustrer ki l'ait fet[18], si[19] renderunt le murdre: XLVI[20] mars.

---

[1] The heading in I is corrupt.   [2] Om. I.   [3] il volge I.
[4] parsuire Hk; persuir I.   [5] li stuverad a c. I.
[6] I; om. Hk.   [7] I adds: u s'il les pot aver.
[8] li [m]etrad I corrupted to liueriad Io; luneral Im.
[9] le quel...haimelborch om. I.   [10] le I.   [11] per I.
[12] sa werre I; sun aveir Hk.
[13] s. seignour (-or Io) warant I, where seign. has probably been carried over from the preceding line.
[14] mettre (meitre Io) I.   [15] d'issi la I.   [16] pot pas puis I.
[17] De murdre I.   [18] pur qui il l'a fait I.   [19] sin I.
[20] XLVII m. I, L.

CAP. 21–22

21. The attachment of livestock: if anyone desires to claim it as stolen, and is willing to give pledge and find surety for prosecuting his claim, he who has possession of it must name his warrantor, if he has one.

§ 1. If, however, he does not have one, he shall name his surety[1] and his witnesses, and produce them at the appointed day and the appointed time, if he has them, and the claimant shall give a pledge with 5 compurgators, and the other shall give the livestock into the hands of his warrantor or his surety, whichever of these he has.

§ 1a. And if he has neither warrantor nor surety but has witnesses that he bought it in the public market and that he does not know whether his warrantor or his pledge is alive or dead, he shall swear to this along with his witnesses with a simple oath[1]. In this way he shall lose his goods (but escape punishment), if they bear witness that he obtained a surety for them.

§ 2. And if he can produce neither warrantor nor witness, he shall lose [the goods] and pay in addition [compensation to the claimant][1] and forfeit his wergeld to his lord. This holds good in the province of Mercia and in the Danelaw.

§ 3. In the province of Wessex he shall not call upon his warrantor until the claimant has put himself under pledge.

§ 4. In the Danelaw the livestock shall be placed in neutral hands[1] until the case has been decided.

§ 5. And if he can prove that it is of his own breeding[1] by means of [witnesses drawn from] three (different) parts[2] of his neighbourhood, he shall have won his case, for when once a man's oath has been accepted it cannot be invalidated[3], according to the law of England.

22[1]. If a Frenchman is slain and the men of the hundred do not seize the slayer and bring him to court within 8 days, in order to prove who has done it, they shall pay the murder-fine, namely 46 marks[2].

23. Si hom volt derehdner cuvenant de terre vers sun seinur, par ses pers de la tenure meimes, qu'il apelerad a testimonie, lui estuverad[1] derehdner, kar par estrange nel purrad pas derehdner.

24. De hume ki plaided en curt, en[2] ki curt que ceo seit, fors la u le cors le rei seit[3], e hom lui met sure k'il ad[4] dit chose qu'il ne voille conuistre, s'il pot[5] derehdner par un[6] entendable hume del plait oant[7] e veant qu'il ne l'averad dit, recovré ad sa parole.

[25[8]. De francplegio.
Omnis qui sibi vult iusticiam exhiberi vel se pro legali et iusticiabili haberi, sit in francplegio.]

26. De quatre[9] chemins, ceo est a saveir Watlingestrete, Er[m]ingestrete[10], Fosse, Hykenild[11], ki en aucun de ces quatre[12] chemins ocist aucun[13] ki seit errant par le pais, u asaut, si enfreint la pais le rei.

27. Si larrecin est truved, en ki terre que ceo seit, e le larrun ovoc, li seinur de la terre e la femme averunt la meité de l'aveir al larrun e les chalenjurs lur chatel, s'il le trovent.

§ 1. E l'autre meited, s'il est trové dedenz sache e soche, si[14] perderad la femme e le seinur l'averad.

28. De stretwarde[15].
De chascuns x[16] hides del hundred un hume dedenz la feste seint Michel e la seint Martin.

§ 1. E si li guardireve averad xxx hides, quite serrad pur sun travail[17].

§ 2. E si aveir trespasse[18] par iloc u il deivent[19] guaiter, e il ne puissent mustrer ne cri ne force que lur fust feite, si rendissent l'aveir[20].

---

[1] *l'est*. I (*lescuv*. Io). [2] *a* I. [3] *est* I. [4] *ait* I.
[5] *ne pot* I. [6] II I; *duos* L. [7] Corrupted to *pleidant* in I.
[8] Om. Hk, I; cf. cap. 20, 3 *a*. [9] III I; *tribus* L.
[10] *Erning'st*. Hk. [11] Om. I, L. [12] Om. I. [13] *home* I.
[14] *sil* I. [15] *strew*. I. [16] *des* Io; cf. *de qualibet hida* L.
[17] *Et wardireve si avrad* xxx *h. quites p. s. t.* I; *gwardereve...habebit* xxx *h. quietas pro labore suo* L.
[18] *trespassent* I. [19] Corrupted to *dement* Im; *denient* Io.
[20] In Hk caps. 20–20, 3 *a* follow, then ECf.

23. If a man wishes to prove against his lord that he has an agreement for his land, he must do so by means of his fellow-tenants whom he summons as witnesses, for he cannot do so by means of strangers.
24[1]. When a man carries on a suit in any court other than that in which the king is present in person, and it is maintained against him that he has said something which he will not acknowledge—if he can prove by means of a trustworthy man, who has seen and heard all the suit, that he did not say it, then the validity of his word shall be admitted[2].
[25[1]. Concerning frankpledge.
Everyone who wishes to be admitted to the benefit of the law and to be qualified to obtain legal rights shall be in frankpledge.]
26. If anyone slays or assaults anyone who is travelling through the country on any of the (following) four highways, namely, Watling Street, Ermine Street, the Fosse Way, the Icknield Way[1], he violates the King's Peace[2].
27. If theft is discovered on anyone's land, no matter whose, and the thief is likewise discovered, the lord of the estate and [the thief's] wife shall have half[1] of his property, and the claimants shall have their goods, if they find them.
   § 1. And with regard to the other half[1], if the theft is discovered in a district over which the lord has rights of jurisdiction, the wife shall lose her share and it shall pass to the lord.
28. The guarding of roads[1].
Every 10 hides of the hundred [shall supply] a man between Michaelmas and Martinmas[2].
   § 1. And even if the Commander of the Watch has 30 hides, his duty shall grant him exemption in this matter[1].
   § 2. And if livestock is taken over[1] the stretch [of road] which it is their duty to watch, and they are unable to prove that they have raised an alarm or that force has been applied to them, they must pay compensation for the stock.

29. Cil qui cu[l]ti[v]ent¹ la terre ne deit l'um travailer, se de lour droite cense noun;

§ 1. ne leist a seignurage departir les cultivurs de lur terre, pur tant cum il pussent le dreit seirvise faire.

30. Les naifs² ki *departet de sa terre ne devient cartre faire nauvrie³ quere* que il ne facent lur dreit service que apend a lour terre⁴.

§ 1. Li naifs qui departet de sa terre dunt il est nez, e vent a autri terre, nuls nel retenget ne li ne se[s]⁵ chatels, enz le facet venir arere a faire soun servise, tel cum a li apend.

31. Si les seinurages ne facent altri gainurs venir a lour terre, la justise le facet.

32. Nullui ne toille a soun seinour sun dreit servise pur nul relais que il li ait fait en arere.

33. Si femme est jugee a mort u a defac[iun]⁶ des membres ki seit enceintee, ne faced l'um justice desqu'ele seit delivere.

34. Si home mort senz devise, si departent les enfans l'erité entre sei per uwel.

35. Si le pere truvet⁷ sa file en avulterie en sa maisoun u en la maisoun soun gendre, ben li laist⁸ ocire l'avultere⁹.

[§ 1¹⁰. Similiter si filius matrem in adulterio deprehendit, patre vivente, licet adulterium occidere.]

36. Si home enpuissuned altre, seit occis u permanablement eissilled.

37. Jo jettai voz choses de la nef pur pour de mort, et de ço ne me poez enplaider, kar leist a faire damage a altre pur pour de mort, quant per el¹¹ ne pot eschaper.

§ 1. E si de ço me mesc[re]ez¹² que pur pour de mort nel feisse, de ço m'esp[u]rj[e]rai¹³.

---

¹ *custinent* I.
² The text here is obviously corrupt; the first part of the phrase may have been carried over from the following sentence. For suggested emendations see Liebermann I. p. 512.   ³ Im; *naiuirie* Io.
⁴ L reads: *Nativi non recedant a terris suis nec querant ingenium unde dominum suum debito servitio suo defraudent.*
⁵ *se* I.   ⁶ *defacum* I.   ⁷ *truitet* Io.   ⁸ *laust oure* Io.
⁹ *la ar.* Im.   ¹⁰ L; om. I.   ¹¹ *parele* Io; *per ele* Im.
¹² Lieb.; *mescez* Io; *viescez* Im; *vieltez* Matzke.   ¹³ *mespriorai* I.

CAP. 29–37   269

29. Those who cultivate the land[1] shall not be harassed except for their legal rent[2].
   § 1. It is not permitted to estate-owners to eject the cultivators from their land, as long as they can perform their legal service[1].
30[1]. Peasants born on estates [must not withdraw from their estates or seek an excuse]* for not carrying out the (form of) legal service which obtains on their estate.
   § 1[1]. If a peasant leaves the estate on which he was born and goes to another estate, no-one shall retain either himself or his goods, but he shall be sent back to perform the service which is incumbent on him.
31[1]. If estate-owners do not make another man's workmen return to their estate, the court shall do so.
32. No-one shall withdraw his legal service from his lord on account of any remission which had been granted to him in the past.
33[1]. If a woman who is pregnant is sentenced to death or to mutilation, the sentence shall not be carried out until she is delivered.
34. If a man dies intestate, his children shall divide the inheritance[1] equally among themselves.
35[1]. If a father finds his daughter in adultery in his own or in his son-in-law's house, he shall have full permission to slay the adulterer(s)[2].
   [§ 1. Similarly if a son finds his mother in adultery during his father's lifetime, he shall have permission to slay the adulterer(s).]
36. If a man poisons another, he shall be slain or sent into permanent exile.
37[1]. I cast your things overboard in fear of death, and you cannot bring a charge against me because of that, for it is permitted to cause loss to another through fear of death, when otherwise there are no means of escape.
   § 1. And if you suspect[1] me of acting otherwise than through fear of death, I shall clear myself of the charge.

* Following L.

§ 2. E les choses qui sunt remises en la nef seient departis en comune sulun les chatels.

§ 3. E si alcun jethed les chatels fors de la nef senz busun, sil rendet.

38. Dous sunt perceners de un erithet¹, e est l'un enplaidé senz l'altre, et per sa folie si pert, ne d[e]it² pur ço l'altre estre perdant qui present ne [f]ud³, kar jose juge[e]⁴ entre eus ne forsjuge pas les altres qui ne sunt a present.

39. Ententivement se purpensent cil qui les jugementz unt a faire, que si jugent cum [il]⁵ desirent quant il dient: "Dimitte nobis debita nostra⁶."

§ 1. Ki tort eslevera u faus jugement fra pur curruz [u]⁷ pur hange u pur aveir, seit en la forfaiture le rei de XL solz, s'il ne pot aleier que plus dreit faire nel so[u]t⁸; si perde sa franchise, si al rei nel pot reachater a soun plaisir.

§ 2. E s'il est en Denelae seit forfait de sa⁹ laxlite, s'il alaier ne se pot que il melz faire ne so[u]t¹⁰.

[40¹¹. Ne quis pro parvo delicto morti adiudicetur.

Prohibemus ne pro parvo forisfacto adiudicetur aliquis homo morti; sed ad plebis castigacionem al[i]a¹² pena secundum qualitatem et quantitatem delicti plectatur. Non enim debet pro re parva deleri factura, quam ad ymaginem suam Deus condidit et sanguinis sui precio redemit.]

41. E nous defendun que l'un Christien fors de la terre ne vende, n'ensurchetut en pais[ni]me¹³.

§ 1. Wart l'um que l'um l'anme¹⁴ ne perde que Deu rechatat de sa vie.

42. E qui dreite lei e dreit¹⁵ jugement refuserad seit forfait envers celi ki dreit ço est a aveir.

¹ d'un crichet Io.   ² dit I.   ³ sud I.   ⁴ juge I.
⁵ Om. Io; si Im.
⁶ In I caps. 41 and 41, 1 follow. The arrangement given here follows the Latin and is that adopted by Thorpe, Schmid and Matzke.
⁷ ne I.   ⁸ sont I.   ⁹ Om. Io.   ¹⁰ solt I.   ¹¹ L; om. I.
¹² alta MS.   ¹³ paismune Im; paisumne Io.
¹⁴ laume Im; lamne Io.   ¹⁵ dreite I.

§ 2. And the things which remained in the ship shall be divided in common according to [the value of] the goods [originally belonging to each person].

§ 3. And if anyone casts the goods out of the ship needlessly, he shall pay compensation for them.

38. If two men are sharers in an inheritance, and one is charged without the other, and loses [the case] through his folly, the other who was not present shall not be a loser because of that, for a judgment given in a case between those concerned cannot affect injuriously others who are not present.

39[1]. Those who have to give judgments shall earnestly take heed that they judge as they themselves desire when they say: "Forgive us our trespasses."

§ 1[1]. He who promotes injustice or pronounces an unjust judgment, as the result of rage or malice or bribery, shall forfeit 40 shillings to the King, unless he can declare on oath that he did not know how to act more justly; he shall lose his right of jurisdiction, unless it be the King's pleasure to allow him to redeem it.

§ 2. And in the Danelaw he shall forfeit his *lahslit*, unless he can declare on oath that he did not know how to do better.

[40[1]. That no-one be condemned to death for a trivial crime.
We forbid the practice of condemning a man to death for a trivial offence, but, for the correction of the public, another penalty [shall be devised] according to the nature and magnitude of the crime; for that which God made in his own image and redeemed at the cost of his own blood should not be destroyed for a trivial matter.]

41[1]. And we forbid anyone to sell a Christian out of the country, especially into heathen lands.

§ 1. Care shall be taken not to destroy the soul which God redeemed with his life.

42[1]. And he who refuses [to observe] just law and just judgment shall forfeit a fine to the party who is entitled thereto[2].

272 THE (SO-CALLED) LAWS OF WILLIAM I

§ 1. Si ço est envers l[e][1] rei, VI liv[re]s[2], si ço est envers cunte, XL solz, si ço est en hundred, XXX solz, e envers touz içous ki curt unt en Engleterre—ço est a[s][3] solz Engleis.

§ 2. E en Denelae, qui dreit jugement refuserad seit en la merci de sa laxlite.

43. E ne face [h]un[4] pleinte a rei d'ici que l'un li seit defaili el hundred u el conté.

44. Ne prenge hum nam [nu]l[5] en conté ne defors, d'ici qu'il eit tres foiz demandé dreit el hundred u el conté.

§ 1. E s'il a la terce fiée ne pot dreit aver, alt a[l][6] conté, e le conté l'en asete le quart jurn.

§ 2. E se cil i defa[l]t[7] de ki il se claime, dunt prenge congé que il pusse nam prendre pur le son lu[in][8] e pref.

45. Ne nul achat le vailiant de IIII den., ne mort ne vif[9], sans testimonie ad IIII hommes u de bur[c][10] u de vile.

§ 1. E [s]e[11] hum[12] le chalange e il n'en[13] ait testimonie, si n'ad nul warant, rende l'um[14] a l'hum[15] soun chatel, e le forfait ait qui aver le deit.

§ 2. E si testimonie ad, si cum nous einz desimes[16], voest les treis f[e]iz[17] e a la quart[e][18] feiz le dereinet u il le rende.

46. Nus ne semble pas raisoun que l'um face pruvance sur testimonie ki conussent ço que entercé[19] est, e que nul nel prust devant le terme de VI meis aprés iço que l'aveir [f]u[20] emblé.

47. E cil qui est redté e testimoniet de deleauté e le plait tres foiz eschuit, e al quart mustrent li sumenour de se[s][21] treis

---

[1] *li* I. [2] *livers* I. [3] *al* I. [4] Lieb.; *l'un* Matzke; *bun* Im; *bon plainte* Io.
[5] *mil* I. [6] *a* I. [7] *defait* I. [8] *lum* I.
[9] *de m., vif* Io. [10] *burt* I. [11] *le* I.
[12] Liebermann suggests the addition of *puis*; cf. *postmodum* L.
[13] *vent* Io. [14] *lun* Im. [15] *al un* Io.
[16] *euiz desunes* Io. [17] *faiz* Im; *foiz* Io. [18] *quart* I.
[19] *entre* Io. [20] *su* I. [21] *se* I.

§ 1. If it is to the king, [he shall pay] £6¹, if it is to an earl, 40 shillings, if it is to a hundred, 30 shillings, and [a similar amount] to all those who have a court² in England—the payment to be made in English shillings.

§ 2. And he who in the Danelaw refuses just judgment shall forfeit a fine equal to his *lahslit*.

43¹. And no-one shall appeal to the king until he fails [to obtain justice] in the hundred or county courts.

44¹. No-one shall make distraint of property either in the county court or outside it, until he has demanded justice three times in the hundred or in the county courts.

§ 1. And if on the third occasion he cannot obtain justice, he shall go to the county court, and the county court shall appoint a day when he shall issue his summons for the fourth time.

§ 2. And if the man against whom he is bringing his charge fails to appear, he shall get leave to make distraint for what is his own both far and near.

45¹. No-one shall buy anything 4 pence in value, either livestock or other property, unless he has 4 men as witnesses either from a town or a village.

§ 1. And if anyone claims it and he has no witnesses and no warrantor¹, the goods shall be given up to the claimant, and the fine shall be paid to the party who is entitled thereto.

§ 2. And if he has witnesses in accordance with what we have declared above, vouching to warranty shall take place three times; and on the fourth occasion he shall prove his ownership of it or deliver it up.

46. We regard it as unjust that a man should claim ownership against the witness of those who recognise the thing vouched to warranty. No-one shall claim ownership in less than six months from the time that the livestock was stolen.

47¹. And if anyone who is accused and against whom evidence of untrustworthiness is given fails three times to attend the court proceedings, and if, at the fourth meeting of the

defautes, uncore le mande l'um que il plege truse e vienge a dreit.

§ 1. E s'il ne volt, sil [v]e[ncu]ist[1] l'um vif u mort, si prenge l'um quanque il ad, e si rende l'um al chalangeur sun chatel, e li sire ait la meité del remenant e le hundred la meité.

§ 2. E si nul parent n'ami ceste justise deforcent, seint forfeit envers l[e][2] rei de vi lib.

§ 3. E quergent[3] le larun, ne[4], en ki poesté il seit trové, n'eit warant de sa vie, ne per defense de[5] plait n'ait mes recoverer.

48. Nuls ne receit hom[e][6] ultre iii nuis, si [c]il[7] ne li command od qui il fust ainz[8].

§ 1. Ne nuls ne lait sun hum[e][9] de li partir pus que il est reté.

49. E ki larun encontre e sanz cri[10] a acient l[e][2] leit aler, si l'amend a la vailaunce de larun, u s'en espurge per plenere[11] lei que il laroun nel sout.

50. E ki le cri orat e sursera, la sursise l[e][2] rei amend u s'en espurget.

51. Si est a[l]cons[12] qui blamet seit dedenz le hundred, e iiii humes le retent, sei xii main s'espurget.

52. E chascun seniour eit soun serjant [en][13] sun plege que, si [um]e[14] le rete, que [il l'][15] ait a dreit el hundred.

§ 1. E si il s'ent[16] fuist dedenz[17] la chalange, li sire rende sun were.

§ 2. E si l'un chalange le seignour que per li s'ent[16] seit alé, si s'escundie sei vi main, e s'il ne pot, envers l[e][2] rei l'ament. E cil soit utlage.

---

[1] *ne vist* I for *uēcuist* = *venquist* (Lieb. following Suchier).
[2] *li* I.   [3] Lieb. suggests that a line may be missing; cf. II Cn. 26.
[4] Lieb. following Matzke; *nen en* I.   [5] *defensed plait* Io.
[6] *hom* I.   [7] *til* I.   [8] *amz* Im; *aniz* Io.   [9] *hum* I.
[10] *qui* Io.   [11] *plevere* Im; *plener* Io.
[12] *asc.* I.   [13] *u* I.   [14] *ne* Im (for *ūe* Lieb.); *si nel r.* Io.
[15] Lieb. following Matzke; om. I.   [16] *seut* Io; *sen* Im.
[17] *suist de duz* Io.

court, the summoners bring forward his three defections, he shall once more be asked to find a surety and appear before the court.

§ 1. And if he refuses, he shall be seized, alive or dead, and all that he has shall be taken, and the value of his goods shall be paid to the claimant, and the lord [of the thief] shall take half of what remains and the hundred half.

§ 2. And if any relative or friend opposes by force this exercise of justice, he shall pay a fine of £6[1] to the King.

§ 3. And they shall search for the thief; and no matter in whose power he is found, he shall have no protection for his life, nor shall he be able to get redress by legal process.

48[1]. No-one shall entertain a man for more than 3 days, unless he is committed to his charge by the man with whom he was formerly serving.

§ 1. And no-one shall let any of his men leave him after an accusation has been brought against him.

49. And if anyone comes upon a thief and of his own accord lets him escape, without raising the hue and cry, he shall make compensation by the payment of the thief's value, or he shall clear himself by the full oath, [asserting] that he did not know him to be a thief.

50. And if anyone hears the hue and cry and neglects it, he shall pay the fine for neglecting it to the king, or clear himself.

51[1]. If there is anyone who has charges brought against him in the hundred court to such an extent that 4 men accuse him, he shall clear himself with 11 compurgators[2].

52[1]. And every lord shall be personally responsible as surety for his servant so that, if an accusation is brought against him, he shall bring him for trial in the hundred court.

§ 1. And if he escapes while he is under the accusation, the lord shall pay his wergeld.

§ 2. And if the lord is accused of being an accessory to his flight, he shall clear himself with 5 compurgators, and if he cannot, he shall pay compensation to the king; and the man shall be an outlaw.

THE CORONATION CHARTER OF HENRY I

Institutiones Henrici regis[1].

[2]Anno incarnationis Dominicae MCI, Henricus, filius Willelmi regis, post obitum fratris sui Willelmi Dei gratia rex Anglorum, omnibus [baronibus et][3] fidelibus suis tam Francigenis quam Anglis[4] salutem.

1. Sciatis me Dei misericordia et communi consilio[5] baronum totius regni Angliae eiusdem regem coronatum esse.

   § 1. Et quia regnum oppressum erat iniustis[6] exactionibus, ego, Dei respectu et amore quem erga vos [omnes] habeo, sanctam Dei aecclesiam inprimis liberam facio[7], ita quod nec[8] vendam nec ad firmam ponam nec, mortuo archiepiscopo sive episcopo sive abbate, aliquid accipiam de dominio aecclesiae vel de hominibus eius donec successor in eam ingrediatur.

   § 2. Et omnes malas consuetudines quibus regnum Angliae iniuste opprimebatur inde aufero, quas malas consuetudines ex parte hic[9] pono.

2. Si quis baronum meorum, comitum sive aliorum qui de me tenent, mortuus fuerit, heres suus non redimet terram suam sicut faciebat[10] tempore fratris mei, sed iusta et legitima relevatione relevabit eam.

   § 1. Similiter et homines baronum meorum iusta et legitima relevatione relevabunt terras suas de dominis suis.

3. Et si quis baronum vel aliorum[11] hominum meorum filiam suam nuptum tradere voluerit, sive sororem sive neptem

---

[1] H, M, Hk; *Magna carta H. I. r. Angliae* Gl; *Carta regis H. I., filii regis Willelmi, de libertatibus concessis Anglis in (sua* Hg) *coronacione; et habuit quilibet comitatus Angliae talem* Sc 2, Hg.
[2] *Anno...f. s. W.* H, Rl; *Henricus r. Anglorum Samsoni episcopo et Ursoni de Abetot et o. b. et f. s. t. F. q. Angligenis de Wirecestrescira salutem* Sc 2; *H. D. g. r. Angliae Hugoni de Boclande vicecomiti (iusticiario Angliae* Alb 1213) *et o. f. s. t. Francis (-cigenis* Alb 1213) *q. Anglis in Her(t)fordscire (iIeref.* Alb) *salutem* Alb.
[3] Om. H, Rl, Haug.   [4] *-icis totius Angliae* Haug.
[5] *c. et assensu* Lond.   [6] *in. occasionibus et* Lond.
[7] *concedo* Haug; *esse concedo* Gl.   [8] *nec eam* Alb, Haug, Br.
[9] *suppono* Q, Sc, Lond.   [10] *facere consueverat t. patris* Alb.   [11] Om. Q.

THE CORONATION CHARTER OF HENRY I

The Statutes of King Henry.

In the year of the incarnation of our Lord 1101[1], Henry, son of King William, after the death of his brother William, by the grace of God King of England, to all his barons and loyal subjects both French and English—greeting[2].

1. Be it known to you that, by the mercy of God and with the full consent of the barons of the whole realm of England, I have been crowned king of the afore-mentioned realm.

    § 1[1]. And because the realm had been harassed by unjust exactions, I, in veneration of God and for the love which I bear towards you all, in the first place establish the liberty of the holy church of God, in such wise that I shall not sell any of the demesne land of the church or let it or, on the death of an archbishop, bishop or abbot, take anything from it, or from the men belonging to it, until a successor enters upon office.

    § 2. And I abolish all the evil practices with which the realm of England was unjustly oppressed, and these evil practices I herewith set down in part.

2. If any of my barons, earls or other tenants-in-chief has died, his heir shall not redeem his land as he did in the time of my brother[1], but he shall pay the just and lawful relief for it.

    § 1. Similarly, the vassals of my barons shall pay the just and lawful relief for their lands to their lords.

3. And if any of my barons or my other vassals wishes to bestow in marriage his daughter or his sister or his niece

sive cognatam, mecum inde loquatur, sed neque ego aliquid de suo pro hac licentia accipiam, neque defendam ei quin eam det, excepto si eam vellet[1] iungere inimico meo.

§ 1. Et si, mortuo barone vel alio homine meo, filia heres remanserit, illam dabo consilio baronum meorum cum terra sua.

§ 2. Et si, mortuo viro[2], uxor eius remanserit et sine liberis fuerit, dotem suam et maritationem[3] habebit, et eam non dabo marito nisi secundum velle suum.

4. Si vero uxor cum liberis remanserit, dotem quidem[4] et maritationem[5] habebit dum corpus suum legitime servaverit, et eam non dabo nisi secundum velle suum.

§ 1. Et terrae et liberorum custos erit sive uxor sive alius propinquarius[6] qui iustius esse debeat[7].

§ 2. Et praecipio ut barones mei similiter se contineant erga filios et[8] filias vel uxores hominum suorum.

5. Monetagium commune quod capiebatur per civitates et comitatus, quod non fuit tempore regis Edwardi, hoc ne amodo sit[9] omnino defendo.

§ 1. Si quis captus fuerit, sive monetarius sive alius, cum falsa moneta, iusticia recta inde fiat.

6. Omnia placita et omnia debita quae fratri meo debebantur condono exceptis rectis firmis meis[10] et exceptis illis quae pacta erant pro aliorum hereditatibus vel pro eis rebus quae iustius aliis contingebant.

§ 1. Et si quis pro hereditate sua aliquid pepigerat[11] illud condono, et omnes relevationes quae pro rectis hereditatibus[12] pactae fuerant[13].

---

[1] *velit* M, Lond; *voluerit* Br; *dare vellet* (*voluerit* 1100) Alb; *nubere voluerit* Gl.
[2] H, Rl; *marito* elsewhere.   [3] *m. suam* Rl; *maritagium* Alb, S.
[4] *suam* Alb, Rs.   [5] *maritagium* Alb, S.
[6] H, Rl; *-quior* Alb, Lond; *-quorum* elsewhere.
[7] H, Rl; *debet* Alb; *debebit* elsewhere.   [8] *vel* Sc 2, Haug, Gl, Sc, T.
[9] *fiat* Alb, Q, Gl.   [10] Om. Sc 2, Hg.
[11] *-git* Haug; *-gerit* Dm, T, Lond.   [12] *hereditationibus* Sc 2, Hg.
[13] H, Rl; *sunt erant* Sc 2, Hg; *erant* elsewhere.

or any [other] female relative he shall consult me on the matter¹, but I shall not take anything from him² in return for my permission, nor shall I forbid him to bestow her in marriage, unless he desires to marry her to an enemy of mine.

§ 1. And if, on the death of a baron or any other vassal of mine, his daughter is left as heiress, I shall bestow her in marriage, with the consent of my barons, along with her land.

§ 2. And if, on the death of her husband, a wife is left and has no children, she shall have her marriage-settlement¹ and dowry², and I shall not bestow her in marriage except in accordance with her wishes.

4. But if the wife is left with children, she shall have her marriage-settlement¹ and dowry as long as she observes continence, and I shall not bestow her in marriage except in accordance with her wishes.

§ 1. And the guardian of the land and children shall be either the wife or some other relative who has a better right.

§ 2¹. And I enjoin upon my barons to act with like moderation towards the sons and daughters and the wives of their vassals.

5. I entirely forbid the continuance of the mint-tax¹ levied on cities and counties as against the practice of King Edward's time.

§ 1¹. If a moneyer or any other person has been seized with false money, the process fitted to the case shall be carried out.

6¹. I remit all pleas and all debts which were owing to my brother, with the exception of my legal rents and the payments which had been agreed upon with regard to the inheritances of others or with regard to property which more justly belonged to others.

§ 1. And if anyone had agreed to pay anything for his inheritance I remit it, and all reliefs which had been agreed upon in order to obtain lawful inheritances.

7. Et si quis baronum vel hominum meorum infirmabitur, sicut ipse dabit vel dare disponet[1] pecuniam suam ita datam esse concedo.

§ 1. Quodsi ipse praeventus armis vel infirmitate pecuniam suam non dederit vel dare disposuerit, uxor sua sive liberi aut parentes et[2] legitimi homines[3] eius eam[4] pro anima eius dividant sicut eis melius visum fuerit.

8. Si quis baronum vel hominum meorum forisfecerit, non dabit vadium in misericordia pecuniae[5] suae, sicut faciebat[6] tempore patris mei vel fratris mei, sed secundum modum forisfacti ita emendabit sicut emendasset retro a tempore patris mei[7] in tempore aliorum antecessorum meorum.

§ 1. Quodsi perfidiae vel sceleris convictus fuerit, sicut iustum fuerit[8] sic emendet.

9. [9]Murdra etiam retro ab illa die qua in regem coronatus fui omnia[10] condono; et ea quae amodo facta fuerint iuste emendentur secundum lagam regis Edwardi.

10. Forestas omni[11] consensu baronum meorum in manu mea retinui[12] sicut pater meus eas habuit.

11. Militibus, qui per loricas terras suas defendunt[13], terras dominicarum carrucarum suarum quietas ab omnibus gildis[14] et omni opere proprio dono meo[15] concedo, ut[16], sicut tam magno [gravamine][17] alleviati sunt, ita equis et armis se bene instruant, ut[18] apti et parati sint ad servitium meum et ad defensionem regni mei.

12[4]. Pacem firmam in toto regno meo pono et teneri amodo praecipio.

---

[1] *-posuerit* Alb; *-posuit* Hl.   [2] H, Rl, Haug, Gl, Alb; elsewhere *aut*.
[3] *h. et gentes* Lond.   [4] Om. Q, Sc.   [5] *totius p.* Q, Sc, Hl, S.
[6] *assuetum erat* Lond.   [7] *vel fratris* Alb 1100; *et fr. mei* Q, Sc.
[8] *sicut erit culpa* Alb.   [9] *De confirmatione legum Edwardi regis* Sc.
[10] *omnino* Sc 2, Hg.
[11] H, Rl; *omni assensu et communi consilio* Lond; *communi con.* elsewhere.
[12] H, Rl, Lond; *ita ret.* elsewhere.
[13] H, Rl, Br, Alb; *deserviunt* elsewhere; *defendunt et des.* Lond.
[14] H, Rl, M, Br; elsewhere *geldis*.   [15] *omnino* added in Lond.
[16] *sicut benignitas mea propensior est in eis, ita michi fideles (-liores) sint et* Q, Lond.
[17] *allevamine* H, Rl.   [18] *ut prompti et* Lond.

7. And if any of my barons or vassals is ill, I grant that his personal property[1] shall be bestowed as he himself bestows it or directs by will for its bestowal.

   § 1. But if he has been prevented by military duty or illness from bestowing his personal property or from directing its bestowal by will, his wife or his children or his relatives and his liege-men[1] shall divide it for the good of his soul as it shall seem best to them.

8. If any of my barons or vassals has committed a misdeed, he shall not forfeit as security the whole of his personal property, as he did in the time of my father or my brother, but he shall make amends according to the nature of the offence, as he did before my father's time in the time of my other predecessors.

   § 1. But if he has been convicted of treason or felony[1], he shall make amends as has been established by law.

9. I likewise remit all murder fines incurred before the day on which I was crowned king, and for those which have been committed since then amends shall duly be made in accordance with the law of King Edward[1].

10[1]. With the full consent of my barons I have retained the forests in my own hands as my father did.

11. To knights who hold their lands by military service[1] I grant, by my own gift, that the lands which they hold in demesne[2] shall be free from all payments and from all labour services, so that, as the result of being freed from so great a burden, they may equip themselves fittingly with horses and arms in order to be prepared and ready for service to me and for the defence of my realm.

12. I establish lasting peace throughout the whole of my realm and enjoin that it be maintained henceforth.

13. Lagam regis Edwardi vobis reddo cum illis emendationibus quibus pater meus eam emendavit consilio baronum suorum.

14. Si quis aliquid de rebus meis[1] vel de rebus alicuius post obitum Willelmi regis, fratris mei, cepit, totum cito sine emendatione reddatur.

§ 1. Et si quis inde aliquid retinuerit, ille super quem inventum fuerit graviter mihi emendabit[2].

Testibus[3]: M. Londoniae episcopo, et Gundulfo[4] episcopo et Willelmo, electo episcopo, et Henrico comite et Simone comite et Waltero Giffardo et Rodberto de Monfort[5] et Rogero Bigoto et Henrico de Portu[6].

Apud[7] [Westmonasterium][8] quando fui coronatus[9].

[1] H, Rl; elsewhere *de meo*.
[2] *Presentis vero ecclesiae monachis libertates, dignitates regiasque consuetudines sibi per cartas regum olim confirmatas concedo* added in Lond, Cust.
[3] *Testibus archiepiscopis, episcopis, comitibus* (om. M, bar. com. Sc), *baronibus, vicecomitibus et optimatibus totius regni Angliae* Q, Sc.
[4] Perhaps wrongly for *G[erardo]* (Lieb.). [5] *Mumf.* Rl.
[6] *M....Portu* H, Rl; *Mauricio Lundoniensi episcopo et Willelmo electo Wintoniensi episcopo et Gerardo Herefordensi episcopo* [*et G[ilberto] abbate Crispino*] *et Henrico comite et Simone comite et Waltero Gifardo et Rodberto de Muntforte et Rogero Bigodo et Eudone dapifero et Roberto filio Hamonis et Roberto Malet* (*et Rog....Malet* om. Gl, Lond; *aliis multis* for *Eu....Malet.* Alb) elsewhere.
[7] *Apud...cor.* om. Alb, Lond. [8] *Londoniam* H, Rl.
[9] *Valete* is added in Sc 2, Haug.

13. I restore to you the law of King Edward with all the reforms which my father introduced with the consent of his barons.

14. If anyone, after the death of King William my brother[1], took possession of anything belonging to me or to any [other] person, it shall be restored immediately in full but without payment of compensation.

> § 1. But if anyone shall thereafter retain anything, he in whose possession it is found shall pay heavy compensation to me.

Witnesses: M[aurice], Bishop of London[1], and Bishop Gundulf[2] and William, Bishop elect[3], and Earl Henry[4] and Earl Simon[5] and Walter Giffard[6] and Robert de Montfort[7] and Roger Bigot[8] and Henry de Port[9].

At Westminster when I was crowned.

HENRY I: DECREE CONCERNING THE COINAGE

Carta eiusdem[1] de moneta falsa et cambiatoribus.

Henricus, rex Anglorum, Samsoni episcopo et Ursoni de Abetot et omnibus baronibus, Francis et Anglis[2], de Wirecestrescira, salutem.

1. Sciatis quod volo et praecipio, ut omnes burgenses et omnes illi qui in burgis morantur, tam Franci quam Angli, iurent tenere et servare monetam meam in Anglia, ut non consentiant falsitatem[3] monetae meae.

2. Et si quis cum falso denario inventus fuerit, si warant[4] inde revocaverit, ad eum ducatur, et si illum[5] inde conprobare poterit, fiat iusticia mea de ipso warant.

    § 1. Si vero non poterit illum[5] probare, de ipso falsonario fiat iusticia mea, scilicet de dextro pugno et testiculis.

    § 2. Si autem nullum warant[4] inde[6] revocaverit, portet[7] inde iudicium, se nescire nominare vel[6] cognoscere[6] aliquem a quo acceperit.

3. Praeterea defendo[6], ne aliquis monetarius denarios[8] mutet, nisi in comitatu suo et hoc coram duobus legittimis testibus de ipso comitatu.

    § 1. Et si in ali[o][9] comitatu mutando denarios[10] captus fuerit, captus sit[11] ut falsonarius.

4. Et nullus sit ausus cambire denarios nisi monetarius.

Teste Willelmo[12] cancellario et Roberto Comite de Mellent et R[odberto] filio Hamonis et R[icardo] de Retuers[13]. Apud Westmonasterium in natale Domini.

[1] *regis Henrici* I, K. [2] *-icis* K. [3] *-te* K. [4] *-nitum* K.
[5] *-ud* K. [6] Om. K. [7] *poterit* K. [8] *-ium* K.
[9] *ali* Sc, K. [10] *-io* K. [11] *si c. s.* Sc, Hg, K.
[12] *-mus* Sc. [13] *Reuers* Hg, K.

HENRY I: DECREE CONCERNING THE COINAGE

Order of Henry I with regard to false money and moneychangers.

Henry, King of England, to Bishop Samson[1] and Urso d'Abetot[2] and all the barons of Worcestershire, both French and English—greeting.

1. Be it known to you that I desire and enjoin, that all burgesses and all those, both French and English, who dwell in boroughs shall swear so to maintain and preserve my money in England that they will countenance no falsification of my money.
2. [1]. And if anyone has been discovered with false money, and has vouched a warrantor for it, the prosecution shall be directed against the latter, and if he [the original defendant] succeeds in proving him guilty, justice in accordance with my laws shall be executed upon the warrantor himself.
    § 1. If, however, he does not succeed in proving him guilty, justice in accordance with my laws shall be executed upon the forger himself, namely, he shall lose his right hand[1] and suffer castration.
    § 2. If, however, he has not vouched a warrantor for it, he shall go to the ordeal[1] to prove that he is unable to name or recognise anyone [as the person] from whom he received it.
3. In addition, I forbid any moneyer to recast money, except in his own county and in the presence of two lawful witnesses from the same county.
    § 1. And if he has been seized recasting money in another county[1], he shall be regarded as a forger.
4. [1]. And no-one shall venture to change money except a moneyer.

Witnesses: Chancellor William[1] and Earl Robert de Meulan[2] and Robert FitzHamo and Richard de Retuers. At Westminster at Christmas.

HENRY I: DECREE CONCERNING THE COUNTY AND HUNDRED COURTS

Carta eiusdem ubi comitatus teneri debet et ubi placita de divisis terrarum[1].

Henricus (Dei gratia)[2] rex Anglorum, Samsoni episcopo et Ursoni de Abetot et[3] omnibus baronibus[4] suis Francis et Anglis[5] de Wirecestrescira[6], salutem.

1. Sciatis quod concedo et praecipio ut amodo comitatus mei et hundreda in illis locis et [e]isdem[7] terminis[8] sedeant sicut sederunt in tempore regis Eadwardi, et non aliter.

2[9]. Et nolo[10] ut vicecomes meus propter aliquod necessarium suum quod sibi pertineat faciat ea sedere aliter.

  § 1. Ego enim, quando voluero, faciam ea satis summonere[11] propter mea dominica necessaria ad[12] voluntatem meam.

3. Et si amodo exurgat placitum de divisione terrarum vel de preocupatione[13], si est inter[14] barones meos dominicos, tractetur placitum in curia mea.

  § 1[9]. Et si est inter vavasores alicuius baronis mei honoris, tractetur placitum in curia domini eorum.

  § 2. Et si est inter vavasores duorum dominorum, tractetur in comitatu.

  § 3. Et hoc duello fiat nisi in eis remanserit.

4. Et volo et praecipio ut omnes de comitatu eant ad comitatus[15] et hundreda sicut fecerunt in tempore regis Eadwardi, nec rem[aneat][16] propter aliquam[17] pacem meam vel quietudinem qui non sequ[a]ntur[18] placita mea et iudicia mea sicut tunc temporis fecissent.

Teste[19]—R[icardo] episcopo Lundoniae et Rogero episcopo et Ranulfo cancellario et R[odberto] comite de Mellent, apud Rading'.

[1] Sc, Hg, K; *Epistola Henrici regis ad omnes fideles suos* T.
[2] Q, Co; om. Sc, Hg, K.   [3] *Sa....Ab. et* om. Q, Co.   [4] *fidelibus* Q, Co.
[5] *-icis* K.   [6] *de W.* om. Q, Co.   [7] *hisdem* Sc, Hg; *isdem* Co.
[8] *terris* K.   [9] Om. Sc, Hg, K.   [10] *volo* Co.   [11] *submoneri* Q, Co.
[12] *-cessitate secundum* Q, Co.   [13] *vel...preoc.* om. Sc, Hg. K.
[14] *interest* K.   [15] *-tum* K.
[16] *remorent* Sc, K; *remaneant* M, Hk.   [17] *aliq. causam* Sc, Hg, K.
[18] *-quuntur* Sc, K; *-atur* M, Hk; *persequatur* T.
[19] *Teste...Rading'* om. Q, Co; *Huius carte transcriptum habui apud Sanctum Augustinum extra Cantuariam* Co.

HENRY I: DECREE CONCERNING THE COUNTY AND HUNDRED COURTS

Order of Henry regarding the places where the County Court and cases concerning the division of lands ought to be held.

Henry, [by the grace of God] King of England, to Bishop Samson and Urso d'Abetot and all his barons in Worcestershire, both French and English—greeting[1].

1. Be it known to you that I grant and enjoin, that henceforth my county and hundred courts shall sit at those times[1] and in those places, when and where they sat in the time of King Edward, and not otherwise.

2. And it is not my wish that my sheriff should make them sit at any other time or in any other place for any business pertaining to himself[1].
   § 1. For I, when I so desire, shall have them summoned, in accordance with my will, a sufficient number of times, in order to transact the business pertaining to the crown.

3. And if henceforth a case arises concerning the division or occupation of lands—if it is between crown barons[1] of mine, the case shall be dealt with in my court.
   § 1. And if it is between the vassals of a crown baron of mine, the case shall be dealt with in their lord's court.
   § 2. And if it is between the vassals of two lords, it shall be dealt with in the county court[1].
   § 3. And the proof shall be by combat, unless they agree to some other mode of proof[1].

4. And I desire and enjoin, that all those belonging to the county shall attend the county and hundred courts as they did in the time of King Edward, and the fact of being under any special peace or protection of mine shall not exempt them from taking part in the cases and decisions of my courts, as they used to do at that time[1].

Witnesses: Richard, Bishop of London, and Bishop Roger[1] and Chancellor Ranulf[2] and Earl Robert de Meulan[3], at Reading[4].

HENRY I: LONDON CHARTER

Item epistola eiusdem omnibus fidelibus suis[1] [de libertate civitatis Lond.][2].

Henricus, Dei gratia[3] rex Angliae[4], archiepiscopo Cantuar[iensi][5] et episcopis et abbatibus et comitibus et baronibus et iusticiis et vicecomitibus et omnibus fidelibus suis, Francis et Anglicis, tocius Angliae—salutem.

1. Sciatis me concessisse civibus meis Londoniarum tenendum Middlesexe ad firmam pro CCC libris ad compotem, ipsis et heredibus suis de me et heredibus meis, ita quod ipsi cives ponent vicecomitem, qualem voluerint, de se ipsis et iusticia[m][6], qualem[7] voluerint, de se ipsis ad custodienda[8] placita coronae meae et ad eadem placitanda; et nullus alius erit iusticia[9] super ipsos homines Londoniarum.

2. Et cives non placitabunt extra muros civitatis pro nullo[10] placito.

    § 1. Et sint quieti de eschot[11] (7 de loth)[12] et de danegeldo et de murdre.

    § 2. Et nullus eorum faciat bellum.

3. Et si quis civium de placitis coronae implacitatus fuerit, per sacramentum quod iudicatum fuerit in civitate, se disrationet homo London.

4. Et infra muros civitatis nullus hospitetur, neque de mea familia neque de alia vi[13] alicui [hospitium][14] liberatur[15].

---

[1] Rs, K. [2] K, om. Rs; *De libertate Lond.* Co, Or. [3] *H. d. g.* om. Cc.
[4] *A. etc.* Cc. [5] Lieb. following Brady and Rymer; *-tuariae* K.
[6] Lieb.; *-ciarium* Cust, Horn; *et ius....ipsis* om. Co.
[7] *quemcunque vel qual.* Cc, El, Horn Cust, E IV.
[8] Rs, El, Cust, E IV; elsewhere *-dum.*
[9] Altered to *-ciarius* K; *-ciarius* elsewhere.
[10] *ullo* Cust, El, E IV, Po.   [11] Lond, Cus; *schot* Horn, Cust, El, E IV.
[12] 7 *de loth (lot)* Rs, Cc, E IV, Horn, Cust, El.
[13] *nisi* Or, Thorpe; *per vim* Po.
[14] Om. Rs, Cc, Cust; superscribed in Horn.
[15] Rs, Cus, Cust; elsewhere *-etur.*

HENRY I: LONDON CHARTER

Letter of the same to all his subjects concerning the freedom of the city of London.

Henry, by the grace of God King of England, to the Archbishop of Canterbury[1] and the bishops, abbots, earls, barons, justiciars, sheriffs and all his loyal subjects, both French and English, throughout the whole of England—greeting.

1[1]. Be it known to you that I have granted Middlesex to my citizens of London to be held on lease by them and their heirs of me and my heirs for £300 paid by tale[2], upon these terms: that the citizens themselves appoint a sheriff[3], such as they desire, from among themselves, and a justiciar[4], such as they desire, from among themselves, to safeguard the pleas of my crown and to conduct such pleas. And there shall be no other justiciar over the men of London[5].

2[1]. And the citizens shall not take part in any case whatsoever outside the city walls.

§ 1. And they shall be exempt from the payment of state taxes[1] and Danegeld[2] and the murder fine[3].

§ 2. And none of them shall take part in trial by combat[1].

3[1]. And if any of the citizens has become involved in a plea of the crown, he shall clear himself, as a citizen of London, by an oath which has been decreed in the city.

4[1]. And no-one shall be billeted within the walls of the city nor shall hospitality be forcibly exacted for anyone belonging to my household or to any other.

5. Et omnes homines Londoniarum sint quieti et liberi et omnes res eorum, et[1] per totam Angliam et per portus maris, de theloneo et passagio et lestagio et omnibus aliis consuetudinibus.

6. Et ecclesiae et barones et cives teneant et habeant bene et in pace socnas[2] suas cum omnibus consuetudinibus, ita quod hospites, qui in soccis hospitabuntur[3], nulli dent consuetudines nisi illi cuius soca fuerit vel ministro suo quem ibi[4] posuerit.

7. Et homo Lond. non iudicetur in misericordia pecuniae nisi ad sa were, scilicet ad c solidos; dico de placito quod ad pecuniam pertineat.

8. Et amplius non sit meskenninge in hustinge neque in folkesimote[5] neque in aliis placitis infra civitatem.

9. Et husting sedeat semel in ebdomada, videlicet die Lunae.

10. Et terras suas[6] et [vadimonia][7] et debita civibus meis habere faciam infra civitatem et extra.

11. Et de terris de quibus ad me clamaverint rectum eis tenebo lege civitatis.

12. Et si quis thelonium vel consuetudinem a civibus[8] Londoniarum ceperit, cives Londoñ. [in civitate][9] capiant de burgo vel de villa, ubi thelonium vel consuetudo capta fuit, quantum homo Londoñ. pro theloneo dedit et proinde de dampno[10] receperit.

13[11]. Et omnes debitores qui civibus debita sua debent, eis reddant[12] vel in[13] Londoniis se disrationent quod non debent[14].

---

[1] Om. Rs, Co, Or, Horn, Cust, E IV.   [2] *sokas* El; *socas* Horn, Cust, E IV.
[3] Rs, Horn; elsewhere *hospitantur*.   [4] *sibi* Co.
[5] *folkesmot* Cust, El, E IV; *-th* Horn; *-mote* elsewhere.
[6] Om. Cc, Cus, Cust, El, E IV.
[7] Horn, Cust, El, E IV, Po; *wardimotum* Rs; *wardemota* Cus; *-motū* Lond.
[8] *civ. meis* Horn, Cust, E IV.
[9] *in c.* Cc, El; om. elsewhere; *vicecomes Lond. namium inde apud Lond. capiat* Po 1155.
[10] *-nacione si* Cc.   [11] Caps. 13, 14 om. El.
[12] *r. in Londonia* Horn, Cust, E IV.
[13] *inde iidem se d.* Cus.   [14] *q. n. d.* om. Cc.

CAP. 5–13   291

5. And all the citizens of London and all their effects shall be exempt and free, both throughout England and in the seaports, from toll and fees for transit[1] and market fees[2] and all other dues.

6. And the churches and barons and citizens shall have and hold in peace and security their rights of jurisdiction along with all their dues, in such a way that lessees who occupy property in districts under private jurisdiction shall pay dues to no-one except the man to whom the jurisdiction belongs, or to the official whom he has placed there.

7[1]. And a citizen of London shall not be sentenced to forfeiture of a sum greater than his wergeld[2], namely 100 shillings, that is to say in a case concerned with monetary compensation.

8. And further there shall be no "miskenning"[1] in a husting or a public meeting or in any other courts inside the city.

9. And the husting[1] shall sit once a week[2], namely on Monday.

10. And I assure to my citizens their lands and the property mortgaged to them and the debts due to them both within the city and outside.

11. And with regard to lands about which they have appealed to me, I shall maintain justice on their behalf, according to the law of the city.

12. And if anyone has exacted toll or tax from citizens of London, the citizens of London within the city shall take[1] from the town or village where the toll or tax was exacted a sum equivalent to that which the citizen of London gave as toll and hence sustained as loss[2].

13[1]. And all those who owe debts to citizens shall pay them or shall clear themselves in London from the charge of being in debt to them.

14. Quodsi reddere noluerint neque[1] ad disrationandum venire, tunc cives[2], quibus debita sua debent[3], capiant[4] in civitatem namia sua vel de [burgo vel villa vel de][5] comitatu in quo manet qui debitum debet.

15. Et cives[6] habeant fugationes suas ad fugandum sicut melius et plenius habuerunt antecessores eorum, scilicet[7] [Ch]iltre[8] e Middelsexe e Sureie.

Teste episcopo Wintoniensi, et Roberto filio Richier.[9] et Hugone Bigot et Alu[redo][10] de Toteneis[11] et Willelmo de Albini[12] et Huberto regis camerario et Willelmo de Munfichet[13] et Hagulfo[14] de Tanei[15] et Johanne Belet et Roberto filio Sawardi[16]. Apud Westmonasterium[17].

[1] *n. quod non debent* Cc, Horn, Cust, E IV.
[2] *civ. Londoniae* Horn, Cust, E IV.   [3] *-ntur* Horn, Cus, Cust, E IV.
[4] *cap. n. s. in civitate London' de b.* Horn, Cust, E IV.
[5] Om. Lond, Cus.   [6] *c. Londoniae* Cust, E IV.
[7] Lond; *sc. in* elsewhere.   [8] *siltre* Lond, Cus.
[9] Rs, Cust, E IV; elsewhere *-her*.
[10] *Aluer̃* Rs; *Aluero* Horn, Cus, Cust; *Alnero* E IV.
[11] *Toneis* Lond; *Coneis* Cus.
[12] *Alb. spiñ* Rs; *Albini Spin'* Cus; *Alba Spina* Cc, Horn, Cust, E IV.
[13] Rs; *Moun.* Cust, E IV; *-cher* Co, Or; *Mont.* elsewhere.
[14] *Hang.* Cust; *Haug.* E IV.   [15] Rs, Cus; *Taney* E IV; *Tani* elsewhere.
[16] Rs, Cus; *Syw.* Cust; *Siw.* elsewhere.
[17] Rs, Co, Horn, Cus, Cust, E IV; *Datum a. W.* elsewhere.

14. But if they have refused to pay or to come to clear themselves, then the citizens to whom they are in debt shall seize their pledges [and bring them] into the city from the [town, village or] county in which the debtor lives.

15[1]. And the citizens shall enjoy as good and full hunting-rights as their ancestors ever did, namely, in the Chilterns, Middlesex and Surrey.

Witnesses: The Bishop of Winchester[1], and Robert FitzRichard[2] and Hugh Bigot[3] and Alfred de Totness[4] and William de Albini[5] and Hubert[6], the King's Chamberlain, and William de Munfichet[7] and Hagulf de Tany[8] and John Belet[9] and Robert FitzSiward. At Westminster.

NOTES TO THE LAWS OF EDMUND AND OF EDGAR

I EDMUND

Preamble. 1. Oda, who was by birth a Dane, became Bishop of Ramsbury in 925–927, and Archbishop of Canterbury in 942 (see Stubbs, *Regist. Sacr. Angl.* p. 25). He seems to have earnestly promoted church reform (see *Constitutiones Odonis*, Spelman, *Concilia*, pp. 415–18, and Wilkins, *Concilia*, I. pp. 212–14) and to have taken a leading part in state affairs (see *Sax. Chr.* Ann. 958 D). His death is recorded in the *Saxon Chronicle* (Ann. 961 A, F) though the date is probably too late (see Plummer, II. p. 153 f.). There is a short Latin life of Oda in Wharton, *Anglia Sacra*, II. pp. 78–87, and in Langebek, *Scriptores Rerum Danicarum*, II. pp. 401–11. References to him are to be found also in the *Vita S. Oswaldi, Angl. Sacr.* II. pp. 191–210, and *Historians of Church of York*, ed. Raine, Rolls Series, I. pp. 399–475; in the *Memorials of St Dunstan*, ed. Stubbs, Rolls Series, pp. 32, 60, 294, 303, 410; and in Wm of Malmesbury, *Gesta Pont.* pp. 20–5, 30, 248, and *Gesta Regum*, I. p. 163.

2. Wulfstan, whose name suggests that he was English by birth, became Archbishop of York in 931 (see Stubbs, *Reg. Sacr. Angl.* p. 26). He figures very prominently in the annals relating to the wars of Edmund and Edgar in the north of England, and appears to have supported the northern kings against the English on several occasions. He was imprisoned by Edred but afterwards reinstated as bishop, either in his own see or at Dorchester (see Plummer, II. p. ix). For further references see *Sax. Chr.* Ann. 943 D, 947 D, 952 D, 954 D, 956 E and 957 D, and *Hist. of York*, ed. Raine, II. p. 339 f.

1. 1. Q translates *Qui plebem Dei docere debent lumen vitae*. For other examples of the use of *læran* with a double acc. see Toller, *Suppl.* p. 601, *s.v.* IV (2 β), V (3). My translation follows Liebermann's.

2. The reading of D, as against H and B, is preferred by Liebermann who points out that what follows would not be prescribed by the canon law. It may be suggested that the presence of *þæt* before *hi* in D is ungrammatical, and points to an (imperfect) correction.

2. 1. Singular or plural? Q translates *decimam*.

2. Cf. In. 4; 61; I As. 4.

3. *Romfeoh* 7 *sulhælmæssan* are mentioned only in D, whereas H, B and Q have simply *ælmesfeoh*. Is it possible that D has differentiated the payments which together make up *ælmesfeoh*?

3. 1. Q adds *sceleratis manibus*.

2. Liebermann prefers *neawiste* (D, B, cf. V Atr. 29; VI, 36) to *ansyne* (H) in view of the use of the word *hired* in II Edm. 4 where this regulation is practically repeated.

3. Liebermann is of opinion that, although the phrase *gyf he cyninges man sy* (B) did not form part of the original text, it conveys

the true interpretation of its meaning; that is to say, that the law was drawn up primarily with reference to the nobles in the king's entourage.

4. This interpretation follows Liebermann (III. p. 125) who points out that the personal action of the bishop might be due to the gravity of the offence or the high rank of the offender.

5. 1. Liebermann's translation is 'gut in Stand halte,' but might not the reference be to the actual restoration of the churches which had been destroyed or had fallen into a dilapidated condition during the Danish wars? Oda himself had Canterbury Cathedral thoroughly repaired (see *Angl. Sacr.* II. p. 83).

2. The churches here referred to are presumably on lands actually belonging to the cathedral or to the bishop himself. For churches on private estates see II Edg. 2.

6. 1. Cf. Af. 1, 1–7; II As. 26.
    2. Cf. II As. 6.
    3. Lit. 'from any portion in God.'

II EDMUND

Preamble. 1. *Eadmund cyning cyð...ðæt ic.* Such transitions from the third person to the first are common in Anglo-Saxon documents of all kinds, cf. I Edw. Pre. 1; Kemble, No. 721; Harmer, *Hist. Docs.* Nos. XX, XXI, and the introduction to Alfred's transl. of the *Cura Pastoralis*.

2. Liebermann prefers this meaning, see his notes on A. and G Pre.[7] and on this passage (III. pp. 84, 127). The phrase is probably equivalent to Af. 4, 2 *ge ceorle ge eorle*.

3. Lit. 'how I could promote most of the Christian religion.' Cf. for uses of *micel* as a neut. subst. with the genitive BT. 683, *s.v.* IV *a*.

§ 1. 1. Cf. the preface of the *Frostathing* Laws (*Norges Gamle Love*, ed. Keyser and Munch, I. p. 121), where King Haakon (1217–63) deplores the many homicides throughout Norway.

1. 1. Cf. Abt. 22 where the term fixed for the payment of the wergeld is only 40 days, and *Be Wergilde*, cap. 6, where the time is left to the decision of the authorities.

§ 1. 1. Liebermann compares with this phrase the continental *meziban*, see Brunner, II. p. 465[17].

§ 3. 1. Cf. II As. 20, 7; *fah wið god*, Beo. l. 811; and see for further references Brunner, I.[2] p. 232.

    2. 1. Cf. Af. 2 f.
        2. Cf. Af. 40.
        3. *i.e.* outlawry and forfeiture of property.
    3. 1. Cf. In. 6 and notes; *Be Wer*. 6.
        2. Cf. In. 70; 76; *Be Wer*. 6.
    4. 1. Cf. I Edm. 3.

2. The words added from Ld (cf. Q: *eum qui sanguinem fundet humanum*) seem to be necessary for the sense.

3. *i.e.* for refuge parallel to the sanctuary provided by the Church.

4. It is to be suspected that the words *on bote befangen* are an addition to the original text, perhaps entered above the line as an alternative to *gebet*. Liebermann suggests (III. p. 127) that Ld's *gebete* is due to a misreading of *gebet l* (*i.e. vel*).

5. 1. Cf. II As. 1, 1–4; 20, 3.

2. Or perhaps 'suppression of fighting' as compared with the suppression of thefts.

6. 1. Liebermann points out that, in view of the penalty, violation of the king's *mund* is probably intended, cf. In. 6.

2. Cf. Norse *heimsókn*, an attack or inroad on a person's home, and the Scots law-term *hamesucken* applied to the same offence. Probably, as Liebermann suggests, the worst kind of *hamsocn* with violence is here referred to. In ordinary cases the penalty incurred seems to have been £5, cf. II Cn. 62.

7. 1. Cf. *Be Wergilde* and see Seebohm, *Tribal Custom*, p. 356 ff.; Phillpotts, *Kindred and Clan*, p. 219 ff.

2. Liebermann translates 'Notable' and says in his notes (III. p. 128) that perhaps 'Gerichtsobere, Schiedsmannen, Rechtsanordner' in particular are meant. He points out that official mediators ('amtliche Vermittler') were known on the continent (see Frauenstädt, *Blutrache*, pp. 47, 106), but the reference here seems more general, namely, to 'men in authority' simply, not to any definitely appointed arbitrators.

3. *Sectan* is a Scandinavian loan word, cf. Norse *sætta*, to reconcile, make peace among.

4. Cf. the Norse law-term *handsal* and the modern German phrase *in die Hand versprechen*, to promise something solemnly.

5. It is difficult to determine whether the *forspeca* is a person who is permanently responsible for the slayer (*i.e.* his *borh*), or whether he is merely a friend whom he has induced to act on his behalf. Liebermann takes the latter view.

§ 1. 1. The omission of the infinitive of motion is common with *mot*, see BT. p. 699, I *b* (2).

2. *Grið* is a Scandinavian loan word. It denotes 'peace' in a limited or localised sense, *i.e.* the sanctuary afforded by special places or the protection granted by a particular person, cf. its compounds *ciricgrið* and *handgrið*, E. and G. 1.

§ 3. 1. Cf. *Be Wer.* 4 and see Pollock, *The King's Peace* (*Oxford Lectures*), p. 77.

2. Cf. Wi. 11 and note; 12; 14.

In *Be Wer.* 4, 1 the amount of the *healsfang* in the case of a wergeld of 1200 shillings is said to be 120 shillings. This is repeated in Hn. 76, 4 *b*, where the sum is stated both in the old currency and in the Norman currency (50 shillings of 12 pence).

The amount of the ceorl's *healsfang* is not stated by any of the earlier authorities but in Hn. 76, 6 *a* and 7 it is said to be 12/6 in Norman currency which would be 30 shillings in the old currency. Liebermann suggests that this is a mistake, due to confusion with the *manbot* payable for a ceorl (see In. 70), and seems to incline to the opinion that the *healsfang* was regularly $\frac{1}{10}$ of the wergeld in the case of the ceorl as well as in that of the thegn. He quotes Leis Wl. 8, 1; 9 where the wergeld of the ceorl is said to be 100 shillings, *i.e.* 1200 pence, both in Mercia and Wessex, and the *healsfang* of the ceorl to be 10 shillings, *i.e.* 120 pence, in both regions. But this assessment of the ceorl's wergeld, if not a mere mistake, is an innovation, as before the Conquest it was 200 shillings, *i.e.* 800 pence in Mercia and 1000 pence in Wessex. The amount fixed for the *healsfang* in Leis Wl. 9 would be correct for Mercian custom before the Conquest if reckoned at 30 (Mercian) shillings. Some evidence for the correctness of this amount as the ceorl's *healsfang* is perhaps given by the custom of Hereford (see DB. I. 179 a, 1), where the heriot of the burgess is said to be 10 shillings, *i.e.* 120 pence. In II Cn. 71, 2 the *healsfang* and the heriot are identified in the case of the '*medeme þegen*' in Wessex, though no heriot is stated for the ceorl.

III EDMUND

Preamble. 1. *Pax* is the Latin word regularly employed to translate the A.S. *frið*, cf. E. and G. Pre.; II Edw. Pre.
2. *Culintonam* is identified by Liebermann with Collumpton (? Cullompton) which in Domesday Book is called *Colitone*. More probably it is Colyton on the Axe (DB. *Culitone*) which was an ancient royal demesne and was situated within a hundred of the same name. Another place of the same name (DB. *Coletone*, now Colyton Raleigh) is slightly to the west on the Otter.
1. 1. Cf. the A.S. phrase *þe ðes haligdom is fore halig, Oath Formulae*, 1; 2. Liebermann suggests that the reference here is probably to a relic of some sort. Oaths were also rendered on the altar (cf. Hl. 16, 2; Wi. 18–21), on the Cross etc. (see Liebermann, II, *Eidesform*, 7 ff.).
2. Liebermann understands this to mean an oath sworn by all the king's subjects, presumably all those who were qualified to take part in the assemblies of the hundred and the county.
3. Liebermann suggests that the original A.S. text read *butan brægde 7 biswice*, cf. I Edw. 1, 5, where, however, the Latin rendering of *butan brægde* is *sine figmento*. The word *controversia* means literally 'dispute.' The words *seductio* and *seditio* are regularly used in juristic Anglo-Latin of the Middle Ages meaning 'treason' (see Pollock and Maitland, *Hist. of Eng. Law*, II. p. 502).
4. It is not clear whether these adverbial phrases qualify the preceding words or are to be taken as parallel to them and like them dependent on *fidelis*.
5. Cf. II Edw. Pre. § 1.
6. This interpretation follows Liebermann's emendation to *a die qua* which certainly gives a better sense.
2. 1. Cf. II As. 20, 2 and 7; VI As. 8, 2.
2. Cf. II Edm. 1, 3 and note.
3. *i.e.* the fine due for insubordination, cf. II As. 20, 2.

4. This is the first mention of the hundred in the Laws. The fact that a fine is made payable to it shows that it was already an organised body.

3. 1. Cf. II Edw. 7.

2. Liebermann suggests that the A.S. text read *se þe to þam hearme geheold* 7 *feormie*, cf. I Edg. 6.

3. Liebermann suggests *warie* (?) *þæt he hine læde* etc. as the reading of the original A.S. text, *i.e.* 'take heed that he bring him' etc. Such a use of *custodire* with *ut* or *ne* is frequent in post-Augustan prose, and for *warian* used intransitively or reflexively with the same sense see BT. p. 1169, *s.v.* I, II *b* and cf. II Atr. 9, 1.

4. 1. Liebermann (II. p. 66) gives the meaning 'der Kopfhaut samt Haaren berauben' and explains the word as a hybrid from *ex* and *tup* (cf. O.E. *topp* and O.F. *estuper*). Scalping was not unknown as a punishment, cf. *hættian*, II Cn. 30, 5; *Sax. Chr.* Ann. 1036 C and note (Plummer, II. p. 215). Presumably in this case only a small part of the scalp is meant.

5. 1. Cf. II As. 10; 12.

2. *hordarii* (*ordalii*) *vel portirevae, i.e.* A.S. *horderes oððe portgerefan*.

6. 1. A.S. *tun*. It is always a question whether this should be translated village, estate or manor. In other passages the word used for estate is generally *land* (Q *terra*), cf. II Edw. 4; V As. 2; II Cn. 73 *a*; 77; 79.

2. A.S. *forsteall*, waylaying, cf. O.F. *guetapens* and see P. and M. II. pp. 455, 463.

3. Liebermann suggests that this phrase, which seems redundant, is the explanation added by the translator of the technical A.S. word *forsteall*.

§ 1. 1. Cf. V As. 2.

§ 2. 1. Cf. *stande þæt spor for þone forað*, V As. 2.

2. Cf. cap. 2³.

7. 1. Cf. III As. 7, and with regard to similar responsibility on the part of the lord among other Teutonic peoples see Brunner, II. pp. 551–4.

2. Is this a definition of *homines suos*?

§ 1. 1. Cf. II As. 20, 1 and 4.

2. Liebermann suggests that the A.S. text read *þa ungetriewan* 7 *tyhtbysigan* (*men*?), cf. III Edg. 7; I Atr. 1, 1; 4; II Cn. 25; 30.

§ 2. 1. Cf. IV As. 7; II As. 25; V As. 1, 2.

2. *i.e. ge eorl ge ceorl*, cf. Af. 4, 2.

3. The penalties do not appear to be specified in the code as it has come down to us.

I EDGAR

1. In all three MSS (*i.e.* B, Q, Cons. Cn.) this ordinance is immediately preceded by two anonymous legal notices *Be Blaserum* and *Be Forfange*.

Preamble. 1. *þæt hundred* is translated 'Hundertgericht' (*i.e.* hundred court) by Liebermann in view of the fact that the hundred appears throughout only in its judicial function, and that the word *hundredesgemot* is employed in III Edg. 5 with reference to this law. In cap. 5, however, it is evidently the geographical district which is meant.

1. 1. *i.e.* the men belonging to the hundred.

2. These provisions give the impression that the hundred was a new thing. This is misleading to a certain extent as the hundred was in existence in the time of Edmund and, in view of III Edm. 2, was already an organised body. The division of the country into hundreds of hides was very much older and is found in the seventh century at least, but there is no evidence for the hundred as a definitely organised unit until the time of Edmund. A monthly public meeting is mentioned in II Edw. 8 which would seem to be the predecessor of the hundred meeting. For a discussion of the relation of the hundred court to the older meeting see Liebermann, II. p. 451, *s.v. Gericht*, 13–13 *n*.

2. 1. The heading is found only in B.

2. Schmid and Liebermann read *on ryd*, the former adding a note 'nicht ganz leserlich im MS.' The writing is in faint red ink in the margin but the reading is clearly *oncryd* (without division). No such word occurs elsewhere but it would seem to be a legitimate abstract formation from *crudan*, similar to *slege* from *slean* or *feng* from *fon*. For the meaning compare Riddle, 4, l. 27 f. *þonne hēah geþring / on cleofu crȳdeð* and *Sax. Chr.* ann. 937 *cread cnear on flot* (Brunanburh, l. 35).

3. Lit. 'the man of the hundred' and 'the men of the tithings,' wrongly translated *hominibus hundredi* and *hominibus decimarum* (*i.e.* tithes) in Q.

The first mention of the tithing in the Laws occurs in VI As. 4, where it apparently refers to the groups of 10 men mentioned in the preceding clause. Such groups seem to have been organised for police purposes. By the time of Henry I the tithing had come to be regarded as a territorial division forming part of the hundred, cf. Hn. 6, 1 *b*. Regarding the history of the tithing see further Liebermann, II, *s.v. Zehnerschaft*; Stubbs, *Const. Hist.* I. pp. 91–6; P. and M. I. pp. 568–71.

4. Cf. II As. 2, 1; VI As. 6, 3.

5. There is no extant law of Edmund's which does state definitely what is to be done with the thief, although it is clear enough from VI As. 1.

§ 1. 1. Cons. Cn. adds *si forte res ipsa furto ablata periit*.

3. 1. Cf. for parallel cases *nylle ridan*, II As. 20, 2; *adire negaverit*, III Edm. 2; *rade forsace*, III Edg. 7, 2.

2. Liebermann translates *dom* as 'Beschluss,' *i.e.* takes it to mean a definite resolution of the hundred.

3. *i.e.* if the accused has failed to prove his ignorance of the affair, cf. *pernegare quod nescivit*, III Edm. 2.

4. Liebermann notes that this fine is not to be confused with the 30 sh. (along with 120 sh. to the king) paid to the hundred according to III Edm. 2. The context does not seem to me to explain

very clearly the difference in the nature of the offence unless it is to be inferred from the words '*ubi fur*' etc. in Edm.
§ 1. 1. x *sol.* Q, *i.e.* Norman shillings.
4. 1. Cf. III Edm. 5.
2. Schmid and Liebermann suggest that *mannes* should be read for *manna*, especially as Q has *hominis hundredi*. The reference would then be to the chief official of the hundred, otherwise the twelve men *gecorene to gewitnesse* mentioned in IV Edg. 5 may possibly be meant.
5. 1. The *hundredesman* (called *hundredes ealdor* in IV Edg. 8, 1) performs the duty ascribed to the reeve in VI As. 8, 4.
§ 1. 1. The fine payable by the *gerefa* was 120 shillings, see VI As. 8, 4. Is it possible that the reeve had jurisdiction over a larger district, *i.e.* several hundreds?
6. 1. Cf. III Edm. 3.
2. *Angylde*, *i.e.* the value of a thing not augmented (or doubled). In this case the reference is not quite clear. It would seem that the person who 'evades the law' has committed theft.
§ 1. 1. Cf. II Cn. 34 which points to the continuance till then of various types of procedure in different parts of the country.
7. 1. The nature of the meetings mentioned in the earlier laws is not specified. It cannot be determined for certain whether such meetings as those mentioned, for example, in Af. 38 are of identical character with those mentioned in II Edw. 8. From this time onwards, as Liebermann observes, we hear of meetings (or courts) of the hundred, the borough, and the county, as well as of the court of the Five Boroughs (*Fif Burga geþincðu*) in the N.E. Midlands. References are also found to joint meetings of several hundreds, *e.g. Liber Eliensis*, ed. Stewart, Bk. II. Chap. 11 (pp. 129–30), Chap. 34 (p. 151).
§ 1. 1. Probably for the carrying out of duties generally, cf. *hlafordes neod* in the Law of the Cambridge Thanes (Thorpe, *Diplomatarium*, p. 611). Q adds *vel infirmitate monstrabili*, cf. *legerbære* (*ibid.*), and see P. and M. II. pp. 562–3.
2. The regular fine payable to the hundred, cf. III Edm. 2; II Cn. 15, 2.
8. 1. The last two regulations seem utterly foreign to the rest of the ordinance both in style and content. It seems probable, as Liebermann suggests, that they were originally anonymous legal notices, similar to *Be Blaserum* and *Be Forfange*, which were appended to the ordinance in the archetype and have been copied in all three MSS as if they formed part of it.
2. The meaning of the word *hoppe* is quite uncertain. It is found as the translation of *bulla* in Alfred's *Orosius*, Bk. IV. Chap. X (see BT. p. 552, *s.v. hoppe*). Liebermann considers it to refer here to the collar which is the distinguishing mark of a dog, but is it not possible that a small disc, presumably inscribed with the owner's particular mark, may have been attached to the collar and may here be described as *hoppe*?
3. No other instance of the form *blæshorn* is noted by Toller (see *Suppl.* p. 96). *Blædhorn* and *blæsthorn* are found elsewhere.

4. Cf. In. 43, 1.

9. 1. Cf. *Be Blas.*: *þæt man...myclade þæt ordal ysen, þæt hit gewege þry pund.* Schmid, following B, reads 7 *to anfealdum an pund.*

II EDGAR

Preamble. 1. Cf. IV Edg. 2; I Cn. Pre.
2. Omitted in D but doubtless in the original text. Cf. for other references to the nation as a whole In. Pre.; III As. Pre.; I Edm. Pre.; IV Edg. Pre.

1. 1. Cf. Wi. 21, 1.

§ 1. 1. Liebermann notes that the rendering of tithes had been enjoined by earlier kings under pain of fines (E. and G. 6; I As.) and excommunication (I Edm. 2), but here for the first time it appears as the definite legal duty of every class of freemen. Edgar's enactments are repeated by his successors, cf. VIII Atr. 7; 8; I Cn. 8, 1 f. etc.

2. At present the name 'minster' is applied to seven cathedrals and large churches in the country (viz. York, Lincoln, Ripon, Beverley, Southwell, Lichfield and Wimborne), and it likewise appears in a good many place-names in the south. Many of these foundations are certainly spoken of as monasteries in early times, though in other cases such evidence is wanting, but this may be due merely to the absence of information.

The reference in this case is taken by Liebermann to be to the parish or mother church (cf. *mater ecclesia,* Q; *mere iglise,* Leis Wl. 1, 1). The reference to the *mæssepreost* in cap. 3, 1 seems to support this view.

3. *geneatland* is land occupied by *geneatas* (free tenants) who are apparently identical with the *gafolgeldan* of the earlier laws (cf. In. 6, 3; 23, 3). Sometimes this land is called *utland* as distinguished from *inland, i.e.* the land kept by the lord of a manor in his own hands.

4. Cf. VIII Atr. 7; I Cn. 8, 2; and cf. also II As. 16 for the plough as a basis of reckoning.

2. 1. Cf. 1 Cn. 11.

§ 2. 1. Offerings from slaves seem to have been voluntary. That they had time at their disposal in which to earn money for themselves, and that they possessed property of their own is evident from Af. 43; II As. 24.

§ 3. 1. Schmid and Liebermann agree that this clause is an addition to the original text, cf. cap. 5, 2 f.

2. Liebermann takes this phrase to mean a fortnight and compares it with Hn. 41, 2 *a*; 59, 2 *b* where the series 7 days, 15 days, 3 weeks, 4 weeks is found, but may not these be due to French reckoning? The ordinary expression for two weeks in England must have been *feowertyne niht* from the beginning. The reason for 15 here may be that dues were not to be paid on a Sunday.

3. 1. Cf. V Atr. 11, 1; VI, 17 f.; VIII, 9 ff.; I Cn. 8 ff.; Wulfstan's Homilies, ed. Napier, pp. 116, 208, 272, 310–11.

2. Cf. In. 4.
3. Cf. I Edw. Pre. and note; II, 5; 5, 2; II As. 5.
§ 1. 1. Cf. IV Edg. 1, 5; VIII Atr. 7; 8; I Cn. 8, 2.
2. Lit. 'let him be directed to the ninth portion,' *i.e.* 'let the next tenth fall to his share' (see BT. p. 967, *s.v.* tæcan, III (2)).
3. Liebermann contrasts this passage with the general direction given in E. and G. Pre. § 2.
4. 1. *heorðpennig* (cf. Wulfstan, pp. 116, 208) seems identical with *Romfeoh*, *i.e.* Peter's Pence (cf. I Cn. 9; Wulfstan, pp. 272, 311), which was a tax of a penny levied on every household.
§ 1. 1. Cf. VIII Atr. 10, 1, where the payment and fine are demanded, without, however, the journey to Rome.
5. 1. Cf. Wi. 9 (where the Sunday rest is apparently reckoned from sunset to sunset); I Cn. 14, 2; Wulfstan, pp. 117, 208. Thurston (*The Mediaeval Sunday*, in *Nineteenth Century*, 46, 1899, p. 40) points out that throughout the Middle Ages and right down to the sixteenth century it was customary, though not obligatory, to stop work when the midday bell rang on Saturday.
§ 2 and § 3. Liebermann is of opinion that these clauses are more likely to have been added to the original text by ecclesiastical scribes in the case of MSS A and D than to have been omitted by such a copyist in the case of MS G.
§ 2. 1. Cf. I As. 4; V Atr. 12, 1; VI, 21; I Cn. 13, 1.
§ 3. 1. Cf. E. and G. 1.
2. Cf. III Atr. 1; V. 15.

III EDGAR

1. 1. In all the MSS there is no break between this code and the preceding one. That they were promulgated at the same meeting of the king and his councillors is apparent, as Liebermann points out, from the absence of any preamble or any mention of the king's name, and from the use of the word *þonne*. A similar arrangement is found in I and II Cn. where the secular part (II Cn.) opens with almost the same formula.
§ 1. 1. Cf. II Edw. 8; I Edw. Pre.; and cf. also I Edg. 7 for a similar combination of clauses taken from Edward's laws.
2. This is repeated in V Atr. 1, 1; VI, 8, 1; II Cn. 1, 1.
3. Alliterative phrases such as this are frequent in the Laws, cf. *mete ne munde*, II Edm. 1, 1; *lufe oððe lage*, III Atr. 13, 3; *ne libbende ne licgende*, II Cn. 24 etc.
§ 2. 1. Cf. VI Atr. 10, 1; II Cn. 2.
2. 1. Cf. II As. 3.
2. This regulation is repeated in II Cn. 17 but without the second phrase *riht abiddan*. Liebermann does not consider, however, that the two phrases express the same idea, and suggests that the former refers to 'die Einlassung in den Prozess,' the latter to 'die Urteilserfüllung' (see III. p. 136). He suggests further that, if it were a case of justice being refused, a penalty would be inflicted on the official presiding over the local court.

304   NOTES TO THE LAWS OF EDMUND AND OF EDGAR

§ 1. 1. See Brunner, II. p. 136, for references to similar mitigation in continental codes of law. Liebermann is of opinion that in England this right probably rested, not with the king alone, but with a special royal court (see II. p. 313, *s.v. Billigkeit*, 4, and *The National Assembly in the A.S. Period*, p. 68), but the evidence for such a court in the tenth century seems to be far from conclusive.

§ 2. 1. As opposed to crimes which are *botleas*, *i.e.* for which no compensation can be paid; cf. III Atr. 1.

3. 1. Cf. II Cn. 15, 1

2. Liebermann is of opinion that the judge referred to is primarily the royal official (*i.e.* in most cases the sheriff), otherwise the duty of exacting the compensation would not fall upon the bishop. He points out, however, that in Leis Wl. 39, 1, where this law of Edgar's is repeated, the punishment threatened is loss of *franchise*, *i.e.* the right of holding a court, and in view of the fact that the penalty mentioned by Edgar is loss of *þegnscipe* not of *scir* or *gerefscipe* concludes that those with the privilege of exercising private jurisdiction are likewise thought of in both cases.

4. 1. There is a curious discrepancy in regard to the reading—a discrepancy which seems to be independent of the general relationship of the MSS. All the texts have *feo* but A, G have *feore* (*vel freme* being written above in A) against D, G₂ with *freme*, while Q has *vita vel commodo*, *i.e. feore oððe freme*. In II Cn. 16 all the A.S. texts have *feo*, A has *feorme*, B *frema*, Ld *feorh*, but Q here has *pecunia vel commodo*, *i.e. feo oððe freme*. Hn. 34, 7 has *vitae iacturam vel honoris detrimentum*, *i.e. feore oððe freme*. Liebermann thinks that the original reading in Edgar's law was probably *feore*, partly because the phrase *feo oððe feore* occurs in E. and G. 12; VIII Atr. 33; II Cn. 40 and *Sax. Chr.* ann. 755, and partly because *freme* is too near in meaning to *feo*, but the reading *feorh* may very well have been taken from E. and G. 12 and the other passages in the Laws in which the reference is not to slander but to robbery or murder, while Hn. 34, 7 makes it clear that *freme* was understood as referring to 'honour' and not to property, cf. Norse *rett*, Irish 'honour-price,' and Welsh *saraad*, Seebohm, *Tribal Custom in A.S. Law*, p. 240.

5. 1. Cf. I Edg. 1.

§ 1. 1. Cf. II Cn. 18.

2. The meaning of this regulation seems to be that, where the county was divided into burghal districts, meetings of these took place three times a year. In districts not so divided county meetings were held twice a year. In all probability there was great local variation. See Ballard, *Domesday Boroughs*, pp. 53, 121; Bateson, *E.H.R.*, 1905, p. 146 ff.; Chadwick, *Anglo-Saxon Institutions*, pp. 220–3.

§ 2. 1. Cf. II Cn. 18, 1.

2. The regulation perhaps applies only to the *scirgemot* (see Chadwick, *op. cit.* p. 223).

3. The Latin version has *doceant*, but probably more than interpretation is meant (see Lieb. III. p. 137).

6. 1. Cf. III As. 7; IV Edg. 3; I Atr. 1; II Cn. 20.

§ 1. 1. Cf. In. 22; *utoðberste* (G) is the older form.

2. *i.e.* the payment of any money compensation due from the delinquent.

§ 2. 1. *ðeof* (A, D, G₂), cf. *latro* (Q), is probably the correct reading.

7. 1. Cf. II As. 20; II Cn. 25.

2. In view of II Cn. 30 *ungetreowe þam hundrede*, Liebermann takes this to refer simply to the members of the court, not to the public at large.

3. *scifte* (D) is a Scandinavian loan word.

4. Cf. II As. 20, 1.

§ 1. 1. Cf. II As. 20, 5 f.; III Edm. 2.

2. Cf. I Edg. 6.

§ 2. 1. Cf. the Scots phrase 'better friend than fremd.'

§ 3. 1. Cf. II Cn. 26.

2. Cf. IV As. 6; III Edm. 2, and compare also the treatment accorded the thief caught *æt hæbbendre hand*, II As. 1.

3. Cf. Af. 4, 2; II As. 4.

4. Liebermann attributes the addition of this clause in D to ecclesiastical influence.

8. 1. Cf. II As. 14; IV Atr. 6; VI, 32, 1; II Cn. 8.

2. See Chadwick, *op. cit.* p. 34 for a table showing the weight of Edgar's coins as compared with those of his predecessors and successors. Matthew Paris, ann. 975 (Rolls Series, I. p. 467), notes the issue of a new coinage at the end of his reign: *deinde per totam Angliam nouam fieri praecepit monetam, quia uetus uitio tonsorum adeo erat corrupta ut uix nummus obolum appenderet in statera*. See Chadwick, *op. cit.* pp. 36, 38[1].

§ 1. 1. The reference may be to measures of capacity, a subject on which unfortunately we have very little definite information for the Saxon period. For notes on the *amber* and the *sester* see Harmer, *Historical Documents*, pp. 73, 79 f.

2. Liebermann suggests that this standard of weight may have been identical with the later 'husting weight' (see Sharpe, *London and the Kingdom*, I. p. 10) and this again may have been meant by the *publicum pondus* of the tenth and eleventh centuries (see Napier and Stevenson, *Crawford Charters*, pp. 77–8).

3. Towards the end of the tenth century London was becoming far more important than Winchester, hence the precedence given it in the later recension of this regulation represented by A, D, G₂. Winchester, noted for its cloth manufacture which dated from very early times, and for its trade in wines, remained a prosperous commercial centre, however, till the thirteenth century. For a short sketch of its history see Kitchin, *Charter of St Giles's Fair*, A.D. *1349*, pp. 8–12.

§ 2. 1. The standard of the wey appears to have varied somewhat, both in the Anglo-Saxon period and later, see Harmer, *op. cit.* p. 73; Cunningham, *Growth of Industry*, p. 130; Bateson, *E.H.R.*, 1899, p. 505.

306 NOTES TO THE LAWS OF EDMUND AND OF EDGAR

2. *deoror*, G, Q. Cunningham, *loc. cit.* and Stone (*L.Q.R.*, 1913, p. 338) accept *undeoror* (the reading of the second recension) and regard this regulation as the earliest fixing a minimum price for wool.

§ 3. 1. This clause is found only in the second recension.

2. D's reading XL *scill.* as against LX *scill.* in A, G₂ is probably a scribal error. Liebermann points out that seller and buyer together pay the regular fine of 120 shillings to the king.

IV EDGAR

Preamble. 1. In F a cross is prefixed, as not infrequently at the beginning of A.S. documents.

2. This beginning is common in wills and other A.S. documents of the tenth and eleventh centuries, see Kemble, Nos. 429, 591, 593, 594, 738, 745 etc.

3. Cf. *Sax. Chr.* ann. 962 A, where a plague and a great fire in London are recorded.

1. 1. Cf. E. and G. 5, 1; I As. 3, where the wrath of God is also threatened for the withholding of ecclesiastical dues.

2. *þæt godcunde*—note the use of the neuter adj. with the article to denote an abstract conception as in Greek and modern German. The phrase is translated: 'He considered the religious question from a secular standpoint' by BT. p. 1195, *s.v. weoroldgewuna*; 'Er betrachtete und erwog das Göttliche [Walten] gemäss weltlichem Gewohnheitsrecht,' by Liebermann (I. p. 207).

§ 1. Cf. II Edg. 1, 1 and note. The Latin version (derived from C) translates *militans, i.e.* it takes *geneat* in its earlier sense. The translation seems to be inexact in many points.

§ 2. 1. See Andrews, *Old English Manor*, pp. 142–3.

2. The Latin version translates *per vim defendere* which Liebermann regards as nearer the meaning than Toller's suggestion 'to withhold wrongfully' (see *Suppl.* p. 24, *s.v. ætstrengan*).

3. Perhaps not to be taken too literally.

§ 4. 1. Saint Dunstan.

2. The reference is probably to the plague, cf. Preamble.

3. Cf. the threat of *eternis baratri incendiis* for the violation of charters, Birch, *Cart. Sax.* 1284, 1297.

4. The reference, primarily at least, is to the fruits of the earth and livestock, cf. I As. Pre.

5. The reference is to II Edg.

6. *mid wedde*, lit. 'pledge,' but apparently used in general with the sense of a pledge expressed in words, cf. the use of the verbs *healdan, brecan, aleogan* with *wedd*, and the regular Latin rendering, viz. *fides, manufirmatio, votum*.

§ 5 *a*. 1. Translated 'erbärmlich' by Liebermann. See Toller, *Suppl.* p. 172, *s.v. earm*, 1 *a*.

2. Liebermann suggests that the word *god* may have been omitted by the scribe, but is this assumption really necessary? The

expression *þæt godcunde* in cap. 1 above rather suggests that the author may have been familiar with foreign (ultimately Greek) constructions. For a short account of the influence of Greek on Old English see Stubbs, *Mem. of St Dunstan*, Intro. p. cxxii. Unfortunately there is nothing of St Dunstan's composition extant which might be compared with these regulations, see Stubbs, *op. cit.* p. cix.

3. It has seemed necessary in translating to insert a phrase to complete the sense.

§ 6. 1. *i.e.*, possibly, among the Danish and Celtic parts of the population as well as among the English, cf. 2, 2.

§ 7. 1. During the reign of Edgar great efforts were made to restore monasticism and to oust secular priests and canons from collegiate churches and cathedrals. For the history of this movement see Hunt, *The English Church from the Foundation to the Norman Conquest*, pp. 326–68.

§ 8. 1. The reference may be specially to the priests of churches in private hands, cf. II Edg. 2 f.

2. 1. The beginning of this section is marked by a cross in F, cf Preamble and note.

2. *i.e.* as opposed to those of the church to which the first section of the ordinance has been devoted.

3. Cf. *æghwær*, cap. 1, 6.

4. Cf. II Edg. Pre.

2 *a*. 1. Cf. I Edg. 2 for a similar reference to Edmund. Liebermann infers either that Edgar's immediate predecessors, Edred and Edwig, left no law concerning the prerogatives of the crown, or that any such law is henceforth to be superseded in favour of the conditions of an earlier time. He points out also that among the extant laws of Edmund there is none bearing particularly upon the royal prerogatives, except possibly III Edm. 1.

2. The word *scipe* occurs elsewhere only in the gloss *scipe vel bigleofa stipendium*, Wrt. Voc. I. 20, 33 (see BT. p. 834, *s.v.*). Is it to be taken here as an abbreviation for *þegnscipes gerihta*?

3. Cf. cap. 12.

§ 1. *lagum*, see BT. p. 615, *s.v. lagu* and cf. Norse *lög*. Liebermann points out that Edgar uses this word only in referring to the constitution of the Danes (cf. cap. 12). In his laws it occurs only in the plural (as in Norse). It may be noted that in Norse it is a neuter pl. but in Æthelred and subsequent laws it appears as a fem. sing. The earlier meanings of the word would seem to be (1) legal conditions affecting a person or community (rights, privileges etc.) similar to *gerihta*; (2) the area within which such conditions were in force, *e.g.* Denelagu, Gulathingslög. In the eleventh century the word acquired its modern significance through the transitional meaning 'regulations' (affecting the condition of a person or community), cf. the phrase *setja lög* (originally *leggja*), meaning probably 'to fix or determine the conditions of.' At this time also it seems to have come into general use throughout the country (cf. *Sax. Chr.* D, ann. 1018 ad fin.), whereas in the tenth century it is used (like *eorl* and *here* in the political sense) only with reference to the Scandinavian districts.

Here and again in cap. 12 below autonomy is specially conceded to the Danes with the reservations expressed in caps. 2, 2; 12, 1; 14, 2. It is not specified, however, within what area this autonomy was to apply, but the reference in cap. 15 to Oslac (who bears the title *eorl*) and to the *here* under his rule seems to indicate that his province (York and the districts dependent on it) is intended. The former (Danish) East Anglian kingdom was under the ealdorman Æthelwine who is coupled with the Mercian ealdorman Ælfhere. This would seem to indicate that this province was not meant to be included. On the other hand we should expect the N.E. Midlands—the district of the Five Boroughs—to be under Danish law since they have a separate code devoted to them in the next reign, viz. III Atr. Possibly this district may have been included in Oslac's province.

§ 1 *a*. 1. Cf. Hl. Pre.; Wi. Pre.; VI As. Pre.
2. Cf. cap. 2.

§ 2. 1. Liebermann points out that Edgar is to be regarded as the first to bring the Danes definitely within the sphere of English law-making since A. and G. and E. and G. are treaties made between the Danes and Wessex and confirming the separate power of each.
2. The reference is perhaps to the Cornish Celts and the Welsh under his rule on the borders of Wales, cf. Birch, 1267: *He (God) hæfð nu gewyld to minum anwealde Scottas 7 Cumbras 7 eac swylce Bryttas 7 eall þæt ðis igland him on innan hæfð.* In this charter Liebermann takes *Cumbras* to refer to Wales (cf. modern Welsh *Cymru*). It may be noted that *Britland* is frequently used for Wales in the eleventh century.

3. 1. Cf. III Edg. 6.
2. Lit. 'both within boroughs and outside.' The Latin version has *in urbe aut rure*, cf. II Cn. 24 *binnan byrig...up on lande*.

4. 1. There is little doubt that the reading XXXVI in F and the Latin version is correct. III and VI are often confused in MSS.

6. 1. The territorial division found in certain counties (the N. and W. Ridings of Yorkshire, Lincolnshire, Leicestershire, Nottinghamshire, Derbyshire and Rutland) corresponding more or less to the hundreds which are found in the southern counties. The term is generally explained from Ed. Conf. 30.

§ 1. 1. Cf. *ungeboht, Oath Formulae*, 8.
2. Cf. cap. 14.

7. 1. *ride*, cf. *utrad*, cap. 8. The use of the verb *ridan* in both clauses implies that the intending purchaser went on horseback.

8. § 1. 1. Presumably the *hundredesman* of I Edg. 2. Maitland (*Domesday Book and Beyond*, p. 147 f.) takes this passage as evidence that the village had no court or magistrate of its own. Probably some sort of informal gathering was held for the allotment of strips etc.

9. 1. Liebermann points out that these herdsmen are evidently slaves since freemen were not subjected to the lash.
10. 1. Liebermann takes this to mean 'in the open country.'
2. *næbbe his* etc. Liebermann translates *his* by 'davon.' The meaning is not clear to me.
11. 1. Probably *and* is used here, as frequently, with the sense of 'or,' cf. I Edm. 3; III Atr. 1, 1. If the livestock has been killed its value is to be set aside from the thief's property and given to the rightful owner (see Liebermann, III. p. 143).
12. 1. Cf. cap. 2, 1.
2. For similar changes of person see II Edm. Pre. and note.
3. For the use of *hyld* elsewhere in the plural see BT. p. 581, *s.v.*
§ 1. 1. This is interpreted as referring to the search for the stolen cattle (see BT. p. 887, *s.v. smeagung*) or else to the inquiry for the unknown owner of the suspected cattle which have been seized (Liebermann). Does it not refer to the whole process of investigation with regard to cattle which have not been reported?
2. Cf. cap. 2, 2.
13. § 1. 1. Liebermann understands this to refer to the lord of the manor or his steward.
14. 1. Liebermann points out that such a provision is not found in the extant laws of Edgar. Presumably the reference is to a lost decree.
2. See Toller, *Suppl.* p. 73, *s.v. beginnan*, II.
§ 2. 1. Cf. 2, 2; 12, 1.
15. 1. The Saxon Chronicle (ann. 966 E) notes *Oslac feng to ealdordome* (*i.e.* of Yorkshire), but the signature *Oslac dux* is found attached to documents of Edgar's as early as 963 (see Birch, 1113). In 975 he was driven into exile. No reason for this banishment is stated in the Chronicle, which mourns his departure in the poem commemorating the death of Edgar. The passage occurs immediately after a reference to the anti-monastic reaction, but we do not know whether the two events were connected. The Chronicle speaks of him in a tone of respect and regret for his departure.
2. The word *here* in A.S. properly means a military force, especially an invading or raiding force, but in Norse it has a political as well as a military sense and it is used in the same way here. Cf. *Sax. Chr.* ann. 921 ad fin.
§ 1. 1. *Ælfhere*, ealdorman of Mercia, whose signature as *dux* or *comes* is found attached to documents from 956 to 982 (see Kemble, 1179-1278), is remembered particularly as the leader of the antimonastic reaction which immediately followed upon the death of Edgar (see *Sax. Chron.* 975 E). It is recorded of him also that he had the body of Edward the Martyr removed and buried with all due honour at Shaftesbury (*ibid.* 980 E). His death is noted in 983 (*ibid.* A, E, C).

A similar account of his career is given in the *Vita S. Oswaldi, Hist. of York*, I. pp. 443 f., 450.

2. *Æthelwine*, son of Æthelstan 'half-king,' followed his father and brother as ealdorman of E. Anglia. His signature as *dux* appears first in 962 (see Birch, 1083). He supported the monastic reforms of Dunstan, Oswald and Æthelwold, thus gaining for himself the title of *Dei amicus*. After the death of Edgar he took an active part along with Byrhtnoth, ealdorman of Essex, in defending the monastic system, and appears as one of the strongest opponents of Ælfhere of Mercia. He died in 992 (see *Sax. Chron.*) and was buried at the monastery of Ramsey which had been founded by Oswald and himself. These incidents of his career are recorded in the *Vita S. Oswaldi, Hist. of York*, I. pp. 428–30, 438, 445–7, 465–9, 474–5.

16. 1. Liebermann takes this to refer to Edgar's councillors.

NOTES TO THE CORONATION OATH

Preamble. 1. Dunstan was Archbishop of Canterbury from 960 till his death in 988 (see Stubbs, *Reg. Sacr. Angl.* p. 28). For the various records of his life and work see Stubbs, *Mem. of St Dunstan*, Rolls Series.
2. Æthelstan, Edred and Edwig were also crowned at Kingston (see Florence of Worcester, ed. Thorpe, ann. 924, 946, 955).
3. Liebermann suggests that something tangible is meant, which the young king laid upon the altar in token of his vow. Edward was only thirteen years of age when he was crowned, Æthelred ten.
1. 1. This phrase is not found in the Latin form of the Coronation oath.
2. Cf. the second Latin recension (the reading of the first recension where it differs from the second is given in brackets): *Haec tria populo Christiano et mihi subdito in Christi promitto nomine (Rectitudo regis est nouiter ordinati et in solium sublimati h. t. precepta p. Ch. sibi subdito precipere).*
§ 1. 1. Cf. the Latin form: *inprimis ut ecclesia dei et omnis populus Christianus ueram pacem nostro arbitrio in omni tempore seruet (pacem seruent in o. t.).*
2. See BT. p. 517, *s.v. healdan*, II.
§ 2. Cf. the Latin form: *Aliud (est) ut rapacitates et omnes iniquitates omnibus gradibus interdicam (interdicat).*
§ 3. Cf. the Latin form: *Tertium ut in omnibus iudiciis equitatem et misericordiam precipiam (precipiat) ut mihi et uobis (sibi et nobis) indulgeat suam misericordiam clemens et misericors deus qui uiuit (q. u.* is omitted in the first recension).

NOTES TO THE LAWS OF ÆTHELRED

I ÆTHELRED

Heading. 1. Cf. Ine, MS B; A. and G., MS B.
Preamble. 1. The plural form in B, in view of the singular verb, is probably incorrect.
    2. Woodstock, a few miles north of Oxford, is described in Domesday Book as a royal forest (see DB. I. 154 b, 2). Oxford, or at least part of it, may have belonged originally to Wessex, but it was in the possession of the Mercians before the great invasion of 866, and may have been annexed by them in the eighth century (see *Sax. Chr.* ann. 777). In lists of the counties dating from the eleventh and following centuries (see Simeon of Durham, ed. Arnold, Rolls Series, II., p. 393; Morris, *O.E. Miscellany*, 1872, p. 146; Gale, *Hist. Angl. SS.* xv. p. 560) it is represented as belonging to Mercia together with Gloucester, Worcester, Hereford, Warwick, Shropshire, Cheshire, Stafford (cf. Lieb. I. p. 552 f.).
    3. Cf. II Edw. 1; VI As. 8, 4 and 7; 12, 4; II Edm. 5; IV Edg. 2; 12, 1; 14, 1; 15; 16; III Atr. Pre.
    4. The sense seems to involve a local use of the phrase, the districts under English law being contrasted with those under Danish law for which special provisions are made in III Atr.
1. 1. Cf. IV Edg. 3.
    § 1. 1. With this clause and those following cf. II Cn. 30–3.
    § 2. 1. Q has *apud Brundonam*. The identification is uncertain as there are many places in England with similar names. Liebermann suggests as possible *Brumdun* (see Kemble, 1322), now Brumdon in Dorset (cf. Parker, *Early Oxford*, p. 394), and *Brumduna* [*Branduna*], now Brundon in Essex (see DB. II. 90 and 90 b)
    2. Cf. III As. 7, 1; *Gerefa*, 7.
    § 3. 1. Hundreds are frequently grouped together in this way, cf. Birch, 1130. where grants of land made to the Abbey of Peterborough (972–992) are stated to have been confirmed at meetings of 2, 3 and 8 hundreds. Liebermann quotes also the case of the Abbey of Ely to which were granted jurisdictional rights (*socna*) over groups of several hundreds (see Birch, 1266, 1267). Instances of hundred-groups are common also in the *Liber Eliensis*, see pp. 123, 130, 133 etc.
    2. Similar regulation of the oath according to the minimum value of the object involved is found in A. and G. 3; I Edw 1, 4; II As. 9.
    § 4. 1. Cf. 1, 1.
    § 5. 1. *i.e.* the regular maximum fine, cf. III Edg. 2, 2.
    2. Cf. 1, 7.
    3. Cf. II As. 1, 3; 20, 4; VI, 1, 4; 12, 2; III Edm. 7, 1; III Edg. 7.

§ 6. 1. The use of head' for 'life' is also found in Norse, e.g. hætta höfði, to risk one's life, *Hávamál*, Str. 106. It is sometimes taken quite literally, as in the stories of Bragi Boddason and Egill Skallagrímsson (see *Egilssaga*, Ch. 59 f.).
In II Cn. 30, 4 we find mutilation instead of capital punishment, cf. In. 18; 37.
§ 7. 1. Cf. III Atr. 6, 2.
§ 8. 1. Cf. I Edg. 6, 1.
§ 9. 1. Cf. 1, 7.
§ 9 a. 1. Cf. In. 22; II As. 1, 1, where the punishment of the thief in similar cases is insisted on but not specified. The formula used here may be compared with those employed in early Norway, e.g. *Egilssaga*, Ch. 57; *Eyrbyggja saga*, Ch. 2.
§ 10. 1. Cf. III As. 7; III Edm. 7.
§ 12. 1. Cf. § 8.
§ 13. 1. Liebermann points out that the wergeld here is the lord's own because, as distinct from the case treated in § 11, the lord in this instance has been an accessory to the man's flight. He refers to Hn. 41, 6–11 where the distinction is clearly expressed, e.g. in 41, 8: *Si accusetur et aufugiat, reddat dominus eius regi weram illius hominis*, and 41, 10: *Si iuramentum frangat ei, reddat weram suam regi; et qui fugit utlaga sit.*
2. 1. The punishment, as Liebermann points out, is more severe than that inflicted by Æthelstan (see II As. 19). For later instances of branding see *E.H.R.*, 1895, p. 726; Bateson, *Borough Customs*, I. 77 f. and note.
2. Liebermann (II. p. 48, Col. 2, No. 5) notes the occasional use of weak declension forms in MS B, e.g. *cyrran* here and in II Cn. 32, 1; *of eardan*, II Cn. 3; *on wintran*, In. 38.
§ 1. 1. Cf. In. 24; VI As. 6, 3; III Edm. 4, where death by hanging is specified.
3. 1. Cf. In. 25; I Edw. 1; II As. 10; 12; VI As. 10.
§ 1. 1. Cf. IV Edg. 11, where the lord takes similar action with regard to stolen cattle.
4. 1. Cf. III Edm. 7, 1; III Edg. 7.
§ 1. 1. With *on ful* (acc. sing. neut.) cf. *on fulan*, II Cn. 33, 1, which Liebermann takes to be dat. pl. The parallel phrase *jaceat in ungildan æcere* occurs in IV Atr. 4.
§ 2. 1. Cf. II As. 1, 5; VI, 1, 3; III Atr. 13; 13, 1.
2. Cf. *forene forstande*, VI As. 1, 4.
§ 3. 1. Cf. IV As. 7.

II ÆTHELRED

Preamble. 1. The well-known Olaf Tryggvason, afterwards King of Norway, 995–1000. Before his acquisition of the throne he spent some years in piracy in the west, cf. *Sax. Chr.* 993 A, 994 E. Detailed accounts of his life, based on tradition, are to be found in Norse literature, especially in Snorri's Saga of Olaf Tryggvason (*Heimskringla*) and in the longer saga of Olaf Tryggvason preserved in the

Flateyjarbók and elsewhere, both of which (the second in an abridged form) have been translated into English. He is also very frequently mentioned in the Islendiga Sögur.

2. Justin, Norse *Josteinn*, was the brother of Ástríðr, the mother of Olaf Tryggvason (see *Olafssaga Tr.* in the *Heimskringla*, Chaps. 58, 102).

3. Guthmund, the son of Stegita, is mentioned by Florence of Worcester, but beyond this nothing definite seems to be known about him.

1. 1. The word *woroldfrið* occurs only in this passage (see BT. p. 1195, *s.v.*). Liebermann understands it to mean an alliance in which the Church as such took no part, the Northmen being still heathen. It seems, however, as if the term might be used to denote the general truce here established, as distinct from the terms concluded by the Archbishop and the ealdormen on behalf of their own districts.

2. The meaning might be 'as a consequence of.'

3. Sigeric was consecrated Bishop of Ramsbury in 985, became Archbishop of Canterbury in 990 and died in October 994 (see Stubbs, *Reg. Sacr. Angl.* p. 30). His signature is found attached to three documents of the year 995 (see Kemble, No. 689 ff.). The first of these records how he pledged land to the Bishop of Dorchester in order to obtain money to pay the Danes, and in its present form is probably not genuine. The second is a record of the restoration of this land to his successor and probably, as Plummer suggests (*Sax. Chr.* II. p. 174), the signatures have been mechanically copied from the preceding document. In the Saxon Chronicle (ann. 991) he alone is mentioned as advising the payment of tribute to the Danes.

4. Between the years 988 and 998 royal charters are invariably attested by *Æthelweard dux* and *Ælfric dux*, their signatures appearing together in the order given. From 993 onwards (*i.e.* after the death of Æthelwine and Byrhtnoth) they always sign at the head of the *duces* (*e.g.* Kemble, Nos. 664 f., 673, 684, 686 ff., 701 etc.). Their respective provinces are named in a document of 997 (Kemble, No. 698), viz. Æthelweard *Occidentalium provinciarum dux* (*i.e.* Western Wessex), Ælfric *Wentaniensium provinciarum dux* (*i.e.* presumably Hants and the adjacent counties). Æthelweard negotiated peace with Olaf also in 994 (see *Sax. Chr.* E). He is identified with the Latin chronicler who styles himself *Patricius Consul Quaestor Ethelwerdus*, and who claims descent from Æthelred I, the brother of Alfred (see *Sax. Chr.* II. p. ci). His chronicle extends to the year 975.

Ælfric continues to sign at the head of the *duces* from 999 to 1009 (see Kemble, Nos. 703, 705 ff., 709 f., 714 f., 1299, 1306). Stevenson (*Crawford Charters*, p. 120) identifies him with the Ælfric whose signature appears among the *duces* from 1012 to 1016 (see Kemble, Nos. 719, 723, 1307 ff.), and both Stevenson and Plummer (*Sax. Chr.* II. p. 323) regard him as the ealdorman Ælfric who fell at Assandun in 1016 (see *Sax. Chr.* E). On two occasions he seems to have played the part of a traitor (see *Sax. Chr.* E, ann. 992, 1003).

5. Such truces seem frequently to have been made between special districts and the invading forces, cf. *Sax. Chr.* ann. 1004 E, F;

1009 E. A similar offer was made to Byrhtnoth, ealdorman of Essex, see *Maldon*, ll. 29–41. Simeon of Durham (*Hist. of Ch. of Durham*, ann. 1018) mentions an earl of Northumbria who apparently made peace and war as he liked, and the case of the warlike Bishop Leofgar might also be quoted (see *Sax. Chr.* ann. 1056 C).

6. Ld reads *under cynges hand*, Q reads *quam sub manu regis superhabebant*. Liebermann accepts B's reading as probably correct. The construction, however, is unusual as *hand* in the sense of power is generally found with the prepositions *to, on, under* (see BT. p. 508, col. 2). For the construction with *ofer* following the word it governs Liebermann refers to BT. p. 730, *s.v. ofer*, III, and quotes *mid Angelþeode ðe he ofer cyning wæs*, Bede, 3, 6.

§ 1. 1. The form *Englaland* apparently came into use about this time replacing the earlier name *Angelcynnes land* (see *Sax. Chr.* II. p. 375). This is its first appearance in the Laws.

2. Cf. for a similar arrangement *Sax. Chr.* ann. 1006 E, 1012 E.

3. The invading force probably wintered in England. The Battle of Maldon which preceded the treaty is ascribed to August 11th by an eleventh century calendar, quoted, with references, by Napier and Stevenson, *Crawford Charters*, p. 88. In *Olafss. Tr.* Chap. 33, there is a romantic story of Olaf's marriage to an Irish princess while he was in England.

§ 2. 1. It is not clear whether *landa* here denotes English provinces or independent neighbouring kingdoms.

2. Does this mean, as Liebermann suggests, that such regions might be warred upon by either party to the truce and their ships and wares seized?

2. 1. *unfriðscyp*, cf. the various compounds of *frið* and *unfrið* in caps. 2 and 3, which seem, as Liebermann points out, to have a special significance in this context. A man belonging to either party to the truce is *friðman*, an Englishman being specially denoted as *Æðelredes cynges friðman* (3, 1). All those outside the truce, but not necessarily enemies, are *unfriðmen*, their provinces are *unfriðland* and their ships *unfriðscipu*. This interpretation seems the most satisfactory in view of 3, 1–3. The Latin rendering of *unfriðmanna* (3, 3) is *pacem non habentium*, although in the preceding clauses (2; 3, 1) *unfriðscip* and *unfriðland* are rendered *navis inimicorum* and *hostilis terra* respectively. Schmid translates *unfriðscyp* as 'ein feindliches Schiff,' *unfriðland* as 'ein friedloses Land,' and *unfrið* here is also taken in its usual sense of 'enemy, hostile' (cf. *Sax. Chr. unfriðflota*, ann. 1000 E, *unfriðhere* ann. 1007 D, 1009 E, *unfriðscip*, 1046 E) by Pollock, *Oxford Lectures*, p. 77 f.

2. Q translates *undrifen* by *non abacta tempestatibus*. Liebermann also takes it to refer to a ship driven to shelter by storm, giving references (*e.g.* Kemble, Nos. 737, 785, 809, 853, 871; Davis, *Reg. Agnorm.* Nos. 109, 177, 203) to show that wrecked goods fell to those possessing rights over the shore upon which they were stranded. The following clause (2, 1), however, suggests that the reference may be to pursuit, presumably by the Vikings who are parties to the truce

and therefore obliged to respect its terms and refrain from violence on land.

§ 1. 1. Cf. *friðman*, 3; 3, 1 and 4. In the north during the tenth and eleventh centuries certain places enjoyed special protection as trading centres, so that merchants from far and wide could bring their goods there without fear of molestation (see Du Chaillu, *Viking Age*, II. p. 210, and cf. *Laxdael Saga*, Ch. 21, where it is said of Ireland: *þetta er fiarri höfnum ok þeim kaupstöðum, er útlendir menn skulu hafa frið*). Such appointment of special havens of refuge, as Liebermann points out, was unknown in England, so that *frið* is to be taken here in the same sense as elsewhere in the treaty.

3. 1. *omnis friðmannus noster*, Q, probably including both parties, cf. the following clause, *Æthelredes cynges friðman*.

§ 1. *unfriðland*, cf. *unfriðscip*, cap. 2 and note.

§ 3. *unfriðmanna*, cf. cap. 2 and note.

§ 4. 1. Cf. Wi. 25; Af. 1, 5; E. and G. 6, 7; also the Swedish phrase *liggi i ungildum akri*.

4. 1. The difference in the readings is noteworthy. Ld's rubric reads *on*, Q *in*.

2. Lit. 'steersman.' It seems to have been the usual practice for the commander to steer the ship, even in the case of kings, cf. *Egilssaga*, Ch. 56.

3. In this construction the chief person is sometimes included in the number and sometimes not—an ambiguity which it is not easy to account for, see BT. p. 933, *s.v. sum*, I *b*, α and β.

4. Liebermann (III. p. 153), in view of the Latin translation *prelocutum erit*, understands the clause to refer to a transaction between an Englishman and a Northman regarding which a dispute has afterwards arisen. It seems more natural, however, to connect it with 3, 3, above.

5. 1. *i.e.* 1200 West Saxon shillings, cf. E. and G. 2, where the same amount is probably intended, and see Chadwick, *A.S. Institutions*, p. 50.

§ 1. 1. A Scandinavian loan word which appears here for the first time in the Laws.

2. A pound was the value of a slave, cf. IV As. 6, 5 f.; Duns. 7. Q has xx sol., *i.e.* shillings of twelve pence according to the Norman reckoning.

§ 2. 1. Cf. In. 13, 1. Liebermann takes *friðbrec* in its usual sense of breach of the peace, not of the truce of 991. Is this really necessary in view of the context?

6. 1. Q (with Ld) has acc. sg. *vivum vel mortuum*.

2. Thorpe and BT. p. 513, *s.v. heafod*, regard *heora nyhstan magas* as object and supply 'or' in front, *i.e.* the burghers are to seize the slayers or their nearest kinsmen. Schmid and Liebermann take the phrase as being in apposition to the subject. This would be more in accordance with A.S. law.

3. The natural meaning of the phrase seems to be 'life for life.' I take the latter part of the sentence from *heora nyhstan magas* as supplementary and suggested by *deade*.

II ÆTHELRED

4. *i.e.* if the town authorities will not take action.
5. Cf. Af. 42, 3 for similar stages of appeal.
6. Liebermann translates 'liege in Friedlosigkeit.'
§ 1. 1. Q's reading *incendiis* would seem to be based on some form like *bærnum* for *brynum* in the A.S. MS source.
2. *gedon wære*, cf. *facta sunt*, Q. Liebermann suggests emending the A.S. reading to *wæren*.
§ 2. 1. Cf. A. and G. 5 and the close of a letter of Pope John XV who shortly before brought about a reconciliation between Æthelred and Duke Richard of Normandy: *et de hominibus regis vel de inimicis suis nullum Richardus recipiat, nec rex de suis sine sigillo eorum* (see *Mem. of St Dunstan*, ed. Stubbs, p. 398; Wm of Malmesbury, *Gesta Reg.*, Rolls Series, I. pp. 192–3).
2. By the end of the tenth century *wealh* is frequently used for 'slave' without any reference to Celtic origin.
7. 1. *landesmann*, *i.e.* Englishman as opposed to a member of the invading force, cf. *twegen landesmenn and an ælþeodig*, Ælfric, *Homilies*, ed. Thorpe, II. p. 26, l. 20.
2. *sceiðman* is derived from *scegð* (O. Norse *skeið*), a light, swift ship of a special kind (see Napier and Stevenson, *Crawford Charters*, p. 128), probably commonly used by the invaders (see Plummer, *Sax. Chr.* II. p. 185), hence the name applied to them, cf. *sæmann, flotman, æscmann* etc.
§ 1. 1. Cf. 5, 2.
§ 2. 1. This is perhaps a note subsequently added to the original document (see Liebermann, III. p. 154). The payment of the tribute demanded preceded the treaty, cf. cap. 1. The sum mentioned here does not correspond to either of the amounts stated in the Saxon Chronicle, viz. £10,000 in 991, £16,000 in 994. Liebermann suggests that various payments may have been added together to give this total and points out that the payment recorded in 991 is qualified as *ærost*. The total amount of money paid out of England during the reign of Æthelred was enormous, and at the present day more of his coins have been found in the Scandinavian countries than in our own (see Keary, *Catalogue of Eng. Coins*, II. p. lxxx ff.; B. E. Hildebrand, *Anglo-Sach. mynt i Svenska k. myntkab.* p. 24).
2. *i.e.* the total sum was paid partly in gold and partly in silver, but the whole sum is to be understood as elsewhere (cf. Birch, 348, 455, 522) in terms of silver.
8. § 1. 1. Cf. § 3.
§ 3. 1. Cf. *Forfang* 3 Q.
§ 4. 1. Cf. cap. 9 where the new regulation is more fully explained.
9. 1. *i.e.* then and not till then.
§ 1. 1. *i.e.* that he obtains trustworthy security from the person against whom he is making the claim, cf. I Edw. 1, 2. The second clause *and beorge þæt he awoh ne befo* seems to introduce another consideration—not connected with the preceding—which the plaintiff has to bear in mind.
§ 2. 1. Cf. In. 53 f.; *Ancient Laws and Institutes of Wales*, p. 209 f. One clause in a London Municipal collection of the time of John

provides for the taking of an oath at the tomb of a dead man regarding the testimony he would have borne if alive, and 'in Manx law until 1609 when a debtor died and no writings remained to prove his debt, the creditor might come to the dead man's grave,...and, with his face toward Heaven and with a Bible on his breast, protest before God and by that book that the dead man owed him the money, and the executors were bound to pay' (see M. Bateson in *E.H.R.*, 1902, p. 488 f.).

§ 3. 1. For other instances of *habban* with a partitive genitive see In. 32; 66; Af. 42, 1 and 3.

2. In view of IV Edg. 11 the culprit might be in danger of losing his life.

§ 4. 1. Cf. I Edw. 1, 5; II As. 9.

2. *propriatio propinquior semper est possidenti quam repetenti,* Q, cf. Hn. 64, 6: *semper erit possidens propior quam repetens.*

III ÆTHELRED

Preamble. 1. Cf. IV Edg. 2, 1 and note.

2. Wantage in Berkshire, a royal manor (see DB. I. 57 a), was the birthplace of Alfred (see Asser, *Life of K. Alfred*, ed. Stevenson, p. 1). An assembly was held there in 997 (see Kemble, 698) and another is recorded (Kemble, 693) *æt Cwicelmes-hlæwe, i.e.* probably Cuckhamsley Hill in the vicinity of Wantage.

3. Q adds *et felicitatis incrementum.*

1. 1. Cf. *cyninges handgrið*, E. and G. 1; VI Atr. 14; I Cn. 2, 2; DB. I. 154 b, 2; 172 a, 1; 252 a, 1; 280 b, 1; 298 b, 2.

2. Cf. *swa hit betst stod*, II Edg. 5, 3. For *fyrmest* in the same sense see X Atr. Pre.

3. See VIII Atr. 1, 1; 1 Cn. 2, 3; II Cn. 64, for lists of crimes which are *botleas.*

§ 1. 1. Cf. Q *vel*; IV Edg. 11 and note.

2. The Five Boroughs (Derby, Leicester, Lincoln, Nottingham, and Stamford) are first mentioned under that name in the Saxon Chronicle, ann. 942 A. They seem to have formed a kind of confederacy, though it is uncertain whether this was in existence before the English Conquest. The whole of this district, more especially the eastern part of it, contained a large Danish population. The twelve lawmen vouched for in Lincoln and Stamford (see DB. I. 336 a and b) and therefore probably to be found in the other towns as well, the division of the land in Domesday Book according to carucates (combined generally in groups of 6 and 12), and the appearance of wapentakes in Lincolnshire, Derbyshire and Nottinghamshire (see Stubbs, *Constit. Hist.* I. p. 103), are all survivals from the period of Danish government. In the Saxon Chronicle, ann. 1015 E, we hear of 'Seven Boroughs' (as a group), the additional two probably being York and Chester (see Plummer, II. p. 193; Hodgkin, *Hist. of England*, I. p. 394).

§ 2. 1. Q's translation (see p. 64[1]) points to a reading *on anre burhge geþincðe*, cf. the reading of H.
2. The fines throughout this law are stated according to Danish standards, cf. A. and G. 2 and E. and G. *passim*. The mark (mörk) contained 8 oran (aurar), while the ora (eyrir) contained sometimes 16, sometimes 20 pence, see IV Atr. 9, 2 and note.
3. Cf. VIII Atr. 4.
2. 1. *i.e.* the persons who make declarations supported by witnesses. Liebermann in his translation takes *cwicon, deadon* as referring to the witnesses but corrects as above (Zeugenführer) in the Addenda to his first volume (see II. p. 757) and in his notes (see III. p. 157) in view of Q's translation: *Et hoc quod per legitimum testimonium monstrabitur, nemo pervertat de vivo plus quam de mortuo*.
§ 1. 1. An instance of the not uncommon A.S. usage of stating prohibitions in a positive instead of a negative form. In such cases it is necessary to insert 'only' in modern English (see Liebermann, II. p. 750, *s.v. Zeugen*, 4 *a*).
2. Cf. cap. 3, 1; *Oath Formulae*, 1; 2; VII Atr. (A.S.), 2, 1; II Cn. 36.
3. 1. *landcop* etc. These words are all collective singular in the original. A more literal translation of *þæt...awende* would be 'shall stand incontrovertible,' cf. *stande unawend*, Kemble, Nos. 868, 895. It should be noted that three of the terms, viz. *landcop, lahcop,* and *witword*, are Scandinavian. The last of these, translated 'asseveration,' appears to have a technical sense in Swedish law, viz. 'the assertion of a right by a party to whom the way to such assertion is legally open,' see Vinogradoff in *H.L.R.* 20 (1907), p. 537. For the form cf. Norse *vitorð*, confidence, cognisance.
Liebermann follows Brunner (*Rechtsge. Germ. Urk.* p. 189), and Vinogradoff (*loc. cit.*), in taking *landcop* to refer to the actual purchase of land, but points out that Schmid (p. 622), BT. (p. 617), Björkmann (*Scandinavian Loanwords*, p. 12), and Hale (*Domesday of St Paul's*, p. xciv) regard it as meaning a tax paid on purchasing land. Jenks (*Law and Politics*, Sec. Ed. p. 213) explains it as the 'payment of a man acquiring land for the witnessing and security furnished by the county.' The fact, however, that the transaction is made incontrovertible seems, as Liebermann points out, to support the view that the actual purchase is referred to.
2. Cf. Vinogradoff (*loc. cit.*): 'the reintegration to one's lawful standing by the payment of a fine.'
3. Liebermann suggests that 'testimony' here may have a technical meaning connected with the acquisition of property, cf. Vinogradoff (*loc. cit.*), also P. and M. II. p. 85. The alliterative phrase *witnum oc wizorþum* is found in Swedish law, see Steenstrup, *Danelag*, p. 190.
§ 1. 1. Cf. II Edw. 2 and perhaps IV Edg. 5, but it is a question whether this council of 12 is not a Scandinavian institution connected, if not substantially identical with, the lawmen. Since from

13, 2 the twelve thegns evidently act as a jury they may be compared with the juries of 12 so frequently mentioned in sagas relating both to Norway and Iceland, e.g. *Egilssaga*, Ch. 56, where three such act in combination, *Eyrbyggja saga*, Ch. 16. In *Gylfaginning*, Ch. 14, the gods themselves are credited with a similar institution (cf. also *Ynglinga saga*, Ch. 2), and there can be no doubt that it was of high antiquity in the north. Its historical connection with the juries of later times is disputed.

  2. Cf. 2, 1.
  3. Cf. Norse *saklauss*.
  4. Cf. Norse *sekr*, accused, guilty (opp. *unsac*), and see BT. p. 806, *s.v. sac*, where no other instance of the use of this adj. is quoted.

 § 2. 1. *qui cum preposito causam habent*, Q.
  2. Cf. 1, 2; 12; 13, 2; 13, 4.
  3. Cf. III Edg. 7, 1.
 § 3. 1. The amount is the same as *lahslit*, cf. E. and G. 3, 2.
 § 4. 1. Cf. I Atr. 1, 1.

4. 1. Cf. I Atr. 1, 2 and 3.
  2. Q has *vadat ad triplex ordalium* which is probably incorrect in view of I Atr. 1, 3.
 § 1. 1. Cf. I Atr. 1, 5–7.
  2. Cf. 4, 2; 5.
 § 2. 1. *þam landrican* is probably to be taken as *dativus commodi*. A more literal translation would be, 'he (the thief) is to go to the ordeal for (the benefit of) the lord of the manor.'
  2. Presumably to the lord of the manor.

5. 1. Cf. I Atr. 3.
  2. Q has *dominus hoc percipiat*; cf. I Atr. 3, 1. The use of the plural in the A.S. text is curious. Liebermann suggests that it may be due to a misreading of the end vowels -*a* and -*o* as -*ā* and -*ō*, *i.e.* as -*an* and -*on*.
  3. Cf. I Atr. 3, 1. In IV Edg. 11 the offence is aggravated by a false oath.

6. 1. Cf. *Be Blas.* 2.
 § 1. 1. Cf. II Atr. 9.
  2. It is not clear what *byrig* means here. Has it the later meaning 'town' (an interpretation which is somewhat favoured by *binnan port* in cap. 7), or is it practically equivalent to the usual *cyninges tun*? Royal manors in the charge of the king's reeves were presumably as a rule fortified, at least in early times. Liebermann translates 'im königlichen [Gericht in reichsunmittelbarer] Stadt.'
 § 2. Cf. I Atr. 1, 7.

7. 1. Cf. In. 20–21, 1.
  2. This sum is forfeited if the plea miscarries, cf. 7, 1.
  3. Cf. 3, 2.
  4. Cf. 6, 1 and note.
 § 1. 1. This interpretation follows Liebermann. Presumably the supposed thief had been slain, cf. ECf. 36–36, 5 (Liebermann, I. p. 666 ff.).
  2. Cf. cap. 7.

8. 1. The only previous reference in the laws which have come down to us is in II As. 14, 1. As over half a century must have elapsed since that time, it seems probable that the reference is to a lost law; cf. the references to a council at Bromdun, I Atr. 1, 2; III, 4.

§ 1. 1. If this is to be taken literally, the right of having moneyers possessed by certain ecclesiastics according to II As. 14, 2 was for a time withdrawn (cf. Parsons, *Brit. Numis. Journal, Sec. Ser.*, Vol. III. p. 9). These rights were restored before the Conquest (see DB. I. 179 a, 1; II. 117 b).

§ 2. Cf. 3, 3.

9. 1. Cf. Bateson, *Borough Customs*, I. p. 59: ownership of cattle attached within the bounds of the city of Waterford about 1300 was to be proved *par pel e par quier*. The hide presumably would be branded with the owner's mark.

§ 1. 1. Cf. 4, 1.

11. 1. Cf. I Atr. 1, 14.

12. 1. As these laws are provincial rather than national it seems probable that the reference is not to actions brought in the king's court but rather to actions brought by the king's representative in other courts, cf. Liebermann's note, III. p. 160: 'eine Fiskalklage durch den öffentlichen Beamten.'

13. 1. A Scandinavian mode of expressing number, cf. *þrennar tylftir* (*Njalssaga*, Ch. 144). The right of refuting charges by means of 36 compurgators is found in London and elsewhere from the twelfth to the fifteenth centuries (see Bateson, *Borough Customs*, I. pp. 37–44; Gross, *Modes of Trial in Mediaeval Boroughs, H.L.R.* 15. p. 695 ff.).

§ 1. 1. Cf. IV As. 6, 3; VI, 1, 2; I Atr. 4, 2.

§ 2. 1. *sámmǽle* is a Scandinavian loan word.

2. If the *þegenas* here mentioned are identical with those mentioned in 3, 1 (this being Liebermann's opinion) it would seem that the votes of more than a bare majority were required. Liebermann suggests the possibility of VIII being a scribal alteration of VII, but Q (*octo*) agrees with H. In the old Norse legal system *tolf þegna dómr* is frequently mentioned (see Maurer, *Altnord. Rechtsgeschichte*, I. (2), p. 181) and in the case of Iceland the rule seems to have been that: *dóm skal ryðja sem* 12 *kvíð* (see Maurer, *op. cit.* v. p. 434). It would seem that in each case the verdict had to be unanimous (see Dasent, *Njalssaga* (1861), p. lvi); there is no mention of a two-thirds majority as here.

3. BT. p. 731, *s.v. oferdrifan*, give only this one instance of its use with the meaning 'to outvote.'

4. Cf. 1, 2; 13, 4.

§ 3. 1. *Cost* is a Scandinavian loan word, cf. Icel. *kostr*.

§ 4. 1. Liebermann takes the phrase to mean 'in spite of that.' BT. p. 605, *s.v. lad* II., translate: 'He that admits or he that offers purgation after that shall pay 6 half-marks.'

14. 1. Cf. the Norse formula *kvaða and krafa*, and see Steenstrup, *Danelag*, p. 184.

2. Q has *heredes*; the original might be either sing. or pl.

15. 1. See P. and M. II. p. 493 f.
2. Cf. ECf. 24, 1.
3. Does this include privilege of sanctuary?
16. 1. Cf. IV Atr. 5, 4.
2. A wood is regarded as a place of secret crime.
3. *i.e.* surreptitiously. According to II As. 14 there were to be no mints except in towns.

This clause is not found in Q and may therefore be an addition due to the scribe of H. In subject-matter it connects with cap. 8 and with the long section on the coinage in IV Atr. There seems no reason to regard it as spurious.

IV ÆTHELRED

1. 1. This is the earliest mention of these names in any extant document (see Lethaby, *London before the Conquest*, p. 86). Stow (*Survey of London*, ed. Kingsford, 1908, I. p. 33) records that he had read that in 1010 the body of King Edmund was brought into London at Cripplegate, 'so-called of Criples begging there,' but in the *Memorials of St Edmund's Abbey* (Rolls Series, I. 43) it is said to have been brought *a via quae Anglice dicitur Ealsegate*. Cripplegate appears also in documents of 1068 and about 1080 (see Davis, *Reg. Agnorm.* Nos. 22, xxvii).

2. 1. This is the earliest mention of this important quay under this name. Lethaby (*op. cit.* p. 92) suggests that it was probably the *Lundentuneshythe* mentioned in a charter of 743-5 (see Earle, *Land Charters*, p. 42). Toll was paid there under Richard I (see Madox, *Hist. of the Exchequer*, I. pp. 775, 778, 779) and under Edward III (see Stow, *op. cit.* p. 206). Stow describes it as 'at this present (*i.e.* 1598) a large watergate, port or harbour for ships and boats commonly arriving there with fish both fresh and salt, oranges, onions and other fruits and roots, wheat, rye and grain of divers sorts.' Its importance as a fish market dates from 1699 (see 10 & 11 William III. c. 24).

§ 1. 1. This is the earliest occurrence of the name 'hulk' quoted in the *N.E.D.* In Ælfric's Glossary it translates *liburna* which is a light, fast-sailing vessel, but in Middle English and later it is the name for a large cargo-ship, a merchantman (see BT. p. 565 *s.v. hulc*). Lorrainers in the twelfth century are described as coming to England in *kiel, hulk u altre nef* (see Bateson, *E.H.R.*, 1902, p. 500).

§ 3. 1. Liebermann suggests that the original may have read *claðtoll.
2. Cf. the twelfth-century regulation: *Mercatores qui Lond' redeunt et afferunt pannos de lino et de lana non debent vendere nisi tantum* III *diebus in ebdomada, scilicet lune, martis, mercurii* (see *E.H.R.*, 1902, p. 717).

Sunday trading was forbidden in E. and G. 7; II As. 24, 1, but these decrees were afterwards abrogated, cf. IV As. 2; VI As. 10. In later times Sunday trading was again forbidden, cf. V Atr. 13, 1;

VI, 22, 1; 44; VIII, 17; I Cn. 15. In the passage quoted above Monday takes the place of Sunday.

§ 4. 1. Old London Bridge which crossed the river to the east of the present bridge has been proved by discoveries of Roman coins, tiles and pottery to be of Roman origin (see Lethaby, *op. cit.* p. 70 f.). It is mentioned in a document of about 970 in connection with a woman who was drowned there for practising pin-sticking witchcraft (see Kemble, 591; Birch, 1131). An interesting description of the bridge as it was about 1014 is found in the *Heimskringla* (*Saga of Olaf the Holy*, Ch. 11).

§ 5. 1. Cf. *Homines Rotomagi qui de ghilda sunt mercatorum sint quieti de omni consuetudine apud Londonium, nisi de vino et de crasso pisce*, Charter of Henry Plantagenet, Duke of Normandy, c. 1150 (see Chéruel, *Rouen pendant l'époque communale*, I. p. 245). The clauses which follow grant to the merchants of Rouen the right of entry to all English markets and also assign to them a special harbour at London which they had held in the time of King Edward, cf. the similar clauses in the Charter of John Lackland, Chéruel, *op. cit.* p. 252 f.

2. Alias *piscis crassus*, *i.e.* whales, porpoises etc. See Du Cange, *s.v. craspiscis*; Round, *Commune of London*, p. 246; Fréville, *Commerce de Rouen*, I. p. 179. Liebermann suggests that the A.S. original may have read *hran(fisc)* or *hwæl*; cf. Icel. *hvalr* (Maurer, *Island*, p. 414).

3. Liebermann suggests that the A.S. text may have read *geriht(o)*.

4. Lit. 'a twentieth part of the fish itself.'

§ 6. 1. Commercial relations between England and Flanders were early established and greatly influenced the industrial development of both countries (see Varenbergh, *Hist. des relations diplomatiques entre le comté de Flandre et l'Angleterre*, pp. 9–12). In the reign of Edgar, according to William of Malmesbury, many foreigners were attracted by his fame to visit England, with evil results for the inhabitants. From the men of Flanders they learned *corporum enervem mollitiem* (see *Gesta Reg.* I. p. 165).

2. Liebermann takes this to mean that they paid toll but no other duty, cf. the clause included among the twelfth-century rules for foreign merchants (Bateson, *E.H.R.*, 1902, pp. 497–8, 500–1): § 8. 'Lorrainers who remain on board their boats and sell their goods there and do not pass Thames Street or the wharves to take up quarters in the city, shall give no other custom (or shewage) except the wine custom, *i.e.* the 'cornage' or pence on every tun.'

§ 7. 1. On the Meuse, N.E. of Namur.

2. Cf. the continuation of the clause quoted above: 'If there is a Lorrainer who wishes to carry his goods up into the town, and passes the wharf and Thames Street, and leaves the ship and takes lodgings in the city, and his goods are gathered together and taken with him, he pays the king's shewage.'

3. A duty to be paid for the privilege of exhibiting their goods in the markets (cf. Du Cange, *s.v. ostensio*, 3). Liebermann

understands it to mean a duty to be paid in place of exhibiting their goods. The technical A.S. term is *sceawung* (see BT. p. 828, *s.v.* VI), and it is frequently included among the list of rights granted by Edward the Confessor in his Charters (see Kemble, 771, 825, 857, 861).

§ 8. 1. The subjects of the Emperor appear to be specially privileged. They have a special clause also in the twelfth-century set of regulations already quoted, viz. § 12: 'The common law of the men of the Emperor of Germany is that they may lodge within the walls of the city of London where they will, except men of Tiel and Bremen and Antwerp, who shall not pass London Bridge unless they will be ruled (?) by the law of London.'

2. Cf. *Geþyncðo*, 6.

3. Probably privileges with regard to trade.

§ 9. 1. *i.e.* wool which is for sale by retail.

2. *unctum*, *i.e. unguentum*, A.S. *smeoru*, as Liebermann points out.

3. Presumably as provision, cf. the twelfth-century regulations quoted above, § 10: 'No Lorrainer may buy more than three live pigs for his table.'

§ 10. 1. Cf. Norse *forkjǫb*, Steenstrup, *Danelag*, p. 378 f., and see Bateson, *E.H.R.*, 1902, p. 718.

2. The construction is difficult to understand. Liebermann suggests that the original (A.S.) may have been elliptical.

3. Liebermann points out that, since they pay toll at Christmas and Easter, German merchants must have wintered in England. According to the twelfth-century rules for foreign merchants no Lorrainer might dwell in the city more than 40 days, unless a storm of wind or some evil delayed him, or he stayed for a debt which was withheld from him, see § 6 (*E.H.R.* 1902, p. 500), and cf. *Lib. Lond.* 9, 1 (Liebermann, I. p. 675). Norwegians and Danes, however, had right of sojourn for a year (*E.H.R.* p. 502).

4. *grisengus pannus* is understood as 'minever' by Schmid, following Du Cange, *s.v. griseum*, and translated 'grey skin' by Ballard (*Domesday Boroughs*, p. 116); *pannus* however, as Liebermann points out, means 'cloth' not 'skin.'

5. Cf. *Lib. Lond.* 8, 1.

6. *i.e.* kegs portable on horseback; *caballinus* is a late Latin word.

§ 11. 1. *i.e.* hampers carried on the back.

§ 12. 1. In Winchester in the time of Henry I every woman selling butter or lard had to pay a penny for *smeargable*, see Round, *Victoria County Hist. of Hants*, I. p. 529.

3. 1. *i.e. tun(es) gerefa*, cf. VII Atr. 2, 5.

2. *praepositus* is the usual word for 'reeve' in Latin documents of the period.

3. *Compellare* translates A.S. *teon*, cf. Af. 17; 33.

4. Cf. *forhealdan*, E. and G. 6, 1.

§ 1. 1. *i.e.* A.S. *tieman* or *cennan*.

IV ÆTHELRED

§ 2. 1. Probably A.S. *forgieldan*. Only one of the five MSS of Q has *et*, but cf. In. 9; 31. Liebermann takes it in this way.
2. Cf. 4, 1.
§ 3. 1. A.S. *kæcepol*, of N. French origin showing Picard *c* corresponding to Central Fr. *ch*, see Skeat, *Academy*, 28 Sept. 1895, p. 252.
2. *Advocare, i.e.* A.S. *tieman*, cf. In. 47; 53; 75; I Edw. 1, 5; II Atr. 9; 9, 4.
4. 1. *i.e.* apparently the king and his councillors.
2. *summam infracturam, i.e.* A.S. *-bryce*. Q does not say what was violated, but the original probably had *mund, borg* or *grið*. Breach of the peace with homicide is probably intended.
3. The word *ungebendeo* or *ungebendro* is obscure and in all probability corrupt. Thorpe (*Glossary, s.v.*) and BT. p. 1106 suggest *ungeboden, i.e.* unsummoned, unbidden, while Steenstrup (*Danelag*, p. 358) takes the phrase as equivalent to *sine licentia placiti* and compares it with the Danish *af þingi unbedhen*. Liebermann suggests that the original A.S. text may have read *gemotes* (*spræce*) *ungebeden* (cf. *placitum* translating A.S. *gemot*, Af. 38 Q; II As. 20 Q; translating *spræc*, I Edw. Pre. Q; also the use of the phrase *rihtes gebeden*, II Cn. 19). His translation is: '[wer] schwerste Verletzung verübt an einem [von ihm noch] nicht zum Rechtsgang aufgeforderten (?).'
4. Cf. Hn. 80, 2 where *forestal* is explained as *in via regis assultus*. Liebermann points out that *forsteall, hamsocn* and *griðbryce* are three of the crimes for which £5 must be paid according to Hn 12, 2; 35, 2; DB. I. 172 *a*, 1; 252 *a*, 1.
5. A Scandinavian expression (*i úgildum akri*), see Steenstrup, *Danelag*, p. 356. The word *úgildr* strictly means that for which no wergeld is paid, and the phrase may therefore mean that he shall lie in the ground used for those for whom no wergeld is paid. On the other hand it is possible that the precise significance originally attaching to the word may have been lost.
§ 1. 1. Cf. Af. 42; II As. 3.
2. Liebermann suggests that, in the original text, these words probably referred to the person attacked and have been misunderstood by the translator.
3. *burhbrece* here can hardly be anything but a corruption of *borgbryce* (cf. Af. 3), as suggested by Schmid and Liebermann. Liebermann points out that the same translator wrote *burgbrece* instead of *borgbrece* also in Hn. 12, 2; 35, 2.
§ 2. 1. Liebermann suggests that the original text probably read *recce freondscipes*.
2. *i.e.* the city authorities.
3. It may be noted that the amount is the same as in the case of the (additional) fine paid to the hundred, see III Edm. 2
5. 1. The change from the first person to the third is curious. Perhaps *we* was omitted in the original which read simply *cwædon*.
2. A.S. *bycgean*, cf. *ungeboht*, unbribed, *Oath Formulae*, 8.

326   NOTES TO THE LAWS OF ÆTHELRED

3. The state of the coins which have come down to us from the reigns of Æthelstan and his successors seems to afford justification for this reproach.

§ 1. 1. *A.S. anes rihtes weorðe*, cf. I Atr. 4, 2; III, 13, 1.

§ 2. 1. From III, 8 it would seem that this expression means the triple ordeal.

§ 3. 1. Cf. II As. 14, 1.
2. Cf. II Atr. 1 Q.

§ 4. 1. Cf. III Atr. 16.

6. 1. For a list of the places possessing a mint in the reign of Æthelred, see Powell, *E.H.R.*, XI. p. 761.

7. § 1. 1. Cf. Wi. 26; 27; In. 6.
2. Cf. 5, 2.

§ 2. 1. The business of exchange was separated from that of coining money by Edward I, see Cunningham, *Growth of Industry*, p. 283.

§ 3. 1. Cf. II Cn. 8, 2.
2. Cf. II As. 9. No oath of nominated compurgators is mentioned elsewhere in IV Atr. Liebermann suggests that *eodem* may be a false translation of *þam*.
3. *i.e.* in 5, 2.

8. 1. Probably tautological, though *comitibus* may be a translation of *eorlum* referring to Danish governors.
2. *utrobique* etc. It is uncertain whether this phrase should be taken with *curam adhibeant* or with *portant per patriam*.
3. The order is noticeable.

9. 1. It is uncertain what towns are meant by the expression *summus portus*, but Liebermann suggests that those named in II As. 14, 2 which had more than one moneyer were probably included among them.

§ 1. 1. *i.e.* in 7, 1?

§ 2. 1. Lit. 'according to the weight for which my money is accepted.'
2. The ore, according to this reckoning, contains 16 pence, a value which is supported by other evidence, see Chadwick, *A.S. Institutions*, pp. 24 f., 412. In Domesday Book an ore of 20 pence is frequently mentioned.

V ÆTHELRED

Heading. 1. The difference in the headings as preserved in the three MSS is noticeable. That in G is the fullest and is probably authentic. It is analogous in form to the heading of VIII Atr. and is specially important as giving the date of the ordinance.

The form *Angolwitena* in G_2 is unusual and is not quoted in BT. Liebermann accepts it as genuine however and parallel to such compounds as *Angelcyning*, *-cynn*, *-cyrice*, *-þeod*, and *Angulseaxe*.

Preamble. 1. The king's name is not mentioned. Cf. I Edg.
2. Cf. I Edm. Pre.; II Edm. Pre.

1. 1. The addition in G_2 is taken over in VI, 1; X, 1.
    2. Cf. VI. 6; VII. 1; IX; I Cn. 1; Wulfstan, *Homilies*, p. 274.
    3. Cf. 34; VI. 1; 42, 2; X. 1; I Cn. 1; 21; *N.P.L.* 47; 67.
    4. Cf. E. and G. Pre. 1; V Atr. 34; VI, 1; VIII, 44; IX; X, 1; *N.P.L.* 47; 67; *Poenit. Ecgberti*, Lib. II. c. 22, IV. 19, ed. Thorpe, *Anc. Laws*, II. pp. 190, 210; *Canons en. under Edgar*, 16, 18, ed. Thorpe, *op. cit.* p. 248. It has been suggested that the influence of the Scandinavian invasions may have caused a recrudescence of heathen practices, but the law may have the Danelaw more especially in view.
    5. Cf. 35; VI. 1; VIII. 44, 1; IX. This is perhaps directed against possible adherents of Sweyn who at this time was generally engaged in hostilities against Æthelred, cf. *Sax. Chr.* The same expression (*an cynedom*) occurs in *N.P.L.* 67, 1.
§ 1. 1. Cf. 23; 33; VI, 8; II Cn. 1.
    2. Cf. III Edg. 1, 1; VII Atr. 6, 1.
    3. Cf. VI. 8, 2; X. 2, 1.
    4. This phrase is of frequent occurrence; cf. 4; 9, 2 etc.
2. 1. Cf. In. 11; VI Atr. 9; VII, 5; II Cn. 3; Wulfstan, pp. 158, 161.
    2. Anselm in 1102 forbade all traffic in slaves: *ne quis illud nefarium negotium quo hactenus homines in Anglia solebant velut bruta animalia venundari deinceps ullatenus facere praesumat* (see Eadmer, *Hist. Novorum*, ed. Rule, Rolls Series, p. 143).
    3. See Chadwick, *Cult of Othin*, p. 27, note 2.
    4. Cf. 3.
3. 1. Cf. VI. 10; II Cn. 2, 1.
    2. Liebermann translates: '[Leben] schonende Strafen.' Does this refer to the substitution of mutilation for capital punishment?
4. 1. Cf. VI. 2; I Cn. 6.
    2. Cf. the classification in VI, 2.
    3. Cf. IV Edg. 1, 7; VI Atr. 2; 41; I Cn. 4, 3; Wulfstan, pp. 120, 179.
5. 1. Cf. VI. 3; Wulfstan, p. 269; and see P. and M. I. p. 434.
    2. Cf. VI. 3 and note.
    3. Lit. 'the word and pledge'—an alliterative phrase which seems to signify a promise formally given and therefore to be regarded as binding.
6. 1. Liebermann suggests that many monks at this time may have been in such a position owing to the destruction of monasteries by the Danes. Cf. however VI. 3, 1 and note.
    2. Cf. 9, 1.
7. 1. Cf. VI. 4.
    2. This is the first occurrence of the term 'canon' in the Laws and, apart from this context, it appears in only one other clause, viz. VI 2 (where V 4 reads *preostas*) repeated in I Cn. 6 *a* (see further J. Armitage Robinson, *St Oswald and the Church of Worcester*, Supplemental Papers of the British Academy, p. 13, and *The Times of St Dunstan*, pp. 170–1).

I understand that the question of the position of canons in the Early Church will be discussed by Miss M. Deanesly in an article on *The Familia at Christchurch, Canterbury*, 597–832, in the forthcoming presentation volume to Professor T. F. Tout.

3. Presumably the prebend which came to him in virtue of his position.

8. 1. Cf. VI, 5; I Cn. 6, 1; Wulfstan, p. 269.

9. 1. Cf. I Edm. 1; IV Edg. 1, 7; VI Atr. 5, 1; VIII, 30; I Cn. 6, 2; Wulfstan, p. 269.

2. A homiletic phrase. The verb may be either indic. or subj. so that it might also be translated, 'let them know full well.'

§ 1. 1. Cf. VI, 5, 3; VIII, 28; I Cn. 6, 2 *a*.

2. Lit. 'in the grave.'

§ 2. 1. Cf. VI, 5, 4.

10. 1. Cf. Wi. 3–6; VI Atr. 11; I Cn. 6, 3.

§ 1. 1. Cf. VI, 13; I Cn. 2, 1; *Be Griðe*, 31.

§ 2. 1. Cf. VI Atr. 15; *N.P.L.* 20–22.

2. Lit. 'enslave.' Liebermann suggests that lay patrons may have been in the habit of subjecting ecclesiastical foundations to secular duties, and quotes the case of Crediton, which in 739 became *causarum fiscalium, rerum regalium, saecularium operum immunis* (see Napier and Stevenson, *Crawford Charters*, p. 2).

3. 'Simony' (see BT. p. 156, *s.v. ciricmangung*), cf. Anselm (1102): *ne ecclesiae aut praebendae emantur.* Lay abbots were common in Scotland in the eleventh century.

11. 1. Cf. E. and G. 5, 1; II Edg. 2, 3; 3; VI, 16–19; 43; VIII, 9–12, 1; I Cn. 8–10; Wulfstan, pp. 116, 208, 310 f.

§ 1. 1. 'Vierzehn Tage' (Liebermann), cf. II Edg. 2, 3 and note.

2. Cf. *Can. Edg.* 54, ed. Thorpe, *Anc. Laws*, II. p. 256. In II Edg. 3 the time fixed is the equinox (*i.e.* September).

3. Cf. I Cn. 12; Wulfstan, pp. 117, 208, 311: *leohtgescot...to Cristes mæssan and to candelmæssan and to eastron*.

12. 1. Cf. II Edg. 5, 2; VI, 20; VIII, 13; I Cn. 13; Wulfstan, pp. 118, 208, 311.

§ 1. 1. Cf. II Edg. 5, 2; VI Atr. 21; I Cn. 13, 1; Anselm (1102): *ne corpora defunctorum extra parochiam suam sepelienda portentur ut presbyter parochiae perdat quod inde illi juste debetur.*

§ 2. 1. Cf. E. and G. 5, 1; VI Atr. 21, 1; VIII, 14; I Cn. 14; Wulfstan, pp. 272, 311.

2. Is the form in D a case of metathesis?

§ 3. 1. Cf. II Edg. 5, 1; VI, 22; 43; I Cn. 14, 1; Wulfstan, pp. 71, 272.

13. 1. Cf. II Edg. 5; VI Atr. 22, 1; 44; I Cn. 14, 2; Wulfstan, pp. 117, 208, 272.

§ 1. 1. Cf. IV Atr. 2, 3 and note; VI, 22, 1; VIII, 17; I Cn. 15; *N.P.L.* 55.

14. 1. Cf. Wulfstan, pp. 117, 208.

2. Cf. VI, 22, 2; I Cn. 16 a. The dates on which these festivals fell were Feb. 2nd, March 25th, August 15th, Sept. 8th (see Piper, *Kalend. Agsa.*, pp. 91, 94).

§ 1. 1. Cf VI, 22, 3; I Cn. 16 a.

2. May 1st.

3. In 1008 Easter fell on March 28th (see Nicolas, *Chronology of History*, Sec. Ed., p. 58).

15. 1. Cf. VI, 22, 4.

2. Cf. II Edg. 5, 3, where a similar expression is employed.

16. 1. Cf. VI, 23, 1 D; I Cn. 17, 1.

2. Edward the Martyr, the elder son of Edgar, was elected king in succession to his father (see *Sax. Chr.* ann. 975 E). In 978 he was assassinated at Corfe (see *Sax. Chr.* A, C; ann. 979 E). In the earliest detailed account of the deed it is said to have taken place when he was visiting his young step-brother, Æthelred, and to have been committed by the thegns belonging to the household and party of his step-mother, Ælfthryth (see *Vita S. Oswaldi*, p. 449 f.). Osbern, writing about 1090, directly attributes the murder to the instigation of Ælfthryth (see *Mem. of St Dunstan*, p. 114), and later writers generally ascribe it to her (see Eadmer, *Mem. of St Dunstan*, p. 215; Fl. of Worcester, I. p. 145; Henry of Huntingdon, Rolls Series, p. 167; Wm of Malmesbury, *Gesta Reg.*, Lib. II. § 162, Rolls Series, I. p. 183). In 980 the body of Edward was removed from Wareham by Ælfhere and buried with all ceremony at Shaftesbury (see *Sax. Chr.* E). Thereafter many miracles were wrought at his tomb (see *Vita S. Oswaldi*, p. 452), and he was regarded both as a saint and a martyr.

17. 1. Cf. II Edg. 5, 1 A; VI Atr. 24; Wulfstan, pp. 117, 208.

18. 1. Cf. E. and G. 9; VI Atr. 25; I Cn. 17; Wulfstan, pp. 117, 208; *Can. Edg.* 24, ed. Thorpe, *Anc. Laws*, II. p. 248.

2. *i.e.* the period preceding the festival of the Nativity, including the four preceding Sundays.

3. *i.e.* January 8th.

4. *i.e.* from the third Sunday before Lent.

19. 1. Cf. VI, 25, 1; I Cn. 17, 2; *Can. Edg.* 23; *Eccles. Insts.* 42, ed. Thorpe, II. pp. 248, 438; Wulfstan, p. 118.

20. 1. Cf. VI, 25, 2; I Cn. 17, 3; *Eccles. Insts.* 42.

21. 1. Cf. VI, 26; Wulfstan, p. 271.

§ 1. 1. Cf. VI, 26, 1; II Cn. 73. At Plumstead in Norfolk the bishop confiscated a widow's land *pro forisfactura quia...nupsit intra annum post mortem viri* (DB. II. 199 a). This rule seems to have been broken by Edmund in his marriage with the widow of Sigeferð (see *Sax. Chr.* ann. 1015 E).

22. 1. Cf. VI, 27; I Cn. 19.

§ 1. 1. Cf. VI, 27, 1; I Cn. 19 (three times in the year). The times for taking communion are given as Christmas, Easter and Whitsuntide in *Excerpt. Egb. Ebor.* 38, ed. Thorpe, *Anc. Laws*, II. p. 103.

§ 2. 1. Cf. Af. 1; VI Atr. 28; I Cn. 19, 1.

23. 1. Cf. VI Atr. 28, 1; I Cn. 19, 2.
24. 1. Cf. VI, 28, 2.
2. Cf. III Edg. 8, 1.
3. Cf. In. 13.
4. *ficunga* G, G$_2$ is emended to *fitunga* (cf. *fit*, strife) by Thorpe and Schmid, but retained by Liebermann in view of *gefic, ficol, befician* and translated 'Betrügereien,' *i.e.* frauds.
25. 1. Cf. Wulfstan, pp. 129 f., 163 f. The alliteration is noteworthy.
2. The distinction between the two lies in the fact that the first is carried out secretly, the second openly (see Brunner, II. pp. 638, 647).
3. Rendered *comesationes, ebrietates* in the Latin paraphrase of VI, 28, 2; *oferfillan*, however, can apparently apply to excess either in eating or drinking (see BT. p. 733 *s.v.*).
4. *hadbrican* may mean 'injuries to the clergy.' Liebermann takes it in this way, cf. II Cn. 6, where Q has *sacrorum ordinum contemptores*. This too is ambiguous. The meaning might also be violation of the rights of the clergy or perhaps violation (by the clergy themselves) of the rules to which they are subject.
26. 1. Cf. VI, 30.
§ 1. 1. Cf. VI, 31; 32, 1 and 3; II Cn. 8; 10; 65.
2. It is to be noted that Æthelred's coins vary greatly with regard to weight, some being only 20 grains, others as much as 27; see Hawkins, *English Silver Coins*, p. 149.
3. The so-called 'Trinoda Necessitas' generally incumbent upon land-owners to whom otherwise large concessions are made, cf. Birch, 335, 346, 348, 400 etc. With regard to *bricbot*, cf. the regulations for the repair of Rochester Bridge, Birch, 1321.
27. 1. Cf. VI, 32, 3; 33.
2. Cf. *Sax. Chr.* ann. 1008 E, an annal which unfortunately is very obscure.
3. *sona* here may perhaps have the meaning 'immediately' (see BT. p. 895 *s.v.*), as otherwise the regulation is extremely indefinite. The Viking raids generally began about that time and continued throughout the summer and autumn.
28. 1. Cf. VI, 35.
2. Lit. 'in which the king himself is present.'
3. The payment of wergeld is frequently found in the Laws as the alternative to the death penalty, cf. Wi. 26; In. 12; 15; Af. 7, 1; VI As. 1, 4. G adds 'and all his property.'
§ 1. 1. This clause is not found either in D or in VI Atr.
29. 1. Cf. I Edm. 3; II, 4; VI Atr. 36; VIII, 42.
2. G has 'and.'
30. 1. Cf. Af. 4 f.; II As. 4; VI Atr. 37.
2. By *þam deopestan* (cf. VI, 37) is probably meant an oath supported by 36 compurgators. Occasionally, as Liebermann points out, much larger numbers are mentioned, generally, however, in cases of dispute regarding the ownership of land, not in

criminal actions (*e.g.* Birch, 379, 1097; *Liber Eliensis*, ed. Stewart, p. 139).
 3. For the reading of MSS G, G$_2$ cf. Af. 4, 1. The amount of the king's wergeld in Wessex is never stated, but the *anfeald wergeld* of the king in Mercia is said to be the equivalent of that of 6 thegns, *i.e.* £120 (see *Be Mircna laga*, 2). It is uncertain whether G's expression means the same thing.
 31. 1. Cf. VI, 38.
  2. *i.e.* his own.
  3. Cf. E. and G. 3, 1 and note.
 § 1. 1. This phrase might also be translated 'has recourse to violence,' cf. II As. 6, 3; VI, 1, 5.
 32. 1. The four clauses which follow are found only in D.
 § 1. 1. Cf. I Edw. 1, 5; II Atr. 9.
  2. The allusions to the west and the north (§ 4) are obscure. For the latter Liebermann refers to *Be Griðe*, 13; 13, 2.
 § 3. 1. Cf. III Atr. 14; *Liber Eliensis*, ed. Stewart, pp. 133, 138 ff., 145, 151.
 § 4. 1. Cf. *sacleas*, III Atr. 3, 1.
 33. 1. Cf. 1, 1; 23; 32; VI, 40; II Cn. 11. This clause is omitted in D.
 § 1. 1. Cf. VI, 40, 1; II Cn. 11, 1.
 35. 1. Cf. cap. 1; VII Atr. 1; Wulfstan, p. 274.
 § 1. 1. This phrase, which is reminiscent of homilies, is not found in G.

VI ÆTHELRED

Preamble. 1. Cf. V Atr. Pre.
 2. Cf. *rædboran, rædwitan,* BT. pp. 782, 784 *s.v.*
 3. The preamble of the Latin paraphrase is noteworthy for the additional information it supplies: *Quodam tempore contigit ut regis Aeþelredi edicto concrepante archipresulumque Aelfeahi et Wulfstani hortatu instigante, universi Anglorum optimates die sancto pentecosten ad locum ab indigenis Eanham nominatum acciti sunt convenire.*
 1. 1. Cf. V, 1 f.; 19; 35.
  2. No other instance of the form *frumræd* is quoted in BT., see p. 342 *s.v.*
  3. Cf. V, 19, also *frið 7 freondscipe*, V, 1, 1.
  4. The Latin paraphrase adds in explanation: [*plebs*] *paganorum incursionibus vel inruptionibus ceterisque calamitatum erumnis pluriformium obprimentibus, a religionis tramite recto anfractibus errabundis exorbitans.*
 2. 1. Cf. V, 4.
  2. This introductory formula corresponds to that in MS G$_2$ of V Atr.
  3. The Latin paraphrase urges abbots and abbesses not to allow any deviation *ab almi norma patris Benedicti*. The Rule of St Benedict was translated into English by Æthelwold, Bishop of Winchester, who was associated with King Edgar and Dunstan in the movement for monastic reform.

3. 1. Cf. V, 5.
  2. The explanation given by the Latin paraphrase is: *per proprium arbitrium egressus vel proprii reatu deliquii expulsus.*
§ 1. 1. Cf. V, 6.
  2. The explanation given by the Latin paraphrase is: *si cuiuspiam monachorum monasterium...cum canonicis vel cum sanctimonialibus* (*i.e.* nuns) *constitutum sit.* After the death of Edgar monks were ejected from many Mercian religious houses in which they had been installed during his reign, see *Sax. Chr.* ann. 975 A, E and note, Plummer, II. p. 163. The reference might also be to monks belonging to monasteries destroyed during the Danish raids.
4. 1. Cf. V, 7.
  2. The Latin rendering is: *Dei hereditate careant.*
5. 1. Cf. V, 8. With the clauses 5–5, 3 cf. Wulfstan, p. 269.
§ 1. 1. Cf. V, 9.
§ 2. 1. Cf. 12, 1; *N.P.L.* 35. Liebermann suggests that this clause, which is not found in V Atr. or in the Latin paraphrase, is an addition of the scribe's.
§ 3 and § 4. Cf. V, 9, 1 f.
6. 1. Cf. V, 34.
  2. Liebermann translates this phrase 'Lieber Mitbürger, Landsmann.' In style it is homiletic, cf. 28; 42.
7. 1. Cf. E. and G. 11; II As. 6; 6, 1; I Edm. 6; Wulfstan, p. 309.
  2. No other instance of the form *scincræftiga(-ca)* is quoted in BT., see p. 833 and cf. *scincræft.*
8. 1. Cf. V, 1, 1.
§ 1. 1. Cf. III Edg. 1, 1; VII Atr. 6, 1; II Cn. 1, 1.
§ 2. 1. Cf. V, 1, 1.
9. 1. Cf. V, 2.
  2. The Latin paraphrase has: *nefas igitur est ut quos Christus sanguinis sui effusione redemit, Judeorum vel gentilium vinculis sint inretiti.* According to Liebermann the Jews of the continent did carry on a slave-trade in the early Middle Ages (see II. p. 527 *s.v. Juden,* 4). In this case however *Jud. vel gent.* may be merely a phrase derived from the Bible.
10. 1. Cf. V, 3.
§ 1. 1. Cf. 52–3.
  2. Cf. III Edg. 1, 2.
§ 2. 1. This clause is not found in V Atr., cf. II Cn. 2 *a.*
11. 1. Cf. V, 10.
12. 1. This clause and the one following are not found in V Atr., cf. I Cn. 7; *N.P.L.* 61–5; Wulfstan, p. 271.
  2. *i.e.* fourth cousins.
  3. Regarding the computation of family relationships in terms of the human body, see Grimm, *D.R.A.* 1899, I. p. 645 ff. The first knee includes descendants of the same grandparents (*i.e.* first cousins), so that relations 'within the fourth knee' are fourth cousins, see Thorpe, *Anc. Laws,* I. p. 257 note *b*; II. p. 19, note 1.

4. Lit. 'as near to him (as this) in secular relationship,' presumably as opposed to 'spiritual' relationship, *i.e.* the relationship entered into by god-parents, etc.

§ 1. 1. *gefæderan* might possibly mean 'fellow-sponsor,' see Toller, *Suppl.*, p. 321, *s.v.*

2. Cf. IV Edg. 1, 4.

13. 1. Cf. V, 10, 1; I Cn. 2, 1; *Insts. of Polity*, 25, ed. Thorpe, *Anc. Laws*, II. p. 338.

14. 1. This clause is not found in V Atr., cf. E. and G. 1; I Cn. 2, 2; *Be Griðe*, 2.

15. 1. Cf. V, 10, 2; *N.P.L.* 20-2

16. 1. At this point MS D begins. With caps. 16-18, cf. V, 11 f.

18. § 1. 1. Cf. II Edg. 3.

19. 1. Cf. V, 11.

20. 1. Cf. V, 12.

21. 1. Cf. V, 12, 1.

§ 1. 1. Cf. V, 12, 2; Wulfstan, pp. 272, 311.

22. 1. Cf. V, 12, 3; I Cn. 14, 1.

§ 1. 1. Cf. cap. 44; V, 13 f.; I Cn. 15 f.; Wulfstan, pp. 117, 208 272; *Lib. Poen. Theodori*, 38 § 6 ff., ed Thorpe, *Anc. Laws*, II. p. 45.

2. These are not mentioned either in V Atr. or in Wulfstan's homilies.

§ 2. 1. With this clause and the next cf. V, 14 f.; I Cn. 16 f.

23. 1. This clause is not found in V Atr.; cf. Wulfstan, p. 272 and a document (doubtful) of about 600 (see Haddan and Stubbs, *Councils*, III. p. 52 f.), where the *jejunia quae S. Gregorius genti Anglorum praedicari praecepit* are given as (1) *in prima hebdomada Quadragesimae*, (2) *in heb. post Pentecosten*, (3) *in plena heb. ante autumnale aequinoctium*, (4) *in pl. heb. ante natale Domini*. On the other hand the *Poen. Ecgberti addit.* 21, ed. Thorpe, *Anc. Laws*, II. p. 234, specifies the dates according to the civil calendar: *on kł Martii, on ðære forma wucan*; *7 kł Junii, on ðære æfteran wucan*; *7 on kł septemb on ðære þriddan wucan*.

§ 1. 1. This clause is found only in D; cf. V, 16.

24. 1. Cf. V, 17.

25. 1. Cf. V, 18 G; I Cn. 17.

2. Cf. Wulfstan, p. 117, l. 14 and note.

§ 1 f. Cf. V, 19 f.

26 f. Cf. V, 21 f.; Wulfstan, p. 271.

27 f. Cf. V, 22 f.; I Cn. 19.

28. 1. Cf. V, 22, 2; I Cn. 19, 1

2. Cf. cap. 6.

§ 1. 1. Cf. V, 23.

§ 2. 1. Cf. V, 24; 25; Wulfstan, pp. 129 f., 163 f.

2. This phrase occurs only in MS G_2 of V Atr.

3. This is the only instance of the word *cyricren* quoted in BT., see p. 189; *Suppl.*, p. 125.

4. The Latin paraphrase adds *rixae, dissensiones, blasphemiae, necromantiae, idolatriae*.

29. 1. This clause is not found in V Atr.
2. This phrase is of frequent occurrence in Wulfstan's sermons.

30. 1. Cf. V, 26; I Cn. 19, 3.

31. 1. Cf. V, 26, 1; II Cn. 8.

32. 1. This clause does not appear in V Atr.; cf. II Cn. 8; Wulfstan, p. 271 f.
2. *bonda* is a Scandinavian loan word, cf. Icel. *bondi*.

§ 1. 1. Cf. III Edg. 8; II Cn. 8.
§ 2. 1. Cf. III Edg. 8, 1; II Cn. 9.
§ 3. 1. Cf. V, 26, 1. The Latin paraphrase reads: *Arcium muri, urbes, oppida, castella, civitates, pontes reparentur...vallis et fossis muniantur et circumvallentur*.

33. 1. Cf. V, 27.

34. 1. This clause is not found in V Atr.
2. *i.e.* £5, cf. VIII Atr. 5, 1.
3. The Latin version reads: *Quicunque aliquam ex novibus per quampiam inertiam vel per incuriam vel neglegentiam corruperit*.

35. 1. Cf. V, 28.
2. The omission of any reference to the death penalty is noticeable.

36. 1 Cf. V, 29.
2. Cf. E. and G. 11.
3. Cf. I Edm. 3; II, 4.
4. As in cap. 35 there is no mention of the death penalty.

37. 1. Cf. V, 30.
2. Cf. *gesoðige*, E. and G. 6, 7.
3. Cf. V, 30 and note. The Latin version reads: *nisi forte maximo iuramento vel fervente ferro excusetur*. It has no mention of the Danelaw.
4. Steenstrup (*Danelag*, p. 226) suggests that clearing by *holmgang*, *i.e.* 'duel,' is meant.

38. 1. Cf. V, 31.
2. In view of the Latin reading: *reddat quod debet legis desertor*, Liebermann suggests that the archetype of VI Atr. may have read *oððe lahslit* (cf. V, 31) and that it may have been consciously omitted by K (which is a Canterbury MS) as not applying to that part of the country.

39. 1. Neither this clause nor the one following is found in V Atr.

40. 1. Cf. II Cn. 11. The Latin text differs curiously here, the clause beginning, *In his itaque et in cunctis iniqua omnia et iniusta quae rex N. una cum optimatibus exterminare decreverat vel mandaverat semper et ubique penitus abiciantur* etc. The singular use of the letter N. for the king's name is noteworthy.

§ 1. 1. Cf. V, 33, 1.

The Latin paraphrase ends here with the addition of the following paragraph: *Haec itaque legalia statuta vel decreta, in nostro conventu sinodali a regi N*. (*Æþelredo* is written above in another handwriting of the eleventh century) *magnopere edicta, cuncti tunc temporis optimates se observaturos fideliter spondebant; idcircoque ego N. (Wulfstanus* cf. *Æþ.* above), *gratia Domini disponente Eboracensium archiepiscopus, eadem ad sequentium memoriam, necnon et ad praesentium vel futurorum salutem, litteris infixi, Domini videlicet proximique dilectione conpunctus.* Does this mean that Wulfstan had drawn up the text (or the translation) or that he was merely charged with its preservation or publication? The marked resemblances between this code and Wulfstan's homilies suggest that the first is the true interpretation. It is pointed out by Liebermann that the extant works of Wulfstan are exclusively in A.S. (see III. p. 168[7]) so that no comparison is possible between the Latin paraphrase of this code and anything of his.

41. 1. Cf. caps. 2; 5. With the section 41–9 cf. Wulfstan, pp. 179, 307 ff.
 2. Lit. 'love celibacy.'
42. 1. Cf. 6; 28.
 2. Cf. 13; I Cn. 2.
The verb *griðian*, derived from the Scandinavian loan word *grið*, begins to appear in the eleventh century (cf. *Sax. Chr.* ann. 1016, 1046, 1068 etc.). It is often found along with the rhyming *friðian*. Liebermann regards the two terms *grið* and *frið* as practically synonymous by the time of Æthelred (see II. p. 642 *s.v. Schutz*, 3 *a*), but suggests that if there is any underlying difference between them, *frið* has the special sense of security against assailants, while *grið* implies the privilege of assuring safety to others.
 3. Cf. 19.
43. 1. Cf. 16; 21, 1; 22.
44. 1. Cf. 22, 1; *Can. Edg.* 19, ed. Thorpe, *Anc. Laws*, II. p. 248.
45. 1. Cf. I Cn. 4; *Be Griðe*, 25; 28; *Hadbot*, 1, 3.
46. 1. Cf. VIII, 6.
47. 1. Liebermann suggests that this clause may have been derived from Exodus Ch. 22, v. 22; cf. Wulfstan, p. 119.
48. 1. Cf. Exodus Ch. 22, v. 21; Wulfstan, p. 119.
 2. *i.e.* no prejudice is to be shown in pronouncing judgment against strangers, cf. II Cn. 35, 1. For regulations regarding the protection extended to strangers, cf. E. and G. 12; VIII Atr. 33; 34; II Cn. 40; *Geþyncðo*, 8.
49. 1. Cf. Wulfstan, pp. 29, 37 f., 67, 73, 112, 144, 179, 274, 282.
 2. Cf. *Be Griðe*, 29; Liebermann suggests Matthew Ch. 7, v. 2 as the origin of this expression, which occurs frequently in homilies.
 3. Cf. Wulfstan, pp. 37, 67, 112, 274, 282; I Cn. 18, 2.
50. 1. The clauses from here to the end are found only in K.
 2. Liebermann suggests that *rihte* here means 'authentic' (echte), on the ground that *Godes laga* cannot be regarded as unjust, but is it necessary to press the logical interpretation of the term?
51. 1. Cf. E. and G. Pre. 2.
 2. Cf. the regulation for the division of tithes in VIII, 6.

3. Lit. 'vain secular pomps.'
4. The meaning might perhaps be 'whatever the gravity of the offence.'
52. 1. Cf. II Cn. 38, 1; *Can. Edg. De Confessione*, 4, ed. Thorpe, *Anc. Laws*, II. pp. 260, 262.
§ 1. 1. Cf. II Cn. 68, 2 f.; *Can. Edg., loc. cit.*; *Eccles. Inst.* 31, ed. Thorpe, *op. cit.* II. p. 428.
2. Cf. Af. 36, 1; II Edw. 4.
53. 1. Cf. 49.

VII ÆTHELRED

Preamble. 1. Liebermann suggests that the incorrect reading *Habam* (M, Hk, Br) may preserve the rudiments of *æt Hatum Baðum* see Birch, 1257, and cf. *Hatabaðum, Sax. Chr.* ann. 972 E). He points out that in this instance the name has apparently been taken over from A.S. as in Latin it regularly appears as *Bathonia* in the twelfth century, a form which was already known in the tenth (see Earle, *Land Charters*, p. 375).
1. 1. Cf. V, 34; 35; VI, 1; Wulfstan, p. 274.
2. Cf. 4; 4, 2; II Edg. 5, 3; V Atr. 15; VI, 22, 4.
§ 1. 1. Cf. 2, 1; VII Atr. A.S. Pre.
§ 2. 1. Cf. VII Atr. A.S. 2, 2.
2. The same phrase occurs in II As. 16 Q where the original is *æt þære sylh*, cf. Wulfstan, pp. 170, 173. The A.S. text has *hide*. Liebermann suggests that the use of the term *carruca* (*i.e. sylh*) may be due to Kentish usage but it is possible that *sulh* may have been in general use popularly. A parallel expression is found in Norse, *e.g. Egilssaga*, Chap. 52: *skilling silfrs af plógi hverjum.*
3. Cf. Wulfstan, *loc. cit.*: *swa gesyfledne hlaf æt hreocendum heorðe, swa elles hwæt, swa witan þonne to ðearfe geræedan hwilum be teoðunge, hwilum be mannes efenwihte, hwilum be freotmen, hwilum an, hwilum oðer.*
§ 3. 1. Cf. VII Atr. A.S. 5.
2. *i.e.* A.S. *hired.*
3. Cf. the A.S. version, cap. 5, which suggests that the reading *hyremannus* has been wrongly substituted for *hiredmannus, i.e.* every member of his household. *hyremannus* would include dependents with houses and holdings who would be personally responsible for their dues.
2. 1. Cf. VII Atr. A.S. 1.
2. Cf. II As. 23; Wulfstan, p. 173, which reads: *to berenan hlafe, to sealte and to grenan wyrtan.*
3. Cf. 2, 3 *a.*
§ 1. 1. Cf. VII Atr. A.S. 2; Wulfstan, pp. 170, 173.
§ 2. 1. Cf. VII Atr. A.S. 2.
§ 2 *a.* 1. This clause does not appear in the A.S. text.
§ 2 *b.* 1. Cf. VII Atr. A.S. 4, 1; Wulfstan, p. 174.

VII ÆTHELRED

§ 3. 1. Cf. Af. 43; Wulfstan, pp. 171, 173, 158 l. 16, note.
  2. This reason for exempting slaves from work is not given in the A.S. version.
§ 3 a. 1. Cf. VII Atr. A.S. 1.
  2. *i.e.* September 29.
§ 4. 1. Cf. VII Atr. A.S. 3; E. and G. 8.
  2. Cf. Wi. 10; 13; 15; E. and G. 8; Wulfstan, p. 172.
  3. Cf. VI Atr. 32; VII Atr. A.S. *bunda*; Wulfstan, p. 172, *bonda*.
  4. Cf. VII Atr. A.S. 3; Wulfstan, p. 172: *þegen mid* xxx *scill'*. Different classes of thegns may be intended, cf. II Cn. 71, but even so the variation between the Latin and the A.S. texts is curious.
  5. Cf. VII Atr. A.S. 4.
§ 5. 1. Cf. VII Atr. A.S. 2, 3.
  2. Cf. *tunesgerefa*, VII Atr. A.S.; *gerefan*, I As. 4; IV Edg. 1, 5.
  3. The heads of the tithings are not mentioned in the A.S. text. Perhaps here, as in I Edg. 2, Q has misunderstood a singular as plural.
  4. Cf. III Atr. 2, 1.
3. 1. Cf. VII Atr. A.S. 6–6, 3.
  2. Cf. *geferræden*, VII Atr. A.S. 6.
  3. Cf. Wi. 1, 1; V As. 3; Can. Ælfric, 20, ed. Thorpe, *Anc. Laws*, II. p. 350.
§ 2. 1. Liebermann regards *singulatim* as a mistranslation of *sundorlice* (cf. VII Atr. A.S. 6, 2) and renders it: '30 Messen besonders für den König, etc.'
4. 1. Cf. II Edg. 1, 1. This section to the end of cap. 7 is not found in the A.S. version.
  2. Cf. VIII, 7; Wulfstan, pp. 116[3], 208[6], 310: *arise seo æcerteoðung a, be ðam ðe seo sulh þone teoðan æcer ær geeode*.
§ 1. 1. Cf. II Edg. 2, 2.
§ 2. 1. *i.e.* Edward, Æthelstan, Edmund and Edgar, cf. E. and G. 6; I As. Pre. 1; I Edm. 2; II Edg. 3; 3, 1; IV, 1, 4 and 6; Wulfstan, p. 113.
5. 1. Cf. V, 2; VI, 9 and notes.
6. 1. Cf. V, 25; VI, 28, 2; II Cn. 7.
§ 1. 1. Cf. III Edg. 1, 1; VI Atr. 8, 1; II Cn. 1, 1.
§ 2. 1. Cf. In. 10.
  2. Liebermann suggests that the original may have read *ær* 7 *æfter*.
§ 3. 1. Cf. for the doubling of a fine in the case of a reeve, DB. I. 262 *b*, 1.
7. 1. *i.e.* A.S. *ælmesfeoh*, cf. I Edm. 2[9].
  2. Cf. cap. 2, 3 *a*.
  3. *i.e.* A.S. *fulwite*, which seems in general to mean a fine of 60 shillings, cf. In. 43; II Edg. 3 (In. 4).
§ 1. 1. Cf. VII Atr. A.S. 8.
  2. *i.e.* in caps. 4; 7.
  3. Cf. cap. 4 f.
  4. Cf. VII Atr. A.S. Pre.

VII ÆTHELRED (A.S.)

Preamble. 1. Cf. VII, 1, 1; 7, 1.
1. 1. Cf. VII, 2; 2, 3 a.
2. 1. Cf. VII, 2, 1; Wulfstan, pp. 170, 173.
§ 1. 1. Cf. Wulfstan, pp. 170, 173.
§ 2. 1. Cf. VII, 1, 2.
§ 3. 1. Cf. VII, 2, 5.
    2. This division into three is not found either in the Latin version or in Wulfstan's homilies; cf. however VIII, 6; *Can. Ælfric*, 24, ed. Thorpe, *Anc. Laws*, II. p. 352.
3. 1. Cf. VII, 2, 4, where similar penalties are inflicted for breach of the fast.
    2. Cf. VII, 2, 4 and note.
4. 1. Cf. VI, 51.
    2. Cf. VII, 2, 4.
    3. Cf. VII, 4 f.; 7, 1.
§ 1. 1. Cf. VII, 2, 2 b.
    2. Cf. 4.
5. 1. Cf. VII, 1, 3.
    2. Cf. *omnis tainus*, VII, 1, 3. The meaning is actualiy 'those who have people under them,' corresponding to the modern idea of employers.
§ 1. 1. Cf. VII, 2, 3; Wulfstan, pp. 171, 173.
6. 1. Cf. VII, 3.
    2. Cf. VII, 3, 2.
§ 1. 1. Cf. VII, 3, 2.
§ 2. 1. Cf. VII, 3; 3, 2.
    2. 'Besonders' (Liebermann), cf. *singulatim*, VII, 3, 2. There may however be a contrast between *sinderlice* here and *ætgædere* in cap. 6, cf. *communiter*, VII, 3.
    3. Cf. VII, 3, 1.
§ 3. 1. Cf. VII, 3, 1.
7. 1. This clause as a whole does not appear in the Latin version, but the ideas expressed in it are found in 1, 1; 2, 1.
8. 1. Cf. VII, 7, 1.

VIII ÆTHELRED

Heading. 1. Cf. V Atr. G. The heading in G, as Liebermann points out, applies only to the portion of the ordinance reproduced there. As regards the date given in D, cf. Wulfstan, p. 156.

Preamble. 1. Liebermann suggests that a secular ordinance was probably issued at the same time and that this statement is due to the scribe who copied only the part dealing with ecclesiastical affairs.

1. 1. Cf. E. and G. 1; II Edg. 1; VI Atr. 14. The first section of the ordinance—the only part which is found in G—begins here and ends with cap. 5, 2; cf. I Cn. 2, 3–3, 2.
§ 1. 1. For *ciricgrið* cf. E. and G. 1; VI Atr. 14.
2. Cf. III Atr. 1; II Cn. 64; Wulfstan, p. 274; *Be Grið̄e*, 13.
3. Cf. E. and G. 6, 6.
4. Does this mean the residence of the king? Cf. II Edm. 2; V Atr. 29; VI 36.
5. Cf. Wi. 26; In. 6; Af. 7; III As. 7, 3; VI, 1, 4; II Edm. 6; III Edg. 7, 3; III Atr. 16; IV, 5, 4; 7, 1 and 3.
2. 1. Cf. Wi. 26; In. 12; 15; Af. 7, 1; E. and G. 6, 5; II As. 1, 4; VI, 1, 4; 12, 2; III Edg. 4; IV Atr. 7, 1; V, 28; I Cn. 2, 4; II, 16; 61; *Be Grið̄e*, 15.
2. Cf. 38; E. and G. Pre. 2.
3. Cf. *bicge him lage (lah)*, III Atr. 3, 3; 8, 2.
§ 1. 1. Cf. Wulfstan, p. 266 f.; *Insts. of Polity*, 2, ed. Thorpe, *Anc. Laws*, II. pp. 304, 306.
3. 1. *i.e.* £5, cf. 5, 1.
2. Phillpotts, *Kindred and Clan*, p. 221, suggests that by *mægbot* payment to the godfather may be meant (cf. In. 76), while Liebermann takes it to mean wergeld (III. p. 183).
3. Cf. In. 70; 76; II Edm. 3; 7, 3.
4. Cf. 4; V Atr. 14, for a similar use of the plural form of the verb with *man*.
4. 1. Cf. *Be Grið̄e*, 13, 1.
2. Liebermann interprets this 'if the man assaulted remains alive,' but it seems rather to be more general in meaning.
3. This offence is not mentioned in this connection either in G or Canute. Liebermann regards it as an insertion of the scribe's, but such a supposition is scarcely necessary if the phrase *be cwicum mannum* means 'if there is no homicide.'
§ 1. 1. Cf. *N.P.L.* 19.
2. Cf. *Be Grið̄e*, 3; 10.
5. 1. Cf. *Be Grið̄e*, 3.
§ 1. 1. Cf. the distinctions made in II Edg. 1, 1–2, 1.
2. As opposed to 1, 1.
3. Cf. Af. 2, 1.
4. Liebermann suggests that *cyninges* is used here simply with the sense of 'highest,' 120 shillings being the highest fixed sum paid as *wite*. The origin of the phrase, however, seems rather to be sought for in the fact that 120 sh. is the regular sum due to the king for insubordination, cf. I Edw. 2, 1; II, 2 etc.
5. Cf. I Cn. 3, 2.
6. The fines are in the proportion 8 : 4 : 2 : 1.
§ 2. 1. Cf. *Had.* 10 Liebermann takes this clause as referring particularly to what precedes, *i.e.* the judgment shall be according to the deed, and the penalty according to the grade of the church, but its verbal agreement with VI, 53 suggests that it may be a general reflection.

6. 1. Cf. VII Atr. A.S., 2, 3; *Can. Ælfric*, 24, ed. Thorpe, *Anc. Laws*, II. p. 352.
    2. Cf. VI, 51
    3. This diminutive seems generally to be used with a depreciatory sense, see BT., p. 1055, *s.v.*
7. 1. Cf. VII, 4 and note.
    2. Cf. II Edg. 3, 1.
    3. Cf. 37; 43.
8. 1. Cf. II Edg. 3, 1; I Cn. 8, 2.
    2. Not mentioned in Edgar.
9. 1. Cf. II Edg. 3; V Atr. 11, 1; VI, 17; I Cn. 8, 1; Wulfstan, p. 116 etc.; *Can. Edg.* 54, ed. Thorpe, *op. cit.* II. p. 256.
10. 1. Cf. II Edg. 4; V Atr. 11; VI, 18; I Cn. 9; *N.P.L.* 57, 1; *Can. Edg.* 54; Wulfstan, pp. 272, 311.
    § 1. 1. Cf. II Edg. 4, 1; I Cn. 9, 1; Wulfstan, *loc. cit.*
11. 1. Cf. II Edg. 3; I Cn. 10; Wulfstan, p. 311.
    § 1. 1. Cf. In. 4 (where the fine is only 60 sh.); I Cn. 10. The same offence is threatened with excommunication in I Edm. 2 and with incurring the wrath of God in IV Edg. 1, 3.
12. 1. Cf. II Edg. 2, 3; V Atr. 11, 1; VI, 16; I Cn. 8, 1; Wulfstan, p. 116 etc.
    § 1. 1. Cf. E. and G. 6, 2, where no set time is mentioned; V Atr. 11, 1; VI, 19; Wulfstan, pp. 116, 208, where light-dues are demanded three times a year; I Cn. 12, where the fixed times are given as Candlemas, Easter and All Hallows; Wulfstan, p. 311, where Christmas is substituted for All Hallows.
13. 1. Cf. V, 12; VI, 20.
14. 1. Cf. E. and G. 5, 1; V Atr. 12, 2; VI, 21, 1.
15. 1. Cf. caps. 8 and 36; E. and G. Pre. § 2; 5, 1; 6–6, 4; II Cn. 48.
16. 1. Cf. II Edg. 5, 1; V Atr. 12, 3; VI, 22.
    2. Cf. E. and G. 7, 1.
17. 1. Cf. IV, 2, 3 and note; V, 13, 1; VI, 22, 1; I Cn. 15.
18. 1. Cf. I Cn. 4; 4, 3; Wulfstan, p. 157: *Godes þeowas syndan mæðe 7 munde gewelhwar bedælde.*
    2. Liebermann translates *weofodþéna* by 'Altardiener.' The phrase *mæssepegnes 7 worldþegnes* in *Norðleoda laga*, cap. 5, rather suggests that the idea may be 'knight of the altar.' In *Insts. of Polity*, 23, ed. Thorpe, *Anc. Laws*, II. p. 336, the term is explained: *weofodþen, þæt is biscop oððe mæssepreost oððe diacon.*
19. 1. This section from cap. 19–cap. 27 is repeated in I Cn. 5–5, 4; cf. Wi. 16–19.
    2. *i.e.* by taking part in the communion service. The administration of the sacrament in this case takes the place of an oath of purgation, see Liebermann, II. p. 263, *s.v. Abendmahlsprobe*, 6; Brunner, II. p. 413[74]; Dahr, *Bausteine*, II. 18; Lea, *Superstition and Force*, pp. 304–11.
22. 1. In this form of ordeal the accused had to clear himself by eating without apparent difficulty a certain quantity (generally 1 ounce) of bread or cheese. In later times the host was used. This

form of ordeal was employed to a certain extent by the Franks and more widely by the Frisians, see Brunner, II. p. 412 f. The story of the death of Earl Godwin in 1053 (see Lea, *op. cit.* p. 301) illustrates the belief in the efficacy of this mode of proof.

23. 1. Cf. II Edw. 6; II As. 1, 3 f.; 6, 1; VI, 1, 4; 9; 12, 1 f.; II Edm. 1, 1 ff. for other references to the part played by the kin of a delinquent.

2. Contrast with this II Edm. 1–1, 3.

24. 1. Cf. *gehádan*, 19, 1 ff.

25. 1. See P. and M. I. p. 433, and cf. Ælfric, *Homilies*, ed. Thorpe, I. p. 398.

26. 1. Cf. II Cn. 41.

27. 1. Cf. E. and G. 3; *N.P.L.* 45.

2. Liebermann points out that, in the laws which show strong ecclesiastical influence, perjury is always regarded as one of the worst crimes, and is classed with murder and sorcery, cf. E. and G. 11; I Edm. 6; V Atr. 24 f.; VI, 7; 28, 2; 36; II Cn. 6.

3. Cf. cap. 28.

§ 1. 1. Schmid and Liebermann follow Thorpe in inserting this phrase from I Cn. 5, 4.

28. 1. With this clause and the two following, cf. V, 9, 1–2; VI, 5, 3–4.

2. Cf. II Cn. 38, 2.

31. 1. With this clause and the one following, cf. V, 4; VI, 2; I Cn. 6 a.

32. 1. Cf. I As. Pre.; VI, 11; IV Edg. 1, 5.

33. 1. With this clause and the two following, cf. II Cn. 40–40, 2 With cap. 33, cf. E. and G. 12; II Cn. 42.

2. Cf. Af. 35–35, 6.

35. 1. Cf. 2, 1. The reading of the MS (*Cristenum mannum...he*) can hardly be correct as it stands. The simplest change is to emend *mannum* to *mannan* as is done in the text on p 126. *Manna* is not a common word in late O.E. although the phrase *þissum mannan* occurs in the *Blickling Homilies*, 247, 18. Liebermann suggests *cyninge* for *mannum* from II Cn. 40, 2.

36. 1. Cf. cap. 15; E. and G. Pre. § 2; *Be Griðe*, 24; *Hadbot*, 11. The alliteration at the beginning of the clause is noteworthy.

2. See BT. p. 1031, *s.v. þær*, II.

37. 1. Alternatively, 'well-known places.'

2. Similar complaints are found in chronicles, biographies and other documents, see Plummer, *Sax. Chr.* II. p. 164 f., and cf. Wulfstan, p. 158[6].

38. 1. Cf. caps. 15; 36.

2. Cf. V, 32, 5.

39. 1. Cf. Wulfstan, p. 157.

40. 1. Cf. E. and G. 11; VI Atr. 7; II Cn. 4.

41. 1. Cf. II Cn. 4, 1.

42. 1. Cf. II Cn. 66 f.

2. Cf. *utlah wið God*, Cn. 1020, 17; Wulfstan, p. 271.

   3. Cf. cap. 2, 1.
   4. The alliteration is noteworthy.
43. 1. Cf. for references to Edmund, I Edg. 2; IV, 2 *a*.
  2. Cf. caps. 7; 37.
  3. Cf. Wulfstan, p. 157.
§ 1. 1. Cf. V Atr. 1; 34; VI, 1; 42; Wulfstan, p. 189.
44. 1. Cf. V, 1; 22; 34; VI, 1; 27; 42; I Cn. 19; 21; *N.P.L.* 47.
§ 1. 1. Cf. V, 1; VI, 1.
  2. Cf. VI, 6; 28; 42.

IX ÆTHELRED

Preamble. 1. Cf. I Atr. Pre.
1. 1. Cf. V Atr. 1; VI, 42.
Concl. 1. *healde* and *holdliche* are both late forms.
  2. Cf. with this concluding sentence V Atr. 34; 35.

X ÆTHELRED

Preamble. 1. Cf. VI, 42.
    2. Cf. II Edm. Pre.
    3. Cf. II Edg. Pre.
    4. Cf. Wulfstan, p. 274.
§ 1. 1. The alliterative phrases in this clause are noteworthy; cf. *Insts. of Polity*, 2; 7, ed. Thorpe, *Anc. Laws*, II. pp. 304, 312; Wulfstan, p. 266.
 § 2. 1. Cf. V, 1, 1; 23; 33; VI, 28, 1; 40.
 § 3. 1. Cf. VI Atr. Pre. and note.
1. 1. Cf. V, 1 G₂; VI, 1.
2. 1. Cf. V, 1, 1; VI, 8–8, 2.

NOTES TO THE LAWS OF CANUTE

CANUTE'S PROCLAMATION OF 1020

1. 1. In 1019 Canute went to Denmark and spent the winter there (see *Sax. Chr.*; Fl. of W., ed. Thorpe, I. p. 182). The exact time of his return is not recorded, but on April 17th he held an assembly at Cirencester (see *Sax. Chr.*; Fl. of W., I. p. 183). The proclamation seems to have been issued soon after his return.

2. The epistolary form in which this document is couched occurs also in one charter of Æthelred's and three of Canute's (see Kemble, III. p. 203; IV. p. 9; Earle, *Land Charters*, pp. 232, 237). Under Edward the Confessor it became common and is regularly employed by the Norman kings (see Maitland, *Domesday Book and Beyond*, pp. 261–5; Stevenson, *E.H.R.* 1912, pp. 5, 8).

3. Lyfing, Archbishop of Canterbury (cf. cap. 3), died in June 1020 (see Stubbs, *Reg. Sacr. Angl.* p. 31), and his successor was not consecrated until November (see *Sax. Chr.* D). The use of the plural here and in cap. 8, therefore, confirms the view that the Proclamation was issued early in 1020. Wulfstan, Archbishop of York, later in the same year consecrated the church founded by Canute at Assandun (generally identified with Ashington), the scene of his victory over Edmund Ironside in 1016 (see *Sax. Chr.* D). He died in 1023 (see *Sax. Chr.* E). Phrases in the proclamation which seem reminiscent of the Laws of Æthelred may therefore be due to the influence of Wulfstan.

4. Thurkil the Tall, who is frequently mentioned both in English and Scandinavian sources, was one of the leading men of the pirate settlement of Jomsburg at the mouth of the Oder, and brother of Sigvaldi the chief of these pirates—a man who played an important part in the time of Sweyn. They are said to have been the sons of a king Strutharald in Skaane (cf. *Saga Olaf Tr.*, *Heimskr.*, Chap. 38; *Jomsvikinga saga*, Chap. 18). He made his first appearance in England in 1009 (see *Sax. Chr.* C; Fl. of W., I. p. 160), and seems to have harried in the south and east for several years. In 1012 however he took service with Æthelred and fought against Sweyn (see *Sax. Chr.* ann. 1013 E). About 1015 he again changed sides (perhaps as the result of the death of a brother, Heming, at the hands of the English; see Larson, *Canute the Great*, p. 67; Napier and Stevenson, *Crawford Ch.*, p. 141), and became one of the most outstanding of Canute's supporters. He took part in the victory over Edmund Ironside at Assandun, and in 1017 was made earl of E. Anglia (see *Sax. Chr.*; Fl. of W., I. p. 181). He signs as *dux* at the head of the magnates of Canute's reign in 1018 and 1019 (see Kemble, vol. IV, pp. 1–9), but in 1021 he was banished (see *Sax. Chr.*; Fl. of W., I. p. 183) and does not seem ever to have returned to

England. In 1023 he was reconciled with Canute and was placed by him over the government of Denmark (see *Sax. Chr.* C). He is said to have perished shortly afterwards (see Wm of Malmesbury, II. § 181; *Vita S. Elphegi*, Langebek, II. p. 453; Larson, *op. cit.* p. 147). By 1026 Ulf, the brother-in-law of Canute, is found governing Denmark.

5. Note that the term *eorl* in the Scandinavian sense now comes into use. It appears to be synonymous here with *ealdormann*, cf. cap. 8.

2. 1. Cf. IV Edg. 16, and the promises made by Æthelred before his return from exile in 1014 (see *Sax. Chr.*).

2. Cf. cap. 8. This expression seems to be used sometimes with the more restricted sense of dues (cf. IV Edg. 1, 4; V Atr. 11; 12, 2; VI, 16; 21, 1; 43; VIII, 14; I Cn. 8; 14), sometimes, as here, with the wider sense of rights, *i.e.* including privileges as well as payments in money or kind, cf. IV Edg. 2 *a*.

3. 1. None of these written injunctions have been preserved.

2. Benedict VIII, see Jaffé-Löwenfeld, *Reg. Pont. Rom.* I. p. 510.

4. 1. It is not quite clear what events are referred to here. Perhaps the most likely explanation is that, both here and in cap. 5, the reference is to the forces which Canute and his father before him had gathered for their invasion of England. There would inevitably be a difficulty in disposing of these forces (drawn from Denmark, Norway and Pomerania) now that the state of warfare which had lasted so many years was brought to an end. For other views on the subject see Liebermann, III. p. 188; Larson, *op. cit.* p. 143 f.

2. Cf. I Cn. Pre. D.

5. 1. Cf. *Sax. Chr.* ann. 1019, 1020.

2. Canute's brother Harold, king of Denmark, seems to have died in 1018 (see Langebek, *Scriptores*, I. p. 159, note) and Canute does not seem to have visited the country until the following year. It is possible that, in the interval while the country was practically kingless, lawlessness and disorder may have spread, and that raids against England were feared. Canute's visit to Denmark secured his recognition as king, and bound the two countries together through the fact of their common allegiance to him.

3. Cf. I Cn. 1.

7. 1. Lit. 'which he has shown for our aid.'

8. 1. Cf. cap. 2.

2. *heom* is dat. sg., cf. Wi. 26, 1; III Edg. 1, 1 D; I Cn. 19 B.

3. Cf. cap. 1 and note.

9. 1. Cf. IV Atr. 8; II Cn. 83. The fact that seven of the eleven earls who appear in the charters issued during the early years of Canute's reign have Scandinavian names (see Larson, *op. cit.* p. 116) may account in some measure for the order observed here. The reference, in view of what follows, is to men of rank and position.

2. Cf. cap. 11; II Cn. 18, 1.

10. 1. Cf. *betsta*, Abt. 75.

11. 1. Cf. Procl. of 1027, cap. 12.

2. Cf. III Edg. 5, 2.
3. Lit. 'do (*i.e.* show) such mercy as...the man may be able to suffer.' If the text is right, *mildheortnesse* would here seem to be equivalent to *forgifnes* in III Edg. 1, 2. Liebermann, however, emends *se* to *þe*—and translates 'solche Milde üben...die man [der Staat] ertragen kann.'
12. 1. Cf. *licgan for*, II As. 3; *for(e)ne forstandan*, I Atr. 4, 2; II Cn. 33, 1 *a*.
2. Liebermann suggests that the triple ordeal may be meant.
13. 1. Cf. *Sax. Chr.* ann. 1018; I Cn. 1 D.
15. 1. Cf. Wulfstan, pp. 266, 298; II Cn. 4 *a*; 5, 1; 6.
2. Cf. Chadwick, *Origin of the English Nation*, p. 339.
16. 1. Cf. VI Atr. 12, 1; I Cn. 7, 1; II. 50, 1.
With caps. 16–17 cf. Wulfstan, p. 271.
18. 1. Cf. II Edg. 5; I Cn. 14, 2; Wulfstan, pp. 117, 208, 210 f., 222, 293; *Can. Ælfric*, 36 (Thorpe, *Anc. Laws*, II. p. 362).
2. Cf. V Atr. 13, 1; VI, 22, 1; 44; *Can. Edg.* 19 (Thorpe, *op. cit.* II p. 248); I Cn. 15; Wulfstan, p. 272; *N.P.L.* 55.
19. 1. Cf. I Cn. 2; *Insts. of Polity*, 25 (Thorpe, *op. cit.* II. p. 340).
2. Cf. II Edg. 5, 1; Wulfstan, pp. 117, 208; V Atr. 12, 3 f.; 14 ff.; 17; VI, 22–24; VIII, 16; I Cn. 14, 1; 16 f.
3. Lit. 'the saints whom'; cf. V Atr. 16; VI, 23, 1; I Cn. 17, 1.
4. Cf. E. and G. 3, 1; *N.P.L.* 11; I Cn. 14, 2 Q.
20. 1. Cf. II Cn. 84, 2.

CANUTE'S PROCLAMATION OF 1027

Preamble. 1. As Canute did not become king of Norway until 1028 (see Larson, *Canute the Great*, p. 239), this title may have been added by a scribe or by the translator (see Lappenberg, *Gesch. v. Engl.* I. p. 476, note 1; Pauli, *Mon. Germ. SS.* XIII. p. 126[10]). Bresslau (*Jahrbücher des d. Reichs u. Konrad II*, vol. II. p. 142, note 1) suggests however that it may have been assumed by Canute even before it was his by rights. This is supported by the Norse tradition given in St Olaf's Saga, *Heimskr.*, ch. 140, although it is not clear what was Canute's justification for such a claim.
2. Steenstrup (*Normannerne*, III. pp. 327–9) and Larson, *op. cit.* pp. 152, 344, emend to *Sclauorum*, but the evidence of coins, on which the title *rex Sueuorum* appears, confirms the reading of the text (see Worsaae, *Danske Erob.* p. 325; Parsons, *Brit. Num. Soc.* Apr. 1914, p. 14 ff.). Parsons suggests that, during the summer of 1027, Canute may have forced his overlordship upon Anund of Sweden.
3. Æthelnoth, Archbishop of Canterbury (see Stubbs, *Reg. Sacr. Angl.* p. 33), was consecrated in 1020 by Wulfstan of York (see *Sax. Chr.*; Kemble, VI. p. 177). He seems to have been greatly beloved and received the title 'the Good' (see *Sax. Chr.* ann. 1038 C).
4. Ælfric, Archbishop of York (see Stubbs, *Reg. Sacr. Angl.* p. 34), was consecrated at Canterbury by Æthelnoth in 1023 (see *Sax. Chr.* F; Fl. of W., I. p. 184). He died in 1051.

5. Cf. cap. 12, also *twelfhynde* 7 *twyhynde*, Procl. of 1020, cap. 1.

2. 1. In the autumn of 1026 Canute was engaged in a campaign against the allied forces of Olaf, king of Norway, and Anund, king of Sweden. For a full account of this campaign see St Olaf's Saga, *Heimskr.*, ch. 160; Saxo, *Gesta Danorum*, ed. Holder, p. 347 f. The Saxon Chronicle records the Battle of Holy River in 1025.

4. 1. Liebermann quotes a similar reference in a charter of Canute's, viz. *Concedo hanc libertatem beato Petro qui potestatem habet in caelo et in terra ligandi itemque solvendi* (see Thorpe, *Dipl.* p. 332).

5. 1. The coronation of Conrad by Pope John XIX took place on Easter Day, March 26th, 1027, during Canute's visit to Rome, and a synod was held on April 6th (see Jaffé-Löwenfeld, *Reg. Pont. Rom.* I. p. 516 f.).

2. Mount Garganus is in northern Apulia.

3. Probably the North Sea is meant, cf. Liebermann, III. p. 191. The phrase 'from Mount Garganus to the sea' perhaps means from the southern to the northern limits of the Empire, although Mount Garganus was actually beyond the frontier.

4. Friendly relations seem to have existed even before this between the Emperor and Canute (see Adam of Bremen, II. Ch. 54; Bresslau, *op. cit.* I. p. 104). The marriage of Canute's daughter Gunnhild and Conrad's son, afterwards Henry III, took place in 1036, after the death of Canute (see Bresslau, *op. cit.* II. pp. 147, 169; Larson, *op. cit.* p. 268 f.).

6. 1. A full account of the route followed by Sigeric, Archbishop of Canterbury 990–4, has been preserved (see Miller, *Die ältesten Weltkarten*, vol. III. p. 156 ff.). It lay through Lucca, Piacenza, Vercelli, Aosta, across the Great St. Bernhard to Lausanne, through Reims and thence to the sea. It may have been this route that Canute had particularly in mind (see Schulte, *Gesch. des mittelalt. Handels u. Verkehrs*, I. p. 67).

2. The reference appears to be to toll-bars or turnpikes. A common meaning of *clausura* is 'mountain pass,' through several of which, including the Great St. Bernhard, pilgrims would have to go, but Canute could not hope to reduce the number of these. Toll-bars were no doubt put up at these passes, but it is hardly to be assumed that they were erected only at such places. Simeon of Durham (Rolls Series, II. p. 157) records of Canute that *in eundo et redeundo... multas per viam clausuras, ubi telon a peregrinis exigebatur, ingenti pretio dato dissipavit*.

3. Rudolf, king of Burgundy, whose territories extended from the Great St. Bernhard nearly to Langres.

4. These documents have not been preserved.

10. 1. The exact date of Canute's birth is not known, but he is generally thought to have been 21 or 22 years of age when he became king of England (see Larson, *op. cit.* p. 108 f.).

11. 1. Cf. *En. Emmae, Mon. Germ. SS.* XIX. p. 520: *(Canute) leges oppressit iniquas, iustitiam et equitatem extulit et coluit*.

12. 1. Cf. I Edw. Pre.

2. *Vicecomites* is the term regularly used in Domesday Book for sheriffs. Liebermann suggests that the original read *scirgerefum*.
    3. Cf. Procl. of 1020, cap. 11.
    4. Cf. *earme* 7 *eadige*, Procl. of 1020, cap. 19.
    5. Cf. II Cn. 69, 1.
13. 1. *i.e.* Norway and Sweden, cf. cap. 2 and note; Procl. of 1020, cap. 6.
14. 1. Cf. Procl. of 1020, cap. 6.
15. 1. Cf. Procl. of 1020, cap. 4.
16. 1. Cf. II Edg. 2, 4; V Atr. 11 f.; VI, 16–18, 1; VIII, 9–11.
    2. Cf. I As. 1, where the date appointed is August 29th.
    3. Liebermann regards *primitiae seminum* simply as a false translation of *ciricsceatt*.
17. 1. For the A.S. *gerefan* glossed *exactores*, see Toller, *Suppl.* p. 393, *s.v. gerefa*.
    2. Cf. *nan forgyfnes*, IV Edg. 1, 5.

I CANUTE

1. Headings are found in MSS A and D, in Inst. and in Cons. Those in A and Cons. are derived from a common ancestor, since both of them refer to Canute as king of Norway, and both end with a similar clause. That in D stands alone, both in its phraseology and in its dating of the ordinance. The MSS of Inst. fall into two groups with two headings entirely different both from each other and from those already mentioned. The heading of the earlier group is entirely general and reads: *Incipiunt quaedam instituta de legibus regum Anglorum*; that of the second entitles Canute king of the English, Danes, Norwegians and Swedes (cf. Procl. of 1027, Pre. and Notes) and describes his ordinance as *lex quae Anglice Danelage est vocata, Latine vero lex Dacorum est interpretata* (see Liebermann, I. p. 279).

2. This phrase seems to be parallel to *gyme se ðe wylle*, cap. 26, and *understande se ðe cunne*, cap. 4, 1. Cons. reads: *legat quilibet utram malit sive secularem legem sive divinam expeditionem*. This heading as a whole seems to be based on the form of the preamble found in G.

Preamble. 1. G and A both read simply *to þearfe*, cf. *sibimet ad regiam dignitatem et expeditionem*, Cons.; Ld however reads: *folc to þearfe*, cf. *ad commune commodum*, Q; *ad profectum totius regni cui preerat*, Inst. Liebermann suggests that *folce* may have been a marginal reading in the archetype. The phrase *him silfum to cynescype* 7 *to þearfe* appears also in II Edg. Pre. D, where the other MSS read *eallum his leodscipe to þearfe*, cf. IV Edg. 2, 1 *a*; *to ealles folces þ.*, Cn. 1020, 8; *þeode þearfe*, I Cn. 1, D.

2. Liebermann (*National Assembly in the A.S. Period*, p. 49) gives a list of 20 assemblies which met at Christmas.

3. For a list of assemblies held at Winchester see Liebermann, *op. cit.* p. 47. Q here contains an addition relating to the translation of the ordinance from English into Latin.

348 NOTES TO THE LAWS OF CANUTE

1. 1. Cf. VI Atr. 1; 6; 42; VII, 1; VIII, 43, 1 ff.; *God lufian*, I Cn. 21; II, 84, 1.

2. It is noteworthy that Canute replaces the general injunctions regarding loyalty, which are frequent in the laws of Æthelred, by the demand for loyalty to himself in person, cf. Procl. of 1020, cap. 5; Procl. of 1027, cap. 16. Cons. omits the king's name, while Q and Inst. omit this injunction altogether.

2. 1. Cf. with cap. 2 ff. *Insts. of Polity*, cap. 25, ed. Thorpe, *Anc. Laws*, II. p. 339 f.

2. Cf. cap. 4; VI Atr. 42. Is *cyrican* to be taken as plural or with the Latin texts (*ecclesiam*) as singular? The following clause rather favours the former interpretation.

3. Cf. Procl. of 1020, cap. 19.

4. Inst. reads: *pro quiete et stabilitate regni sui proque salute corporis et animae suae* (*i.e.* the king's).

§ 1. 1. Cf. VI Atr. 13; *Be Griðe*, 1; 31; Wulfstan, p. 266.

§ 2. 1. Cf. VI Atr. 14; *Be Griðe*, 2; Wulfstan, pp. 266, 275.

2. *i.e.* with homicide, cf. VIII Atr. 1, 1; *Nor. Grið*, 1.

3. Cf. *botleas*, cap. 2, 3; III Atr. 1. Forfeiture of property generally accompanies loss of life, cf. Af. 4; 4, 2; II As. 20, 3; V Pre. § 3; VI, 1, 1 and 5; IV Edg. 11; V Atr. 28 G; VI, 37; VIII, 42; II Cn. 57; DB. I. 154.

4. Cf. VIII Atr. 1, 1 and note.

§ 3. 1. Cf. VIII Atr. 1, 1; *Be Griðe*, 15.

2. *talem locum aut hominem requirat ut...*, Inst.

§ 4. 1. Cf. with this clause and the one following, VIII Atr. 2; 3.

3. 1. Cf. VIII Atr. 4.

3 a. § 1. 1. With this clause and the next, cf. VIII Atr. 5 f.

§ 2. 1. *principales ecclesiae sicut episcopatus et abbatiae* is the reading of Inst. except in one MS which classes *abbatiae* along with *canonicatus* as *mediocres ecclesiae*.

2. With this clause, which is an addition in G, cf. *Be Griðe*, 11 (drawn from Af. 3), and note the discrepancy between it and cap. 6: *on Cantwara lage cyning 7 arcebiscop agan gelicne and efen dyrne mundbryce*.

3. Cf. Af. 3; II Cn. 58, 1; 62 G. Inst. adds: *secundum certe legem Danorum octo libras*.

4. Liebermann suggests that collegiate foundations are probably meant, cf. *canonicatus*, Inst.

4. 1. Cf. VIII Atr. 18; *Hadbot*, 1; 1, 3; *Be Griðe*, 28.

2. Translated *sanctuaria*, Q; *reliquias sanctorum*, Inst.; *sacra*, Cons.

§ 1. 1. With this clause and the two following, cf. *Insts. of Polity*, cap. 19, ed. Thorpe, *Anc. Laws*, II. p. 326.

§ 2. 1. The alliteration is noteworthy.

2. Cf. Bede, ed. Plummer, I. p. xiii; Wulfstan, p. 144.

§ 3. 1. Cf. cap. 6 *a*; V Atr. 4; VI, 2; 41; *Be Griðe*, 19, 1; Wulfstan, pp. 120, 179.

5. 1. With caps. 5–5, 2 *d*, cf. VIII Atr. 19–25.

I CANUTE

    2. *de latrocinio aut de incantatione vel de aliqua huiusmodi (simili) re*, Inst.
5 *a*. § 3. 1. With this clause and the next, cf. VIII Atr. 27 f.
6. 1. Cf. V Atr. 4; VIII, 31.
    2. Q reads *quicumque in ordine clericatus constituti*; Inst. *unusquisque, cuiuscumque ordinis aut sexus sit.*
6 *a*. 1. Cf. V Atr. 4.
    § 1. 1. Cf. VI Atr. 5; Wulfstan, p. 269
        2. Cf. II Cn. 84, 3.
        3. Cf. caps. 7, 3; 18 *b*; 25, also IV Edg. 1, 4; VI Atr. 12, 1.
    § 2. 1. With this clause and the next, cf. V Atr. 9 f.
    § 2 *a*. 1. The Scandinavian *lagu* here replaces the *riht* of Canute's source.
    § 3. 1. Cf. V Atr. 10.
        2. Cf. cap. 4, 3.
        3. Cf. caps. 7, 2 f.; 24; Procl. of 1020, cap. 15 f.; II Cn. 50–52, 1; 54–5.
7. 1. With caps. 7–7, 3, cf. VI Atr. 12 f.
    § 1. 1. *commatrem vel filiolam*, Q.
    § 2. 1. This clause is not found in Æthelred.
    § 3. 1. *and that...wife* is not found in Æthelred. Concerning marriage customs during the A.S. period see *Be Wifmannes Beweddunge*; Hazeltine: *Geschichte der Eheschliessung nach A.S. Recht.*
        2. Inst. reads: *eaque sola, dum vivit, sana et infirma, sit contentus*. With regard to the matrimonial entanglements of Northumbrian magnates a few years earlier, see Simeon of Durham, *De Obsessione Dunelmi*, Rolls Series, I. p. 215 ff.
8. 1. With this clause and the one following, cf. VI Atr. 16 f.
    § 2. 1. Cf. II Edg. 3, 1; VIII Atr. 7 f.
9. 1. With this clause and the two following, cf. VIII Atr. 10–11, 1.
    2. Q reads: *in festo sancti Petri ad vincula*, i.e. August 1st (cf. *in principio Augusti mensis*, Inst.), as distinct from the general festival of St Peter celebrated on June 29th, see Hastings, *Encycl. of Religion and Ethics*, Vol. v. p. 850.
    § 1. 1. Cf. Hn. 11, 3.
        2. Note that A reads 220 sh. here and in 10, 1.
10. § 1. 1. Cf. Hn. 11, 4.
11. 1. With this clause and the two following, cf. II Edg. 2 ff.
    2. Translated *in hereditate sua*, Q; *in alodio suo*, Inst.; *in sua libera terra*, Cons.
12. 1. With caps. 12–14, 1 cf. VI Atr. 19–22.
    2. Liebermann suggests that the last part of the clause, which is found in Ld, Q, Inst. and Cons., may have been missed in G and A because of the repetition of *ealswa*.
13. 1. Cf. Wulfstan, pp. 118, 208.
14. 1. *fyrðrige*, G, cf. Wulfstan, p. 311; *friðige*, A; cf. V Atr. 12, 2; VI, 21, 1.
    With caps 14–16, cf. Procl. of 1020, caps. 8; 19; Procl. of 1027, cap. 16.

§ 1. 1 Cf. V Atr. 12, 3; VI, 22; VIII, 16.
§ 2. 1. Cf. II Edg. 5 etc.; Wulfstan, pp. 117, 208.
   2. *sicut a sacerdote nuntiatae*, Q, cf. II Edg. 5, Q.
15. 1. With this clause and the one following, cf. VI Atr. 22, 1.
16. 1. Cf. II Edg. 5, 1; VI Atr. 22, 3; 23; Procl. of 1020, cap. 19; II Cn. 46.
16 *a*. 1. Cf. VI Atr. 22, 2 f.
§ 1. 1. Lit. 'unless anyone has had it prescribed to him.' Inst. reads: *preceptum pro publica penitentia*.
   2. Note G's addition, which means literally 'a week after the twelfth Mass day.'
17. 1. Cf. VI Atr. 25; Wulfstan, pp. 117, 208.
§ 1. 1. Cf. V Atr. 16; VI, 23, 1.
§ 2. 1. With this clause and the next, cf. VI Atr. 25, 1 f.
18 *a*. 1. Cf. II Cn. 68; Wulfstan, p. 113.
18 *b*. 1. Cf. Wulfstan, p. 114; *Dream of the Rood*, l. 107 ff.
   2. The meaning of *anfeald* is presumably not to be taken too literally.
   3. Cf. Wulfstan, pp. 94, 114.
§ 1. 1. Cf. VI Atr. 1.
§ 2. 1. Cf. VI Atr. 49; Wulfstan, pp. 37, 144, 282.
§ 3. 1. Cf. V Atr. 3; VI, 9–10; II Cn. 2, 1; 30, 5.
19. 1. Cf. VI Atr. 27 f.
heom is dat. sg., cf. Wi. 26, 1; III Edg. 1, 1; Procl. of 1020, cap. 8.
§ 1. 1. Cf. VI Atr. 28.
   2. Cf. VI Atr. 6 etc.; VIII, 44, 1. Q reads *quisquis amicus Dei*.
§ 2. 1. Cf. VI Atr. 28, 1; II Cn. 1; *En. Emmae, Mon. Germ. SS.* XIX. p. 520.
§ 3. 1. Cf. VI Atr. 30; II Cn. 84, 1 and 6.
20. 1. With this clause and the two following, cf. Wulfstan, pp. 74, 119.
   2. Cf. *Oath Formulae*, 1.
§ 2. 1. Liebermann compares this with *Episcopus*, 10 (see I. p. 478).
   2. Cf. *formanig, foroft*, BT., p. 315.
21. 1. Cf. II Cn. 84, 1 and 4 *a*; Wulfstan, p. 307.
22. 1. Cf. *Can. Edg.* 22, ed. Thorpe, *Anc. Laws*, II. p. 248; *Can. Ælfric*, 23, *ibid*. p. 351; Ælfric, *Homilies*, ed. Thorpe, I. p. 274; II. p. 604; Wulfstan, pp. 33, 39, 301 f., 307.
   2. *geleornige...geleornian*. This verb appears to be used in somewhat different senses here—intrans. in the former case, trans. in the latter. The passive idea ('receive instruction') is not actually contained in the first case, but in practice instruction would probably be involved.
§ 3. 1. Cf. *Ancren Riwle*, ed. Morton, London, 1853, p. 28.
§ 4. 1. This clause is in the form of a rhetorical question, cf. *Be Griðe*, 27.
§ 5. 1. G reads somewhat differently: 'After his death he cannot rest in the company of Christians nor in a hallowed grave nor can he be entitled to receive the sacrament while he is alive here.' Wulfstan, p. 307, agrees with B and A.

2. Q has *in requie sanctorum* (possibly as the result of misunderstanding the A.S. text), Cons. has *in sanctificata requie*. Is *requies* used here meaning 'churchyard'?
23. 1. Cf. Wulfstan, p. 307 f.
2. Cf. V Atr. 25; VI, 28, 2.
24. 1. Cf. Wulfstan, *loc. cit.*
2. Cf. V Atr. 25; VI, 28, 2; Procl. of 1020, cap. 15; II Cn. 6; Wulfstan, p. 298. Cons. misunderstands the word *ǽwbryce* and translates it *qualibet legis transgressione* both here and in II, 6.
25. 1. Cf. Wulfstan, p. 308.
26. 1. With caps. 26–26, 4, cf. *Insts. of Polity*, 6, ed. Thorpe, *Anc. Laws*, II. p. 310.
2. Cf. II Cn. 84, 4; Ælfric, *Homilies*, ed. Thorpe, II. p. 74.
§ 1. 1. With what follows to the middle of § 3, cf. *Insts. of Polity*, 19, ed. Thorpe, II. p. 326. From § 1 to the end, cf. Wulfstan, p. 191.
2. The same metaphor is used in II Cn. 84, 2.
§ 3. 1. Lit. 'man-wolf,' cf. *virlupus*, Cons., *i.e.* a man who can assume at will the form of a wolf, see Grimm, *Teutonic Mythology*, transl. Stallybrass, pp. 1093–7. Mogk[1] regards the form *werewulf* (for *werw.*) as parallel to *weregild* (for *werg.*), cf. In. 33 H; Af. 7, 1 E; II Cn. 61.
§ 4. 1. Cf. *Be Griðe*, 20.
2. Cf. Wulfstan, pp. 191, 309.

II CANUTE

Preamble. 1. Cf. III Edg. 1.
2. Liebermann, in view of the form *minan* (cf. *ðissan*, cap. 4 *a*), takes *ræd* in the sense of 'council' (see Toller, *Suppl*, p. 683, *s.v.* V) and regards Canute therefore as the first to speak of a 'unified body of state counsellors' (see *National Assembly*, p. 12). For late forms of the gen. pl. such as *witenan*, see Sievers, *A.S. Gram.* §§ 276, note 4; 304, note 2. In spite of the difficulty of explaining *minan* as a gen. pl. adjectival form (except, perhaps, as due to the influence of the following noun), I am inclined to think that the whole phrase is simply equivalent to *mid witena geþeahte*, cf. II Edm. Pre.; II Edg. Pre.; VIII Atr. Pre.; I Cn. Pre.
1. 1. Cf. V Atr. 1, 1; Procl. of 1020, cap. 15; I Cn. 19, 2.
2. Cf. cap. 75, 1.
§ 1. 1. Cf. III Edg. 1, 1; VI Atr. 8, 1.
2. 1. Cf. VI Atr. 10, 1.
2. Liebermann takes this to mean 'forfeits his life' (see I. p. 309), but *deope* would then seem unnecessary.
2 *a*. 1. Cf. VI Atr. 10, 2.
§ 1. 1. Cf. VI Atr. 10.
2. Cf. 30, 5.
3. Cf. I, 18, 3.
3. 1. Cf. VI Atr. 9; VII, 5.

---

[1] *Beiträge zur Gesch. d. deutschen Sprache u. Lit.*, Vol. 21, p. 575 f.

352 NOTES TO THE LAWS OF CANUTE

  2. Liebermann translates *ealles to swiðe* as 'allzu rasch,' but is it not rather used elliptically, meaning 'as is done far too much'? It can hardly have been intended at this time to give legal sanction to the practice at all.

  3. With regard to the form *eardan*, see I Atr. 2 and note.

4. 1. Cf. VIII Atr. 40.

4 a. 1. Cf. E. and G. 11; VI Atr. 7.

  2. *sagae vel incantatrices*, Q; *incantatores et incantatrices*, Inst.

  3. Cf. caps. 5, 1; 56.

  4. *Deo et hominibus publice satisfaciant*, Inst.

§ 1. 1. Cf. VIII Atr. 41.

  2. Cf. *utlah wið God*, Procl. of 1020, cap. 17.

§ 2. 1. Cf. Wulfstan, pp. 26, 115, 204, 310.

5. § 1. 1. See Bede, ed. Plummer, II. p. 59 f., for a list of the references in Bede and elsewhere to heathen practices such as idolatry, sacrifices, etc. Idolatry was first forbidden by law by Erconbert of Kent (640–664), see Bede, Lib. III. ch. 8, while Wihtred also inflicts penalties upon those who make offerings to devils (see cap. 12 f.). No further references to heathen practices appear in the Laws until the period of the Danish settlement, cf. V Atr. 1 and note. References to the worship of idols, divination, etc. appear also in *Poen. Theod.* 27 (ed. Thorpe, *Anc. Laws*, II. pp. 32–4); *Poen. Egb.* II. 22, IV. 19 (*ibid.* pp. 190, 210); *Dial. Egb.* XV. (*ibid.* p. 94); *Can. Edg.* 16 (*ibid.* p. 248); Wulfstan, pp. 12, 303; *N.P.L.* 48; 54.

  2. For the use of this expression in apparently heathen poetry see *Hákonarmál*, Strophe 21, ed. Kershaw, *A.S. and Norse Poems*, p. 108.

  3. *on blote*, G, B; *on hlotæ*, A. Q has *in sacrificio...in sorte*, apparently translating both. Two texts of Q add after *sacrificio* (*id est secundum ritum Suuanorum*). For the continuation of heathen observances in Sweden after the kings had become Christian see Kershaw, *Stories and Ballads*, p. 141 ad fin., also *Heimskr., Saga Sigurðar, Eysteins ok Olafs*, Chap. 28; Adam of Bremen, IV. Ch. 26 f.

  4. Cf. Norse *frett*, an inquiry of gods or men about the future.

6. 1. Cf. Wulfstan, pp. 26, 114.

Note the alliteration characteristic of legal formulae in late A.S. times.

  2. Cf. E. and G. 11; I Em. 6; V Atr. 24 f.; VI, 7; 36; Procl. of 1020, cap. 15.

  3. *legis transgressores*, Cons., cf. I, 24.

7. 1. The alliteration is again noteworthy.

§ 1. 1. Cf. E. and G. 11; VIII Atr. 40.

8. 1. Cf. VI Atr. 31–32, 1.

  2. Both are actually singular. Inst. translates *bondan* by *pauperibus hominibus*, cf. VII Atr. 2, 4 and note. In reality, however, the Norse word *bondi* denotes any free members of the community, whether rich or poor, other than persons in official positions.

§ 1. 1. I have followed Q, Cons. and Liebermann in taking *ðara handa* as singular. Inst., followed by Thorpe, takes it as plural. In view of what follows, however, and of II As. 14, 1, most probably one hand only is meant. In caps. 30, 4; 48, 1 both are to be forfeited.

§ 2. 1. Cf. IV Atr. 7, 3.
2. It is noteworthy that, about this time, a great deal of false money was produced, not in England but in Scandinavia. Canute's money is of a very much lighter standard than that of previous kings, but is not bad, see Chadwick, *A.S. Institutions*, p. 33.
3. Inst. reads: *purget se triplici purgatione, sacramenti aut igniti ferri*, cf. IV Atr. 7, 3; Cons. reads: *p. s. t. purgamine*, one MS adding, *cum* XLII[bus] *legalibus hominibus nominatis, et iuret se tricesima et sexta manu*, cf. Leis Wl. 15, 1. The expression probably does refer to an oath of 36 compurgators, cf. the Anglo-Scand. phrase *mid þrinna xii* in III Atr. 13, which suggests that the normal mode of exculpation was by the oath of 12 compurgators.
9. 1. Cf. VI Atr. 32, 2.
10. 1. Cf. VI Atr. 32, 3; II Cn. 65.
11. 1. With this clause and the one following, cf. VI Atr. 40 f.
12. 1. *gerihta* means rights of jurisdiction as well as the profits of jurisdiction, cf. IV Edg. 2 *a*.
2. Cf. *griðbryce*, cap. 15.
3. Generally, from the time of IV Atr. 4, *mundbryce, hamsocn* and *forstal* are classed together, the fine for each being £5, cf. Hn. 12, 2; 35, 2; DB. I. 154 *b*, 2; 172 *a*, 1; 179 *a*, 1; 252 *a*, 1.
4. Cf. In. 51; II Cn. 65; 77; Kemble, IV., Nos. *771, *785, *809, 853, 874.
5. Cf. Canute's grant to the Archbishop of Canterbury, Earle, *Land Charters*, p. 232.
13. 1. *i.e.* a deed which would legally involve outlawry; cf. the Norse phrase *göra utlaga verk*.
2. Probably we are to understand 'no-one but the king,' cf. one MS of Q which reads, *pacis emendatio in solius regis consistat imperio*.
§ 1. 1. Cf. I Atr. 1, 14.
§ 2. 1. Cf. II As. 20, 8.
2. Cf. cap. 66, 1, where the penalty is much more severe.
3. Cf. II As. 20, 8, where, however, the MSS have *flyman* (*flymene*, Ld). I do not understand the forms *flema, fleame*. Toller, *Suppl.* p. 224, *s.v. fleam*, apparently takes the latter as a form (? dative) of *fleam*, but is not *on* required in that case? Liebermann suggests that the word *gangende* is understood and that the form *fleame* is instrumental.
15. 1. Cf. cap. 12.
2. *i.e.* a fine for fighting which has resulted in the shedding of blood, cf. II Edm. 3; *Be Wergilde*, 6. It covers, therefore, cases both of wounding and of slaying.
15 *a*. 1. The term *friðleas* does not occur elsewhere, see Toller, *Suppl.* p. 268 *s.v.*
2. Cf. II Edw. 5, 2.
§ 1. 1. Cf. III Edg. 3; Leis Wl. 39, 1; Hn. 13, 4; 34, 1.
2. Cf. *Sax. Chr.* ann. 1052 C, D: *Frencisce men...unlage rærdon*

7 *undom demdon*. For the opposite of these terms, see cap. 15, 2: *rihte lage* 7 *rihtne dom*.
  3. With the reading of B and G, cf. V As. 1, 3; with that of A (*his weores*), cf. II As. 17.
  4. Cf. III Edg. 3; *Duns.* 3, 3.
  § 1 *a*. 1. Judging from *N.P.L.* 51–53, the amount paid as *lahslit* depended upon the rank of the delinquent, viz. a king's thegn paid 10 half-marks, a landowner 6 half-marks, and an ordinary freeman 12 ores. Caps. 51–53 of *N.P.L.* are used by Inst. at this point.
  § 2. 1. Cf. Leis Wl. 42 f.; Hn. 34, 3.
    2. The regular fine payable to the hundred, cf. III Edm. 2.
  16. 1. Cf. III Edg. 4; Hn. 34, 7.
    2. The texts show three different readings of this phrase, viz. (1) *feo o. freoma*, B, cf. G (*o. freme*), Q (*pecunia vel commodo*), Cons. (*censu aut commodo*); (2) *feo o. feorh*, Ld, cf. Inst. (*pecuniam aut vitam*); (3) *feo o. feorme*, A. Liebermann takes *freoma*, B, as a late form of *freme* (see Toller, *Suppl.* p. 264, *s.v. fremu*), and suggests that the scribe of A had in mind the alliterative phrase *feoh* 7 *feorm* (see Toller, *Suppl.* p. 213, *s.v. feorm*). Here as in III Edg. 4 (see note) I have adopted the reading *feo o. freme* (*freoma*).
  17. 1. Cf. III Edg. 2; Leis Wl. 43.
  § 1. 1. Cf. III Edg. 5.
    2. Does this mean 30 shillings?
  18. 1. Cf. III Edg. 5, 1.
    2. This phrase, which appears only in B, has perhaps been taken over from the preceding clause.
  § 1. 1. Cf. III Edg. 5, 2.
  19. 1. Cf. In. 9; II As. 3, and see Bigelow, *Hist. of Procedure in England*, p. 205.
    2. *Nam* is a Scandinavian loan word which here makes its first appearance in the laws.
    3. See BT. p. 836, *s.v. scir*, III. Liebermann, following Bigelow, *op. cit.*, takes it to mean the shire court (Grafschaftsgericht).
  § 2. 1. I have taken the phrase *ge heonan* etc. to mean either the shire court or the hundred court. Liebermann in his translation ('von hier und da') apparently follows Q which has *abhinc et inde*; cf. also Leis Wl. 44, 2.
  20. 1. I have accepted Schmid's punctuation as giving the better sense. For a different reading see Liebermann, I. p. 322, cap. 20 f.
    2. Note the difference in the MS readings. Inst. has *si occisus fuerit* which agrees with that in B and A; Q has *si quis eum affligat* (*accuset*) which agrees with that in G. Liebermann suggests that the original text may have contained both readings, since *lade wyrðe* suits that in G and Q, *weres wyrðe* that in B, A, Inst.
    3. Cf. *on borh* near the end of the clause. Liebermann regards the terms *teoðung* and *borg* as practically synonymous in Canute's usage of them and as representing the system later known as frankpledge. *on teoðunge* is translated *in plegio* in Inst., cf. *in plegio liberali*, Hn. 8, 2; *in francplegio*, Leis Wl. 25.

II CANUTE

§ 1. 1. *stræc* is rendered *potentes sive fortes* in Q; *fortes* in Inst.; *austerus* in Cons. Schmid has 'mächtig,' Liebermann 'gewaltig.'
   2. Lit. 'a man of his' or 'one of his men.'
22. 1. Lit. 'who has never been frequently accused.'
   2. To complete the A.S. formula *him* has to be understood, *i.e. him naðer ne burste*, etc., cf. I Atr. 1, 2.
   3. Liebermann takes this to mean that the compurgators must be found by the accused within the hundred to which he belongs, cf. A, *innan his hundrede*.
   4. Cf. I Cn. 5, 4.
§ 1. 1. Lit. 'the simple oath shall be chosen.' In this case the accused is not allowed to nominate his own compurgators.
§ 1 *a*. 1. *forað* means lit. 'preliminary oath,' *i.e.* the oath sworn by the accuser in beginning his action.
   2. Inst. explains more fully the difference between a simple oath of accusation and a triple one: *simplici sacramento...hoc est accipiat duos et sit ipse tertius...triplex...accipiat quinque et sit ipse sextus*.
§ 3. 1. For previous exceptions to this rule, see V As. 2; III Edm. 6, 2.
23. 1. Cf. I Edw. 1, 1 ff.; I Edg. 4, 1; II Atr. 8
§ 1. 1. Lit. 'that they are bearing true testimony on his behalf that he acquired it legally in accordance with what, etc.'
24. 1. Liebermann, following Inst. (*rem mortuam vel iacentem*) and Cons. (*quicquam tam vivum quam mortuum*), explains *licgende* as 'todte Fahrhabe,' *i.e.* dead stock, see Plummer, *Sax. Chr.* II. p. 115, BT. p. 637, *s.v. licgan*, I. (end), where other examples of the use of the term are quoted. Q renders the phrase *mobile vel immobile*.
   2. Cf. In. 25; Af. 34; I Edw. 1; II As. 12; 13, 1; IV As. 2; VI, 10; IV Edg. 6.
§ 1. 1. No other instance of the word *æftergild* is quoted in BT. (see p. 11, *s.v.*). It is translated *secundam solutionem* in Q; *tantum valens* in Inst.; *persolutam* in Cons. Liebermann takes it to mean a payment equal to the value of the goods, cf. the use of *persolvere* in IV Atr. 3, 2; II Cn. 63 (where it translates *forgyldan* in the three Latin texts).
§ 2. 1. It is difficult to understand the exact meaning of *ahnian* here and in the following clause; cf. however Leis Wl. 45, 2 f. The difficulty with regard to § 3 is increased by the peculiar use of *sculan*, perhaps due to its being a negative sentence.
25. 1. With this clause and those following, cf. III Edg. 7–7, 3.
27. 1. Cf. Bateson, *Borough Customs*, II. p. 9. In Iceland it would seem from the Sagas that such a practice was very common, *e.g. Njalssaga*, Chap. 64.
28. 1. Cf. Hl. 15; II Edw. 7; II As. 22.
§ 1. 1. Cf. II As. 22, 2.
29. 1. Cf. In. 36; IV As. 6, 3.
   2. Probably exculpation by means of the oath of 12 compurgators is meant.

30. 1. Cf. I Atr. 1, 1.
2. Cf. *adeo suspectus...ut*, Cons. This use of *and* is rare and is not recognised in dictionaries. It is somewhat parallel, however, to its use after *gelice* and compounds of *efen*, etc., see Toller, *Suppl.* p. 38, *s.v. and*, IV.
§ 1. 1. *i.e.* (apparently) 'from the present time onwards.' The words are taken from I Atr. 1, 2, with the substitution of Winchester for Bromdun.
§ 2. 1. With this clause and the one following, cf. I Atr. 1, 3 f.
§ 3 *b*. 1. Cf. I Atr. 1, 5.
§ 4. 1. Cf. I Atr. 1, 6. Here again as in 8, 1 (cf. III Atr. 8; 16; IV, 5, 4) Canute replaces capital punishment by maiming. With regard to the infliction of this type of punishment by Canute, see *Sax. Chr.*, ann. 1014.
§ 5. 1. Cf. III Edm. 4; *Sax Chr.*, ann. 1036 C.
§ 6. 1. With the section from § 6–cap. 31, cf. I Atr. 1, 7–1, 10.
31 a. § 1. 1. With the clauses from here to 32, 1, cf. I Atr. 1, 11–2, 1.
§ 2. 1. Cf. *utlah wið eal folc*, cap. 30, 9. Both phrases are used to indicate that the outlawry is not limited to the district over which the jurisdiction of the court extends, cf. III Atr. 10.
32. 1. *ðeofman*, B, A; *ðeowman*, G. Liebermann points out that a similar confusion of *w* and *f* in MS B occurs in the word *stoddeowe* in Af. 9, 2.
33. 1. With this clause and the three following, cf. I Atr. 4–4, 3.
36. 1. Cf. II As. 26.
2. *ðara hánda* here, as in cap. 8, 1, is to be taken as sing. in view of the alternative, cf. Af. 71 and note.
§ 1. 1. Cf. II As. 26; I Cn. 5, 3.
37. 1. Cf. II As. 10, 1.
2. For the payment of *healsfang* as a fine, cf. Wi. 11; 12; 14; VI Atr. 51; II Cn. 45, 1.
38. 1. Cf. cap. 47.
§ 1. 1. Cf. VI Atr. 52; II Cn. 68, 1 *a*.
§ 2. 1. Cf. Wulfstan, p. 275.
39. 1. Cf. *Theod. Poen.* 3 § 11, ed. Thorpe, *Anc. Laws*, II. p. 5.
§ 1. 1. Cf. 41, 2.
40. 1. Cf. E. and G. 12; VIII Atr. 33.
§ 1. 1. Cf. VIII Atr. 34.
§ 2. 1. Cf. VIII Atr. 2, 1; 35.
41. 1. Cf. VIII Atr. 26.
2. Cf. VIII Atr. 18 and note.
42. 1. Cf. VIII Atr. 33 f.
2. Cf. *N.P.L.* 23.
43. 1. Cf. E. and G. 4, 2.
44. 1. Cf. E. and G. 5.
45. 1. Cf. E. and G. 9, 1.
§ 1. 1. Cf. Wi. 11 as contrasted with In. 3, 2; E. and G. 7, 1.
§ 2. 1. Cf. In. 3, 1; E. and G. 7, 1; 8.
§ 3. 1. Cf. In. 3; E. and G. 7, 2.

46. 1. Cf. E. and G. 8.
§ 2. 1. Cf. *ibid.*; VII Atr. 2, 4.
47. 1. Cf. Af. 5, 5; 40, 2.
    2. Cf. DB. I. 262 *b*, 1.
48. 1. Cf. E. and G. 6, 4.
    2. Probably 120 shillings, cf. I Cn. 10, 1.
§ 1. 1. Cf. E. and G. 6, 5.
    2. Taken as sing. by Q and Inst., plural by Cons. In E. and G. the fine is the man's wergeld, and as one hand is equal in value to half the wergeld Liebermann concludes that both are meant here.
§ 2. 1. Cf. E. and G. 6, 6 and note.
    2. Schmid, followed by Liebermann, regards *hearme* as a metathesised form of *hreame* (cf. *cum clamore*, Q, Inst.), but see the note to E. and G., *loc. cit.*
§ 3. 1. Cf. E. and G. 6, 7.
49. 1. Inst. reads: *Quicunque violaverit ordinem, sicut est aut monachum aut presbyterum aut aliquem ordinatum verberaverit aut aliquid huiusmodi fecerit...ita emendet* etc. For *hadbryce*, cf. V Atr. 25; VI, 28, 2; II Cn 6; Wulfstan, pp. 130, 164.
50. 1. Cf. I Edm. 4; V Atr. 25; VI, 28, 2; I Cn. 24; II, 6.
51. 1. Cf. E. and G. 4; VI Atr. 12; I Cn. 7; *N.P.L.* 61, 1.
52. 1. Cf. VI Atr. 39.
53. § 1. 1. See P. and M. II. p. 367.
54. 1. Cf. *Poen. Theod.* 19 § 8, ed. Thorpe, *Anc. Laws*, II. p. 17; *Conf. Egb.* 14, *ibid.* p. 142.
§ 1. 1. Cf. *Can. Edg., Mod. poenit.* 17, *ibid.* p. 270; *Poen. Egb.* II. 9, *ibid.* pp. 184, 186; *Poen. Theod.* 19 § 33, *ibid.* p. 20.
55. 1. Cf. Wi. 4.
56. 1. This clause seems tautological. For a parallel translation to the one I have given, see BT. p. 698, *s.v. morð*, III. For another version see BT. p. 763, *s.v. open.*
§ 1. 1. *i.e.* a suspicion which has to be proved.
    2. Cf. cap. 53, 1. Liebermann suggests that the decision with regard to the penalty may have rested with the bishop in this case because of the belief that the death of an enemy was frequently brought about by magical arts.
57. 1. Cf. Af. 4, 2; V Atr. 30; VI, 37; II Cn. 26; 64.
58. 1. With this clause and the two following, cf. Af. 3; *Be Griðe*, 11.
§ 1. 1. In *Norðleoda laga*, 2 the wergeld of an *æþeling* is stated to be the same as that of an archbishop.
59. 1. Cf. In. 6; Af. 7; *Be Griðe*, 15.
    2. Cf. *huse*, Ine; *healle*, Af.
60. 1. Lit. 'pay for him.'
    2. Cf. Abt. 24; Af. 35; 35, 6.
61. 1. Lit. 'perpetrates to the full a breach of the peace,' *i.e.* probably, by committing homicide.
§ 1. 1. Lit. 'half perpetrates,' *i.e.* probably, without the taking of life; cf. for a similar distinction I Cn. 2, 3; 3. Ld reads *ran wyrce*, *i.e.* commits robbery.

358 NOTES TO THE LAWS OF CANUTE

62. 1. Cf. II Edm. 6; IV Atr. 4; 4, 1; II Cn. 12; 15.
2. Compare G's addition here with that in I Cn. 3, 2.
§ 1. 1. Cf. IV Atr. 4.
63. 1. Cf. In. 9; 31. This translation follows Liebermann, but see Toller, *Suppl.* p. 243, *s.v. forgildan*, II a.
2. Liebermann regards G's addition as probably representing actual practice.
64. 1. This list is probably due to Scandinavian influence, see Steenstrup, *Danelag*, p. 262 f.
2. The difference between *hamsocn* and *husbryce* seems to be that the latter involves destruction or damage to the house itself, see Brunner, II. p. 653[23].
3. Cf. II As. 6, 2, and see P. and M. II. p. 492 f; *Pleas of Gloucester*, ed. Maitland, n. 216.
4. Cf. Af. 4, 2; III Edg. 7, 3; II Cn. 26; 57; 77.
5. Cf. III Atr. 1; VIII, 1, 1; I Cn. 2, 3.
65. 1. Cf. V Atr. 26, 1; VI, 32, 3; II Cn. 10; *Rect.* 1.
§ 1. 1. Cf. I Edm. 5; Birch, no. 599, where one condition attached to a grant of land made by the Bishop of Winchester to a certain Beornulf in 902 is that every year help shall be given *to þære cyrican bóte*.
66. § 1. 1. Cf. VIII Atr. 42.
68. 1. Cf. I Cn. 18 a f.
§ 1. 1. With this clause and those following, cf. VI Atr. 52 ff.
69. § 1. 1. Cf. Procl. of 1027, cap. 12.
§ 2. 1. The reference is doubtless to the last few words of the preceding clause. The case suggested is that of a reeve who tries to treat the voluntary payment there mentioned as a compulsory tax.
2. *crafian* is a Scandinavian loan word.
70. 1. See P. and M. I. p. 312 ff.
71 a. § 1. 1. *i.e.* those whose personal lord is the king—the barons of later times, cf. Leis Wl. 20, 1.
§ 2. 1. The reference is no doubt to medial thegns, *i.e.* those not under the immediate lordship of the king—the vavasours of Leis Wl. 20, 2, cf. *Be Leode Geþincðum*, cap. 3.
§ 4. 1. Lit. 'if he has relations with the king to a higher degree (than others).' *furðor* here is an adverb.
§ 5. 1. This reference to wealth is peculiar to B. The phrase *læsse maga* (cf. A. and G. 3), which is common to all the texts, would seem to have the same meaning as *medemra ðegna* (MSS. G, A) in § 2.
72. 1. Cf. III Atr. 14; V, 32, 3, and 5 D.
73. 1. Cf. V Atr. 21, 1; VI, 26, 1.
73 a. 1. Cf. *Wifmannes Beweddung*, 4; DB. II. 199 a.
§ 2. 1. Cf. cap. 52; and see P. and M. II. p. 427.
74. 1. Cf. *Wifmannes Beweddung*, 1; Earle, *Land Charters*, p. 228, where the marriage contract between a certain Godwine and his prospective father-in-law Byrhtric is given.

II CANUTE

76. 1. Cf. In. 57.
2. I cannot understand *arefned*, the reading of B. Liebermann suggests that it is a mistake for *arefsed*.
§ 1. 1. Cf. In. 7; 7, 1; 57.
§ 1 *a*. 1. The form *tægan* is unusual and does not occur elsewhere, see BT. p. 972, *s.v. teah*.
§ 1 *b*. 1. Cf. In. 57.
§ 2. 1. Cf. Wulfstan, p. 158, and the complaint made by Christian III of Denmark in 1537 (Phillpotts, *Kindred and Clan*, p. 82).
77. 1. Cf. V Atr. 28; VI, 35; Wulfstan, p. 275.
2. Cf. *Sax. Chr.* ann. 999; *Rect.* 1, 1.
§ 1. 1. Cf. cap. 13, 1.
78. 1. Does *ut of lande* mean 'abroad,' or, in view of 77, 'at sea'?
79. 1. The phrase employed with this sense throughout Domesday Book is *defendere pro*, see Maitland, *DB. and Beyond*, p. 55.
80. § 1. 1. Lit. 'Let every man leave my hunting alone where I wish to have it preserved,' see BT. p. 568, *s.v. huntnað*.
In this case the full penalty probably means 120 shillings, the fine for insubordination to the king.
81. 1. Cf. III Atr. 3; *N.P.L.* 67, 1.
2. The exact significance of the word *dryncelean* is uncertain. It is regarded by Steenstrup (*Danelag*, p. 187) as equivalent to the Scandinavian *drekkulaun*, *i.e.* land bestowed as a gift by the king in return for hospitality (see also Amira, *Nordgerm. Oblig.* II. p. 619). It seems possible, however, that a gift of 'drink-money' may have marked the successful conclusion of a bargain, see *Anglia*, 33 (1910), p. 134; Gierke, *Schuld und Haftung*, p. 368 f. In the twelfth century 1 penny had to be paid as drink money (*beverache*) by a buyer of land at Whitby, see Bateson, *Borough Customs*, II. p. 81.
83. 1. With this clause and the two following, cf. II As. 25, 2.
84. 1. With this clause and the next, cf. I Cn. 21.
§ 2. 1. Cf. I Cn. 26, 1–3.
§ 3. 1. Cf. I Cn. 6, 1; 25.
§ 4. 1. Cf. I Cn. 26.
§ 4 *b*. 1. Cf. I Cn. 19, 3.
§ 5. 1. Cf. I Cn. 26, 4 B.

NOTES TO THE LAWS OF WILLIAM I AND OF HENRY I

WILLIAM I: LONDON CHARTER

1. 1. Cf. Procl. of 1020, Pre. and note.
2. William was consecrated Bishop of London in 1051 and died in 1075 (see Stubbs, *Reg. Sacr. Angl.* p. 36).
3. Cf. Wl. ep. Pre., and see Round, *Geoffrey de Maundeville*, p. 439.
4. Cf. II As. 12; III Atr. 7.
2. 1. *i.e.* the bishop as the representative of the ecclesiastical authority and the mayor as the representative of the secular.
3. 1. Liebermann's view that this clause is intended to assure the retention of property in private possession without any danger of confiscation by the Crown seems in keeping with the general tone of the Charter. Ballard, who regards it as referring to cases of intestacy, gives other instances from town charters (see *British Bor. Charters*, p. 74 f.).

WILLIAM I: REGULATIONS REGARDING EXCULPATION

1. Cf. In.; I Edm. H. Liebermann points out that the form *asetnysse* might be sing. Cf. *gewitnysse, -nesse* in II Cn. 23, 1; 37.
1. 1. *orneste* is a Scandinavian loan word, see BT. p. 766, *s.v. orrest*; Steenstrup, *Danelag*, p. 227; Sax. Chr. ann. 1096 and note.
2. Schmid, followed by Liebermann, takes *dóm* here in the sense of 'ordeal,' cf. *judicium* translating *iren* in caps. 2; 3, also in Wl. ep. 4, 1 f.; Hn. 18; 45, 1 *a*; 49, 6; 92, 13; DB. II. 110 *b*; 146 *b* etc. Such an interpretation is possible, especially as the phrase *Godes dóm* meaning 'ordeal' is found in *Jud. Dei*, VIII. 2, 2 (Liebermann, I. p. 415). There is evidence that the ordeal was frequently employed as a mode of proof by Normans as well as by Englishmen (see Bigelow, *Placita A.N.* p. xii f., also pp. 30, 34, 38, 40 ff.; P. and M. I. p. 74), but, since there is no mention of it otherwise in connection with Normans in the decrees attributed to William I, it is perhaps better to keep the sense of *dom* noted in Toller, *Suppl.* p. 154, *s.v.* VIII.
§ 1. 1. See P. and M. I. p. 90. In Hn. 18 the statement occurs: *Francigena si compellatur iuret se sexto.*
2. § 1. 1. No other instance of the use of this word is quoted in BT. (see p. 898, *s.v.*); cf. *gespelia*, VIII Atr. 2, 1; 42.
§ 2. 1. Cf. Hn. 59, 15.

§ 3. 1. It is noteworthy that compurgation was not mentioned as a possible mode of proof in cap. 2.

3. 1. The form *utlaga* probably represents the dat. pl. of the adjective with final *-n* omitted; cf. *utlagan þ.*, cap. 3, 1. Q however translates the phrase *utlagariae rebus* and therefore regards it as the genitive of an abstract noun.

§ 2. 1. Apart from here the word occurs only in Ælfric, *Homilies*, ed. Thorpe I. p. 260, l. 29, where it clearly means 'inviolate' (see BT. p. 1104, *s.v. unfored* and *unforodlic*). Q reads *plano iuramento* (*non in verborum observantiis*), cf. *sacramento non fracto*, Wl. art. 6, 3, and similar expressions in Hn. 64, 1; 2 a; 3 a; 4; 6. The type of oath represented seems to be one the validity of which did not depend on the exact pronouncement of a prescribed formula, phrase by phrase. For the opposite (*iuramentum fractum, frangens* etc.) see Hn. 64, 1; 1 c; 1 f; 2; 4; 6. Similar expressions are quoted from Old French and Norman sources by Brunner (see II. 427; *Forschungen*, p. 327 f.). He explains this provision of William's as intended to free the Norman from the necessity of repeating an oath, dictated to him in English, which he would probably not understand (see *Zeitsch. d. Savigny Stiftung, Germ. Abt.* XVII. p. 128; *Political Science Quarterly*, XI. p. 537). For similar importance attached to the exact pronouncement of a prescribed formula in the Viking Age, see *Njalssaga*, ch. 23.

THE EPISCOPAL LAWS OF WILLIAM I

Preamble. 1. Ralph Bainard appears in Domesday Book as a tenant-in-chief holding lands in Hertfordshire and Essex (I. 138 a, 2; II. 68 b). His signature is found attached to a (spurious) charter granted by Wm I (see Davis, *Reg. Agnorm.* *88), and he appears as sheriff of Essex about 1080 (see Davis, *op. cit.* 122, *181, 211).

2. Geoffrey de Maundeville held lands in Hertfordshire, Middlesex and Essex (see DB. I. 139 b, 2; 129 b, 1; II. 57 b; Round, *Geoffrey de Maundeville*, p. 37). His name appears frequently in documents issued by Wm I and Wm II (see Davis, *op. cit.* p. 149), and at some unknown date he held office as sheriff, not only of London and Middlesex (see Round, *op. cit.* pp. 142, 354), but also, as it would appear from later charters, of Essex and Hertfordshire as well (see Round, *op. cit.* pp. 150, 166).

3. Peter de Valognes held lands in Hertfordshire and Essex (see DB. I. 140 b, 2; II. 78), and his name appears frequently in documents of Wm I and Wm II (see Davis, *op. cit.* p. 153). He held office as sheriff of Hertfordshire about the year 1086 (see DB. I. 141 a, 1).

4. Davis (see n. 93) is of opinion that this notification was sent to Ralph Bainard as sheriff of Essex, Geoffrey de Maundeville as sheriff of Middlesex, and Peter de Valognes as sheriff of Hertfordshire, but Liebermann suggests that these three counties may have been grouped together and their affairs as a whole managed by the three magnates here named.

5. The preamble of the copy intended for the diocese of Lincoln reads: 'William, by the grace of God king of England, to the earls and sheriffs and all the French and English who hold lands in the diocese of Bishop Remigius—greeting.'
1. 1. Stigand was deposed on April 11th, 1070 and Lanfranc consecrated as Archbishop of Canterbury on August 29th. Ealdred, Archbishop of York, died on September 11th, 1069 and was succeeded by Thomas, consecrated in 1070 (see Stubbs, *Reg. Sacr. Angl.* pp. 35, 38).
2. 1. This expression may have a wider significance and the reference may be to ecclesiastical jurisdiction in general. Liebermann translates it by 'kanonisches Recht,' cf. *ad regimen animarum*, and see P. and M. I. p. 75².
2. *i.e.* the public secular court, cf. *popularia placita quod Angli vocant hundred*, Inst. II. 17.
3. § 1. 1. Cf. *wrecan*, VIII Atr. 2, 1; 35; II Cn. 40, 2.
§ 2. 1. Cf. *oferhyrnesse seu lahslite pro unaquaque vocatione episcopo reddant*, Synodus Lanfranci, April 1076, quoted by Liebermann, I. p. 485ᶠ.
4. 1. The title *praepositus* (A.S. *gerefa*) is applied to the governor of any district smaller than a county.
2. *i.e.* one who has a court of his own.
§ 1. 1. The meaning might be 'except in the presence of an official of the bishop's,' cf. Liebermann, I. p. 485ᵍ; ECf. 9: *Assit ad iudicium minister episcopi*.

THE TEN ARTICLES OF WILLIAM I

Preamble. 1. Cf. Inst. Cn. heading.
The French version reads: *Ici sunt escrites les leys et les custumes ke li reys Willame establit en Engleterre, pus ke il aveit la terre conquise.*
2. Cf. Leis Wl., heading; ECf. Pre.
1. 1. Cf. V Atr. 1; VI, 1; VII, 1; I Cn. 1; Inst. Cn. 1; Cons. Cn. 1.
The French version reads: *Tut al comencement comandat il ke la Christienté e les custumes de seint eglise e ses dreiz e ses franchises fussent mainteneues.*
2. Liebermann points out that, in genuine decrees of William I and his sons, the term *Franci* or *Francigenae* is always employed, cf. Wl. lad *passim*; Wl. Lond. 1; Hn. cor. Pre.; Hn. mon. Pre.; 1; Hn. com. Pre.; Hn. Lond. Pre.
2. 1. Cf. III Edm. 1. Such a demand on the part of William is confirmed by the evidence of the *Sax. Chr.* ann. 1086.
2. Liebermann, following Brunner (II. p. 62 ³⁴), draws attention to the resemblance between the form of this oath and the West Frankish *sacramentum fidelium (laicorum)* of 858 and 872 (see *Mon. Germ. Legum.* I. pp. 457, 518).
3. Cf. *ge on sæ ge on lande*, II Edw. Pre. 1; II Cn. 78 and note; and see Brunner, I.² p. 190.
3. § 1. 1. The French version has *li sires al homicide*, *i.e.* the lord of the slayer, which Liebermann regards as incorrect.

2. The time set is 7 days according to Hn. 75, 6 a; 91, 1; 92, 3 and 5; 8 days according to Leis Wl. 22 and ECf. 15.

3. Cf. Leis Wl. 22; Hn. 13, 2; 91, 1; ECf. 15, 2. This sum, however, seems to have been very rarely exacted. Those mentioned in the Pipe Rolls vary and are generally much smaller (see Stubbs, *Lect. Early Hist.* p. 72; P. and M. II. p. 487). According to Hn. 91, 1; ECf. 15, 6 f., 40 marks went to the king and 6 to the kin of the slain man.

§ 2. 1. Payment in the first instance is exacted from the *manerium* on which the body has been found according to Hn. 91, 2; from the *villa* according to ECf. 15, 2, and only when their property proves insufficient does the hundred become responsible for what remains (Hn. 91, 2 a; ECf. 15, 4). An exception is made in the case of a royal manor (see Hn. 91, 3). The hundred, however, appears as primarily responsible in Leis Wl. 22; Hn. 75, 6 a; 91, 1 b and 4; *Dial. de Scacc.* I. x, p. 26 a; and also in the cases recorded in the early Pipe Rolls (see Stubbs, *op. cit.* p. 71). Minute directions regarding the murder-fine are given in Hn. 91 ff., 92 ff.

4. 1. Lit. 'shared in the payment of taxes,' *i.e.* had become naturalised. It seems best to take this clause in connection with cap. 3, a noteworthy distinction being made by William between his own followers and men of French birth who had settled in England during the previous reign.

2. The French version, following the reading *persolvat*, has *rende le murde solum la ley des Engleis*.

3. William was at Gloucester in 1072, 1081, 1082, 1085 and 1086 (see Osbern, *Vita Dunstani*, ed. Stubbs, p. 75; Davis, *Reg. Agnorm.* p. xxii; n. 288 a).

5. 1. Cf. I Edw. 1; II As. 13, 1; II Cn. 24.

2. Cf. *pannus usatus*, ECf. 38. The regulation is apparently intended to prevent the sale of stolen goods. It is suggested by Liebermann that the MS variants of *vetustam* are due to a misreading of such a form as *vet'tam* in the archetype. The French version has *nule chose de ailurs aportée (i.e. rem vectam) ne fust receue ne vendue ne achatée sanz plegage* etc.

6. 1. Cf. Wl. lad 2.

2. A Scandinavian loan word which occurs only here (cf. Wl. art. retr. 12) and in II Cn. 61, 1 Ld.

3. The French version has *par chaut fer*.

§ 1. 1. Cf. Wl. lad 2, 1, where a substitute is mentioned for the combat only, not for the ordeal. The French version has *autre...ke il conbate pur lui*.

§ 2. 1. Cf. Wl. lad 2, 2, where, however, payment is mentioned only in the case of the Frenchman.

2. The reading LX found only in one MS agrees with Wl. lad.

§ 3. 1. Cf. Wl. lad 3, 1 f.

2. Liebermann points out that this is a mistake on the part of the compiler, as no Englishman could refuse trial by ordeal.

3. Cf. Wl. lad 3, 2 and note. The French version reads simply *serement*.

7. 1. Cf. Leis Wl. Pre.; Hn. cor. 13.
8. 1. Cf. II Cn. 20 Inst., where *plegium* is used to translate Canute's *teoðung*.

8 a. 1. The French version takes this clause and the following one together and reads: *gardent ses pleges ke il rende ço ke ert chalengé e si se eslajent par serement, ke il ne seurent nule tricherie en luy ki est eschapet, seit demandez al hundred e al cunté cil vers ki l'un parolet, si cum nos ancestres esgarderent.*

§ 1. 1. Cf. I Edg. 1; II Cn. 17, 1; Hn. com. 1, 4.
§ 2. 1. Cf. II As. 20; III Edg. 7; II Cn. 25; Leis Wl. 47.
    2. The value of an ox was 30 pence, see VI As. 3; 6, 2; 8, 5; also *N.P.L.* 59 as compared with VIII Atr. 10, 1.
§ 3. 1. Cf. II Cn. 25, 1.
    2. *i.e.* A.S. *oferhyrnes* (120 shillings), cf. II As. 20; III Edm. 6, 2; II Cn. 15, 2, where the same fine is exacted for contempt of court or refusal to comply with the law.

9. 1. Cf. V Atr. 2; VI, 9; VII, 5; II Cn. 3; Leis Wl. 41.
    2. The French version reads: *hors del pais ne de la terre, come li Engleis feseint jadis.*

10. 1. Cf. V Atr. 3; VI, 10 f.; II Cn. 2, 1; Leis Wl. 40.

WILLELMI ARTICULI RETRACTATI

1. 1. Cf. ECf. 33 (Liebermann, I. p. 660ᶜ).
3. 1. The two words *protectio* and *pax* express practically the same idea.

§ 1. 1. With the marginal note (*De Englecherie*) in the two MSS Co and Or, cf. Hn. 75, 6 b; 92, 9 a.

5. 1. Cf. Hn. cor. 11, where, however, the reference is to knights (*milites*) only.
7. 1. Cf. II Cn. 9.
8. 1. See P. and M. I. pp. 282–90.
    2. Cf. Hn. cor. 11; *Assize of Arms* (1181), ed. Stubbs, *Select Charters*, p. 183.
9. 1. Cf. Wl. art. 2; ECf. 32 A, 5 f. (Liebermann, I. p. 655); Stubbs, *Lect. Early Hist.* p. 67.
10. 1. Liebermann suggests that the reading *venditam* (for *vetitam*) which occurs in Co and Or is probably taken from the *vendatur* of the preceding line.
11. 1. *forum* has probably the same meaning as *mercatum*, cf. ECf. retr. 39, 2, where *in foro regio* replaces *in mercatis*, ECf. 39, 2 (Liebermann, I. p. 670).
15. § 1. 1. Cf. Hn. 78, 1.
16. 1. Cf. Glanville, v. cap. 5, and see P. and M. I. p. 649.
    2. The noun here seems to have the sense 'claim,' cf. the frequent use of the verb *calumniare* with the same meaning, *e.g.* Wl. art. 8, 3; *Liber Eliensis*, ed. Stewart, II. Chap. 46, 124; DB. I. 2 a, 1; 36 b, 2.
17. 1. Cf. Wl. art. 10; Leis Wl. 40 L.

THE (SO-CALLED) LAWS OF WILLIAM I

Preamble. 1. Translated *leges et consuetudines* in the Latin version. The phrase is regarded by Liebermann as meaning laws and unwritten customs, cf. the use of the word *custume* in cap. 3.
2. Translated *concessit* in L. Perhaps, however, an earlier sense of O.F. *graanter, creanter* is to be understood here, namely 'assure' or 'confirm' (see Godefroy, *s.v.*; Du Cange, *s.v. creantare*). Liebermann translates it 'zusicherte.'
3. Cf. Wl. art. heading.

1. 1. Cf. I Cn. 2.
2. *pacem et immunitatem ecclesiae sanctae concessimus*, L.

§ 1. 1. Cf. I Cn. 3, 2.
2. *i.e.* Norman shillings, corresponding to Canute's £5.
3. These sums in Norman shillings of 12 pence correspond to Canute's 60 shillings and 30 shillings respectively, calculated (wrongly) at 4 pence to the shilling, *i.e.* according to the Mercian system, cf. cap. 11, 1.

2. 1. *i.e.* £5, the regular West Saxon and Mercian fine, cf. Af. 3; II Cn. 58; Hn. 12, 2; 35, 2; 79, 4.
2. Cf. Hn. 80, 11 *a*; *hamsoken vel hamfare est insultus factus in domo*, Bromton, ed. Twysden, *Hist. Angl. Scriptores decem*, col. 957.
3. *i.e.* the Norman equivalent of the O.E. *forsteal*, see P. and M. II. p. 468.
4. Cf. DB. I. 179 *a*, 1; 252 *a*, 1.

§ 1. 1. Cf. VII Atr. 6, 3; Hn. 51, 4.
§ 2. 1. Cf. *ures hlafordes grið*, III Atr. 13.
2. Cf. DB. I. 280 *b*, 1; 336 *b*, 1.
§ 2 *a*. 1. 40 (Norman) shillings are equivalent to 120 Mercian shillings, 50 (Norman) shillings to 120 W. Saxon shillings; so that the fine in both cases is that due for insubordination.
§ 3. 1. O.E. *cyninges þegn*, cf. II Cn. 71, 3.
2. Cf. O.E. *sacu* (V Atr. 19; VI, 25, 1; I Cn. 17, 2); also *socn* (III Atr. 11; II Cn. 71, 3).
3. Grants of toll are found in documents dating from early in the eleventh century, *e.g.* Kemble, 726 (*theloneum aquarum*); *737 (*thel. omnium navium*).
4. O.E. *team, i.e.* the right to hold processes involving vouching to warranty and to receive the payments forfeited in such cases. The phrase *toll and team* occurs in a document of about 1020 (see Earle, *Land Charters*, p. 236) and is regularly found from about the middle of the eleventh century following *sac* 7 *soc* and preceding *infangentheof*, cf. Kemble, *785, 813, 829, 830, 843.
5. *i.e.* the right to hang thieves caught with the stolen goods upon them.
§ 4. 1. If the ore is taken as equivalent to 20 pence, the sum paid to the plaintiff is 20 Norman shillings, cf. cap. 3, 1.

3. 1. 'innerhalb seiner Verbürgung' (Liebermann). Bartsch (*Chrestomathie de l'ancien français*, 10th ed. p. 39) and Matzke (*Lois de*

Guillaume le Conquérant, p. 4), following I, read *et il s'en fuie dedenz [le terme], sun plege si averad* etc.

2. Cf. ECf. 15, 1; 23, 2. In the case of a person *ultra mare* the time granted is 6 weeks and 1 day, cf. Hn. 41, 2 *b*.

3. Cf. cap. 49; IV As. 6, 3; II Cn. 29.

§ 1. 1. Cf. III Edm. 3; I Edg. 6.

2. Cf. cap. 2, 4 and note.

3. Cf. the town law of Waterford (about 1300): *De latronibus... se il soit lays homme...chelui qi le pendra avera son meillor drap ou iiiid.* (Bateson, *Borough Customs*, I. p. 53). In Torksey about 1345 also two payments of 4 pence were made to the *ballivus* by a prisoner who had been acquitted (*ibid.* II. p. 37).

4. The value of the *maille* is given as half a denar by La Curne and Du Cange (*s.v. mallia*).

5. Presumably this small sum goes to the gravedigger. The payments here specified are those which the persons concerned would have received, if the man had been convicted and put to death.

6. *i.e.* 120 Mercian shillings, the fine for insubordination, cf. 2, 2 *a*; 4, 1.

§ 2. 1. *i.e.* £5, the fine for breach of the king's protection in Wessex, cf. Af. 3; II Cn. 58.

§ 3. 1. Cf. III Atr. 7; 7, 1.

§ 4. 1. Cf. caps. 5, 2; 6, 1.

4. 1. The first part of the word *hengwite* is probably connected with O.E. *hengen*, a prison, the fine being one exacted for failing to keep a criminal in custody. The form *hangwite* is also common and is interpreted in the twelfth and thirteenth centuries as a fine incurred for having hanged a thief without trial (cf. *Munim. Gildhal.*, ed. Riley, II. p. 732; *Liber Rub. Scacc.*, ed. Hall, III. p. 1036). It occurs among the list of privileges granted by Edward the Confessor in two (spurious) charters, see Kemble, Nos. *809, *825.

2. In view of what follows in § 1 this seems to refer to the payment of the 10 shillings.

5. 1. The Latin version reads *praepositus hundredi*.

2. The Latin version adds *vel cuiuscumque generis averia vagantia*.

3. The Latin version reads *dabit praeposito*.

4. The sums mentioned here do not agree with those in *Forfang*, caps. 1; 2; 3, 1.

§ 2. 1. It seems to be assumed here, and in cap. 6, 1, that the man who has taken charge of the livestock or property is one with some sort of a court.

6. 1. Cf. cap. 21, 5. As regards later procedure see ECf. 24 ff.

7. 1. *i.e.* 30 Mercian shillings. In In. 70, the sum payable as *manbot* for a *twyhynde* man is given as 30 shillings, *i.e.* 150 pence according to the W. Saxon money system.

2. Cf. Hn. 70, 2 and 4. This sum represents the value of the slave (cf. II Atr. 5, 1; Hn. 70, 7).

8. 1. *i.e.* 1200 shillings in each case, cf. II Atr. 5; *Be Wergilde*, 1; *Be Mircna laga*, 1, 1; Hn. 70, 1; 76, 4 *a*.

§ 1. 1. According to the older laws the wergeld of a commoner was 200 shillings both in Mercia and in Wessex, *i.e.* 800 pence in the one case, 1000 pence in the other, cf. A. and G. 2; *Be Wergilde*, 1, 1; *Að*, 1.

9. 1. *i.e.* $\frac{1}{10}$ of the villein's wergeld.

2. The corruptions of *healsfang* in both Hk and I show that by 1100 the origin and meaning of the term had been forgotten.

§ 1. 1. The sums equated with the stallion, bull and boar seem very high. Liebermann suggests that, in the case of the two latter, the Mercian shilling of 4 pence may be meant.

10. 1. With this clause and the two following, cf. the twelfth-century custumal of Preston, Bateson, *Borough Customs*, I. p. 30; *E.H.R.* 1900, pp. 498, 505 f.

2. The Latin version reads: *lichfe, quantum scilicet in curam vulneris impendit*; cf. *læcefeoh þam læce gylde,* Ps. Egb. Confess., cap. 22 (Thorpe, *Anc. Laws*, II. p. 148).

3. Cf. 14, 3; *ne for hete ne for hole, Oath Formulae*, 4; and see P. and M. II. p. 588.

§ 1. 1. Cf. Abt. 59 f.; 67, 1; Af. 45 f.

2. No other instance of this word is noted by BT., see p. 817, *s.v.* It is derived by Steenstrup from the Scandinavian *sarbætr* (see *Danelag*, p. 315), meaning the compensation paid for inflicting a wound upon anyone.

3. The explanation given in the text applies to *sar*, which in O.E. means 'pain,' but is incorrect for the compound *sarbot*, see preceding note.

4. The sums in Af. are 2 sh. and 1 sh., *i.e.* 10 pence and 5 pence respectively.

§ 2. 1. Cf. Hn. 36, 2 ff.

2. The Latin reads: *si amici consulerent,* cf. Steenstrup, *Danelag,* p. 317.

11. 1. Cf. Abt. 69; Af. 71 and note; II Cn. 36, and see Brunner, II. p. 635.

§ 1. 1. The penalty for cutting off the thumb is 30 shillings (*i.e.* 150 pence) according to Af. 56; Hn. 93, 15; see Brunner, *loc. cit.*

2. The sums payable for the index and ring fingers are the same as those in Af., but those for the middle and little finger are different, cf. Af. 56–60; Hn. 93, 15–19. The shilling, however, is again the Mercian one of 4 pence.

§ 2. 1. The sums payable for the nail of the middle and ring fingers are 2 sh. and 4 sh. respectively according to Af. (*loc. cit.*), and that for the nail of the little finger is 1 sh. (*i.e.* 5 pence).

13. 1. Cf. II Cn. 15, 1 *a*.

14. 1. Liebermann explains this form as due to the frequent misunderstanding of *iuramentum planum* as *iur. plenum*, which resulted in the substitution of *plein* for *plain* (see Liebermann, I. p. 502[a]).

§ 1. 1. Cf. II Cn. 65.
§ 3. 1. Cf. cap. 10.
   2. Cf. *Oath Formulae*, 8.
15. 1. Cf. Godefroy, *s.v. moustier*.
   2. Lit. 'room,' cf. Lat. *camera*, but Liebermann takes it as referring to a treasury. This use is recognised by Du Cange (*s.v. camera*, 3). 'Estate office' is probably the nearest modern equivalent.
§ 3. 1. This type of ordeal seems to have been regarded as more disgraceful than the iron ordeal. *Jud. Dei*, xv, which deals with the water ordeal, has a marginal note which reads *propter rusticos*, cf. Glanville, xiv. 1, 8: *per ferrum calidum, si homo liber, per aquam, si fuerit rusticus* (see Liebermann, I. p. 427, Nos. xv^b, xvi^b).
16. 1. Liebermann is of opinion that the original text probably read *vilain*, cf. I and L (*villanus*). The compensation payable to the commoner in Wessex was 6 sh. (*i.e.* 30 pence), cf. In. 6, 3 (*gebur*); Af. 39 (*ceorl*).
17. 1. Cf. ECf. 10.
   2. Lit. 'stock at pasture,' cf. O.E. *feldhryþer, -oxa* (Toller, *Suppl.* p. 209, *s.v.*).
17 a. 1. Lat. *bordarii*; see Vinogradoff, *English Society*, pp. 456–60.
   2. Lat. *bubulci*, cf. Rect. 12: *oxanhyrde*, Lat. *bubulcus*. The meaning here may be 'ploughmen,' see Vinogradoff, *op. cit.* p. 464. Liebermann translates it 'Rinderhirten.'
17 b. 1. Cf. ECf. 10.
§ 2. 1. With this clause and the one following, cf. VIII Atr. 10, 1; I Cn. 9, 1.
§ 3. 1. This sum is equal to 120 (Mercian) shillings.
19. 1. Cf. Abt. 43 (where the penalty is 50 sh.); Af. 47; 71; Hn. 93, 5 (in all of which it is 66$\frac{2}{3}$ sh. of 5 pence). Liebermann suggests that 70 sh. here may represent a rounding of the sum in Af. In any case Mercian shillings of 4 pence are meant.
§ 1. 1. Littré emends the reading *remis* to *remese*, *i.e. restée* (see Dictionary, *s.v. prunelle*).
20. 1. With this clause and the three following, cf. II Cn. 71 *a*–71, 2, and see P. and M. I. p. 312 ff.
   2. The number of shields and lances is half that in II Cn. 71 *a*, and the money payment is omitted.
§ 2. 1. Cf. *medemra ðegna (ðegen)* II Cn. 71 *a*, 2. No local distinctions are made with regard to this payment.
§ 3. 1. See Vinogradoff, *Villainage*, pp. 160, 162; *Growth of Manor*, p. 347.
§ 3 *a*. 1. Cf. cap. 25. The difference in the texts is noteworthy.
§ 4. 1. See Neilson, *Customary Rents*, p. 88 f. (*Oxford Studies in Social and Legal History*, ed. Vinogradoff, vol. II); Bateson, *E.H.R.* 1900, p. 502.
21. § 1. 1. Cf. Scandinavian *hjemmelborh*.
§ 1 *a*. 1. Cf. cap. 14.
§ 2. 1. Cf. II Cn. 24, 1 and note. Liebermann interprets it as a payment equal to the value of the goods.

§ 4. 1. Cf. Bateson, *Borough Customs*, II. p. xlix; *en owele mayn, Yearbooks*, ed. Maitland, III. p. 124; *in equali manu*, P. and M. II. p. 164[3].

§ 5. 1. Cf. II As. 9; II Atr. 9, 4; *Oath Formulae*, 3, 4.
    2. Cf. cap. 6.
    3. For a note on the practice known as *a sacramento levare*, see P. and M. II. p. 162.

22. 1. Cf. Wl. art. 3, 1 f. and notes.
    2. Cf. Wl. art. 3, 1; 47 marks in I and L.

24. 1. Cf. Hn. 31, 4; 49, 4, and see P. and M. II. p. 669.
    2. Cf. the Latin phrase *responsum suum recuperare* which occurs in a law of 1194 relating to Pontefract, see Bateson, *Bor. Customs*, I. p. 162.

25. 1. Cf. 20, 3 *a* and note.

26. 1. These are the O.E. names applied to certain Roman or, in some cases perhaps, pre-Roman roads. The name Watling Street is applied to several such roads in different parts of the country. The chief of these, which is presumably meant here, is the one which runs through Wroxeter, Wall near Lichfield, Dunstable, London, and hence by Canterbury to the Kentish ports. Ermine Street is no doubt the Great North Road from London through Godmanchester and Lincoln and on into Yorkshire. The Fosse Way ran through Lincoln, Leicester and Bath to Axminster. By the Icknield Way is probably meant a road of somewhat winding course, mainly pre-Roman, leading from East Anglia through Newmarket and Dunstable, across the Thames at Streatley and south-west into Dorset.
    2. See Pollock, *The King's Peace*, L.Q.R. I. (1885), p. 46; *Oxford Lectures*, p. 81; P. and M. II. p. 463 f.

27. 1. In In. 57; VI As. 1, 1 the wife takes one-third of the thief's property.
§ 1. 1. Liebermann takes this to mean the half which otherwise fell to the wife.

28. 1. Liebermann notes that an official called the *Stretbidel* is found in Winchester under Henry I, see *E.H.R.* XIV. (1899), p. 423.
    2. Cf. ECf. 39, 1: *clamabant cives...quod circa festum sancti Martini emebant animalia sine plegio ad faciendas suas occisiones contra natale Domini*.
§ 1. 1. Does this mean that he shall be exempt from active participation in the guarding of the roads?
§ 2. 1. See P. and M. II. p. 526 f.

29. 1. *i.e.* peasants with holdings of their own, cf. In. 67.
    2. Cf. 20, 4, and for other references to the payment of rent (O.E. *gafol*) see In. 6, 3; 23, 3; 44, 1; 59, 1; 67; *Rect.* 2; 4, 1 and 5; 5, 1.
§ 1. 1. For a list of such services see *Rect.*, also Vinogradoff, *Growth of the Manor*, p. 287; *Villainage*, pp. 174, 284; Andrews, *Old English Manor*, p. 158 ff.

30. 1. The French text of this clause is very corrupt. Liebermann, following Matzke, reads: *Les naifs ki departent de la terre ne deivent cartre faire n'avurie quere*, which he translates: 'Die [hörigen] Einge-

borenen, welche aus dem Landgut fortziehen, sollen nicht Urkunde machen, noch Schutzherrschaft aufsuchen.' He also suggests c[un]tre [se]i[nu]r a[vu]rie; castel franc (i.e. 'eine Freiburg') quere as possible readings, see III. p. 290; 1. p. 512 (last two lines of note). My translation follows the reading of the Latin version.

§ 1. 1. Cf. In. 39; II Edw. 7; II As. 22; III, 4; IV, 4; II Cn. 28.
31. 1. See Maitland, *DB. and Beyond*, p. 51.
33. 1. The following section, from cap. 33 to cap. 38, shows the influence of Roman Law, see Vinogradoff, *Roman Law in Mediaeval Europe*, pp. 52, 84.
34. 1. Liebermann is of opinion that the whole of the heritable property of the deceased is meant. Pollock and Maitland suggest that the reference may be to 'movables' only, see II. p. 267.
35. 1. See P. and M. I. p. 102^1; II. p. 484.
2. The form *avultere* may be either sing. or plural, cf. *adulterium* in § 1; DB. I. 1 a, 2.
37. 1. See P. and M. II. p. 159. The use of the first person is contrary to Anglo-Norman legal usage.
§ 1. 1. Liebermann supports his emendation by reference to a similar clause in the Laws of Oléron: *s'ilz ne le creent mie...sera le mestre cru par son serement* (ed. Twiss, *Black Book of the Admiralty*, II. 218, 220).
39. 1. Cf. II Cn. 2 a.
§ 1. 1. With this clause and the one following, cf. II Cn. 15, 1 f.
40. 1. Cf. II. Cn. 2, 1.
41. 1. With this clause and the next, cf. II Cn. 3.
42. 1. With this clause and the two following, cf. II Cn. 15, 2 f.
2. See P. and M. II. p. 666 f.
§ 1. 1. In II Cn. 15, 2 the fine is 120 (W. Saxon) shillings, *i.e.* £2½.
2. This class is not mentioned in Canute. Liebermann regards its inclusion here as proof of the growth of private jurisdiction.
43. 1. Cf. III Edg. 2; II Cn. 17.
44. 1. With this clause and the two following, cf. II Cn. 19 ff.
45. 1. With this clause and the three following, cf. II Cn. 24–24, 3.
§ 1. 1. There is no mention of a warrantor in Canute's regulations; cf. caps. 21–21, 3 above.
47. 1. With this clause and the two following, cf. II As. 20; III Edg. 7; II Cn. 25 ff.
§ 2. 1. £6 again represents Canute's fine of 120 shillings, cf. 42, 1 above.
48. 1. With this clause and the three following, cf. II Cn. 28–29, 1.
51. 1. Cf. II Cn. 30.
2. Canute demands the triple ordeal in such a case.
52. 1. With this clause and the two following, cf. II Cn. 31–31, 2.

THE CORONATION CHARTER OF HENRY I

Preamble. 1. The date as it appears in H and Rl is incorrect, cf. last line of text.
2. According to the statement of Richard of Hexham (ed. Howlett, Rolls Series, III. p. 142) a copy of this charter was placed in the royal

treasury at Winchester. Liebermann suggests that the preamble of such a copy may be represented here (see Introduction).
1 § 1. 1. With regard to William II's treatment of vacant bishoprics, see Freeman, *William Rufus*, II. pp. 565–7.
2. 1. Cf. *Sax. Chr.* ann. 1100, where it is said of Wm II: *ælces mannes gehadodes 7 læwedes yrfenuma beon wolde*.
3. 1. With regard to the phrase *loqui cum rege* see Freeman, *Norman Conquest*, v. p. 46.
2. This promise does not seem to have been kept by Henry, see P. and M. I. p. 325.
§ 2. 1. *i.e.* the money or property settled upon her by her husband, see Du Cange, *s.v. dos* (2).
2. *i.e.* the money or property brought by the wife from her own family, see Du Cange, *s.v. maritagium*; N.E.D., *s.v. maritage*.
4. 1. Instances of the withdrawal of the marriage-settlement from a widow on her remarriage are fairly frequent in the Middle Ages, see P. and M. II. p. 422.
§ 2. 1. Cf. cap. 2, 1.
5. 1. The *monetagium* was a tax introduced into England by the Norman kings. In Normandy it took the form of a triennial payment made by every household to the Duke and intended, in part at least, to prevent a frequent change of coinage (see Du Cange, *s.v.*). There is some difference of opinion as to the form it took in England. It is generally supposed, however, to have been a payment directed to the same ends as the *monetagium* in Normandy (see Ashley, *Economic Hist.* p. 168; Round, *E.H.R.* 1903, p. 313). Brooke (*Athenaeum*, Feb. 3, 1912, p. 134) regards it as a tax imposed by Wm I upon shires and boroughs for the right to maintain their local mints.

Liebermann points out that the *monetagium* appears in Domesday Book (generally as a payment reserved by the king, cf. I. 336 *b*, 1) although it cannot be regarded as a pre-conquest levy. Anglo-Saxon practice is regularly represented by the payment made by moneyers to the king on the receipt of new dies following a change in the coinage, see DB. I. 172 *a*, 1; 252 *a*, 1; 262 *b*, 2.
§ 1. 1. Cf. Hn. mon. 2. According to Eadmer, *Hist. Novorum*, ed. Rule, p. 193: *Nullus qui posset depraehendi falsos denarios facere aliqua redemptione quin oculos et inferiores corporis partes perderet juvari valeret*; cf. Wm of Malmesbury, *Gesta Reg.* Lib. v, § 399 (Rolls Series, II. p. 476): *Nullum falsarium quin pugnum perderet*. See also P. and M. II. p. 504 f.
6. 1. According to Eadmer, *op. cit.* p. 31 f., William II made similar promises during an attack of illness in 1093.
7. 1. *i.e.* as distinct from property in land.
§ 1. 1. See P. and M. II. pp. 333, 356.
8. § 1. 1. See P. and M. II. p. 514.
9. 1. Liebermann suggests that Henry probably means to include here the reforms introduced by his father, cf. cap. 13. The murder-fine (*murdrum*) appears only after the Conquest.

10. 1. In 1087 Wm II, in order to obtain the support of the English, *geatte mannan heora wudas and slætinge*, see *Sax. Chr.* E and cf. Wm of Malmesbury, *Gesta Reg.* Lib. IV, § 306, Rolls Series, II. p. 361.

11. 1. Round, *E.H.R.* 1901, p. 729, compares with this the French equivalent for a knight's fee, viz. *fief d'hauberc*.

2. *i.e.* A.S. *inland*, see Vinogradoff, *Law Q. Review*, 21 (1905), p. 251.

14. 1. *i.e.* during the interregnum from 2–5 August.

Witnesses. 1. Maurice, Bishop of London, consecrated Henry as king, see Freeman, *William Rufus*, II. p. 681.

2. Bishop of Rochester.

3. William Giffard, ordained Bishop of Winchester on 11 August, 1107 (see Stubbs, *Reg. Sacr. Angl.* p. 41).

4. Henry, Earl of Warwick, was a staunch supporter of Henry I in his claim to the throne, see Wm of Malmesbury, *Gesta Reg.* Lib. v. § 393 (Rolls Series, II. p. 470); Freeman, *op. cit.* II. p. 348.

5. Simon, Earl of Northampton, appears as a witness to a document issued by Henry in 1111; see Rymer, *Foedera*, I. p. 8.

6. Probably Earl of Buckingham, see Davis, *Reg. Agnorm.* No. 320.

7. Robert de Montfort frequently appears as a witness to charters issued in the two preceding reigns, see Davis, Index.

8. Roger Bigot appears as seneschal (*dapifer*) under Wm II and held this office until his death in 1107 (see Davis, p. xxiv).

9. Henry de Port held lands in Hampshire (see Davis, Nos. 377, 379). For his appearance elsewhere as a witness to charters issued by Henry, see Rymer, *Foedera*, I. p. 10; Wm of Malmesbury, *Gesta Reg.*, Rolls Series, II. p. 522.

DECREE OF HENRY I CONCERNING THE COINAGE

Preamble. 1. Bishop of Worcester.

2. Sheriff of Worcestershire under Wm I, Wm II and Henry I, see Wm of Malmesbury, *Reg. Pont.* Lib. III. § 115 (end), Rolls Series, p. 253; Davis, *Reg. Agnorm.* Index; Round, *Feudal England*, pp. 309, 313, 423.

2. 1. With this clause and the two following, cf. Hn. cor. 5, 1 and note, also IV Atr. 7 f.

§ 1. 1. Cf. II As. 14, 1; IV Atr. 5, 3; II Cn. 8, 1; *Sax. Chr.* ann. 1125 and note (Plummer, II. p. 301 f.).

§ 2. 1. *i.e.* of iron, cf. II As. 14, 1.

3. § 1. 1. Such a course of action would suggest a desire for secrecy, cf. III Atr. 16; IV, 5, 4.

4. 1. Cf. IV Atr. 7, 2.

Witnesses. 1. William Giffard (cf. Hn. cor.) became chancellor under Wm II and remained in office until 1101 (see Davis, *E.H.R.* XXVI. (1911), p. 87).

2. Robert de Meulan, Robert FitzHamo, and Richard de Retuers were all staunch supporters of Henry in 1100, see Wm of Malmesbury, *Gesta Reg.* Lib. v. § 394 (Rolls Series, II. p. 471). The two last named died in 1107 (see Fl. of W., II. p. 57).

DECREE OF HENRY I CONCERNING THE COUNTY AND HUNDRED COURTS

Preamble. 1. Cf. Hn. mon. Pre.
1. 1. Cf. I Edg. 1; III, 5 f.; II Cn. 17, 1; 18; Wl. art. 8, 1.
2. 1. *i.e.* the regular business of the court, the proceeds of which passed to the sheriff, in return for a fixed sum paid to the king.
3. 1. *i.e.* tenants-in-chief.
§ 2. 1. Liebermann points out that a few years later such a case was tried in the court of the defendant's lord, cf. Hn. 25, 2.
§ 3. 1. More literally, 'unless it has been stopped on their part.' Davis (*E.H.R.* 1913, p. 425) translates it 'unless the combat be impeded on their part.'
4. 1. Exemption from attendance was frequently granted by charter, see P. and M. I. p. 537 f.
Witnesses. 1. Bishop of Salisbury.
2. Ranulf became chancellor sometime during the year 1107 (see Davis, *E.H.R.* XXVI. (1911), p. 89).
3. Cf. Hn. mon.
4. Henry founded an abbey at Reading and his body was buried there.

HENRY I: LONDON CHARTER

Preamble. 1. William of Corbeuil was Archbishop of Canterbury from 1123–36 (see Stubbs, *Reg. Sacr. Angl.* p. 43).
1. 1. For a repetition of this clause see Liber Albus (*Munim. Gildhal. Lund.* I. p. 14) and King John's Charter of 1199 (*ibid.* II. p. 249 f.).
2. Cf. Ballard, *Borough Charters*, p. 220.
3. O.E. *portgerefa*, cf. Davis, *Reg. Agnorm.* Nos. 15, 265. Liebermann points out that the privilege of electing their own sheriff was granted to several other towns in the twelfth century, see Ballard, *op. cit.* pp. 242–4.
4. This privilege was granted to Coventry and Colchester in 1181 and 1189 respectively (see Ballard, *op. cit.* p. 242).
5. The names of several holders of this office under Stephen are given by Round, *Commune of London*, pp. 98 f., 108 f., 113, 116–8. By the time of Henry II it seems to have disappeared.
2. 1. Cf. the case of Newcastle in the time of Henry I (Ballard, *Borough Charters*, p. 115).
§ 1. 1. The phrase *scot and lot* is generally used of the burdens shared in common by the members of a township, see Vinogradoff, *Growth of the Manor*, pp. 196, 274 f. In this instance it seems to be

used in a more specialised sense (cf. the use of *scot* alone) to mean taxes levied by the state.

2. Cf. Hn. cor. 11

3. Exemption from the payment of this fine was frequently granted to boroughs and monasteries, see Ballard, *Borough Charters*, p. 150 f.; Davis, *Reg. Agnorm.* Nos. xxv, 202; Maitland, *Pleas of Gloucester*, p. xxx.

§ 2. 1. In exceptional cases trial by combat was apparently resorted to in London as well as in other similarly privileged boroughs, see Gross, *Trials in Mediaeval Boroughs (Harvard Law Review*, xv. p. 694); Bateson, *E.H.R.* 1902, p. 723; Ballard, *op. cit.* p. 132 ff.

3. 1. See Gross, *loc. cit.* p. 695 ff.

4. 1. Cf. Ballard, *op. cit.* p. 87. For an interpretation which follows the reading *nisi* (which is not accepted as correct by Liebermann), see Stubbs, *Lectures on Early History*, p. 125.

5. 1. See Du Cange, *s.v. passagium*.

2. See Gross, *Gild Merchant*, ii. p. 409, *s.v. lestageum*; N.E.D., *s.v. lastage*. Exemption from the payment of these dues was frequently granted to other towns in the twelfth and following centuries, see Gross, *op. cit.* i. p. 9; ii. pp. 178, 183, 191, 211, 251; Ballard, *Borough Charters*, pp. 180–90.

7. 1. Cf. Hn. cor. 8.

2. Cf. III Edg. 2, 2.

8. 1. The meaning is that advantage is no longer to be taken of a mistake in pleading. Formerly, if detected, it might lead to the infliction of a heavy fine by the court or might be used by the pleader's opponent to gain a judgment in his own favour. See Bateson, *Borough Customs*, ii. pp. cxlix ff., 1–4.

9. 1. The word *husting* is of Scandinavian origin, see Steenstrup, *Danelag*, p. 176. It occurs in the *Sax. Chr.* ann. 1012, where the reference is to a meeting held by the Danish invaders, but later it is regularly used, as here, to mean a court of the citizens of London.

2. In the thirteenth and fourteenth centuries the husting met fortnightly, see *Mun. Gildhal.* i. p. 86; ii. p. 334.

12. 1. This process is technically known as *withernam*, see Bateson, *Borough Customs*, i. pp. 119–25.

2. Liebermann compares with this the similar phrase in the Colchester Charter of 1189: *quantum de damno per hoc habuerit*.

13. 1. Cf. Ballard, *Borough Charters*, p. 143 f.

15. 1. For examples of similar rights granted to other towns in the twelfth century, see Ballard, *op. cit.* p. 83.

Witnesses. 1. Probably either William Giffard, Bishop of Winchester, 11 Aug. 1107–25 Jan. 1129 (see Stubbs, *Reg. Sacr. Angl.* p. 41), or Henry of Blois, ordained 17 Nov. 1129 (see Stubbs, *op. cit.* p. 44).

2. See Round, *Geoffrey de Maundeville*, p. 370[1]. He appears as a witness to charters issued by Stephen, see Round, *op. cit.* pp. 11, 13 f., 262 f.

3. Hugh Bigot appears as a witness to a charter of 1131 (see

Round, *op. cit.* p. 265) and is a prominent figure in Stephen's reign and later (see Round, *op. cit.* Index).

4. A great Devonshire land-owner, see Round, *Feudal England*, p. 327.

5. Two men of this name are distinguished as Wm de Albini, Brito (*i.e.* the Breton), and Wm de Albini, Pincerna (*i.e.* the Butler) respectively (see Round, *King's Serjeants*, p. 141). The latter was present at Stephen's Easter court of 1136 (see Round, *Geof. Maund.* p. 262 f.). His son, who bore the same name, succeeded to his father's office.

6. Round suggests that the person meant is Albericus [de Vere], see Davis, *Reg. Agnorm.* p. xxv, while Lappenberg, *Gesch. v. Engl.* II. p. 215, suggests Herbert, see Davis, *loc. cit.*; *Chr. Abing.* II. 52, 116. Liebermann notes, however, that a *Hubertus camerarius* is vouched for before 1147, see Rymer, *Foedera*, I. p. 15.

7. Holder of a fief in Essex, see Round, *Feudal England*, pp. 253, 257.

8. Hagulf (Hasculf) de Tany is mentioned in a charter of the Empress, 1141, see Round, *Geof. Maund.* p. 91.

9. Sheen was held by the Belet family by the serjeanty of Cutlery, see *E.H.R.* 1902, p. 485.

INDEX

Abbess. Abbesses shall order their lives aright, VI Atr. 2
Abbey. Of sanctuary in an abbey, Leis Wl. 1, 1
Abbot
    Abbots shall order their lives aright, VI Atr. 2 = VIII 31, 1 = I Cn. 6 *a*
    Abbots shall submit to their duty, VI Atr. 4
    The king's reeves shall support abbots in their temporal needs, VIII Atr. 32
Accessory, accomplice '*gewita*'
    If a priest be the accessory of thieves, VIII Atr. 27 = I Cn. 5, 3
    Everyone over 12 years of age shall swear that he will not be a thief's accomplice, II Cn. 21
Adultery, assault, illicit unions, etc. '*hæmed*,' '*unrihthæmed*,' '*adulterium*,' '*avulterie*,' '*sibleger*'; vb. '*forlicgan*,' '*niednæman*,' '*purgir*,' etc.
    Of intercourse with a nun and adultery, I Edm. 4
    All Christian men shall avoid illicit unions, V Atr. 10 = VI 11 = I Cn. 6, 3
    Of violations of marriage, V Atr. 25 = VI 28, 2
    Prostitutes shall be driven from the land, VI Atr. 7 = II Cn. 4 *a*
    If anyone does violence to a widow, VI Atr. 39 = II Cn. 52
    If the protection of the church is broken by illicit intercourse, VIII Atr. 4
    An end shall be put to incest, Cn. 1020, 15
    Illicit unions shall be abhorred, I Cn. 24
    Adulterers shall make amends or depart, II Cn. 6
    If anyone commits adultery, II Cn. 50
    If anyone commits incest, II Cn. 51
    If anyone does violence to a maiden, II Cn. 52, 1
    No woman shall commit adultery, II Cn. 53
    If a married man commits adultery, II Cn. 54
    If foreigners will not regularise their unions, II Cn. 55
    If anyone assaults the wife of another man, Leis Wl. 12
    If anyone assaults a woman, Leis Wl. 18; 18, 2
    If a father finds his daughter in adultery or a son his mother, Leis Wl. 35 f.
Advocate '*forspeca*'; II Edm. 7 f.
Æftergild 'supplementary payment'; II Cn. 24, 1
Ægilde 'without the payment of compensation'; V Atr. 31, 1 = VI 38; II Cn. 48, 3; 62, 1
Æht 'property,' 'goods,' 'possessions'; IV Edg. 1, 2; II Atr. 3, 1 ff.; V Atr. 29; VI Atr. 36; 51; II Cn. 51; 70; 76; 77; 78
Ælæte 'a divorced woman'; VI Atr. 12, 1 = I Cn. 7, 1
Æðeling 'a member of the royal family'; II Cn. 58, 1
Agwait purpensé 'premeditated waylaying'; Leis Wl. 2. See *Forsteall*.
Altar '*weofod*.' See also *Weofodbot*, *Weofodþegn*.
    Of the pledge laid upon Christ's altar, Cor. Oath Pre.
    Of the brotherhood prostrate before the altar of God, VII Atr. (A.S.) 6, 3
Andaga 'appointed day'; II Edg. 4, 1; VIII Atr. 42; II Cn. 19, 1
Angild 'the unaugmented value of goods,' I Edg. 6; III Atr. 4, 1. Used adverbially, III Edg. 7, 1
Archbishop
    Archbishop Oda and Archbishop Wulfstan, I Edm. Pre.
    The injunction of the King and the Archbishop, IV Edg. 1, 4
    Archbishop Sigeric, II Atr. 1
    King Canute greets his archbishops, Cn. 1020, 1
    Archbishop Lyfing, Cn. 1020, 3
    The king prays his archbishops to be zealous with regard to the rights of the Church, Cn. 1020, 8
    £3 shall be paid to the archbishop in Kent for *mundbryce*, I Cn. 3, 2
    £3 shall be paid for violation of an archbishop's protection, II Cn. 58, 1

INDEX

Army *'fierd'*
  If anyone deserts an army which is under the personal command of the king, v Atr. 28 = vi 35
  If anyone deserts any other army, v Atr. 28, 1
  If anyone is guilty of a capital deed of violence while serving in the army, ii Cn. 61
Arson *'bærnet'*
  Arson is one of the crimes which is *botleas*, ii Cn. 64
Attach *'befon'*
  If anyone attaches what he has lost, ii Atr. 8; 8, 2
  Vouching to warranty shall always take place where the property has first been attached, ii Atr. 8, 4; 9
  He who attaches his goods shall have trustworthy security and beware of attaching wrongly, ii Atr. 9, 1
  If manorial lords attach livestock acquired without surety, iii Atr. 5
  Of the witnesses required to declare whence a man acquired the stock attached in his possession, ii Cn. 23
  If any property is attached and its possessor has no such witnesses, ii Cn. 24, 1

Bailiff *'bydel'*
  If a lord repeatedly claims his rent through his bailiffs, iv Edg. 1, 2
Bana 'slayer,' 'murderer'; ii Atr. 6; ii Cn. 56; *dædbana, rædbana*, viii Atr. 23 = i Cn. 5, 2 *b*
Banweorc 'homicide'; v Atr. 32, 4
Baptism *'fulluht'*
  He who will not learn the Pater Noster may not stand sponsor to another man at baptism, i Cn. 22, 6
Baron *'barun,' 'baro'*
  A baron shall have 10 shillings as compensation for breach of his protection, Leis Wl. 16
  The heriot of a baron, Leis Wl. 20, 1
  Greeting from Henry I to all his barons, Hn. cor. Pre.
  He has been crowned king with the full consent of the barons, Hn. cor. 1
  If any of the king's barons has died, Hn. cor. 2
  Of the vassals of the king's barons, Hn. cor. 2, 1
  If any of the king's barons wishes to bestow his daughter in marriage, Hn. cor. 3
  If, on the death of a baron, his daughter is left as heiress, Hn. cor. 3, 1
  Of the king's injunction to his barons to act with moderation towards their vassals, Hn. cor. 4, 2
  If any of the king's barons is ill, Hn. cor. 7
  If any of the king's barons has committed a misdeed, Hn. cor. 8
  With the full consent of his barons the king has retained the forests in his own hands, Hn. cor. 10
  Of the reforms introduced by Wm I with the consent of his barons, Hn. cor. 13
  Greeting from Henry I to all the barons of Worcestershire, Hn. mon. Pre.; Hn. com. Pre.
  If a case arises between crown barons, Hn. com. 3
  If a case arises between the vassals of a crown baron, Hn. com. 3, 1
  Barons shall have and hold their rights of jurisdiction, Hn. Lond. 6
Befon. See Attach
Bell *'belle'*
  A cow's bell shall be worth a shilling, i Edg. 8
  Part of the money paid as amends for religious offences shall be applied to the purchase of bells, vi Atr. 51
Bishop *'bisceop,' 'evesque'*
  Of the bishops present at King Edmund's assembly at London, i Edm. Pre.
  Of legal penalties prescribed by the bishop, ii Edm. 4
  The bishop's reeve, ii Edg. 3, 1 = viii Atr. 8 = 1 Cn. 8, 2
  The bishop of the diocese shall be present at the County Court, iii Edg. 5, 2 = ii Cn. 18, 1

Bishop, *continued*
   The bishops as the guardians of souls, IV Edg. 1, 8
   In the case of an action brought by a bishop 12 ores shall be deposited as security, III Atr. 12
   Bishops shall submit to their duty, V Atr. 4 = VI 2, 2 = I Cn. 6 *a*
   No-one shall turn out a minister of the church without the bishop's consent, V Atr. 10, 2
   The primary ordinance of the bishops, VI Atr. 1
   Money paid as compensation for religious offences shall be applied in accordance with the direction of the bishops, VI Atr. 51
   A priest shall make amends as the bishop prescribes for him, VIII Atr. 27 = I Cn. 5, 3
   King Canute prays all his diocesan bishops (*leodbiscopas*) to be zealous with regard to the rights of the church, Cn. 1020, 8
   Of instruction with regard to amends for wrong-doing given by the bishops, Cn. 1020, 9
   Just judgments shall be pronounced with the cognisance of the bishops, Cn. 1020, 11
   The bishops declare that severe amends must be made for the violation of oaths and pledges, Cn. 1020, 14
   He who withholds Peter's Pence or church dues shall give them to the bishop, I Cn. 9, 1; 10, 1
   The bishops are God's heralds, I Cn. 26
   The bishops are the shepherds of the divine flocks, I Cn. 26, 3
   Half a delinquent's wergeld shall be divided between the lord and the bishop, II Cn. 36
   Of the fine due to the bishop for sacrilege, II Cn. 42
   The case of a man in holy orders shall be reserved for the bishop's decision, II Cn. 43
   An adulterer shall make amends as the bishop directs him, II Cn. 54, 1
   William, Bishop of London, Wl. Lond. 1
   A bishop shall have 20 shillings as compensation for breach of his protection, Leis Wl. 16
   A fine of 30 pence shall be paid to the bishop for withholding Peter's Pence, Leis Wl. 17, 3

Blæshorn 'horn for blowing'
   A horn for blowing shall be worth a shilling, I Edg. 8

Blot 'sacrifice'
   The compassing of death by sacrifice is forbidden, II Cn. 5, 1

Boar; equivalent to 5 shillings, Leis Wl. 9, 1

Boc 'book,' 'Canon Law'
   The servants of God shall apply themselves to their books and prayers, VI Atr. 41
   Part of the money paid as compensation for religious offences shall be applied to the purchase of books, VI Atr. 51
   If a member of the priesthood orders his life according to the teaching of the Canon Law, VIII Atr. 28

Bocland 'land held by title-deed'
   If a thegn has a church on the land which he holds by title-deed, II Edg. 2 = I Cn. 11
   If anyone does the deed of an outlaw and has land held by title-deed, II Cn. 13, 1
   If a man who deserts his lord on an expedition has land held by title-deed, II Cn. 77, 1

Boctale 'the directions contained in the Canon Law'
   Ecclesiastical amends shall always be exacted in accordance with the directions contained in the Canon Law, II Cn. 38, 2

Bonda 'householder'
   Public security shall be promoted in such a way as shall be best for the householder, VI Atr. 32 = II Cn. 8
   A householder, if he does not render a penny or the value of a penny, shall pay 30 pence, VII Atr. (A.S.) 3

Bonda, continued
    When a householder has dwelt all his time free from claims and charges, II Cn. 72
    If a householder has been cited before his death, II Cn. 72, 1
    No wife can forbid her husband (*bunda*) to deposit anything in his cottage, II Cn. 76, 1 *b*

Borg. See Surety

Borgbryce 'violation of protection'
    Of the compensation for *borgbryce* to be paid to the king, archbishop, etc., II Cn. 58

Borhleas 'without surety'; III Atr. 5

Borough. See *Burg*

Bot
  i. Improvement, remedy
    Of the remedy for the plague which has ravaged the country, IV Edg. Pre.
    Of the improvement (promotion) of public security, IV Edg. 14, 1 I Atr. Pre.; III Pre.; v 26, 1 = VI 31 f. = II Cn. 8; of the improvement of the coinage, v Atr. 26, 1 = VI 31; 32, 1 = II Cn. 8; of general improvement, VIII Atr. 38 f.
  ii. Amends, compensation; see also *Mægbot*, *Manbot*; II Edm. 4; II Edg. 4, 2 III Edg. 1, 2; 3; I Atr. 1, 6; 2, 1 = II Cn. 32, 1; II Atr. 6, 1; 7, 1; v Atr. 20 = VI 25, 2 = I Cn. 17, 3; v 29; VI 36; 50; VIII 1, 1; 2; 3 = I Cn. 2, 3 ff. VIII 36; II Cn. 30, 4; 38, 2; 41, 2

Botleas 'for which no compensation can be paid'
    Breach of the peace which the king establishes in person shall be *botleas*, III Atr. 1
    Homicide committed within the walls of a church shall be *botleas*, VIII Atr. 1, 1 = I Cn. 2, 3
    Crimes which are *botleas*, II Cn. 64

Botwyrpe 'for which compensation can be paid'
    No man shall forfeit more than his wergeld for any offence which is *botwyrpe*, III Edg. 2, 2
    Amends for violation of the protection of churches of different grades in cases which are *botwyrpe*, VIII Atr. 5, 1 = I Cn. 3, 2

Brycgbot 'the repair of bridges'; v Atr. 26, 1; VI 32, 3; II Cn. 10; 65

Bull; equivalent to 10 shillings, Leis Wl. 9, 1

Burg
  i. *cyninges burg* 'a fortified royal manor (?)'
    If anyone flees for sanctuary to the *c. b.*, II Edm. 2
    Every vouching to warranty and every ordeal shall take place in the *c. b.*, III Atr. 6, 1
  ii. borough, town
    Every man shall be under surety whether he lives within a borough or in the country, IV Edg. 3
    A body of standing witnesses shall be appointed for every borough, IV Edg. 3, 1; 4; 5
    Every man shall transact business in the presence of these witnesses in a borough or in a wapentake, IV Edg. 6; 10
    Concerning a breach of the truce in a borough or in the open country, II Atr. 5, 2; 6
    For an untrustworthy man compurgators for the triple oath shall be selected from the district under the jurisdiction of the borough (court), II Cn. 22, 1
    No-one shall buy anything over 4 pence in value in a borough or in the open country, unless he has 4 men as witnesses, II Cn. 24 = Leis Wl. 45
    The various boroughs shall have one law with regard to exculpation, II Cn. 34
    All boroughs shall be watched and guarded, Wl. art. retr. 6
    No market or fair shall be held except in boroughs etc., Wl. art. retr. 11
    All those who dwell in boroughs shall discountenance falsification of money, Hn. mon. 1

380 INDEX

Burg, continued
  ii. borough, town, *continued*
    If toll or tax has been taken by a borough from citizens of London, Hn. Lond. 12
Burgbot 'the repair of fortifications'; v Atr. 26, 1; vi 32, 3; ii Cn. 10; 65
Burggemot
  The borough court shall be held three times a year, iii Edg. 5, 1 = ii Cn. 18
Fif burga geþincð, 1 burggeþincð
  Concerning breach of the peace established in the court of the Five Boroughs or in that of one borough, iii Atr. 1, 1 f.
Burgman, burgeis, burhwaru; ii Atr. 6; iv 2, 10; Wl. Lond. 1; Leis Wl. 17 *b*

Canon
  Canons shall maintain regularity and celibacy in their foundations, v Atr. 7 = vi 4
  Canons shall revert to a proper discharge of their duties, vi Atr. 2 = 1 Cn. 6 *a*
Castle '*castellum*'
  All castles shall be guarded every night, Wl. art. retr. 6
  Of markets held in castles etc., Wl. art. retr. 11
Ceap 'goods,' 'property,' etc.
  All goods shall be bought or sold in the presence of witnesses, iv Edg. 6
  Two or three men shall be present as witnesses at every transaction (*ceap*), iv Edg. 6, 2
  Of a man who sets out to make a purchase (*ceap*), iv Edg. 7
  If he makes a purchase unexpectedly, iv Edg. 8
  Of the purchase made by God at a great price, v Atr. 3 = vi 10 = ii Cn. 2, 1; i Cn. 18, 3
Ceapgield 'the value of goods'; i Edg. 2, 1; iii Edg. 7, 1 = ii Cn. 25, 1; iv Edg. 11; i Atr. 1, 7 = ii Cn. 30, 6; Wl. art. 8, 3
Celibacy, continence '*clænnes*'
  Those in holy orders shall observe celibacy, i Edm. 1
  The servants of God, by virtue of their purity, shall intercede for us with God, iv Edg. 1, 7
  The monk who has no monastery shall observe celibacy, v Atr. 6 = vi 3, 1
  The priest who observes celibacy shall obtain the favour of God, v Atr. 9, 1 = vi 5, 3 = i Cn. 6, 2 *a*
  Canons shall maintain celibacy in their foundations, v Atr. 7 = vi 4
  The servants of God shall practice celibacy, vi Atr. 5 = 41 = i Cn. 6, 1
Ceorl 'husband'; ii Cn. 53; 73, 2
Chapel '*feldcirice*,' '*chapele*'
  Of amends for the violation of the protection of a country chapel, viii Atr. 5, 1 = i Cn. 3, 2
Child
  The property of a man who dies intestate shall be divided among his wife and children, ii Cn. 70
  The wife and children of a householder who has dwelt free from claims and charges, ii Cn. 72
  Of the treatment of a child in the cradle, ii Cn. 76, 2
  Every child shall be his father's heir, Wl. Lond. 3
Christ; v Atr. 2 = vi 9 = ii Cn. 3; vi Atr. 41; vii (A.S.) 2, 1; viii 2 = i Cn. 2, 4; viii Atr. 2, 1; 15 = 36; 37; 38; 42; i Cn. 2, 1; 4, 2 f.; 22, 2; the law of Christ, v Atr. 31 = vi 38
Christian, Christianity; i Edm. 2; 3; ii Edm. Pre.; ii Edg. 5, 2; iv 1; v Atr. 1 = vi 1 = x 1 = i Cn. 1; v Atr. 2 = vi 9; v 4 = vi 2; v 10 = vi 11; v 10, 1 = vi 13; v 19 = vi 25, 1; v 22 = vi 27 = i Cn. 19; v 34; vi 5, 2; 10; 12–13; 40 = ii Cn. 11; vi 41; 42; viii 2, 1; 7; 35 = ii Cn. 40, 2; vi Atr. 42; x Pre. f.; Cn. 1020, 17; i Cn. 2, 1 f.; 4; 6 *a*; 21; 22 f.; 22, 5 f.; ii 54, 1
Christmas '*midwinter*'
  Trial by ordeal etc. forbidden from the Advent till a fortnight after Christmas, v Atr. 18
  The ordinance drawn up during the holy Christmas season, i Cn. Pre.

INDEX 381

Christmas, *continued*
  No man need fast from Christmas to the Octave of Epiphany, I Cn. 16, 1
Church '*cirice*,' '*mynster*,' '*ecclesia*,' '*iglise*'
  All God's churches should be well put in order, I Edm. 5
  If anyone flees for sanctuary to a church, II Edm. 2
  God's churches shall be entitled to all their prerogatives, II Edg. 1
  All tithes shall be paid to the old churches (*mynstrum*), II Edg. 1, 1
  The case of a thegn's church, with or without a graveyard, II Edg. 2 f. = I Cn. 11 f.
  If anyone refuses to pay tithes, the tenth part shall be taken, without his consent, for the church to which it belongs, II Edg. 3, 1 = VIII Atr. 8 = I Cn. 8, 2
  Payment for the souls of the dead shall be rendered to the church to which it is due, II Edg. 5, 2 = V Atr. 12, 1 = VI 21 = I Cn. 13, 1
  Every right of sanctuary possessed by the church (*cyricgriđ*) shall be maintained, II Edg. 5, 3
  True peace assured to the church of God, Cor. Oath 1, 1
  All churches shall be under special protection, V Atr. 10, 1 = VI 13 = I Cn. 2, 1
  No-one shall oppress the church or make it the object of improper traffic (*ciricmangunge*) or turn out a minister of the church (*ciricđen*), V Atr. 10, 2 = VI 15
  Every right of sanctuary within the walls of a church (*cyricgriđ*) shall remain inviolate, VI Atr. 14 = I Cn. 2, 2
  The security and sanctity of the churches of God shall be maintained (*cyrican griđian* 7 *friđian*), VI Atr. 42 = I Cn. 2
  Part of the money paid as compensation for religious offences shall be applied to the repair of churches (*cyricbot*) and to the purchase of ecclesiastical vestments (*cyricwæd*), VI Atr. 51
  Every one shall go barefoot to church, VII Atr. (A.S.) 2
  The penny or the value of a penny given as dues shall be brought to church, VII Atr. (A.S.) 2, 3
  Slaves shall be exempt from work in order to attend church (*ciricsocn*), VII Atr. (A.S.) 5, 1
  The churches of God shall exercise their right of protection to the full, VIII Atr. 1
  Amends for the violation of the protection of the church, etc., VIII Atr. 1, 1; 3–5, 1 = I Cn. 2, 3 and 5; 3–3, 2
  The protection of Holy Church shall be inviolable, Leis Wl. 1
  If anyone has laid hands on a man who has sought a mother church (*mere iglise*), Leis Wl. 1, 1
  He who withholds Peter's Pence shall pay it through the court of Holy Church, Leis Wl. 17, 2
Church dues '*ciricsceatt*,' '*consuetudo*'
  Every Christian man shall pay church dues, I Edm. 2
  Every church due shall go to the old church, II Edg. 2, 2 = I Cn. 11, 2
  Every church due shall be rendered by Martinmas, II Edg. 3 = VI Atr. 18, 1 = VIII 11 = Cn. 1027, 16 = I Cn. 10
  Church dues are payments which men are in duty bound to render, IV Edg. 1, 3
  All men for love of God shall give their church dues, VII Atr. 4
  All church dues shall be rendered to the mother church, VII Atr. 4, 1
Clemency; II Cn. 68, 2. See also Leniency, Mercy, Mitigation
Coinage. See Money
Commoner '*twyhynde*,' '*ignobilis*'; Cn. 1020, 1; 1027, 12
Confession, confessor '*scrift*,' '*scriftspræc*'; vb. '*andettan*'
  A homicide shall do penance as his confessor directs him, I Edm. 3
  Every Christian man shall go frequently to confession and freely confess his sins, V Atr. 22 = VI 27
  Men shall confess their misdeeds, VI Atr. 1
  Confession of misdeeds shall be made to confessors, I Cn. 18, 1
  He who falls into sin shall make amends according to his confessor's advice, I Cn. 23
  If a condemned man desires confession, II Cn. 44

INDEX

Corsnæd 'ordeal of consecrated bread'; VIII Atr. 22; 24; I Cn. 5, 2 *a*; 2 *c*
County '*scir*,' '*comitatus*,' '*cunté*'
    The county court (*scirgemot*) shall be held twice a year, III Edg. 5, 1 = II Cn. 18
    King Edgar shall possess his royal prerogatives in every county, IV Edg. 2 *a*
    If a man vouched to warranty is in another county, II Atr. 8, 1
    The number of weeks' adjournment granted in order to find a man vouched to warranty shall be in proportion to the number of counties named, II Atr. 8, 3
    The conditions under which no-one shall make distraint of property either within the shire or outside it, II Cn. 19 = Leis Wl. 44
    The action of the shire court on the fourth occasion, II Cn. 19, 1 = Leis Wl. 44, 1
    If, with the cognisance of the shire, a man has performed the services demanded from a landowner, II Cn. 79
    If a baron has to pay a fine in the county court, Leis Wl. 2, 3
    No-one shall appeal to the king, unless he fails to obtain justice in the county court, Leis Wl. 43
    Order of Henry regarding the places where the county court (*comitatus*) ought to be held, Hn. com. Heading; 1–2, 1
    A case between the vassals of two lords shall be dealt with in the county court, Hn. com. 3, 2
    All those belonging to the county shall attend the county court as they did in the time of King Edward, Hn. com. 4
Court '*gemot*,' '*curt*,' '*plait*,' '*placitum*.' See also under 'County,' 'Hundred'
    In the hundred as in other courts every case shall be treated in accordance with the public law, I Edg. 7
    If anyone who has a bad reputation fails to attend the court-meetings three times, III Edg. 7 = II Cn. 25; Leis Wl. 47
    A court shall be held in every wapentake, III Atr. 3, 1
    Concerning the man who in court tries to protect himself or one of his men by bringing a countercharge, II Cn. 27
    Livestock which is claimed shall be brought for decision to the court of the man who had taken it into his care, Leis Wl. 5, 2 = 6, 1
    30 shillings shall be paid as a fine to all those who have a court in England, Leis Wl. 42, 1
    A case between crown barons shall be dealt with in the king's court, and one between the vassals of a crown baron in their lord's court, Hn. com. 3 f.
Cow; Leis Wl. 5; 20, 3
Crown '*corona*,' '*curune*'
    Of the islands, provinces and countries which appertain to the crown, Wl. art. retr. 1
    Of the peace and dignity of the crown, Wl. art. retr. 9
    Of the pleas belonging to the king's crown, Leis Wl. 2
    A justiciar shall be appointed by the citizens of London to safeguard the pleas of the crown, Hn. Lond. 1
    If a citizen has become involved in a plea of the crown, Hn. Lond. 3
Cyrað 'an oath of nominated jurors'; IV Atr. 7, 3

Dane, Danish
    Of the maintenance of the rights of the laity among the Danes, IV Edg. 2, 1
    Of a measure which shall apply to the whole nation, English, Danes and Britons, IV Edg. 2, 2
    Of the constitution to be observed by the Danes, IV Edg. 12
    Of the penalty in a particular case to be fixed by the Danes, IV Edg. 13, 1
    If an Englishman slay a Dane or a Dane an Englishman, II Atr. 5
    If an Englishman slay a Danish slave or a Dane an English slave, II Atr. 5, 1
    If a Dane defies the law of God, etc., Cn. 1020, 9
    Canute, King of the Danes, I Cn. Heading and Pre.
    Of cases in which *lahslit* shall be paid in a Danish district, II Cn. 45, 3; 46; 48
    The heriot of a king's thegn among the Danes, II Cn. 71, 3
    The compensation to be paid by a Dane for violation of the law, II Cn. 83

Danegeld
   The citizens of London shall be exempt from the payment of Danegeld,
      Hn. Lond. 2, 1
Danelaw, VI Atr. 37; II Cn. 15; 15, 1 a; 15, 3; 62; 65; Leis Wl. 2, 2; 2, 3 f.; 3, 3;
   17, 1; 21, 2 and 4; 39, 2; 42, 2
Day '*dæg*'; II Edm. 7, 3; VII Atr. (A.S.) 1; 5, 1; 6; 6, 2; *se halga dæg* (Sunday)
   V Atr. 13, 1 = VI 22, 1 = Cn. 1020, 18 = 1 Cn. 15, 1; *his yldrena dagum*, III Atr. 1;
   dæges (adv. gen.), I Cn. 6 *a* = 25; *leohtan dæge* (in daylight), III Atr. 15;
   meaning 'date,' I Edg. 7, 1; I Cn. 9, 1; 10, 1; meaning 'lifetime,' III Atr. 14;
   II Cn. 72; 79; Wl. Lond. 2, 3
   Domesdæg, endedæg, I Cn. 25; *freolsdæg*, II Edg. 5; V Atr. 18 = VI 25 = I Cn.
   17; II Cn. 45 f.; 45, 3; *haligdæg*, II Cn. 45, 1; *lifdæg*, VIII Atr. 37; *lenctendagas*,
   I Cn. 17; *mæssedæg*, II Edg. 4; 5; V Atr. 16 = VI 23 = I Cn. 17, 1; I Cn. 14, 2;
   (*riht*)*ymbrendagas*, V Atr. 18 = VI 25 = I Cn. 17
Deacon
   If a simple accusation is brought against a deacon who lives according to a
      rule, VIII Atr. 20 = I Cn. 5, 1
   A secular priest shall clear himself in the same way as a deacon, VIII Atr. 21 =
      I Cn. 5, 2
Dead, death
   Of a delinquent who shall be seized, alive or dead, III Edg. 7, 1 = II Cn. 25 *a* =
      Leis Wl. 47, 1
   Of the withholding of dues which leads to sudden death in this life and the
      death to come in hell, IV Edg. 1, 4
   Of a case in which the slayers shall be taken, alive or dead, II Atr. 6
   If anyone vouches a dead person to warranty, II Atr. 9, 2
   Of the compensation in a case of breach of the peace in an alehouse, if a man
      is slain (*æt deadum menn*), III Atr. 1, 2
   Of declarations which shall be incontrovertible, whether the persons concerned
      be alive or dead, III Atr. 2
   Christian men shall not be condemned to death for trivial offences, V Atr. 3 =
      VI 10 = II Cn. 2, 1
   If a man departs intestate through sudden death, II Cn. 70
   If a householder had been cited before his death, II Cn. 72, 1
   The heriot of a thegn shall include his father's horse as it was on the day of
      his death, Leis Wl. 20, 2
   If a man does not know whether his warrantor is alive or dead, Leis Wl. 21, 1 *a*
   If a woman who is pregnant is sentenced to death, Leis Wl. 33
   Of things cast overboard in fear of death, Leis Wl. 37 f.
Deaðscylde 'a capital crime'; II Cn. 43
Deaðscyldig 'condemned to death'; II Cn. 44. See also 'Life'
Denial, deny '*andsæc*,' '*ætsacan*,' '*oðsacan*'
   The men chosen as witnesses shall swear that they will never deny any of the
      things of which they have been witnesses, IV Edg. 6, 1
   The captain of a ship shall deny a charge of theft, II Atr. 4
   An Englishman charged with theft or homicide by a Viking and a fellow-
      countryman shall not be entitled to make any denial, II Atr. 7
   Denial is stronger than accusation, II Atr. 9, 3
   If anyone denies the charge of breaking the fast of Lent, II Cn. 47, 1
Denmark; Cn. 1020, 5; Cn. 1027, Heading
Devil
   Of the priest driving away devils, I Cn. 4, 2
   No spoiler is so evil as the devil, I Cn. 26, 2
   Devilish deeds shall be guarded against, V Atr. 25 = VI 28; I Cn. 23
   Of the shepherd who delivers his flock from devils, II Cn. 84, 2 *a*
Dog '*hund*'
   A dog's collar (*hoppe*) shall be worth a shilling, I Edg. 8
Dom 'decree,' 'decision,' 'judgment,' 'verdict'
   II Edm. 6; I Edg. 3; III Edg. 1, 1 = II Cn. 1, 1; 3; IV Edg. 2, 1 *a*; 12, 1; Cor.
   Oath 1, 3; III Atr. 13, 2 f.; VI Atr. 10, 1; 52; 53; VIII Atr. 5, 2; Cn. 1020, 11;
   I Cn. 18, 2; II Cn. 2 *a*; 8, 2; 15, 2; 35, 1; 43; 68, 1 *c*; 84, 1 *a*

Domboc; II Edg. 3; 5
Door
  Concerning the case of a man setting his spear at another man's door, II Cn. 75
Dowry '*maritatio*'; Hn. cor. 3, 2; 4
Dryhten 'the Lord,' *i.e.* 'God'; IV Edg. 1, 3; V Atr. 6 = VI 3, 1; 53; VIII 7; I Cn. 4, 1; 6, 3; II 84; 84, 3; 84, 4 *b*
Dryncelean; II Cn. 81
Due, right, prerogative '*gerihte*,' '*consuetudo*,' '*rectitudo*'; IV Edg. 2 *a*; II Cn. 20; Wl. art. 4; Hn. Lond. 5; 6; 12; ecclesiastical dues(*Godes* or *godcunde gerihta*), IV Edg. 1, 4 and 6; V Atr. 11 = VI 16 = I Cn. 8; V 12, 2 = VI 21, 1 = VIII 14; VI 43; VII 4, 1; 7, 1; VII (A.S.) 8; I Cn. 14; II Cn. 48; rights of the church, Cn. 1020, 2; 8

Ealdorman
  The ealdorman shall be present at the county court, III Edg. 5, 2 = II Cn. 18, 1
  The ealdormen, Ælfhere and Æthelwine, IV Edg. 15, 1
  The ealdormen, Æthelweard and Ælfric, II Atr. 1
  The penalty for breach of the peace established by the ealdorman in the court of the Five Boroughs, III Atr. 1, 1
  Ealdormen shall be on the watch for coiners, IV Atr. 8
  The ealdormen shall support the bishops, Cn. 1020, 8
  If anyone violates the protection of an ealdorman, II Cn. 58, 2
  Ealdormen shall take part in providing for the protection of cities, etc. against malefactors, Wl. art. retr. 6
Ear
  Witnesses shall declare that they are speaking the truth in accordance with what they heard with their ears, II Cn. 23, 1
  A man who has committed a serious crime shall have his ears cut off, II Cn. 30, 5
  A woman who has committed adultery shall lose her ears, II Cn. 53
Earl '*eorl*,' '*comes*,' '*cunte*'
  Earl Oslac, IV Edg. 15
  The case of an action brought by an earl, III Atr. 12
  Earl Thurkil, Cn. 1020, 1; 9
  An earl shall receive 60 shillings as the fine due to him, II Cn. 15, 2
  An earl's heriot, II Cn. 71 *a*
  An earl shall receive 40 shillings as the fine due to him, Leis Wl. 42, 1
  Earl Henry and Earl Simon, Hn. cor., Witnesses
  Earl Robert de Meulan, Hn. mon.; Hn. com., Witnesses
  Greeting from Henry I to his earls, Hn. Lond. Pre.
Easter
  Plough-alms shall be rendered 15 days after Easter, II Edg. 2, 3 = V Atr. 11, 1 = VI 16 = VIII 12 = I Cn. 8, 1
  Trial by ordeal etc. forbidden from the Septuagesima till a fortnight after Easter, V Atr. 18 = VI 25 = I Cn. 17
  No fast is enjoined at the festival of Philip and James because of the Easter festival, VI Atr. 22, 3 = I Cn. 16 *a*
  Warships shall be made ready soon after Easter, VI Atr. 33
Ecclesiastics. See also Bishop, Priest
  An assembly both of the ecclesiastical and secular estates, I Edm. Pre.
  Those in holy orders (*þa halgan hadas*) shall observe celibacy, I Edm. 1
  Of the advice of councillors both ecclesiastical and lay, II Edm. Pre.; V Atr. Pre.
  The servants of God shall live a pure life, IV Edg. 1, 7
  The servants of God shall submit to their duty, V Atr. 4
  No minister of the church shall be turned out without the bishop's consent, V Atr. 10, 2 = VI 15
  Violations of holy orders (or injuries to the clergy), V Atr. 25 = VI 28, 3
  The servants of God shall obey God, etc., VI Atr. 5
  The servants of God shall be protected, VI Atr. 45
  Every cleric shall sing 30 psalms, VII Atr. 2, 2 *a*
  All men, both clerics and laymen, shall turn zealously to God, VII Atr. (A.S.) 7
  If a man in holy orders is charged with vendetta, VII Atr. 23

Ecclesiastics, *continued*
  If an attempt is made to deprive a man in orders of his goods or his life, etc., VIII Atr. 33 f. = II Cn. 40 f.
  King Canute sends greetings to all his subjects, nobles and commoners, ecclesiastics and laymen, Cn. 1020, 1
  If anyone, whether a man in orders or a layman, defies the law of God, Cn. 1020, 9
  The whole nation, ecclesiastics and laymen, shall keep the law of Edgar, Cn. 1020, 13
  All Christian men should protect members of the clergy, I Cn. 4
  The various ranks in holy orders should be recognised, I Cn. 4, 3
  Injurers of the clergy shall make amends, II Cn. 6
  If anyone binds or beats or insults a man in holy orders, II Cn. 42
  If a man in holy orders places his life in jeopardy by committing a capital crime, II Cn. 43
  If anyone injures a member of the clergy, II Cn. 49
  Spiritual teachers shall be obeyed, II Cn. 84, 1–4 *a*
Enemy, foe '*feond*,' '*hostis*,' '*inimicus*'
  Victory over their foes shall be sought from God, VII Atr. 7, 1; VII (A.S.) Pre.
  All freemen shall defend King William's lands against his enemies, Wl. art. 2; Wl. art. retr. 2
  Cities etc. shall be guarded on all sides against enemies, Wl. art. retr. 6
England, English, etc.
  King of England (or the English), V Atr. Pre.; VIII Pre.; Cn. 1027, Heading; Sp. I Cn. Heading and Pre.; Wl. ep. Pre.; Wl. art. Pre.; Hn. cor. Pre.; Hn. mon. Pre.; Hn. com. Pre.; Hn. Lond. Pre.
  Districts under English law (*æfter* or *on Engla lage*), I Atr. Pre.; VI 37; VIII 5, 1 = I Cn. 3, 2; II Cn. 15, 1 and 2; 62; 65; in an English district (*mid Englum*), II Cn. 45, 3; 46; 48
  The additions made by Edgar to the laws of his ancestors shall be observed among the English, IV Edg. 2, 1 *a*
  A measure which shall apply generally, to the English, Danes and Britons, IV Edg. 2, 2
  If a hostile fleet harry in England, II Atr. 1, 1
  If a region afford protection to any of those who harry in England, II Atr. 1, 2
  If an Englishman slay a Dane or a Dane an Englishman, II Atr. 5
  If an Englishman slay a Danish slave or a Dane an English slave, II Atr. 5, 1
  The sum paid out of England to the Viking fleet, II Atr. 7, 2
  St Edward's festival shall be celebrated throughout England, V Atr. 16 = I Cn. 17, 1
  The ordinance agreed upon by the English councillors, VI Atr. Pre.
  Greetings from the king to his subjects in England, Cn. 1020, 1; Wl. lad Pre.
  The secular ordinance which shall be observed over all England, II Cn. Pre.
  Violation of the law by a Dane or an Englishman, II Cn. 83
  Modes of defence for an Englishman, Wl. lad; Wl. art. 6–6, 3
  Peace and security shall be maintained among both English and Normans, Wl. art. 1 = Wl. art. retr. 1
  All freemen shall be loyal to the king both in and out of England, Wl. art. 2 = Wl. art. retr. 2
  The case of Frenchmen who had been admitted to the status of Englishmen, Wl. art. 4
  Additions to the existing laws made for the benefit of the English nation, Wl. art. 7
  English terms and modes of reckoning, Leis Wl. 5; 11, 1 f.; 19; 42, 1
  Concerning the case in which a man's oath cannot be invalidated according to the law of England, Leis Wl. 21, 5
  Those with a court in England, Leis Wl. 42, 1
  People both French and English, Wl. Lond. 1; Hn. cor. Pre.; Hn. mon. Pre.; 1; Hn. com. Pre.; Hn. Lond. Pre.
Escape '*losian*,' '*utaberstan*,' '*uthleapan*,' '*eschaper*,' '*s'en fuir*'
  If anyone does wrong and escapes, III Edg. 6, 1

386 INDEX

Escape, *continued*
    Such precautions shall be taken against thieves that very few of them may escape, IV Edg. 2, 2
    If an accused man escapes and avoids the ordeal, I Atr. 1, 7=II Cn. 30, 6; I Atr. 1, 11=II Cn. 31, 1
    If his lord is accused of advising him to escape, I Atr. 1, 8=II Cn. 30, 7; I Atr. 1, 12=II Cn. 31, 1 *a*
    If anyone of his own accord lets a thief escape without raising the hue and cry, II Cn. 29=Leis Wl. 49
    If anyone who is accused of larceny or robbery and who is under surety to appear before the court escapes, Leis Wl. 3
    Of how it is permitted to cause loss to another through fear of death when otherwise there is no means of escape, Leis Wl. 37

Excommunication
    Anyone who refuses to pay church dues shall be excommunicated, I Edm. 2
    Those who commit perjury and practise sorcery shall be cast out for ever from the fellowship of God, I Edm. 6
    If an excommunicated man remains anywhere near the king, V Atr. 29
    If anyone sells a man out of the country, he shall be shut out from the blessing of God and of all the saints, VII Atr. 5
    If a monk or a priest becomes an utter apostate, he shall be excommunicated, VIII Atr. 41
    He who keeps an excommunicated man under his protection, VIII Atr. 42
    If anyone marries a professed nun or a woman under religious vows, he shall be an outcast before God and cut off from the whole community of Christians, Cn. 1020, 17
    Those who are cast out from the fellowship of God, II Cn. 4, 1
    If anyone slays a minister of the altar, he shall be excommunicated, II Cn. 39
    If anyone unlawfully maintains an excommunicated man, II Cn. 66 f.

Exculpation. See also Denial, Oath
    i. *(Ge)clænsian*
        How a man shall clear himself when property is attached in his possession, II Atr. 8, 1 f.
        How a man who vouches a dead person to warranty shall clear himself, II Atr. 9, 2
        If anyone seeks to clear a thief, III Atr. 7
    ii. *(Ge)cyðan, alaier*
        Of the declaration on oath of a judge who has given a false judgment, III Edg. 3=II Cn. 15, 1; Leis Wl. 39, 1 f.
        Of declarations made with the support of witnesses, III Atr. 2
        Of the declaration of witnesses who are acting on behalf of a man who is vouching to warranty, II Cn. 23, 1
    iii. *(Ge)ladian, lad, escundire, espurgir*
        How a man accused of abetting a delinquent to escape shall clear himself, I Edg. 6, 1; I Atr. 1, 8 f.=II Cn. 30, 7 f.; I Atr. 1, 12 f.=II Cn. 31, 1 *a* and 2; Leis Wl. 52, 2
        How a lord may clear one of his men, III Atr. 4
        How a man accused of helping one who has broken the king's peace shall clear himself, III Atr. 13
        How exculpation shall not be permitted after a case has been decided by amicable agreement, III Atr. 13, 4
        How a man who plots against the king's life shall clear himself, V Atr. 30= VI 37
        How a priest who lives according to a rule shall clear himself, VIII Atr. 19 f.= I Cn. 5 f.
        How a deacon who lives according to a rule shall clear himself, VIII Atr. 20 f. =I Cn. 5, 1 f.
        How a secular priest shall clear himself, VIII Atr. 21=I Cn. 5, 2
        How a member of the priesthood shall clear himself, VIII Atr. 22=I Cn. 5, 2 *a*
        How a man in holy orders who is charged with vendetta shall clear himself, VIII Atr. 23 f.=I Cn. 5, 2 *b* and 2 *c*

INDEX

Exculpation, *continued*
  How a priest charged with false witness etc. shall clear himself, VIII Atr. 27, 1 = I Cn. 5, 4
  How a man who protects a thief shall clear himself, Cn. 1020, 12
  How a reeve accused of permitting the coining of false money shall clear himself, II Cn. 8, 2
  How a man who harbours a fugitive shall clear himself, II Cn. 13, 2
  How a man in the Danelaw shall clear himself of a charge of false judgment, II Cn. 15, 1 *a*
  Every freeman who desires to have the right of exculpation shall be in a tithing, II Cn. 20
  Every trustworthy man shall be entitled to clear himself by the simple oath of exculpation, II Cn. 22
  How cases involving a simple or a triple oath of exculpation shall be begun, II Cn. 22, 1 *a*
  How a man who lets a thief escape without raising the hue and cry shall clear himself, II Cn. 29; Leis Wl. 49
  How a man who neglects the hue and cry shall clear himself, II Cn. 29, 1; Leis Wl. 50
  The various boroughs shall have one law with regard to exculpation (*ladunge*), II Cn. 34
  How a man who slays a minister of the altar shall clear himself, II Cn. 39
  How a minister of the altar who commits a serious crime shall clear himself, II Cn. 41, 1
  How a man who binds or beats a man in holy orders shall clear himself, II Cn. 42
  How a man who causes a breach of the fast of Lent shall clear himself, II Cn. 47, 1
  If the attempt to refute a charge of adultery fails, II Cn. 53, 1
  If a man charged with murder fails to clear himself, II Cn. 56, 1
  How a Frenchman who is accused by an Englishman shall clear himself, Wl. lad 1, 1
  How an Englishman shall clear himself, Wl. lad 2, 3; 3
  How a man entitled to the benefit of the law shall clear himself of a charge of theft, Leis Wl. 14
  How those who have been previously accused shall clear themselves, Leis Wl. 14, 1
  How anyone accused of breaking into a church or a treasury shall clear himself, Leis Wl. 15 f.
  How a man suspected of acting otherwise than through the fear of death shall clear himself, Leis Wl. 37, 1
  How a man who is accused by 4 men at once shall clear himself, Leis Wl. 51

Extopare. See *Hættian*

A slave who has committed theft shall have (part of) his scalp removed, III Edm. 4

Eye '*eage*,' '*oil*'
  Witnesses shall declare that they are speaking the truth in accordance with what they saw with their eyes, II Cn. 23, 1
  A man who has committed a serious crime shall have his eyes put out, II Cn. 30, 5
  If anyone knocks out a man's eye, Leis Wl. 19
  If he destroys the sight without displacing the pupil (*la purnele*), Leis Wl. 19, 1

Fæhðbot 'compensation incurred by vendetta'
  No monk may lawfully either demand or pay *fæhðbot*, VIII Atr. 27 = I Cn. 5, 2 *d*

Fast '*fæsten*'
  Every fast shall be rigorously observed, II Edg. 5, 1; V Atr. 12, 3; 15 = VI 22 = VIII 16 = I Cn. 14, 1; 16; Cn. 1020, 19
  St Mary's festivals shall be honoured first with fasting and afterwards with festivity, V Atr. 14 = VI 22, 2 = I Cn. 16 *a*

25-2

Fast, *continued*
    Fasting shall be observed at the festival of every apostle except that of Philip and James, v Atr. 14, 1 = vi 22, 3 = 1 Cn. 16 *a*
    Fasts shall be observed according to the highest standards of the past, v Atr. 15 = vi 22, 4
    Breaches of fasts (*fæstenbryce*), v Atr. 25 = vi 28, 2
    The mercy of God shall be invoked by fasts, vii Atr. 1, 1
    Every adult Christian shall fast for three days, vii Atr. 2 = vii (A.S.) 1
    Slaves shall be exempt from work so that they can fast the better, vii Atr. 2, 3 = vii (A.S.) 5, 1
    The case of a fast being broken, vii Atr. 2, 4
    The food which each person would otherwise have enjoyed shall be distributed after the fast, vii Atr. (A.S.) 4, 1
    The conditions in which a man in holy orders who is charged with vendetta shall have recourse to fasting, i Cn. 5, 2 *c*
    If a freeman breaks a legally ordained fast, ii Cn. 46
    If a slave does so, ii Cn. 46, 2
    Lenctenfæsten, the fast of Lent, i Cn. 16
    Riht fæsten(dæg), a legally appointed fast day, i Cn. 17; ii Cn. 46

Father
    King Edgar's claim to the prerogatives which his father had, iv Edg. 2 *a*
    Every child shall be his father's heir after his father's death, Wl. Lond. 3
    The heriot of a *vavassur* to his liege lord is his father's horse, etc., Leis Wl. 20, 2
    If a father finds his daughter in adultery, Leis Wl. 35

Fear '*ege*'
    Every witness shall swear that he will never, through fear, deny any of the things of which he has been witness, iv Edg. 6, 1
    Mercy and leniency shall be shown towards those who have need of them, through the fear of God, vi Atr. 53
    The status of the priesthood shall be respected through the fear of God, viii Atr. 18
    The various ranks in holy orders shall be recognised and distinguished through the fear of God, i Cn. 4, 3
    All men should have the fear of God in their hearts, i Cn. 25
    If anyone desires to turn from lawlessness, mercy shall be shown to him, through the fear of God, ii Cn. 67
    Greater leniency shall be shown in imposing penance upon the weak than upon the strong, through the fear of God, ii Cn. 68, 1

Feoh 'property,' 'money'
    If anyone tries to accuse another man falsely so that he is injured either in property or reputation, iii Edg. 4 = ii Cn. 16
    Every witness shall swear that he will never, for money, deny any of the things of which he has been witness, iv Edg. 6, 1
    Of the tribute paid by the king to the Viking fleet, ii Atr. 1
    Of moneyers who are accused of striking false money, iii Atr. 8
    The improvement of the coinage (*feos bot*), v Atr. 26, 1 = vi 31 f. = ii Cn. 8
    Of monetary compensation (*feohbot*) paid as amends for religious offences, vi Atr. 51
    Concerning the money received as payment for neglect of dues, vii Atr. (A.S.) 4
    If an attempt is made to deprive a man in orders or a stranger of his goods (*feoh*) or his life, viii Atr. 33 = ii Cn. 40

Feohfang 'bribery'; ii Cn. 15, 1
Feormfultum 'purveyance'; ii Cn. 69, 1
Festival '*freols*,' '*freolsdæg*,' '*freolstid*,' '*freolsunge*,' '*heahfreols*,' '*feste*'
    Every Sunday shall be observed as a festival, ii Edg. 5 = Cn. 1020, 18 = i Cn. 14, 2; v Atr. 13 = vi 22, 1
    A fast shall be observed every Friday, unless it be a festival, ii Edg. 5, 1 = v Atr. 17 = vi 24 = i Cn. 16 *a*
    Festivals shall be duly observed, v Atr. 12, 3 = vi 22 = viii 16 = i Cn. 14, 1
    All St Mary's festivals shall be zealously honoured, v Atr. 14 = vi 22, 2

Festival, *continued*
    Concerning the celebration of the festival of every apostle and that of Philip and James, v Atr. 14, 1 = vi 22, 3
    Trial by ordeal and the rendering of oaths forbidden during festivals, v Atr. 18 = vi 25 = i Cn. 17
    Breaches of festivals (*freolsbryce*), v Atr. 25 = vi 28, 2
    Lawlessness should be avoided at sacred seasons and in sacred places (*freolstídan 7 on freolsstowan*), ii Cn. 38
    No condemned man should be put to death during the Sunday festival, ii Cn. 45
    Regulations regarding work during a church festival, ii Cn. 45, 1–3
    Of the guarding of roads between Michaelmas and Martinmas, Leis Wl. 28
Field
    Every man shall be entitled to hunt in the fields on his own property, ii Cn. 80
Fierd. See Army
Fierdfaru 'military service'; ii Cn. 65
Fierdscip 'warship'; vi Atr. 33; 34
Fierdung (i) 'the provision (equipment) of military forces'; v Atr. 26, 1 = vi 32, 3 = ii Cn. 10
    (ii) 'campaign'; ii Cn. 78
Fierdwite 'the fine for neglect of military service'; ii Cn. 12; 15
Fighting
    Of the distress caused by the manifold illegal deeds of violence (*gefeoht*) in the country, ii Edm. Pre. 1
    No fine for fighting (*fihtwite*) shall be remitted, ii Edm. 3
    If a man included in the truce fights, ii Atr. 3, 4
    Concerning breach of the protection of a church by fighting (*feohtlac*), viii Atr. 4 = i Cn. 3
    In the Danelaw the king has the receipt of fines for fighting, ii Cn. 15
    No condemned man shall be put to death on Sunday, unless he flees or fights, ii Cn. 45
    Concerning a breach of the fast of Lent by fighting, ii Cn. 47
    Concerning those who fight at the king's court, ii Cn. 59
Finger
    The fines for injuries to a man's fingers, Leis Wl. 11, 1 f.
Flight '*fleon*' (vb.), '*fleam*,' '*fliema.*' See also under Outlaw
    If a man included in the truce flees, ii Atr. 3, 4
    Concerning everyone who is a fugitive (outlaw) in one district, iii Atr. 10
    How the priest puts devils to flight, i Cn. 4, 2
    Concerning the man who harbours a fugitive, ii Cn. 13, 2
    No condemned man shall be put to death on Sunday, unless he flees, ii Cn. 45
    Concerning excommunicated persons (*Godes flieman*), ii Cn. 66
    Concerning the man who deserts his lord on an expedition, ii Cn. 77
Folc 'people,' 'nation'; iv Edg. 15; Cor. Oath 1; 1, 1; i Atr. Pre.; 1, 9 *a*; 4 = ii Cn. 33; v Atr. 3; 10, 1; vi 6; 13; 41; vii (A.S.) 1; viii 36; Cn. 1020, 8; 11; i Cn. 4, 1 and 3; 26, 3; ii 2, 1; 65, 1; 69; *folce ungetriewe*, unworthy of public confidence, iii Edg. 7 = ii Cn. 25; *folces men*, laymen, iv Edg. 1, 3; *folcgemot*, public meeting, v Atr. 13, 1 = vi 22, 1; i Cn. 15; *folcisc gemot*, vi Atr. 44; *folcisc mæssepreost*, secular priest, viii Atr. 21 = i Cn. 5, 2; *folcriht*, public law, ii Edm. 7; i Edg. 7; iii 1, 1; vi Atr. 8, 1; ii Cn. 1, 1; *folces fyrdscip*, national warship, vi Atr. 34; *folcfrig*, possessing the rights of a freeman, ii Cn. 45, 3
Foot
    Of the case in which a malefactor shall have his feet cut off, ii Cn. 30, 4
    If a man cuts off another man's foot, Leis Wl. 11
Foreað; ii Cn. 22, 1 *a* and 3. See Oath
Forefang; Leis Wl. 5
Foreigner. See also Stranger
    Foreigners, if they will not regularise their unions, shall be driven from the land, ii Cn. 55
Forene (*forstandan, -fon, -licgan*); i Atr. 4, 2 = ii Cn. 33, 1 *a*; Cn. 1020, 5; 12

Forfeit

i. *Forwyrcan, forfaire*
No man shall forfeit more than his wergeld, III Edg. 2, 2
A man who does a deed involving outlawry shall forfeit his *bocland*, II Cn. 13, 1
A man who assaults another man's wife shall forfeit his wergeld, Leis Wl. 12
He who assaults a woman shall suffer castration, Leis Wl. 18; 18, 2

ii. *Þolian*
Those in holy orders who fail to observe celibacy shall forfeit their worldly possessions and burial in consecrated ground, I Edm. 1
Anyone taking vengeance on a man other than the actual delinquent in a case of vendetta shall forfeit all he possesses, II Edm. 1, 3
Anyone who commits *mundbryce* or *hamsocn* shall forfeit all he possesses, II Edm. 6
A man who fails to obey the law four times shall forfeit all that he possesses, I Edg. 3, 1
A man who refuses three times to pay Peter's Pence shall forfeit all he possesses, II Edg. 4, 3
A judge who gives a false judgment shall forfeit his *þegnscipe*, III Edg. 3 = II Cn. 15, 1
A man who does not give notice of livestock which he has purchased shall forfeit it, IV Edg. 8, 1; 9; 10
If he makes a false statement with regard to it he shall forfeit his head and his possessions, IV Edg. 11
A man who deposits his goods in a house in common with those of *unfriðmenn* shall forfeit them, II Atr. 3, 3
Canons who do not maintain regularity and celibacy in their foundation shall forfeit their endowment, V Atr. 7 = VI 4
A priest who commits grievous crime shall forfeit his ecclesiastical office and be banished, VIII Atr. 26 = II Cn. 41
A priest who commits perjury etc. shall forfeit both the society and the friendship of those in holy orders and also every kind of privilege, VIII Atr. 27 = I Cn. 5, 3
He who violates the protection of the church or that granted by the king shall forfeit both land and life, I Cn. 2, 2
He who coins false money shall forfeit his hand, II Cn. 8, 1
He who swears a false oath on the relics shall forfeit his hand or half his wergeld, II Cn. 36
A woman who commits adultery shall forfeit both her nose and her ears, II Cn. 53
A widow who remarries within a year shall forfeit her morning-gift and all her first husband's property, II Cn. 73 a

iii. *Scyldig beon*
A man who seeks to accuse another man falsely shall forfeit his tongue, III Edg. 4 = II Cn. 16
Moneyers who work in secret places shall forfeit their lives, III Atr. 16
He who deserts an army shall forfeit 120 sh., V Atr. 28, 1
He who plots against the king shall forfeit his life, V Atr. 30 = VI 37 = II Cn. 57
A man who marries a professed nun shall forfeit all that he possesses, Cn. 1020, 17
He who promotes injustice etc. shall forfeit 120 sh. or *lahslit*, II Cn. 15, 1 f. = Leis Wl. 39, 1 f.; 42, 2
He who refuses to observe just laws shall forfeit a fine, II Cn. 15, 2 = Leis Wl. 42
He who is guilty of robbery shall forfeit his wergeld, II Cn. 63
A reeve who demands a fine unjustly shall forfeit his wergeld, II Cn. 69, 2
A man who marries a widow within a year from the death of her first husband shall forfeit his wergeld, II Cn. 73, 1
He who violates the law shall forfeit his wergeld, II Cn. 83

Forfeit, *continued*
  iv. *Misericordia* (cf. *merci*, Leis Wl. 42, 2)
    No baron or vassal shall forfeit the whole of his personal property as security, Hn. Cor. 8
    No citizen of London shall be sentenced to forfeiture of a sum greater than his wergeld, Hn. Lond. 7

Forsacan 'to refuse,' etc.
  Concerning the man who harbours a delinquent after his kinsmen have disclaimed him, II Edm. 1, 2
  Concerning the man who ignores the authority of the hundred, I Edg. 3
  If anyone refuses to ride against a man who fails three times to attend the court meetings (*ða rade forsacan*), III Edg. 7, 2 = II Cn. 25, 2
  No one shall refuse to accept the established coinage, IV Edg. 8 = II Cn. 8
  Concerning the man who refuses to observe just laws and just judgments, II Cn. 15, 2
  If an Englishman declines trial by combat, Wl. lad 1, 1

Forsteall 'violent opposition.' See *Agwait purpensé*
  No obstacle shall be placed in the way of the investigation with regard to stolen cattle, III Edm. 6
  If anyone offers obstruction to the law of Christ or of the king, V Atr. 31 = VI 38
  The fine for *forsteall* is one of the payments to which the king is entitled, II Cn. 12

Forword 'agreement'; II Atr. Pre.

Frankpledge
  Everyone who wishes to retain the status of a freeman shall be in a frankpledge, Wl. art. 8
  All villeins shall be in frankpledge, Leis Wl. 20, 3 *a*
  Everyone who wishes to obtain the benefit of the law etc. shall be in frankpledge, Leis Wl. 25

Free, freedom, freeman '*freo*,' '*franc*,' '*liber*,' '*frigman*'
  Concerning the church dues from free households, II Edg. 2, 2 = I Cn. 11, 2
  Every freeman shall have a trustworthy surety, I Atr. 1 = II Cn. 20
  If an Englishman slays a Dane, both being free men, II Atr. 5
  Concerning the injustice of representing one's men to be either freemen or slaves, II Cn. 20, 1
  If a freeman works during a church festival, II Cn. 45, 1
  If a freeman breaks a legally ordained fast, II Cn. 46
  Freemen and slaves must be carefully distinguished, II Cn. 68, 1 *b*
  All freemen shall affirm by oath that they will be loyal to King William, Wl. art. 2 = Wl. art. retr. 2
  Concerning the procedure in setting free a slave, Wl. art. retr. 15, 1
  Concerning *manbot* for a freeman, Leis Wl. 7
  If a freeman is accused of theft, Leis Wl. 14
  A freeman in the Danelaw who has livestock worth half a mark shall pay Peter's Pence, Leis Wl. 17, 1

Fremu 'reputation'; III Edg. 4 = II Cn. 16

Friday
  A fast shall be observed every Friday, unless it be a festival, II Edg. 5, 1 = V Atr. 17 = VI 24 = I Cn. 16 *a*

Friend
  A man who commits homicide may pay composition for it with the help of his friends, II Edm. 1
  The hostility of the king and of all his friends, II Edm. 1, 3
  The friends of a dead man may clear him according to the law, II Atr. 9, 2 f.
  Of a case in which no compensation shall be paid for a man's death to any of his friends, V Atr. 31, 1
  Of an appeal made to the friends of the king and his councillors, VI Atr. 6; VIII 44, 1
  Of an injunction addressed to the friends of the king and his councillors, VI Atr. 28 = I Cn. 19, 1
  Everyone who is the friend of God shall pursue the miscreant who violates the protection of the church, VIII Atr. 1, 1 = I Cn. 2, 3

INDEX

Friendless
   If an accusation is brought against a member of the priesthood who is friendless, VIII Atr. 22 = I Cn. 5, 2 *a*
   Concerning friendless men who are accused, II Cn. 35 f.
Friendly
   Friendly greetings from the king, Cn. 1020, 1; Wl. Lond. 1; Wl. lad Pre.
Friendship
   Cases in which the penalty is forfeiture of the king's friendship, IV Edg. 1, 5; Cn. 1020, 11
   Peace and goodwill (lit. 'friendship') shall be duly maintained in the country, V Atr. 1, 1 = VI 8, 2 = X 2, 1
   A priest who commits certain crimes shall forfeit both the society and the friendship of those in holy orders, VIII Atr. 27 = I Cn. 5, 3
   Of the injunction given by the king to his reeves to uphold the rights of abbots, if they wish to obtain his favour (lit. 'friendship'), VIII Atr. 32
Friđ
   i. Public security, maintenance of law and order, II Edm. 5; IV Edg. 2; 12, 1; 14, 1; 15; 16; I Atr. Pre.; III Pre.; V 1, 1 = VI 8, 2 = X 2, 1; V 26, 1 = VI 31 f. = II Cn. 8; Cn. 1020, 3; II Cn. 13
   ii. Truce between the English and the Danes, II Atr. 6, 1; 7, 2; *woroldfriđ*, a general truce, II Atr. 1; *friđburg*, a town included in the truce, 2, 1; *friđmal*, the terms of the truce, Pre.; *friđman*, a man included in the truce, 3; 3, 1; 3, 4; *friđbrec*, a breach of the truce, 5, 2; 6
   iii. Protection, sanctuary, II Atr. 2–3, 3; III 15; *friđbena*, a suppliant for protection, V 29; VI 36; *friđsocne*, sanctuary, VIII 1, 1 = I Cn. 2, 3; *friđleas*, outlawed, II Cn. 15 *a*; *friđlice*, V Atr. 3 = VI 10 = II Cn. 2, 1
Friđian, II Atr. 1, 2; VI 42 = 1 Cn. 2; 4; Cn. 1020, 12; II Cn. 80, 1
Frumgyld 'first instalment'; II Edm. 7, 3
Fugitive. See Flight
Fulwite 'full fine,' i.e. probably 120 sh., II Cn. 48 f.

Gafol 'rent,' 'tribute'; IV Edg. 1, 1 f.; VIII Atr. 43
Gefædere, VI Atr. 12, 1 = I Cn. 7, 1
Gefera 'companion'; VIII Atr. 24 = I Cn. 5, 2 *a* (fellow-ecclesiastics); II Cn. 35, 1; 77
Geferræden 'the fellow-members of a religious foundation'; VII Atr. (A.S.) 6
Geferscipe 'society'; VIII Atr. 27 = I Cn. 5, 3
Gehada 'fellow-ecclesiastic'; VIII Atr. 19, 1–20, 1 = I Cn. 5 *a*–5, 1 *a*
Gemana 'fellowship'; V Atr. 9 = VI 5, 1 = I Cn. 6, 2; VIII Atr. 27 = 1 Cn. 5, 3; I Cn. 22, 5
Gemot 'meeting,' 'court'; I Edg. 7; III Edg. 7 = II Cn. 25; I Atr. 1, 2 = III 4 = II Cn. 30, 1; III Atr. 3, 1; VI Atr. 44; VIII 37; II Cn. 27; 82
(*Ge*)*neatland* 'land held by tenants'; II Edg. 1, 1; *geneatman* 'tenant'; IV Edg. 1, 1
Geogođ 'youth,' 'young livestock'; II Edg. 3; V Atr. 11, 1 = VI 17; VI 52 = II Cn. 68, 1 *b*; VIII Atr. 9; I Cn. 8, 1
Geunsođian 'to refute'; III Edg. 4 = II Cn. 16
Gewitnes
   i. 'Cognisance'; I Edg. 4; IV 8; 10; I Atr. 1, 14; VII (A.S.) 2, 3; Cn. 1020, 11; II Cn. 75, 1; 79
   ii. 'A witness'; IV Edg. 3, 1; 4; 6, 1; 7; 9; 10; I Atr. 3; II 9, 2; III 2 f.; II Cn. 23–24, 2
   iii. 'Testimony'; IV Edg. 14; III Atr. 3; V 24 = VI 28, 2; VIII 27 = I Cn. 5, 3; II Cn. 23, 1; 37
   iv. 'Compurgator, Compurgation'; Wl. lad 1, 1; 2, 3
Gewrit; IV Edg. Pre.; 15, 1; Cor. Oath Pre.; Cn. 1020, 3; Wl. lad Pre.
Gift
   Concerning the gift made by a lord of what he has the legal right to bestow, III Atr. 3
God; I Edg. 2; IV 1, 4; Cor. Oath 1, 3; V Atr. 1 = VI 1; 6 = IX 1 = X 1 = I Cn. 1; V Atr. 3 = VI 10; V 5 = VI 3; V 6 = VI 3, 1; V 26 = VI 30; VI 41; 51; VIII 3; 22; 24 = I Cn. 5, 2 *c*; 35 = II Cn. 40, 2; 38; 40; 43 f.; X Pre.; Cn. 1020, 14–16;

INDEX 393

God, *continued*
  I Cn. 2, 5; 4, 2 f.; 5, 2 *a*; 7; 18 *a*; 18, 2 f.; 20, 1; 22, 1–4; 26; 26, 4; II Cn. 36, 1; 45, 1; 84, 1–2 *a*; 84, 4 *b*–6; Wl. Lond. 5; Leis Wl. 41, 1; favour of God, v Atr. 9, 1 = VI 5, 3; VIII 32; I Cn. 6, 2 *a*; II 23, 1; fear of God, VI Atr. 53; VIII 18; I Cn. 6, 3; 25; II 67; 68, 1; glory of God, II Edg. Pre.; Cn. 1020, 3; I Cn. Heading and Pre.; help of God, Cn. 1020, 4–7; love of God, VII Atr. (A.S.) 4 f.; I Cn. 18; II 68, 1; mercy of God, VIII Atr. 7; Cn. 1020, 7; 20; wrath of God, v Atr. 8 = VI 5 = I Cn. 6, 1; *for Gode 7 for worolde*, III Edg. 1, 2 = VI Atr. 10, 1 = II Cn. 2; v Atr. 1, 1 = VI 8, 2 = X 2, 1; v Atr. 4 = VI 2, 1; v Atr. 9, 2 = VI 5, 4; v 33, 1 = VI 40, 1 = II Cn. 11, 1; VI Atr. 8; 36; 39; 53; VIII 38; II Cn. 38, 1; *ge wið God ge wið men*, VIII Atr. 1, 1 = I Cn. 2, 3; VIII Atr. 27 = I Cn. 5, 3; II Cn. 39, 1; 41, 2; 54; *Godes bebod*, IV Edg. 1; *Godes lagu*, VI Atr. 12, 1; 42; 50; VIII 30; 43; Cn. 1020, 9; I Cn. 7, 3; 19, 3; 21; 26; II 84, 1; *Godes riht*, III Edg. 5, 2 = II Cn. 18, 1; v Atr. 26 = VI 30 = I Cn. 19, 3; II Cn. 1; 75, 1; *Godes fliema*, I Edm. 6; *Godes utlaga*, VIII Atr. 42 = II Cn. 4, 1; *utlah wið God*, Cn. 1020, 17; II Cn. 39; *Godes cirice*, I Edm. 5; II Edg. 1; Cor. Oath 1, 1; VI Atr. 42 = I Cn. 2; VIII Atr. 1; *Godes hus*, I Edm. 5; I Cn. 4; *Godes gerihta*, IV Edg. 1, 4; 5 *a*; 6; v Atr. 11 = VI 16 = I Cn. 8; VI Atr. 21, 1 = VIII 14 = I Cn. 14; VIII Atr. 43; Cn. 1020, 2; 8; *Godes grið*, v Atr. 10, 1 = VI 13 = I Cn. 2, 1; v 21 = VI 26; *Godes ciricgrið*, VIII Atr. 1, 1 = I Cn. 2, 2 and 3; *Godes dæl*, I Edm. 6; *Godes folc*, I Edm. 1; *Godes ordal*, II Cn. 35; *Godes þearfa*, VI Atr. 46; VIII 6; *Godes weofod*, VII Atr. (A.S.) 6, 3

Godbot; VI Atr. 51
Godcund; (*bot*), II Edm. 4; v Atr. 29; VI 50; 52; II Cn. 38, 2; 68, 1 *c*; (*bydel*), II Cn. 84, 4; (*gebed*), I Cn. 22, 3; (*geriht*), II Cn. 48; (*had*), I Edm. Pre.; II Pre.; (*lagu, rihtlagu, lar*), v Atr. 10; VIII 36; x Pre. 1; I Cn. 6, 3; (*heord*), II Cn. 26, 3; (*lareow*), VI Atr. 42; I Cn. 21; II 84, 1; (*neod*), VI Atr. 51; (*ðearf*), I Cn. 26; *þæt godcunde*, IV Edg. 1
Godcundlice (adv.); VIII Atr. 5 = I Cn. 3, 1
Godlar; I Cn. 23
Gold
  22,000 pounds in gold and silver paid to the Viking fleet, II Atr. 7, 2
  Everyone shall go to church without gold or ornaments, VII Atr. (A.S.) 2
  A coiner shall not redeem his hand either with gold or with silver, II Cn. 8, 1
  The heriot of an earl shall include 200 mancuses of gold; that of a king's thegn who stands in immediate relationship to him, 50 mancuses of gold, II Cn. 71 *a*, 1 and 4
Goods. See *Æht, Ceap, Feoh*
Grave '*græfe*,' '*leger*'
  Payment for the souls of the dead shall be rendered before the grave is closed, v Atr. 12 = VI 20 = VIII 13 = I Cn. 13
  A priest who observes celibacy shall enjoy the privileges of a thegn *ge on life ge on legere*, v Atr. 9, 1 = VI 5, 3 = VIII 28
Graveyard '*legerstow*'; II Edg. 2; 2, 1 = I Cn. 11; 11, 1; VIII Atr. 5, 1 = I Cn. 3, 2
Grið 'peace,' 'protection,' 'security'; III Edm. 7, 1; III Atr. 1, 1 f.; VIII Atr. 1; II Cn. 82; *Godes (Cristes, cynges, folces) grið*, v Atr. 10, 1 = VI 13 = I Cn. 2, 1; v Atr. 21 = VI 26; III Atr. 1; 13.
Griðbryce; VIII Atr. 4, 1 = I Cn. 3 *a*; VIII Atr. 5, 1 = I Cn. 3, 2; II Cn. 15
Griðian; VI Atr. 42; I Cn. 2; 4
Guilty
  i. *Ful*
    Concerning a freeman found guilty at the triple ordeal, I Atr. 1, 5 = II Cn. 30, 3 *b*; 30, 4; III Atr. 4, 1
    Concerning a slave found guilty at the ordeal, I Atr. 2 = II Cn. 32
    If a man who seeks to clear a thief prove guilty at the ordeal, III Atr. 7, 1
  ii. *Sac*
    The twelve leading thegns and the reeve in the wapentake court shall swear that they will never shield a guilty man, III Atr. 3, 1

394   INDEX

Guilty, continued
  iii. *Scyldig*
    Concerning the man who by his veracity brings just doom upon the guilty, IV Edg. 14
    If stolen goods have been deposited by a man in his wife's storeroom, chest, or cupboard, she shall be held guilty, II Cn. 76, 1 *a*
    Concerning the custom of treating a child in the cradle as if it were guilty, II Cn. 76, 2

Had 'estate,' 'rank'
  i. With a general sense
    King Edmund's assembly of the ecclesiastical and secular estates, I Edm. Pre.
    Unrighteous deeds shall be put an end to among all classes of society, Cor. Oath 1, 2
    Men of every estate (the reference may be to members of the clergy) shall submit to their duty, V Atr. 4 = VI 2 = I Cn. 6; VIII Atr. 31
    The higher the privileges of a man's rank, the more fully shall he make amends for his sins, VI Atr. 52 = II Cn. 38, 1
  ii. With reference to the clergy
    Those in holy orders (*þa halgan hadas*) shall observe the celibacy befitting their estate whether they are men or women (*swa werhades swa wifhades*), I Edm. 1
    Concerning the priest who will not do what befits his order, V Atr. 9, 2 = VI 5, 4
    A priest who perpetrates crime shall be deprived of his ecclesiastical office (or rank), VIII Atr. 26 = II Cn. 41
    A priest should observe the laws of God as properly befits his estate, VIII Atr. 30
    All Christian men shall protect the members of the clergy (*hadas griðian 7 friðian*), I Cn. 4
    The various ranks in holy orders shall be recognised and distinguished, I Cn. 4, 3
    The fine for injury inflicted upon a member of the clergy shall be regulated according to the rank (*had*) of the injured man, II Cn. 42; 49

Hadbreca 'an injurer of the clergy'; II Cn. 6
Hadbryce 'violation of holy orders'; V Atr. 25 = VI 28, 3, or possibly, in view of II Cn. 49, 'injury inflicted upon the clergy'
Hadian 'to consecrate'
  No widow shall be too hastily consecrated as a nun, II Cn. 73, 3
(*Ge*)*hadod man* 'a man in orders,' II Cn. 40; 41; 42; 43; *g. nunne* 'a professed nun,' Cn. 1020, 16; *g. witan* 'ecclesiastical councillors,' V Atr. Pre.
Hættian. See *Extopare*
  A man who has perpetrated very serious crime shall have (part of) his scalp removed, II Cn. 30, 5
Haligdom 'holy things,' *i.e.* in general probably 'relics'
  A man shall appear as witness to such things only as he is prepared to swear to on the relics, III Atr. 2, 1
  The twelve leading thegns and the reeve in the wapentake court shall swear on the relics, III Atr. 3, 1
  All shall go out with the relics, VII Atr. (A.S.) 2, 1
  All Christian men shall maintain the security and sanctity of holy things, I Cn. 4
  If anyone swears a false oath on the relics, II Cn. 36
Hamsocn 'an attack on, or forcible entry into, a man's house,' cf. *hemfare*, Leis Wl. 2
  The penalty for *hamsocn* shall be forfeiture of all a man's possessions, II Edm. 6
  A man who is slain while committing *hamsocn* shall lie in an unhonoured grave, IV Atr. 4
  Payment of *hamsocn* one of the dues to which the king is entitled, II Cn. 12; 15
  The fine for *hamsocn* in districts under English law and in the Danelaw, II Cn. 62

INDEX

Hand '*hand*,' '*manus*,' '*main*,' '*puing*'
  i. Ordinary use
    Concerning oaths sworn on the relics given into a man's hand, III Atr. 2, 1; 3, 1
    He who coins false money shall forfeit his hand, II Cn. 8, 1
    A man proved guilty for the second time in the triple ordeal shall have his hands cut off, II Cn. 30, 4
    A man who swears a false oath on the relics shall lose his hand, II Cn. 36
    A man who resists by force the payment of ecclesiastical dues and wounds anyone shall redeem his hands from the bishop or lose them, II Cn. 48, 1
    If a man cuts off another man's hand, Leis Wl. 11
    The value of the thumb is half that of the hand, Leis Wl. 11, 1
  ii. Special phrases. See also *Handgrið*
    On hand syllan, to give security, II Edm. 7 f.; II Atr. 8; *on handa standan* (used of necessity or hostility), to be urgent, to threaten, I Edg. 2; VII Atr. (A.S.) 6, 2; Cn. 1020, 4; (used of goods), to have in one's possession, II Atr. 9, cp. *on handa habban*, *aveir entre mains*, II Atr. 9, 3; Leis Wl. 21; *ofmanian to ðæs cynges handa*, on the king's behalf, III Edg. 3; *hand ofer habban*, to have control over, II Atr. 1; *æt bisceopes handa onfon*, to act as sponsor at confirmation, I Cn. 22, 6; *to handa forwyrcan*, to forfeit into someone's hands, II Cn. 13, 1 = *gan to handa*, to pass into someone's hands, 77, 1; *metre main en*, to lay hands on, Leis Wl. 1, 1; *metre en uele main*, to place in neutral hands, Leis Wl. 21, 4
  iii. With the sense of 'person'; III Edm. 3; II Atr. 8, 1; *jurer*, *s'escundire*, *s'espurger sei siste* (*duzime*, *trente-siste*) *main*, to clear oneself with 5 (11, 35) compurgators, Leis Wl. 14, 3; 21, 1; 52, 2; 3; 14, 1; 15; 51; 15, 1

Handgrið; VI Atr. 14 = I Cn. 2, 2; III Atr. 1

Hang
  The leader of a number of slaves who commit theft shall be hanged, III Edm. 4

Harbour (vb.)
  If the kinsman of a slayer harbours him, II Edm. 1, 2
  Neither of the parties to the truce shall harbour a slave etc. belonging to the other party, II Atr. 6, 2
  If anyone harbours a fugitive, II Cn. 13, 2
  If anyone harbours an outlawed man, II Cn. 15 *a*

Head '*heafod*,' '*teste*'
  A man who makes a false statement with regard to the purchase of cattle shall forfeit his head, IV Edg. 11
  A man who is found guilty for the second time at the triple ordeal shall not be able to make any amends except by his head, I Atr. 1, 6
  Similarly in the case of a slave, I Atr. 2, 1 = II Cn. 32, 1
  In the case of breach of the truce (with homicide) the nearest relatives of the slain men shall take head for head, II Atr. 6
  A man who kills a cow shall keep the head for three days, III Atr. 9
  Of the payments made in lieu of the head of a thief who has escaped, Leis Wl. 3, 1 ff.
  Compensation for a wound on the head, Leis Wl. 10, 1

Healsfang, II Edm. 7, 3; VI Atr. 51; II Cn. 37; 45, 1; 60; 71, 2; Leis Wl. 9

Heathen, heathen practices '*hæðen*,' '*hæðendom*,' '*hæðenscipe*,' '*pagani*,' '*paisnime*'
  Christian men shall not be sold out of the land, least of all to the heathen, V Atr. 2 = VI 9; II Cn. 3; Leis Wl. 41
  All heathen practices shall be renounced, V Atr. 1; 34 = VI 1; 6 = VIII 44 = IX Expl. = X 1
  A mass and a collect against the heathen shall be sung daily, VII Atr. 3 f.
  Heathen practices forbidden and defined, II Cn. 5 f.

Heimelborh 'surety'; Leis Wl. 21, 1 f.

Heir *'yrfenuma'*
  Concerning the heir of a dead man who can answer a charge brought against him, II Atr. 9, 2
  No one shall bring an action against the heirs of a man who has been free from claims and charges during his lifetime, III Atr. 14
  If a householder has been cited before his death, his heirs shall answer the charge, II Cn. 72, 1
  The heirs of a man who falls during a campaign shall succeed to his land, II Cn. 78
  Every child shall be his father's heir after his father's death, Wl. Lond. 3
Hengwite 'a fine for neglecting to arrest a thief'; Leis Wl. 4
Here
  i. Invading force, Viking fleet, II Atr. Pre.; 1; 1, 2; 3, 1; 7, 2; VII (A.S.) Heading
  ii. Used in a political sense, IV Edg. 15
Hergian, to harry; II Atr. 1, 1 f.; *hergung*, II Atr. 6, 1
Heriot
  If a man dies intestate his lord shall take no more than his legal heriot, II Cn. 70
  Heriots shall be fixed according to the rank of the person concerned, II Cn. 71
  The heriot of an earl, a king's thegn, etc., II Cn. 71 *a*–71, 5; Leis Wl. 20–20, 4
  Every widow shall pay the heriots within twelve months, II Cn. 73, 4
  The heriots of a man who falls during a campaign shall be remitted, II Cn. 78
Hide. See 'Scourging'
  A man who kills a cow shall keep the hide for 3 days, III Atr. 9
  Of the fine if he disposes of it before that, III Atr. 9, 1
Hide (of land)
  From every hide a penny or the value of a penny shall be given as dues, VII Atr. (A.S.) 2, 2
  A halfpennyworth of wax shall be paid from every hide three times a year as light dues, I Cn. 12
  Every 10 hides shall supply a man for guarding the roads, Leis Wl. 28
  The case of the commander of the watch if he has 30 hides, Leis Wl. 28, 1
Highway
  Violation of the king's peace on the four highways (*chemins*), Leis Wl. 26
  Concerning the guarding of roads (*stretward*), Leis Wl. 28
Homicide. See Slaying, Wergeld
Hordarius 'treasurer'; III Edm. 5
Horse
  An earl's heriot shall include 8 horses, that of a king's thegn 4, that of an ordinary thegn 1, that of a king's thegn among the Danes 2, II Cn. 71 *a*–71, 4
  If anyone has taken horses into his care, Leis Wl. 5
  A stallion is the equivalent of 20 shillings, Leis Wl. 9, 1
  The heriot of an earl shall include 8 horses, that of a baron 4, that of a thegn his father's horse, that of a villein shall be a horse, if it is the best animal that he has, Leis Wl. 20–20, 3
House, household, home
  No one who commits homicide shall have right of access to the king's household (*hired*), II Edm. 4
  Concerning the church dues from every free household (*heorð*), II Edg. 2, 2 = I Cn. 11, 2
  When a man who has had to take his Peter's Pence to Rome comes home (*ham*), II Edg. 4, 1 f.
  No one shall apply to the king, unless he fails to command justice at home, III Edg. 2
  When a man who makes a purchase comes home, IV Edg. 7 f.
  Every lord shall be surety for the men of his household (*hiredman*), I Atr. 1, 10 = II Cn. 31
  If a man included in the truce bears his goods into a house in common with those of men not included in the truce, II Atr. 3, 3
  Every member of a household shall give a penny as alms, VII Atr. (A.S.) 5

INDEX

House, *continued*
    Every freeman, whether he has an establishment of his own (*heorðfæst*) or not, shall be in a tithing, II Cn. 20
    Concerning those who fight at the king's court (*hired*), II Cn. 59
    Assaults upon houses (*husbryce*) one of the crimes which are *botleas*, II Cn. 64
    A widow who remarries within a year shall lose her possessions, unless she is willing to return home, II Cn. 73, 2
    If a man sets his spear at the door of another man's house, II Cn. 75
    If a man carries stolen goods home to his cottage, II Cn. 76
    If a father finds his daughter in adultery in his own or in his son-in-law's house, Leis Wl. 35

Hundred
    30 shillings shall be paid as a fine to the hundred, III Edm. 2; II Cn. 15, 2; Leis Wl. 42, 1
    The ordinance concerning the administration of the hundred, I Edg. Heading
    The chief official of the hundred shall be informed when the pursuit of a thief is urgent, I Edg. 2
    Half of the thief's property (when the value of the stolen goods has been deducted) shall be given to the hundred, I Edg. 2, 1; III Edg. 7, 1; II Cn. 25, 1; Leis Wl. 47, 1
    30 pence shall be paid to the hundred as a fine for ignoring its authority, I Edg. 3
    No-one shall keep strange cattle except with the cognisance of the men of the hundred, I Edg. 4
    If one hundred follow up a track into another hundred, I Edg. 5
    In the hundred (court) every case shall be treated in accordance with the public law, I Edg. 7
    The hundred court shall be attended as previously ordained, III Edg. 5; II Cn. 17, 1
    A body of standing witnesses shall be appointed for every hundred, IV Edg. 3, 1; 5
    If a man does not give notice within 5 days of livestock which he has acquired, the villagers shall inform the head of the hundred, IV Edg. 8, 1
    If he announces that he bought it with the cognisance of the men nominated as witnesses in a hundred, IV Edg. 10
    A lord who is defending one of his men shall choose as compurgators two trustworthy thegns within the hundred, I Atr. 1, 2 = II Cn. 30, 1
    If the oath is forthcoming the accused man may clear himself by an oath supported by compurgators found within three hundreds, I Atr. 1, 3 = II Cn. 30, 2
    No-one shall appeal to the king, unless he fails to obtain justice within his hundred, II Cn. 17
    No-one shall make distraint of property until he has appealed for justice three times in the hundred court, II Cn. 19 = Leis Wl. 44
    Every freeman over 12 years of age shall be within a hundred, II Cn. 20
    Every trustworthy man shall be entitled to clear himself within the hundred by the simple oath of exculpation, II Cn. 22
    For an untrustworthy man compurgators for the simple oath shall be selected within three hundreds, II Cn. 22, 1
    The hundred court shall determine the way in which a man who has tried to bring a countercharge against his opponent shall meet the original charge, II Cn. 27
    If anyone has forfeited the confidence of the hundred, II Cn. 30
    A member of a lord's household shall answer a charge within the hundred in which he is accused, II Cn. 31 *a*
    No pleas affecting episcopal jurisdiction shall be held in the hundred court, Wl. ep. 2
    The whole hundred in which a murder has been committed shall assist in paying the murder-fine, Wl. art. 3, 2
    All hundreds shall be watched and guarded, Wl. art. retr. 6

Hundred, *continued*
    If a Frenchman is slain and the men of the hundred do not seize the slayer, Leis Wl. 22
    Every 10 hides of the hundred shall supply a man for guarding the roads, Leis Wl. 28
    If anyone has charges brought against him by four men at once in the hundred court, Leis Wl. 51
    Every lord shall bring an accused servant for trial in the hundred court, Leis Wl. 52
    The hundred court shall sit as it did in the time of King Edward, Hn. com. 1
    The hundred court shall be attended as it was in the time of King Edward, Hn. com. 4

Hunting
    Hunting expeditions shall be abstained from on Sunday, VI Atr. 22, 1 = I Cn. 15, 1
    Every man shall be entitled to hunt on his own property, II Cn. 80
    Everyone shall avoid hunting on the king's preserves, II Cn. 80, 1
    The citizens of London shall enjoy as good and full hunting-rights as their ancestors did, Hn. Lond. 15

Husband. See *Ceorl*

Husl, huslgang 'holy communion,' 'sacrament,' 'eucharist'
    Everyone shall prepare himself frequently for receiving the sacrament, V Atr. 22, 1 = VI 27, 1 = I Cn. 19
    A priest shall clear himself by the holy communion, VIII Atr. 19 f.; 22 = I Cn. 5; 5, 2 *a*
    The power of the priest when he hallows the eucharist, I Cn. 4, 2
    A man who does not have true belief in God cannot be entitled to receive the sacrament, I Cn. 22, 5

Husting; Hn. Lond. 8; 9

Idol
    The worship of idols forbidden, II Cn. 5, 1

Ierfe 'cattle,' 'livestock'; I Edg. 2, 1; 4

Ierfenuma. See Heir

Informer '*melda*'
    A cow's bell, a dog's collar and a horn for blowing are all reckoned as informers, I Edg. 8

Injuries
    If anyone attacks or injures a man who is taking sanctuary, II Edm. 2
    If anyone seeks to accuse another man falsely so that he is injured either in property or in reputation, III Edg. 4 = II Cn. 16
    Concerning the man who assaults an innocent person on the king's highway, IV Atr. 4
    Concerning injurers of the clergy, II Cn. 6; 49
    If a man who resists the payment of ecclesiastical dues wounds anyone, II Cn. 48, 1
    If a man wounds another and has to pay compensation, Leis Wl. 10 ff.
    If a man cuts off another man's hand or foot or any of his fingers, Leis Wl. 11 ff.

Inland 'demesne land'; II Edg. 1, 2

Innocent
    Of a man who by giving true witness saves the innocent (*unscyldig*), IV Edg. 14
    The twelve leading thegns and the reeve shall swear that they will not accuse any innocent (*sacleas*) man, III Atr. 3, 1
    Christian men who are innocent of crime (*unforworhte*, *i.e.* who have not forfeited their lives) shall not be sold out of the land, V Atr. 2 = VI 9
    Of the practice of bringing an accusation against a guiltless man (*unsac*), V Atr. 32, 4

Insubordination '*oferhiernes*,' the fine for; IV Atr. 6; II Cn. 29, 1

Insult
    If a man in orders or a stranger is insulted, VIII Atr. 33
    If anyone deeply insults a man in holy orders, II Cn. 42.

INDEX 399

Iron. See Ordeal

Judge (nn. and vb.), judgment *'dema,' 'deman,' 'dom,' 'juger,' 'jugement'*
 The decision as to whether a delinquent's life shall be spared shall rest with the king, II Edm. 6
 Every man shall be awarded just decisions, III Edg. 1, 1
 Of a judge who gives a false judgment, III Edg. 3
 Of a verdict given by the thegns, III Atr. 13, 2
 He who judges another man shall consider what he himself desires, VI Atr. 10, 2; Leis Wl. 39
 Of careful discrimination in forming a judgment, VI Atr. 52; 53; II Cn. 68, 1 c
 The king's reeve shall pronounce just judgments, Cn. 1020, 11
 The same sentence shall be passed upon the reeve who permits the coining of false money as upon the coiner, II Cn. 8, 2
 Of the fine(s) payable by the man who refuses to observe just judgments, II Cn. 15, 2; Leis Wl. 42; 42, 2
 Of a man who is more severe in pronouncing judgment upon a friendless man than upon one of his friends, II Cn. 35, 1
 The case of a man in orders who has committed a capital crime shall be reserved for the bishop's decision, II Cn. 43
 The bishop shall pronounce the judgment in cases of adultery and of murder, II Cn. 53, 1; 56, 1
 Greater leniency shall be shown in passing judgment upon the weak than upon the strong, II Cn. 68, 1
 Spiritual teachers shall lead men to the judgment where God shall judge every man, II Cn. 84, 1 a
 No case concerning spiritual jurisdiction shall be brought forward for the judgment of laymen, Wl. ep. 2
 He who gives a false judgment shall forfeit his wergeld, Leis Wl. 13
 The sentence of death or mutilation shall not be carried out on a woman while she is pregnant, Leis Wl. 33
 A judgment cannot affect those not involved in the case, Leis Wl. 38
 Of the man who pronounces an unjust judgment as the result of rage or malice or bribery, Leis Wl. 39, 1

Jurisdiction
 No one shall have jurisdiction (*socn*) over a king's thegn except the king, III Atr. 11
 The heriot of a king's thegn who possesses rights of jurisdiction, among the Danes, II Cn. 71, 3
 A double fine shall be paid by a sheriff who does injury to the men in his jurisdiction, Leis Wl. 2, 1
 If an accusation is brought against a baron who possesses rights of jurisdiction, Leis Wl. 2, 3
 If theft is discovered in a district over which the lord has rights of jurisdiction, Leis Wl. 27, 1
 A man who promotes injustice shall lose his right of jurisdiction, Leis Wl. 39, 1
 Churches and barons etc. shall enjoy their rights of jurisdiction, Hn. Lond. 6

Justice. See *Riht*

Kin, kindred, kinsman *'cynn,' 'mægð,' 'mæg,' 'parent,' 'propinquarius'*
 Of the part played by the kindred on both sides in a case of homicide, II Edm. 1, 1–3; 7 f.
 A homicide shall be denied access to the king's household until he has set about making reparation to the kin, II Edm. 4
 If a kinsman refuses to ride against a man who has failed 3 times to attend the court meetings, III Edg. 7, 2 = II Cn. 25, 2 = Leis Wl. 47, 2
 Of a case in which the nearest relatives of the slain men shall take head for head, II Atr. 6
 Of the way in which the kinsmen of a dead thief may clear him, III Atr. 7, 1
 A Christian man shall not marry among his own kin within 6 degrees of relationship, VI Atr. 12 = I Cn. 7

Kin, *continued*
  Of the payment of compensation to the kin of a slain man (*mægbot*), VIII Atr. 3 = I Cn. 2, 5; II Cn. 39
  A man in holy orders who is charged with vendetta shall clear himself with the help of his kin, VIII Atr. 23 f. = I Cn. 5, 2 *b* and 2 *c*
  Of a monk who leaves the law of his kindred behind, VIII Atr. 25 (*mæglagu*) = I Cn. 5, 2 *d* (*mægðlagu*)
  The king shall act as the kinsman of a man in orders or a stranger, VIII Atr. 33 = II Cn. 40
  Of parricides (*mægslagan*), Cn. 1020, 15
  The property of a widow who remarries within a year shall pass to the nearest relatives (*þa nyxtan frynd*) of her first husband, II Cn. 73 *a*
  The relatives and orphans shall share the wergeld of a slain man after the *healsfang* has been paid, Leis Wl. 9
  The guardian of a dead man's land and children shall be the widow or some other relative, Hn. cor. 4, 1
King '*cyning*,' '*rei*'
  Conditions under which delinquents are forbidden to come anywhere near the king, I Edm. 3; V Atr. 29; VI 36
  Of incurring the hostility of the king, II Edm. 1, 3
  Of the king's *mund*, II Edm. 6; 7, 3; VIII Atr. 3; I Cn. 3, 2; II 42; of his protection (*grið, handgrið, borh*) III Atr. 1; VI 13; 14; 26; I Cn. 2, 1; II 58; of his peace, Leis Wl. 2; 2, 2 f.; 26
  Cases in which mitigation of the penalty involved rests with the king, I Edg. 3, 1; III 3 = II Cn. 15, 1 = Leis Wl. 39, 1; III Edg. 7, 3; III Atr. 16; VIII 1, 1 = I Cn. 2, 3; I Cn. 2, 2
  Of compensation and fines payable to the king, I Edg. 5, 1; II 4, 1 f.; III 3 = II Cn. 15, 1 = Leis Wl. 39, 1; III Edg. 7, 2 = II Cn. 25, 2; VI Atr. 34; VIII 2 = I Cn. 2, 4; VIII Atr. 10, 1 = I Cn. 9, 1; I Cn. 3, 2; II Cn. 12; 14; 15; 15, 2 = Leis Wl. 42, 1; II Cn. 33, 2; 37; 42; 44, 1; 63; 65; Wl. lad 2, 2; Leis Wl. 2, 4; 3, 1 ff.; 17, 3; 47, 2; 50; 52, 2; the king's fines which fall to the sheriff, Leis Wl. 2, 2 *a*
  Of forfeiture of property to the king, Cn. 1020, 17; II Cn. 13, 1
  Concerning appeals to the king, III Edg. 2; II Cn. 17 = Leis Wl. 43
  Every case of vouching to warranty and every ordeal shall take place in a royal manor (*cyninges burg*), III Atr. 6, 1
  The case of an action brought by the king, III Atr. 12
  If anyone deserts an army which is under the personal command of the king, V Atr. 28
  If anyone plots against the king, V Atr. 30 = VI 37 = II Cn. 57
  If anyone opposes the law of the king, V Atr. 31
  Complaint that the laws of the king have been disregarded since the days of Edgar, VIII Atr. 37
  The duty of a Christian king, VIII Atr. 2, 1 = 35 = II Cn. 40, 2
  Permission for the payment of compensation for homicide within a church granted by the king, VIII Atr. 3 = I Cn. 2, 5
  The relation of the king to a man in orders or a stranger, VIII Atr. 33; 34 = II Cn. 40
  Of the compensation assigned to Christ and the king, VIII Atr. 37; 38
  The term for extending protection to an excommunicated man is fixed by the king, VIII Atr. 42
  The king alone shall have the power to grant an outlaw security, II Cn. 13
  Of the king's court, Leis Wl. 2, 1; 17, 3; of that in which he is present in person, Leis Wl. 24
  Of the king's crown, Leis Wl. 2
  Of the king's reeves, II Edg. 3, 1 = VIII Atr. 8 = I Cn. 8, 2; III Atr. 1, 1; 7; II Cn. 33
  Of the king's thegns, III Atr. 11; II Cn. 71, 1; 71, 3 f.
  Of the heriot of an earl which falls to the king, Leis Wl. 20

Lad. See Exculpation; I Atr. 1, 9 = II Cn. 30, 8; I Atr. 1, 13 = II Cn. 31, 2; III Atr. 13; 13, 4; VIII 27, 1 = I Cn. 5, 4; Cn. 1020, 12; II Cn. 8, 2; 22, 1 *a*; 29; 42; 47, 1; 53, 1; 56, 1

Lagu 'law,' etc.
  Concerning the constitution (*laga*) determined upon by the Danes, IV Edg. 2, 1;
    12; 13, 1
  Æthelred's laws (*lage*, pl.?), I Atr. Heading
  The constitutions enacted by King Æthelred and his councillors at Wantage,
    III Atr. Pre.
  Cases in which the accused must pay 12 ores in order to obtain the benefit of
    the law (*bicgan him lage*), III Atr. 3, 3; 8, 2
  If a thegn has two alternatives before him—amicable agreement or legal
    proceedings (*lufe oðð̄e lage*), III Atr. 13, 3
  Justice (*lage, laga*) shall be promoted and injustice (*unlage, -laga*) suppressed,
    V Atr. 1, 1 = VI 8 = X 2 = II Cn. 1
  The laws of the church (*godcunde laga*), V Atr. 10 = VI 11 = I Cn. 6, 3; the law(s)
    of God, VI Atr. 12, 1 = I Cn. 7, 3; VI Atr. 42 = I Cn. 21; VI Atr. 50; VIII 30;
    43 f.; Cn. 1020, 9; II Cn. 84, 1; the laws of Christ, VIII Atr. 37
  Regulations applying to districts under English law (*on Engla lage*), VI Atr. 37;
    VIII 5, 1 = I Cn. 3, 2; II Cn. 15, 2; 62; 65
  Concerning a very just rule, VI Atr. 49
  The penalty to be paid for violation of the law(s) of men (of the king),
    VI Atr. 50; II Cn. 83
  Precepts and laws shall be upheld, X Atr. Pre., 2
  The law of Edgar, Cn. 1020, 13
  Cases which are provided for by the (established) law, II Cn. 15 a; 31 a; 75, 2
  The boroughs shall have one law with regard to exculpation, II Cn. 34
  The citizens of London shall be entitled to the rights (*laga*) which they had
    in the time of King Edward, Wl. Lond. 2
  Concerning Norman law, Wl. lad 1, 1
  Of the law of King Edward, Hn. cor. 9; 13
Lahcop 'the purchase of legal rights'; III Atr. 3
Lahslit; V Atr. 31; VI 51; II Cn. 15, 1 a = Leis Wl. 39, 2; II Cn. 15, 3 = Leis Wl.
    42, 2; II Cn. 45, 3; 46; 48; 49
Land
  Of a delinquent who shall be outlawed unless the king allow him to remain in
    the country, I Edg. 3, 1
  Those included in the truce shall enjoy protection on land or water, II Atr. 3
  Peace and goodwill shall be maintained within the land, V Atr. 1, 1 = VI 8, 2
  Christian men shall not be sold out of the land, V Atr. 2 = VI 9 = II Cn. 3
  Every injustice shall be cast out of the land, V Atr. 23 = VI 28, 1 = I Cn.
    19, 2
  Of things to be attended to throughout the country, V Atr. 26, 1
  Of the only way to obtain improvement in the condition of the country,
    V Atr. 33, 1 = VI 40, 1 = II Cn. 11, 1
  An appeal to the whole nation to defend the country, V Atr. 35
  Wizards etc. shall be driven from the land, VI Atr. 7 = II Cn. 4 a
  Of the purification of the land, VIII Atr. 40 = II Cn. 4; 7, 1
  A man who defies the law of God or the king shall be driven from the country
    or crushed, if he remains in the country, Cn. 1020, 10
  A man who violates the protection of the church or of the king shall lose both
    land and life, I Cn. 2, 2
  Every illegality shall be eradicated from the land, II Cn. 1
  Apostates and excommunicated men shall depart from the land, II Cn. 4, 1
  Foreigners, if they will not regularise their unions, shall be driven from the
    land, II Cn. 55
  If a widow remarries within a year, the relatives of her first husband shall
    take his land, II Cn. 73 a
  Concerning the man who deserts his lord on an expedition either by sea or by
    land, II Cn. 77
  Concerning the heriots of a man who falls during a campaign within the
    country or abroad, II Cn. 78
  Concerning the man who has performed the services demanded from a land-
    owner on expeditions either by sea or by land, II Cn. 79

R.   26

Land, *continued*
  The legal heriot of those who hold their land by the payment of rent, Leis Wl. 20, 4
  If a man wishes to prove that he has an agreement for his land, Leis Wl. 23
  If theft is discovered on anyone's land, Leis Wl. 27
Land; I Edg. 6, 1; III Atr. 10 (district); II Atr. 1, 2 (region); II Cn. 24 (open country)
Landcop 'purchase of land'; III Atr. 3
Landrican 'lord of the manor'; III Atr. 4, 2; I Cn. 8, 2
Lechefeo 'payment for medical attendance'; Leis Wl. 10
Leniency. See also Clemency, Mercy, Mitigation
  Mercy and leniency and forbearance shall be shown towards those who have need of them, VI Atr. 53
  Greater leniency shall be shown in passing judgment upon the weak, II Cn. 68, 1
Lestagium, Hn. Lond. 5
Liblac 'sorcery'; I Edm. 6
Life, live, etc.
  Of the duty of those in holy orders to teach God's people by the example of their life, I Edm. 1
  Of the power of the king over life and death, II Edm. 6; III Edg. 1, 3; III Atr. 16; VIII 1, 1; I Cn. 2, 2 and 3; II 59
  Of a delinquent who shall be seized alive or dead, III Edg. 7, 1 = II Cn. 25 a = Leis Wl. 47, 1
  Of a lord's power over the life of his *geneatman*, IV Edg. 1, 2
  Of incurring sudden death in this present life, IV Edg. 1, 4
  The servants of God shall live a pure life, IV Edg. 1, 7
  Of inheriting eternal life, IV Edg. 1, 8
  Of King Edgar's assurance of goodwill as long as his life lasts, IV Edg. 12; 16
  Of the circumstances in which an Englishman's life shall be spared, II Atr. 3, 3
  If a man vouches a living person to warranty, II Atr. 8, 1
  Of clearing a dead man as he himself would have been obliged to do had he been alive, II Atr. 9, 2 f.; II Cn. 72, 1
  If a man dwells on his property free from claims and charges during his life, III Atr. 14
  Of the souls bought by Christ with his own life, V Atr. 2 = VI 9 = II Cn. 3; Leis Wl. 41, 1
  Of living according to a rule, V Atr. 4 = VI 2 = VIII 31, 1 = I Cn. 6 a; of those who live according to a rule, VIII Atr. 19 f.; 20 f. = I Cn. 5 f.; 5, 1 f.; VIII Atr. 32; of a secular priest who does not live according to a rule, VIII Atr. 21 = I Cn. 5, 2
  The priest who observes celibacy shall enjoy the privileges of a thegn during his life, V Atr. 9, 1 = VI 5, 3 = VIII 28
  Cases involving forfeiture of life, V Atr. 30 = VI 37 = II Cn. 57; Cn. 1020, 11; II Cn. 26 f.; 61; 77; Leis Wl. 47, 3
  An appeal to all to defend their lives and their country, V Atr. 35
  Abbots and abbesses shall order their lives aright, VI Atr. 2
  A Christian man shall remain with one wife as long as she lives, VI Atr. 12, 1 = I Cn. 7, 3
  Of men who are guilty of forsaking their wives and taking others while these are still alive, VI Atr. 5, 2
  If a priest misdirects his life, VIII Atr. 29
  Men of every estate shall live such a life as befits them, VIII Atr. 31
  If an attempt is made to deprive a man in orders or a stranger of his life, VIII Atr. 33 = II Cn. 40
  Of those who rendered tribute to God as long as they lived, VIII Atr. 43
  Hostility from Denmark no longer to be feared during King Canute's life, Cn. 1020, 5
  God who liveth and reigneth for ever, Cn. 1020, 20
  Concerning the reward for what we have done in our lifetime, I Cn. 18 b
  Concerning the things of which a man has need, both for this life and for the life to come, I Cn. 22, 3

Life, *continued*
 Of the purchase of anything over 4 pence in value, either livestock or other property (*libbende oððe licgende, mort u vif*), II Cn. 24 = Leis Wl. 45
 If a man departs from this life intestate, II Cn. 70
 The heirs of a householder shall answer a charge brought against him as he himself would have done had he been alive, II Cn. 72, 1
 An evildoer shall have protection for his life, if he makes his way to a church, Leis Wl. 1
 The attachment of livestock (*vif aveir*), Leis Wl. 21
 If a man does not know whether his warrantor or his pledge is alive or dead, Leis Wl. 21, 1 *a*
Light dues '*leohtgescot*'
 Light dues shall be paid 3 times in the year, V Atr. 11, 1 = VI 19 = I Cn. 12; at Candlemas, VIII Atr. 12, 1
Lord '*hlaford*,' '*seignur*.' See also *Dryhten*
 Of the proportion of a thief's property which shall be given to his lord, I Edg. 2, 1 = III 7, 1 = II Cn. 25, 1 = Leis Wl. 47, 1
 Of a man prevented from attending a court-meeting by a summons from his lord, I Edg. 7, 1
 Of the man discovered in treason against his lord, III Edg. 7, 3 = II Cn. 26; II Cn. 64
 If any tenant neglects the payment due to his lord, IV Edg. 1, 1 f.
 Of the part taken by a lord in clearing one of his men, I Atr. 1, 2 = III 4 = II Cn. 30, 1
 Of the payment of a delinquent's wergeld to his lord, I Atr. 1, 5 = II Cn. 30, 3 *b*; I Atr. 1, 7
 If the lord is accused of advising the delinquent to escape, I Atr. 1, 8 = II Cn. 30, 7
 Every lord shall be responsible as surety for the men of his household, I Atr. 1, 10 = II Cn. 31; for his servant, Leis Wl. 52
 If a man is accused and escapes, his lord shall pay his wergeld to the king, I Atr. 1, 11 = II Cn. 31, 1 = Leis Wl. 52, 1
 If the lord is accused of advising him to escape, I Atr. 1, 12 = II Cn. 31, 1 *a* = Leis Wl. 52, 2
 If he fails to clear himself, he shall pay his own wergeld to the king, I Atr. 1, 13 = II Cn. 31, 2
 Concerning gifts by a lord of what he has a legal right to bestow, III Atr. 3; II Cn. 81
 An accused man shall pay 20 ores to the lord of the manor who shall make him go to the ordeal, III Atr. 4, 1 f.
 References to 'our lord,' *i.e.* the king, V Atr. 1, 1–5; 32; 32, 5
 Every lord shall give a penny for each member of his household who has nothing himself, VII Atr. (A.S.) 5
 Of Canute's promise to be a gracious lord, Cn. 1020, 2
 Of the reward of men who are faithful to their lord, I Cn. 20 f.
 Of the duty of every lord towards his men, I Cn. 20, 2
 Of witnesses who desire to obtain the favour of their lord, II Cn. 23, 1
 If anyone insults a man in holy orders, he shall pay to his lord the full fine for breach of his *mund*, II Cn. 42
 A lord who compels his slave to work during a festival shall pay *lahslit* or a fine, II Cn. 45, 3
 Of plotting against a lord, II Cn. 57
 If a man dies intestate, his lord shall take no more than his legal heriot, II Cn. 70
 Concerning the man who deserts his lord, II Cn. 77
 Concerning the man who falls before his lord, II Cn. 78
 10 ores shall be paid to the lord of the manor to which an accused man belongs, Leis Wl. 2, 4
 Concerning the payment of *manbot* to the lord of a slain man, Leis Wl. 7
 The man who assaults another man's wife shall forfeit his wergeld to his lord, Leis. Wl. 12

404　INDEX

Lord, *continued*
>Concerning the payment of a penny on the part of a lord which shall free his labourers etc. from Peter's Pence, Leis Wl. 17 *a*; 17, 1
>The heriot of a *vavassur* to his liege lord, Leis Wl. 20, 2 f.
>The heriot of a villein, Leis Wl. 20, 3
>A man who can produce neither warrantor nor witness with regard to livestock in his possession shall forfeit his wergeld to his lord, Leis Wl. 21, 2
>If a man wishes to prove against his lord that he has an agreement for his land, Leis Wl. 23
>The lord of an estate on which theft is discovered shall have half the thief's goods, or all of them, if he has rights of jurisdiction, Leis Wl. 27 f.
>No-one shall withdraw his legal service from his lord, Leis Wl. 32

Lorica, used of tenure by military service; Hn. cor. 11

Loyal, loyalty, etc.
>Concerning the oath of fidelity to King Edmund, III Edm. 1
>Appeal to all men loyally to support one royal lord, v Atr. 35 = VI 1 = VIII 44, 1 = IX Expl.
>King Canute shall be loved with due fidelity, I Cn. 1
>All men shall be faithful and true to their lord (the king), I Cn. 20 f.
>Greetings from the king to his loyal subjects, Wl. ep. Pre.; Hn. cor. Pre.; Hn. Lond. Pre.
>All freemen shall affirm by oath that they will be loyal to King William, Wl. art. 2 = Wl. art. retr. 2

Mægbot; VIII Atr. 3 = I Cn. 2, 5. See Kin

Mæglage, mægðlage; VIII Atr. 25; I Cn. 5, 2 *d*

Mæð 'rank,' 'status'; of churches, VIII Atr. 4, 1 = I Cn. 3 *a*; VIII Atr. 5 = I Cn. 3, 1; of members of the clergy, VIII Atr. 18; I Cn. 4; 4, 3; II Cn. 42; 49; *be mæðe* = in proportion, VI Atr. 10, 1; 53 = VIII 5, 2; VIII 27, 1 = I Cn. 5, 4; II Cn. 51; 70, 1

Magician; VI Atr. 7

Maiden
>If anyone does violence to a maiden, II Cn. 52, 1
>No maiden shall ever be forced to marry a man whom she dislikes, II Cn. 74

Manbot 'compensation for a slain dependent'
>No *manbot* shall be remitted, II Edm. 3
>Of the time allowed for the payment of *manbot*, II Edm. 7, 3
>Of the payment of *manbot* in the case of a man slain in a church, VIII Atr. 3 = I Cn. 2, 5
>Of the amount to be paid as *manbot*, Leis Wl. 7

Mancus; II Cn. 71 *a*; 71, 1; 71, 4

Mark; Wl. art. 3, 1; Leis Wl. 17 *b*; 17, 1; 22

Market
>Concerning the toll on hens and eggs when they come to the market, IV Atr. 2, 11
>A list of places where markets shall be held, Wl. art. retr. 11
>If a man has witnesses (to prove) that he bought certain livestock in the public market (*al marché le rei*), Leis Wl. 21, 1 *a*

Martinmas
>Every church due shall be rendered by Martinmas, II Edg. 3 = VI Atr. 18, 1 = VIII 11 = I Cn. 10

Mass
>Every priest shall say mass for the king and his people, VII Atr. (A.S.) 6, 1
>One mass shall be said daily in every religious foundation (during a period of great distress), VII Atr. (A.S.) 6, 2
>A priest who lives according to a rule shall say mass to clear himself of a charge, VIII Atr. 19 = I Cn. 5

Mass-priest. See Priest

Measure(ment) '*gemet*'
>There shall be one system of measurement throughout the country, III Edg. 8, 1

Measure(ment), *continued*
    False measures shall be done away with, v Atr. 24 = vi 28, 2
    Measures shall be corrected, vi Atr. 32, 2 = ii Cn. 9
Mercy. See also Clemency, Leniency, Mitigation
    Of mercy in the decision of cases, Cor. Oath 1, 3
    Of the establishment of merciful punishments, v Atr. 3 = vi 10 = ii Cn. 2, 1
    Of the mercy which shall be shown to those who have need of it, vi Atr. 53
    Of obtaining the mercy of God, vii Atr. (A.S.) Pre.; Cn. 1020, 20
    Thankfulness for the mercy of God, Cn. 1020, 6 f.
    Of the mercy to be shown to anyone who desires to turn from lawlessness, ii Cn. 67
Miskenning; Hn. Lond. 8
Mitigation
    Of mitigation of the law to be obtained from the king, iii Edg. 2, 1
    Of the infliction of mitigated penalties, Cn. 1020, 11
    Of mitigation for the protection of the general public, ii Cn. 69
Monastery. See *Mynster*
Monetagium 'mint-tax'; Hn. cor. 5
Money, moneyers '*mynet*,' '*mynetere*,' '*moneta*,' '*monetarius*.' See also *Feoh*
    One coinage shall be current throughout the country, iii Edg. 8 = vi Atr. 32,1 = ii Cn. 8
    Every moneyer who is accused of striking false coins shall go to the triple ordeal, iii Atr. 8
    No-one except the king shall have a moneyer, iii Atr. 8, 1
    Every moneyer who is accused shall pay 12 ores in order to obtain the benefit of the law, iii Atr. 8, 2
    Moneyers who work in secret places shall forfeit their lives, iii Atr. 16 = iv 5, 4
    Coiners (*falsarii*) and those who bribe them to falsify good money shall incur the same punishment, iv Atr. 5 f.
    Coiners shall lose a hand, iv Atr. 5, 3
    No-one shall refuse pure money wherever it has been coined, iv Atr. 6
    Of coiners who circulate bad money, iv Atr. 7 ff.
    Town-reeves who have been the accessories of coiners shall incur the same punishment, iv Atr. 7, 3
    A watch shall be kept for those who coin base money, iv Atr. 8
    Moneyers shall be fewer in number, iv Atr. 9
    Of the production of pure money of the proper weight, iv Atr. 9, 1
    Every weight shall be stamped according to the standard employed in the king's mint, iv Atr. 9, 2
    If a moneyer or any other person has been seized with false money, Hn. cor. 5, 1
    The decree of Henry I concerning the coinage, Hn. mon.
    No falsification of money shall be countenanced by those who dwell in boroughs, Hn. mon. 1
    If anyone has been discovered with false money, Hn. mon. 2
    No moneyer shall recast money except in his own county, Hn. mon. 3 f.
    No one shall venture to change money except a moneyer, Hn. mon. 4
Monk
    Monks shall submit to their duty and live according to their rule, v Atr. 4 = vi 2 = viii 31, 1 = i Cn. 6 *a*
    Concerning monks who are out of a monastery, v Atr. 5 = vi 3
    Concerning monks who have no monastery, v Atr. 6 = vi 3, 1
    Concerning the celebration of special masses in every college of monks, vii Atr. 3, 2
    If a monk becomes an utter apostate, viii Atr. 41
Month
    A man who commits homicide shall pay compensation within twelve months, ii Edm. 1
    If his surety can lay hold of a thief within twelve months, iii Edg. 6, 2
    Every widow shall remain without a husband for twelve months, v Atr. 21, 1 = vi 26, 1 = ii Cn. 73

406   INDEX

Month, *continued*
  Every widow shall pay her heriots within twelve months, II Cn. 73, 4
  His surety shall have respite for a month and a day to seek a man who has committed larceny or robbery, Leis Wl. 3
  No one shall claim ownership of livestock in less than six months from the time that it was stolen, Leis Wl. 46
Morning-gift
  A widow who remarries within a year shall lose her morning-gift, II Cn. 73 a
Mund, mundbora, mundbryce
  If the kindred of a man who has committed homicide give him neither food nor shelter (*mund*), II Edm. 1, 1
  Violation of the king's *mund*, II Edm. 6
  Of the establishment of the king's *mund*, II Edm. 7, 3
  The fine for breach of the king's *mund*, VI Atr. 34; VIII 3 = I Cn. 2, 5; VIII Atr. 5, 1 = I Cn. 3, 2; II Cn. 12; 42
  Compensation for breach of a lord's *mund*, Leis Wl. 18, 1
  The king shall act as the protector of a man in orders or a stranger, if he has no other, VIII Atr. 33 = II Cn. 40
Murder '*morð*,' '*morðweorc*'
  Murders shall be put an end to, V Atr. 25 = VI 28, 2; Cn. 1020, 15
  Those who secretly compass death (*morðwyrhtan*) shall be driven from the land, VI Atr. 7 = II Cn. 4 a
  Concerning the conditions under which those who secretly compass death shall be allowed near the king, VI Atr. 36
  The secret compassing of death (*morðweorc*) forbidden, II Cn. 5, 1
  If anyone dies by violence and it becomes evident that it is a case of murder, II Cn. 56
  Murder which cannot be denied is one of the crimes which are *botleas*, II Cn. 64
  If a Frenchman summon an Englishman for murder, or an Englishman a Frenchman, Wl. art. 6
Murdre 'the murder-fine for the death of a Frenchman'; Leis Wl. 22; Hn. cor. 9; Hn. Lond. 2, 1
Mutilation. See Ear, Eye, etc.
Mynster
  i. Monastery, V Atr. 5 f. = VI 3 f.; VIII 32; *mynstermunuc*, a monk belonging to a monastery, VIII Atr. 25 = I Cn. 5, 2 d
  ii. Church, II Edg. 1, 1; 2, 2 = I Cn. 11, 2; II Edg. 3, 1 = VIII Atr. 8 = I Cn. 8, 2; V Atr. 12, 1 = VI 21 = I Cn. 13, 1; *heafodmynster*, principal church, VIII Atr. 5, 1 = I Cn. 3, 2; *medemra mynster*, church of medium rank, *ibid.*; *mynsterclænsung*, purification of a church, VIII Atr. 3 = I Cn. 2, 5
  iii. Religious foundation, V Atr. 7 = VI 4; VII Atr. (A.S.) 6; 6, 2

Nail. Compensation for injuries to, Leis Wl. 11, 2
Nam 'distraint'; II Cn. 19 = Leis Wl. 44; 44, 2; Hn. Lond. 14
Neighbour
  A man who makes a purchase shall inform his neighbours either before or after, IV Edg. 7; 8, 1; 10
Nied, neod 'need,' 'necessity,' etc.
  If the need is urgent in the case of pursuing a thief, I Edg. 2
  The duties of military service etc. shall be attended to when the need arises (for the common need), V Atr. 26, 1 = VI 32, 3 = II Cn. 10
  Concerning the need for frequent exhortation, VI Atr. 42
  Payments for the needs of religion shall take the place of payments to the secular authorities, VI Atr. 51
  In every religious foundation a mass shall be said daily because of the pressing need of the time, VII Atr. (A.S.) 6, 2
  Of Canute's assurance that the Danes are ready to help the English if they have need of it, Cn. 1020, 6
  Concerning the duty of priests to make intercession for the needs of the people, I Cn. 4, 3

Nied, continued
  Everyone who recites the Pater Noster makes supplication to God for everything of which a man has need, I Cn. 22, 3
  A man is entitled to clemency when he acted as he did from compulsion (*for neode*), II Cn. 68, 2
Niedan 'to compel'
  If a lord compels his slave to work during a church festival, II Cn. 45, 3
  No woman or maiden shall be forced to marry a man whom she dislikes, II Cn. 74
Niedgafol; IV Edg. 1
Niedmage 'a blood relation'; VI Atr. 12 = I Cn. 7
Niednæman; VI Atr. 39; II Cn. 52 f.; 73, 2. See Adultery.
Niedpearf 'special necessity'; I Cn. 15
Niedwyrhta 'an involuntary agent'; VI Atr. 52, 1 = II Cn. 68, 2
Niht
  Healsfang shall be paid 21 days after the establishment of the king's *mund*, 21 days after that *manbot*, and 21 days after that the first instalment of the wergeld, II Edm. 7, 3
  Plough alms shall be rendered 15 days after Easter, II Edg. 2, 3 = V Atr. 11, 1 = VI 16 = VIII 12 = I Cn. 8, 1
  A man who has made a purchase of livestock shall inform his neighbours about it within 5 days, IV Edg. 8, 1 f.
  A man shall keep the hide and the head of a cow which he has killed for 3 days, III Atr. 9
  Trial by ordeal and the rendering of oaths are forbidden (from the Advent till a fortnight after Christmas and) from the Septuagesima till a fortnight (15 days) after Easter, V Atr. 18 = VI 25 = I Cn. 17
  No-one shall entertain a man for more than 3 days, II Cn. 28 = Leis Wl. 48
  A man who has slain a minister of the altar shall begin to make amends within 30 days, II Cn. 39, 1
  If a minister of the altar has committed homicide he shall begin to make amends within 30 days, II Cn. 41, 2
Nihtes 'by night'; VI Atr. 41; I Cn. 6 *a*; 25
Noble '*twelfhynde,*' '*nobilis.*' See also under Earl
  Nobles and commoners, III Edm. 2; Cn. 1020, 1; Cn. 1027, Heading; 12
Nose
  A man who has committed a grave crime shall have his nose cut off, II Cn. 30, 5
  A married woman who commits adultery shall lose her nose, II Cn. 53
Nun '*nunne,*' '*myncenu*'
  He who has intercourse with a nun, I Edm. 4
  Monks and nuns (*minicena*), priests (canons) and women under religious vows (*nunnan*) shall submit to their duty, V Atr. 4 = VI 2 = I Cn. 6 *a*
  A Christian man must never marry a professed nun, VI Atr. 12, 1 = I Cn. 7, 1
  If anyone injures a nun, VI Atr. 39
  No one shall marry a professed nun or a woman who has taken religious vows, Cn. 1020, 16

Oath
  Of declarations on oath made by those who have given a false judgment, III Edg. 3; II Cn. 15, 1
  Each of the men chosen as witnesses shall take an oath, IV Edg. 6, 1
  Of the oath sworn by a lord in support of the assertion that an accused man has failed neither in oath nor in ordeal, I Atr. 1, 2 ff. = II Cn. 30, 1 ff.
  The rendering of oaths is forbidden at certain seasons, V Atr. 18 = VI 25 = I Cn. 17
  Every Christian man shall abide by his oath, V Atr. 22, 2 = VI 28 = I Cn. 19, 1
  If a man is accused of plotting against the king he shall clear himself by means of the most solemn oath, VI Atr. 37
  If an accusation is brought against a member of the priesthood and he has no-one to support his oath, VIII Atr. 22 = I Cn. 5, 2 *a*
  If a priest be concerned in perjury (*mæne að*), VIII Atr. 27 = I Cn. 5, 3

408 INDEX

Oath, *continued*
    Concerning the amends which must be made to God for the violation of oaths, Cn. 1020, 14
    Everyone over 12 years of age shall take an oath that he will not be a thief, II Cn. 21
    Every trustworthy man who has never failed either in oath or in ordeal shall be entitled to clear himself by the simple oath of exculpation, II Cn. 22
    Of the choice of compurgators for an untrustworthy man in cases involving a simple or a triple oath, II Cn. 22, 1
    Concerning oaths of accusation, either simple or triple, II Cn. 22, 1 *a*–22, 3
    If anyone lets a thief escape without raising the hue and cry, he shall clear himself with the full oath, II Cn. 29 f.
    If anyone swears a false oath on the relics and is convicted, II Cn. 36 f.
    Of the circumstances in which a Frenchman may clear himself with an oath supported by compurgators, Wl. lad 1, 1
    Of the case in which a Frenchman may defend himself by a comprehensive oath (*mid unforedan aðe*), Wl. lad 3, 2 = Wl. art. 6, 3 (*sacramento non fracto*)
    A freeman who is entitled to the benefit of the law shall clear himself by the simple oath of exculpation, Leis Wl. 14
    Those who have been previously accused shall clear themselves by the oath with selected compurgators (*par serment numé*), Leis Wl. 14, 1
    A man who is accused of breaking into a church or a treasury shall clear himself by the triple oath, Leis Wl. 15; 15, 2
    A man who does not know whether his warrantor is alive or dead shall swear to this with a simple oath, Leis Wl. 21, 1 *a*
    When once a man's oath has been accepted it cannot be invalidated, Leis Wl. 21, 5

Oferhiernes. See Insubordination

Ordeal '*ordal*,' '*isen*,' '*juise*,' '*jugement*,' '*judicium*'
    The iron for the triple ordeal shall weigh 3 pounds, I Edg. 9
    A man of bad reputation shall go to the triple ordeal, I Atr. 1, 1
    Of a man whose lord asserts that he has failed neither in oath nor in ordeal, I Atr. 1, 2 = III 4 = II Cn. 30, 1
    If the lord's oath is supported, the accused shall choose either the simple ordeal or an oath, I Atr. 1, 3 = II Cn. 30, 2
    If the oath is not supported, the accused shall go to the triple ordeal, I Atr. 1, 4 = II Cn. 30, 3
    If the man evades the ordeal, I Atr. 1, 7 = III 4 = II Cn. 30, 6
    If the owner of the goods fails to appear at the ordeal, III Atr. 4, 2
    Every accuser shall have the choice of whichever ordeal he desires for the accused—either ordeal by water or by fire, III Atr. 6
    If the accused flees from the ordeal, III Atr. 6, 2
    If a man engaged in circulating false coin is accused, he shall clear himself by the full ordeal, IV Atr. 5, 2
    Town-reeves who have been accessories to the circulation of false money shall clear themselves by the same ordeal, IV Atr. 7, 3
    Trial by ordeal is forbidden at certain seasons, V Atr. 18 = VI 25 = I Cn. 17
    Of trustworthy men who have never failed either in oath or in ordeal, II Cn. 22
    In the case of untrustworthy men, compurgators shall be selected or they shall go to the ordeal, II Cn. 22, 1
    Of the mode of opening a case which involves the triple ordeal, II Cn. 30, 3 *a*
    If a friendless man or a stranger is accused, he shall go to prison and wait there until he goes to the ordeal, II Cn. 35
    If anyone plots against the king, he may prove himself innocent at the triple ordeal, II Cn. 57
    An Englishman may defend himself by the ordeal of iron, Wl. lad 2 = Wl. art. 6; Wl. lad 2, 3
    In all charges involving outlawry an Englishman shall clear himself by the ordeal of iron, Wl. lad 3
    No layman shall make a man undergo trial by ordeal without the authority of the bishop, Wl. ep. 4, 1

Ordeal, *continued*
    Trial by ordeal shall not take place anywhere except as appointed by the bishop, Wl. ep. 4, 2
    If an Englishman declines to prove a charge against a Frenchman by ordeal, Wl. art. 6, 3
    A man who has been previously accused and who cannot find compurgators shall clear himself by the ordeal, Leis Wl. 14, 2
    A man who is accused of breaking into a church or a treasury and who cannot find compurgators shall go to the triple ordeal, Leis Wl. 15, 2
    If he has previously paid compensation for theft, he shall go to the water ordeal, Leis Wl. 15, 3
    If a man who has been discovered with false money has not vouched a warrantor for it, he shall go to the ordeal, Hn. mon. 2, 2
Ores; III Atr. 1, 2; 3, 3; 4, 1 f.; 5; IV 9, 2; Leis Wl. 2, 3 and 4
Orf 'livestock,' 'cattle': IV Edg. 8; 8, 1; 9 ff.; 13; 14; I Atr. 3, 1; II 7; III 5
Ostensio; IV Atr. 2, 7
Outlaw, outlawry '*fliema*,' '*utlah*,' '*utlaga*'
    He who ignores the authority of the hundred four times shall be in danger of being outlawed, I Edg. 3, 1
    Of a thief who shall be treated as an outlaw by the whole nation, I Atr. 1, 9 *a* and 13 = II Cn. 30, 9; 31, 2 = Leis Wl. 52, 2
    If the Vikings slay 8 Englishmen, they shall be treated as outlaws, II Atr. 7, 1
    Everyone who is an outlaw in one district shall be an outlaw everywhere, III Atr. 10
    If anyone does the deed of an outlaw, II Cn. 13
    If anyone feeds or harbours the fugitive, II Cn. 13, 2
    If anyone maintains or harbours an outlawed man, II Cn. 15 *a*; 66, 1
    If anyone slays a minister of the altar, he shall be outlawed, II Cn. 39
    Unless a minister of the altar who has committed a grave crime begins to make amends within 30 days, he shall be outlawed, II Cn. 41, 2
    If anyone who resists the payment of church dues kills a man, he shall be outlawed, II Cn. 48, 2
    In all charges involving outlawry an Englishman shall clear himself by the ordeal of iron, Wl. lad 3
    If an Englishman brings a charge involving outlawry against a Frenchman, Wl. lad 3, 1
    Godes utlaga, VIII Atr. 42; II Cn. 4, 1; *utlah (-laga) wið God*, Cn. 1020, 17; II Cn. 39; *Godes fliema*, II Cn. 66. See Excommunication
Ox; Leis Wl 5; 20, 3

Palfrey; Leis Wl. 20; 20, 1
Passagium; Hn. Lond. 5
Pax, pais 'peace,' 'protection'
    Every man shall act as surety for all those who are under his protection, III Edm. 7
    All the men who came with Wm I or have followed him to England shall enjoy the benefit of his peace and protection (*pax et quies*), Wl. art. 3
    The protection of holy church shall be inviolable, Leis Wl. 1
    Of the man who violates the king's peace, Leis Wl. 2; 2, 2; 26
    Lasting peace (*pax firma*) established by Henry I, Hn. cor. 12
    The fact of being under any special peace or protection of the king's shall not exempt anyone from attending the court meetings, Hn. com. 4
Penny
    Peter's Pence (*Romfeoh*), I Edm. 2; V Atr. 11, 1 = VI 18 = VIII 10 = I Cn. 9; Cn. 1027, 16; Leis Wl. 17–17, 2
    30 pence shall be paid to the hundred as a fine for neglect of its authority, I Edg. 3
    Every hearth-penny shall be paid by St Peter's Day, II Edg. 4
    He who has failed to make payment by the appointed time shall (take it to Rome and) pay 30 pence in addition, II Edg. 4, 1 f.; VIII Atr. 10, 1 = I Cn. 9, 1; Leis Wl. 17, 2 f.

Penny, *continued*
   Of the clearance from a charge of theft in the case of an object over 30 pence in value, I Atr. 1, 3 = II Cn. 30, 2
   From every plough-land (hide) a penny or the value of a penny shall be given as dues, VII Atr. 1, 2 = VIII (A.S.) 2, 2
   Every member of a household shall give a penny, or his lord shall give it for him, VII Atr. 1, 3 = VIII (A.S.) 5
   A poor freeman who breaks the prescribed fast shall pay 30 pence, VII Atr. 2, 4
   Every householder who does not give his penny shall pay 30 pence, VII Atr. (A.S.) 3
   Every penny shall be distributed for love of God, VII Atr. (A.S.) 4
   No one shall buy anything over 4 pence in value unless he have witnesses, II Cn. 24
   A man who acts as surety for a thief who escapes shall pay 4 pence to the jailer and a farthing for the spade, Leis Wl. 3, 1
   A man shall pay 8 pence, as a maximum sum, in return for the care taken of strayed livestock, Leis Wl. 5 f.
   Of fines of 8 pence and 4 pence for wounds, Leis Wl. 10; 11, 2
   Of the English reckoning of 4 pence to the shilling, Leis Wl. 11, 1
   The fine for breach of a sokeman's protection is 40 pence, Leis Wl. 16
   He who possesses livestock of the value of 30 pence shall pay Peter's Pence, Leis Wl. 17
   The payment of 1 penny on the part of a lord shall free his labourers, etc., Leis Wl. 17 *a*; 17, 1
Perjury, perjurers
   Those who commit perjury shall be cast out for ever from the fellowship of God, I Edm. 6
   Horrible perjuries shall be got rid of, V Atr. 25 = VI 28, 2
   Perjurers shall be zealously driven from the land, VI Atr. 7
   Perjurers who remain anywhere near the king shall be in danger of losing their possessions, VI Atr. 36
   If a priest be concerned in perjury, VIII Atr. 27 = I Cn. 5, 3
   The deeds of perjurers should be got rid of, Cn. 1020, 15
   Perjurers shall submit and make amends, II Cn. 6
   Concerning perjury, II Cn. 36
Pig
   If anyone has taken pigs into his care, Leis Wl. 5 f.
Pledge '*wedd*,' '*weddian*,' '*gwage*.' See also under Frankpledge, Surety
   The slayer shall pledge himself to pay the wergeld of the slain man, II Edm. 7, 1
   Of the solemn declaration (*wedd*) of the councillors at Wihtbordestan, IV Edg. 1, 4 f.
   Of the pledge laid upon Christ's altar by the king, Cor. Oath Pre.
   Of the sums paid as security (*wedd*) by a man of bad reputation, III Atr. 3, 2; by a man who seeks to clear a thief, III Atr. 7; in an action brought by the king, an earl, a bishop or a thegn, III Atr. 12
   Confirmation by word and by pledge, V Atr. 1
   Of the vows (*word* 7 *wed*) rendered by a monk to God, V Atr. 5 = VI 3
   Every Christian man shall abide by his oath and his pledge, V Atr. 22, 2 = VI 28 = I Cn. 19, 1
   Of the amends which must be made to God for the violation of pledges, Cn. 1020, 14
   A man who claims strayed livestock shall give pledge and find surety (*gwage e plege*), Leis Wl. 5, 2; 6, 1
   If anyone desires to claim livestock as stolen and is willing to give pledge and find surety for prosecuting his claim, Leis Wl. 21 f.; 21, 3
Plough
   Payment of church tithes shall be made from all land under the plough, II Edg. 1, 1 = VIII Atr. 7 = I Cn. 8, 2
   From every plough-land (*carruca*) a penny or the value of a penny shall be given, VII Atr. 1, 2
   Plough-alms, I Edm. 2; II Edg. 2, 3 = V Atr. 11, 1 = VI 16 = VIII 12 = I Cn. 8, 1

INDEX

Poor
  In the phrase 'rich and poor' (*earm 7 eadig*), III Edg. 1, 1; IV 1, 4; 2; 2, 2; 15, 1; VI Atr. 8, 1 = II Cn. 1, 1; Cn. 1020, 19
  The poor of God (*Godes þearfan*), VI Atr. 46; VIII 6
  Concerning the maintenance of the indigent, VI Atr. 51
  Concerning the fine payable by a poor freeman (*liber pauper*) for breach of the prescribed fast, VII Atr. 2, 4
  Concerning the distribution of food among the needy, VII Atr. (A.S.) 4, 1

Pope
  A priest who commits homicide shall travel as a pilgrim as far as the Pope appoints for him, VIII Atr. 26 = II Cn. 41
  Concerning the injunctions brought by Archbishop Lyfing from the Pope, Cn. 1020, 3

Pound
  A fine of half a pound shall be paid for ignoring the authority of the hundred three times, I Edg. 3, 1
  Of an oath equivalent to a pound in value, I Atr. 1, 3 = II Cn. 30, 2
  25 pounds shall be paid for a Dane or an Englishman who is slain, and 1 pound for a slave, II Atr. 5 f.
  Of the payment of 22,000 pounds in gold and silver to the Viking fleet, II Atr. 7, 2
  Of the payment of fines for breach of protection, viz. 5 pounds to the king, VIII Atr. 5, 1; I Cn. 3, 2; II Cn. 13, 2; 58; 62; 3 pounds to an archbishop or a member of the royal family, II Cn. 58, 1; 2 pounds to a bishop or an ealdorman, II Cn. 58, 2
  Heriots of 2 pounds, II Cn. 71, 2 and 5; 4 pounds, 71, 3
  Of the payment of 3 pounds to the king by a Frenchman who has been defeated in the trial by combat, Wl. lad 2, 2
  Of the payment of 144 pounds in the Danelaw for violation of the king's peace, Leis Wl. 2, 2
  Of the payment of fines of 4 and 7 pounds to the king for a thief who has escaped, Leis Wl. 3, 2 f.
  The wergeld of a thegn—20 pounds in Mercia, 25 pounds in Wessex, Leis Wl. 8
  Of the payment of 6 pounds to the king for refusing to observe just law and just judgment, Leis Wl. 42, 1
  Of the payment of 300 pounds to the king for the lease of Middlesex, Hn. Lond. 1
  The iron for the triple ordeal shall weigh 3 pounds, I Edg. 9

Priest. See also Ecclesiastics
  Of the payments made by a thegn to his priest, II Edg. 2, 1
  Of the action taken by the mass-priest of a church when anyone refuses to pay tithes, II Edg. 3, 1 = VIII Atr. 8 = I Cn. 8, 2
  Of the enforcement of their duties upon priests, IV Edg. 1, 8
  Priests shall submit to their duty, V Atr. 4
  Priests admonished to guard against incurring the wrath of God, V Atr. 8; 9 ff. = VI 5–5, 4 = I Cn. 6, 1 ff.
  Every priest shall say mass for the king and his people on the three days prescribed for fasting and prayer, VII Atr. (A.S.) 6, 1
  The status of the priesthood shall be respected, VIII Atr. 18
  If an accusation is brought against a priest who lives according to a rule, VIII Atr. 19 f. = I Cn. 5 f.
  If an accusation is brought against a secular priest, VIII Atr. 21 = I Cn. 5, 2
  If an accusation is brought against a member of the priesthood who has no friends, VIII Atr. 22 = I Cn. 5, 2 *a*
  If a priest commits homicide, VIII Atr. 26
  If a priest is concerned in false witness or perjury, VIII Atr. 27 = I Cn. 5, 3
  If a member of the priesthood orders his life aright, VIII Atr. 28
  If a priest becomes an utter apostate, VIII Atr. 41
  Of the celebration of the saints-days enjoined by the priests, Cn. 1020, 19
  Wonderful are the things which a priest is able to do, I Cn. 4, 1 ff.

Priest, *continued*
  Concerning the duty of the priests to provide for the safety of the divine flock, I Cn. 26, 3
  If anyone slays a priest, II Cn. 39 f.
  If a priest (a minister of the altar) commits homicide, II Cn. 41 f.
Prison
  A friendless man or a stranger who cannot produce a surety shall go to prison if he is accused, II Cn. 35
Protection. See *Frið, Grið, Mund*

Rædbana
  If a man in holy orders is charged with having instigated homicide, VIII Atr. 23 = I Cn. 5, 2 b
Rank. See *Had, Mæð*
Reeve *'gerefa,' 'praepositus,' 'provost'*
  No one shall make a purchase unless he have the high reeve (*summus praepositus*) as witness, III Edm. 5
  The king's reeve (or the reeve of the lord of the manor) and the bishop's reeve shall act together in exacting tithes from a man who has refused to render them, II Edg. 3, 1 = VIII Atr. 8 = I Cn. 8, 2
  The king's injunction to his reeves to carry out the regulations of his ordinance, IV Edg. 1, 5
  If any of the king's reeves offers any indignity either to the villagers or their herdsmen, IV Edg. 13, 1
  A lord may delegate to his reeve the duty of supporting one of his men who has been accused, I Atr. 1, 2 = II Cn. 30, 1
  No one who holds land by title-deed shall pay compensation unless in the presence of the king's reeve, I Atr. 1, 14
  The king's reeve shall place under surety a man who is regarded with suspicion, I Atr. 4 = II Cn. 33
  Concerning breach of the peace which the king's reeve establishes in the court of the Five Boroughs, III Atr. 1, 1
  Concerning the arrest of men of bad repute against whom the reeve is taking proceedings, III Atr. 3, 2
  If anyone seeks to clear a thief, he shall deposit 50 of silver with the king's town-reeve, III Atr. 7
  Of 12 compurgators nominated by the reeve, III Atr. 13
  If the town-reeve (*portireva*) or the village reeve (*tungravius*) accuses anyone of having withheld toll, IV Atr. 3
  Town-reeves who have been accessories to the circulation of false money shall incur the same punishment as coiners, IV Atr. 7, 3
  The village reeve shall be one of the witnesses to the carrying out of the prescribed alms-giving and fasting, VII Atr. 2, 5
  The money paid as dues shall be divided in three in the presence of the village reeve, VII Atr. (A.S.) 2, 3
  The injunction of the king to his reeves to support abbots in all their temporal needs, VIII Atr. 32
  The injunction of the king to his reeves to govern justly, Cn. 1020, 11
  If a reeve is accused of permitting the coining of false money, II Cn. 8, 2
  Of the king's injunction to his reeves to provide for him from his own property, II Cn. 69, 1 f.
  Greetings from King William to Geoffrey, Mayor of London, Wl. Lond. 1
  Reeves are forbidden to interfere with the jurisdiction which belongs to the bishop, Wl. ep. 4
  If any mayor (*provost*) does injury to the men in his jurisdiction, Leis Wl. 2, 1
Refectory *'beodern'*; V Atr. 7 = VI 4
Relatives. See Kin
Remission
  Of the remission allowed in the case of compensations, III Edg. 1, 2
  Of cases in which there shall be no remission of the prescribed punishment, IV Edg. 1, 5; 9

INDEX 413

Remission, *continued*
  The heriots of a man who falls during a campaign shall be remitted, II Cn. 78
Riht (nn.). See also *Unriht*
  i. Justice
    Every man shall do justice to his fellow, I Edg. 1
    No one shall apply to the king unless he fails to command justice at home, III Edg. 2
    A thief shall be delivered up to justice by his surety, III Edg. 6, 2
    Of justice promised in the decision of all cases, Cor. Oath 1, 3
    A suspicious character shall be brought to do justice to those who have charges against him, I Atr. 4 = II Cn. 33
    A man who vouches a dead person to warranty shall show that he is acting justly, II Atr. 9, 2
    If a man offers resistance to the course of justice, V Atr. 31, 1
    Every man should show the justice to others which he desires should be shown to him, VI Atr. 49
    If anyone refuses to render church dues, he shall be brought to justice by a civil penalty, VIII Atr. 15
    By the appointment of civil laws to uphold the principles of religion many are forced to submit to justice, VIII Atr. 36
    Evil-doers shall be brought to justice, VIII Atr. 40
    Earl Thurkil is enjoined to bring evil-doers to justice, Cn. 1020, 9
    No one shall make distraint of property until he has appealed for justice three times, II Cn. 19 f.
    Concerning the injustice of claiming ownership of property where there is evidence that fraud is involved, II Cn. 24, 3
  ii. Law, etc.
    The procedure according to public law (*folcriht*) in a case of vendetta, II Edm. 7
    A thief shall receive his deserts (*riht*), I Edg. 2
    If anyone evades the law and escapes, I Edg. 6
    Every case shall be treated in accordance with the public law, I Edg. 7
    God's churches shall be entitled to all their prerogatives, II Edg. 1
    Every man shall obtain the benefit of the (public) law, III Edg. 1, 1 = V Atr. 1, 1 = VI 8, 1 = X 2 = II Cn. 1, 1
    No one shall apply to the king unless he cannot obtain the benefit of the law, III Edg. 2
    If the law is too oppressive, III Edg. 2, 1
    The bishop and the ealdorman shall direct the observance of both ecclesiastical and secular law (*Godes riht ge woruldriht*), III Edg. 5, 2 = II Cn. 18, 1
    Every man shall have a surety who shall keep him to the performance of every legal duty, III Edg. 6 = I Atr. 1 = II Cn. 20
    Those who take the part of delinquents shall incur the same penalty, I Atr. 4, 2 = II Cn. 33, 1 *a*; III Atr. 13, 1
    There shall be no interference with gifts by a lord of what he has a legal right to bestow, III Atr. 3
    A priest who observes celibacy shall enjoy the privileges of a thegn (*þegnriht*), V Atr. 9, 1 = VI 5, 3
    The law of God shall be zealously cherished, V Atr. 26 = VI 30 = I Cn. 19, 3
    If anyone offers obstruction or open opposition to the law (*lahriht*) of Christ or of the king, V Atr. 31 = VI 38
    The king's reeves shall help abbots everywhere to obtain their rights (dues?), VIII Atr. 32
    If anyone defies the law of God or secular law, Cn. 1020, 9
    A man who is not within a tithing shall not be entitled to any of the rights of a freeman (*freoriht*), II Cn. 20
    If anyone insults a man in holy orders, he shall make amends in accordance with the law, II Cn. 42
    Of a delinquent who shall be outlawed and pursued with hostility by all those who wish to promote law and order, II Cn. 48, 2

Riht, continued
  ii. Law, *continued*
      If he brings about his own death by setting himself against the law, II Cn. 48, 3
      If anyone desires to turn from lawlessness to observance of the law, II Cn. 67
      Concerning the case in which a man shall be clear of any charge of complicity according to the law of God, II Cn. 75, 1

Mid rihte 'justly,' 'lawfully,' etc.
  Rich and poor shall possess what they have lawfully acquired, IV Edg. 2, 2
  Livestock acquired without security and witnesses shall be seized and kept until it is known who is the rightful owner, I Atr. 3, 1
  The friends of a dead man may clear him according to the law, II Atr. 9, 2
  Canons shall maintain regularity in their foundations, V Atr. 7
  Priests have no right to marry, V Atr. 9 = VI 5, 1 = I Cn. 6, 2
  Concerning widows who lead a respectable life, V Atr. 21 = VI 26
  Every Christian man shall order his words and deeds aright, V Atr. 22, 2 = VI 28 = I Cn. 19, 1
  He who seeks to observe God's law aright shall remain with one wife as long as she lives, VI Atr. 12, 1 = I Cn. 7, 3
  Judgment, following the principles of justice, shall always be in accordance with the nature of the deed, VIII Atr. 5, 2
  No monk may lawfully either demand or pay any compensation incurred by vendetta, VIII Atr. 25
  Concerning a member of the priesthood who observes the laws of God as properly befits his estate, VIII Atr. 30
  Every man shall treat his fellow justly, VIII Atr. 44, 1
  Every church is rightly in the protection of Christ, I Cn. 2, 1
  Of the things which a priest is able to do if he is duly pleasing to his lord and serves Christ as he ought, I Cn. 4, 1 f.

Riht (adj.), *rihte* (adv.), *rihtlice, ariht*
  Those who commit perjury and practise sorcery shall undertake the prescribed penance, I Edm. 6
  Every man shall be awarded just decisions, III Edg. 1, 1 = II Cn. 1, 1
  A judge who gives a false judgment shall declare on oath that he did not know how to give a more just decision, III Edg. 3 = II Cn. 15, 1
  Concerning the man who by his veracity brings just doom upon the guilty, IV Edg. 14
  The captain of a ship shall prove that he was justified in taking certain goods, II Atr. 4
  Concerning the man who is putting forward a just claim to certain property, II Atr. 9
  Justice (*riht lagu, rihte laga*) shall be promoted and peace and goodwill duly maintained, V Atr. 1, 1 = VI 8 = X 2 = II Cn. 1
  Concerning what is right in the case of a canon who refuses to observe regularity and celibacy, V Atr. 7 = VI 4
  All Christian men shall duly observe the laws of the church, V Atr. 10
  Concerning what is best (*rihtast*) with regard to payment for the souls of the dead, V Atr. 12 = VI 20 = VIII 13 = I Cn. 13
  Festivals and fasts shall be duly observed, V Atr. 12, 3 = VI 22
  At holy festivals, as is fitting, there shall be peace and concord, V Atr. 19
  One God shall be duly loved and honoured and one royal lord shall be supported with due fidelity, VI Atr. 1
  Men should have a right belief in the true God and duly keep the true Christian faith, VI Atr. 42
  Concerning a very just rule, VI Atr. 49
  Concerning the man who violates the just decrees of God or of man, VI Atr. 50
  Concerning the division of tithes in accordance with the principles of justice, VIII Atr. 6
  Every Christian man shall duly render his tithes to his lord, VIII Atr. 7
  If anyone refuses to make due rendering of his tithes, VIII Atr. 8

INDEX 415

Riht, continued
  Concerning the duty most incumbent upon a Christian man (king), VIII Atr. 35 = II Cn. 40, 2
  Concerning the true Christian religion, VIII Atr. 44
  Each man shall love his fellow with true fidelity, VIII Atr. 44, 1
  Concerning the king's desire to promote the just interests of the royal authority and to ordain most justly the conditions which should be observed, X Atr. Pre.
  Concerning Canute's declaration that he will not fail to support just secular law, Cn. 1020, 2
  Concerning the results of loyal support of the king, Cn. 1020, 5
  Concerning Canute's injunction to his reeves to govern justly, pronounce just judgments and inflict such mitigated penalties as the bishop may approve, Cn. 1020, 11
  Concerning what justly befits all Christian men, I Cn. 4
  Every lord should treat his men justly, I Cn. 20, 2
  Every Christian man should apply himself until he can understand the true belief, I Cn. 22 f.; 22, 4
  Concerning the man who refuses to observe just laws and just judgments, II Cn. 15, 2
  Every man shall attend the hundred court whenever he is required by law to attend it, II Cn. 17, 1
  Concerning the man who must meet his opponent's charge as the hundred court shall determine, II Cn. 27
  If a freeman breaks a legally ordained fast, II Cn. 46
  Of Canute's command to his reeves to provide for him in accordance with the law, II Cn. 69, 1
  If a man dies intestate his lord shall take no more than his legal heriot, and his property shall be strictly divided, II Cn. 70 f.
  Concerning the law which the king considers right in a certain case, II Cn. 75
  A very just division shall be made of the property left by a man who falls during a campaign, II Cn. 78
Robbery '*ran*,' '*reaflac*,' '*roberie*,' etc.; '*reafian*' (vb.)
  Robbery by all classes of society forbidden, Cor Oath 1, 2
  If a man robs another in daylight, III Atr. 15
  Robberies shall be got rid of, V Atr. 25 = VI 28, 2
  If the protection of the church is broken by robbery, VIII Atr. 4 = I Cn. 3
  Robbers shall be made an end of, II Cn. 4, 2
  Robbers shall incur the wrath of God, II Cn. 7
  If anyone causes a breach of the fast of Lent by robbery, II Cn. 47
  If anyone is guilty of robbery, II Cn. 63
  Concerning *ran*, by which the English mean open robbery which cannot be denied, Wl. art. 6
  If anyone in Mercia is accused of robbery, Leis Wl. 3
Romfeoh 'Peter's Pence.' See Penny
Rule '*regol*'
  The servants of God shall live according to their rule, V Atr. 4 = VI 2 = I Cn. 6 *a*
  Concerning every monk who is out of a monastery and is not observing a rule, V Atr. 5 = VI 3
  Canons shall maintain regularity and celibacy as their rule prescribes, V Atr. 7 = VI 4
  If an accusation is brought against a priest who lives according to a rule, VIII Atr. 19 f. = I Cn. 5 f.
  If an accusation is brought against a deacon who lives according to a rule, VIII Atr. 20 f. = I Cn. 5, 1 f.
  If an accusation is brought against a secular priest who does not live according to a rule, VIII Atr. 21 = I Cn. 5, 2
  A monk leaves the law of his kindred behind when he accepts monastic rule, VIII Atr. 25 = I Cn. 5, 2 *d*
  Abbots and monks shall live more according to a rule, VIII Atr. 31, 1

Rule, *continued*
   Of assisting abbots to remain in their monasteries and live according to their rule, VIII Atr. 32

Sammæle 'unanimous'
   A verdict in which the thegns are unanimous shall be held valid, III Atr. 13, 2
Sanctuary. See *Frið*
Sarbot 'compensation for a wound'; Leis Wl. 10, 1
Scalp. See *Extopare, Hættian*
Sceiðman 'Viking'; II Atr. 7
Scot, in the phrase 'lot and scot'; Wl. art. 4; Hn. Lond. 2, 1
Scourging
   Of a case in which the herdsmen of a village shall undergo the lash, IV Edg. 9
   A slave who breaks the prescribed fast shall undergo the lash, VII Atr. 2, 4
   A slave who does not render his penny shall undergo the lash, VII Atr. (A.S.) 3
   If a slave works during a church festival he shall undergo the lash, II Cn. 45, 2
   If a slave eats during a fast he shall undergo the lash, II Cn. 46, 2
Security. See Pledge, Surety
   Of the security given by the slayer, his advocate, and the kin of the slain man in a case of vendetta, II Edm. 7 f.
   If anyone seeks to clear a thief he shall deposit 100 [of silver] as security, III Atr. 7
   Of the security which shall be deposited in the case of an action brought by the king, an earl, a bishop or a thegn, III Atr. 12
   A baron who commits a misdeed shall not henceforth forfeit as security the whole of his personal property, Hn. cor. 8
Sheep, shepherd
   A man shall keep the hide and head of a sheep for 3 days, III Atr. 9
   If anyone has taken sheep into his care, Leis Wl. 5 f.
   Of a shepherd who will be considered failing in his trust, I Cn. 26, 1
   Of the shepherds whose duty it is to guard people against the spoiler, I Cn. 26, 3
   Of the shepherd who shall lead his flock to the kingdom of God, II Cn. 84, 2 f.
Shield
   The heriot of an earl shall include 8 shields, that of a king's thegn 4, that of a king's thegn in the Danelaw who stands in intimate relationship to the king 2, II Cn. 71 *a*; 71, 1; 71, 4
   The heriot of an earl shall include 4 shields, that of a baron 2, that of a thegn of lower rank 1, Leis Wl. 20–20, 2
Ship
   If a hostile fleet (*sciphere*) harry in England, II Atr. 1, 1
   If a merchant ship (*ceapscip*) enters an estuary, II Atr. 2
   If a subject of King Æthelred's comes to a region to which the truce does not apply, protection shall be afforded to his ship and to all his goods, II Atr. 3, 1 f.
   If anyone has been robbed of his goods and he knows the ship by which it has been done, II Atr. 4
   The fitting out of ships (*scipfirðrunga, -forðunga*) shall be carried out as diligently as possible, V Atr. 27 = II Cn. 10
   The provision of naval forces (*scipfyrdunga*) shall be diligently undertaken, VI Atr. 32, 3
   If anyone damages a national warship (*folces fyrdscip*), VI Atr. 34.
Shire. See County
Sibb
   i. Relationship
      A Christian man shall not marry among his own kin within six degrees of relationship (*sibfæce*) or with the widow of a man as nearly related to him as this, VI Atr. 12 = I Cn. 7
      If anyone commits incest, he shall make amends according to the degree of relationship, II Cn. 51 f.
   ii. Peace
      True peace is assured to the church of God and to all Christian people, Cor. Oath 1, 1

Sibb, continued
  ii. Peace, *continued*
    At holy festivals there shall be peace and concord (*som* 7 *sib*) among all Christian men, v Atr. 19 = vi 25, 1 = i Cn. 17, 2
Silver
  Of the sum paid in gold and silver to the Viking fleet, ii Atr. 7, 2
  A coiner shall not redeem his hand in any way either with gold or with silver, ii Cn. 8, 1
Sin; iv Edg. 1; v Atr. 22 = vi 27; vi 1 = 42 = x 1 = i Cn. 18, 1; vi Atr. 52; Cn. 1020, 19; i Cn. 23; 25; ii 6
Sister
  Of incest with a sister, ii Cn. 51, 1
  If a baron or any other vassal of the king's wishes to bestow his sister in marriage, Hn. cor. 3
Slave
  If a number of slaves commit theft, iii Edm. 4
  If a slave is found guilty at the ordeal, i Atr. 2 = ii Cn. 32
  If an Englishman slays a Danish slave or a Dane an English slave, ii Atr. 5, 1
  If a slave breaks the prescribed fast, vii Atr. 2, 4
  If a slave does not render his dues, vii Atr. (A.S.) 3
  Slaves shall be exempt from work on the three stated days, vii Atr. (A.S.) 5, 1
  A part of the tithes received by the church shall be assigned to poverty-stricken slaves, viii Atr. 6
  Of the injustice of representing one's men to be either freemen or slaves, ii Cn. 20, 1
  If a slave works during a church festival, ii Cn. 45, 2
  If a lord compels his slave to work during a church festival, ii Cn. 45, 3
  If a slave eats during a fast, ii Cn. 46, 2
  Distinction must carefully be made between freemen and slaves, ii Cn. 68, 1 *b*
  If anyone desires to set free one of his slaves, Wl. art. retr. 15, 1
  If slaves have remained for a year and a day without being claimed, Wl. art. retr. 16
  The *manbot* for a slave shall be 20 shillings, Leis Wl. 7
Slaying
  If anyone sheds the blood of a Christian man, i Edm. 3 = ii Edm. 4
  A homicide shall not be allowed burial in consecrated ground, i Edm. 4
  If anyone slay a man, ii Edm. 1-1, 3
  Concerning the procedure in a case of homicide, ii Edm. 7-7, 3
  The leader of a band of slaves who commit theft shall be slain, iii Edm. 4
  If any man slays outright anyone engaged in an investigation with regard to concealed cattle, iv Edg. 14
  A suspicious character who has no surety shall be slain, i Atr. 4, 1 = ii Cn. 33, 1
  Of the case in which no compensation shall be paid for a man included in the truce, if he is slain, ii Atr. 3, 4
  If an Englishman slays a Dane or a Dane an Englishman, ii Atr. 5 f.
  If 8 men are slain, ii Atr. 5, 2 f.
  Concerning the slaughter which took place before the truce was made, ii Atr. 6, 1
  If an Englishman is charged with having slain anyone, ii Atr. 7
  If the Vikings slay 8 Englishmen, ii Atr. 7, 1
  Every moneyer who is guilty of striking false coins shall be slain, iii Atr. 8
  Of malefactors who shall lie in unhonoured graves, if they are slain, iv Atr. 4
  Homicides shall be avoided, v Atr. 25 = vi 28, 2
  If a man brings about his own death by opposition to the law, v Atr. 31, 1 = vi 38 = ii Cn. 48, 2 f.
  Of the unjust practice of bringing accusations of homicide against a guiltless man, v Atr. 32, 4
  If proved homicides remain anywhere near the king, vi Atr. 36
  If anyone violates the protection of the church by committing homicide within its walls, viii Atr. 1, 1 = i Cn. 2, 3

Slaying, *continued*
  If a man in holy orders is accused of having committed or instigated homicide, VIII Atr. 23 = I Cn. 5, 2 *b*
  If a priest commits homicide, VIII Atr. 26 = II Cn. 41
  Concerning every freeman who desires to be atoned for by the payment of compensation, if he is slain, II Cn. 20
  If anyone slays a priest, II Cn. 39
  If a man who commits *hamsocn* is slain, II Cn. 62, 1
  If an Englishman summons a Frenchman to trial by combat for homicide, Wl. lad 1 = Wl. art. 6
  If any of the men who came to England along with, or after, Wm I is slain, Wl. art. 3, 1
  The slaying of anyone for any offence is forbidden, Wl. art 10 = Wl. art. retr. 17
  If a Frenchman is slain, Leis Wl. 22
  If anyone slays anyone who is travelling on the four highways, Leis Wl. 26
  If a man poisons another, he shall be slain, Leis Wl. 36
Smeremangestrae 'women who deal in dairy produce'; IV Atr. 2, 12
Sorcery '*liblac*'; I Edm. 6
Soul
  Concerning the counsel taken for the welfare of their own souls and those of the people under their charge by the archbishops, etc., I Edm. Pre.
  Concerning payment for the souls of the dead (*sawlsceat*), II Edg. 5, 2; v Atr. 12 f. = VI 20 f. = VIII 13 = I Cn. 13 f.
  Of a man who curtails what is due to God to the ruin of his soul, IV Edg. 1, 5 *a*
  Concerning the guardians of men's souls, IV Edg. 1, 8
  Concerning the good of the souls of all men, IV Edg. 15
  Care shall be taken not to destroy the souls which Christ redeemed, V Atr. 2 = VI 9 = II Cn. 3
  Of a Christian man who seeks to save his soul from hell-fire, VI Atr. 12, 1 = I Cn. 7, 3
  Of the salvation of men's souls, I Cn. 2
  Of the spoiler who desires to do harm to the souls of men, I Cn. 26, 2
  Of preserving the soul from injury, II Cn. 30, 5
Spade
  Of the payment of a farthing for the spade, Leis Wl. 3, 1
Spear
  The heriot of an earl shall include 8 spears, that of a king's thegn 4, that of a king's thegn among the Danes who stands in intimate relationship to the king 2, II Cn. 71 *a*; 71, 1; 71, 4
  Concerning the case of a man who sets his spear at another man's door, II Cn. 75
Stranger '*ælþeodig mann*,' '*fremde*.' See also Foreigner
  If anyone, either kinsman or stranger, refuses to ride against a delinquent, III Edg. 7, 2 = II Cn. 25, 2
  Strangers and men come from afar should not be vexed or oppressed, VI Atr. 48
  If an attempt is made to deprive a stranger of his goods or his life, VIII Atr. 33 = II Cn. 40
Sunday
  Sunday shall be observed as a festival from noonday on Saturday till dawn on Monday, II Edg. 5 = Cn. 1020, 18 = I Cn. 14, 2
  The festival of Sunday shall be rigorously observed and marketings and meetings shall be abstained from, V Atr. 13 f. = VI 22, 1 = 44 = VIII 17 = Cn. 1020, 18 = I Cn. 15
  No condemned man shall be put to death during the Sunday festival, II Cn. 45
Surety '*borg*'
  A man who has committed homicide shall find a surety for the payment of the wergeld (*wæreborh*), II Edm. 7, 2
  Every man shall act as surety for his men, III Edm. 7
  All men of ill repute who have been frequently accused shall be placed under surety, III Edm. 7, 1

Surety, *continued*
  Every (free) man shall have a surety, III Edg. 6 = IV Edg. 3 = I Atr. 1 = II Cn. 20
  The duties of a surety, III Edg. 6, 1 f.; I Atr. 1, 7
  A man who has failed to attend the court meetings three times may still find a surety, if he can, III Edg. 7
  Of a case in which a man shall appoint trustworthy sureties, I Atr. 1, 5
  Every lord shall be personally responsible as surety for the men of his own household, I Atr. 1, 10 = II Cn. 31 = Leis Wl. 52
  No-one shall buy or sell unless he have a surety and witnesses, I Atr. 3
  The king's reeve shall place a suspicious character under surety, I Atr. 4 = II Cn. 33
  If he has no surety, I Atr. 4, 1
  A man in whose possession property is attached shall furnish surety that he will produce his warrantor, II Atr. 8
  He who attaches his goods shall have a trustworthy surety, II Atr. 9, 1
  If anyone has livestock acquired without surety, III Atr. 5
  A priest who has been concerned in false witness or perjury or has been the accessory of thieves shall find surety, VIII Atr. 27
  If anyone swears a false oath on the relics, he shall find surety, II Cn. 36, 1
  A man who claims stolen or strayed livestock shall find surety (*plege*), Leis Wl. 5, 2; 6, 1; 21
  The defendant in a case of attaching livestock shall name his surety (*heimelborch*), Leis Wl. 21, 1
  If he has neither warrantor nor surety, Leis Wl. 21, 1 *a*
Sword
  4 swords shall be included in the heriot of an earl, 2 in that of a king's thegn (baron), 1 in that of a thegn among the Danes who stands in intimate relationship to the king, and 1 in that of a *vavassur*, II Cn. 71 *a*; 71, 1; 71, 4; Leis Wl. 20 ff.

Theft
  Concerning immunity from thefts, II Edm. 5
  If a number of slaves commit theft, III Edm. 4
  Men shall go in pursuit of thieves, I Edg. 2
  If the case be that of a thief, III Edg. 6, 2
  The life of the proved thief shall be in the power of the king, III Edg. 7, 3 = II Cn. 26
  Of a measure directed against thieves, IV Edg. 2, 2
  A man whose statement concerning the acquisition of livestock proves false shall be regarded as a thief, IV Edg. 11
  If a man's lord swears on his behalf that he has never paid compensation as a thief (*ðeofgyld*), I Atr. 1, 2 = III 4 = II Cn. 30, 1
  Of a thief who shall be treated as an outlaw by all the nation, I Atr. 1, 9 *a* = II Cn. 30, 9
  Neither of the two parties to the truce shall harbour a thief pursued by the other party, II Atr. 6, 2
  If an Englishman is charged with having stolen cattle, II Atr. 7
  Of a case where a man, in whose possession certain goods are found, will be held guilty of theft, II Atr. 9, 3
  Thefts shall be got rid of, V Atr. 25 = VI 28, 2
  Public security shall be promoted in such a way as shall be worst for the thief, VI Atr. 32 = II Cn. 8
  If a priest be the accessory and accomplice of thieves, VIII Atr. 27 = I Cn. 5, 3
  If anyone protects a thief, Cn. 1020, 12
  Thieves shall be made an end of, II Cn. 4, 2
  Everyone over 12 years of age shall swear that he will not be a thief or a thief's accomplice, II Cn. 21
  In a case of open theft the delinquent shall never save his life, II Cn. 26, 1
  If anyone comes upon a thief and lets him escape, II Cn. 29; Leis Wl. 49

420　INDEX

Theft, *continued*
  Theft which cannot be disproved is one of the crimes for which no compensation can be paid, II Cn. 64
  If anyone carries stolen goods home to his cottage, II Cn. 76
  No protection shall be extended to a notorious thief, II Cn. 82
  If an Englishman summons a Frenchman to trial by combat for theft, Wl. lad 1
  Of the exercise of summary justice upon a thief caught in the act, Leis Wl. 2, 3
  Of an oath in support of a plea of ignorance that a certain man was a thief, Leis Wl. 3
  If a thief's surety can find him within a year and a day, Leis Wl. 3, 4
  If a man captures a thief against whom no hue and cry has been raised, Leis Wl. 4
  If a man accuses another of theft, Leis Wl. 14
  If a man has previously paid compensation for theft, Leis Wl. 15, 3
  If theft is discovered on anyone's land and the thief likewise, Leis Wl. 27
  If theft is discovered in a district over which the lord has rights of jurisdiction, Leis Wl. 27, 1
  Of the search for a thief, Leis Wl. 47, 3
Thegn
  Of the fine payable by a thegn for refusing to comply with the law, III Edm. 7, 2
  Payment of tithes shall be made both from the thegn's demesne land and from that held by his tenants, II Edg. 1, 1
  If a thegn has a church on his *bocland*, II Edg. 2 = I Cn. 11
  Of dealing with a man who refuses to render his tithes, whether he be under the lordship of the king or of a thegn, II Edg. 3, 1 = VIII Atr. 8 = I Cn. 8, 2
  A judge who gives a false judgment shall be in danger of forfeiting for ever his rank as a thegn (*þegenscip*), III Edg. 3 = II Cn. 15, 1
  The king and his thegns shall enforce upon the priests the duties prescribed by the bishops, IV Edg. 1, 8
  The king's thegns shall keep their rank during King Edgar's lifetime, IV Edg. 2 *a*
  Of the right of investigation with regard to a thegn's livestock, IV Edg. 13
  A lord who is supporting one of his men shall take an oath along with two trustworthy thegns, I Atr. 1, 2 = III 4
  A lord who is accused of advising his man to escape shall choose 5 thegns as his compurgators, I Atr. 1, 8; I, 12 = II Cn. 31, 1 *a*
  Of the oath taken by the twelve leading thegns in the wapentake court, III Atr. 3, 1
  No-one shall have jurisdiction over a thegn of the king except the king himself, III Atr. 11
  In the case of an action brought by a thegn, 6 ores shall be deposited as security, III Atr. 12
  Of the verdict given by the thegns, III Atr. 13, 2
  Of a case where a thegn has two alternatives, III Atr. 13, 3
  A priest who observes celibacy shall enjoy the wergeld and privileges of a thegn, V Atr. 9, 1 = VI 5, 3 = VIII 28 = I Cn. 6, 2 *a*
  Every thegn shall render a tithe of all that he has, VII Atr. 1, 3
  In the case of a fast being broken, a thegn of the king's shall pay 120 shillings, VII Atr. 2, 4
  If a thegn does not render his dues, he shall pay 30 shillings, VII Atr. (A.S.) 3
  If a thegn has a trustworthy man to give his oath of accusation for him, II Cn. 22, 2
  The heriot of a king's thegn, II Cn. 71, 1 and 3 f.
  The heriot of an ordinary thegn, II Cn. 71, 2
  The wergeld of a thegn, Leis Wl. 8
Thumb
  The value of the thumb is half that of the hand, Leis Wl. 11, 1
Tihtbysig 'of bad reputation'; III Edg. 7; I Atr. 1, 1; III 3, 2 and 4; II Cn. 22; 25; 30
Tithe
  Of the injunction to every Christian man to pay tithes, I Edm. 2
  All tithes shall be paid to the old churches, II Edg. 1, 1

Tithe, *continued*
   A thegn who has a church on his *bocland* shall pay to it a third part of his tithes, II Edg. 2 = I Cn. 11
   Of the dates fixed for the rendering of tithes, II Edg. 3; v Atr. 11, 1 = VI 17 = VIII 9 = I Cn. 8, 1
   If anyone refuses to render tithes, II Edg. 3, 1 = VIII Atr. 8 = I Cn. 8, 2
   Of the misfortune merited through the withholding of tithes, IV Edg. 1
   Of the audacity of laymen in refusing to render tithes, IV Edg. 1, 3
   Everyone shall render tithes, IV Edg. 1, 4
   All men shall give their rightful tithes, VII Atr. 4
   Men of position shall pay tithes, VII Atr. (A.S.) 5
   Of the division of tithes, VIII Atr. 6
   Every Christian man shall duly render his tithes, VIII Atr. 7
   The tithe of animals and of fruits shall be paid before Canute's return to England, Cn. 1027, 16

Tithing
   The chief officials of the tithings shall be informed in a case of theft, I Edg. 2
   No-one shall keep strange cattle except with the cognisance of the chief official of the tithing, I Edg. 4
   The heads of the tithings shall be witnesses that the prescribed alms-giving and fasting are carried out, VII Atr. 2, 5
   Every man shall be in a tithing, II Cn. 20

Toll
   Of the toll paid by various ships at Billingsgate, IV Atr. 2–2, 2
   Of the payment of toll for cloth, IV Atr. 2, 3
   Of the toll for fish and wine, IV Atr. 2, 4 f.
   Of the foreigners who exhibited their goods and paid toll, IV Atr. 2, 6 f.
   Of the toll paid by subjects of the Emperor, IV Atr. 2, 10
   Of the toll paid for hens and eggs, IV Atr. 2, 11
   Of the toll paid by dealers in dairy produce, IV Atr. 2, 12
   If a man is accused of having withheld toll, IV Atr. 3–3, 3
   Of English travellers to Rome harassed by unjust tolls, Cn. 1027, 6
   If an accusation is brought against a baron who has rights of toll, Leis Wl. 2, 3
   The citizens of London shall be free from toll, Hn. Lond. 5
   If anyone has exacted toll from citizens of London, Hn. Lond. 12

Tongue
   A man who seeks to accuse another man falsely shall be in danger of forfeiting his tongue, III Edg. 4 = II Cn. 16

Town, town-reeve '*port*,' '*portgerefa*.' See also Borough, *Burg*
   The town-reeve shall be present as witness when a man purchases or receives strange cattle, III Edm. 5
   A man who seeks to clear a thief shall deposit a certain sum with the king's town-reeve, III Atr. 7
   If the town-reeve accuses anyone of having withheld toll, IV Atr. 3
   Of the man who within the town commits *hamsocn*, IV Atr. 4
   If he values the goodwill of the town, IV Atr. 4, 2
   Of traders who bring defective money to the town, IV Atr. 7
   Of town-reeves who have been accessories to such a fraud, IV Atr. 7, 3
   Of the duty of those who have charge of towns, IV Atr. 9, 2
   Geoffrey, Mayor of London, Wl. Lond. 1

Track
   Of tracking stolen cattle, III Edm. 6 ff.

Trader
   Of traders who circulate money which is defective in quality and weight, IV Atr. 5; 7 ff.

Treason, treachery
   Of the man who has been discovered in treason against his lord, III Edg. 7, 3 = II Cn. 26
   Treachery towards a man's lord is one of the crimes which are *botleas*, II Cn. 64

422   INDEX

Treasurer, treasury
    The treasurer may act as witness when a man purchases or receives strange
        cattle, III Edm. 5
    If anyone is accused of breaking into a treasury, Leis Wl. 15
Trustworthy
    Of a man who must be thoroughly trustworthy, I Edg. 4
    Every freeman shall have a trustworthy surety, I Atr. 1
    Of the oath of a lord along with two trustworthy thegns (men), I Atr. 1, 2 =
        II Cn. 30, 1
    A delinquent who is found guilty shall appoint trustworthy sureties, I Atr. 1, 5
    He who attaches his goods shall have a trustworthy surety, II Atr. 9, 1
    If trustworthy witnesses establish a man's ownership of certain goods,
        II Atr. 9, 4
    Concerning trustworthy men, II Cn. 22
    If a thegn has a trustworthy man to give his oath of accusation for him,
        II Cn. 22, 2
    No-one shall vouch to warranty, unless he have trustworthy witnesses, II Cn. 23
    No-one shall buy anything over 4 pence in value, unless he have trustworthy
        witnesses, II Cn. 24
    The buying or selling of livestock is forbidden, except before trustworthy
        witnesses, Wl. art. 5
    If a man who is accused can produce witnesses to prove his trustworthiness,
        Leis Wl. 14
    Of the nomination of trustworthy men by the court to act as an accused man's
        compurgators, Leis Wl. 14, 1; 15 f.
    Twelfhynde 7 *twyhynde* 'nobles and commoners,' III Edm. 2; Cn. 1020, 1
Twelfth Night
    Ordeals and oaths are forbidden from the Advent till the eighth day after
        Twelfth Night, I Cn. 17
    Twelve. Periods of 12 months, II Edm. 1; III Edg. 6, 2; VI Atr. 26, 1 = II Cn. 73;
        II Cn. 73, 4; twelve-fold compensation, VIII Atr. 11, 1; freemen over 12 years
        of age, II Cn. 20; 21; oaths of 12 men, II Cn. 48; Leis Wl. 3; 14, 1; 15
Twibote 'double compensation'; II Cn. 47

Unanimous '*sammæle*'; III Atr. 13, 2
Undrifen 'not pursued'; II Atr. 2
Unforeda (*að*) 'comprehensive'; Wl. lad 3, 2. See Oath
Unfriðland, -mann, -scip 'not included in the truce'; II Atr. 2; 3, 1; 3, 3
Ungilde 'without the payment of compensation'; II Atr. 3, 4. See *Ægilde*
Unlagu 'injustice.' See also *Unriht*
    Injustice shall be zealously suppressed, V Atr. 1, 1 = 33 = VI 8 = X 2 = II Cn. 1
    Hateful injustices shall be strictly avoided, V Atr. 24 = VI 28, 2
    There shall be an end to unjust practices, V Atr. 32
    Constant thought shall be taken how to suppress every injustice, VI Atr. 40 =
        X Pre., 2 = II Cn. 11
    Of the man who promotes injustice, II Cn. 15, 1
    If one man unjustly disarms another, II Cn. 60
Unmaga 'weak'
    The strong (*maga*) and the weak are not alike, VI Atr. 52
    The weak and the strong cannot bear an equally heavy burden, II Cn. 68, 1 *a*
Unmihtig 'of small means'; II Atr. 9
Unriht (adj. and nn.); *unrihtlic*
    Concerning manifold illegal deeds of violence, II Edm. Pre., 1
    Unrighteous deeds are forbidden, Cor. Oath 1, 2
    Of the escape of a man who has done wrong, 1 Atr. 1, 8 = II Cn. 30, 7
    Of the man who has in his possession property to which he is not entitled,
        II Atr. 9
    No-one shall make the church an object of improper traffic, V Atr. 10, 2 = VI 15
    Every injustice shall be zealously cast out, V Atr. 23 = VI 28, 1 = I Cn. 19, 2
    Concerning the process of attacking property by which many people have
        been unjustly oppressed, V Atr. 32, 1

INDEX 423

Unriht, continued
 Of an unjust practice stopped by the king, v Atr. 32, 5
 Of the suppression of injustice, v Atr. 33, 1 = vi 40, 1; Cn. 1020, 3; ii Cn. 1; 7, 1
 An end shall be put to all unjust practices, vi Atr. 32, 2 = ii Cn. 9
 Of restraining other men from wrongdoing, vi Atr. 42
 All shall cease from evil, ix Atr. 1
 Of an evildoer (*unrihtwisan*) who shall be brought to justice, Cn. 1020, 9
 Every form of unrighteousness shall be put away, Cn. 1020, 15
 Of an injustice which is no longer permitted, ii Cn. 20, 1
 Lawlessness is not permitted at any time, ii Cn. 38
 Of the amends required for lawless behaviour, ii Cn. 38, 1
 If anyone unlawfully maintains an excommunicated person, ii Cn. 66
 If anyone desires to turn from lawlessness to observance of the law, ii Cn. 67
Unrihthæmed; v Atr. 10 = vi 11 = i Cn. 6, 3; viii Atr. 4; i Cn. 24. See Adultery
Unstranga 'weak'; ii Cn. 68, 1

Vendetta
 A man who has committed homicide shall himself alone bear the vendetta, ii Edm. 1
 If any of his kinsmen harbour him thereafter, he shall incur the vendetta, ii Edm. 1, 2
 The authorities must put a stop to vendettas, ii Edm. 7
 If a man in holy orders is charged with vendetta, viii Atr. 23 = i Cn. 5, 2 *b*
 No monk who belongs to a monastery may either demand or pay any compensation incurred by vendetta, viii Atr. 25 = i Cn. 5, 2 *d*
Vengeance
 If any member of a slain man's kindred take vengeance on any man other than the actual delinquent, ii Edm. 1, 3
 No-one shall avenge the injuries done before the truce, ii Atr. 6, 1
 A Christian king (man) shall avenge offences against Christ (God), viii Atr. 2, 1 = 35 = ii Cn. 40, 2
 The king shall avenge injuries done to a man in orders or a stranger, viii Atr. 34 = ii Cn. 40, 1
Village '*tun*,' '*villa*,' '*vile*'
 When stolen cattle is being tracked, thorough investigation shall be made at the village, iii Edm. 6
 Of a case in which a man shall act with the cognisance of the village to which he belongs, iv Edg. 8
 If he fails to do so, the villagers shall inform the head of the hundred, iv Edg. 8, 1
 Of the right of investigation granted to villagers, iv Edg. 13
 If any one offers indignity to the villagers, iv Edg. 13, 1
 If a man who has been robbed makes the deed known in 3 villages, iii Atr. 15
 If a village-reeve accuses anyone of having withheld toll, iv Atr. 3
 The village-reeve shall be one of the witnesses to the carrying out of the prescribed alms-giving and fasting, vii Atr. 2, 5
 The village-reeve shall be one of the witnesses to the division of the money received as dues, vii Atr. (A.S.) 2, 3
 No-one shall buy anything over 4 pence in value, unless he has 4 men as witnesses, either from a town or from a village, Leis Wl. 45
 Of the sum to be exacted from a town or village which has demanded toll from citizens of London, Hn. Lond. 12
Villein
 The wergeld of a villein in Mercia and Wessex, Leis Wl. 8, 1
 The heriot of a villein, Leis Wl. 20, 3
 All villeins shall be in frankpledge, Leis Wl. 20, 3 *a*
Vouching to warranty '*team*,' '*tieman*,' '*geteama*'
 Of the circumstances in which a man is permitted to vouch to warranty, i Edg. 4, 1
 Of producing a warrantor, ii Atr. 8
 If a living person is vouched to warranty, ii Atr. 8, 1

Vouching to warranty, *continued*
  Vouching to warranty shall always take place where the property has first been attached, II Atr. 8, 4; 9
  A man who attaches his goods shall have trustworthy security in every case of vouching to warranty, II Atr. 9, 1
  If anyone vouches a dead person to warranty, II Atr. 9, 2 f.
  If, in the course of vouching to warranty, anyone accepts, and does not carry the process any further, II Atr. 9, 4
  Every vouching to warranty shall take place in a royal manor, III Atr. 6, 1
  No man shall be entitled to vouch to warranty unless he has trustworthy witnesses, II Cn. 23; 24, 1
  Vouching to warranty shall take place three times, II Cn. 24, 2
  Of a baron who possesses rights of vouching to warranty, Leis Wl. 2, 3
  If anyone has been discovered with false money and has vouched a warrantor for it, Hn. mon. 2

Wapentake
  Of buying and selling in a wapentake, IV Edg. 6
  Of compensation for breach of the peace established in a wapentake, III Atr. 1, 2
  A court shall be held in every wapentake, III Atr. 3, 1
  Of the money paid as security to the wapentake by men of bad repute, III Atr. 3, 2
  Of the money paid to the wapentake in order to obtain the benefit of the law, III Atr. 3, 3
  Wapentakes shall be guarded against malefactors, Wl. art. retr. 6
Warranty, warrantor. See Vouching
Water. Of the ordeal by water, III Atr. 6
Weapon
  The heriot of an ordinary thegn shall include his weapons, II Cn. 71, 2
  If a man lays any weapons in a place where they might remain quietly, II Cn. 75 f.
Weight
  Of the establishment of a uniform standard of weight, IV Edg. 8, 1
  Untrue weights shall be done away with, V Atr. 24 = VI 28, 2
  Weights shall be corrected, V Atr. 32, 2 = II Cn. 9
Weofodbot 'sacrilege'; II Cn. 42
Weofodpegn 'a minister of the altar'; VIII Atr. 18; 22 = I Cn. 5, 2 *a*; VIII Atr. 28; II Cn. 39; 41
Wergeld
  Of the payment of compensation to the full amount of the slain man's wergeld, II Edm. 1; 7, 1 ff.
  No-one shall forfeit more than his wergeld for any offence for which compensation may be paid, III Edg. 2, 2
  A man who is in danger of losing his tongue may redeem himself with his wergeld, III Edm. 4 = II Cn. 16
  Of the payment of a delinquent's wergeld to his lord, I Atr. 1, 5 = II Cn. 30, 3 *b*; I Atr. 1, 7 = III 6, 2 = II Cn. 30, 6; I Atr. 1, 9 = II Cn. 30, 8; to the king, I Atr. 1, 9 *a* = II Cn. 30, 9; I Atr. 11 = II Cn. 31, 1
  Of the payment of the lord's wergeld to the king, I Atr. 1, 13 = II Cn. 31, 2
  Of the payment of the full wergeld if less than 8 men are slain, II Atr. 5, 2
  Of a deserter who runs the risk of forfeiting his wergeld, V Atr. 28
  Of the payment of wergeld for opposition to the law of Christ or the king, V Atr. 31 = VI 38
  Of the money received by the payment of wergeld, VI Atr. 51
  Of the payment of wergeld in order to obtain the legal right to offer compensation, VIII Atr. 2 = I Cn. 2, 4
  If anyone lets a thief escape, he shall make compensation by the payment of his (*i.e.* the thief's) wergeld, II Cn. 29
  If anyone swears a false oath on the relics, he shall lose his hand or half his wergeld, II Cn. 36

Wergeld, *continued*
  Of the payment of wergeld as compensation for injury to one of the clergy, II Cn. 49
  Of the payment of wergeld for incest, II Cn. 51
  Of the payment of wergeld for violence done to a widow or a maiden, II Cn. 52 f.
  Of the payment of half a man's wergeld as compensation for binding him, II Cn. 60
  Of the forfeiture of wergeld for a capital deed of violence, II Cn. 61
  Of the payment of wergeld to the king as compensation for unlawfully maintaining an excommunicated person, II Cn. 66
  Of the forfeiture of his wergeld by a man who has married a widow within a year, II Cn. 73, 1
  The wergeld of a thegn, Leis Wl. 8
  The wergeld of a villein, Leis Wl. 8, 1
  The payment of wergeld, Leis Wl. 9 f.
  Of the payment of half a man's wergeld for cutting off his hand or his foot, Leis Wl. 11
  Of the payment of wergeld for assault, Leis Wl. 12
  Of the payment of wergeld for a false judgment, Leis Wl. 13
  Of the forfeiture of a man's wergeld to his lord as the result of his inability to produce either warrantor or witness, Leis Wl. 21, 2
  Of the payment of a delinquent's wergeld by his lord, Leis Wl. 52, 1
  No citizen of London shall forfeit a sum greater than his wergeld, Hn. Lond. 7
Widow
  Of widows who lead a respectable life, v Atr. 21 = vi 26
  Every widow shall remain without a husband for a year, v Atr. 21, 1 = vi 26, 1 = II Cn. 73
  A Christian man must not marry the widow of a near relation, vi Atr. 12 = I Cn. 7
  If anyone does violence to a widow, vi Atr. 39 = II Cn. 52
  Of oppressing the widow and the orphan, vi Atr. 47
  If a widow re-marries within a year, II Cn. 73 *a*–73 *a*, 2
  No widow shall be too hastily consecrated as a nun, II Cn. 73 *a*, 3
  Every widow shall pay the heriots for her husband within 12 months, II Cn. 73, 4
Wife
  No Christian man shall marry a near relative of his first wife's, vi Atr. 12 = I Cn. 7
  No Christian man shall have more wives than one, vi Atr. 12, 1 = I Cn. 7, 3
  If anyone has a lawful wife (*rihtwif*), II Cn. 54. 1
  Of a wife's share in her husband's property if he dies intestate, II Cn. 70, 1
  If a householder has dwelt free from claims and charges, his wife shall be unmolested by litigation, II Cn. 72
  If stolen goods have been put (by a thief) under his wife's lock and key, II Cn. 76, 1 f.
  No wife can forbid her husband to deposit anything he likes in his cottage, II Cn. 76, 1 *b*
  He who assaults the wife of another man, Leis Wl. 12
  Of a wife's share in her husband's property if he commits theft, Leis Wl. 27 f.
Witan
  i. Authorities, II Edm. 7; II Atr. 9; v 16 = vi 23, 1 = I Cn. 17, 1; v Atr. 30; *woruldwitan*, secular authorities, v Atr. 51 = VIII 36; VIII 43
  ii. Councillors, II Edm. Pre.; II Edg. Pre.; IV Edg. 1; 1, 4 f.; 2, 1 *a*; 14; I Atr. Pre. = IX Pre.; II Pre.; III Pre.; v 1, 1; 2–5; vi Heading; Pre.; 2 f.; 8; 9 f.; VIII Pre.; 6; x 2; I Cn. Heading; Pre.; II Cn. Pre.
Wite 'fine'; II Edg. 3 = VIII Atr. 9; II Edg. 5 = VIII Atr. 12; IV Edg. 8, 1; I Atr. 1, 7 = II Cn. 30, 3 *b*; I Atr. 1, 14; v 31 = vi 38; vi 51; VII 7; VIII 5, 1 = I Cn. 3, 2; VIII Atr. 7; II Cn. 17, 1; 24, 1; 45, 3; 48 f.; 49; 51; 69, 2
  Fihtwite, II Edm. 3; II Cn. 15; *fierdwite*, II Cn. 12; 15; *hengwite*, Leis Wl. 4; *woroldwite*, VIII Atr. 17
Wiðertihtle 'counter-charge'; II Cn. 27

426 INDEX

Witness. See *Gewitnes*
    Testimonie, Leis Wl. 6; 14; 21, 1 ff.; 23; 45 ff.; 46; 47
Woman
  No woman shall commit adultery, II Cn. 53
  No woman shall ever be forced to marry a man whom she dislikes, II Cn. 74
  If anyone assaults a woman, Leis Wl. 18 ff.
  a woman who is pregnant is sentenced to death, Leis Wl. 33
Wound. See Injuries

For EU product safety concerns, contact us at Calle de José Abascal, 56–1°, 28003 Madrid, Spain or eugpsr@cambridge.org.

www.ingramcontent.com/pod-product-compliance
Ingram Content Group UK Ltd.
Pitfield, Milton Keynes, MK11 3LW, UK
UKHW010852060825
461487UK00012B/1076